The
END
of
RACISM

Principles for a Multiracial Society

DINESH D'SOUZA

THE FREE PRESS

New York   London   Toronto   Sydney   Tokyo   Singapore

The Free Press
A Division of Simon & Schuster Inc.
1230 Avenue of the Americas
New York, N.Y. 10020

Printed in the United States of America

printing number

1 2 3 4 5 6 7 8 9 10

Text design by Carla Bolte

Library of Congress Cataloging-in-Publication Data

D'Souza, Dinesh
    The end of racism: principles for a multiracial society /
Dinesh D'Souza.
        p.   cm.
    Includes bibliographical references (p.   ) and index.
    ISBN 0-02-908102-5
    1. Racism—United States.   2. United States—Race relations.
3. Pluralism (Social sciences)—United States.   I. Title.
E.185.615.D75   1995
305.8'00973—dc20   95-18300
                                                        CIP

For my darling wife

DIXIE

who makes my life complete.

CONTENTS

PREFACE

I do not undertake this investigation of racism and multiculturalism as an unbiased observer. I am a first generation immigrant to the United States who became a citizen in 1991. East Indians have been in this country since 1789, when a Salem minister, Reverend William Bentley, recorded "a tall black Sikh walking down Derby Street in his blue turban, long white tunic, loose trousers and red sash." There are now almost a million Indian immigrants in this country, and like many of them I have a sense of appreciation for the opportunity and freedom which America provides, although like Cordelia in Shakespeare's *King Lear,* mine is a loyalty that eschews extravagant profession.

My inclinations are strongly antiracist and sympathetic to minorities. My family endured European colonialism in India for many generations, and my great-grandfather was killed by the British army for alleged insubordination. In the United States I am no stranger to xenophobia, prejudice, and discrimination. I also feel a particular debt to the civil rights movement, whose campaign on behalf of black equality helped to expand rights and opportunities for all citizens. Yet I am not an uncritical cheerleader for every parade that carries the minority banner. As a partisan of the cause of equal rights in America, I seek to offer constructive criticism that will provide a firmer ground for true liberty and equality for all citizens. In this book I try to be fair to all groups, including the majority. Some of my best friends are white.

I feel especially qualified to address the subject of multiculturalism, because I am a kind of walking embodiment of it. I was born in Bombay, India in 1961. My family is Catholic; our ancestors were converted to Christianity by Portuguese missionaries many generations ago. Although my parents are named Allan and Margaret, since I was born in post-independence India I was given a Hindu name which literally means "god of the sun." (My sister is named Nandini, which means "holy cow.") I studied in schools run by Spanish Jesuits who spoke several languages; in addition to English, I also learned Hindustani and a regional dialect, Marathi. Since 1978, I have lived in many parts of this country: in Arizona, New Hampshire, New Jersey, and now Virginia. For my senior year, I attended public high school in Arizona where one half of the students were of Mexican origin. During my freshman year at Dartmouth College, I roomed with a young African American from Bedford-Stuyvesant in New York. I am married to a Protestant woman named Dixie, who was born in Louisiana and raised in California and whose ancestry is English, Scotch Irish, German, and American Indian. Our newborn daughter, Danielle, is, well, beyond racial classification.

It is not hard to see that I have a personal stake in the American experiment to establish a multicultural society free of the humiliations and injuries of racism. Moreover, I believe that I bring a unique and perhaps enlarged perspective to a subject that could benefit from some new and different points of view. Black and white Americans live with many bizarre features of race relations which they accept as perfectly natural because they are familiar. By excavating beyond the usual digging sites and applying a new angle of vision, I hope to make helpful discoveries.

As a "person of color," I enjoy an element of ethnic immunity that enables me to address topics with a frankness that would be virtually impossible on the part of a white male. I believe this is part of what is wrong with the American race debate, which excommunicates many participants whose cooperation is essential to develop just principles for the emerging multiracial society. I hope that, by addressing some of the taboo issues in the right tone, I can help bring the offstage discussion of race into public view, narrow the parameters of the unspeakable, and clear the ground for a deeper and wider inquiry.

At the same time, I recognize that minorities too must endure vicious attacks and name-calling for dissenting from the political agenda promoted by civil rights groups. During my travels to hundreds of schools and colleges over the past several years, I have heard African Americans called Uncle Toms, Aunt Tomassinas, Aunt Jemimas, House Negroes, Oreos, Incognegroes, Afro-Saxons, and Negrophobic blacks. I have heard Asian dissenters called coconuts (yellow on the outside, white on the inside) and Uncle Tongs. American Indians who stray off the ideological reservation are denounced as Uncle Tomahawks. After a recent debate I was approached by a fellow Indian who urged me to "decolonize your mind." When I asked him which part of my speech he disagreed with, he said none of it, but he was gravely troubled by my "real views." Clearly he saw my stated positions as epiphenomenal and distinguishable from my nefarious hidden thoughts. As this example illustrates, minority activists routinely suspect freethinkers like me of selling out our own cause and confirming the suspicions of white racists.

There is some truth to this "sleeping with the enemy" charge. This book includes a good deal of criticism of the contemporary civil rights movement; it rejects the viability of a monolithic minority agenda, and allows the possibility of competing visions of minority progress. Undoubtedly some of my arguments will give ammunition to enemies of equal rights. However, the alternative is to acquiesce in an incoherent vision of civil rights and an ultimately regressive political agenda, and to impose as well a regime of self-censorship so comprehensive that one is prevented from making legitimate arguments for fear that illegitimate use may be made of them. This kind of "sensitivity" does no one any good. At the same time, I accept my obligation to distinguish my principled positions from the ground occupied by bigots, and to attack racism no matter what its source.

As a self-described conservative, I also acknowledge that the political right has a mixed-to-poor record in supporting civil rights during the 1950s and 1960s. Jack Kemp spoke wisely when he said in a 1994 interview, "We Republicans had a great history, and we turned it aside. We should have been there on the freedom marches and bus rides." Since I was born in 1961, I obviously took no position on the Civil Rights Act of 1964 or the Voting Rights Act of 1965. Yet even though this book makes clear my reservations about some aspects of the movement led by Martin Luther King, if I had been old enough at that time I would have wholeheartedly supported his agenda. This is also true of many young conservatives today.

But the issue is not who was right then, but what is the right course of action now. My main conclusion in this book is that most of our basic assumptions about racism and civil rights are either wrong or obsolete. Because I am committed to the liberal goals of a just and inclusive society, my objective is not to strengthen old bigotries, but to discover a stronger basis for the principles of liberty and equal rights in this multiracial society. My ultimate purpose is to restore a basis for liberal hope in an atmosphere of deepening despair, and to enable the crusade against racism to recover the moral high ground it has lost.

ACKNOWLEDGMENTS

This book would not have been possible without the help of my research assistants, Nita Parekh and William Tell, who set up interviews, prepared questions, checked facts, and offered valuable suggestions and criticism. I am also indebted to the following persons who assisted me with leads and comments: James and Gloria Brubaker, Erick Brubaker, Larry Burks, Terry Eastland, Michael Fumento, Michael Greve, Holly Grzeskowiak, Gertrude Himmelfarb, Michael Keenan Jones, Adam Meyerson, David Murray, Ranna Parekh, Jonathan Rauch, Thomas Riley, James Sharf, Scott Walter, Wilcomb Washburn, and Gordon Wood. *The End of Racism* is based on extensive scholarly research and personal interviews. The research is cited in the notes; where no citation appears, the comment is based on a personal interview. I am grateful to the American Enterprise Institute for giving me the time and research facilities to write this book, and to its president, Christopher DeMuth, for reading the manuscript in several drafts. I wish to thank the John M. Olin Foundation and its executive director, James Piereson, for research support and encouragement. My editor at The Free Press, Adam Bellow, worked closely with me throughout the preparation of the manuscript. Raphael Sagalyn helped shape the concept for the book and managed my business affairs. Finally, I owe more than I can say to my wife Dixie, whose patience, love, and suggestions enabled me to put my best effort into this study. Since her birth in January 1995, little Danielle has contributed coos and smiles that I have found immensely inspirational.

1

THE WHITE MAN'S BURDEN

The Collapse of Liberal Hope

The world is white no longer, and it will never be white again.
—James Baldwin[1]

A generation after the civil rights movement, Americans are once again engaged in a radical rethinking of their attitudes toward race, and major changes in public policy are imminent. The choice is whether to preserve the existing structure of race-based policies or opt for a completely different approach. The moment of decision cannot be avoided: not to choose is to decide in favor of the status quo and to perpetuate current problems. Yet before adopting a course that will determine the future of race relations into the twenty-first century, Americans must step back from the sound and fury long enough to ask some fundamental questions about race and racism.

The public mood is not conducive to such prudent statesmanship. Indeed the crisis of American race relations is evident from the volatile combination of confusion and anger that characterizes the public debate. Both sentiments arise from a deep chasm of understanding that now separates whites and blacks. Many whites have become increasingly scornful of black demands, and vehemently reject racial preferences. Most blacks, by contrast, support affirmative action as indispensable to fighting the

1

enduring effects of white racism. On other racial issues as well, from the Los Angeles riots to the O.J. Simpson case, blacks and whites seem to view each other across a hostile divide. There is a political chasm as well: increasingly the Republican party is becoming the party of whites, while the Democratic party is beholden to its African American voting base. If these political and racial divisions are exacerbated, we are likely to witness a further decomposition of the bonds that hold the country together. Thus America's historically unprecedented attempt to construct a truly multiracial society may be doomed to fail.

This book is an attempt to explain and reconcile the perception gap between whites and blacks by resolving what appears to be the fundamental issue in dispute: is America a racist society? Deeply distressed by the continuing failure of blacks as a group to succeed in America, many scholars and social activists allege that all talk of racial progress is an evasion or a mirage. They assume that racism is not a departure from American ideals but a true expression of them, that the nation's institutions are ineradicably tainted by racism, and that racism may be an intrinsic part of the human or at least the Western psyche, so that we may never be able to transcend it. The dominant view today is that race is a social reality or, as African American scholar Cornel West puts it, "race matters"; therefore the only viable response is to institutionalize race as the basis of public policy. In the face of such pessimism, this book advances the view that Cornel West is wrong, that racism can be overcome, and that a serious attempt to do so must first involve revising our most basic assumptions about race. Specifically, I question and reject the following widely shared premises that shape the conventional wisdom about racism, as well as America's civil rights laws.

- Racism is simply an irrational prejudice, a product of ignorance and fear.
- Slavery was a racist institution, and the Constitution's compromise with slavery discredits the American founding as racist and morally corrupt.
- Segregation was a system established by white racists for the purpose of oppressing blacks.
- In American history, racism is the theory and discrimination is the practice.
- The civil rights movement represented a triumph of justice and enlightenment over the forces of Southern racism and hate.
- Although Martin Luther King, Jr. helped to secure formal rights for blacks, white racism has become more subtle and continues its baleful influence through institutional structures.
- The civil rights leadership is committed to fighting racism and building

up the economic and cultural strengths of blacks, especially the poorest ones.

- Affirmative action is a policy that assures equal opportunity for disadvantaged African Americans and other minorities.
- Multiculturalism unites blacks and nonwhite immigrants in a common struggle against white racism.
- Blacks and other persons of color cannot be racist because racism requires not just prejudice but also power.
- Racism is the main obstacle facing African Americans today, and the primary explanation for black problems.

BLACK RAGE

The three main features of the nation's racial crisis are the phenomena of black rage, white backlash, and liberal despair.

In 1992, a white congressional aide working for Senator Richard Shelby of Alabama was accosted at his home in Washington, D.C., and shot to death. A few weeks later, Edward Evans, a young black man, was arrested. Two friends of Evans testified that they saw him shoot the young staffer. One of them said that Evans harbored strong antiwhite sentiments and promised he was going to kill a white man. The material evidence against Evans, presented at trial, seemed overwhelming. Yet although eleven jurors, including five blacks, initially agreed that Evans was guilty of murder, one African American woman, Velma McNeil, refused to convict. A frustrated white jury foreman claimed to the judge that "one juror" was simply unwilling to give credence to the prosecution's evidence against Evans. He also stated later that, during jury deliberations, McNeil told fellow jurors that the exoneration of Los Angeles police officers who beat black motorist Rodney King showed the systematic bias of the judicial system against blacks. Juror McNeil denied that her refusal to find the defendant guilty was based on race, pointing instead to possible contradictions in the statements given by the two eyewitnesses. The consequence was a hung jury, and the judge was forced to declare a mistrial. A *Washington Post* photograph shows McNeil emerging from the courtroom, smiling, chatting, and embracing a relative of the accused.[2]

If juror McNeil's reluctance to convict a fellow African American was at least in part motivated by race, the incident is striking in that it reveals two paradigmatic cases of black rage: a poor black man, consumed with racial resentment, seeking to vent his hostility on a white man; and a middle-class black woman, perhaps equally alienated from society, using the system to settle a score against whites as a group. Black rage is also part of the undertow of the O.J. Simpson trial, where the defense seems to seek to capitalize on the antagonism of black jurors toward white policemen in order to win a hung jury or an acquittal. Both cases point to the justice system's vulnerability to racial politics. This is hardly a new problem: during the first half of this century in the segregated South, blacks were routinely victimized by racist policemen, prosecutors, judges, and juries. What is new is that, for the first time, whites may find it difficult to receive justice in many inner cities such as Washington, D.C., and Los Angeles which are fertile grounds for black rage. As African American legal scholar Randall Kennedy points out, "One dissenter is all that it takes to prevent a conviction."[3]

The Constitution guarantees citizens the right to a jury of our peers, but in a racially polarized society, who are our peers? If justice is simply a matter of whose ethnic perspective prevails, neither African Americans nor whites can expect fairness when juries are mainly composed of members of the other group. This issue goes far beyond the criminal justice system. In a liberal society it is fair rules, a sense of common citizenship, and respect for reason that constitute the means to adjudicate disputes and conflicts of interest. Black rage, to the extent it affects the judicial process, is alarming because it defies prevailing norms of civility and rationality. Unchecked, such sentiments lead to fanaticism, riots, and even a possible physical conflict between the races.

These concerns are not entirely speculative. In 1990, a black alderman from Milwaukee, Michael McGee, worked to organize African Americans in several cities into a black militia that was arming itself for war against "property" if its demands for $100 million in racial reparations were not met within five years. "The only way to get respect is to be willing to use violence," said McGee. "I'm talking . . . bloodshed and urban guerrilla warfare." Inner-city blacks routinely applaud McGee's remarks, and McGee claims that more than a thousand have signed up for training in his militia.[4]

On December 7, 1993, Colin Ferguson, a Jamaican immigrant living in Brooklyn, converted his racial antagonism against white society into an occasion for mass murder. Ferguson boarded a commuter train from Manhattan and proceeded to shoot passengers at point blank range, killing six and wounding nineteen. Notes found in his possession suggested that Ferguson had a vendetta against whites and what he called "Uncle

Tom Negroes" whom he suspected of plotting against him. Remarkably, a *National Law Journal* survey showed that 68 percent of African Americans were persuaded by the argument of Ferguson's lawyers that white racism drove him to his crazed rampage. Yet Ferguson himself rejected this defense, claiming that he was being framed by racist policemen and prejudiced eyewitnesses. Although Ferguson was later convicted of murder, Martin Simmons, a black scholar at New York University, termed him "a hero" and observed, "I have colleagues who tell me they're putting his picture on the wall next to Malcolm X." African American psychiatrist Alvin Poussaint wondered aloud "why there haven't been more blacks who have exploded because of the mistreatment that they have received at the hands of white people."[5]

Another well-known example of black anger was the savage beating administered to white truckdriver Reginald Denny in the aftermath of the Rodney King case. The Los Angeles riots themselves showcased the resentment of poor blacks and Hispanics who burned and looted without a hint of embarrassment or remorse. African American scholar Cornel West termed the riots, in which more than fifty people died and four thousand were injured, a "display of justified social rage."[6] Black rapper and activist Ice T struck an even more defiant note.

> The most peaceful time I ever experienced in South Central was during the riots. While everybody was looking for fires, we walked through the streets. Kids were setting shit on fire, people were smiling. Everybody was shaking each other's hands, feeling a camaraderie. It was as if the people had taken the city back.[7]

Anticipating many such outbreaks in the future, some black leaders have adopted something like a martial posture. "Basically, we're at war," declares publisher and author Haki Madhubuti.[8] In *Young, Black and Male in America,* Jewelle Taylor Gibbs predicts that African American rage will eventually find violent expression in the suburbs. "The violence which young black males now direct mainly against the black community . . . will inevitably erupt and spread throughout urban and suburban America."[9] Legal scholar Derrick Bell says:

> We should appreciate the Louis Farrakhans while we've got them. While these guys talk a lot, they don't actually do anything. The new crop of leaders are going to be a lot more dangerous and radical, and the next phase will probably be led by charismatic individuals, maybe even teenagers, who urge

that instead of killing each other, they should go out in gangs and kill a whole lot of white people.[10]

Both a prediction and a warning, Bell's statement suggests that multiracial societies depend on a radius of trust between groups, and that is now gone. His remarks make one wonder whether white flight to the suburbs can restore the peace or merely postpone the inevitable. Sister Souljah, Al Sharpton, and Louis Farrakhan are the bellicose prophets of black rage in America today. Like Bell, they combine threats of anarchy with forecasts of racial apocalypse. And while their appeal is mainly to poor blacks, there are signs that many successful black professionals identify with these voices of militancy, and share in the racial resentment directed against whites. Middle-class blacks, Ellis Cose writes in *The Rage of a Privileged Class,* suffer from "deeply repressed rage. . . . They are at least as disaffected and pessimistic as those struggling at society's periphery."[11] Other recent books such as Brent Staples's *Parallel Time,* Jill Nelson's *Volunteer Slavery,* and Nathan McCall's *Makes Me Wanna Holler* convey this same molten anger. Given the intensity of black rage and its appeal to a wide constituency, whites are right to be nervous.

Black rage is a response to black suffering and failure, and reflects the irresistible temptation to attribute African American problems to a history of white racist oppression. Despite substantial progress over the past few decades, African Americans continue to show conspicuous evidence of failure—failure in the workplace, failure in schools and colleges, and failure to maintain intact families and secure communities. Taken together, these hardships and inadequacies virtually assure that blacks will not achieve equality of earnings and status with other groups anytime soon. Even more seriously, they threaten to destroy poor black communities and endanger the economic and physical integrity of society as a whole.

- The annual income of African Americans who are employed in full-time jobs amounts to about 60 percent of that of whites.
- The black unemployment rate is nearly double that of the whole nation.
- One third of blacks are poor, compared with just over 10 percent of whites.
- One half of all black children live in poverty.
- The infant mortality rate for blacks is more than double that of whites.
- The proportion of black male high school graduates who go on to college is lower today than in 1975.
- More young black males are in prison than in college.

- Homicide is the leading cause of death for black males between the ages of fifteen and thirty-four.
- Although African Americans make up 12 percent of the population, they account for more than 35 percent of all AIDS cases.
- The life expectancy of black men is sixty-five years, a rate lower than any other group in America and comparable to that of some Third World countries.
- Nearly 50 percent of all African American families are headed by single women.
- More than 65 percent of black children born each year are illegitimate.[12]

What, if not racism, has caused these terrible problems? Alvin Poussaint attributes black afflictions to enforced victimization of a nation with a "record of flagrant racial prejudice."[13] Author John Edgar Wideman rhetorically asks, "Do black newborns die at three times the rate of white babies because of some factor intrinsic to blackness or because being black means they're treated by society as only one-third as valuable as white newborns?"[14] Activist William Cavil explodes, "I don't understand, if there's not some conspiracy going on, how every group has managed to flourish and get ahead except African Americans."[15] Sister Souljah charges that "racism has turned our communities into war zones, where we are dying every day."[16]

The case for holding white racism and its historical legacy responsible for the contemporary hardships of blacks is a strong one. Film producer Spike Lee argues that "when you're told every single day for four hundred years that you're subhuman, when you rob people of their self-worth, knowledge and history, there's nothing worse you can do."[17] As Lee suggests, unlike other immigrants, African Americans did not come to this country voluntarily; they were brought here in chains. Slavery lasted for more than two and a half centuries, during which most blacks found their lives largely bent to the wills of their masters. African American scholar Gerald Early writes that "every single black life today is tied inextricably to the tragedy of slavery."[18] Afrocentrist Molefi Asante invokes the enduring consequences of slavery to argue that whites should pay monetary reparations, estimated in some cases at several hundred thousand dollars per family, to compensate for "wages that our ancestors lost that we now require for a new start in life."

Others go beyond slavery to attribute African American problems to the residual effects of segregation and discrimination during the twentieth century. "Young people forget, but I am old enough to know that not long ago blacks were basically non-citizens in this country," remarks Margaret Bush Wilson, former chairman of the National Association for the Advancement of Colored People (NAACP). Like many others, Wilson views segregation as an American form of apartheid, which imposed indescribable deprivation and humiliation on blacks. For much of this century most black men were forced to work in degrading menial jobs, such as janitoring and field work. Black women had few occupations open to them other than cleaning and cooking in white households. Historian John Hope Franklin says, "Many young blacks are angry because they do not believe that we have come very far. And there are times when I have to agree with them."

As Franklin's remarks imply, many blacks view racism not as a thing of the past, but as a continuing force which brutally limits the aspirations of African Americans today. Many contemporary examples support this suspicion. In 1993 Christopher Wilson, a thirty-one year old black man, was abducted, robbed, and set on fire by two white men who shouted racial slurs and applauded his cries for help. The Southern Poverty Law Center reported numerous horrific hate crimes that year: two white men placed a rope around a black man's neck and burned a cross to terrorize him; a group of Skinheads cornered a black man whom they beat and tortured; two white bikers assaulted an interracial couple; a white man picked a fight with a black neighbor who was married to a white woman, and stabbed a Hispanic passerby who attempted to stop the fight.[19]

Although hate groups are less visible today, African Americans point out that such groups continue to spread their toxic message in America. Most people are familiar with David Duke's past as a Nazi and Ku Klux Klan leader, but the world he claims to have left behind continues without him. In northern Idaho, white supremacist Richard Butler runs a Christian Identity church whose members are preparing for a racial Armageddon, an apocalyptic final struggle between whites on behalf of God and nonwhites on behalf of Satan. From his pulpit decorated with racist paraphernalia, Butler preaches that "the Bible is the family history of the white race." Butler warns that white intermarriage with Jews or blacks results in "mulatto zombies."[20] Many commentators have seized upon the recent bombing of an Oklahoma City federal building to argue that white racist extremists continue to pose a serious threat to American institutions and public safety.

Civil rights activists complain that even apart from the indignities of white supremacist groups, blacks on a routine basis suffer racial discrimination in getting a job, being promoted, applying for a loan, seeking justice from the police or the courts, even in getting a taxi or being served at a restaurant. As far as minorities are concerned, Jesse Jackson protests, "All the evidence I know says there's not a level playing field."[21] For example, numerous accusations of racism have been registered against the national restaurant chain Denny's. Robert Norton, a white employee, reports that as young black customers approached the doors one evening he saw Denny's employees rush to lock the doors. Although they claimed the restaurant had closed, Norton reports that the doors were promptly opened for white customers when the blacks left. At various Denny's restaurants across the country, African Americans were reportedly subjected to regular demands for prepayment, minimum purchase requirements, gratuities added to the bill, denials of advertised free birthday meals, back-room seatings, and scandalously rude service.[22]

In addition to these documented incidents, many African Americans argue that white racism now operates in the form of "code words" and institutional standards that disguise deeply bigoted sentiments that dare not speak their name. "It is unlikely that racism is declining in the United States," Alphonso Pinkney writes. "The most obvious cases of gross discrimination and segregation have somewhat abated, but the basic racism remains."[23] Ralph Wiley argues, "When they want to say *niggers,* they say *crime.* When they want to say *niggers,* they say *welfare.* When they want to say *niggers,* they say *drugs.*"[24] Summing up both the direct and indirect evidence for the pervasiveness of bigotry, political scientist Ronald Walters said at a recent lecture, "Look at Bensonhurst. Look at Howard Beach. Look at Susan Smith blaming a black man for abducting her children when she drowned them herself. If white racism is not to blame for black problems, you tell me what is."

WHITE BACKLASH

For many whites, in contrast, America does not have a race problem but rather a black problem. Most whites seem to acknowledge historical oppression inflicted upon blacks, but some raise questions about its contemporary significance. At a talk in which I raised the issue, one high school senior scornfully responded, "Slavery ended a long time ago. My ancestors were in Palermo at the time. I'm tired of being lectured about how I'm somehow responsible for slavery." Similarly, while many people concede the injustice of segregation, surveys show that most whites believe systematic oppression came to a halt with the civil rights era of a generation ago, when major laws were passed to guarantee legal equality by outlawing discrimination in schools, housing, and the workplace. Many whites seem convinced that racism is flourishing today, not in American society but in the imaginations of black activists.[25]

The appropriate remedy for existing discrimination, most whites seem to believe, is for the government to enforce the principle of color blindness or race neutrality. Preferences based on color or ancestry are now strongly opposed by a majority of whites and an overwhelming percentage of white males.[26] Such preferences, critics of affirmative action argue, compound the evil of discrimination by multiplying it. "Count me among those angry men" opposed to race-based policies, says Thomas Wood, one of the sponsors of California's Proposition 196, a measure on the 1996 ballot which outlaws preferential treatment in hiring, college admissions, and government contracting. Wood adds, "I was once passed over for a teaching job because I was told I was white and male. It didn't count that I was the most qualified."[27] San Francisco fire fighter Ray Batz conveys the exasperation of many whites over demands for what they perceive as special treatment. "Some minority firefighters have been promoted four times. I don't think anyone needs four legs up. That's madness."[28] Arnold O'Donnell, whose construction company has lost out to minority firms despite submitting bids at lower cost, protests, "You give a handful of firms a preference every single day, not once to get them started, but year after year. It's just a giveaway to those firms."[29] Other critics of affirmative action have been less reserved. "Rejoice you crybaby niggers," wrote the author of an anonymous flier distributed at the University of California at Berkeley. "When I see you in class it bugs the hell out of me because you're taking the seat of someone qualified."[30]

Understandably enough, such rhetoric causes African American leaders to treat resistance to preferential treatment as itself a resurgent form of racism. Yet such opposition is not confined to whites; some African American scholars have repudiated affirmative action, and an increasing number of younger blacks seem ambivalent about it. Many whites now seem contemptuous of what they view as unfair and exaggerated accusations made by hypersensitive blacks. Conservative columnists have taken up the cause of white backlash. "Are we willing to permit ourselves to become a country with permanently coddled minorities?" Mona Charen asks.[31] Tony Snow writes that racial preferences are a "divisive nuisance" and that charges of racism amount to nothing more than "playing the race card."[32] In a similar vein, Patrick Buchanan asserts, "Words like racist have lost their power to intimidate. No one is cowed anymore."[33] As the rhetoric of leading politicians like Robert Dole, Pete Wilson, and Phil Gramm suggests, the Republican party hopes to make white opposition to racial preferences a catalyst for massive voter defections from the Democrats.

As the de facto party of whites, the GOP seems increasingly responsive to growing majority concerns about high levels of nonwhite immigration. Each year some 800,000 legal immigrants and an unknown number of illegals enter the country. Unlike in the past, most immigrants do not come from Europe, but from Asia, Africa, and most of all, Latin America. These demographic trends have dramatically altered the complexion of states such as California, Texas, and Florida. If these trends continue, by the year 2050 whites will make up just 50 percent of the national population. Hispanics would be the largest minority, more than 20 percent and, counting illegals, possibly closer to 25 percent; blacks would be around 15 percent, and Asians near 10 percent.[34] Many whites are acutely uncomfortable about what one observer has called "the browning of America." A substantial majority of Americans is resolutely opposed to current levels of immigration.[35]

Once relegated to the fringe, the anti-immigration cause has gathered mainstream recognition and national momentum, even without moderating its harsh rhetoric. Books such as Peter Brimelow's *Alien Nation,* Richard Lamm and Gary Imhoff's *The Immigration Time Bomb,* Lawrence Auster's *The Path to National Suicide,* and Leon Bouvier's *Peaceful Invasions: Immigration and Changing America* warn that many of the new immigrants cannot be assimilated. In *The Immigration Invasion,* Wayne Lutton and John Tanton charge that "the United States has become a welfare magnet to people around the world" and that "over time, work places become colonized by aliens to the degree that Americans are not welcome."[36] Warning that public schools are now "mandated to teach in at least 42 different languages," that many jurisdictions now administer driving tests in multiple languages, and that hundreds of voting districts are now required to provide voting ballots in Spanish, the national organization U.S. English has developed a large constituency behind the concept of a constitutional amendment establishing English as the national language.[37] The founder of the group insists that owing to their higher birth rates, immigrants are out-breeding other Americans: "Those with their pants up are going to be caught by those with their pants down."[38]

The nativists are cultural environmentalists of a sort: they insist on protecting the ecology of traditional mores and morals, and they fear overpopulation and contamination from too many newcomers and aliens. A Florida resident says, "The politicians are so busy giving away our tax money to Cubans, Haitians and anyone else who feels like coming here, there won't be anything left for us and our children."[39] Illustrating mainstream hostility to Hispanic immigration, the *New York Times* cited an outburst from Emma Tropiano, a senior citizen and member of the Allentown, Pennsylvania city council. "They've brought all their bad habits here, and they want Allentown to wave our hankies and say: that's fine! We *enjoy* having litter and graffiti and shopping carts all over the place and old sofas on the porches. These kids are all over the streets. If they like it here so much, why do they destroy property? Why do they act disrespectful to the elderly?"[40] And racist groups like the Ku Klux Klan seem to be attempting a revival by trumpeting the nativist cause. "There never will be peace in America as long as whites are forced to live among the colored savages," Klansman Robert Shelton has proclaimed. "The one and only solution is America for the white man. We are at war in America. Look at the color of your skin—that is your uniform."[41]

In 1994, white backlash found scholarly support in Richard Herrnstein and Charles Murray's controversial book *The Bell Curve.* By asserting that blacks and Hispanics were on average less intelligent than Caucasians and Asians—deficiencies alleged to be possibly inherited—Herrnstein and Murray supplied what to many angry whites must have sounded like an appealing explanation for why groups differ in academic performance and economic achievement. Although *The Bell Curve* met with furious denunciation—"dishonest," "creepy," "indecent," "shabby," "politically ugly," and "Nazi" were some of the epithets used[42]—the book became a runaway best-seller, attracting hundreds of thousands of readers. Could it be that Herrnstein and Murray were articulating truths that many whites privately believe? After all, the liberal insistence that the races are identical in ability seems to conflict with commonsense observation and must be accompanied by an elaborate rationale for why blacks are doing relatively poorly in America, for why black crime and illegitimacy rates are vastly higher than those of whites and Asians, for why the predominantly white nations of the world are the most prosperous, for why much of Asia and Latin America are expanding economically while most of Africa remains in a state of economic and political chaos. By contrast, Herrnstein and Murray's view appears to succeed by the logic of Occam's razor: a natural hierarchy of racial abilities would predict and fully account for such phenomena.

If Herrnstein and Murray are right, the hope for a society in which all groups compete on equal terms is an illusion. The possibility of such intrinsic differences raises old and ugly prospects: eugenic schemes to ensure survival of the fittest, millions of black boys and girls stigmatized as incapable of learning, orphanages for children from broken or impoverished families, a revival of certain forms of segregation and racial discrimination. Nor are these fanciful or hypothetical proposals. Reflecting a newly emboldened racial consciousness, conservative columnist Samuel Francis in a recent article urges that whites begin a "reconquest of the United States" by deporting all illegal aliens "and perhaps many recent legal immigrants," repealing all civil rights protections for minorities, imposing forced birth control on welfare mothers, and providing incentives for whites to have more children and minorities to stop reproducing.[43] Although these sentiments cannot be taken as representative of whites in general—certainly few would express themselves this way—nevertheless discontentment over affirmative action and Third World immigration appears to be solidifying what sociologist Robert Blauner terms "a dominant white racial identity."[44] White backlash is now a political juggernaut that threatens to reverse the liberal immigration and civil rights policies of the past generation, and to further polarize the races in this country.

LIBERAL DESPAIR

Once optimistic about their ability to heal the historical rift between the races, many white liberals now seem cynical and gloomy about America's capacity for racial reconciliation and progress toward a society free of racism. In the 1950s and 1960s, liberals supported the two bedrock principles of the civil rights movement: desegregation, epitomized by the *Brown v. Board of Education* decision, and nondiscrimination, written into law in the Civil Rights Act of 1964. Support for these measures was premised on the assumption that racism was a form of ignorance and fear, and that as whites regularly associated with blacks their prejudices and stereotypes would dissolve and enlightened tolerance would replace irrational antipathy. Similarly, many white liberals claimed that since racism was a mechanism for enforced group inequality, the elimination of discrimination could be reasonably expected to generate over time a racial equality of performance and rewards. The early 1960s witnessed a high degree of confidence that the race problem would soon be solved. In 1962 sociologist Arnold Rose argued that by the end of the century the forces generating racial inequality "will be practically eliminated" and racism would decline to the "minor order" of reciprocal prejudices among Catholics and Protestants.[45]

A generation later, Rose's prediction sounds absurdly naive. Contrary to many people's hopes, it is fairly clear that liberal enlightenment has failed. During the 1970s and early 1980s many whites fiercely resisted measures like busing which were designed to promote increased contact between the races; more recently, liberals have discovered to their amazement that many blacks too reject integration and prefer to associate with their own kind. Today this fact is made obvious by the existence of black fraternities, black sororities, black student unions, black proms, black professional associations, black political caucuses, and black suburban enclaves.[46] "There is something of a movement in the African American community away from integration," remarks black scholar David Bositis.[47] Historian David Garrow adds that "there is less integrationist sentiment in black America now than at any time since King's death."[48]

Rejecting another liberal refrain from the civil rights era, over the last few decades the black leadership has moved away from its embrace of color-blind laws; this group now supports policies which discriminate in favor of minorities with a view to increasing their representation in the work force and political institutions. Although ambivalent about racial quotas, many liberals supported preferences that they viewed as benignly and temporarily designed to assure genuine equality of opportunity. Yet of late white liberals have watched in dismay as the majority of Americans reject affirmative action, and African American leaders bitterly denounce this rejection as insensitive if not racist. Absent racial preferences, Cornel West writes in *Race Matters,* "it is a virtual certainty that racial and sexual discrimination would return with a vengeance." Columnist Carl Rowan accuses opponents of affirmative action of "apoplectic spasms of bigotry" which seek to "roll the clock back to a time of segregation and rabid racial discrimination." Willie Brown, speaker of the California Assembly, denounces Proposition 196 as "totally and completely racist." In hyperbole that conveys the depth of emotional attachment to affirmative action, Jesse Jackson accuses California Governor Pete Wilson and supporters of color-blind policies of being contemporary incarnations of slaveowners and segregationists, and Congressman Charles Rangel likens plans to eliminate race-based programs to Hitler's policies for extermination of the Jews. Even moderate voices like Representative John Lewis declare that to save preferential policies, "we've got to do battle again." And Congressman Kweisi Mfume warns that affirmative action advocates will not "go down quietly" and that the battle could "tear this country apart."[49]

Frustrated by these escalating tensions, many white liberals now argue that the civil rights movement succeeded in assuring formal equality but not meaningful equality. In this view, Martin Luther King, Jr., was successful in confronting legal segregation and discrimination, but the real adversary, white racism, remains as dangerous as ever. Indeed, many liberals warn that racism is now more threatening, because it has gone underground where it operates in subtle ways to thwart black aspirations. Liberal scholars have devised an extensive vocabulary which seeks to perform the difficult task of uncovering disguised and hidden forms of white racism. There is "intentional racism" which is deliberate and "unintentional racism" which is subconscious.[50] In varying degrees, racism can be identified as "blatant," "subtle," or "covert."[51] Racism as practiced by white ethnics is called "crypto-racism" or "neoracism."[52] "Dominative racism" refers to direct Southern-style bigotry as contrasted with "aversive racism" which is epitomized by Northern-style coldness and avoidance of blacks. Neither must be confused with "metaracism," defined as the racism generated by modern technology.[53] "Process racism" refers to procedures that generate racially disparate outcomes.[54] "Kinetic racism" is defined as racism which "manifests itself by nonverbal means."[55] Moreover, racism can be understood as "malignant racism," "benign racism," or "benevolent racism."[56] And racism comes in stages: the "oral phase," the "anal phase," and the "phallic-oedipal phase."[57] A bigoted preference for one's own culture becomes "cultural racism."[58] Progressives who highlight positive images about blacks, thus ignoring serious problems faced by the community, are said to be guilty of "enlightened racism."[59] Finally there are "feel-good racism" and "well-intentioned racism" which infect everyone who continues to benefit from the nation's legacy of racial inequality.[60]

Despite a major social project to educate whites about racism, many liberals have been saddened to discover in recent years that whites seem uninterested in the self-analysis needed to unmask covert forms of bigotry; on the contrary, most whites seem increasingly hostile to all measures that seek to assure greater equality for blacks as a group. Even more significant, liberals have been stunned during the past few decades to see a virtual disintegration of the norms of community in the inner cities, where a substantial segment of the black population seems not to have gained anything from the civil rights movement. Who would have predicted that America's cities, once monuments to the vitality of cosmopolitan civilization, would include battle zones governed by youth gangs who live on crime, prostitution, and drug sales, only marginally restrained by the law, operating within a culture whose cardinal rules seem to be power and pleasure?

Inner-city neighborhoods in some major cities resemble the scenes of Third World countries. Stores are boarded up, windows are broken, nothing seems to work, and many people do not seem to have anything to do. Many areas seem to have lost all institutions except the church, the liquor store, the gas station, and the funeral home. The streets are irrigated with alcohol, urine, and blood. "Never before have we witnessed such violence in the black community," says Congressman John Lewis, a veteran of the civil rights movement. Jesse Jackson sums up the painful reality: "If whites shoot blacks, we want to riot. If blacks shoot whites, whites want revenge and capital punishment. If blacks shoot blacks, no one cares."[61] In this Hobbesian world, violence is now a normal part of daily existence, and residents are not surprised to hear the sound of gunfire or the screams of the bereaved. Mothers regularly see their sons arrested and taken to prison. Drug and alcohol addiction have reached epidemic proportions. Gangs conduct a vigorous traffic in crack cocaine, punctuated by murders. Children lose their innocence at an early age and are initiated into a culture of hardened street attitudes, slang expression, flamboyant ritual, and ghetto chic. Very few have fathers who take care of them or provide guidance for responsible manhood. Many people do not support themselves but receive their subsistence checks from welfare programs. In *Do or Die,* journalist Leon Bing reports on reasons given by gang members for killing people:

> "Cause I don't like his attitude."
> "Cause of the way he walk."
> "Cause he try to get with my lady."
> "Cause he give me no respect."
> "Cause he a disgrace."
> "Cause he wearin' the wrong color."
> "Cause I don't like him."
> "Cause he said somethin' wrong."
> "Cause he look at me funny."[62]

Many African American communities seem physically and culturally isolated from the rest of the country. Behavior that would be regarded as pathological anywhere else is considered routine, and sometimes glamorous, in the ghetto. African American scholar Julius Lester diagnoses the problem as nihilism, "a condition without precedent in black American history because even during slavery blacks had hope."[63] Despite their outward bravado, many black adolescents understand the desperation of their condition. "Go ahead and kill us," one of the Los Angeles rioters told a reporter. "We're already dead."[64] How can racism not be implicated in the sufferings of the black underclass? Consequently some white liberals have found themselves reluctantly propelled toward the position, held by many African Americans, that racism is deeply embedded in the nation's institutions and culture, so that there is no realistic hope of overcoming it. Here are some expressions of the mood of despair shared by many white liberals and black activists.

"Racism is as healthy today as it was during the Enlightenment," argues Nobel laureate Toni Morrison. "It has assumed a metaphorical life so completely embedded in daily discourse that it is perhaps more necessary and more on display than ever before."[65]

Legal scholar Richard Delgado advances his law of racial thermodynamics: "There is change from one era to another, but the net quantum of racism remains exactly the same. Racism is neither created nor destroyed."[66]

After the *Brown* decision, recalls black sociologist Kenneth Clark, who offered crucial testimony for that case, "I felt that this was the beginning of major positive changes in race relations." But now, confronting the social breakdown in many black communities, Clark poignantly writes, "Reluctantly I am forced to face the likely possibility that the United States will never rid itself of racism."[67]

"We are a racist society," Joel Kovel writes in *White Racism*. "Racism is ultimately indivisible from the rest of American life. It is a streamlined and reconstituted racism. Freed of the grosser manifestations of prejudice, the system remains all the more racist because the basic mechanisms for racial degradation are not only still in place, but indeed are strengthened."[68]

Author Derrick Bell remarks that "what we designate as racial progress is not a solution. It is a regeneration of the problem in a particularly perverse form. . . . Racism is an integral, permanent and indestructible component of this society. Americans achieve a measure of social stability through their unspoken pact to keep blacks on the bottom."[69]

"Everybody of Caucasian descent believes that we belong to a superior strain," political scientist Andrew Hacker writes. "Most white people believe that persons with African ancestries are more likely to carry primitive traits in their genes. . . . I may believe this and hate myself for believing it. I don't see how I can say it's in so many other people and not in me."[70]

Legal scholar Charles Lawrence sums up the emerging consensus of leading liberals. "Racism in America is much more complex than either the conscious conspiracy of a power elite or the simple delusion of a few ignorant bigots. . . . It arises from the assumptions we have learned to make about the world, ourselves and others, as well as from the patterns of our fundamental social activities. . . . To the extent that this cultural belief system has influenced all of us, we are all racists."[71]

THE MULTICULTURAL SOLUTION

Multiculturalism is the contemporary paradigm of liberal antiracism. By offering a broad vision that links the struggles of blacks with those of nonwhite immigrants, multiculturalism seems to unify the political left today in much the same way that anticommunism once provided the cement that kept the right together. Thus advocates of multiculturalism typically downplay incidents of internecine conflict between minorities; in their view, African Americans, Mexicans, Koreans, and even women and homosexuals are collective victims of bigotry based on race, gender, and sexual orientation. Consequently multiculturalists argue that these groups should jointly militate against racism, sexism, and homophobia.

In its most comprehensive expression, multiculturalism offers a wide-ranging critique of prevailing political and cultural institutions. Multiculturalism springs from the premise that Western civilization in general, and American institutions in particular, are fundamentally racist because they elevate Eurocentric or "white" standards and values over those of other cultures. What multiculturalists call the "dominant white culture" did not prevail because of its greater appeal; it prevailed largely through racist oppression visited upon minority cultures. Thus the multicultural project is to seek equality or parity in all respects for minority cultures. Multiculturalism is a political movement based on a denial of Western cultural superiority.

As the name suggests, multiculturalism is a doctrine of culture—the multiplicity of cultures. At its deepest level, the intellectual premise of multiculturalism is cultural relativism. In this context, relativism means that all cultures are basically equal. No culture can be said to be better or worse than any other. Cultures are just different, and we must learn to cherish their differences. All cultures are equally entitled to respect. Finally, the standards for evaluating or criticizing a culture must come from within that culture. Relativism dictates that cultures are not entitled to impose their values on others. "Each human culture is so unique," argues anthropologist Renato Rosaldo, that "no one of them is higher or lower, greater or lesser than any other."[72]

The logic of cultural relativism leads directly to proportional representation, which is the underpinning of American civil rights law. Since racial minorities in this country are presumed to constitute distinct cultural groups, relativism generates an expectation of group equality. The government applies an antidiscrimination standard that presumes that, in the absence of discrimination, all groups should be represented in the work force at roughly their proportion in the population. If a company is sued for racial discrimination in hiring, the government or the courts may ask, Why is your company only 5 percent Hispanic when Hispanics are 10 percent of the surrounding population? According to current law, the company is presumed guilty of illegal discrimination. The logic of group equality applies not just to hiring but also to promotion—all companies at all levels are expected to generate the specified racial balances. As Labor Secretary Robert Reich recently complained, "The world at the top of the corporate hierarchy still does not look like America."[73]

Traditionally, American companies are at liberty to hire people at all levels based on their ability to perform. The merit system is under attack, however, whenever it fails to produce the results dictated by proportional representation. Activists argue that merit has been and frequently continues to be a cover for racist exclusion. Drawing on relativism, critics scornfully ask, Whose standards? The argument is that merit is simply that which the dominant culture defines as such; as Deval Patrick, head of the civil rights division of the Justice Department, puts it, minorities refuse to be "trapped in someone else's stereotype."[74] Consequently, advocates of proportional representation contend that merit standards should be adjusted when possible and abandoned if necessary to secure racially balanced results. Moreover, proportional representation extends beyond employment to virtually all sectors of public life. If blacks are 10 percent of the population in a state, the government and the courts expect that in order to be represented as a group, blacks should make up roughly 10 percent of elected officials. If they do not, then the Voting Rights Act can be invoked to reshape electoral districts in such a way that the election of black representatives is virtually assured. In other words, ballot procedures are modified to assure a proportional outcome.

It is easy to see how this logic becomes irresistible. All public policies generally produce results that can be challenged on the basis of proportional representation. Consequently, any policy that does not meet the relativist standard is denounced for its "disparate impact." Whenever recruitment is involved, activists demand that preferences be used to ensure adequate places for "underrepresented groups." Cultural relativism thus becomes the basis for the thoroughgoing racialization of society—a project that is necessary, advocates argue, to combat the effects of deeply entrenched forms of white racism. As Michael Omi and Howard Winant cynically observe, "Race will *always* be at the center of the American experience."[75] In this logic, since racial categories cannot be transcended, they must be institutionalized. "Since race created the problem," African American scholar Franklin Jenifer contends, "it has to be part of the solution."[76]

There is now a civil rights establishment in place that aggressively fights for proportional representation in every sphere of American life. Included in this establishment are such well-funded and influential groups as the National Association for the Advancement of Colored People (NAACP), the National Council for La Raza, the Mexican-American Legal Defense Fund, the Alliance for Justice, People for the American Way, Lawyers' Committee for Civil Rights Under Law, the American Civil Liberties Union, Japanese American Citizens League, National Black Caucus of State Legislators, National Conference of Black Mayors, National Congress for Puerto Rican Rights, National Congress of American Indians, and the National Education Association. More than a hundred civil rights groups unite behind a formidable coalition called the Leadership Conference on Civil Rights, which includes not just racial minorities but feminist and homosexual rights groups as well. Proportional representation is institutionally promoted and enforced by government agencies such as the Equal Employment Opportunity Commission (EEOC), the Office of Federal Contract Compliance Programs (OFCCP), the civil rights divisions of the Justice Department and the Education Department, and the affirmative action apparatus that exists throughout the public sector.

Cultural relativism also provides the intellectual framework that governs multicultural education in the schools and universities. Here multiculturalism is intended as a comprehensive form of antiracist pedagogy. In this analysis the traditional curriculum is inherently biased in favor of the historical, scientific, mathematical, philosophical, and literary accomplishments of Western civilization. "Eurocentrism," defined as an emphasis on the achievements of white males, becomes the newest form of racism. Multicultural advocates argue that the Eurocentric curriculum inferiorizes other cultures and injures the self-esteem of minority students. Using the example of American Indians, the Latin American writer Eduardo Galeano alleges, "Throughout America, the dominant culture acknowledges Indians as objects of study, but denies them as subjects of history: the Indians have folklore, not culture; they practice superstitions, not religions; they speak dialects, not languages; they make handicrafts, not art."[77]

Many multicultural advocates seek a complete renovation of the curriculum, not to eliminate Western influence but to promote among students an enhanced respect for all cultures. At the same time, advocates of multiculturalism seek to expose students to the European crimes of racism, sexism, slavery, imperialism, and colonialism which are alleged to have produced unjust concentrations of power among white men. Activists demand that students learn about each group's victimization at the hands of Europeans: native Americans were genocidally exterminated, Mexicans were colonized and reduced to farm laborers, Asians were excluded and subjected to unjust internment and discrimination. While highlighting the crimes of the West, multicultural advocates seek to emphasize the achievements of non-Western and minority cultures so young people will recognize that they are in no way inferior.

Finally, cultural relativism provides the basis for a strong challenge to American assimilation. Why, activists demand to know, should minority groups surrender their cultures, which are no less legitimate than European culture, and dissolve into a melting pot which may include racist ingredients? They argue that the classical liberal notion of individual rights and the traditional American notion of patriotism premised on a common culture are largely obsolete. They seek to preserve, cherish, and strengthen their ethnic identities, which are said to be the basis of their deepest fulfillments. "Our diversity," argues political scientist Ronald Takaki, "is at the core of what it means for us to be Americans." Thus group membership becomes a central basis for identity and rights.

So a new liberal paradigm is emerging which seeks a transformation of basic American institutions. It seeks to implement new rules of political organization, new regulations for the work force, new approaches to education, indeed a new American dream and a new way of life. It demands a future in which power, resources, and cultural authority are equally or proportionally divided between racial groups, a future predicated upon what diversity consultant Thomas Kochman terms "the decline and fall of the white male."[78]

AN ALTERNATIVE VISION

This book examines the credibility of the claim that racism is to blame for black failure and tests the viability of the multicultural vision being promoted to fight Eurocentrism and institutional racism. My conclusion is that antiracism, in its current form, is intellectually bankrupt and may have run its course. Thus the contemporary phenomena of black rage, white backlash, and liberal despair are part of the debris of a liberal intellectual edifice that is now imploding. Virtually all the contemporary liberal assumptions about the origin of racism, its historical significance, its contemporary effects, and what to do about it are wrong. In a sense, pessimists like Andrew Hacker and Derrick Bell are right: liberal hope is dead. The only questions are how a seemingly noble vision went awry, and whether there are grounds for a restoration of a realistic liberal belief in a solution to the race problem. Here are some of the issues I examine and—admittedly in condensed and simplified form—some of my main findings.

Is racism a Western idea? Yes. Contrary to popular impression, racism is not universal. Indeed there are no clear examples of racism anywhere in the world before the year 1500 A.D. Racism arose in the West during the modern era as a rational and eventually scientific ideology to explain large differences in civilizational development that could not be explained by environment. Thus racism originated not in ignorance and fear but as part of an enlightened enterprise of intellectual discovery. The good news is that since racism had a beginning, it is conceivable that it may have an end.

Was slavery a racist institution? No. Slavery was practiced for thousands of years in virtually all societies: in China, India, Europe, the Arab world, sub-Saharan Africa, and the Americas. In the United States, slave-owning was not confined to whites: American Indians and free blacks owned thousands of slaves. Thus slavery is neither distinctively Western nor racist. What is uniquely Western is the abolition of slavery. The American founders articulated principles of equality and consent which formed the basis for emancipation and the civil rights movement.

Why did white liberals and black activists abandon color blindness as a basis for law and policy? The civil rights movement in which both groups participated embodied from the outset the assumptions of cultural relativism: the presumed equality of all cultures or groups. Martin Luther King, Jr., emphasized one serious problem faced by blacks (racial discrimination) while ignoring another equally serious one (cultural deficiencies) which inhibited black competitiveness. Thus equal rights for blacks could not and did not produce equality of results. Consequently, many liberals and civil rights activists invoked equality of results to prove that white racism continues unabated. They supported affirmative action and racial preferences in order to fight the effects of past and present racism.

Why have charges of racism multiplied while clear evidence of racism has declined? There is now in place a civil rights establishment which has a vested interest in making exaggerated accusations of racism. Promiscuous charges of bigotry are used to cajole and intimidate whites into acquiescing in programs which financially and politically benefit the civil rights establishment. If racism were to disappear, many of these activists and bureaucrats would be out of a job.

Why is the black underclass worse off while the black middle class is better off? As the main beneficiary of affirmative action, blacks with better skills and motivation have moved out of their old neighborhoods, taking with them middle-class norms and social and financial resources. Consequently, in the inner city, civilizing institutions such as the church and small business have greatly eroded. Moreover, the civil rights establishment has a vested interest in the persistence of the underclass, because the scandalous pathologies of poor blacks create the public sympathy that legitimizes continuing subsidies to the black middle class.

Can blacks be racist? Yes. Many liberals find it difficult to recognize black racism because they are ideologically committed to view it as a mere reaction to white racism. In fact African American racism is a coherent ideology of black supremacy, promoted in Afrocentric courses and institutionally embodied in the Nation of Islam. In an increasingly meritocratic society, black racism becomes a rationalization for black failure. Thus African American antagonism is most vehemently directed against groups such as Jews and Asian Americans that have no history of persecuting blacks but that outcompete them.

Does contemporary liberalism have a future? No. Many white liberals are so embarrassed by low levels of academic performance and high levels of criminal and antisocial behavior by blacks, that they are destroying liberal institutions such as free speech, race neutrality, the legal presumption of innocence, and equal rights under the law in order to compel equal results for racial groups. Ultimately white liberals are trapped in a logic in which they must blame themselves for African American problems, and condone the demise of their cherished principles in order to camouflage black failure.

Is racism the main problem facing blacks today? No. The main contemporary obstacle facing African Americans is neither white racism, as many liberals claim, nor black genetic deficiency, as Charles Murray and others imply. Rather it involves destructive and pathological cultural patterns of behavior: excessive reliance on government, conspiratorial paranoia about racism, a resistance to academic achievement as "acting white," a celebration of the criminal and outlaw as authentically black, and the normalization of illegitimacy and dependency. These group patterns arose as a response to past oppression, but they are now dysfunctional and must be modified.

Are you saying that racial discrimination no longer exists? On the contrary. Evidence for the old discrimination has declined, but there are many indications that black cultural pathology has contributed to a new form of discrimination: rational discrimination. High crime rates of young black males, for example, make taxi drivers more reluctant to pick them up, storekeepers more likely to follow them in stores, and employers less willing to hire them. Rational discrimination is based on accurate group generalizations that may nevertheless be unfair to particular members of a group.

If racism is not the main problem for blacks, what is? Liberal antiracism. By asserting the equality of all cultures, cultural relativism prevents liberals from dealing with the nation's contemporary crisis—a civilizational breakdown that affects all groups, but is especially concentrated among the black underclass. Many liberals continue to blame African American pathologies on white racism and oppose all measures that impose civilizational standards on the grounds that they are nothing more than "blaming the victim." Meanwhile, the pathologies persist unchecked.

Can you really demonstrate any of this, and if so, what should be done about it? Read the book.

2

IGNOBLE SAVAGES

The European Origins of Racism

Can the Ethiopian change his skin, or the leopard his spots?
—*Jeremiah* 13:23

The contemporary mood of frustration and pessimism about racism springs from the conviction that American society may never be able to get rid of it. Perhaps, after all, racism is a universal staple of the human psyche, or at least so deeply ingrained in Western consciousness that it is now ineradicable. In order to see whether this melancholy view is warranted, let us turn our basic assumptions about racism into questions. One widespread assumption is that racism is a form of ignorance. "Racism is basically irrational," argues historian Ronald Takaki. "I would say it arises out of ignorance of the Other—of those who are different." Ignorance is thought to result in fear. "Naturally we are afraid of what we don't understand," maintains John Hope Franklin. And what we fear we are said to hate. "You cannot have racism without hostility," says Alvin Poussaint. "I see it as a malignant condition." Poussaint points to two characteristics of the racist: he concocts stereotypes which are false generalizations about other people, and he develops prejudices or irrational hostilities against them.

Contemporary scholars offer three conflicting theories to account for the origin of racism. One is that racism is a universal problem. "What society can claim to be free of racism?" sociologist Todd Gitlin asks rhetorically. "It arises out of a primordial instinct, which is tribalism or xenophobia." An alternative view is that racism is a product of slavery, and developed out of the need to rationalize enslavement. "Slavery seems to have fixed the notion of black inferiority in the minds of us whites," Andrew Hacker suggests. A third claim, made by some black nationalists and Afrocentrists, is that racism is a peculiarly Western or white pathology that is embedded in the English language. A writer for the *Los Angeles Times* contends, "Many of us fall victim to racism because the language we use keeps it alive."[1] Frantz Fanon argued that for English-speaking people "the torturer is the black man, Satan is black, one talks of shadows, when one is dirty one is black. . . . In Europe, whether concretely or symbolically, the black man stands for the bad side of the character."[2] Could it be a coincidence, activists like Fanon ask, that we have terms such as blackmail, blackball, black Mass, blacklist, black magic, black market, black sheep, and blackguard, all of which suggest wickedness, disgrace, or corruption, whereas whiteness is perennially associated with purity and goodness? Even the term "white lie," Paula Rothenberg points out in her textbook *Racism and Sexism,* refers to an untruth "not intended to cause harm."[3] And Christine Bolt regards it as highly significant that "in English literature, the most famous black beauty is not a human, but a horse."[4]

Despite some disagreements over the origins of racism, many contemporary sources agree about the best way to fight it. "I don't think we'll ever be rid of racism, but we can try to control its effects through education," Hacker says. "Racists are sorely in need of enlightenment," remarks Poussaint, adding, "We need to raise their consciousness." Philosopher Richard Rorty recommends sympathetic exposure to the lives of strangers, in order to diminish white insecurities that lead to racism.[5] Black political scientist Ronald Walters argues that "since people are taught to hate, educators have a responsibility to try and counter that socialization." African American scholar Charles Willie contends that racists require a kind of therapy: "It is the unique responsibility of educators to diagnose the problem and prescribe the treatment, just like a doctor in an epidemic."[6]

In fact, racism is not a universal staple of the human condition. Racism did not always exist in the West. Nor is racism a product of slavery. Moreover, racism is not part of the English language, and terms like "blackmail" and "black sheep" have nothing to do with racism. An examination of the historical record reveals that racism did have a beginning. Although it can be found in embryonic form among the Chinese and the Arabs in the late Middle Ages, racism is a modern and Western ideology. Racism developed prior to slavery although it was later reinforced by slavery. Far from being the product of irrationality, fear and hatred, racism developed in Europe as a product of Enlightenment, part of a rational and scientific project to understand the world. Racism was inspired by the European voyages abroad, which produced an unprecedented project to classify and rank the diversity of the world's plants, animals, and peoples. For European travelers, missionaries, and ethnologists, racism provided a coherent account of large civilizational differences that could not be attributed to climate and were thus considered intrinsic. Racism originated as a theory of Western civilizational superiority.

WHAT IS RACISM?

It is hard to disagree with Andrew Hacker's claim that "something called racism obviously exists,"[7] but what exactly does racism mean? It is not unusual to see the term used in various ways, but the basic definition remains clear: racism is an ideology of intellectual or moral superiority based upon the biological characteristics of race. Moreover, racism typically entails a willingness to discriminate based upon a perceived hierarchy of superior and inferior races. According to *Webster's New World Dictionary,* racism is a "doctrine or teaching . . . that claims to find racial differences in character and intelligence, that asserts the superiority of one race over another, that seeks to maintain the supposed purity of a race," as well as "any program or practice of racial discrimination or segregation based on such beliefs."[8] Most scholarly and popular definitions of racism concur.[9] Martin Luther King, Jr., defined racism as a "doctrine of the congenital inferiority and worthlessness of a people."[10] A common definition is given by George Fredrickson in *White Supremacy:*

> Racism is a mode of thought that offers a particular explanation for the fact that population groups that can be distinguished by ancestry are likely to differ in culture, status and power. Racists make the claim that such differences are due mainly to immutable genetic factors and not to environmental or historical circumstance.[11]

From these definitions the main features of racism emerge. In order to be a racist, you must first believe in the existence of biologically distinguishable groups or races. Second, you must rank these races in terms of superiority and inferiority. Third, you must hold these rankings to be intrinsic or innate. Finally, you typically seek to use them as the basis for discrimination, segregation, or the denial of rights extended to other human beings.

The prevailing view, shared by virtually everyone who writes about the topic, is that racism (like sexism or homophobia) is a product of irrational antipathy. This notion of racism as a kind of pathology or dementia is a crucial and virtually uncontested core of the modern psychological portrait of the racist. Yet this assumption raises an historical dilemma: if racism is a product of ignorance, fear, and hate, why is it the case that beliefs most people would unhesitatingly consider racist were shared by many of the most enlightened, courageous, and humane figures in America and in the West until only a few decades ago? It is hard to deny that many of the most eminent European and American religious leaders, philanthropists, philosophers, scientists, and statesmen were, by modern criteria, outright racists. One may say that racism was the conventional wisdom of the past several centuries, just as antiracism is the conventional wisdom now. Nothing could be more ridiculous than to imagine that three of the leading philosophers of Western civilization—Hume, Kant, and Hegel—were cowed and blinded by simple superstitious fright. They weren't "threatened" by blacks. Consequently we must ask: why did they believe what they did? Here are their views:

> I am apt to suspect the Negroes, and in general all the other species of men, to be naturally inferior to the whites. There never was any civilized nation of any other complexion than white, nor even any individual eminent in action or speculation. No ingenious manufactures among them, no arts, no sciences. . . . Such a uniform and constant difference could not happen, in so many countries and ages, if nature had not made an original distinction betwixt these breeds of men.
>
> —David Hume, 1748[12]

> The Negroes of Africa have received from nature no intelligence that rises above the foolish. The difference between the two races is thus a substantial one: it appears to be just as great in respect of the faculties of the mind as in color.
>
> —Immanuel Kant, 1764[13]

The Negro race has perfect contempt for humanity. Tyranny is regarded as no wrong, and cannibalism is looked upon as quite customary and proper. . . . The polygamy of the Negroes has frequently for its object the having of many children, to be sold, every one of them, into slavery. . . . The essence of humanity is freedom. . . . At this point we leave Africa, not to mention it again. For it is no historical part of the world; it has no movement or development to exhibit.

—Georg Hegel, 1837[14]

For mainstream scholars today, these views pose an intellectual problem, not because they place revered Western thinkers in a bad light, but because they call the widely shared premises of modern antiracism into question. Is it possible that everything we take for granted about racism is itself a product of unquestioned assumption, of irrational prejudice? Challenging the popular view, historian Oscar Handlin argues that "racism grew out of truth-seeking explorations into the nature of man and of human society."[15] Winthrop Jordan, author of *White Over Black,* a classic account of European racial attitudes, says that "racism developed in conjunction with Enlightenment, not in resistance to it." Let us investigate whether these assertions are true, and whether much of what we think we know about race is false.

THE UNKINDNESS OF STRANGERS

Irrationality, fear, and hatred are all human qualities and, as such, universal. Consequently if racism were a product of unreasonable insecurity and hostility, we would expect to find it in virtually all societies. In fact, scholars vehemently disagree about whether racism is universal. Perhaps the predominant group maintains that it is, while other scholars argue that its origins are Western, locating them in the ancient Greeks or in transatlantic slavery. Consider some statements of the claim that racism is universal.

- Joel Kovel in *White Racism* suggests that "racist phenomena are ubiquitous throughout history" and that "racial hatred is built into human nature."[16]
- Racism is "an ancient form of behavior that is probably found worldwide," the French scholar Tzvetan Todorov asserts.[17]
- Harvard paleontologist Stephen Jay Gould suspects that racial prejudice is "as old as recorded history."[18]

• In a well-known textbook, Thomas Gossett claims to have discovered racist sentiments in the ancient civilizations of Egypt, China, India, and Greece.[19]

How could we possibly know whether racism exists and has existed in every society? No one who espouses the universal view of the origins of racism has made a systematic historical study to identify the presence of racism in all human cultures. Typically, scholars make a kind of grand global survey, foraging for facts that seem to suggest animus and conflict between groups, which they cite to demonstrate the universality of racism.

• Some Chinese historians of the Han dynasty in the third century B.C. describe their encounters with savage people "who greatly resemble the monkeys from whom they are descended."[20] The Chinese of the T'ang period seem to show unmitigated contempt for the nakedness and primitivism of the dark islanders of the south.[21]
• In ancient India, the invading Aryans described themselves as "nobly born" and the dark-skinned natives as Anaryan (not-Aryan) or "dasa" (slave), a fact which seems to give the Indian caste system a racial character.[22]
• The majestic Zulus in Africa have historically linked other tribes with wild beasts, and describe the rival Sothos as "those having the color of a yellowish claypot."[23]
• Muslim travelers during the Middle Ages frequently made derogatory comments about blacks; one was the eleventh century scholar Sa'id al-Andalusi, who found Ethiopians and Nubians "fickle, foolish, ignorant, and lacking in self-control."[24]

These examples seem to establish decisively the presence of color consciousness in various cultures of the ancient world. They also indicate that some Chinese, Indians, Zulus, Greeks, and Muslims did not practice the modern art of euphemism: they spoke with brutal candor about aliens and outsiders. We may reasonably conclude that convictions of superiority seem to be widely held by ancient societies. But do these adverse sentiments amount to racism? We know that many ancient cultures noticed racial differences, and also held their own society to be superior. But it remains to be seen whether people in the ancient world linked physical differences to cultural superiority.

Is the Indian caste system racist? At first glance, the system displays many of the features that would be expected in a racist society. The caste system is hierarchical and hereditary. Lower castes are stigmatized as inferior. There are strict prohibitions on social contact between members of higher and lower castes. But here is the crucial problem: all the members of the various castes—brahmin, kshatriya, vaishiya, and shudra—belong to the same race. In other words, the caste system erects religious and social distinctions among people who share similar features and could not be easily distinguished simply on the basis of appearance. The caste system may have initially entailed a color hierarchy, in that the conquering Aryans were lighter than the indigenous Dravidians, but those differences were greatly blurred by the effects of climate and intermarriage, so that caste, as it evolved, largely detached itself from physical features. Many Indians today, as is the case in other parts of the world, retain a general esthetic preference for light skin in choosing a marriage partner. But Indian scholars agree that it makes no sense to speak of members of various castes as belonging to different races. Deploring the tendency of Western scholars to interpret the caste system through their familiar framework of racism, Rabindranath Tagore, India's Nobel laureate, wrote, "There was no *racial* difference between Brahmin and Kshatriya." Moreover, Hindus typically ascribe caste status not to biological features but to good or bad actions performed in a previous life.[25]

The other examples prove equally problematic. The ancient Chinese were highly xenophobic, regarding their "Middle Kingdom" as the center of the universe, and all foreigners as worthy sycophants and worshippers at the feet of the Chinese emperor, who ruled with a "mandate from heaven." Reflecting the relatively high state of Chinese civilization, for centuries members of the Chinese ruling class regarded Europeans as barbarians. The problem with pronouncing this attitude to be racist, however, is that the Chinese were just as hostile to the Japanese, the Koreans, and other subjugated Asian peoples who looked very much like them, as they were toward foreigners who were white and brown and black. The Chinese never developed a racial hierarchy among peoples or a specifically biological basis for claims of superiority. The Chinese, we may say, did not discriminate based on race: they held themselves to be superior to everyone.[26]

The Zulus, a conquering force in southern Africa, were famously ethnocentric, regarding their own group as the center of the universe. But so were the Sothos, the Dinka, the Fulani, the Wolof, the Hausa, and many other African nations.[27] Moreover, the differences italicized in tribal conflict typically had nothing to do with color, since that quality the combatants had in common. For instance, the main physical trait dividing the feuding Tutsi and Hutu tribes of modern Rwanda and Burundi is height.

The Muslim writer Sa'id al-Andalusi's views about Ethiopians and Nubians must be placed in the context of his even harsher appraisal of white Europeans, particularly Slavs. "Their temperaments are frigid, their humors raw . . . they lack keenness of understanding and clarity of intelligence, and are overcome by ignorance and dullness, lack of discernment, and stupidity."[28] Typical of Muslim writing in the Middle Ages, al-Andalusi's work comments harshly on all communities that are perceived not to possess the civilizing light of Islam, regardless of their race or color. Al-Andalusi is entirely in the tradition epitomized by a tenth century Islamic writer:

> The people of Iraq have sound minds, commendable passions, balanced natures, and high proficiency in every art, together with well-proportioned limbs, well-compounded humors, and a pale brown color, which is the most apt and proper color. They are the ones who are done to a turn in the womb. They do not come out with something between blond, blanched and leprous coloring, such as the infants dropped from the wombs of the women of the Slavs and others of similar light complexion; nor are they overdone in the womb until they are burned, so that the child comes out black, murky, malodorous, stinking, and crinkly-haired, with uneven limbs, deficient minds, and depraved passions, such as the Ethiopians and other blacks who resemble them. The Iraqis are neither half-baked dough nor burned crust, but between the two.[29]

Today, of course, such theorizing is rare, but it was widespread in the ancient world. Anthropologists have discovered precisely the same account of the origins of skin color in African and American Indian cultures—only in each case the details are adjusted so that the ideal complexion belongs to the group espousing the belief.[30]

ETHNOCENTRISM VERSUS RACISM

What emerges from these examples is a crucial distinction that anthropologists and historians make between racism on the one hand, and tribalism or ethnocentrism on the other. While racism refers to the hierarchal ranking of human beings based on biological characteristics, tribalism and ethnocentrism are nothing more than an intense preference for one's own group over strangers. Ethnocentrism comes from the Greek word *ethnos,* which means "people" or "nation." Ethnic groups are usually related by blood, kinship, or a common history, but these ties do not have to be racial—frequently they are not. Nationality, religion, shared traditions, and mere geographical proximity are much more common denominators for tribalism and ethnocentrism than is race. While racism is necessarily rooted in biology, ethnocentrism is typically rooted in culture.

Tribalism and ethnocentrism are universal. All human communities from the beginning of time, whether primitive or advanced, Western or non-Western, are self-centered, culturally narcissistic, and regard strangers with caution, if not aggression. Confusing what is natural with what is conventional, we are all tempted to establish our own ways as the norm for all humanity, and to regard the customs of others as outlandish, unnecessary, even absurd.[31] Nor do our sympathies easily extend to strangers: as the Russian proverb has it, "The tears of strangers are only water." Predictably one finds ethnocentrism in highly advanced civilizations which look condescendingly upon their more primitive neighbors,[32] but it is equally characteristic of simple and primitive peoples. Anthropologist Ruth Benedict points out that the formula "I belong to the elect" is characteristic of agrarian and premodern societies, many of whose tribal names, in their own languages, mean "human beings" or "men," in contrast to outsiders, who are regarded as less than human, and eligible for hunting or enslavement.[33] Sociologist Orlando Patterson writes, "The words tribesmen have for strange peoples always emphasize their non-humanity."[34] Tribalism may therefore be described as a strong group loyalty, which we feel in varying degrees for our family, our children, our close relatives, our religious group, our country of origin.[35] Groups, like individuals, tend to be self-interested; ethnocentrism parallels egocentrism. This group feeling creates solidarity among inhabitants of a community, which many scholars argue is a necessary basis for defense of the group and cooperation among its members.[36]

Some scholars maintain that ethnocentrism is a survival instinct rooted in evolutionary biology.[37] In *The Selfish Gene,* Richard Dawkins argues that kinship and fellow-feeling among groups has a Darwinian function: it is an expression of genetic self-perpetuation that forms the basis for natural selection.[38] Pierre Van Den Berghe argues that "nepotism between kinsmen" is an evolutionary mechanism for individual and group survival.[39] Other scholars such as Bradford Cornell argue that ethnocentrism serves a cultural purpose. Cornell's argument is that ethnocentrism springs from the human recognition that it is easier to make distinctions among those whose appearance, habits, and culture are recognizable; foreigners are all alike in their unfamiliarity. "As a result," Cornell argues, "when making key decisions such as selecting a mate or choosing friends, a person is likely to draw from the population of similar individuals."[40] Whether biological or cultural, anthropologists are virtually unanimous in proclaiming tribalism, along with supernaturalism and the incest taboo, to be a universal characteristic of human communities.[41]

Ethnocentrism and tribalism are typically accompanied by provincialism or narrow-mindedness, and xenophobia, or fear of foreigners, but these too are not the same as racism. Conflicts between Serb and Croatian, Sikh and Hindu, Basque and Spanish, Protestant and Catholic, English and Irish, Turk and Armenian are undoubtedly tribal conflicts characterized by ethnocentric loyalties, yet the groups pitted against each other have the same skin color and belong to the same race. Some of the greatest wars in history, including the American Civil War, the Hundred Years War in Europe, the 1948 Hindu-Muslim massacres in India, the Indochina hecatomb of the 1970s, and two global wars in the twentieth century have largely been wars involving internecine conflict between people who shared a common race and (to some extent) cultural ancestry. Thus although racism may be viewed as a subset of tribalism, the two are conceptually distinct.

Similarly racism and anti-Semitism are quite different, a distinction often missed because both are associated with Adolf Hitler, who was both a racist and an anti-Semite. Let us briefly examine the history and origins of anti-Semitism to show how it is an ideology separate from racism. In the ancient world, Jews were recognized as a tribe, like many others. The Romans persecuted Jews, but they persecuted Christians even more.[42] Later, over a period of centuries, Christians persecuted Jews, not on account of their race but on account of their religion, which was viewed as responsible for deicide as well as a blasphemous rejection of Christ, the messiah. For the most part, during the Middle Ages, Jews who converted to Christianity were received as full members of the church.[43] We see an indication of this in Shakespeare's *Merchant of Venice:* Shylock's daughter converts to Christianity and is fully accepted by the community.

In the modern era, anti-Jewish sentiment became secularized. Many scholars trace the roots of secular anti-Semitism to fifteenth century Spain. On March 31, 1492, shortly after defeating the Moors and recapturing Granada, King Ferdinand of Aragon and Queen Isabella of Castille sought to consolidate Christian influence in their domain by expelling the Jews from Spain. The queen's expulsion decree applied to the 300,000 Jews who did not practice the Christian faith and was motivated by theological antagonism. But many Jews avoided the edict by converting to Christianity, or at least outwardly professing the Catholic faith. Privately, a large number continued to practice Judaism.[44] Increasingly, the Spanish people, the church, and the monarchy suspected the so-called new Christians of covert infidelity. These fears predated the edict: as early as 1480 a number of well-known new Christians were caught holding a seder on the first night of Passover. According to Solomon Grayzel in *The History of the Jews,* Jews began to be accused of being "not loyal Christians, but secret Jews."[45] As a result, new laws were passed restricting and discriminating against Jews not on account of their faith but on account of their blood. The new Christians were called "marranos" which meant "pigs." This was "a new kind of anti-Semitism," writes David Brion Davis, in which marranos "were never free from persecution as crypto-Jews."[46] For the first time, historian Robert Wistrich argues, European Christians adopted an attitude "which held that Jewish blood was a hereditary taint which could not be eradicated by baptism."[47]

Since then, there have been many outbreaks of secular anti-Semitism, notably in France during the late nineteenth century as evidenced in the infamous Dreyfus case. In such cases, Jews were no longer terrorized because of their religious views but because of who they were. Hitler's Holocaust was, of course, the culmination of the demonization of the Jews, leading to a campaign of genocide. Yet the Jews of Germany belonged to the same white race as their oppressors, and features used to caricature Jews, such as a long nose, were the features that the Nazis used to identify Aryans. Precisely because Jews enjoyed a kind of protective coloration and could not be easily distinguished from other Germans, the Nazis were compelled to use yellow stars, tattoos, and other insignia to mark them for discrimination and extermination.[48] Even though anti-Semitism and racism are forms of dehumanization, both have distinctive careers in Western history. At crucial points, as we will see, these careers intersect. But in general, as Abraham Foxman, national director of the Anti-Defamation League of B'nai B'rith, argues, anti-

Semitism is unique. "Jews are a religious and a cultural group, not a racial group," Foxman argues. "Our persecutors come in all colors." In recognition of this distinction, this study at several points covers the subject of anti-Semitism where relevant, but it is primarily an examination of the distinguishable phenomenon of racism.

In short, those who assert that racism is universal and can be detected in all societies throughout history are wrong. While we have located considerable evidence of tribalism, ethnocentrism, and anti-Semitism, these do not amount to racism. The us-against-them mentality is universal, but it is often based on differences of religion, tradition, and other social features, not on biology. Sociologist Pierre Van Den Berghe rightly concludes: "Racism, unlike ethnocentrism, is not a universal phenomenon. Only a few human groups have deemed themselves superior because of the content of their gonads."[49]

RACISM AND SLAVERY

If racism is not strictly universal, perhaps it originated, as some scholars suggest, as an ideological handmaiden of slavery.[50] Marxist scholars frequently argue that racism arose as a convenient system for the Western bourgeoisie to justify the merchandizing and exploitation of black Africans.

- Eric Williams in *Capitalism and Slavery* claims that slavery developed entirely for economic reasons: "Slavery was not born of racism; rather, racism was the consequence of slavery."[51]
- In *The African Slave Trade* Basil Davidson writes that "race contempt crept in when free men could justify their material interests by the scorn they had for slaves."[52]

Popular writers such as Salman Rushdie and Lerone Bennett echo these sentiments.[53] On one point these writers are surely right: over time in America, the practice of slavery supported and perpetuated racism. It is not hard to see how white Americans who enslaved Africans for hundreds of years would develop a doctrine of inferiority to rationalize the oppression. Once transatlantic slavery developed, as Winthrop Jordan argues, a symbiotic and mutually reinforcing relationship evolved between slavery and racism.[54] But it does not follow that slavery can account for the *origin* of racism. Indeed racism burgeoned and flourished in Europe from the fifteenth through the twentieth century even in places such as the Scandinavian countries where there were few slaves, or none at all. Traveling in America during the early nineteenth century, Alexis de Tocqueville observed that hostility to blacks was much stronger in the states where slavery was virtually extinct than in the slaveholding regions.[55] The black abolitionist Frederick Douglass agreed: "Prejudice against color is stronger North than South."[56] Racial bias against blacks seems to have existed before transatlantic slavery and indeed to have constituted one of the reasons that Europeans chose to transport Africans as slaves to the new world. It is surely significant, after all, that Europeans did not persist in enslaving Indians or other groups but ended up with an exclusively black slave population.

Racism is habitually equated with slavery today because the two practices evolved together in America. But in this respect the American experience is historically unique. As Orlando Patterson demonstrates in *Slavery and Social Death,* slavery is a universal institution:

> Slavery has existed from the dawn of human history right down to the 20th century, in the most primitive of human societies and in the most civilized. There is no region on earth that has not at some time harbored the institution. Probably there is no group of people whose ancestors were not at one time slaves or slaveholders.[57]

Slaves were usually acquired by kidnapping, as payments of tribute, debt, and taxation, and by inheritance. People sometimes sold themselves or their children into slavery to relieve poverty and starvation. By far the most common method of acquiring slaves was by taking captives in war. Indeed in many societies slavery was regarded as the humane alternative to the accepted practice of killing captives: frequently the male combatants were slain, and women and children spared for use as concubines and slaves. Hardly a European invention, slavery of this sort was widely practiced in Asia, Africa, and the Middle East.

The ancient Sumerians, Babylonians, Egyptians and Assyrians all practiced slavery, and defined slaves as property. Indian temples regularly used slaves, and India's oldest legal treatise, the Laws of Manu, which dates to the second century B.C., prescribes slavery as a punishment for failure to pay a fine. The Greeks and Romans employed slaves as domestic servants, craftsmen and artisans, common laborers, gladiators and soldiers. In ancient Burma, northern Europe, and the Near East, slaves were also used as articles of trade and sometimes as a form of currency in place of money. The ancient Chinese used both domestic and imported slaves and customarily buried them alive with their deceased masters.[58]

Yet although the Chinese, the Indians, the Greeks, the Romans, the Arabs, black Africans, and native Americans all placed human beings into bondage, the remarkable fact about slavery in the ancient world is that it had little or nothing to do with race.[59] Indeed scholars of the subject conclude that most of the slaves in ancient India, China, Europe, and Africa belonged to the same race as their owners.[60] Of the total slave population in the five centuries before Christ, the largest number were probably white slaves.[61] The term "slave" actually derives from the term "Slav," a reference to the large number of white slaves captured from that region of Central Europe.[62] In Greece and Rome, black Ethiopians were so highly prized that they were often spared manual labor and reserved for personal service or for entertainment roles as dancers and jugglers.[63] During the Middle Ages, in the cosmopolitan slave markets of Baghdad and Constantinople, traders erected platforms for the display of black slaves, white slaves, brown slaves, and yellow slaves.[64] In Europe, during this period, black slaves were relatively rare, were often treated better than Muslim slaves, and sometimes commanded a higher price.[65] In Renaissance Italy, where white slaves were numerous and easy to obtain, young black boys were sometimes kept as pets by wealthy families in Mantua and Milan.[66]

Slaves were inevitably degraded on account of their social status.[67] As was the practice everywhere, slaves suffered the physical pain and psychic humiliation of being subject to the arbitrary will of another. The suggestion that any society practiced "benign slavery," Patterson declares, is a myth promoted by those who would seek to justify systematic oppression. Rather, Patterson argues that the universal status of the slave was one of "social death," a total deprivation of honor, not on account of race or color, but on account of slave status. It is true that slaves were slightly better off in societies where they bore a physical likeness to their masters. The reason is that if they ever escaped or were emancipated, they could often be integrated into the free population, without continuing to endure the stigma of slavery. And manumissions, although hardly typical, were frequent in the ancient world; sometimes they were the main technique of assimilation of captive peoples.[68] In a careful study, Patterson found no relation between racial differences and the slave manumission rate.[69] Surveying the historical record on slavery and racism, Pierre Van Den Berghe concludes, "Slavery has often existed without a trace of racism. Conversely, racism can develop and persist in the absence of slavery."[70]

WERE THE ANCIENT GREEKS RACIST?

A third possibility for the origin of racism, promoted mainly by Afrocentric scholars, is that racism is a uniquely white ideology which can be traced to the beginnings of Western civilization. Afrocentrist Na'im Akbar proclaims racism "a Euro-American pathology."[71] Marimba Ani contends that "racism is endemic to European history," arising out of a white "supremacist ideology" that has proved fearful and aggressive "since its inception in the Indo-European hordes of the North."[72] Michael Bradley in *The Iceman Inheritance* argues that whites have a historic proclivity for racism which has caused most of the world's problems:

> Racism is a predisposition of but one race of mankind—the white race. Nuclear war, environmental pollution, resource rape . . . all are primary threats to our survival and all are the results of peculiarly Caucasoid behavior, Caucasoid values, Caucasoid psychology. There is no way to avoid the truth. The problem with the world is white men.[73]

These formulations are somewhat extreme, but this does not mean they are wrong. We can verify the charge that racism has always existed among whites by investigating the racial attitudes of the Greeks, the Romans, and early Christians—three of the most formative influences on the West. The question of whether these groups were racist is examined in two books, *Blacks in Antiquity* and *Before Color Prejudice,* by the African American scholar Frank Snowden.[74] An emeritus professor of classics at Howard University, Snowden is perhaps the leading scholar in the United States on how blacks were viewed in ancient civilization. Analyzing the literary, numismatic, artistic, and archaeological evidence of encounters between Europeans and Ethiopians in the ancient Mediterranean, Snowden argues that despite the awareness of color differences in the ancient world, differences that were acknowledged and discussed in frank and sometimes pungent fashion, neither the ancient Greeks nor the early Christians espoused anything resembling a theory of racial superiority. Indeed, by and large the two groups espoused a positive view of the African blacks they knew best—the Ethiopians.

For Homer, blacks were the blameless of the gods. Diodorus mentioned their widespread reputation for religious piety. Seneca found them notable for their courage and love of freedom. Lucian noted that in astrological knowledge they were the wisest of men. Herodotus, the first European to comment on the physical appearance of Ethiopians, described them as the most handsome of men. Martial noted that while he was pursued by a woman whiter than a swan, he sought the affections of one blacker than pitch. Snowden quotes a Greek epigrammatist, Asclepiades, "Gazing at her beauty I melt like wax before the fire. If she is black, what is that to me? So are coals, but when we burn them, they shine like rosebuds." Snowden concludes that manumissions were open to black slaves as much as slaves of any other color.

Like countless other peoples, the Greeks were ethnocentric and regarded aliens as "barbarians," an onomatopoeia apparently derived from the incomprehensible bar-bar-bar sound made by foreigners. Yet the epithet applied to anyone who could not speak Greek, and who was therefore considered primitive.[75] The Greeks did not describe as barbarians anyone on account of their skin color, and Snowden says there is no evidence that blacks were systematically associated with unintelligence. Strabo, he points out, concluded that the most barbarian people in the world were the Irish. Similarly, Martin Bernal remarks in *Black Athena* that Greeks, although haughty about their own accomplishments, were curious about and respectful of black Ethiopians, whereas they considered northern Europeans to be utterly lacking in the rudiments of civilization.[76] Eventually, as Edward Gibbon chronicles, those snow-white barbarians from the north would plunder and destroy Greco-Roman civilization.

The Greeks were well aware of variations in features and skin color, Snowden says. They certainly did not confuse Egyptians and Ethiopians; in fact, Snowden maintains that they could distinguish between the physical characteristics of dark-skinned Asians and black Africans. Like many other people in the ancient world, however, the Greeks were what we may call environmentalists: they typically attributed differences of appearance and of custom to the influence of geography and climate. Ptolemy found some of the habits of black Africans primitive, but blamed them not on natural deficiencies but on the enervating and oppressive temperature of the region. In general, the Greeks attributed the dark skin of the Ethiopian to the sun's heat, as the famous legend of Phaeton illustrates. Apparently Phaeton, son of the sun god Helios, insisted on borrowing his father's fiery chariot for a day. He lost control of the horses and drove the chariot too close to the earth in some parts, charring the inhabitants black; in other places he steered too far from land, so that the people turned pale from the cold.[77]

Among the Greek poets, Snowden found instances of good-natured joking about differences of color and appearance. Miscegenation, he says, was sometimes a subject of comedy, typically about the master who came home to discover that his wife had produced a brown infant who looked suspiciously like his house servant. Plutarch relates the case of a Greek woman whose black baby caused her to be accused of adultery, but the controversy subsided when an investigation of her lineage revealed that she was the great-granddaughter of an Ethiopian. Snowden argues that the ancients typically did not frown on intermarriage between whites and blacks, that black skin was not a sign of inferiority, and that Greeks and Romans noted differences of color and appearance in their paintings and literature but attached no particular moral or social significance to it. "The ancients," Snowden concludes, "are a model on which we could start to reform our own racially intoxicated society."

One of the clearest expressions of the Greek understanding of racism and slavery is evident in the work of Aristotle. "It is clear that some are by nature free, and others are by nature slaves," Aristotle writes in *The Politics*, "and for these latter the condition of slavery is both beneficial and just."[78] This statement is sometimes cited as an early expression of Western prejudice. Aristotle also denounces virtually all non-Greeks as barbarians. Yet although he supports the institution of slavery, Aristotle distinguishes between natural slavery and conventional slavery, recognizing that many foreign people are enslaved purely as a result of accidents such as shipwreck, kidnapping, or being captured in wars. Aristotle makes a crucial distinction between free men who are capable of being citizens and slaves who are by nature incapable of assuming personal and civic responsibilities. Aristotle writes, "There is an interest in common between master and slave . . . when they are by nature fitted for this relationship, but not when the relationship arises out of the use of force."[79]

In justifying slaves and condemning barbarians, Aristotle shows no interest in group differences of appearance or color. His theories of servitude and citizenship are ethnocentric, but they have no racial basis. Indeed Aristotle reserved some of his harshest cultural observations for Northern Europeans, the English in particular, whom he regarded as "incapable of ruling over others" and "wanting in intelligence and skill."[80]

Rather, like many Greek thinkers, Aristotle drew a basic distinction between civilization and barbarism. Since human beings are naturally social, Aristotle believed that the uncivilized person lacked virtue. "He is the most savage, the most unrighteous, and the worst in regard to sexual license and gluttony."[81] Aristotle viewed civilization as a rare phenomenon, only made possible by the most favorable circumstances, including the right arrangement of society and government. For Aristotle the Greeks represented the highest stage of civilization, but Aristotle thought that captured and enslaved non-Greeks were capable of civilization with the training provided by Greek life.

Like Plato, Aristotle makes another crucial distinction: between what is natural and what is conventional. The human ability to speak is natural, for example, but the particular languages we speak are conventional—the product of custom and early training. Familiar with the diversity of human customs, Aristotle argued that the civilized life requires that we learn to live "in accordance with nature." This requires a philosophical inquiry into human nature and its constitutive purpose. The tension between nature and convention (which we now call "nurture" or "environment") in explaining human and racial differences has persisted throughout Western history. For Aristotle, nature offers a crucial basis for the critique of convention—for deciding whether our traditional or customary ways of living can be rationally and morally justified. Despite his justification of slavery, Aristotle's distinction between natural and conventional slavery provides the basis for *resistance* to slavery, since Aristotle only defends a certain type of slavery. Indeed others in the ancient world, the Sophists and later the Stoics, classified slavery as an entirely conventional institution, sustained only by might, not right. The playwright Euripides acknowledged that slaves were often superior in talent and character to their masters. The cynic Diogenes affirmed this point: when captured by pirates in Crete and taken to be sold, he pointed to a Corinthian buyer and pleaded, "Sell me to him, he needs a master."[82]

In the Christian era which supplanted the classical one in Europe, scholars have found lots of evidence of prejudice and hostility, so that Christianity today is routinely criticized for encouraging, if not inventing, racism, sexism, and homophobia, and providing a spiritual justification for slavery and colonialism. Forrest Wood's *The Arrogance of Faith* is a wholesale assault on a religion that Wood alleges "has been fundamentally racist in its theology, organization and practice." Yet Wood's findings seem to surprise even the author. "In none of the biblical passages directly or obliquely sanctioning slavery could one find a specific reference to race or color," he writes. Moreover, "Despite the association of darkness with all that was evil and demonic, early Christians did not, in fact, exhibit a negative attitude toward black people generally."[83]

For Christians, the primary distinction was between the believer and the infidel.[84] As Saint Augustine (who was himself an African) emphasizes, distinguishing between the "City of God" and the "City of Man," it is through the instrument of conversion that all may be equal as children of God and as citizens in Christian civilization.[85] Indeed the religious commitment of the early Christians generated a passionate universalism, reflected in Paul's letter to the Galatians, "There is neither Jew nor Greek, there is neither bond nor free, there is neither male nor female, for ye are all one in Christ Jesus."[86] For the convert to the faith, racial and even cultural differences were superseded by Christian brotherhood. No group was excluded: as Martin Bernal has pointed out, early Christian and medieval illustrations routinely portray one of the magi who came to worship the infant Christ as black.[87]

This brings us to the issue of color symbolism. The early Christians appropriated pagan images of the sun as a source of life, and light as a symbol of divinity. Blackness is regularly deployed in the Bible and early Christian writings as a sign of evil and sin. Frank Snowden argues, however, that in contrast to contemporary prejudices about color, for the early Christians the symbolic attachment of darkness and evil in no way implied that black people were cast outside the orbit of salvation or Christian acceptance. Origen, one of the fathers of the early Christian church, argued that human souls are initially black like the Ethiopians, but through divine redemption all souls can be brightened. In fact Origen contrasts the Ethiopian's natural hue, caused by the heat of the sun, with blackness in the soul, caused by sin and dereliction. In the same vein, Augustine urged Christians to go to the remotest corners of the world, including darkest Ethiopia, to spread the light of the Christian message.[88]

We may therefore conclude that the Greeks, Romans, and early Christians made crucial distinctions—between nature and custom, between civilization and barbarism, between salvation and damnation—that would later be invoked to justify racism. But there is no racism in the distinctions themselves, nor can the ancient and early Christian societies of the West be rightly accused of color prejudice.

THE CHINESE AND ARAB VIEW OF BLACKS

It should not be imagined that the absence of racism in the ancient world can be easily explained by the lack of civilizational contact between peoples. In fact, such contacts have existed for two millennia. Human beings have never lived in total cultural isolation; from time immemorial, they have ventured beyond immediate borders to conquer, to trade, to spread their religion and culture, to resettle, and to seek adventure. In the first century before Christ, the famous Silk Roads were opened which eventually extended from China to northern India; to Persia; to Mesopotamia; to Egypt; to the Roman empire. Over the next several centuries, merchants in China, India, Europe, and North Africa engaged in a sophisticated cosmopolitan trade which included horses, wool, silk, lacquer, pearls, glass, and precious gems.[89]

Yet such early contacts did not generate widespread convictions of intrinsic superiority, mainly because these civilizational exchanges in the ancient world were transacted between nations that had developed the economic, military, and cultural resources to project across continental chasms. As pointed out by William McNeill and Jerry Bentley, who have studied early cross-cultural encounters, only the richest and most powerful civilizations of the period could sustain trade and contact over great distances. The most primitive cultures remained in relative isolation, except when they were invaded and occupied. Most people ventured abroad to trade and to conquer. Yet even the merchants and combatants could not have been unaware of the fragility of their enterprise, which carried such risks that no one could possibly consider any military or trade advantage to be enduring or permanent.[90] There was no shortage of arrogance on the part of the Arabs, Europeans, Indians, and Chinese, but no group was strong enough to entirely dominate the others, and so their hubris was tempered by respect among rivals of comparable strength. This began to change in the modern world, when Western science and technology provided a decisive and seemingly irreversible advantage.

Alvin Poussaint identifies racism with Europeans' "deep fear of Africa," the result, he contends, of "white projection" of the "unacceptable impulses in themselves."[91] In Poussaint's view whites have a regrettable tendency to take their own bad qualities and deposit them on others, especially blacks. But before the rise of the modern West, there were the great civilizations of the Arabs and the Chinese, which were the most advanced in the world in the late Middle Ages, and it would be interesting to explore what people from those cultures thought about Africa. Like the Christians, the Muslims have traditionally distinguished between believers and infidels. Early Islamic scholars contrasted *dar al-Islam,* the abode of Islam, with *dar al-harb,* the abode of unbelievers and perpetual conflict.[92] Bernard Lewis writes in *Race and Slavery in the Middle East:*

> The Koran expresses no racial or color prejudice. Like every other society, the ancient Middle Eastern peoples harbored all kinds of prejudices and hostilities against those whom they regarded as the Other. But the Other was primarily someone who spoke another language or professed another religion.[93]

Between the tenth and the fifteenth centuries, the Arabs made numerous journeys both by land and sea to sub-Saharan Africa. Muslim travel accounts of the period show a condescending attitude toward blacks, but also toward other groups perceived as unenlightened and culturally inferior. For a Persian writer, black Africans are "distant from the standards of humanity," for which he mainly blames the sun's heat.[94] Another comments harshly about the coarse bodies and bad odor of black women.[95] At the same time, Muslim writers expressed no less derogatory views of Europeans. The Muslim geographer Mas'udi found the Franks and Slavs of Europe to be the ultimate barbarians, and they became paler, grosser, and dumber the further north one went. He blames this on the absence of the sun's heat.[96] Perhaps tiring of temperature as an explanation, another Muslim traveler of the period attributes the stupidity of the Sicilians and Italians to their gross habit of eating onions.[97]

Two of the most famous travel accounts of black Africa are those of Ibn Battuta, an inveterate chronicler of cultural differences, and Ibn Khaldun, the leading historian and thinker of the Muslim world in the late Middle Ages. Touring in Mali, one of the largest empires of black Africa in the fourteenth century, Battuta is impressed to see complete safety and many signs of Muslim religiosity; on the other hand, he does not like to see so many naked women, and he cannot understand "the reprehensible practice among many of eating carrion, dogs and asses." Battuta also journeyed a good deal in Europe, where he was also unimpressed by the level of culture, for which he blamed excessively cold weather and infidel faith.[98]

For Ibn Khaldun, black Africans are "close in character to dumb animals. Most of them dwell in caves and thickets, live in savage isolation, and eat each other." Not to be exclusive, Khaldun adds, "The same applies to the Slavs." We are amazed to find in Ibn Khaldun's writings stereotypical perceptions of black Africans that most people would identify as distinctively American. More than five hundred years ago, Khaldun wrote in his *Muqaddimmah,* "We have seen that Negroes are in general characterized by levity, excitability and great emotionalism. They are found eager to dance whenever they hear a melody." Yet Khaldun has an environmental explanation: the tropical climate. Whenever he gets into his hot bath, Khaldun reminds his readers, he feels like singing![99] Yet one cannot find in Khaldun's writings any doctrine of intrinsic biological superiority. The most we can say is that Khaldun implies for whatever reason that there is a large and possibly unbridgeable civilizational gap between the high culture of the Arab world and the primitivism of black Africa. Khaldun compares blacks to animals with great regularity, and at times he distinguishes between white and black slaves, hinting that the latter may be especially suited to servitude.[100]

Bernard Lewis argues that Islamic attitudes toward blacks underwent a gradual and yet unmistakable change between the Middle Ages and the early modern period. The conventional wisdom that evolved in the Arab world was that blacks were incorrigibly primitive, thus unequipped for civilization and better suited for slavery and servitude. For the first time, color seems to become a badge of inferiority. There are an increasing number of derogatory Muslim references to the color black, which is associated with primitivism and stupidity. This harsh view is epitomized in a description of slaves by the Egyptian writer al-Abshihi in the early fifteenth century. "Is there anything more vile than black slaves, of less good and more evil than they?" he asks. To support his low opinion, the writer invokes the saying, "When the black slave is sated, he fornicates. When he is hungry, he steals." Arabs continued to domesticate European and Asian slaves in the early modern period, but for the first time they used what Lewis terms "racial specialization": black slaves are reportedly given the most menial and degrading tasks; they occupy the lowest rung of the slave hierarchy. One of the Arab terms for slave, *abid,* slowly comes to mean "black slave," and is eventually used to refer to blacks in general.[101]

Another navigating people of the late Middle Ages, the Chinese, arrived on the coast of Africa several times between the eleventh and the fifteenth centuries, especially during the famous voyages spearheaded by Cheng-ho during the Ming period, 1405–1433. Hailing from perhaps the richest, most learned and most technically skilled civilization on the planet for a thousand years, Chinese sailors, like the Arabs, were struck by what they viewed as the barbarism of southern Africa, and speculated that Africans seemed incapable of developing an advanced society. As early as the eighth century, an official of the T'ang dynasty, Du Huan, found himself transported as a war captive to black Africa, probably the region now called Eritrea. His impressions, preserved as a *Record of My Travels,* were decidedly unfavorable. The blacks he found to be "uncouth," lacking in respect for their parents, and promiscuous to the point of practicing incest. (Huan was almost certainly mistaken about incest, which anthropologists today say is a virtually universal taboo. Some sociobiologists now argue that this taboo has an evolutionary and genetic foundation.) A later expedition by Chinese sailors produced scary and fantastic accounts of African divination, including reports of magicians who could change themselves into beasts and birds. J. J. L. Duyvendak in *China's Discovery of Africa* cites reports about Africa preserved in Ming court histories which suggest a subsistence economy. "They live in solitary and dispersed villages. The customs are very simple. The mountains are uncultivated. Fish are caught in the sea with nets." A nineteenth century account by the geographer Xu Jiyu corroborates numerous European reports: black Africans "appear as if they were living in the most ancient times. . . . They were unable to develop a civilization by themselves."[102]

Although there is little doubt of their religious and cultural ethnocentrism, the Arabs and the Chinese seem not to have developed a systematic ideology of racism. What the Arab and Chinese encounters with Africa illustrate is the acute arrogance that goes with relative political, economic, military, and technological strength. All cultures are ethnocentric and begin with notions of supremacy, but powerful cultures who encounter simpler and weaker societies are strengthened in their convictions. When civilizational superiority is attributed to biology or nature, racism is the result.

THE CIVILIZATION GAP

It is difficult for us to uncover the origins of European racism because we see the world through the prism of our own prejudices and terminology. Many people operate out of a paradigm of cultural relativism according to which all cultures are presumed equal; if this is dogmatically held to be so, then any effort to explain cultural superiority and inferiority becomes inherently unnecessary, if not perverse. Even the term "race," which we use so freely today, did not come into general use until the eighteenth century. Etymologists themselves aren't sure, but the term "race" may have derived from an Arabic word *ras,* which means "head" or "beginning."[103] Yet "race" did not become a biological category, adorned with the respectability of science, until the nineteenth century. Moreover, right into the twentieth century the term "race" has been used in different senses, sometimes suggesting nationality, sometimes religion or ethnicity, or the species itself: "the German race," "the Tamil race," "the Celtic race," "the Jewish race," "the human race."[104] It was even customary to refer to a "race of animals" or a "race of birds."[105]

Similarly, today Western technology has spread all over the world, homogenizing it to some extent, and generating in many areas the comforts of modern mechanization and a cosmopolitan awareness of how other people live. The issue of civilizational superiority seems less important because to some extent we live in a global civilization strongly influenced by the West. But this was not the scenario confronting Europeans between the sixteenth and the nineteenth centuries. Like the Chinese and the Arabs before them, what the European cognoscenti—the small population of explorers, travelers, soldiers, and missionaries who formed opinions on these matters—encountered and sought to explain was a widespread and conspicuous primitivism.

The early European travelers were, by our standards, gullible about the rest of the world. Even in the early modern period, many of them embodied attitudes that were a product of the medieval age. Numerous reports of strange sea monsters that arose in the Middle Ages inhibited superstitious Portuguese sailors many decades later. Medieval Europeans also believed in "wild men" who lived in trees, and in trumpet-blowing apes.[106] Writing in the fourteenth century, the traveler and physician Sir John Mandeville testified that, beyond the Holy Land, Europeans could expect to find dog-headed men and natives whose testicles hung down to the ground.[107] Columbus himself fully anticipated finding "people born with tails" and other prodigies.[108] Other explorers such as Walter Raleigh, Francisco de Orellanna and John Swan displayed similar credulity.[109]

Yet these Europeans did not approach Asia, Africa, and the Americas with hostile preconceptions. On the contrary, they were generally respectful and envious of the achievements of many foreign cultures. Much of the European fascination with the Far East was fired by the travel accounts of the Venetian explorer Marco Polo, who died in 1323 after serving in the court of the Great Khan, and left behind alluring (and somewhat exaggerated) catalogs of Oriental wealth.[110] The Portuguese did not navigate the African coast in search of slaves; they wanted to find a way to the spice treasures of Asia.

Some Europeans had a religious motive for going to Africa. Marco Polo in his *Travels* also left behind a tantalizing report of a Christian prince living at the edge of the Muslim world; for more than three hundred years, Europeans would search for this elusive Prester John, who was widely believed to be black.[111] Moreover, Europeans were magnetically attracted by legends of African gold. In 1324, the black king of Mali, Mansa Musa, who was a convert to Islam, made a famous pilgrimage to Mecca, reportedly traveling in a procession of five hundred slaves, each one carrying a staff of pure gold.[112] Musa's glittering display of wealth made him a legend in the Arab world and Europe for at least three centuries. Equally appetizing were the travel accounts of Leo Africanus, a famous chronicler who in 1510 left a generally glowing account of prosperity and higher learning in Timbuktu, a black territory fertilized by Muslim influence.[113]

Whatever their shortcomings and mixed motives, the Europeans who voyaged abroad were the historical instruments of a major world transformation: the advent of modernity. Up until the late Middle Ages there were several civilizations of comparable military, economic, and political strength—Chinese, North African, Indian. But between the sixteenth and the nineteenth centuries, this relative equilibrium began to change, and Europe emerged decisively as the most vibrant and powerful civilization.[114] European strength was indicated by increased production of goods, which generated rising standards of living; by increases in the population, owing to a declining death rate; by an increase in knowledge; and by military sophistication, which reflected both wealth and the application of new inventions. The reasons for Western hegemony are complex, but essentially the rise of Europe is connected to the evolution of three systems: science, representative self-government, and capitalism.

The rudiments of human curiosity, participation in public affairs, and the trading impulse are obviously universal traits. But the West developed specific institutional channels for these human proclivities—for instance, universities, parliamentary systems, joint stock companies—and specific mechanisms for formulating and adjudicating political, economic, and general information—for instance, elections, the free market, the scientific method.[115] These developments produced not simply a different way of fighting wars or building cathedrals, but a radically new way of seeing the world, and man's place in it. No longer did the best minds in Europe think that they lived in an "enchanted world," governed by mysterious spirits; rather, they were increasingly convinced that the universe operated according to rational laws, discernible to the human mind unassisted by divine revelation.[116]

The rise of Europe is connected with powerful ideas that we are now fully conversant with, but which were then entirely new: the idea of a coherent and intellectually accessible world, the idea of progress.[117] For the first time, in the West, it was possible to envision man exercising dominion over the elements—the "conquest of nature." For the first time, it seemed plausible to think of history as having a secular purpose and technology as the engine of irreversible progress. Francis Bacon's hope, that a new kind of knowledge would enable "the relief of man's estate," an increasing triumph over the elements, was being realized. Thus Europeans began to think of their own society as moving ahead, while other groups remained stagnant.[118]

Europe between the sixteenth and the nineteenth centuries was a rich, powerful, increasingly self-conscious, and rapidly changing civilization. Several other societies had produced important inventions—the Chinese, for example, invented printing and the compass, the number system came from India and was wrongly called "Arabic numerals" because the Arabs brought it to Europe. Europeans knew that Muslim scholars in Toledo and elsewhere had preserved much of the learning of the classical world that made possible the humanist Renaissance of Petrarch, Rabelais, and Leonardo da Vinci. Christian theology, which was largely influenced by Neoplatonism, suddenly encountered the revolutionizing challenge of Aristotelian philosophy, lost to Christendom but preserved in the Islamic world. Yet civilizational development does not always accrue to the originators or even the preservers of ideas, but to those who employ them in creative ways. European civilization was able to use foreign ideas and innovations, along with its own, to transform itself, while the institutions of other societies remained relatively unchanged. For example, printing had virtually no effect in changing Chinese society because the presses were controlled by the court; in Europe, the advent of printing dramatically altered many people's way of life. The Reformation is inconceivable without it.

One reason for the growth of European power and influence is that Europeans developed the scientific method which produced not simply a plethora of inventions, but what William McNeill calls "the invention of invention," a systematic process for building on knowledge, and for correcting mistakes, that no other culture possessed, and that was simply alien to the ancient world.[119] Europe was also in the midst of political and social revolutions, which introduced for the first time the idea of representative self-government on a wide scale. In short, before the fifteenth century it made no sense to speak of Europe, only of medieval Christendom. But when Columbus sailed, the concept of Western civilization was beginning to coalesce.[120] And between the fifteenth and the nineteenth centuries, the West made a swift and irreversible transition from a traditional society to a modern society. Enlightenment would help to produce Western success, and also Western racism.

THE EMBARRASSMENT OF PRIMITIVISM

For the Europeans who first voyaged abroad, much of the rest of the world came as a shock for which they were poorly prepared. Early modern accounts, such as Richard Hakluyt's sixteenth century *Principal Navigations* or Samuel Purchas's seventeenth century *Purchas His Pilgrimage* and *Hakluytus Posthumus,* convey the stupefaction of the Europeans who encountered distant and unfamiliar peoples. Europeans who were even then making a transition into the modern era found themselves genuinely amazed and horrified at other cultures which appeared virtually static, confined from time immemorial in the nomadic or the agrarian stage. The consequence was that many Europeans viewed the nonwhite peoples of Africa, the Americas, and elsewhere as savages and barbarians, "beyond the pale of civilization," to borrow Metternich's phrase.

Significantly, it was the Portuguese who arrived on the shores of black Africa and not black Africans who voyaged to Europe. The Portuguese had the three-mast ship, the compass, the quadrant, the astrolabe, navigation charts, and a comparatively good knowledge of winds, currents, stars, and latitudes. The Portuguese knew, as did educated Europeans of the time, that the earth was not flat. When the Portuguese sailed abroad in the second half of the fifteenth century, they left an emerging modern European civilization which had almost a hundred universities; which had several hundred printing presses and some fifteen thousand book titles in circulation; which had cannons and body armor and gunpowder; which used modern business methods such as checks, bills of exchange, insurance, and double-entry bookkeeping; which had mechanical clocks and precision instruments; which had harnessed the power of wind and water to grind grain, crush ore, mash pulp for paper, saw lumber and marble, and pump water, which had built Gothic cathedrals.[121] This technical head start would soon produce a very large gap between Europe and the rest of the world. The enormous European lead is suggested by just a few European inventions and technological advances of the period, a list which could be vastly multiplied: the microscope (1590), the telescope (1608), the barometer (1643), the pendulum clock (1656), the thermometer (1714), the spinning jenny (1770), the steam engine (1781), vaccination (1796), the electric battery (1800).[122]

Essentially what happened, partly by historical accident, is that between the sixteenth and the nineteenth centuries, the most advanced civilization in the world crashed into the shores of sub-Saharan Africa and the Americas, two regions which were, by European standards, incomparably primitive. In many of the tribes of southern Africa and the Americas, the natives had no numbers that went beyond one or two. The Europeans, increasingly skeptical and rationalistic in their outlook, became disdainful of cultures that insisted upon patterning behavior on the miraculousness of everyday life: one could converse with rocks, daily events were controlled by ancestral spirits, dancing and shouting made it rain, diseases could be cured by wearing masks, women could give birth to animals, and so on.[123]

Southern Africa and the Americas were not the most primitive cultures in the world. Indeed between the sixth and the fifteenth centuries, Africa saw the rise of the kingdoms of Ghana, Mali, and Songhai which were large, rich in gold, and politically integrated. Foreigners frequently visited the trading centers of Benin and Kanem-Bornu. Undoubtedly it was a black African people who constructed the great monuments, including an ancient temple, in Zimbabwe. Parts of southern Africa enjoyed the benefits of Muslim literacy and learning. Ethiopia retained an ancient Christian civilization.[124] In the Americas, the Maya, Inca, and Aztec civilizations were impressive for their sophisticated knowledge of the seasons and stars, an advanced calendar, elaborate techniques of weaving and ornamentation, and architectural brilliance that amazed the Spanish.[125] Africa and the Americas were undoubtedly more developed than some of the monsoon forests of southeast Asia, some of the steppe and forest zones of northern Eurasia, and the islands off the coast of India and Australia, such as Tasmania and the Andaman and Nicobar islands, which were still in the paleolithic stage when Europeans arrived there in the eighteenth and nineteenth centuries.[126]

According to Robert Hughes in *The Fatal Shore,* before the Europeans arrived the aborigines of the Australias "had not invented the bow and arrow." Some tribes "had no conception of agriculture—they neither sowed nor reaped." The Iora people never washed themselves, but "spent their lives coated with a mixture of rancid fish oil, animal grease, sand, dust and sweat." The aborigines had "no property, no money . . . no farming, no houses, clothes, pottery, or metal. . . . They had no idea of stock-raising. They saved nothing, lived entirely in the present." One common form of courtship was for a man to "fix on some female of a tribe at enmity with his own . . . stupefy her with blows on her head, back, neck . . . then drag her streaming with blood . . . till he reaches his tribe."[127] Anthropologist Robert Edgerton gives an equally riveting account of Tasmania. Men hunted with wooden spears and by hurling rocks at the heads of animals. Women too foraged for food, typically prying shellfish off rocks, digging up roots, or clubbing possums and seals to death. Tasmanians traveled virtually naked except for kangaroo skins slung over their shoulders. "In all the entire Tasmanian inventory of manufactured goods came to no more than two dozen items." Amazingly, Edgerton points out, Tasmanians could not take advantage of the ocean surrounding their island, because although they once learned how to fish, they forgot or gave up the practice. Thus many Tasmanians perished of starvation despite the availability of a plentiful food source all around them. Nor did they know how to build boats or rafts in order to communicate with other islands. Tasmanian medicine consisted mainly of "slashing the patient with deep cuts until the victim was covered with blood." Edgerton proclaims much of Tasmanian culture "frankly maladaptive."[128]

What the Australian and Tasmanian examples illustrate is the extreme civilizational disadvantage imposed by relative isolation. Apart from the availability of natural resources,[129] the main reason for the relative underdevelopment of Africa, the Americas, and many other parts of the world, compared with China, India, Europe, and the Arab world, seems to be geographical separation. Civilization is largely a product of cultural interaction and shared knowledge. Yet the Americas were cut off from the rest of the world by the Atlantic and Pacific oceans. Black Africa is largely partitioned from North Africa by the Sahara desert. It is true that camels could be used to cross the desert with great difficulty, but the camel is not native to southern Africa. Camels only came into general use for desert journeys around the fourth century A.D.[130] The Arabs were the first to use dromedaries imported from Asia for large-scale caravans across the Sahara. Similarly American Indians did not enjoy the advantages either of the horse or cattle until the Spanish brought them from Europe; consequently, native tribes were compelled to use inefficient modes of transportation, such as llamas and domesticated dogs.[131] "Other cultures could pick up things from traders and missionaries and foreign visitors," remarks historian Philip Curtin. "The sub-Saharan Africans, like some of the Indian tribes, had to invent everything for themselves."

Three of the crucial instruments for a society to rise above the meager subsistence level are the wheel, the plow, and writing. One of the decisive human inventions for improving the efficiency of labor, the wheel is one of the oldest of civilizational resources. Every advanced civilization depended on it, and its invention is usually credited to ancient Mesopotamia, where there is evidence of its use before 3500 B.C.[132] But more than 5000 years later, the wheel was unknown in virtually all of black Africa, and also in pre-Columbian America, although strangely enough the wheel did exist in Mexico, where it was only used as a toy.[133] An essential instrument for the human transition from hunter-gatherer society to some form of settled agriculture, the plow was first used in ancient Sumeria around 3500 B.C.[134] Virtually no community in the Americas nor black Africa knew about the plow until Europeans introduced it in the modern era.[135] Every generation builds upon the knowledge of its ancestors largely because of the invention of writing, which is a mechanism for storing and accumulating knowledge, without which societies are forced to rely on the foibles of memory. "The lack of writing," African philosopher Kwasi Wiredu observes with characteristic understatement, "is a definite handicap in the preservation and enhancement of a philosophical tradition."[136] Also first encountered in Sumeria around 3500 B.C.,[137] writing became the foundation for learning in both the East and the West. But with the exception of Mayan hieroglyphics, writing was unknown in the Americas, even to the relatively advanced Aztecs; the Incas frequently communicated through the use of knotted threads.[138] In black Africa, literacy was confined to small enclaves: Islamic outposts such as Timbuktu, the Christian culture in Ethiopia.[139]

It is impossible, even for scholars hostile to the West, to deny the civilization gap.[140] African sources such as the 1837 autobiography of a former slave, Olaudah Equiano, confirm it.[141] The African scholar Francis Deng remarks that traditional Africa had a "subsistence economy and a simple tribal way of life." Some black activists such as Aime Cesaire even seek to make a virtue out of necessity, declaring African superiority on the grounds of primitive chic. "Hurrah for those who never invented anything, who never explored anything, who never discovered anything."[142] For some white and African American scholars, however, the civilization gap and specifically the low level of African development are sources of acute embarrassment. Consequently many scholars attempt to downplay civilizational differences or offer euphemisms to explain them away.

• Christine Bennett in *Comprehensive Multicultural Education* argues that "early writings of Muslim scholars . . . provide evidence that African civilization was as advanced, or more so, than contemporary Europeans."[143] As we have seen, the writings of many Muslim scholars contradict Bennett's account.

• African American anthropologist Johnnetta Cole writes that the early modern Europeans who reached Africa produced "glowing reports of Africans as stately, well-mannered, highly civilized people."[144] A few accounts do convey respect for the traditional mores of Africans, but there is virtually no record of European reports of advanced civilization in sub-Saharan Africa.

• Historian Gary Nash argues that "the culture gap between European and African societies was not very large when the two peoples met." Elsewhere, Nash modifies this claim to assert that civilizational differences "were not so great as is usually imagined." Applying a lowest-common-denominator mode of comparison, Nash cites the existence of "art, social organization and cultural traditions" both in Africa and the West to imply rough civilizational parity.[145]

• Anthropologist Marvin Harris generously grants that African and American Indian civilizations were "fully comparable" with the civilizations of Egypt, Mesopotamia, and the Indus Valley. True, but Harris is comparing African and American Indian levels of development between the fifteenth and the nineteenth centuries with ancient civilizations which had reached those levels several thousand years earlier.[146]

Since contemporary scholars do not like to think of cultures as superior or inferior, advanced or backward, the very subjects of primitivism and progress, of development and underdevelopment, frequently generate discomfort and even indignation. Only a few historians such as Philip Curtin and William McNeill will say publicly that there were only small enclaves of learning and achievement in sub-Saharan Africa or the Americas. Curtin and McNeill estimate that the most advanced communities of American Indians and African blacks were between one and four thousand years behind the West in technological development. Historian J. M. Roberts is bold enough to state that a large number of peoples whom the Europeans encountered for the first time were virtually "still living in the stone age."[147]

THE COLLAPSE OF ENVIRONMENTALISM

Alexis de Tocqueville remarks that the historical results are usually beneficial when a civilizationally inferior power overwhelms a culturally superior power by force. The reason is that the barbaric victors can then acknowledge their cultural deficiencies, and learn from the society they have subdued.[148] For example, when the Romans supplanted the Greeks as the primary force in southern Europe, Romans acknowledged Greek cultural superiority, as suggested by the Roman poet Horace: "Captive Greece enslaved her fierce captor." Similarly the primitive hordes from northern Europe who sacked Rome over time embraced the Christian faith and acquired, however partially, the essentials of Greco-Roman civilization. The Mongol swordsmen who overran China, India, Europe, and the Middle East inevitably encountered superior cultures and assimilated into them.

By contrast, the Europeans of the modern era were both the more advanced civilization and the conquering power, which resulted, as Tocqueville warned, in uninhibited arrogance on the part of the victors and the total degradation of the vanquished. Europeans from ancient times were familiar with themes of civilizational superiority, and had generally attributed them to climate—the theory we have called environmentalism. Racism developed when the environmental explanation was found by many Europeans to be untenable. Neither skin color nor lack of scientific and intellectual achievement could be plausibly blamed on the soil or the sun. Thus atmospheric theories fell into disrepute.

Along with the Arabs, many Europeans had argued that blackness derives from the sun's heat. The eminent naturalist Comte de Buffon insisted at the end of the eighteenth century that Africans were blackened by the sun, and then passed on blackness as a hereditary feature to their descendants. Buffon predicted that if Negroes were brought to cold countries, over a few generations their skin would lighten.[149] It did not take very long for Europeans to realize the error of that assumption. Europeans also noted, with some chagrin, that the darkest people in Africa were the Wolof living near Cape Verde, not the Africans nearest the Equator. It came as a further surprise that Negro children born in Europe did not come out white. Nor did whites who lived and worked in the West Indies and other tropical zones turn black. When the English and French in America went north, where the climate was cooler, they were confident that they would find Indians with lighter skin; again, this expectation was proven wrong.[150] Many Europeans who followed the path of Columbus to the Americas also believed that the primitive condition of the native Indians was largely the result of their living close to the line of the Equator. As Englishmen and Frenchmen moved northward, many of them expected to see Indian civilization improve in temperate and cooler climates. This turned out not to be the case. Indeed, in some respects, the pattern was reversed. The most advanced Indian civilization was centered in the relatively hot environs of Mexico city; as the French moved north into what is now Canada, they found nothing of comparable sophistication.

It is important to recognize that Europeans were entirely convinced, based on the Bible, that all humans were simultaneously created by God and had inhabited the earth for the same amount of time.[151] How to explain why one people had palaces and cathedrals and technology to explore the seas and the heavens, while other peoples rowed about in canoes and shot blowdarts at each other? Europeans found it difficult to give an explanation for why, over the same period, one society seemed to have accomplished so much and other societies so little. Europeans have also had a long tradition of regarding noble and base qualities to be hereditary. This was part of the justification for a hereditary monarchy and aristocracy. In much of European literature we see suggestions that physical form is revealing, if not determinative, of qualities of character and intelligence. "Let me have men about me that are fat," Julius Caesar says. "Yond' Cassius has a lean and hungry look . . . such men are dangerous." Finally, long before Darwin there is a European anthropomorphic habit of linking human beings and animals, and devising intermediaries such as mermaids and centaurs believed to share human and animal attributes. For all these reasons, it was not difficult for many Europeans to biologize their perceptions of the civilizational inferiority of other cultures. Philip Curtin writes:

> Europeans could now see and measure their superiority—in factory production, agricultural yields, or the cost of transportation by railway or steamship. While superiority feelings had once rested on little more than religious arro-

gance and ordinary xenophobia, they could now be buttressed by demonstrable superiority in power and knowledge. . . . Culture prejudice slid off easily toward color prejudice.[152]

Many Europeans began to assert, with increasing frequency and confidence, that the attributes of race, color, and human achievement are intrinsic. Some people are simply superior to others by nature. And since race and color appear to be hereditary, and since Europeans could not help noticing that they were white and the people they considered barbarian were dark-skinned, they concluded that there must be some relationship between physical attributes or race and civilizational achievement. Moreover, they came increasingly to believe that these racial inequities must be dictated by nature or history or even by God. Thus it was that European racism came into the world.

WHO IS THE FAIREST ONE OF ALL?

Although European convictions of intrinsic superiority are perhaps understandable in this context, there remains an interesting puzzle: both American Indians and Africans were viewed by Europeans as hopelessly primitive, but Europeans only singled out one group, Africans, for dehumanization. A clue to the different way Europeans perceived the two groups is provided by their names. The term "Indian" is a geographical term, reflecting the mistaken belief of Columbus that he had arrived in the Indies. The term "Negro" is racial, and refers to the color black. Why, then, did Europeans distinguish between Indians and blacks, regarding the former as backward but the latter as not really human?

Certainly Europeans condescended to American Indians, who were routinely described as savages. There is a good deal of bestial imagery in Spanish and later French and English accounts of Indians, who are likened to jungle animals in their primitivism and brutality. Indians too were enslaved in the Americas. At the same time, however, European hostility is frequently complemented by genuine admiration. The Indian may be a savage but he is a "noble savage."[153] In many ways, the Indians looked like Europeans and reminded them of their own ancestral past. Some argued that the Indians were the descendants of the Lost Tribes of Israel.[154] When the Europeans vanquished the Indian, they drowned their spoils of conquest with tears of contrition.[155] Even if partly insincere, these homages to the greatness of a disappearing people are entirely absent from European discussion of black Africa. George Fredrickson writes in *White Supremacy* that owing to differences in stature and appearance, the so-called Hottentots "struck Europeans as so outlandish that there was some doubt whether they were fully human."[156]

Taken as a whole, the record suggests that in the minds of Europeans, the Indian was dehumanized, but he was not animalized, he was not considered part of the world of beasts. All of this is in stark contrast with the collective European perception of black Africa that would coalesce between the sixteenth and the nineteenth centuries. This contrast dates back to the debates at the University of Salamanca in the sixteenth century over the question of whether Indians had souls and natural rights; the church and the Spanish court concluded that they did. It never occurred to anyone to debate seriously these matters in connection with black Africans. Indeed the basic humanity and natural rights of Negroes did not become an issue in Europe until two centuries later.[157] Despite the inferiorization of both black Africans and American Indians on account of large civilizational gaps between them and Europeans, the white man saw Indians as original human beings, innocent of Christianity but capable of being instructed, savage in customs but worthy of being civilized. This same white man increasingly saw black Africans as degraded beneath the standards of humanity, corrupt in religion to the point of being in league with the devil, incorrigibly barbarian to the point where slavery seemed appropriate to their natures.

Puzzling over the reasons for these anomalies, scholars such as David Brion Davis and Winthrop Jordan have conducted detailed research into European attitudes. From this work, three explanations emerge, one overlooked largely because it is so obvious, two of them acknowledged by these authors. The obvious explanation is natural environment, the perennial recourse of the ancients to account for human differences. Europeans saw the Americas and Africa very differently: as a result, they grew favorably disposed to the former, and increasingly hostile to the latter. Columbus encountered the Indians first in the Bahamas and then on other Caribbean islands, some of the most beautiful parts of the world. His natural reaction, echoed by many subsequent voyagers, was that he was in the garden of Eden.[158] Many Europeans were captivated by the Americas, which they saw as a land largely uninhabited, a land flowing with milk and honey, a land of long beaches, ideal climate, abundant fruits, and singing birds. As Daniel Defoe's *Robinson Crusoe* suggests, the conflict between the desire to settle the continent, combined with a haunting fear of corrupting its natural beauty, impressed itself powerfully on the European mind. Increasingly, Europeans thought about settlement; to many, it sounded like paradise, a prospect for which it was worth leaving Europe. By contrast, Africa was virtually uninhabitable to Europeans, whose primary interest in it was confined to gold and slaves. Their constitutions could not endure the insects and disease, to which black Africans had developed immunities. The climate was for the most part intolerably hot, they considered the continent already inhabited, and they feared the hazards of impenetrable forest, powerful warrior clans, snakes and wild animals. Europeans had no interest whatsoever in venturing deep into Africa, let alone living there. To many, it sounded like hell.

A second critical reason for European differentiation between blacks and Indians is the white man's association of African primitivism with the negative connotations of the color black. This point has been widely misunderstood. In contemporary racial debates, many are fond of pointing out the linguistic implications of the term "black." The *Oxford English Dictionary* definition describes blackness as "deeply stained with dirt, soiled, dirty, foul, malignant, deadly, baneful, disastrous, sinister, iniquitous, atrocious, horrible, and wicked." This definition, however, is given before the sixteenth century, when Europeans had virtually no exposure to black Africa at all.[159] Winthrop Jordan and other scholars have shown that contrary to the conventional wisdom which views racism as engraved in the English language, the European association of black with darkness and evil long precedes any application to black Africans. All the familiar English metaphors—black sheep in the family, a black mark against one's name, black as the color of death, to blackball or blackmail—evolved independently of racism. So did the religious symbolism of white as the color of angels, and black as the color of the devil.[160] We see a hint of this in Shakespeare, where Iago warns Desdemona's father about Othello: Desdemona is being "covered with a Barbary horse," indeed, "an old black ram is tupping your white ewe."

Europeans, however, are not uniquely disposed to attach benign significance to their own skin color. Extensive research by historians and anthropologists has shown that the color symbolism of white and black is universal. Many scholars suspect that it originates in the basic distinction between darkness and light.[161] We can therefore reappraise black imagery as used by the ancient Greeks and Romans, and medieval Christians and Muslims. By itself, such imagery does not prove racism at all. But Jordan suggests that, combined with the perception of black

Africans as extremely primitive, the term "black" begins to be associated with civilizational backwardness in a way that it never was in the premodern world. In the European mind, Africa truly becomes what Joseph Conrad termed the "heart of darkness."

A third and final reason which inspired the distinction between black Africans and American Indians derives from an historical coincidence. It turns out that Englishmen discovered black Africans as a group in the same place and at the same time that they discovered an animal they had never encountered before: the chimpanzee or two-legged ape, which they called an orang-outan.[162] Many writers bent on scientific classification and journalistic speculation found it irresistible to make a linkage between the two, assuming that two-legged apes were the product of sexual intercourse between the monkey and the African. In the middle of the seventeenth century, reports about chimpanzees and orang-outans circulated in Europe and America. During the 1690s, Edward Tyson, an anatomist from the Royal Society of London, argued that there were astonishing similarities in the muscle and skeleton structure between apes and human beings. He dissected a chimpanzee, which he mistook for a "pygmy." Amazed at the human qualities of this unique creature, Tyson maintained that the so-called pygmy occupied an intermediate position between beasts and men on the Great Chain of Being.[163] Tyson was no scandal-mongering journalist; he was a reputable scientist. As Audrey Smedley points out, in some ways his theories foreshadowed the "missing link" debates of evolutionary biologists two centuries later.[164]

Many European travelers placed these accounts of black Africans in the context of lascivious discussions of sexuality. Undoubtedly African sexual mores shocked Europeans throughout the seventeenth and eighteenth centuries. Moreover, information from black Africa continued to be scarce, and travel accounts undoubtedly italicized perceived differences for the purpose of titillating the folks back home. Subsequent research has shown that African sexual customs were not laissez-faire, although they seemed so to many Europeans, who viewed blacks as furnaces of libidinal passion. Thus although many African tribes outlawed adultery, it was customary in some of them for a man to show hospitality by offering his wife or daughter for the night.[165] To the European mind, these kinds of accounts conveyed debauchery pure and simple. Black sexuality was regarded as purely animalistic, and no report seemed too farfetched to win adherents, or at least to inspire lurid fascination. To make matters worse, some African tribes espoused a mythology which traced their own origins to the union of women with animals.[166] Scholars like Jordan and Davis cite numerous travel reports which confirm early European perceptions of black Africans. Traveling the circumference of the African coast in the seventeenth century, Richard Jobson reported on "the enormous size of the virile member among the Negroes." Jobson invokes this observation as "infallible proof" that blacks are descended from Noah's son, cursed in his loins for uncovering his father's nakedness.[167] Another fantastic but influential account of blacks came not from Africa but from a traveler in Jamaica, Edward Long, in 1774. Playing on the morbid fascination of his European readers, Long narrated spellbinding accounts of iniquitous huts, to which African apes carried black women. Long took into account the possible skepticism of some in his audience in his conclusion, "Ludicrous as the opinion may seem, I do not think that an orang-outan husband would be any dishonour to a Hottentot female."[168]

If black Africans were debased by these perverse links, monkeys gained by being elevated to the level of men. Indeed the very term "orang-outan" derives from the Malay word meaning "man of the woods."[169] The scientist Buffon had reported that chimpanzees could be taught to eat dinner with a knife and fork. Lord Monboddo, a firm believer in men with tails, was a kind of champion of the rights of animals; orang-outans, he insisted, were entirely rational beings who happened to live in a primitive state of nature, untainted by civilization. Edward Long himself insisted that apes came in different varieties, and the more intelligent among them could learn to speak a little and to "perform a variety of menial domestic service," just like blacks.[170]

THE NATURE OF SUPERIORITY

Far from being ignorant and fearful, the early European racists were the most learned and adventurous men of the age, and their views developed as a rational and increasingly scientific attempt to make sense of the diverse world that was for the first time being encountered as a whole. Environmentalism, which the ancient Greeks and many others used to explain human differences, was intellectually discredited along with much of the other cosmology and biology of the ancients. We see evidence of racism, complete with rejection of environmentalism, in the greatest thinkers of the Enlightenment. Hume, Voltaire, Montesquieu, Kant, and Hegel were among the many who entertained racist views, although these did not make up the main part of their philosophy.

David Hume, in his famous description of barbarism in Africa and around the world, examines the possibility that black inferiority is not inherited but imposed by slavery. Hume dismisses that explanation on the grounds that the descendants of slaves and "low people" all over Europe have proved that they can rise above their ancestral histories and achieve literary, mathematical, and scientific distinction, whereas the backwardness of black Africans seems to him comprehensive and apparently ineradicable. "In Jamaica," Hume writes, "they talk of one Negro as a man of parts and learning, but it is likely he is admired for very slender accomplishments, like a parrot, who speaks a few words plainly."[171] Similarly Immanuel Kant is skeptical that black inferiority is the sole product of unfortunate circumstance. "Among the whites," he observes, "people constantly rise up from the lowest rabble and acquire esteem through their superior gifts."[172]

But for the classic expression of European racism we must turn to the French diplomat and scholar Joseph Arthur de Gobineau, who is today unknown or considered the embodiment of wickedness, but who was a friend and respected correspondent of Tocqueville and in some respects one of the most learned exponents of the *Zeitgeist* of the nineteenth century. Nowhere is the racist worldview more comprehensively stated than in Gobineau's *The Inequality of Human Races,* published in 1853. When Gobineau sent his book to Tocqueville, he received only mild dissent about the soundness of his theories, although Tocqueville strongly protested their demoralizing effect.[173] But such warnings could hardly be expected to deter Gobineau, a deep pessimist, who feared that currents of race-mixing and democratic ideas of equality were diluting Teutonic blood and destroying the greatness of the Aryan aristocracy.[174] Gobineau was also an acquaintance of Josiah Nott, an apologist for slavery who publicized Gobineau's views in the American South, and of the philosopher Friedrich Nietzsche and the composer Richard Wagner, both of whom shared Gobineau's love of aristocracy of birth and his hatred of equality. Gobineau was an elitist and an eccentric, but his racism made him a man of his time, elevated to high posts and widely admired. Even the *Encyclopaedia Britannica* echoed his views.[175] Moreover, his influence would prove lasting: in the twentieth century, Gobineau was one of Adolf Hitler's favorite authors and his works were popular textbooks in the schools of Nazi Germany.

Gobineau drew on the discoveries made by Orientalists such as

William Jones that there was a common Aryan source for Indo-European languages such as Sanskrit, Persian, Greek, Latin, and German. Gobineau argued that the highest aspirations of humanity were embodied in these Aryans, a single white family of Germanic peoples who had infused European and even Asian culture with its brilliance and vigor.[176] Gobineau writes that the existence of advanced and backward races—the former who live by codes of civility, ingenuity, and technological comfort, the latter who live by laws of force at a subsistence level—proves that some races are naturally superior to others. This superiority, Gobineau stresses, applies to races as groups, not to individuals. Considering the environmental account of human differences, Gobineau sarcastically writes, "The humidity of a marsh, I suppose, will produce a civilization which would inevitably have been stifled by the dryness of the Sahara." Gobineau quickly proceeds to rebut such a notion.

> In spite of wind and rain, cold and heat, sterility and fruitfulness, the world has seen barbarism and civilization flourishing everywhere on the same soil. The brutish fellah is tanned by the same sun as scorched the powerful priest of Memphis; the learned professor of Berlin lectures under the same inclement sky that once beheld the wretched existence of the Finnish savage.

If environmentalism is true, Gobineau asks, why have some groups endowed with rich natural resources nevertheless failed to produce a comparable civilization to that of Europe? "So the brain of a Huron Indian contains in an undeveloped form an intellect which is absolutely the same as that of the Englishman or the Frenchman!" he explodes. "Why, then, in the course of the ages, has he not invented printing or steam power?" Gobineau suggests that "nowhere is the soil more fertile, the climate milder, than in certain parts of America. There is an abundance of great rivers, the gulfs, the bays, the harbours, are large, deep, magnificent, and innumerable. Precious metals can be dug out almost at the surface of the ground." And the same is true for large parts of Africa. So where, Gobineau asks, is the American Indian or African version of Caesar, Newton, Charlemagne, and Homer?

> We often hear of Negroes who have learned music, who are clerks in banking houses, and who know how to read, write, count, dance, and speak like white men. People are astonished at this, and conclude that the Negro is capable of everything! I will not wait for the friends of equality to show me such and such passages in books written by missionaries or sea captains, who declare that

some Wolof is a fine carpenter, some Hottentot a good servant, that some Kaf-fir dances and plays the violin, that some Bambara knows arithmetic. . . . Let us leave these puerilities, and compare together not men but groups.

The equality of the races could be expected to produce a rough civilizational equality among cultures, Gobineau writes. "Early in the world's history, they would have gladdened the face of the earth with a crowd of civilizations, all flourishing at the same time." Gobineau argues that the historical record refutes such political expectations. In fact, he contends, it is whites who have developed modern civilization, while other people have proved at best adept imitators. Civilization, Gobineau argues, depends not on mere mimicry. "No one has a real part in any civilization until he is able to make progress by himself, without direction from others." In rhetoric that is bound to offend contemporary ears, Gobineau defies his readers to cite one example of a black civilization satisfying these criteria, or even one truly great scientific invention accomplished solely by a black African. "I will wait long for the work to be finished," he says, "I merely ask that it may be begun. But it has never been begun; it has never even been attempted."[177]

In the twentieth century, many of these racist ideas would come under ferocious assault, both on intellectual and moral grounds. Eventually the antiracist view would prevail, and racism would be redefined to suit the politics of a new age. But it is important to recover the origin of racism, because it teaches us that racism had a beginning both in space and in time. Whatever its later career, racism began as part of a rational project to understand human differences. Racism originated as an assertion of Western cultural superiority that was eventually proclaimed to be intrinsic. From the ancient world we get a glimpse of societies that respected nature rather than seeking to subdue and conquer it; that were aware of physical differences but attached no importance to them—perhaps a model for a better society than the one we have now. In any event, there is no historical warrant for the extreme pessimism which holds that racism has always existed and will always exist. Painful though we may find it to read what people in earlier centuries had to say about others, it remains profoundly consoling to know that racism had a beginning, because then it becomes possible to envision its end.

3

AN AMERICAN DILEMMA

Was Slavery a Racist Institution?

Good gracious! Anybody hurt?
No'm. Killed a nigger.
Well, it's lucky because sometimes people do get hurt.
—Mark Twain[1]

Although slavery ended in the United States more than a century ago, its legacy continues to be disputed among scholars and to underlie contemporary debates about public policy. The reason for the controversy is that slavery is considered the classic expression of American racism, and its effects are still viewed as central to the problems faced by blacks in the United States. The effect of slavery, African American scholar Michael Eric Dyson writes, "continues to exert its brutal presence in the untold sufferings of millions of everyday folk."[2] Other scholars such as Johnnetta Cole and Alphonso Pinkney agree.[3] Andrew Hacker writes, "Must it be admitted at the close of the twentieth century, that residues of slavery continue to exist? The answer is obviously yes."[4]

For Hacker, slavery is responsible for the high levels of black residential separation from whites today.[5] Stephen Steinberg writes in *The Ethnic Myth* that "ghettos are nothing less than the shameful residue of slavery."[6] Alvin Poussaint blames slavery for contributing to high rates of black births out of wedlock.[7] Patricia Williams, Molefi Asante, and others assert that slavery is responsible for many of the social pathologies in the black community, such as chronic homelessness, single-parent households and youth violence.[8] Scholars and activists also argue that slavery has undermined contemporary black identity, causing many African Americans to internalize racist stereotypes invented by slaveowners, and even to fear a possible restoration of slavery. The case of legal scholar Patricia Williams illustrates how slavery continues to shape black identity, as she imagines herself as a slave, sexually exploited by a ruthless Southern planter.[9] Cornel West argues that slavery has produced in African Americans "an airborne people" still consumed with "self-contempt, self-hatred, self-affliction, and self-flagellation."[10] Adopting a more extreme position, Derrick Bell contends that for blacks, the restoration of slavery is a real possibility. "Slavery is . . . a constant reminder of what white America might do."[11]

Thousands of black activists are now resolutely pressing for Congress or the courts to direct whites to pay African Americans reparations to place them in the financial position they would occupy if slavery had never occurred.[12] Although some whites may imagine that they are already paying, in the form of affirmative action, welfare, and other transfer payments, black economist David Swinton insists that more money is needed to "restore lost capital to repair the damage that was done to our wealth and business ownership by years of discrimination and slavery."[13] Bernard Boxill argues that while no blacks today were alive during slavery, they are fully entitled to inherit the stolen wealth that their forefathers produced.[14] Referring to a thwarted Reconstruction proposal by Thaddeus Stevens, Henry Louis Gates argues that "had each slave got 40 acres and a mule, race relations in America would be completely different."[15] Reparations is not a new idea,[16] but as the problems of the black underclass persist, it seems to be gaining momentum within the African American community. Hundreds of organizations now exist to promote the concept, which is supported by the Nation of Islam, civil rights leaders such as Jesse Jackson and Coretta Scott King, Afrocentric scholars such as Molefi Asante, celebrities such as Spike Lee and the rap group Public Enemy, and several members of the Black Caucus such as Representative John Conyers. In 1994, many African Americans took reparations seriously enough to act upon it. According to the Internal Revenue Service, more than twenty thousand African Americans refused to pay taxes, writing "exempt" on the grounds that the descendants of slaves should receive money from rather than pay money to the government.[17] The I.R.S. disallowed the claims, but black activists pledge to fight what they see as racist resistance to just demands. They point out that Congress a few years ago paid reparations to Japanese families unjustly interned during World War II, and that Germany has paid reparations for the Holocaust. Reparations proposals vary in their projected costs.

- The National Coalition of Blacks for Reparations (N'Cobra) suggests that blacks be exempted from income taxes in perpetuity.
- A Tacoma, Washington activist computes that whites owe each black family $198,149, which is the value of forty acres and a mule in 1865, plus the interest that would have accrued over the past 130 years.
- Roger Ransom and Richard Sutch calculate that the value of unpaid income to the slaves amounts to $3.4 billion. "The present value of that exploitation would be over $17 billion."
- Two other scholars, Larry Neal and James Marketti, offer more generous estimates: $1.4 trillion and $4.7 trillion, respectively.
- Black nationalist Haki Madhubuti is less precise. "The amount we are owed is in the trillions of dollars."[18]

KUNTA KINTE'S STORY

Reparations is an issue because slavery seems to be the wound that never healed—the moral core of the oppression story that is so fundamental to black identity today. The case for holding slavery responsible for black America's contemporary problems depends crucially on a vivid narrative that is promulgated by countless textbooks, novels like Toni Morrison's *Beloved,* and popular films and TV shows like "Roots" and its sequels. This dramatic portrait keeps slavery very much alive in the minds of Americans, guaranteeing, as T. S. Eliot put it, "not only the pastness of the past, but its presence."[19] Alex Haley's *Roots* has been largely exposed as fiction rather than history,[20] yet the broad outlines of Haley's narrative remain imprinted on the American psyche.

According to the prevailing view, slavery was a racist institution that extracted so much suffering that it qualifies as a kind of American holocaust. In a book that is controversial among scholars but closely echoes the popular image, Stanley Elkins argues that slaves lived in a kind of concentration camp atmosphere which was so psychically debilitating that it infantilized slaves, destroyed their resources of moral autonomy, taught many of them to embrace their oppression and even their oppressors, and fostered the well-founded stereotype of Sambo, the slave who is childish, servile, and contented.[21] The conventional wisdom holds that slaves suffered indescribable material deprivations including inadequate food, clothing, and medical attention; that masters subjected slaves to continuous floggings, brandings, and mutilations; that owners declared open season on the wives and daughters of slaves, producing innumerable unacknowledged mulattoes; that the system as a whole was characterized by wholesale disregard for the life and well-being of slaves. African American scholar Bell Hooks observes that slavery was characterized by "sexual sado-masochism," represented by "the master who forced his wife to sleep on the floor as he nightly raped a black woman in bed."[22] No wonder that bitterness generated by recollections of slavery has turned a generation of black scholars and activists against the nation's founding—against identification with America itself.

• Jefferson didn't mean it when he wrote that all men are created equal," remarks John Hope Franklin. "We've never meant it. The truth is that we're a bigoted people and always have been. We think every other country is trying to copy us now, and if they are, God help the world." Franklin argues that by betraying the ideals of freedom "the founding fathers set the stage for every succeeding generation of Americans to apologize, compromise and temporize on those principles."[23]

• Nathan Huggins in *Black Odyssey* condemns the American framers for establishing not freedom but "a model totalitarian society." Huggins faults the framers for refusing to mention the words "slave" or "slavery" in the Constitution, in an effort to "sanitize their new creation" and avoid "the deforming mirror of truth." The founding, he concludes, was simply "a bad way to start."[24]

• Speaking on the two hundredth anniversary of the Constitution, former Supreme Court Justice Thurgood Marshall refused to "find the wisdom, foresight and sense of justice exhibited by the framers particularly profound. The government they devised was defective from the start." Marshall urged that instead of jingoistic celebration, Americans should seek an "understanding of the Constitution's defects," its immoral project to "trade moral principles for self-interest."[25]

Is it true that American slavery was a racist institution? That it reflected a uniquely Western form of iniquity? That whites were the oppressors and blacks were the victims? That slaves were subjected to virtually uninterrupted brutalization and dehumanization? That white slaveowners produced innumerable illegitimate offspring by raping slave women? That blacks were robbed of their culture? That contemporary black illegitimacy and inner-city poverty can be traced to the legacy of slavery? Must we agree with the abolitionist William Lloyd Garrison who charged that far from being a beacon for the world, the American founding was a "covenant with death," an "agreement with hell," and a "refuge of lies," an appraisal endorsed by the great black leader Frederick Douglass?[26] Is the black scholar Eric Williams right to question even the motives of abolitionists, whom he accuses of being racists who only involved themselves in the antislavery cause for reasons of economic and political expediency?[27] It is time to reappraise the contemporary narrative about slavery, to sort out the myths from the realities.

OF HUMAN BONDAGE

Although U.S. Senator Bill Bradley articulates the conventional view that "slavery was our original sin,"[28] in fact there was nothing original about Americans practicing slavery. Not only was slavery extensively practiced in the ancient world, as we have seen, but in the modern era slavery was prevalent in Africa, the slave trade was actively promoted by the Arabs, American Indians owned slaves, and there were even thousands of black slaveowners in America. In this sense, American slavery was hardly a peculiar institution.

The practice of whites owning slaves developed in the United States in congruence with universal practices, indeed consistent with prevailing Western institutions which held millions of whites in various degrees of unfreedom. In this context it is not hard to understand Charles Pinckney's amazement, during the debates over the American founding, over questions about the morality of slavery. "If slavery be wrong," Pinckney erupted, "it is justified by the example of all the world."[29] It makes sense to speak of the problem of slavery in the West, where it has been a problem. But in this respect the Western experience is unique. In most parts of the world, slavery was uncontroversial for the simple reason that the concept of freedom simply did not exist. "Indeed there was no word for freedom in most non-Western languages before contact with Western peoples," Orlando Patterson writes.[30]

Prior to the development of a modern Western notion of freedom, most people lived in a world shaped by what David Brion Davis terms "the normal network of kinship ties of dependency, protection, obligation and privilege," a system that included various forms of patronage and servitude.[31] Nathan Huggins writes that slavery evolved in a social system radically different from our own, one that considered servants and laborers as "base people," that used hunger and beating as a "goad to productivity," that maintained discipline through "maiming, dismemberment . . . torture, the rack, beheading, burning at the stake, impaling." Between white laborers and black slaves, Huggins writes, "the differences were more in degree than in kind."[32] Historian Oscar Handlin writes that in Europe, as in much of the world, the antithesis of the term "free" was not "slave" but "unfree," and the vast majority of people lived under conditions of partial or no freedom. Involuntary bondage was common: "a debtor could be sold at an outcry," vagrants and vagabonds frequently had their labor sold for a term to the highest bidder, criminal offenses were routinely punished with sentences of forced public service, "sometimes for life."[33] Many whites became indentured servants in America: they bound themselves to a planter or company for four to seven years in return for which they received free passage across the Atlantic and some start-up provisions.[34] Like English servants, bondsmen in America were frequently bought and sold, or used as gambling stakes; "Under such circumstances," writes historian Gordon Wood, "it was often difficult for the colonists to perceive the distinctive peculiarity of black slavery."[35]

Even the notion that slaves had no rights and served entirely at the will of the master was familiar: wives and children were widely considered to be the property of husbands and fathers. Until the eighteenth century, not many Europeans had moral qualms about slavery, and the very few who wrestled with their consciences usually prevailed. That slavery contradicted no important social value for most people around the world can be seen by a brief examination of Arab, American Indian, and African slavery. In the Arab world, which was the first to import large numbers of slaves from Africa, the slave traffic was truly cosmopolitan. Slaves of every hue and origin were sold in open bazaars. Manuals were compiled offering consumer guidance for slave buyers. Many slaves were castrated to meet the high demand for slave eunuchs, who were especially sought by wealthy and aristocratic Arabs to safeguard their harems. The Arabs also had a specialized market in homosexual slaves, and slave boys for use in pederasty.[36] The Arabs played an important middleman role in the transatlantic slave trade, and contemporary research suggests that between the seventh and the nineteenth centuries they transported about fourteen million black slaves across the Sahara and the Red Sea—a larger number than were shipped to the Americas.[37]

Native Indians practiced slavery on each other, long before Europeans arrived to practice it on them. For several tribes in the American northwest, slaves comprised between 10 and 15 percent of the population.[38] The Cherokee employed "slave catchers" to retrieve wounded combatants from other tribes, although the Cherokee preferred to kill enemies rather than take them captive.[39] In some Indian tribes, slaveowners proved how wealthy they were by how much they could afford to consume and waste: large numbers of slaves were routinely killed in potlatch ceremonies.[40] Among the Tupinamba of Brazil, who adopted an especially harsh version of this practice, slaves were segregated from the community, then subjected to ceremonial denunciation and abuse, then taunted with the possibility of escape, then ritually hunted down, massacred, and eaten.[41]

Some white liberal scholars such as Gary Nash downplay African slavery, insisting that "the scale of it was small and it involved personal service, often for a limited period of time."[42] But Nash's account, for which he provides no evidence, is contradicted by recent studies which show that slavery was widespread in Africa from antiquity. The three powerful medieval kingdoms of Ghana, Songhai and Mali all relied on slave labor. Nor were these slaves exclusively black Africans: the emperor Mansa Musa, for example, purchased Turkish slaves for his court in Mali. White Europeans who were shipwrecked off the west coast of Africa were also enslaved. The Ashanti of West Africa customarily enslaved all foreigners. Claims of the benign quality of African slavery are hard to square with such reports as slaves being tortured at the discretion of their owners, or executed *en masse* to publicly commemorate the deaths of the kings of Dahomey.[43]

Far from being limited in scope, African slavery was both widespread and uncontroversial. Paul Lovejoy argues that "in the American context, slavery was introduced from the outside and always relied on the importation of slaves" while "in Africa slavery evolved from indigenous institutions."[44] Indeed in a recent study, John Thornton shows that slavery was far more deeply embedded in Africa than in Europe because Europeans recognized land as the primary source of private wealth whereas "slaves were the only form of private, revenue-producing property recognized in African law."[45] No wonder that tribal chiefs in Africa, working through Arab middlemen, were able to sell millions of blacks to Europeans. The transatlantic slave trade required a vast increase in volume, but no fundamental modification of the institutions and values of Africa.[46] According to Basil Davidson in *The African Slave Trade:*

> The notion that Europe altogether imposed the slave trade on Africa is without any foundation in history. . . . Those Africans who were involved in the trade were seldom the helpless victims of a commerce they did not understand: on the contrary, they responded to its challenge. They exploited its opportunities.[47]

Contrary to popular belief, Europeans did not typically invade African tribes to chase down and capture slaves.[48] Many slaves purchased by Europeans were already slaves in Africa. Warfare and kidnapping for the purpose of acquiring slaves was a specialty of African kingdoms such as Dahomey, Ashanti, Sierra Leone, Gambia, and the Congo. As middlemen, the Arabs frequently participated in slave raids. At times African raids reached such a point that Europeans complained about unpredictability: "the Negro who sold you slaves last month might find himself captured and sold a few days later."[49]

Income from the slave trade made many African chiefs and tribes rich. Smaller African states on the Gold Coast urged Europeans to construct forts to protect the valuable merchandise from raids by inland African kingdoms.[50] Perhaps African complicity in the slave trade is epitomized in the proposition advanced to Europeans by an African chief in the early nineteenth century: "We want three things: powder, ball and brandy; and we have three things to sell: men, women and children."[51] The grim reality of the African slave trade between Africa and America was summed up by Zora Neale Hurston, the great black writer of the Harlem Renaissance, in the early part of the twentieth century:

> The white people held my people in slavery here in America. They had bought us, it is true, and exploited us. But the inescapable fact that stuck in my craw was: my people had sold me. . . . My own people had exterminated whole nations and torn families apart for a profit before the strangers got their chance at a cut. It was a sobering thought. It impressed upon me the universal nature of greed and glory.[52]

WHO OWNED BLACK SLAVES?

The popular conception seems to be that American slavery as an institution involved white slaveowners and black slaves. Consequently, it is easy to view slavery as a racist institution. But this image is complicated when we discover that most whites did not own slaves, even in the South; that not all blacks were slaves; that several thousand free blacks and American Indians owned black slaves. An examination of these frequently obscured aspects of American slavery calls into question the facile equation of racism and slavery.

This is hardly to deny the well-known facts about the North American slave trade. The first Africans came to North America in 1619, probably as indentured servants,[53] although the Spanish and the Portuguese had an elaborate system of slave plantations which had already lasted a century by this time.[54] By the end of the seventeenth century, strengthened by the racism that Europeans imported into the Americas, black indentured service metamorphosed into slavery.[55] Over the next three and a half centuries, approximately ten million black slaves, mainly from the West Coast of Africa, would find their involuntary home in the New World.[56] During the late seventeenth and eighteenth centuries the importation of North American slaves grew exponentially, so that by the first U.S. census of 1790, no fewer than 697,000 Negroes, almost one fifth of the entire population, were bound in perpetual servitude.[57] In 1860, on the eve of the Civil War, the number of black slaves would exceed four million, making African bondage one of the central institutions of American history. Yet most whites in the United States did not own slaves. In 1790, the number of slaveowning families in America was as high as 25 percent, but by 1850, the number declined to 10 percent. Even in the South, less than one third of free white families owned slaves on the eve of the Civil War.[58] "The typical Southerner," writes Kenneth Stampp, "was not only a small farmer but a non-slaveholder."[59]

Whites were not the only Americans to own black slaves. Indian tribes such as the Choctaws, Chicasaws, Cherokees, Creeks and Seminoles all owned black slaves.[60] Seminole slaveowners were relatively tolerant, and over time there was considerable intermarriage between Indians and blacks, generating an Afro-Indian community in the state of Florida by the nineteenth century.[61] By contrast, Cherokee slaveholders were notoriously harsh. According to Theda Perdue in *Slavery and the Evolution of Cherokee Society,* the Cherokee gave up enslaving other Indians by the time of the American Revolution and only kept black slaves. Cherokee law protected property rights in African slaves, and the *Cherokee Phoenix* carried announcements and advertisements for slaves in the early nineteenth century. Most Cherokee owners had fewer than ten black slaves apiece, but some held more than fifty, such as the half-breed Joseph Vann, who in 1835 employed 110 Negroes on his plantation and in his distillery. The Cherokee, who were excellent trackers, also volunteered their services to catch black runaways for white owners, although some plantation owners were reluctant to employ Cherokee slavecatchers, because they frequently killed their fugitives.[62] Another slaveowning tribe, the Choctaw, elected to fight on the side of the American South during the Civil War. Although slavery was abolished in most of the United States after the defeat of the Confederacy, the Choctaw and other tribes continued to keep slaves until 1866, when these tribes signed a treaty with the U.S. government in which they reluctantly agreed to suspend the practice.[63]

Just as with Indians, free blacks in the United States were permitted to own slaves, except in two states, Delaware and Arkansas.[64] Thus even as many of their other rights were legally withheld, free blacks continued to enjoy property rights. It is important to recognize that at no time in American history were all blacks slaves. From the beginning, there was a substantial proportion of free Africans in America. Between the American revolution and the Civil War free blacks made up approximately 10 percent of the total black population; in 1860, for example, there were almost half a million free blacks, 50 percent of whom lived in the South.[65] Some free blacks were former slaves and, once manumitted, they could accumulate income and property by marketing skills they once used on the plantation. Many free blacks worked as blacksmiths, carpenters, brick masons, tailors, shoemakers, and butchers. Over the years, a small but sizable segment of the free black population acquired the economic resources to purchase property, including black slaves.[66] As early as the 1640s, around the time that whites began to enslave blacks, there is proof of a black man, Anthony Johnson, owning a slave of his own race.[67] The Virginia courts upheld the right of blacks to own other blacks as early as 1654; other states followed this precedent. In 1833 the Supreme Court affirmed Negro slaveholding. With relatively few exceptions, up until the Civil War, blacks enjoyed the same legal rights as whites and Indians to hold black slaves. There was no legal right to enslave whites.[68]

Black slaveownership began benignly enough. Starting in the late seventeenth century, a number of Southern states either forbade or placed restrictions on slave emancipation. By the late eighteenth and early nineteenth centuries, it was typically required that a plantation owner who manumitted his slaves had to pay to transport them out of the state.[69] These restrictions were intended to discourage emancipation, and to limit the free Negro population in the American South. Between 1750 and 1850, a substantial community of free blacks was able to accumulate sufficient income and savings to buy the freedom of family members, relatives, and friends who were still enslaved. But due to emancipation restrictions, they ended up purchasing and thus owning these blacks. For some, selfish interests soon set in, and some free blacks chose to put their slaves to work.[70]

African American historian Carter G. Woodson cites several cases of husbands who bought their wives to ensure their good behavior and commitment to work. One Negro shoemaker in Charleston, he reports, purchased his wife for $700, but finding her unsatisfactory he sold her a few months later for $750.[71] What began as an example in noble humanitarianism ended up as an institution in which free blacks debased their African kinsmen, sometimes their own relatives, into chattel slavery. Many free blacks purchased other blacks for no liberating end but simply to enjoy the benefits of being slaveowners; in Ira Berlin's words, "They showed little sympathy for the slave and had few qualms about the morality of slavery."[72] During the first half of the nineteenth century, some blacks owned Southern slave plantations right alongside their white counterparts; some owned slaves jointly with whites; others rented slaves from white neighbors.[73] Black slaveowners were not above competing with whites for wealth in slaves, advertising in newspapers for the recovery of runaways, or suing whites for the return of slaves belonging to them.[74]

Black slaveholding was most widespread in Louisiana, fairly common in South Carolina, and not unusual in Texas, Florida, Mississippi, and several other states.[75] In North Carolina around 1830, for example, only eight blacks owned a total of twenty-five slaves, whereas in South Carolina more than three hundred black slaveholders—a majority of free Negro heads of household—owned in excess of two thousand slaves.[76] In Louisiana, records from various parishes in 1830 show 753 persons of color registering as slaveowners, with twenty-five owning ten or more slaves apiece, and more than a hundred persons owning between five and ten slaves. At that time, the mulatto Augustin Metoyer commanded a family dynasty that boasted no less than 287 slaves. Another Negro family in 1851 purchased an estate in Iberville Parish with ninety-one slaves. Adolph Reggio, a black sugar planter, possessed forty-three slaves. The mulatto freeman Martin Donate owned his wife, seven children, and eighty-nine other slaves. The black entrepreneur Madame Cecee McCarty, who imported foreign goods for sale in Louisiana, owned thirty slaves whom she used in her sales force. Black planter Andrew Durnford owned about seventy-five African slaves and complained about the laziness of his "rascally Negroes." Records from Louisiana parishes in 1830 show that at least seventeen other free blacks owned more than thirty slaves each.[77]

In *Black Masters,* Michael Johnson and James Roark document the remarkable story of William Ellison, a free Negro planter and cotton gin maker in South Carolina, who owned over a hundred slaves. Themselves descended from slaves, the Ellison family proved to be no different as owners than white planters. Ideologically, Ellison was "no more anti-slavery than they were—namely, not at all." He treated his slaves severely, and some complained of brutality. His slaves were reputed to be the worst fed and most poorly clothed in the area. When his funds ran a bit low, he did not hesitate to break up families by selling slave girls to whites. The authors write:

> Despite his own history, Ellison did not view his shop and plantation as halfway houses to freedom. He never permitted a single slave to duplicate his own experience. Nothing suggests that he wrestled with a moral dilemma. Everything suggests that Ellison held his slaves to exploit them, to profit from them, just as white slaveholders did.[78]

Although William Ellison was not typical, he was not the wealthiest black planter in the country, nor the owner of the most slaves. This distinction belonged to a Louisiana widow named C. Richard and her son P. C. Richard, who together in 1860 owned 152 slaves. Much more typical of Negro slaveowners were several cases recorded in Charleston: Maria Weston, the wife of a mulatto machinist, who owned fourteen slaves; a wood merchant named Richard Dereer, who with his brother owned twenty slaves; and James Drayton Johnson, who owned three slaves.[79] When the Civil War broke out, the Ellison family defended its property by backing the Confederacy. So did a number of other black slaveowners in South Carolina and Louisiana. One black planter boasted of his plans to take Abraham Lincoln captive and run up the Confederate flag at the U.S. Capitol. Others contributed funds and resources to the Southern cause. Eventually, writes Gary Mills in his study of the Cane River Negro elite, "The free mulatto slaveowners suffered heavy financial losses with the Union victory."[80]

How extensive was black slaveholding in the American South? Not extensive, by comparison with white slave ownership, but extensive enough to be morally disturbing. Three distinguished scholars—historian Kenneth Stampp of Berkeley, African American scholar John Sibley Butler of the University of Texas at Austin, and Abram Harris of Howard University—agree that in 1830 there were more than 3,500 American black slaveowners who collectively owned more than 10,000 black slaves.[81]

Although facts about black slaveowners are undisputed, it is probably the case, as Larry Koger writes, that "most Americans, black and white, believe that slavery was a system exclusively maintained by whites to exploit black people." Even scholars do not emphasize black slaveownership, David Brion Davis says, because it "does not fit the conventional narrative—it confuses the morality tale." Indeed acutely chagrined about the subject, some scholars seek to dismiss black slavery as nothing more than a case of free Negroes buying their relatives. This claim is refuted by Koger's study of South Carolina, which found that more than 80 percent of black slaveowners were light-skinned mulattoes, while 90 percent of the slaves they owned were dark-skinned. The two groups, Koger argues, were hardly "kinfolk."[82] Nor can it be argued that black slaveowners took slaves as a consequence of internalizing white slaveowners' racial stereotypes. There is no reason to believe that, virtually unique among the peoples of the world, black masters were forced into slaveownership and would have abstained from it absent social pressures. Indeed such a view takes away from blacks their free will, perhaps the most important indicator of their emancipated status.

Certainly this chapter in the history of American slavery does not alter the big picture. The institution of black-run plantations was modest in comparison to the magnitude of white slaveownership. Yet its existence proves that history seldom draws clear lines between oppressors and victims. The acquiescence, indeed participation, of black slaveowners in the institution of slavery confirms that American slavery, like slavery around the world, bore no necessary link to racism, and that in America, as elsewhere, human beings of all races are capable of serious moral crimes in the name of expediency and self-interest.

WHY RACISM?

As the example of black slaveowners suggests, American slavery was not established because of racism but for the purpose of profit. There was work to be done building the new world, and slavery provided the unpaid labor to do the job. As Winthrop Jordan argues, racism may have influenced the European decision to seek black slaves in Africa,[83] but it can hardly be the main or only reason. Scholars are fairly unanimous that African slaves were purchased and transported to America for reasons of convenience and economic gain.[84] Nor can the spread of racism in America be explained by the factors leading to its origin in Europe. It is preposterous to imagine that the vast majority of Americans devoted any time whatsoever to contemplating the civilization gap between the West and the dark-skinned part of the world. How, then, did the speculations of a relatively small number of naturalists, travelers, missionaries, and diplomats become part of the conventional wisdom of the American people for more than two hundred years, persisting into the twentieth century?

Marxist scholars such as Eugene Genovese have a powerful answer. "Race relations did not determine the patterns of slavery in the new world; the patterns of slavery . . . determined race relations."[85] The Marxist view is that racism developed and spread in America as an ideology to rationalize the enslavement and oppression of blacks by a white master class. Fortified by racism from the beginning, American slavery itself became a catalyst for the institutionalization of bigotry.[86] This view draws on the insight that C. R. Boxer popularized: "One race cannot systematically enslave members of another for centuries without acquiring a conscious or unconscious feeling of racial superiority."[87] That is why, in many ancient cultures, it was customary to brand or tattoo slaves to confirm their social stigma.[88] But in the United States no such measures were necessary.[89] Africans were chosen for slavery in part because they were considered inferior as a race. They already wore a racial uniform, which itself became the mark of slavery, and even later a stigma of shame and inferiority.

The Marxist view contains a good deal of truth. Even though not all blacks in America were slaves, and not all slaves in America were black, over time these nuances became blurred, and in crucial respects racism and slavery became synonymous, at least in perception if not in operation. The consequence was a virtually inseparable association in the American mind between the degradation of slavery and the degradation of blackness. As the *Daily Intelligencer,* an Atlanta newspaper, put it in 1860, "Whenever we see a Negro, we presuppose a master, and if we see him in what is commonly called a free state, we consider him out of his place."[90] Yet the Marxist account leaves an unanswered question: what economically exploitative purpose does racism serve by plaguing and tor-

menting the free black population? Moreover, why did white racism toward blacks far exceed racism toward American Indians, even though
some Indians too were slaves in America? These questions are illuminat-
ed by considering the differences between black slavery and Indian slavery in the United States, and between slavery in the United States and
slavery in Latin and South America. Scholars who study Caribbean and
South American slavery agree that the system was extremely harsh, in
some respects harsher than in the United States.[91] Reporting to absentee
owners in Spain and Portugal, ruthless overseers wielded the lash over gi-
gantic plantations of Africans, working them with little apparent concern
for their health or longevity. The slave mortality rate was far higher in
Latin America than in the United States.[92] The reason South American
slaves could be worked to death is that there were countless others to replace them; thus slaves were disposable, a kind of human fodder.

Yet partly through the influence of the Catholic Church, Latin American slave laws were far more humane than those in the United States.[93]
Nowhere in the United States was marriage legal for slaves, whereas
slaves in Latin America had a legal right to marry and receive the sacra-
ments. Also, as Brazilian scholars like Gilberto Freyre and Florestan Fernandes have shown, because of the church's emphasis on family unity,
slave families in Latin America had specific rights, including legal protections against arbitrary dissolution. By contrast, slaveowners in the United
States had full discretion over whether to break up families and separately sell parents and children.[94] Every American slave state except South
Carolina had laws against miscegenation, and although the practice occurred it was regarded as publicly shameful. In Latin America, because of
the small number of white women who settled in the Spanish colonies,
black concubinage was everywhere legal, public, even moderately respectable.[95] In fact, according to Stanley Elkins, miscegenation was generally considered a good thing in Latin America because it had a
whitening effect, whereas it was generally considered a bad thing in the
United States because it had a darkening effect.[96]

Manumissions were easier, as a matter of both law and practice, in
Latin America. Some American states severely restricted the right of
masters to free their slaves, fearing the presence of a resentful class of
free blacks among the white population. But Latin American slaves were
often permitted to accumulate private savings and to purchase their own
freedom. Indeed it was customary, especially in Cuba, to regard slaves
who had paid one-third or one-half of their price to their owners as one-

third or one-half free and consequently entitled to that proportion of their own free time.[97] The consequence of the Latin American system was the gradual emergence of a free colored class, which was considered neither white nor black, but named for the specific proportion of white and black and Indian blood. Latin Americans were classified variously as mestizos, mulattoes, zambos, quadroons, and octoroons.[98] Indeed it was common throughout Latin America for masters to free their offspring by slave women. The child of a slave inherited his father's freedom, not his mother's servitude. In the United States, by contrast, the progeny of master and slave usually remained slaves. Servitude was inherited through the mother, and the child typically ignored and repudiated by the father.[99] Thus the United States gradually embraced a doctrine unique in the history of slavery: all children with any recognizable black ancestry would be considered black.[100] There was no question of gradation or what Carl Degler of Stanford terms the "mulatto escape hatch."[101] To be white meant, *de jure* if not *de facto,* to be a thoroughbred European, uncontaminated by a single drop of Negro blood.[102] Even after slavery, the one-drop rule would ensure that blacks, as a group, would remain distinct and distant from whites, who could think of themselves as a ruling class.[103]

None of this means that no enduring hierarchy developed in Latin America. It did, but it was primarily a social and not a racial hierarchy. The colored class emerged as a buffer zone, an intermediary between pure whites and pure blacks; in many countries, the colored class became the national majority. Dark skin continued to carry some stigma, but it was entirely possible to erase this through wealth, political status, and intermarriage with others of lighter skin. Racial tensions persist today in Brazil, Cuba, and other Latin American countries, but the racial legacy of slavery there is unquestionably less stark than in the United States.[104]

Scholars have struggled to explain why the North American and the South American slave systems evolved so differently. No doubt many factors are responsible, including religious and cultural differences. But an often-overlooked cause for the racial difference lies in the radically different systems of government. Spain and Portugal, which maintained South American colonies, were rigid monarchies. From the seat of government to the church, presided over by the Holy Inquisition, freedom defined as the right of self-government and the right to determine one's own life simply did not exist. Consequently Spanish and Portuguese plantation owners did not have to explain to anyone, or even to themselves, why they were enslaving large numbers of Africans, depriving them of liberty, and stealing the fruits of their labor. Slavery was a practice that seemed entirely reasonable for social and economic life, and one that did not contradict any of the institutions in their home countries. In short, South American slaveowners were under very little obligation to justify or rationalize slavery.

By contrast, the United States in the late eighteenth century became a free society with a liberal democratic creed. Inspired by the words of a Southern slaveholder, Thomas Jefferson, these people fought a revolution in order to secure the proposition that "all men are created equal and endowed by their Creator with certain inalienable rights." In an early draft of the Declaration, Jefferson specifically excoriated King George for violating the basic rights of human beings by "carrying them into slavery."[105] Duncan MacLeod writes that "the very term slavery was among the most frequent in the Revolutionary vocabulary. The war was seen as essentially a battle against political servitude."[106] It is not easy for a society revolting in the name of liberty and equality to justify slavery. The British Tory Samuel Johnson summarized the dilemma. "How is it that we hear the loudest yelps for liberty among the drivers of Negroes?"[107]

Many Americans found a way to resolve the contradiction. All men are created equal, blacks are being bought and sold in America, therefore blacks must not be men. After all, if blacks are men, and all men are created equal, then blacks are entitled to the same rights as whites, including the right not to be held in captivity. Consequently the premise of black humanity must be denied in order to sustain slavery. This explains the contorted logic of the infamous *Dred Scott* decision of 1857 in which the Supreme Court invoked black inferiority to exclude slaves from constitutional protection, and pronounced slave ownership as a fundamental property right.[108]

The doctrine that slaves were legally equivalent to property generated both legal and human contradictions. In fact, slave laws implicitly recognized the humanity of slaves by holding them accountable for their actions. Nathan Huggins writes, "A pig in the corn was not a thief; a slave in the smokehouse was. A horse that trampled the life from a cruel master was no murderer; a slave who struck out against brutality was."[109] Moreover, masters who engaged in sexual relations with slaves also presumed their humanity—otherwise their behavior would constitute not merely fornication, but bestiality.

So the Marxist argument is essentially correct: the ideology of racial superiority, which originated to explain civilizational differences, became consolidated in America as a convenient rationalization for continuing oppression. What some Marxist scholars seem to miss is that racism in America was not an economic but a *moral* justification. Although they limited the franchise to propertied white males, the American founders were not insincere in proclaiming their allegiance to principles of liberty and equality. Precisely because they cherished those principles, they found it necessary to believe in the inhumanity of blacks. Southerners who were in the forefront of the American Revolution and were no less committed than Northerners to the principles of the Declaration and the Constitution, found themselves in a particular quandary as they administered their forced-labor plantations. Racism in the American South served to rationalize and justify behavior that flatly contravened the nation's political ideals. The consequence, Winthrop Jordan writes, is the emergence of a new category of consciousness: Americans began to regard themselves not merely as English, or as Christian, but as white.[110]

If Americans did not believe in equality, then racism would serve no ideological or material purpose. "Racism represents a contradictory resurgence in egalitarian society of what finds direct expression as hierarchy in caste society," Louis Dumont writes.[111] Racism, therefore, flourished in the interregnum between the principles of the Constitution and its pragmatic concession to the institution of slavery. Far from being proof of distinctive American evil, racism is a peculiar reflection of the moral conscience of America, and of the West. It reflects the oppressor's need to account for the betrayal of his highest ideals. Despite the ignominious career of racism as a justification for exploitation, in all of human history, only the white man has felt compelled to provide such a justification. Paradoxically, those who indulged in racism thereby revealed their humanity, even as they disregarded the humanity of others.[112] The very existence of racism implies that, from the very outset, slavery existed uncomfortably and anomalously with Jeffersonian principles.

THE RED AND THE BLACK

Earlier we saw that from the outset American Indians were, despite their perceived primitivism, less vulnerable to white racism. A further reason that Indians escaped the worst virulence of European and American racism is that whites found it difficult, if not impossible, to maintain them as slaves. "Negroes were considered draft animals, Indians wild animals," writes native American writer Vine Deloria.[113] Ironically Europeans came to regard the American Indian's apparent unsuitability for slavery to be a mark of nobility. Obviously one of the first projects of the European settlers was to try to enslave the indigenous people of America, and many Indians were captured and put to work. Yet Indian slavery soon proved unsatisfactory, which is why the settlers found it necessary to get involved in the long-distance African trade. Over time the enslavement of Indians in the United States eroded to the point of insignificance, and slavery came to be associated entirely with African people.

One reason that Europeans found it difficult to enslave Indians was the "noble savage" idea that caused whites to admire and envy the red man. The European fundamentally considered the Indian, for all his darkened hues, to be a kind of uncivilized white man. In fact, the color of the Indian was often dismissed as insignificant, and some trappers maintained that it resulted from the Indian practice of smearing himself with bear grease and other cosmetics.[114] Thus, European racism toward Indians was moderated from the outset. But the main reason for Europeans losing their appetite for enslaving Indians was prudential. Many Indians came from fierce tribes which vowed and sometimes secured vengeance. Europeans wanted to maintain amicable relations with tribes, with whom they traded furs, linens, rifles, alcohol, and other goods. Moreover several Indian tribes were nomadic hunters, and European planters found it exasperating to the point of impossibility to accustom them to the intensive work of settled agriculture. Finally Indians proved quite adept at escaping, and when this happened they faded into the landscape; it was extremely difficult to retrieve runaway Indians who knew the territory.[115] By contrast, Africans could run but they could not easily hide.

Although content to enslave Indians to get work done, Europeans in general considered Indian slavery a temporary expedient to accelerate the native's transition to civilization. When Indians proved resistant to slavery, many of them dying from disease, resistance, and strain, some Europeans attributed this to the nobility of the Indian character, which they concluded was not naturally disposed to slavery. Many whites liked and respected Indian qualities; Winthrop Jordan comments that it is no historical accident that the Indian, and not the Negro, ended up on the old American five-cent piece.[116] Even today one finds legacies of the white man's admiration: high school teams called the Indians, Braves, and Seminoles, or cities with names like Cheyenne and Sioux City.

Nothing better illustrates the presence of racism than attitudes and laws affecting miscegenation, and here too the Indian found himself favored over the African. While whites portrayed blacks as grossly promiscuous and declared sexual contact with them abominable and unlawful, they showed no comparable public revulsion toward relationships with Indians.[117] Although they would probably have regarded it as unthinkable for blacks, several of the most distinguished Americans of the colonial period—Patrick Henry, John Marshall, Robert Beverley, William Byrd, Thomas Jefferson—all recommended intermarriage as an excellent way to overcome white prejudices against Indians and integrate them into civilized society.[118]

Although slavery and racism are not intrinsically related, as we have seen, what distinguished the American experience from the rest of the world was the evolution over time of racial slavery, specifically black slavery. The American institution of slavery became driven and maintained by the assumptions of racial superiority. Yet over time racism developed into an ideological system with institutions of its own. As one scholar puts it, "Eventually a black skin was taken as a natural outward sign of inward mental and moral inferiority."[119] Since the dehumanization of black slaves can be ascribed to their slave status rather than their color, nowhere can the impact of American racism be better seen than in the treatment of free blacks in this country.

During the period between the American Revolution and the Civil War, most states either by law or social compulsion prevented free blacks from voting. In a number of northern states they were prohibited from giving testimony in cases where a white person was involved. Frequently, free blacks found themselves systematically segregated from the white community, even in the northern states. Most lived in black areas of town, nicknamed "Little Africa," "New Guinea," and "Nigger Hill." Many found all but the most menial and low-paying jobs closed to them. Some states burdened them with special taxes. Free blacks and slaves were generally not permitted to marry. In virtually all states intermarriage with whites was strictly outlawed. Some jurisdictions made it a crime for free blacks to travel without identification, or to keep guns or dogs without license, or to consort with slaves, or to meet in large groups even for school or church. Finally, all free blacks were exposed to the discretionary indignities of whites, with little recourse to courts of law or any other forum of grievance. If free blacks could not pay their debts or violated the law, they sometimes risked being sold into slavery.[120]

TAKING CARE OF BUSINESS

Although scholars continue to debate whether slavery was a profitable institution, the question becomes clearer if we specify: profitable for whom? Obviously slavery was profitable for slaveowners, which is why they adopted it. As scholars never tire of pointing out, slavery existed because there was work that needed to be done, and plantation owners preferred that it be done without pay. Slaves were a kind of "human tool," as Orlando Patterson puts it. They cost money to buy and to maintain, but as property they were conveniently exempt from wages and salaries. The Southern plantation system preceded slavery, but it made the transition from employing paid workers to slaves for the simple reason that black slaves were cheaper. "The money which procured a white man's services for ten years could buy a Negro for life."[121] It cost $200 on average to buy a slave at the beginning of the 19th century; by 1860 the cost ranged from $1,400 to $2,000.[122] These were not trifling amounts of money in those days, but they entitled slaveowners to a man or woman's entire life of service. Although white slaveowners described themselves as patriarchs and aristocrats, administering a system pleasantly detached from the injustices and greed of Northern capitalism—a claim endorsed by some scholars—Walter Rodney sensibly points out that it strains credulity to think that slave traders and plantation owners "were so dumb that for centuries they absorbed themselves in a nonprofit venture."[123] Slave labor enriched the slaveowner and served as the foundation of the plantation economy of the southern states.[124]

At the same time, what was good for the slaveowner was not necessarily good for the South. Slavery insulated that region of the United States from the vital economic information conveyed by a wage and price system. Thus when labor became expensive in the North, business began to move toward consolidation, mechanization, and other techniques of improved efficiency. While the North invested in innovation and invention, the South languished.[125] Whatever needed to be done, the slaves were there to do, and nobody, least of all the slaves, was in any particular hurry.

The paradoxical conclusion is that slavery in the United States was profitable for the planters, yet simultaneously retarded the industrial development of the plantation society. Until recently, the South remained the most economically backward part of the country.

In the mid 1970s, the scholarly debate on the material life of black slaves was dramatically changed with the publication of Robert Fogel and Stanley Engerman's *Time on the Cross*. Previous generalizations about the slave livelihood were largely partial and anecdotal: excerpts from slave diaries, reports of abuse by masters, a handful of plantation records from this or that state. Based on a systematic review and computer analysis of tens of thousands of farms, drawn from census data, invoices of sales, and Southern plantation records—a technique called cliometrics—Fogel and Engerman made some astonishing claims. They argued that slaves were in general relatively well treated by masters. Whippings were infrequent. The slave diet was better than that of many white workers in the North and many more in Europe. Slaves often lived in better quarters than Northern laborers. They worked shorter hours and fewer days. A noticeable number of masters did not typically expropriate all the earnings of slaves; instead, they permitted slaves to retain a percentage of their product, so that many slaves could accumulate private property and capital. Slaveowners only infrequently broke up slave families by selling off wives, although they more readily sold children. Masters did not typically cohabit with the wives and daughters of slaves, nor did they breed large regiments of mulatto children; on the contrary, they encouraged the family unit which remained basically intact.[126]

In presenting their findings about slavery, Fogel and Engerman stated their intention to "expose many myths that have served to corrode and poison relations between the races."[127] But the authors soon discovered that, when it comes to slavery, good news is unwelcome. Few contemporary scholars, least of all African Americans, are interested in conclusions that mitigate the historical sins of the slaveholders and reduce the magnitude of the sufferings of the slaves. After an initial burst of favorable publicity, Fogel and Engerman came under obstreperous attack from scholars who accused them of being morally insensitive, and from black activists who accused them of being racists. Writing in *The New Republic*, Allan Lichtman charged Fogel and Engerman with offering a "benign portrait of slavery," a work that was "susceptible to racist interpretations." Christopher Dell in *The Nation* fumed that the authors appeared "as the friends of slavery," presenting findings according to which "slavery can appear to be a kind of happy picnic lunch."[128]

As these remarks indicate, the greatest concern of Fogel and Engerman's critics was that the two scholars were giving scholarly support to ancient plantation stereotypes of the happy slave, singing in the cotton field, getting along famously with his compassionate master.[129] This Southern perspective is represented by the husband of Mary Boykin Chesnut, who always complained that slaves ate his hogs and meat but hardly did any work. Asked if he had a problem with runaways, he snorted, "Never. It's pretty hard work to keep me from running away from them."[130] Actually, Fogel and Engerman's critics had a point. Reading *Time on the Cross* by itself, slavery appears such a relatively mild business that one begins to wonder why Frederick Douglass and so many others ever tried to escape. Fogel and Engerman's statistical work frequently does obscure the day-to-day hardships of slavery, which are more apparent by scrutinizing the fates of particular individuals, not simply mathematical tables. Proclaiming the new findings inconclusive, critics of Fogel and Engerman resuscitated example after example from the old literature of slave hardship and abuse.[131] One undoubtedly positive result of the debate was that a number of reputable scholars undertook new research, seeking for Fogel and Engerman either vindication or their own time on the cross.

Two decades later, a great deal has been published on the subject, and scholars are beginning to converge on the facts about slavery, as they can best be determined given inevitable limitations of data. The emerging consensus of this scholarship is that slaves were, in material terms of diet, health, and shelter, slightly better off than northern industrial workers, and far better off than workers in much of Europe. Oddly, the slave's complete dependence gave the master the responsibility for providing him and his family with food, clothing, shelter, and medical attention; however partial or inadequate these provisions, no free workers enjoyed a comparable social security system from birth until death. Indeed Eugene Genovese in *Roll, Jordan, Roll* concludes that the vast majority of the world's population probably did not then live and eat as well as the slaves did in the South a hundred years ago.[132] Slaves who worked in urban areas as skilled craftsmen enjoyed much greater freedom, often choosing their own housing, and paying a share of their earnings to their owners, keeping the rest for themselves.[133] "Slaves came to expect Sundays off," Nathan Huggins writes. "Holidays, especially Christmas, were almost everywhere occasions for parties and entertainment. There would be extras like whisky, cake and dances."[134]

In Latin America slaves were often worked to death by overseers who were paid a percentage of the crop, so that they had every incentive to maximize production and none to keep the slaves healthy. But American plantations were relatively small, and owners typically played a direct role in management. Because slaves were expensive, masters treated them as valuable possessions. Thomas Sowell points out that masters often hired immigrants, especially Irishmen, to do work that was considered unsafe for slaves, such as draining infested swamps, cutting trees, building railroads, or tending combustible boilers.[135] The Northern traveler Frederick Olmstead was told by an Alabama riverboat owner, "The niggers are worth too much to be risked here; if the Paddies are knocked overboard or their backs break, nobody loses anything."[136]

Of all the slaves shipped from Africa to the New World, only a small fraction, about 7 percent, came to the United States.[137] Yet this relatively small imported population of approximately 400,000 would multiply by 1860 to a slave total of more than four million, making the U.S. slaves the only group in the Americas to multiply itself.[138] The life expectancy of slaves in the South was only slightly lower than that for slaveowners.[139] Their average diet, although acknowledged by Robert Fogel to be nutritionally inadequate in some respects, nevertheless gave them a mortality rate comparable to many Western Europeans.[140] Certainly this is a reflection of the material treatment of slaves.

Journeying in the United States during the 1830s, the French writer Gustave de Beaumont compared the circumstances of Indians and Negroes in America to those of the Irish in Europe. "I have seen the Indian in his forests and the Negro in his chains, and thought, as I contemplated their pitiable condition, that I saw the very extreme of human wretchedness, but I did not then know the condition of unfortunate Ireland."[141] Visiting Ireland in the 1840s, the former slave turned abolitionist Frederick Douglass agreed; he was so appalled that he was almost "ashamed to lift my voice against American slavery."[142] Slaves in the United States suffered no dietary deprivation comparable to the Irish potato famine, in which one million people perished from hunger.[143]

But these are comparisons of deprivation with extreme deprivation. As Beaumont's remarks make clear, slaves may have lived less miserably than others, but they did live miserably. They typically rose at four or five in the morning, they worked between twelve and sixteen hours a day, their meals were tasteless or unappetizing, their living quarters drab and inadequate, their medical care was poor, their religious and social lives were entirely subordinate to their work routines. As the testimony of several former slaves indicates, the institution was excruciating to endure because of its debilitating monotony and boredom, its elaborate paraphernalia of rules and regulations, and its routinized neglect of those aspects of life which raise the human being above the level of a beast.[144] Slaves were purposefully condemned to an existence as a hewer of wood and a drawer of water, so that others could live fuller, more comfortable lives.[145]

If many slaves were fortunate to have kind or moderate owners who did not ill treat them, this is because the corrupt system did not erode all that was Christian and decent in the Southern master class. Moreover, if it was customary for planters to offer special rewards to slaves such as extra holidays, better meals, even small cash payments, this was mainly for the purpose of getting work out of them. If whippings were not used promiscuously on well-run plantations, this was because they had been administered often enough to have a deterrent effect. If wounds and mutilations and injuries to slaves were not the norm, this was partly because masters knew that injuries and visible scars reduced the efficiency and future marketability of the slave. If masters did not routinely rape and abuse slave women, this was largely to avoid a collapse of morale among slave families, not to mention the possibility of murderous retaliatory attacks from slave men.[146]

The point is that all these terrible things happened, and happened often. If they did not occur more frequently, that is partly because of the religious and ethical sensibilities of masters, but mostly because it was not in the interest of the owners to carry the abuse of slaves too far. Remember that the defining characteristic of the slave was that he was legally classified as property. Most people, and Southern planters were no different, try to take care of their property, not because they care about its feelings, but because they don't want it to spoil or depreciate. In the words of one plantation journal, "Men, like animals, cannot work unless there is furnished to them the necessary comforts which by nature they require."[147] In summary, the American slave *was* treated like property, which is to say, pretty well.

THE PSYCHIC WOUND OF SLAVERY

Despite the fact that scholars have refuted much of the popular conception of slavery as a form of physical mass torture, the conventional image
of the institution remains true insofar as the most heinous legacy of slavery was not its material deprivations but its psychological and social injuries. The testimony of three of the most perceptive observers suggests
the depth of slavery's psychic burden. Tocqueville reports in the early
nineteenth century that masters had improved the physical condition of
slaves quite a bit, yet the plight of the slave never improved because
"they have spiritualized despotism and violence."[148] A few years later,
Frederick Douglass denounced slavery as not only the theft of a man's
labor but, more painful, the "murder of his soul,"[149] a process of dehumanization by which "a man was transformed into a brute."[150] Reflecting
on slavery early in the twentieth century, the African American scholar
W. E. B. Du Bois acknowledged that slaves shared the hardships of many
common laborers in the mines and sweatshops of the world:

> But there is a real meaning to slavery different from that we may apply to the
> laborer today. It was in part psychological, the enforced personal feeling of in-
> feriority, the calling of another Master, the standing with hat in hand. It was
> the helplessness. It was the defenselessness of family life. It was the submer-
> gence below the arbitrary will of any sort of individual.[151]

It is perhaps understandable why masters would seek to extract the
maximum labor of slaves, but why would they degrade them in this manner? The reasons lie in the very nature of slavery. As Orlando Patterson
argues, slavery is not a voluntary condition, yet morally in his failure to
resist to his last breath, the slave is the person who has chosen a debased
life over an honorable death. Consequently, slaves throughout the world
have been considered to be persons without honor.[152] Moreover, the
practice of slavery accustoms masters to dealing with human beings as
commodities. In the United States, as elsewhere, slaves were auctioned
in open markets, bred and sometimes branded like cattle, wagered in
card and dice games, presented as gifts at social events, and deeded to
others in wills.[153] Since the law treated slaves as things rather than people, many masters showed little desire to honor their psychological and
social needs, or even to acknowledge that they had any.

The effects of this institutionalized callousness on the slaves were cat-
aclysmic. Any material security that came from the expectation that their

masters would feed and clothe them was overwhelmed by the psychic in-security that came from the knowledge that their masters could sell their common-law wives or children at any time. Such sales were not typical; in a review of the evidence, one scholar estimates that one-quarter to one-third of slave marriages were broken up in this way. But in no South-ern state were such sales illegal, and they were frequent enough to be a source of perennial anguish.[154] The indignities imposed on slave women must have been excruciating for them to bear, and for their men and children to behold. Females of every age were often required to strip to the waist, or even to take all their clothes off, for display and inspection at auction. Whether the practice was frequent in some places or rare in others, in no state was the rape of a slave woman a crime by law. The consequence, for the slaves, was a tremendous physical and emotional vulnerability.[155]

Although many states had laws against wantonly cruel treatment, blacks were not allowed to testify in court and white juries proved ex-tremely reluctant to convict. Slaves were not permitted to strike a white man, and there were actually laws on the books recommending that slaves be chastised for rudeness and insolence. Especially in areas of heavy slave concentration, local statutes made it illegal for slaves to leave the area, carry sticks or weapons, or gather in large numbers, even to lis-ten to a sermon, outside the presence of a white man. Although never fol-lowed consistently in practice, the logic of regarding slaves as chattel implied that there were few legal restrictions on what masters could do, including flog or maim them. As one Virginia assembly put it: how can a man be prevented from mistreating his own property?[156]

Even slaves not subjected to these brutal whims were demeaned by their masters who kept them ignorant and illiterate, allowing their minds to atrophy. Many states made it illegal for masters to teach slaves to read and write, fearing the implantation, however unwitting, of ideas of freedom into their heads.[157] In addition to all this, there were the discretionary in-dignities, sometimes deployed by masters for their own amusement and to keep black slaves in their places. Virtually all slaves were given only a first name, and not permitted a surname or family name. Grown men were ad-dressed as "boy" to italicize their subordinate status. Frequently, slaves were not told their own age.[158] And masters with a special taste for malice gave their slaves improbable and absurd names, such as Colonel, Senator, Apollo Belvedere, Napoleon Boneyfidey Waterloo, Ananias, Piddlekins, Lady Adeliza Chimpanzee and Prince Orang Outan.[159]

OUT OF AMERICA

The Negro has been formed by this nation, for better or worse,
and does not belong to any other—not to Africa, and certainly not
to Islam.

—James Baldwin[160]

Slavery is routinely blamed for having stolen from American blacks their
culture, yet as a result of slavery, American blacks lost their ancestral tribal affiliations but gained a culture. Contrary to the claims of some Afrocentrists, this culture is not African, but Afro-American. The cumulative
social effect of slavery was to uproot Africans from their original home,
to foster the development of a unique new culture under the strains of
oppression. Thus like other ethnic groups blacks have recognizable
group traits. They did not import these from abroad, but developed
them in the United States. The camaraderie generated by this common
culture is suggested by African Americans who call each other "brother"
or "sister," even when they are not related. Like all cultures, Afro-American culture under slavery developed unique strengths and weaknesses,
some of which may have endured long after slavery was abolished, perhaps even to the present day.[161]

Scholars continue to debate the persistence of African beliefs and customs among American slaves. Scholars seeking to build a case for contemporary black nationalism and African pride have labored hard to
locate African religious beliefs, tribal ways, and folk history and literature
among American slaves. Many such examples have been located, sometimes in the United States but predominantly in South America and the
Caribbean.[162] One scholar, J. L. Dillard, argues that Black English, the
urban dialect spoken by many African Americans, has etymological roots
in "survivals from West African languages."[163] Yet the case for a substantial African heritage in the United States remains problematic. American
slaves did not come from a single area or nation in Africa. They came
from hundreds of different tribes, speaking literally hundreds of different languages, and adhering to a varied array of customs and beliefs.[164] It
is only a slight exaggeration to say that the only thing they had in common was the color of their skin. Thus it seems farfetched for African
Americans today to allege that whites have stolen from them a shared
African culture that not even their ancestors possessed. Yet coming from
heterogeneous cultures, Africans in the United States entered a relatively

homogenous culture decisively shaped by Europe, Protestantism, and the distinctive American experience.[165] Unlike in South America and the Caribbean, where plantations commonly employed several hundred or even thousands of slaves, blacks in the United States were typically placed on family-owned plantations with small numbers of slaves.[166] As a result, African mores such as voodoo, conjuring, and witchcraft endured much better in the large slave communities of Brazil and the West Indies. In the United States, by contrast, slaves were unable to preserve over the generations anything more than fragments of African memory.

As black scholar E. Franklin Frazier describes, the shock of displacement to a new land was soon followed by a struggle for social adjustment and survival. Africans could not continue to speak in their native language, for not only their masters but also other slaves from other tribes would not understand them. So the slaves learned English, although of a broken, pigdin variety. African religions lasted longer, but even these were typically treated as barbarous by slaveowners and sometimes had to be practiced in secret. Over time, many slaves converted to the religion of their masters, and residual African beliefs were synthesized with the new faith.[167]

Although slaves in the United States were stripped of their African heritage, through their own creative response and resistance to slavery they fashioned over time a new and distinctive style and ethos. This is not to suggest that black slaves entirely reinvented themselves, only that from a common African background they created a new American culture. Some of their distinctive cultural affinities, such as the centrality of music and dance, are clearly traceable to Africa, but of course they now sang in English, about topics more pertinent to American slavery than to tribal life— the melancholy of oppression or the hope of Christian salvation.[168] The culture of American slaves was *sui generis;* as many studies have shown, black slaves reoriented their African identities to their special situation in the new country.[169] Thus there does not seem to be much substantial African content in black culture in the United States today. America has Polish-Americans, Irish-Americans, and Italian-Americans, but no Yoruba-Americans or Wolof-Americans. The contemporary invocation of African heritage has its ideological rationale, and it accurately points to a place of origin, but historically it seems to be a misnomer for the uniquely American cultural identities of the descendants of black slaves.

What did Africans make of themselves in America? In sharp contrast to their tribal and communal past, they discovered the virtues of individuality, which was a desperate and eventually triumphant defense of personal dignity against the commonplace assaults of slavery. Right from their earliest experience in the United States, black slaves began to develop distinctive ways of walking, of talking, of telling jokes and stories. As if to assert their unique individual identities, some slaves took to eccentric habits like carrying a cane or cocking their hat. Slaves developed widely different personalities on the plantation: the playful Sambo, the sullen "field nigger," the dependable Mammy, the sly and inscrutable trickster.[170] Some of these personality types are still recognizable.

Slaves developed a communal life too, much of it built around the two central institutions of the black church and the black family.[171] For a people oppressed, a deep religious faith helped to create autonomous spiritual space that even the master had to respect, and it offered hope that the travails of the slaves would someday end; in the touching words of the spiritual, "I'd rather be in heaven settin' down."[172] The slaves embraced the white man's Christianity, but they did not make the white man's distinction between salvation in the next world and liberation in this one. Slaves identified with Christ as the suffering victim who would rise again, and they invested this-worldly hopes in scriptural themes of deliverance and the promised land: "Let my people go."[173] Led by Richard Allen and Absalom Jones, some blacks withdrew from white pews and founded their own churches, such as the African Methodist Episcopal Church.[174] Even today, black churches have a distinct style and sound.

Slavery did not destroy the black family. In claiming that it did, W. E. B. Du Bois, E. Franklin Frazier, Kenneth Stampp, and Daniel Patrick Moynihan seem to overstate their case.[175] These scholars are certainly right that slavery placed enormous pressure on the monogamous family. Because men had no special responsibility or ability to provide for others, the black family was never as patriarchal as the white family. During slavery the only distinction between legitimate and illegitimate children was conventional, not legal. In *The Negro American Family,* W. E. B. Du Bois estimated the black illegitimacy rate in 1900, a few decades after emancipation, to be around 25 percent, compared with a white illegitimacy rate of less than 2 percent.[176] Ever since that time, single-parent and illegitimacy rates for black families have always been higher than those for white families. Who can deny that this is partly a consequence of slavery?

Yet the black family outlasted slavery. As Herbert Gutman documents in *The Black Family in Slavery and Freedom,* despite countless assaults and depredations, blacks struggled to preserve their families during slavery.

Even when old ones were broken up, they started new ones, a process that Eugene Genovese terms "sequential polygamy." After emancipation, many former slaves searched the countryside to reunite broken homes and lost relatives. In the early part of the twentieth century, there is clear evidence of a two-parent black family building upon the foundation of that institution under slavery. Gutman found that in many areas, the duration and stability of marriages were about the same for blacks and whites of similar socioeconomic background. Both in the rural South and the urban North, Gutman found that "the typical Afro-American family was lower-class in status and headed by two parents." Even in Harlem between 1905 and 1925, Gutman found few female-headed families.[177]

The worst decay in the two-parent black family unit seems to have occurred not during slavery or as a result of slavery, but much later and for different reasons. Nor is there any evidence that as a consequence of slavery, blacks condoned illegitimacy as acceptable within the community. For the decline and fragility of the contemporary black family, the institution of slavery bears only a minor responsibility.

CULTURE OF IRRESPONSIBILITY

Slavery as a system can legitimately be blamed for a culture of self-defeating and irresponsible attitudes and behavior among black Americans. Whether that culture persists today is arguable; that it developed under slavery, and as a result of slavery, seems well established in the evidence. This raises an awkward question: were white stereotypes of blacks, dating back to the late nineteenth and early twentieth centuries, partly accurate?

For an institution so widespread, and one that lasted for more than two hundred years, slavery in the United States inspired very few revolts. In this respect, Denmark Vesey and Nat Turner were aberrations.[178] This has disappointed some scholars such as Herbert Aptheker, who have been looking for slaves to behave like an American proletariat, but it is hardly surprising: slaves were outnumbered and outgunned, and revolts were virtually guaranteed to fail. As an alternative to revolution, however, slaves did develop numerous strategies of resistance. Over time, these consolidated into predictable modes of thought and action, recognized by masters and slaves alike, and internalized into the routines of slave culture.

Three aspects of the slave culture of resistance stand out. One revolves around a series of measures to avoid, postpone, and minimize work. Masters decried it as sloth and laziness, but for slaves it was a creative technique to abstain from toiling for rewards that would primarily benefit someone else. Slaves were certainly driven to their labors by various inducements and threats, but understandably they did no more than absolutely necessary to secure their small benefits and defer the master's wrath. This phenomenon has been observed of slaves in the United States and elsewhere.[179] "Nothing could stop the dogged slave from doing just as little and as poor work as possible," writes W. E. B. Du Bois. "All observers spoke of the fact that the slaves were slow and churlish; that they wasted material and malingered in their work. Of course they did. They might be made to work continuously, but no power could make them work well."[180] Elsewhere Du Bois reflects upon "the peculiar contribution which the Negro made to labor" in the United States and comes up with a surprising answer: "the thing that is usually known as laziness."[181] Techniques for avoiding or at least deferring work included moving in very slow motion, taking long breaks and pauses, breaking tools to create an interruption, setting fire to property, and feigning sickness.[182] When such strategies went undetected, they were a source of exhilaration and even prestige among slaves, who came to attach a high value to the ethic of work avoidance, an attitude captured in the defiant slave song:

I'se Wild Nigger Bill
Frum Redpepper Hill,
I never did wo'k,
An' I never will.[183]

Of course slavery influenced the work habits of masters no less than slaves. In *The Mind of the South,* first published in the 1940s, W. J. Cash noticed a lackadaisical approach to punctuality and hard work in the South which he attributed to the legacy of slavery. Since the families of white masters did very little work, over the generations they developed cultural patterns of sloth and an aristocratic self-image that glorified idleness.[184]

Another practice that was widely followed and won high praise among slaves was theft. Again, from the slave's point of view, what is the harm of stealing something that you have worked for, and to which you feel entitled by right, but which is taken from you by force, as part of an institution that you regard as fundamentally unjust? "The white man's laws against theft," Kenneth Stampp writes, "were not supported by the slave's code."[185] Slaves did not lack a moral code; as Eugene Genovese argues, they regarded stealing from each other as wrong and worthy of punishment, but stealing from the master's provisions as justifiable and commendable.[186] Moreover, theft by slaves revealed the contradiction at the heart of slavery, for here was a case of property stealing property! In the words of Frederick Douglass:

> To be sure, this was stealing . . . but in the case of my master it was a question of removal—taking his meat out of one tub and putting it in another. At first he owned it in the tub, and last he owned it in me.[187]

The third, and perhaps most broadly shared, part of resistance culture among slaves was the high prestige and valorization of the "bad nigger." The master might regard him as defiant and uppity, but for many slaves he carried all the appeal of the outlaw taking on the corrupt establishment. Since the regime itself was unlawful and scandalous, the "bad nigger" demonstrated his open contempt for law and his own ability to scandalize. He was a small-scale revolutionary, always threatening to poison the master, or stalking his wife, or setting fire to the barn at night. If the slaves spoke of a runaway as a "ba-ad nigger," the implication was that the phrase meant the opposite of what was said.[188]

This renegade archetype, cultivated under slavery, persisted well into the twentieth century. Numerous black folk tales dramatize and sometimes romanticize this roguish character. Richard Wright acknowledges that the tortured crimes of Bigger Thomas in his classic novel *Native Son* are based on an enduring "bad nigger" image that, in Bigger's mind, became indistinguishable from reality.[189] The famous story called "Stagolee" begins with the statement, "Stagolee was undoubtedly and without question the baddest nigger that ever lived." The story goes on to describe Stagolee's drinking, cardplaying, womanizing, and criminal exploits, all with an air of naughty appreciation.[190] And in Spike Lee's film, the young Malcolm X is presented as a "bad nigger." His pimping and criminality are integrated into a playful and amusing musical routine. The implication is that there is nothing wrong with the "bad nigger," it's the system that makes him bad. Even today, among many blacks, the term "bad" is often used in a context that makes it clear that what is meant is "good."[191] Orlando Patterson writes:

> There was a distinct underclass of slaves . . . who lived fecklessly or dangerously. They were the incorrigible blacks of whom the slaveowner class was forever complaining. They ran away. They were idle. They were compulsive

liars. They seemed immune to punishment. . . . We can trace the underclass, as a persisting social phenomenon, to this group.[192]

For better or worse, it seems hard to deny that blacks, many of whom are racially mixed, have nevertheless shaped, out of the debris of oppression, a distinctive ethnic identity which goes back to slavery. This ethnic identity is distinguished from a racial identity in the sense that the former is cultural, the latter biological. Black culture is of course partly Southern culture, and among poorer blacks, lower-class culture. Yet it remains possible that ethnicity, rather than race, may partly account for black patterns of behavior that advance or inhibit the aspirations of African Americans today.

WHO KILLED SLAVERY?

If America as a nation owes blacks as a group reparations for slavery, what do blacks as a group owe America for the abolition of slavery? This question is not frivolous, because while slavery is not a distinctively Western institution, what is distinctively Western is the campaign to end slavery. Many people have of course resisted being captured and sold as slaves, but no society, including all of Africa, has ever on its own account mounted principled opposition to human servitude.[193] In all the literature condemning Western slavery, however, few scholars have asked why a practice sanctioned by virtually all people for thousands of years should be questioned, and eventually halted, by only one.[194] "No civilization once dependent on slavery has ever been able to eradicate it, except the Western," J. M. Roberts writes.[195]

Paradoxically, nowhere else in the world but in America is the legacy of slavery a contemporary issue; the American Constitution is condemned as a document that basely compromised with slavery, and the framers are routinely denounced for being racist hypocrites. The irony is compounded by the recognition that the prevailing view of the Constitution as pro-slavery was precisely that of Justice Taney in the *Dred Scott* decision. By contrast, Abraham Lincoln strongly denied Taney's view and Lincoln's position came to be enthusiastically embraced by the greatest black leader of the nineteenth century, Frederick Douglass. It is to the debates over the legitimacy of slavery in the West that we must turn to decide whether Taney and many twentieth century scholars are right, or whether Lincoln is right.

The Southern defense of slavery only developed as a coherent ideology in the eighteenth and nineteenth centuries, because for the first time, slavery came under strong attack. Throughout history, slavery had very few defenders for the simple reason that it had no critics. The institution was uncontroversial, and that which is established and taken for granted does not have to be justified. It would be unthinkable for Muslims to launch an antislavery crusade, Bernard Lewis writes, because slavery is specifically permitted by the Koran and the prophet Muhammad owned slaves.[196] The American South was virtually unique among slave societies in history in that it produced a comprehensive pro-slavery ideology.[197] In part this was because slavery was under assault to a degree unrivaled anywhere else in the world.[198]

The simplest defense for slavery is economic necessity; as Chancellor William Harper casually observed in 1837, "If there are sordid, servile and laborious offices to be performed, is it not better that there should be sordid, servile and laborious beings to fill them?"[199] This argument is based on a kind of domestic *Realpolitik:* someone has to do the dirty work, so why not them rather than us? Harper's argument is based on an implicit premise: whites in the South are in a position to compel blacks to perform menial but necessary tasks. It is force, rather than right, that keeps the system of slavery in place.

Southerners were familiar with a European tradition, going back to the Crusades, which held that it was permissible to enslave pagans but not Christians. In response to this, the leading forces in the South formulated an identical justification: Africans were heathens, so that slavery would serve as a kind of moral education to introduce them to Christianity. But there was a serious flaw in this argument: once slaves embraced the Christian faith of their masters, other excuses became necessary in order to justify keeping them in servitude. Here many Southern divines intervened to offer a racist rationale. They promulgated a dubious interpretation of a story in the book of Genesis in which Noah curses the descendants of his son Ham, who impudently looked upon his father's nakedness. Thus, in this account, the children of Ham were condemned to blackness and future enslavement. This argument too was absurd: in fact, the Bible nowhere states that the children of Ham were black. But since slavery proved such an expedient institution, for a long time there was little challenge to this innovation in biblical exegesis.[200]

It was only when the institution of slavery came under moral assault for betraying the Declaration of Independence and for betraying Christian charity by treating human beings as chattel, that many Southern apologists such as John Calhoun, James Henry Hammond, Edmund Ruffin, George Frederick Holmes and George Fitzhugh responded by formulating an audacious defense of slavery as a positive good.[201] Southerners like James Hammond and George Fitzhugh repudiated the Jeffersonian doctrine of equality as, in Hammond's words, "ridiculously absurd." Fitzhugh tastelessly quipped that blacks "have a natural and inalienable right to be slaves."[202]

As articulated in *DeBow's Review* and other Southern journals, the case for slavery depended on a paternalistic worldview in which Negroes, like women and children, occupied positions in an organic society commensurate with their limited moral and intellectual abilities. Eugene Genovese writes in *The Slaveholders' Dilemma,* "Southerners from social theorists to divines to politicians to ordinary slaveholders and yeomen insisted fiercely that emancipation would cast blacks into a marketplace in which they could not compete and would condemn them to the fate of the Indians or worse."[203] Although defenders of slavery were right about the harshness of Northern capitalism, their paternalistic vision foundered in that the community of interests that could generally be presumed between husband and wife, or between parents and children, could not be presumed between master and slave.

Oddly enough, Southern pro-slavery thought contained an implicit defense of democracy—for whites. As Alexander Stephens put it in 1861, "With us, all the white race, however high or low, rich or poor, are equal in the eyes of the law. Not so with the Negro. Subordination is his place."[204] Pierre Van Den Berghe terms this racial system "Herrenvolk democracy," because it extends full rights to the master class but denies rights to subordinate classes on account of their presumed inferiority.[205] Southern paternalism was supported not simply by slaveowners, who had a vested material interest in such an ideology, but also by many poor whites because it offered an important psychological benefit: racial self-esteem. The Southern doctrine of Negro inferiority automatically extended to whites, even those who were destitute and ignorant, membership in an exclusive racial club and a social position above that of all blacks, both slave and free. Edmund Morgan argues in *American Slavery, American Freedom* that the racial defense of Southern slavery strengthened, among whites, the conviction that despite conspicuous differences of wealth and position they were equal just as the Declaration of

Independence posited.[206] Racism, in other words, became a source of white social status.

The Southern defense of slavery ultimately came down to a very old Western argument, one found in Plato's *Republic:* the wise should rule over the unwise. During the Lincoln-Douglas debates, Stephen Douglas defended the right of states to decide for themselves whether they wanted slavery in precisely these terms:

> The civilized world has always held that when any race of men have shown themselves to be so degraded by ignorance, superstition, cruelty, and barbarism, as to be utterly incapable of governing themselves, they must, in the nature of things, be governed by others, by such laws as are deemed to be applicable to their condition.[207]

WISDOM AND CONSENT

We may think Stephen Douglas's view to be crude and hateful, but Abraham Lincoln did not. He agreed with Douglas: it is absurd to construct a regime in which the wise do not rule; surely no one wants to be governed by the mediocre or the foolish. In fact this raises a problem with democracy that the American founders and Lincoln all recognized: how can the wise, who are by definition the few, be reliably identified and chosen to rule by the many? Representative government is based on the hope that the majority will exercise their power on behalf of right: that they will choose others to govern who are wiser than themselves. Yet modern democracy introduces a crucial qualification to the claim of the wise to rule: such rule is only legitimate when it is vindicated by popular consent. The majority is not always the best judge of what is wise, but most people do recognize their own interests. Hence representative democracy is a "mixed regime," which seeks to reconcile the claims of right and expediency.

This debate is the crucial backdrop to an examination of the antislavery movement of the eighteenth century, because it provided the context and indeed the moral terms for the debate. Martin Klein writes that for the first time in all of recorded history, slavery came under attack in Europe and America in the eighteenth century.[208] Absent what David Brion Davis terms "a bizarre radicalism" first among religious Protestants and then among political reformers, slavery may never have been seriously challenged and could well have persisted to the present. The two principles that would form the basis for the first serious challenge to the institution of slavery and the doctrine of black inferiority are both encapsulated in the Declaration of Independence: the Christian belief that all persons are children of God and equal in His eyes, and the distinctively modern European political conception that all human beings enjoy a natural right to freedom and self-government that can only be abridged by their consent.[209]

Neither of these principles was formulated to deal with slavery, and for a very long time they were not thought to be relevant to it. After all, as Southern writers pointed out, the Bible appears to sanction slavery and Christ mounted no political campaign against it. Biblical passages extolling human equality in God's sight were interpreted as referring to the spiritual equality that obtained in the perfection of the next world, not to the political and social hierarchy that was deemed necessary to govern sinful human beings in this one. As for the idea of natural rights, it can be found in embryonic form in Greece as early as the fifth century B.C. The Sophists held that slavery was not natural but conventional, but they stopped short of invoking a right not to be enslaved. As we saw earlier, Aristotle defended slavery, although he distinguished between slaves "by nature," who lacked the capacity to govern themselves, and slaves "by accident," who happened to be enslaved owing to debt or captivity.

Only in the modern period, under the influence of Hobbes, Locke, and others, did Europeans conceive of freedom as encompassing the right to self-rule. Although Hobbes argued for absolute monarchy, his philosophy broke with the thought of the ancients in asserting that the wisdom of the king is only legitimate when it is ratified by the consent of the governed; all else is tyranny.[210] Despite his own allowances for slavery, which he described as "nothing else but the state of war continued between a lawful conqueror and a captive," Locke articulated a theory of property rights—"Every man has a property in his own person; nobody has any right but to himself; the labor of his body, and the work of his hands are properly his"[211]—that was flatly inconsistent with forced servitude. Eventually these principles worked themselves out in the minds of Europeans and helped to produce an antislavery position.

In the second half of the eighteenth century, a small but militant group of religious and political activists began to apply the doctrine of equality more broadly and concretely in order to reform the injustices of this world, what David Brion Davis terms "a sacralization of social progress."[212] Tocqueville wrote:

We have seen something absolutely without precedent in history—servitude abolished, not by the desperate effort of the slave, but by the enlightened will of the master. . . . It is we who have given a definite and practical meaning to the Christian idea that all men are born equal, and applied it to the realities of this world.[213]

The first group to mount an organized campaign against slavery was the Society of Friends, the Quakers, first in Europe in the second half of the seventeenth century, then in the United States. Ignoring passages in the Bible that had been invoked to justify slavery, leading Quakers such as George Fox in England, and John Woolman and Anthony Benezet in the United States, emphasized that spiritual freedom, man's capacity to choose the good in his quest for moral perfectibility, required freedom of choice in this life. Slavery, according to this view, represented the moral imprisonment of God's children and thus was wrong, even blasphemous. Drawing on the religious energies of the Great Awakening, the first of a series of revival movements that would energize America between the mid eighteenth century and the end of the nineteenth, many evangelical Protestants began to embrace a similar interpretation. They applied Christ's injunction—do unto others as we would have them do unto us—directly to the relationship between slaveowners and slaves. Their antislavery convictions grew stronger in the late eighteenth century in op-position to secular and anticlerical philosophes and freethinkers who de-clared slavery to be a rational system based on empirical evidence of the natural inferiority of blacks. Such scientific arguments, David Brion Davis writes, "enabled orthodox Christians to make a defense of Africans a defense of religion itself."[214]

In 1772, Lord Mansfield issued a landmark decision in Britain abol-ishing slavery on English soil. In 1833, thanks to the abolition campaign of Granville Sharp, Thomas Clarkson, and especially William Wilber-force, slavery was outlawed throughout the British empire. Economic motives undoubtedly contributed, but scholars now generally agree that religious and political principles were indispensable in achieving the end of servitude.[215] Antislavery victories soon spread to France, which for-bade slavery in its territories in 1848, and to other European nations as well.[216] In a bizarre development, tribal leaders in Gambia, the Congo, Dahomey, and other African nations that had prospered under the slave trade sent delegations to London and Paris to vigorously protest the abo-lition of slavery.[217] The rulers and merchants of Senegal demanded and secured classification as a "protectorate" rather than a "colony" so they could continue as slave traders. "Africans felt that the rules of their traditional life had been called into question," Mohamed Mbodj writes, "by initiatives which destabilized the bases of their society."[218]

Of course it is impossible to identify the typical African view of antislavery. Perhaps the fairest generalization is that no Africans opposed slavery in principle, they merely opposed their own enslavement. One English activist, who led a campaign to suppress slavery in the Sudan, found Africans unreceptive to his pleas and pressures. "It was in vain that I attempted to reason with them against the principles of slavery—they thought it wrong when they were themselves the sufferers, but were always ready to indulge in it when the preponderance of power lay upon their side."[219] Eventually, the British example backed by diplomatic and even military measures eradicated slavery in all foreign areas of European influence.

In America, although there were many abolitionists who shared prevailing prejudices against blacks, the abolitionist movement contained the first antiracists. Leading abolitionists felt the force of the argument that blacks were civilizationally inferior and incapable of ruling themselves. Consequently, many abolitionists conceded present black inferiority but revived the environmental explanation for it. Black inferiority, they said, is no justification for slavery; rather, it is the product of slavery itself.[220] Some abolitionists endorsed the idea of helping blacks to resettle in Africa, but those who recognized the implausibility of such schemes attempted to show that blacks were capable of living as free people. In order to directly rebut the Southern argument that blacks were better off being ruled by their betters, abolitionists began a slow but relentless quest for intelligent blacks who would be standing refutations of theories of intrinsic inferiority.[221]

Opponents of slavery had three prime exhibits to demonstrate the intellectual capacity of Negroes: Phillis Wheatley, the Negro poet; Benjamin Banneker, the black mathematician and scholar; and Frederick Douglass, the runaway slave and later statesman and orator. For many Americans, it was so unbelievable that a black person could produce a serious work of literature that eighteen eminent whites (including John Hancock, who signed the Declaration of Independence, and Thomas Hutchinson, the governor of Massachusetts) offered an "attestation to the publick" testifying that, upon examination, the poems were verified to be Wheatley's own work and that she was indeed a full-blooded black woman.[222] Additionally, abolitionists stressed the physical and mental sufferings of slaves in order to recruit humanitarian sentiment on behalf of emancipation; no one was more successful in this than Harriet Beecher Stowe, author of *Uncle Tom's Cabin,* published in 1852. Perhaps the most influential political tract of the nineteenth century, Stowe's sentimental novel was credited by Lincoln for turning the North irrevocably against slavery, setting the stage for the confrontation that ended with the Civil War.

WOLF BY THE EARS

The only distinction between freedom and slavery is this: in the former state, a man is governed by the laws to which he has given his consent; in the latter, he is governed by the will of another.

           —Alexander Hamilton[223]

Justice Taney's argument in *Dred Scott,* that the American founders were hypocrites who produced a pro-slavery regime, an opinion shared by many contemporary scholars, rests on the apparent contradiction between stated ideals and actual practice. It seems hard to explain how a slaveowner like Thomas Jefferson could declare that "all men are created equal." Nor is it obvious how fifty-five men in Philadelphia, some thirty of whom were slaveowners themselves, could proclaim antislavery principles while endorsing a document that would permit slavery to continue in the Southern states. This is the force behind Taney's insistence that these men could not have meant what they said. Taney's interpretation that the Constitution secures no rights for blacks leads directly to the contemporary suggestion that the founders were motivated not by noble ideals but by crass self-interest.

That the American founders were self-interested it is impossible to deny. Thomas Jefferson owned some two hundred slaves and did not free them; George Washington freed his slaves, but only upon his death.[224] Yet the case of Jefferson is revealing: far from rationalizing plantation life by adopting the usual Southern arguments about the happy slave, Jefferson the Virginian vehemently denounced slavery as flatly inconsistent with justice. "I tremble for my country when I realize that God is just."[225] Jefferson recognized that blacks were not slaves "by nature," only by convention. Although he agreed with the enlightened scientific view of his time—that blacks were probably inferior to whites in capacity—Jefferson expressed his hope that black accomplishment would prove his suspicions wrong.[226] (Jefferson's empirical observations about black inferiority were not shared by Benjamin Franklin or Alexander Hamilton.)[227] Moreover, Jefferson strongly denied that possible black intellectual or civilizational inferiority justified white enslavement. "Whatever be their talents, it is no measure of their rights."[228] Consequently the only rationale for Jefferson not freeing his slaves is expediency. "Justice is in one scale, and self-preservation in another."[229]

The dilemma of Jefferson and the American founders may be summarized as follows: they fully recognized that a democratic society depends not just on wisdom, but also on consent. Consequently, there is no justification whatsoever for ruling another human being without his consent. Blacks are human beings, and in possession of natural rights. Slavery is therefore against natural right and should be prohibited. But how? Here is where Jefferson and the founders faced two profound obstacles. The first was that virtually all of them recognized the degraded condition of blacks in America. Whatever the cause of this condition, the framers recognized that it posed a formidable hurdle to granting to blacks the rights of citizenship. By contrast with monarchy and aristocracy, which only require subjects to obey, self-government requires citizens who have the moral and civilizational capacity to be rulers.

Jefferson also recognized the existence of intense and widespread white prejudices against blacks which seemed to prevent the two alien peoples from coexisting harmoniously on the same soil. While Jefferson agonized over the problem, Madison proposed a strange but bold scheme for solving the nation's multiracial dilemma: the government, he suggested, might take the land it had acquired from the Indians, sell it to the new European immigrants, and use the money to send blacks back to Africa.[230] The concept of relocating blacks in Africa was later endorsed in principle by Lincoln and retained its appeal among many whites and some blacks until the Civil War.[231]

The deference of Jefferson and the American founders to popular prejudices strikes many contemporary scholars as excessive. Some suggest that popular convictions simply represented a frustrating obstacle that the founders should have dealt with resolutely and forcefully. In a democratic society, however, the absence of the people's agreement on a fundamental moral question of governance is no mere technicality. The case for democracy, no less than the case against slavery, rests on the legitimacy of the people's consent. To outlaw slavery without the consent of the majority of whites would be to destroy democracy, and thus to destroy the very basis for outlawing slavery.

The men gathered in Philadelphia confronted a dilemma. For them to sanction slavery would be to proclaim the illegitimacy of the American Revolution and the new form of government based on the people's consent; yet for them to outlaw slavery without securing the people's consent would have the same effect. In practical terms as well, the choice facing the men gathered in Philadelphia was not to permit or to prohibit slavery. Rather, the choice was either to establish a union in which slavery was tolerated, or not to have a union. Any suggestion that Southern states could be persuaded to join a union and give up slavery can be dismissed as unlikely. As Eugene Genovese writes, "If the Constitution had not recognized slavery, the Southern states would never have entered the union."[232] Thus the accusation that the founders compromised on the Declaration's principle "all men are created equal" for the purpose of expediency reflects a grave misunderstanding. The founders were confronted with a competing principle, also present in the Declaration: governments derive their legitimacy "from the consent of the governed." Both principles must be satisfied, and where they cannot, compromise is not merely permissible but morally required.

The American framers found a middle ground not between principle and practice, but between antislavery and popular consent. Not only are these closely related principles, but in a philosophic sense, they are the same principle. How did the framers seek to mediate between their rival claims? By producing a Constitution in which the concept of slavery is tolerated, in deference to consent, but nowhere given any moral approval, in recognition of the slave's natural rights. Indeed nowhere in the document is the term "slavery" used. Slaves are always described as "persons," implying their possession of basic rights. The founders made concessions to slavery as a matter of fact but not as a matter of right.[233] In addition, the framers produced a Constitution that nowhere acknowledges the existence of racial distinctions, thus producing a document that transcended its time and provided a charter for a better future.[234]

None of the supposed contradictions that contemporary scholars have located in the American founders were unrecognized by them. Many of the framers justified their toleration for slavery on prudential grounds: in the 1770s and 1780s they had reason to believe that slavery was losing its commercial appeal. In this they were wrong: Eli Whitney's invention of the cotton gin in 1793 (which the founders could not possibly have anticipated) revived the demand for slavery in the South. Even so, the test of the founders' project is the practical question: did the Declaration of Independence and the Constitution strengthen or weaken the institution of slavery?

The intellectual and moral ferment that produced the American Revolution, Gordon Wood argues, should be judged by its consequences. Before 1776, slavery was legal in every state in America. Yet by 1804 every state north of Maryland had abolished slavery, either immediately or gradually; Southern and border states prohibited further slave importations from abroad; and Congress was committed to outlawing the slave trade in 1808, which it did. Slavery was no longer a national but a sectional institution, and one under moral and political siege. "Before the revolution, Americans like every other people took slavery for granted," Wood says. "But slavery came under indictment as a result of the same principles that produced the American founding. In this sense, the Civil War is implicit in the Declaration of Independence."

Garry Wills praises Lincoln for "correcting the Constitution without overthrowing it."[235] Wills implies that Lincoln ingeniously manipulated the history and language of the founding compromise with slavery to justify an antislavery result the founders never intended. This is praise that Lincoln would have probably regarded as an insult, both to the American founders and to him. Moreover, it is questionable that Wills knows what the founders did or did not intend, since as a starting point he dismisses the possibility that when they articulated antislavery principles they meant what they said. Abraham Lincoln was the most perceptive student of the American founding in his time or since. He not only understood clearly the framers' dilemma, but knew that he had inherited it. The principle of majority rule is based on Jefferson's doctrine that "all men are created equal," yet what Harry Jaffa terms the crisis of the house divided arises when the majority denies that "all men are created equal," that is, denies the basis of its own legitimacy.[236] Lincoln was presented with two concrete options: working to overthrow democracy, or working to secure consent through persuasion.

Conscious that he too must defer, as the founders did, to prevailing prejudices, Lincoln nevertheless sought to neutralize those prejudices so they did not become a barrier to securing black freedom. In a series of artfully conditional claims, Lincoln paid ritual obeisance to existing racism while drawing even racists into his coalition to end slavery.[237] Lincoln made these rhetorical concessions because he knew that the possibility for securing antislavery consent was far better in his time than in the 1780s. In one of the clearest commentaries on the Declaration, Lincoln observed:

> They intended to include all men, but they did not intend to declare all men equal in all respects. They did not mean to say all were equal in color, size, intellect, moral developments or social capacity. They defined with tolerable distinctness in what respects they did consider all men created equal—equal in certain inalienable rights. They did not mean to assert the obvious untruth, that all were then actually enjoying that equality, nor yet, that they were about to confer it immediately upon them. . . . They meant simply to declare the *right,* so that the *enforcement* of it might follow as fast as circumstances should permit.[238]

By working through rather than around the democratic process, Lincoln justified the nation's faith in the untried experiment of representative self-government. In vindicating the slave's right to rule himself, Lincoln also vindicated the legitimacy of democratic self-rule. And Lincoln's position came to be shared by Frederick Douglass, who once denounced the Constitution but who eventually came to the conclusion that it contained antislavery principles. "Abolish slavery tomorrow, and not a sentence or syllable of the Constitution need be altered." Slavery, he concluded, was simply a "scaffolding to the magnificent structure, to be removed as soon as the building is completed."[239]

It took a civil war to destroy slavery, and with it much of the infrastructure and economy of the South, between 1860 and 1865. More than half a million whites died in that war, "one life for every six slaves freed," C. Vann Woodward reminds us.[240] Although the question of slavery in the United States was ultimately resolved by force, for Lincoln as for Douglass, the greatest white and black statesmen of the time, the triumph of the union and the emancipation of the slaves represented not the victory of might over right, but the reverse; justice had won over that of expediency and the principles of the American founding had at long last prevailed.

THE PRICE OF FREEDOM

Whatever its functional relevance in a world utterly different from our own, slavery was a moral crime. People should not own other people. Unfortunately the practice of slavery persisted into the twentieth century in many parts of Asia, Africa, and the Middle East: Saudi Arabia and Yemen outlawed it only in 1962. According to the British Anti-Slavery International, which monitors the institution worldwide, it continues today, practiced covertly in Southeast Asia, Latin America, and the Arab world. In Mauritania alone, nearly 100,000 people are estimated to be enslaved.[241]

The abolition of slavery did not entail the abolition of racism. As George Fredrickson puts it, "The slaveholding mentality . . . remained the wellspring of white supremacist thought and action long after the institution that originally sustained it had been relegated to the dustbin of history."[242] At the same time, abolition constitutes one of the greatest moral achievements of Western civilization. The reason for the acceptability of slavery prior to the eighteenth century is that the idea of freedom simply did not exist in an applied and comprehensive sense anywhere in the world.

It is understandable that American blacks, on discovering the circumstances in which their ancestors were brought to this country, would feel at best a qualified patriotism. But upon reflection this ambivalence may be unwarranted. Africans were not uniquely unfortunate to be taken as slaves; their descendants were uniquely fortunate to be born in the only civilization in the world to abolish slavery on its own initiative, without the slaves being in a position to revolt and gain their own independence. For Zora Neale Hurston, the black feminist writer, the legacy of slavery is one of opportunities for the future, not unceasing submersion in the past.

> From what I can learn, it was sad. Certainly. But my ancestors who lived and died in it are dead. The white men who profited by their labor and lives are dead also. I have no personal memory of those times, and no responsibility for them. Neither has the grandson of the man who held my folks. . . . I have no intention of wasting my time beating on old graves. . . . I do not belong to the sobbing school of Negroes who hold that nature somehow has given them a low-down dirty deal and whose feelings are all hurt about it. . . . Slavery is the price I paid for civilization, and that is worth all that I have paid through my ancestors for it.[243]

A similar position was elaborated by Booker T. Washington, who was born a slave but went on to become the most powerful black statesman and educator in the United States:

Think about it: we went into slavery pagans; we came out Christians. We went into slavery pieces of property; we came out American citizens. We went into slavery with chains clanking about our wrists; we came out with the American ballot in our hands. . . . Notwithstanding the cruelty and moral wrong of slavery, we are in a stronger and more hopeful condition, materially, intellectually, morally, and religiously, than is true of an equal number of black people in any other portion of the globe.[244]

Washington's argument, echoing earlier writings of the poet Phillis Wheatley,[245] is that slavery proved to be the transmission belt that nevertheless brought Africans into the orbit of modern civilization and Western freedom, so that future generations of black Americans would be far more free and prosperous than their former kinsmen in Africa.[246] Washington's conclusion seems hard to deny: slavery was an institution that was terrible to endure for slaves, but it left the *descendants* of slaves better off in America.

What do Americans today owe blacks because of slavery? The answer is: probably nothing. If there is a social debt, it is to the slaves, and the slaves are dead. It makes little sense to say that the United States has an obligation to place African Americans in the economic and social position they would occupy "but for" slavery, since "but for" slavery they would probably be worse off in Africa. More precisely, "but for" slavery they would not exist. Frederick Douglass, who better than anyone else understood the lasting harms inflicted by slavery, argued that it entitled blacks to nothing more than the freedom to help themselves.[247] "Our oppressors have divested us of many valuable blessings and facilities for improvement and education, but thank heaven, they have not yet been able to take from us the privilege of being honest, industrious, sober and intelligent."[248]

African Americans, indeed all Americans, should learn about the tragic crime of slavery. An understanding of the complexity of this history should prove the futility of drawing up ancestral balance sheets or selling indulgences that appeal to (misplaced) white guilt. A rich country like America should seek to help its most disadvantaged members, not because of what their ancestors endured, but because they deserve a chance to reach their full potential here and now. Although slavery remains an inextricable part of American history, excessive national self-flagellation carries moral dangers, as the writer Leon Wieseltier points out:

In the memory of oppression, oppression perpetuates itself. The scar does the work of the wound. That is the real tragedy: that injustice retains the power to distort long after it has ceased to be real. It is a posthumous victory for the oppressors, when pain becomes a tradition. This is the unfairly difficult dilemma of the newly emancipated and the newly enfranchised: an honorable life is not possible if they remember too little, and a normal life is not possible if they remember too much.[249]

4

THE INVENTION OF PREJUDICE

The Rise of Liberal Antiracism

At some future period, the civilized races of man will almost certainly exterminate and replace the savage races throughout the world.
—Charles Darwin[1]

Our contemporary understanding of race and racism is the product of an intellectual revolution that took place in the early part of this century, establishing the foundations for the civil rights movement. Just as the antislavery movement of the nineteenth century delegitimized and eventually banned servitude, the antiracist cause of the twentieth century made racism a four-letter word and the racist an object of public contempt. The abolitionists, let us recall, fought slavery in the name of equal rights under God and under the law. Many of them fought against racism, but many more accommodated themselves to it. The intellectual forefathers of contemporary liberalism are not Abraham Lincoln and Frederick Douglass; rather, they are a small but influential group of twentieth century anthropologists who shaped our academic and popular assumptions about race.

The popular view of race is admirably expressed by Anna Quindlen in the *New York Times:* "Each generation finds its own reasons to hate." "There are gradations of imperfectly raised consciousness." "Attitudes can range from the uninformed to the unconscious to the genuinely bigoted." "Years and years of rage and racism, measured now in angry words and broken glass."[2] In similar terms, the United Church of Christ asserts that "racism permeates most of our institutions" and that "as a result of racial discrimination, all over the U.S. there are quiet riots in the form of unemployment, poverty, social disorganization, family disintegration, housing and school deterioration, and crime."[3] The *New York Times* and the United Church of Christ are reflecting what a few years ago seemed—and, for many people, still seem—like liberal certainties. Racism is based on ignorance. Ignorance generates "prejudices" and "stereotypes." Such predispositions lead to irrational fear. Fear produces "hate." Hate produces "discrimination." Although racism comes in degrees, the racist is basically an ignorant and hateful person, largely responsible for the sufferings of minorities and the despair of the inner cities. Riots, in this view, are not merely the work of rioters but a consequence of the accumulated and justified resentments produced by white racism. The liberal solution is twofold: education, to raise the consciousness of the racist; and civil rights laws, to help minorities overcome the destructive effects of racial discrimination.

Yet these remedies have been in place for more than a generation now, and America's race problems seem as intractable as ever. Despite a generation of liberal policies, we seem no closer to the age of antiracist enlightenment. The current confusion reveals itself in the way that crucial terms now baffle even those who frequently use them. "I don't like to use the word *stereotypes,* because it's negative," remarks diversity consultant Thomas Kochman, adding that "I call accurate generalizations about groups *archetypes.* Stereotypes are racist but archetypes are not racist." Remarks black sociologist Troy Duster, who teaches at Berkeley, "We have one word, *racism,* that stretches to include everything from lynching to somebody frowning at you in a restaurant. When I ask black students what they mean when they claim this university is a racist place, they often don't know what to say."[4]

In order to penetrate this confusion, it is helpful to explore the intellectual origins of liberal antiracism, which provided the basis for the civil rights movement. Although it seems obvious to many today that people should not judge others based on race because race is merely a surface trait revealing no deep or fundamental differences, a few decades ago it was equally obvious to intelligent and progressive thinkers that, as Harvard psychologist William McDougall wrote in 1921, "races differ in intellectual stature, just as they differ in physical stature."[5] So powerful was this earlier consensus that the term "racist" did not even exist before the twentieth century, and only came into popular use during the 1930s to describe the Nazis.[6]

What, then, is the source of the contemporary liberal premises that "racism is the symbol and sum of all oppression"[7] and that the racist is a hateful ignoramus who is sorely in need of enlightenment, if not therapy? The new paradigm reflects a revolution in the commonsense understanding of human differences. It is the product of a heated debate in the early part of this century, after which one progressive view totally vanquished another, even to the point of redefining the earlier view as inherently malicious and stupid, so that no humane and enlightened person could adopt it.[8] The earlier understanding was based on a distinction between barbarism and civilization, and on an evolutionary model in which biological groups called races were seen to occupy ascending places in a hierarchy. The new paradigm is based on cultural relativism, which in this form denies that race is a meaningful natural category and holds that all cultures are equal. According to this now-entrenched view, no group may be considered superior or inferior, group differences are largely the product of environment and specifically of unjust discrimination, all attempts to attribute intrinsic qualities to groups reflect ignorance and hatred, so that the mission of sound policy is not to civilize the barbarians, but to fight racism and discrimination. It is worth contrasting some expressions of the old orthodoxy and the new.

• Thomas Huxley, a friend of Darwin and a strong defender of his theory of evolution, wrote at the turn of the century: "No rational man, cognizant of the facts, believes that the average Negro is the equal, still less the superior of the average white man."[9]

• E. L. Godkin, editor of *The Nation,* denounced nonwhite immigrants as inherently inferior and unassimilable. "In truth," he said, "there is no corner of our system in which the ignorant foreign voter may not be found, eating the political structure, like a white ant."[10]

• The socialist writer Jack London, author of *The Call of the Wild,* argued:

Socialism is not for the happiness of all men, but for the happiness of certain kindred races . . . so that they may survive and inherit the earth to the extinction of the lesser weaker races. Will the Indian, the Negro, or the Mongol ever conquer the Teuton? Surely not! All that the other races have not, the Teuton has. We are a race of doers and fighters, of globe-encirclers and zone conquerors.[11]

• Margaret Sanger, the founder of Planned Parenthood, coined the slogan "More children from the fit, less from the unfit." In language that many of her contemporary admirers would probably like to forget, she described blacks and Eastern European immigrants as "a menace to civilization" and "human weeds." Concerned that American blacks might protest Planned Parenthood's special "Negro Project" aimed at promoting sterilization, Sanger wrote to an associate, "We do not want word to get out that we want to exterminate the Negro population."[12]

Today many writers, even if they know little about science, describe these nineteenth and early twentieth century views as "pseudoscientific" racism.[13] Yet the term "pseudoscientific" seems an unjust characterization of views that represented the best scientific knowledge of the time.[14] Is Newtonian physics "pseudoscientific" because it has been replaced by Einsteinian physics? The nineteenth century consensus reflected not only the latest advances in Darwinian biology, but also the highest ethical ideals of the most enlightened sectors of society. It was a progressive view. Opposition to it was considered to be a sign of ignorance or religious dogmatism. Today's liberal ideology, however, is drawn from a different mold. One widely shared contemporary notion is that race is not a natural but a purely conventional category, what scholars call a "social construct."

• Henry Louis Gates writes, "Race as a meaningful criterion has long been recognized to be a fiction."[15]

• Tzvetan Todorov announces, "Whereas racism is a well-attested phenomenon, race itself does not exist."[16]

• Naomi Zack writes in *Race and Mixed Race,* "The concept of race does not have an adequate scientific foundation."[17]

• Joel Williamson maintains that "scientific scholars generally agree that there is actually no such thing as race."[18]

• Eugenia Shanklin writes in *Anthropology and Race,* "Race is a concept that exists in our minds, not in our bodies. . . . I have grown weary of explaining to my students that there is no such thing as race."[19]

Contemporary scholars also argue that civilizational and cultural achievements, where they do exist, cannot be ascribed to race. In a twentieth century version of environmentalism—the revival of the ancient Greek attribution of cultural differences to the vagaries of custom and circumstance—the anthropologist Marvin Harris writes that "few in-formed scientists" would be willing to attribute the "temporary techno-logical superiority" of Europe and North America to racial or genetic factors.[20] In a similar vein, Claude Lévi-Strauss writes:

> If the cultural contributions of Asia, Europe, Africa or America are distinctive
> . . . the fact is to be accounted for by geographical, historical and sociological
> circumstances, not by special aptitudes inherent in the anatomical or physio-
> logical makeup of the black, yellow or white man.[21]

Indeed the conventional wisdom in social science today goes beyond a separation of race and culture to deny the existence of a universal "human nature," and to argue that all social achievement is the product of culture. Since each culture has its own unique integrity, this view holds, there are no cross-cultural or transcendent standards for judging groups to be superior or inferior. Clifford Geertz asserts that "there is no such thing as a human nature independent of culture," and that social scientists should engage in "thick description" that eschews cultural com-parison: they should seek "not to generalize across cases but to general-ize within them."[22] Writing in 1947, anthropologist Melville Herskovits articulated this perspective in terms that will sound recognizable:

> The inevitable basic questions enter: Whose good? Whose bad? Whose
> means? Whose ends? Evaluations are relative to the cultural background out
> of which they arise. . . . The very definition of what is normal or abnormal is
> relative to the cultural frame of reference. In studying a culture . . . one does
> not judge the modes of behavior one is describing; rather, one seeks to un-
> derstand the sanctions of behavior in terms of the established relationships
> within the culture itself.[23]

The consequence of a denial of transcultural standards is that the dis-tinction between civilization and barbarism collapses, so that in both schol-arly and popular writings today, terms such as "savage" and "civilized," "primitive" and "advanced," "inferior" and "superior" typically appear in quotation marks, suggesting that these are questionable and discredited notions.[24] Here is a sample from Andrew Hacker's *Two Nations*:

> Since Europeans first embarked on explorations, they have been bemused by
> the "savages" they encountered in new lands. In almost all cases, these "prim-
> itive" peoples were seen as inferior to those who "discovered" them.[25]

Much of contemporary social science is now dedicated to combating the possibility of cultural superiority and promoting appreciation of other groups as not inferior, only different. As African American scholar John-netta Cole observes in an anthropology textbook:

> Studying . . . other complex societies helps us correct stereotypes and mis-conceptions about tribal societies. It is also a means of countering ethnocen-trism, the assumption that one's own way of life is superior. It puts brakes on the tendency to view attitudes and behavior patterns of others as inherently "inferior," "weird" and "exotic."[26]

Since these sorts of statements are so familiar that they appear obvi-ous, few have bothered to question them. Yet as economist John May-nard Keynes once said, common sense is but dead theory.[27] The reason we have to reopen the early twentieth century debate is to recover the first principles behind the prevailing liberal premises about racism. Only then can we determine if they are sound, and whether current civil rights policies are constructed on a firm foundation.

WHAT'S IN A NAME?

According to contemporary liberal thinking, racial classifications serve no rational purpose except perhaps when they are used to help blacks and other minorities overcome a history of discrimination. If it is true that race is a conventional category that is arbitrarily employed by venomous whites for the purposes of irrational discrimination, then racism is indeed based on ignorance and hate and the prevailing view is sound. But start-ing in the eighteenth century and culminating in the nineteenth century, leading scientists and progressive thinkers viewed race as a valid biologi-cal category, pointing to distinctions in nature which corresponded to civ-ilizational differences between human populations. If this earlier view is right, then it is entirely possible that prejudices might be prudent, stereo-types might contain elements of truth, and racial discrimination may be warranted under some circumstances.

Southern defenders of slavery in the eighteenth and nineteenth cen-turies would have found preposterous the suggestion that they were in any way ignorant of blacks. Much of their indignation at Northern inter-ference stemmed from a heartfelt conviction that proximity gave them up-close insights into the Negro, while the Yankees, in their view, were moralists blinded to reality. Even Southerners like Thomas Jefferson who did not defend slavery expressed what they considered to be rational doubt, as opposed to ignorant prejudice, about the capacity of blacks. "Jefferson was more convinced than many other slaveowners about the white man's intellectual superiority," Eugene Genovese says, adding, "The reason is that his science was up to date. Many of his peers relied on the Bible."

The existence of new sources of support for racism is suggested by the fact that the abolition of slavery did little to diminish white convictions of black inferiority—indeed, as Tocqueville foresaw, American racism grew stronger after emancipation.[28] One might expect Southern hostility to blacks to increase, as it did in the aftermath of the region's defeat in the Civil War, yet scholars note the paradox of rising racism in the North as well. "When the nation freed the slaves," Joel Williamson writes, "it also freed racism."[29] Nancy Stepan notes the irony that in Europe, "just as the battle against slavery was being won, the war against racism was being lost. The Negro was legally freed, but in the British mind he was still mentally, morally and physically a slave."[30] No doubt, as Tocqueville observed, attitudes of white superiority could be expected to outlast slavery, yet how to explain his observation that antiblack sentiment in America was strongest in states which never had slavery?[31]

The reason is that, both in the Northern states and in Europe, racism received added reinforcements from a discipline that represented perhaps the most undisputed source of the superiority of Western civilization: science. Scientific racism developed out of a major European project in the eighteenth and nineteenth centuries to explore, map, classify, and understand the natural world. Physicists were uncovering the principles of the earth and its place in the heavens, chemists were probing the secrets of matter, so biologists and naturalists too searched for law and order in the workings of the animal and human world. In no sense can this European project be considered a product of obscurantism or fear; on the contrary, it represented a bold intellectual enterprise to dispel ignorance.

The problem faced by Western scientists and naturalists was a genuine one. In the eighteenth and nineteenth centuries, it was axiomatic in Europe and the United States that apart from enclaves of civilization, the majority of the population in the nonwhite world was plunged in barbarism. "With the expansion of industrial civilization," writes George Stocking in *Race, Culture and Evolution*, "the widening visible gap between savage man and civilized European was no longer so easy to be bridged."[32] It was equally obvious that these people looked very different from whites: they seemed to belong to different anatomical groups. The scientific enterprise of the period was devoted to investigating the intuition that these two phenomena—barbarism and racial difference—were closely related. Drawing on new techniques in biology, anthropology, psychology, and genetics, scholars in Europe and the United States developed an elaborate racist paradigm in which race became the central determinant of human character, culture, and history.[33] And the credibility of scientific racism was strengthened by the contribution of science to modern technology, and to a widening of the civilization gap between Europe and the rest of the world. "One could debate the merits of monarchical as opposed to parliamentary government or the advantages of monotheism over animism," Michael Adas writes. But in science and technology, he adds, Western "superiority was readily demonstrable, and the European advantage over other peoples grew at an ever increasing pace."[34]

Oddly enough, scientific racism was not mainly directed against blacks. Rather, it provided a biological rationale for whites in the Northern states to inferiorize and exclude other minorities: Chinese, Japanese, Asian Indians, Mexicans, even white immigrants who came from Central and Eastern Europe. Starting in the mid-nineteenth century, whites mobilized on racial grounds to halt Chinese and Japanese immigration. In the early twentieth century, for the first time in American history, the U.S. Congress passed a series of laws restricting immigration based on race, laws that were not overturned until the 1960s. Scientific racism did not create most of the hostility to immigrants, which arose out of a desire to avoid economic competition, but by suggesting that the new immigrants were congenitally deficient, science provided a scholarly justification for policies that would otherwise have to be defended solely on grounds of self-interest.

Racism had previously been drawn in the stark tones of black and white, and relied on a weak appeal to Scripture or an intuitive appeal to civilizational differences; science provided it with a new evolutionary rationale and an elaborate hierarchy of races. Now for the first time it would be possible to engage in scholarly racial taxonomy: whites would be Caucasoids, Asians and American Indians would be Mongoloids, and blacks would be Negroids. Further, Caucasoids could be ranked as Nordic, Alpine, and Mediterranean, in that order. Two crucial questions, therefore, are where do these categories come from and how were they used for the purposes of racist exclusion? These questions have a direct bearing on the contemporary debate about Americanization, multiculturalism, and the "melting pot."

Toward the end of the seventeenth century, a French doctor named François Bernier published an article in Paris claiming an intellectual breakthrough. "The geographers up until this point have divided the world only according to the different countries or regions," he said. Bernier's new system called for classification based on facial appearance and body types. Based on his new method, Bernier suggested four categories: Europeans, whom he did not bother to describe because they would be familiar to his readers; Far Easterners, whom he found peculiar in their facial slant and their apparent eye impediment; blacks, who have wooly hair, thick lips, and very white teeth; and Lapps, the author's least favorite group, who have faces similar to those of bears, and are "quite frightful."[35]

Although Bernier may have made the very first effort to classify mankind based on the emerging but still inchoate new category of "race," he inaugurated an enterprise widely taken up in Europe in subsequent decades. The first major scientist to attempt racial classification was Carolus Linnaeus, a Swedish botanist, whose *Systemae Naturae,* published in 1735, did not just organize human types but also placed them in the context of a wider kingdom of living things. Linnaeus assumed that animal and human types were basically fixed and unchangeable. He classified man with other mammals, and broke down human types into four groups: Homo Europaeus, Homo Asiaticus, Homo Africanus, and Homo Americanus. He also added some miscellaneous categories, such as "wild men," dwarfs, troglodytes, and "lazy Patagonians." For Linnaeus, Europeans were "governed by laws," native Americans were "regulated by customs," Asians were "ruled by opinions," and Africans were "governed by caprice."[36]

A couple of decades later, Georges-Louis Leclerc Buffon, a naturalist and opponent of slavery, published a widely read *Natural History* which may have first introduced the term "race" into the scientific lexicon. Comte de Buffon recognized the difference between species, which could not mate with each other and reproduce, and varieties within a species, which could. An advocate of the unity of the human species, Buffon's categories for man included Laplanders, Mongolians, Southern Asiatics, Europeans, Ethiopians, and Malays. Assuming the color white to be the norm, Buffon blamed the vagaries of climate for other skin tones. Commenting that certain African tribes could not count beyond the number three, Buffon implied that this primitivism would disappear in a more temperate climate.[37]

The term "Caucasian" was first used by Johann Blumenbach, a German professor of medicine writing between the 1770s and 1790s, and one of the founders of modern anthropology. He speculated, wrongly as it turned out, that Europeans originated in the area of the Caucasus mountains of Russia. Yet his term remained in use, and soon went from scholarly to popular currency. Based on his study of human skulls, Blumenbach identified five races for man: Caucasoid, Ethiopian, Mongoloid, American, and Malay. Blumenbach's classification had a lasting influence, in part because his categories neatly broke down into the familiar colors: white, black, yellow, red, and brown. Like Linnaeus and Buffon, Blumenbach endorsed the biblical account of a single creation and of the unity of man—any observed defects in human types he blamed on "degeneration" caused by climate and circumstance.[38]

These early attempts at racial taxonomy would be superseded in the early nineteenth century by Georges Cuvier's threefold division of humans into Caucasians, Mongolians and Negroes[39]—which is even today the most commonly used classification. But in the eighteenth century scientific techniques established a powerful framework, supported by religion, for organizing the conspicuous variety of the human species. Because they endorsed the concept of simultaneous creation for man and the animals, set forth in the biblical account of Adam and Eve in the book of Genesis, this group later became known as "monogenists." They were so described in opposition to a rising school of thought, whose adherents claimed that the best explanation for large differences between human populations was that the races belonged to separate species. This group came to be known as "polygenists." The debate between monogenists and polygenists is worth examining because it reflects the triumph of scientific racism over the religious and political doctrine that human beings are, as the Declaration of Independence has it, "created equal." Moreover, this debate—which still rages in modified form in scientific circles—is an important precursor to Darwin's theory of evolution, which would provide the strongest possible justification for modern racism, and the most dangerous obstacle to any liberal effort to affirm the equality of the races.

ONE SPECIES OR MANY?

Neither monogenists nor polygenists were, by contemporary standards, egalitarian in their understanding of human differences. While the monogenists advocated the unity of man, they were reluctant to deny gradations of civilizational achievement among human populations, and virtually none of them endorsed the idea of political or social equality. Polygenists went much further: they could not imagine any kinship of blood between races "separated from each other by such profound mental, moral and physical differences," in Nancy Stepan's words.[40] While monogenists tended to believe that races were the product of changes in climate or civilization, polygenists regarded race as essentially fixed and unalterable.

In 1774 such a polygenist argument was advanced to considerable acclaim by Lord Henry Homer Kames who, seeking to avoid the wrath of the churches, argued that the separation of the races into different species occurred not at creation but at the time of the building of the Tower of Babel, when God permitted a "change of constitution" in various human groups, partly as a punishment for vanity, partly to enable them to cope with different environments, circumstances, and languages.[41] A few years later an English surgeon, Charles White, unabashedly dispensed with religious orthodoxy. Arguing that the variety of the human species was simply too great to be explained by climate, White identified what he called a "regular gradation" of mammals from the European to the Asiatic to the Negro to the orang-outan to the monkey. To bolster his argument for separate lines of creation, White employed an analysis of "facial angles" as well as measurements of the sizes of heads and even genitals. "That the Penis of an African is larger than that of a European," he concluded, "has I believe been shown in every anatomical school in London. Preparations of them are preserved in most anatomical museums, and I have one in mine."[42]

The polygenist position gathered strength in the early nineteenth century because of the monogenists' apparent inability to show how climate and environment could possibly explain conspicuous differences, not just in color but in height, body shape, hair, eyes and, other features among Africans, native Americans, Asian Indians, Chinese, and Europeans. Moreover, European freethinkers such as Voltaire, Saint-Simon, and Giordano Bruno seized on the idea of separate creation and intrinsic black inferiority as a polemical weapon against the Christian churches.[43] The French philosopher Saint-Simon dismissed the environmental explanation for racial differences as absurd. "The Negro, because of his basic physical structure, is not susceptible, even with the same education, of rising to the intellectual level of Europeans."[44] Montesquieu seemed to agree, and Voltaire asserted that only religious dogmatism stood in the way of the scientific conclusion that Negroes and whites belonged to different species, and that the mental capacity of blacks was such that "they seem formed neither for the advantages nor the abuses of philosophy."[45]

The polygenists were consistently opposed by the Christian churches, and by scientific critics as well. In the United States, a major attack against polygenism was launched by Samuel Stanhope Smith, a theologian who would later become president of the College of New Jersey, now Princeton University. In his *Essay on the Causes of the Variety of Complexion and Figure,* Smith focused on what monogenists consistently considered the Achilles heel of the polygenist position: the question of offspring. If racial groups actually belonged to different species, he asked, did it not contradict the laws of science for them to be able to mate and have children? But it was a matter of common scientific knowledge that such cross-breeding could and did take place. Consequently, the polygenist argument must be fallacious. Smith placed himself directly in the tradition of Linnaeus, Buffon, and Blumenbach. There were no separately created races, he argued, just the human race. Smith pointed out that whites in colder climates such as northern Europe had paler skin than whites in warmer climates. He even claimed that blacks in America were less savage in appearance and behavior than those in Africa, and that blacks who were "house Negroes" had lighter skins and more agreeable features than "field Negroes." To him, this proved that climate and circumstance regulated the human appearance, and if blacks remained in the United States and were treated well, over time they would turn white.[46]

The debate between monogenists and polygenists raged during the first half of the nineteenth century, as the study of race became institutionalized in scientific societies in Europe and North America. One important reason polygenism gained a strong following was the work of Samuel Morton, a Philadelphia doctor and professor of anatomy who was described by the *New York Tribune* in the mid-nineteenth century as the leading scientist in the world. Morton buttressed the polygenist position with craniometry—the science of measuring heads in order to estimate brain size. He began his skull collection in the 1820s, and had more than a thousand in his possession. Today Morton's popular reputation is suspect, mainly as a result of Harvard paleontologist Stephen Jay Gould's debunking of Morton's experiments in *The Mismeasure of Man.*[47] Yet in the scientific community Gould's refutation is itself controversial: one scholar who analyzed the disputed data concluded that Gould's conclusions were distorted by ideological bias while "Morton's research was conducted with integrity."[48] In any event, Morton was highly regarded in Europe and America during his time, because unlike many previous writers who based their racial theories on travel accounts and speculation, Morton brought to polygenism a degree of empiricism and scientific rigor which seemed, for many observers, to settle the argument.[49]

In his two major studies, *Crania Americana* (1839) and *Crania Aegyptiaca* (1844), Morton revealed his basic methodology, which was to rank races by the relative sizes of their brains. He took skeletons of different groups—Europeans, American Indians, Negroes, and Asians—filled them with mustard seed, then poured the seed into a graduated cylinder, and tabulated the skull volume in cubic inches. Then he repeated the experiment using lead shot instead of mustard seed. Through a wide use of samples and many repetitions he claimed to have virtually eliminated statistical error. Based on this information, presented in excruciating detail, Morton concluded that the racial hierarchy had been discovered: Europeans at the top, Asians and American Indians in the middle, blacks at the bottom.[50]

Curiously, polygenism found a more receptive audience in the North than in the South. After all, the implications of polygenism, with its supposition that blacks were simply a lesser species, were a far stronger justification for racism and slavery than monogenism, which conceded black inferiority but denied that it was intrinsic. The reason that Southerners eschewed polygenism was because it blatantly contradicted the biblical account of creation. Some scholars of the history of race have noted the irony that the leading apologists for slavery in the South were inhibited, by their religious convictions, from using polygenist ammunition against their Northern enemies.[51] Indeed the Reverend John Bachman of Charleston, a resolute monogenist, accused polygenists of trying "to degrade their servants below the level of those creatures of God to whom a revelation has been given, and for whom a savior died."[52] Yet a few shrewd Southerners learned to use biblical rationalizations for black inferiority at home, and polygenist arguments against Northern opponents.

The most influential of these was Josiah Nott, an Alabama physician who studied craniology under Morton. An advocate of the view that under slavery in the American South, the Negro had "reached his highest level of civilization,"[53] Nott convinced his friends at the *Southern Quarterly Review* and *DeBow's Review* to gave him a major forum to publicize Morton's research, as a result of which Morton's work attracted the in-

terest of the leading Southern defender of slavery, South Carolina Senator John C. Calhoun.[54] In 1854, Nott and a co-author named George
Gliddon produced *Types of Mankind,* an eight-hundred-page polemic
which denounced "biblical dunces" who persisted in adhering to monogenism. Placing himself firmly in the tradition of Copernicus and Galileo,
Nott argued that "the charge of heresy cannot destroy hieroglyphical
facts." Based largely on Morton's research, Nott and Gliddon alleged
that the Negro's brain was one tenth smaller than that of Europeans, that
his facial angle was more acute, and that continued intermixing between
Negroes and whites would over time generate sterile or deformed offspring—just as the mating between the horse and the ass produces the
mule. This "muleology," as one scholar terms it, was broadly accepted in
the South (in fact the term "mulatto" derives from the Spanish and Portuguese word for "mule") and *Types of Mankind* became a best-seller,
going through nine editions during the rest of the nineteenth century.[55]

By the middle of the century, whites who wished to espouse a doctrine
of Negro inferiority found their views supported by the latest trends in
Western science. Soon they would discover an even more comprehensive
rationale for bigotry, which was provided by Charles Darwin. Today many
writers make a strenuous effort to distance Darwin from racism, cite his
record as an opponent of slavery, and blame the racism that subsequently
took his name on an unscientific "social Darwinism" which is generally
branded as a distortion of the theory of evolution.[56] But as we are about
to see, Darwin thought otherwise.

OUR ARBOREAL ANCESTORS

The controversy between monogenists and polygenists was settled in
favor of the former with the publication of Darwin's *The Origin of Species*
and *The Descent of Man.* Both Darwin and Samuel Morton were working
on the same scientific problem: how to account for variations in animal
species. Morton's research led him in the direction of hybridization—he
thought it possible that species could mate and produce offspring of a
new and distinct type. But Darwin accounted for variation with his principle of natural selection, in which the groups most adapted to their environment survive and others perish. Darwin's theory of evolution, which
would become canonical wisdom in the natural sciences, viewed racial
groups as competitors in an ongoing mammalian struggle for survival. Yet
Darwin could not understand what evolutionary pressures would pro-

duce racial differentiation. Thus although races could be viewed as incipient species, Darwin emphasized the virtual certainty that mankind belonged to a single group and descended from common ancestors.[57] The polygenists were sorely disappointed. One leading scholar said that acceptance of Darwinism was contingent on freeing the theory from its monogenist implications.[58] Yet Josiah Nott took consolation from Darwin's denial of divine creation: "The man is clearly crazy, but it is a capital dig into the parsons."[59]

On the one hand Darwinism dealt a blow to the racism that seemed inherent in polygenism. As Harvard biologist Asa Gray noted in a review of Darwin's work, "The very first step backward on the evolutionary scale makes the Negro and the Hottentot our blood relations."[60] Moreover, nowhere did Darwin compare blacks or nonwhite peoples to apes; he recognized, based on observation, that superficial resemblances notwithstanding, the thin lips, tan color and copious body hair of apes brought them into closer clinical resemblance to whites than to Negroes. On the other hand, Darwin appeared to offer a new and perhaps more powerful ground for belief in the existence of race as a natural category and in the inferiority of the colored races, and that was the concept at the heart of evolution: natural selection. Quite deliberately, Darwin subtitled his *Origin of Species* "The Survival of Favored Races in the Struggle for Life." Endurance and success on earth, Darwin suggested, could be attributed to the ability of races to adapt themselves to the threats and challenges of the natural environment. Here, then, was an entirely secular and scientific explanation for the civilizational achievements of Europeans, and for the relative backwardness of other peoples: whites were simply in the evolutionary vanguard, and the backward races were the unfit peoples on their way out. George Stocking writes, "The primitive and the savage were now associated with the apelike and the animal not simply by analogy but by derivation."[61]

Moreover, Darwin seemed to have largely refuted the theory, advanced by the French naturalist Lamarck, that traits acquired by one generation could be passed down to the next. Darwin showed that evolution occurred not through the inheritance of acquired traits but through the elimination of the unfit. This scientific discovery had social implications, because it appeared to suggest that racial groups which did not show the highest traits of civilization could not be expected to acquire and transmit them to their children. On the contrary, inferior groups would remain inferior, and so would their descendants. Progress depended on superior groups perpetuating themselves, and inferior groups ceasing to exist. Natural selection, Darwin maintained, "is the doctrine of Malthus applied to the whole animal and vegetable kingdom."[62] As the resources of the world became scarce, Darwin argued, the stronger animals would prevail and the weaker would die out. This applied just as much to human beings as to other animals. And Darwin left no doubt that he felt the process was for the best.[63] In *The Descent of Man,* published in 1871, Darwin for the first time specifically applied his theory to race. He asserted categorically that races differ physically, temperamentally, and intellectually.[64]

Arguing that "extinction follows chiefly from the competition of tribe with tribe, and race with race," Darwin found that "when civilized nations come into contact with barbarians, the struggle is short."[65] He predicted that as a result of continuing evolution, higher races like the Caucasian would develop into more advanced species while barbaric races like Negroes and Australian aborigines would be eliminated. Even in the West, Darwin worried, "We civilized men do our utmost to check the process of elimination: we build asylums for the imbecile, the maimed, the sick, we institute poor laws." From an evolutionary point of view, Darwin found this solicitude "highly injurious to the race of man," and recommended, "There should be open competition . . . the most able should not be prevented by laws or customs from succeeding best and rearing the largest number of offspring."[66] Although his theory was biological and not cultural, Darwin seemed confident that there was a correspondence between biological characteristics and civilizational achievement, and that primitive peoples of his time were at the evolutionary stage of European society thousands of years earlier.[67] Viewing with amazement the primitives of South America, "absolutely naked and bedaubed with paint," Darwin commented, "Such were our ancestors." Darwin insisted that the barbarism of the native suggested his evolutionary continuum with beasts, and he compared the native's "hoarse, guttural and clicking" sounds with dogs barking and chickens clucking.

> Viewing such men, one can hardly believe that they are fellow-creatures, and inhabitants of the same world. . . . The difference between savage and civilized man is the difference between a wild and tame animal, and part of the interest in beholding a savage is the same which would lead everyone to desire to see the lion in his desert, the tiger tearing his prey in the jungle, or the rhinocerous wandering over the wild plains of Africa.[68]

In fact, Darwin declared that he would as soon be descended from the baboon as from the savage who "delights to torture his enemies, offers up bloody sacrifices without remorse, treats his wives like slaves, knows no decency, and is haunted by the grossest superstitions."[69] In the raucous debate that erupted between Darwin and Christian believers in divine creation, Darwin's defenders frequently argued that it was not so implausible to regard man as related to the ape and pointed to "lower" types of men such as blacks as possible "missing links."[70] In a strong defense of Darwinism, Thomas Huxley proclaimed in 1865:

> It is simply incredible that our prognathous relative . . . will be able to compete successfully . . . in a contest which is to be carried out by thoughts and not by bites. . . . The highest places in the hierarchy of civilization will assuredly not be within the reach of our dusky cousins.[71]

Social Darwinism as an idea actually preceded Darwin. Its roots can be found in the progressive doctrines of the Enlightenment, such as Condorcet's *Sketch for an Historical Picture of the Progress of the Human Mind,* published in 1795, which forecast an upward spiral of human development, spearheaded by reason, toward perfection. In the nineteenth century Auguste Comte argued that the history of man's intellectual development proceeds through three stages: theological, metaphysical, and scientific or positivist. These views rendered believable the notion of a principle of gradation, a hierarchy of the world's peoples on a civilizational ladder, even a scale of value for individuals within Western civilization.[72] Darwin's theory of evolution helped to give that concept a racial cast and a scientific justification. Primitive peoples were in a kind of evolutionary infancy; they could not be related to Western civilization less in space than in time. For Europeans, they represented "the way we were." Unfortunately, they were laggards on the civilizational ladder and thus marked for defeat and extinction. Liberals in the nineteenth century supported evolution because, in historian Carl Degler's words, "Evolution . . . was actually another word for progress."[73]

The strongest opponents of Darwinism and its social implications were, of course, Christians who espoused divine creation and the special dignity of man. There is no question that many of these Christians themselves harbored convictions of black inferiority. But in their paradigm it was God who was held accountable for natural differences, a belief that humanized blacks and moderated racism. Indeed the eminent British naturalist Alfred Russel Wallace, who discovered natural selection concurrently with Darwin, later recoiled from the atheist and racist implications of evolution as a direct result of his conversion to spiritualism. For the rest of his life Wallace insisted that a purely material evolution accurately described the workings of the universe, but that the mind of man was created by a supernatural intelligence. At the same time, he strongly defended the equal potential of human beings and condemned racism.[74]

If God does not exist, Dostoyevsky warns, everything is permitted. The secularism and racism embodied in Darwin prevailed, and increasingly race began to replace religion as the gnostic key to history.[75] Essentially, Darwin helped to legitimize the racist application of the principle that "might is right." This was not a new idea: Thrasymachus defended the concept against Socrates in Plato's *Republic*. But it was an idea that had been reviled and opposed by many in the West for the next two millennia in the name of morality and religion. Now it had returned, carrying a scientific imprimatur, and to oppose it was to stigmatize yourself as a religious fanatic or an ignoramus.

THE NATIVISTS ARE RESTLESS

The Darwinian influence in European and American scholarship soon became pervasive.[76] In the late nineteenth and early twentieth centuries, it would have been difficult to throw a stone into the corridors of American academia and not hit a racist.

• In England, Darwin's cousin and soulmate Sir Francis Galton in 1869 published his *Hereditary Genius: An Inquiry Into Its Laws and Consequences* in which he warned, "Much more care is taken to select appropriate varieties of plants and animals . . . than to select appropriate types of men."[77] Widely regarded as the intellectual godfather of intelligence testing, Galton also championed the cause of human improvement through selective breeding, a process he called eugenics, a word he coined from the Greek term meaning "well born."[78]

• The architect of Social Darwinism, Herbert Spencer, first used the two terms most closely associated with the idea of evolution, the "struggle for existence" and the "survival of the fittest."[79] These terms soon entered the scholarly as well as the popular vocabulary. Spencer and his protégés were insistent hereditarians, attributing poverty, pauperism, crime, and other social ills not to social causes but to inherited defects. They argued that the social contract did not replace but only camouflaged the harsh doctrine of survival of the fittest that obtained in nature, so that promises of human rights and equality were absurd attempts to regulate the laws of evolution that would end up restricting human progress.[80] Spencer exercised a strong influence on the emerging discipline of sociology in America.[81]

• Writing in the late nineteenth century, the Italian physician Cesare Lombroso drew on Darwin's linkage of man and beast to suggest that within civilized society there exist bestial types characterized by thick skulls, large jaws, sloping foreheads, and large ears who are biologically predisposed to become criminals. Lombroso's theory that criminals could be identified by their physical traits was controversial from the outset, but it became widely known throughout the European world.[82]

• In Germany, one of Darwin's strongest defenders, the biologist Ernst Haeckel, developed his "biogenetic law" which held that the development of children from infancy through adolescence to maturity directly parallels the development of societies from primitivism through barbarism to civilization. Other European scholars suggested that precisely this racial pattern of development is replicated in the evolution of the class structure of modern industrial societies. In academic parlance, ontogeny recapitulates phylogeny.[83]

• In the United States, two of the founders of modern anthropology, E. B. Tylor and Lewis Henry Morgan, became exponents of cultural stages in human evolution. In his book *Ancient Society* Morgan divided societies into three main stages: savagery, barbarism, and civilization. Morgan's influential formulation held that savages lived nomadically and promiscuously, barbarism came with the invention of settled agriculture and the extended clan, and civilization was reached with the development of writing, civil government, and the monogamous family.[84]

Social Darwinism quickly filtered down to the popular level. Prevailing scholarly notions of cultural evolution became a powerful rationale for activists who were unsettled by high levels of immigration to the United States in the late nineteenth and early twentieth centuries. It also provided the impetus for eugenics—a program to ensure survival of the fittest within America by designating people as unfit and discouraging them from having children, possibly by sterilization. The fevered nativism of the period is echoed in books like Charles Josey's *Race and National Solidarity,* Houston Stewart Chamberlain's *The Foundations of the 19th Century,* and Lothrop Stoddard's infamous tracts, *The Rising Tide of*

Color Against White World Supremacy and *The Revolt Against Civilization: The Menace of the Under Man.* Fairly typical of nativist polemics was *Our Country,* a bestseller published in 1885 by a progressive clergyman, Josiah Strong, which argued that nonwhite immigrants were corrupting Anglo-Saxon civilizational virtues.[85]

Nativism and economic protectionism are not, in themselves, racist. American employers and employees are likely to have fought for their interests regardless of the color of those threatening their economic security. Many unions, for example, sought to keep nonwhite workers out of the country to protect collective-bargaining privileges for white workers already here.[86] Moreover, anti-immigrant bias was frequently motivated by hostility to Catholicism, socialism, and the cultural practices of the new immigrants; these sentiments may be described as ethnocentric or tribal, but they are not racist. Racism became an issue when the alleged cultural deficiencies of aspiring nonwhite immigrants were biologized. Scientific racism became the foundation of the nativist movement because it offered a rationale for restricting immigration for Asians, Mexicans, and even Eastern and Central Europeans. After all, if the new immigrants constituted a "yellow peril" and "brown peril," endangering social progress in America, they they could be excluded in good conscience and without naked appeals to self-interest. Moreover, if their inferiority was natural rather than cultural, then assimilation could not be expected to remedy deformities which were regarded as incorrigible. Thus, biological inferiority was repeatedly invoked to justify immigration restrictions that might otherwise be regarded as unchristian, morally reprehensible, and contrary to the American principles of openness to immigration, self-determination, and free markets. Traveling under the passport of the latest discoveries in biology and ethnology, nativists argued that it made no evolutionary sense to treat inherently different peoples alike. Mexicans after the Treaty of Guadelupe Hidalgo in 1848, the Chinese and Japanese in the second half of the nineteenth century, and Italians, Slovaks, and Jews in the early twentieth century all suffered from these campaigns of exclusion.[87]

The anti-immigrant crusades began with a campaign against the Chinese in California. The Chinese first came in substantial numbers to work in the mines, where gold was discovered in the 1840s. Many could not find the jobs they wanted, but they started to work as cooks, laundrymen, fishermen, shoemakers, cigar makers, tenant farmers, and menial workers. Starting in the 1860s, thousands of Chinese found work as laborers on the great western railroads. As is also the case today, the Chinese had a reputation for frugality and hard work. As Ronald Takaki documents in *Strangers from a Different Shore,* when the Chinese began to succeed in America, they experienced a strong reaction from white workers.[88] Responding to pressure from labor activists and nativist groups like the Asiatic Exclusion League, and supported by the claims of the intelligentsia, politicians militated for an end to Chinese immigration on the grounds that the "Mongolian hordes" were overrunning the country and taking jobs away from American citizens. Gangs of union workers and vandals launched periodic assaults on the Chinese community, and in 1876, the California legislature termed the Chinese "impregnable to all the influences of our Anglo-Saxon life."[89] In 1879, President Rutherford B. Hayes warned that "the present Chinese invasion is pernicious and should be discouraged." In Darwinian terms he added, "Our experience in dealing with the weaker races, the Negroes and Indians, is not encouraging."[90] In 1882, the U.S. Congress passed its first immigration exclusion act aimed at keeping the Chinese out of America. "For the first time in American history," writes Ronald Takaki, "Congress restricted immigration on the basis of race."[91] Some Chinese continued to get through, so the U.S. government passed more laws in 1888 and 1892 to close any loopholes.[92]

Soon attention turned to the Japanese, who were not very numerous but whose number was growing around the turn of the century. Under pressure from activist groups such as the California Oriental Exclusion League and the Immigration Restriction League, the U.S. government in 1908 entered into a Gentleman's Agreement with Japan which sharply curbed immigration from that country.[93] Asian immigration was a tiny fraction of total immigration to America, yet it attracted disproportionate, virtually obsessive attention from white nativists. Asian Indian immigration was infinitesimal, yet Indians too suffered attempts at restriction. The Asiatic Exclusion League made repeated reference to "the immodest and filthy habits of the Hindoos . . . their lack of cleanliness, petty pilfering, and insolence to women," and Samuel Gompers, president of the American Federation of Labor, noted:

> Sixty years contact with the Chinese, twenty five years experience with the Japanese, and two or three years of acquaintance with the Hindus should be sufficient to convince an ordinarily intelligent person that they have no standards by which a Caucasian may judge them.[94]

MELTING POTS AND SALAD BOWLS

The scientific racists ranked cultures hierarchically and linked them to race. Consequently, cultural evolutionism became implicated in a vitriolic American dispute about immigration and Americanization, one that closely parallels the contemporary debate about multiculturalism and assimilation. Today's argument focuses on whether immigration should be curtailed, and whether immigrants should be expected to dissolve their ethnic identities in a "melting pot" or common culture. Historians like Arthur Schlesinger, Jr., view assimilation as the crucible of a shared citizenship and warn of the dismal alternative: a cauldron of racial resentment.[95] By contrast, some scholars allied with multiculturalism allege that assimilation is a racist ideology. Toni Morrison suggests that it provides a mechanism for immigrants to develop racist attitudes toward African Americans. "They displace what and whom they can. When they got off the boat, the second word they learned was *nigger.* A hostile posture toward resident blacks must be struck at the Americanizing door before it will open."[96] Stanley Fish writes:

> *Common values. National unity. American character. One people. A single nation. Assimilation.* These are now the code words and phrases for an agenda that need no longer speak in the accents of the Know-Nothing party of the nineteenth century or the Ku Klux Klan of the twentieth.[97]

Let us try to view the argument that erupted in the late nineteenth and early twentieth centuries through the lens of these ideological perspectives. Then, as now, there were massive increases in immigration which seemed to threaten political institutions and the economic security of native workers. The two debates are not only analogous; in some respects, they are the same debate. Immigration to the United States in the 1990s is high, but in proportional terms it is lower than immigration levels at the turn of the last century.[98]

Before 1820, immigration was extremely modest: about ten thousand persons per year, and only eight million immigrants entered the country between 1840 and 1880. Between 1880 and 1930, however, the United States attracted some 25 million immigrants, more than at any previous time in its history. The new settlers, moreover, came predominantly from eastern and southern Europe: Italians, Poles, Russian Jews, Slovaks, Czechs, Hungarians, and Lithuanians, among others.[99] The immigrants congregated in sections of major cities that often came to be named after them: Chinatown, Little Italy, and the Jewish ghetto. They established ethnic enclaves. They started up hundreds of foreign-language newspapers. Between 1880 and 1900 New York grew from 2 to 3.5 million residents; Detroit, Cleveland, and Milwaukee doubled in size; and Chicago tripled. By 1920 half of the U.S urban population was foreign born or second generation immigrant. In the cases of the Portuguese, the Italians, the Lithuanians, and the Poles, only about 50 percent of the newcomers could speak English.[100]

Toni Morrison seems to exaggerate the extent to which immigrants were welcomed as full citizens on account of their whiteness. In fact, drawing on scientific racism, nativists invoked a hierarchy among whites, so that millions of Eastern and Central European immigrants faced opposition far greater than that faced by nonwhite immigrants today. Americans have traditionally embraced the concept that this is a nation of immigrants, but they have not always embraced the immigrants themselves. Being white, by itself, offered no insurance against racist exclusion. The language employed to warn against white immigrants sounds like a racist description of American blacks; the immigrants were described as "hirsute, low-browed, big-faced persons of obviously low mentality . . . clearly they belong in skins, in wattled huts at the close of the great Ice Age."[101]

In the mid-nineteenth century, the Irish were caricatured in the cartoons of Thomas Nast as simian creatures, good for nothing more than brawling and alcoholism. Irish immigrants suffered the taunts, humiliation, and violence of the Know-Nothings,[102] a powerful movement of exclusionists whose platform during the 1850s was not racism but anti-Catholicism. Immigrants like the Irish, warned Francis Walker, head of the American Economic Association, are "beaten men from beaten races, representing the worst failures in the struggle for existence."[103] Irish immigrants endured signs in major cities, "No Irish Need Apply." One writer recommended, "The best remedy for whatever is amiss in America would be if every Irishman should kill a Negro and be hanged for it."[104] In some northern states, employers would specify that they were willing to hire blacks, but not Irishmen.[105] Only gradually, as the Irish gained political power, were they incorporated into the American mainstream, along with earlier immigrants from Germany, England, and Scotland.[106]

Nor did immigrants rapidly melt into some hypothetical WASP pot.

On the contrary, many cherished their religious and ethnic identity, viewing themselves not as white but as German and Irish and Polish and Catholic and Protestant. Will Herberg argues in *Protestant, Catholic, Jew* that America worked as a kind of "triple melting pot" in which immigrants were expected to retain the religious associations they inherited at birth. "Almost from the beginning," Herberg writes, "the structure of American society presupposed diversity and substantial equality of religious associations."[107] The melting pot was never the only dominant symbol; it always coexisted with other images, such as Horace Kallen's metaphor of an American orchestra in which different instruments, each of distinct sound, harmonize together to make beautiful melodies.[108] The reality of American immigration has always fallen somewhere in between assimilation and cultural pluralism. Thus there is nothing new about contemporary metaphors such as the American "mosaic" or "salad bowl." They describe a reality which existed even a century ago.

As early as the eighteenth century, German immigrants, for example, insisted upon setting up their own schools, refused to intermarry and even interact with the English and the Irish, and spoke to one another in German. Benjamin Franklin complained of the Germans in Pennsylvania that "instead of learning our language, we must learn theirs, or live as in a foreign country."[109] It was only over several generations that the Germans and other immigrants assimilated. Moreover, in the process they changed American culture. Contributions that once seemed foreign or identifiably ethnic eventually came to seem distinctively American. Hamburgers and pizza, once considered odd importations from Germany and Italy, are now considered to be authentically American cuisine. Hot dogs were introduced as a novelty by a German immigrant named Antoine Feuchtwanger in the 1880s; today they are eaten with relish on the Fourth of July and at baseball games, and few Americans consider them to be a form of ethnic cuisine.[110] In contemporary America, it is not uncommon to see German Americans eat pizza, Latinos drink Budweiser, and African Americans enjoy Chinese food.

When immigrants arrived *en masse* in New York at the turn of the century, there were concerns about how America could digest approximately one million newcomers per year, with jobs in the cities increasingly scarce and many of the immigrants unable to speak English. Given the unprecedented magnitude of the transformation of the American population, these concerns were legitimate and cannot be automatically ascribed to

Coolidge agreed, proclaiming a slogan that many would probably endorse today: "America must be kept American."[123] The consequence, writes Stephen Jay Gould, was "one of the greatest victories of scientific racism in American history."[124] Congress and the White House worked together to implement a series of immigration laws that were explicitly racial in seeking to exclude yellow people from the Orient, brown people from India and north Africa, and even whites of sunkissed complexion from Eastern and Southern Europe. After imposing some restrictions—a literacy test in 1917 and a skills test in 1921—Congress in 1924 passed a landmark Immigration Act which sharply restricted immigration totals, virtually ended Asian immigration, and imposed national origin quotas designed to preserve the prevailing ethnic composition of the country. The implication of what Reed Ueda terms a "discriminatory hierarchy of quotas" was that northwestern Europeans, who were less eager to emigrate, were now welcome, whereas nonwhites and other Europeans, who wanted to come, were not.[125]

Life was also getting increasingly uncomfortable for immigrants already in the United States. Nativists and bigots produced books and pamphlets warning against intermarriage. In *The Biological Basis of Human Nature,* H. S. Jennings cautioned that "when diverse races are crossed, the offspring may well develop combinations of parts that lack complete harmony. A large body may be combined with small kidneys, or large teeth in a small jaw." Hybrids, Jennings concluded, were simply "badly put-together people."[126] Inspired by Mendel's discoveries in genetics, eugenic societies such as the National Conference on Race Betterment, the Eugenics Record Office, and the American Breeders Association were formed. The latter group included some of the nation's leading natural and social scientists: David Jordan, a biologist and president of Stanford University; Charles Henderson, a sociologist at the University of Chicago; geneticist Charles Davenport. Their goal was not specifically racial, although given the findings of scientific racism it has a clear racial effect. In this atmosphere, there is no race-neutral way to read the words of one eugenic manifesto which sought to reduce "the menace to society of inferior blood."[127] Nor was this mere rhetoric. Sixteen states passed sterilization laws and in the famous 1927 Supreme Court case of *Buck v. Bell,* a young woman was forcibly sterilized by the state and Justice Oliver Wendell Holmes approvingly declared, "Three generations of imbeciles are enough."[128]

FIGHTING RACISM WITH RELATIVISM

Atahualpa was accused of idolatry, polygamy and incest, which was
equivalent to condemning him for practicing a *different* culture.
                                            —Eduardo Galeano[129]

In the nineteenth century racism went largely unchallenged, but during
the first half of the twentieth century, a new generation of scholars, many
of them Jewish immigrants, rose to positions of authority and respect in
American universities. Hostile to Anglo-Saxon nativism and sympathetic
to blacks, these scholars subjected scientific racism to withering criticism.[130] They did so by reviving the ancient dispute between nature and
nurture—a tension that goes back to the Greeks, defines the philosophy
of Rousseau, and remains central to the American race debate. The new
generation of immigrant scholars began by insisting that there was no
proof that race differences were intrinsic; rather they were probably the
product of environment. They proceeded to question whether human
groups could be ranked hierarchically as savage, barbarian, and civilized.
Questioning the standards that would be used to make such a classification, they adopted a relativist position: standards are in the eye of the
beholder, so that Western criteria should not be used to evaluate non-
Western cultures. Eventually some articulated a strong form of cultural
relativism: all cultures are equal. Some went beyond relativism to insist
that non-Western cultures were morally superior to Western civilization,
because they were closer to nature.

In 1928, a young anthropologist named Margaret Mead published
Coming of Age in Samoa, a book which sold millions of copies in more
than a dozen languages and established itself as one of the most influential works in early twentieth century social science. Mead became virtually a household name in America, and perhaps the most famous
anthropologist in the world. *Coming of Age in Samoa,* according to anthropologist Sherwood Washburn, "influenced the way people were
brought up in this country."[131] Mead was a special kind of cultural relativist, who believed that Western standards should not be used to judge
other cultures, but who argued that the West could learn from other cultures which were, at least in some respects, superior. For Mead, the
Samoans were a contemporary example of Rousseau's noble savages:
they were people whom Westerners could envy and try to emulate. They
were not racial inferiors but cultural superiors. They lived a life that was

one with nature and free of guilt. Mead concentrated on the sexual virtues of the Samoans.

> They laugh at stories of romantic love, scoff at fidelity . . . believe explicitly that one love will quickly cure another . . . adultery does not necessarily mean a broken marriage . . . divorce is a simple, informal matter. . . . Samoans welcome casual homosexual practices. . . . In such a setting, there is no room for guilt.[132]

This message of liberation from civilizational hangups was very much one that many Americans wanted to hear. Mead's work corroborated a new romantic ethos which celebrated the social and sexual freedom of the noble savage and deplored the constraining cage of civilization. Mead's appeal was not what she wrote about Samoa but what she implicitly preached to America. By making outlandish practices in Samoa seem familiar, Mead made familiar Western practices seem outlandish. Mead attacked traditional American concepts of morality and perversion: her message was that Americans were too repressed and guilt-ridden about sex, and could enjoy the fruits of free love if they would go native like the Samoans. Reviewing Mead's book, Freda Kirchwey wrote in *The Nation,* "Somewhere in each of us, hidden among our most obscure desires, is a South Sea island promising freedom and irresponsibility."[133] Charles Peters, editor of the *Washington Monthly,* recalls, "I remember reading Mead when I was a young man. I read her as telling me that it was okay to get laid. Her cultural relativism, or whatever you call it, seemed like a small price to pay for freedom." Mead was one of the first apostles of the sexual revolution in the United States.

In 1934 another famous anthropologist, Ruth Benedict, published *Patterns of Culture,* which became one of the most popular nonfiction books of the decade, selling over a million copies. George Stocking credits this book with helping win public acceptance for a new "anthropological idea of culture."[134] Benedict went on to publish numerous well-known works such as *Race and Racism* and *The Chrysanthemum and the Sword.* Like Margaret Mead, Benedict argued that human behavior was shaped primarily by nurture rather than nature. *Patterns of Culture* celebrated human malleability and possibility: Americans could burrow beneath the apparently strange customs of other peoples and learn wonderfully liberating things from them. Cultural relativism was advanced by Benedict as a recipe for tolerance, openness, and emancipation—a very attractive liberal message for the times.[135]

Mead and Benedict were in fact academic colleagues at Columbia

University, and shared a lesbian relationship.[136] Both were students of Franz Boas, a Jewish immigrant from Germany who was the founder of the American Anthropological Association and chairman of the most influential departments of social science in the United States. Although Boas is mainly known today through the influence of his disciples, his own impact on American scholarship has been enormous, surpassing that of famous European anthropologists like Bronislaw Malinowski and Claude Lévi-Strauss, and in some ways rivaling that of Marx, Darwin, and Freud. Carl Degler writes, "The Boas influence upon American social scientists can hardly be exaggerated."[137] Another scholar maintains that "it is possible that Boas did more to combat race prejudice than any person in history."[138]

An immigrant who came to the United States from Germany in 1886, Boas left behind a country and a continent increasingly prey to anti-Semitism, which he felt keenly as a Jew. In the United States, Boas, whose own politics were left-leaning,[139] carefully began to mobilize against the entrenched nativism of the Anglo-Saxon school who dominated American universities. He was preparing for a measured yet devastating assault on nineteenth century cultural evolutionism. Boas first established his academic footing at Columbia University, and then cultivated a new cohort of scholars—some of them black, several of them Jewish, many of them women and immigrants—who would go on to distinguish themselves in the social sciences and transform the assumptions of American scholarship. These scholars amplified Boas's views and prosecuted a full-scale intellectual war against scientific racism. By the 1930s, they were winning the intellectual battle. By the 1940s, their influence was manifest on American public opinion. Their achievement was to deprive scientific racism of its reputation both for being progressive and for being scientific. Thanks in large part to this one man and his students, the country entered a new era.[140]

RACE AND CULTURE

Scientific racism was based on two premises: cultures can be ranked according to a linear scale of savage, barbarian, and civilized; and cultural achievement is a reflection of racial characteristics. Boas accepted biological evolution but denied cultural evolution. He emphasized that differences in civilizational achievement were not the result of races adapting to their natural environment, but of cultures adapting to their social environment. Boas questioned the relationship between race and culture, producing studies to show that cultural differences were the product of environment rather than biology. Boas also criticized the notions of cultural superiority and inferiority, arguing that such evaluation is a relative matter. Boas urged that American social scientists describe other cultures rather than judge them. He advocated historical particularism, a system in which each culture is studied on its own terms as an integral and functional whole.

Boas's alienation from the industrialized West is evident as early as 1883, even before he came to the United States. Boas made a field trip that year to Baffinland, where he was struck by the harmony of Eskimo life and began to ask himself whether what he regarded as civilization was simply a Western bias against the natural way of life. Echoing Rousseau's critique of bourgeois civilization, Boas implied that a savage existence may be freer and more authentic. Then he proceeded to relativize Rousseau's critique: neither the savage nor the civilized lifestyle is superior, indeed such evaluations will vary depending on the perspective and values of the observer. Boas wrote in his diary of the trip:

> I often ask myself what advantages our "good society" possesses over the "savages." The more I see of their customs, the more I realize that we have no right to look down upon them. Where amongst our people would you find such true hospitality? Here, without the least complaint, people are willing to perform every task demanded of them. . . . For me the most important result of this trip lies in the strengthening of my point of view that the idea of a "cultured" individual is merely relative.[141]

In America, Boas secured a teaching appointment at Columbia, where he began work in a familiar field, craniometry, but with the objective of showing limitations in the arguments of the scientific racists. Between 1908 and 1909 Boas supervised a massive government-funded study of more than 18,000 immigrants, some of them recent arrivals, others who had lived in the United States for years. With the aid of research assistants, Boas measured their heads and bodies, computing cephalic indexes. In his report, he emphasized the revolutionary nature of his findings. Boas claimed that for each immigrant group, the cranial index and body type changed according to its duration in the United States. Indeed immigrants from generally dolichocephalic, or long-skulled, groups tended to develop rounder heads the longer they stayed in America, and immigrants from brachycephalic, or short-skulled, groups found their heads getting longer. What Boas had found was not merely change in the cranial index, but also convergence. Since their parents and ancestors did not show these traits, Boas argued that the changes could "only be explained as due directly to the influence of environment." Moreover, the results showed, contrary to the scientific racists, that "all the evidence is now in favor of a great plasticity of human types."[142]

Boas outlined his views denying the importance of nature and emphasizing the influence of culture in several books, including *The Mind of Primitive Man,* published in 1911 and now considered a classic. Boas argued that the development of Western civilization was not the consequence of intrinsic genius on the part of the white race but simply owing to favorable circumstances. Other cultures could not be termed inferior, he declared, only different. He questioned the practice of scientific racists who compared existing peoples from undeveloped cultures to the Europeans' ancient ancestors.[143] Challenging the credibility of the Social Darwinists, Boas specifically criticized Herbert Spencer's argument that groups could be deemed backward from an evolutionary point of view. Spencer had made a passing reference to the inattentiveness of American Indians. Based on his studies of the Kwakiutl of Vancouver Island, Boas responded that the Indians gave trifling answers to European questions because they were uninterested in them; in fact, their conversation was highly animated and engaged. Boas was right to point out Spencer's biased assumptions, yet his own study of the Kwakiutl, although impressive for its detail, sought to portray his subjects in a positive light by carefully avoiding any references to abhorrent Kwakiutl practices such as slavery.[144]

Denying the allegations of the scientific racists that American blacks were naturally inferior to whites, Boas argued that such conclusions were premature because of the burdens imposed by slavery and oppression. He advocated conditions of equal opportunity that would permit blacks to reach their potential.

> We do not know of any demand made on the human body or mind in modern life that anatomical or ethnological evidence would prove to be beyond the powers of the Negro. There is every reason to believe that the Negro, when given facility and opportunity, will be perfectly able to fulfill the duties of citizenship as well as his white neighbor.[145]

Boas's arguments were greatly strengthened because of a kind of linguistic revolution he launched in American social science by his novel use of the term "culture." Before the nineteenth century, European writers spoke only of "civilization." The term civilization comes from the Latin word *civis* meaning citizen. Used in the singular, civilization implies a certain form of government and a certain level of achievement. In the nineteenth century, Matthew Arnold used the term "culture" in contrast with "civilization." For Arnold culture was the corpus of liberal learning apart from the mechanized and homogenized work of industrial civilization. The word culture comes from the Latin term *cultura* meaning to grow or cultivate. "Culture" arises out of "agriculture." Arnold used culture in an elevated sense, however: culture was represented by the high traditions of Athens and Jerusalem. It was "the study of perfection . . . the best that has been known and thought." To say that someone is cultured in the Arnoldian sense implies that he is educated in morals and taste.[146]

Boas, however, used a new definition, one that was initiated by the English anthropologist Edward Tylor, who defined culture as the "knowledge, belief, arts, morals, customs and any other capabilities and habits acquired by man as a member of society."[147] This was a less demanding and more inclusive definition according to which the term "uncultured" was essentially meaningless. Only some people may be considered to have civilization, but all people in the Boasian sense have culture, in that they have customs and beliefs. Accordingly, anthropologists now began to speak not of culture in the singular but of cultures in the plural.[148] Through the democratization of the term, Boas found it much easier to suggest the essential relativity of cultures, and to define the task of anthropology as that of examining cultures on their own terms, rather than trying to compare their levels of development on a single scale of evaluation. Over time, even Americans who did not espouse relativism began to speak of "culture" in the Boas sense of the term, which is the way we commonly use the term today.[149]

Historically, one of the strongest arguments for Western civilizational superiority has been the spectacular political and economic successes of modern industrial society. According to George Stocking in *The Ethnographer's Magic,* Boas qualified but never abandoned his belief in the concepts of modernity, technology, rationality, and civilization.[150] He did not claim that groups had demonstrated the same levels of achievement, only that these differences were due to culture and circumstance; groups probably had the same inherent potential.[151] Boas was not a strict cultural relativist, although he moved increasingly in that direction over the years.[152] He emphasized that his main argument with the scientific racists was not that they were wrong, but that their case was unproven.[153]

SAMOAN TALL TALES

As often happens with an influential teacher, however, Boas's students extended his principles to construct a radically new framework for understanding race in the modern world.[154] The names of Boas's students at Columbia University read like a Who's Who of early American anthropology: Margaret Mead, Ruth Benedict, Otto Klineberg, Kenneth Clark, Melville Herskovits, Theodosius Dobzhansky, Alfred Kroeber, Robert Lowie, Edward Sapir, L. C. Dunn, Isidor Chein, Gene Weltfish, and Ashley Montagu. Under his careful direction, these young scholars undertook projects that would decisively shape their field, as well as influence American public attitudes and policy. Many of Boas's students developed their teacher's concept of culture into a comprehensive ideology of relativism. In its radical form, this relativism did not merely assert the difficulty of understanding other cultures but insisted that there is no rational basis for judging them and consequently that all cultures should be considered essentially equal and equally deserving of respect.

• Alfred Kroeber and Robert Lowie insisted that culture should be studied entirely independent of biology or heredity, which went far beyond anything Boas wrote.[155]

• Ruth Benedict argued the inevitability of Western scholarly ethnocentrism in evaluating other cultures: "The seeing eye is not a mere physical organ but a means of perception conditioned by the tradition in which its possessor has been reared."[156]

• Margaret Mead virtually denied that human nature had anything to do with heredity: "Human nature is almost unbelievably malleable, responding . . . to contrasting cultural conditions."[157]

• Otto Klineberg even offered relativism as a moral imperative: "Feelings of superiority are not conducive to good human relations."[158]

• Perhaps the clearest exposition of the strong form of cultural relativism was given by Melville Herskovits.

> Cultural relativism is a philosophy that recognizes the values set up by every society to guide its own life, and that understands their worth to those who live by them, though they may differ from one's own. Instead of underscoring differences from absolute norms that, however objectively arrived at, are nonetheless the product of a given time and place, the relativistic point of view brings into relief the validity of every set of norms for the people who have them.[159]

The Boas school sought both to defend this doctrine and to give it practical application. The triumph of the Boasians is illustrated by the success achieved by his most prominent student, Margaret Mead. Mead's famous trip to Samoa in 1925–1926 was suggested and shaped by Boas, who convinced Mead to become an anthropologist in the first place. Prior to her Samoan adventure, Boas instructed Mead that her "most important contribution" would be to show the "psychological attitude of the individual" was a product of the pressure of the general pattern of culture." Boas also implied to Mead that the awkward adolescent phase of sexual adjustment (which Freud attributed to repression) might be a kind of Western peculiarity, not shared by Samoans and other truly emancipated peoples.[160] What Mead wanted to find, and what her teacher wanted her to find, perhaps not very surprisingly, is exactly what she did find. Her response to Samoans was like that of Montaigne to the cannibals of his day: "One very beautiful thing about their marriages is that whereas our wives anxiously keep us from enjoying the friendship and kindliness of other women, their wives are equally anxious to procure just those favors for their husbands."[161] In an introduction to Mead's *Coming of Age in Samoa,* Boas spelled out Mead's corroboration of his hypothesis: "Much of what we ascribe to human nature is no more than a reaction to the restraints put upon us by our civilization."[162]

In fact, Mead's portrait of Samoa was misleading, if not substantively false. Samoan students studying at American colleges in later years would angrily denounce her for misrepresenting and distorting their culture.[163] Another leading anthropologist, Derek Freeman, documented that Mead was wrong on virtually every claim she had made about Samoa. While Mead had claimed that Samoans were free of jealousy and psychological remorse over sexuality, in fact repression and guilt were pervasive in Samoan culture. Mead insisted that free love was generally accepted, but Freeman pointed out that bridal virginity was regarded as indispensable and even publicly tested by the groom's family. Mead wrote that adultery was considered harmless by the Samoans, but Freeman documented that adultery, once punished in Samoa by death, was listed in the Samoan legal code during the 1920s as a crime punishable by a fine and a year's imprisonment or both. Mead had claimed to be struck by the absence of suicide, whereas Freeman showed that suicides were frequent in Samoa at the time, and were reported regularly in the local newspapers. Mead had written that rape was foreign to the Samoan mind, but Freeman showed that rape rates in Samoa were several times higher than in the United States, indeed "among the highest in the world." Mead's account was so scandalously in error, Freeman concluded, that it constitutes the worst case of "self-deception in the history of the behavioral sciences." He argued that the best explanation for how she could have gone so far wrong is that "as a kind of joke" she had been "deliberately misled by her adolescent informants." Freeman located one of Mead's sources, Fa'apua'a Fa'amu, who confirmed that she and her girlfriends were so chagrined by Mead's prurient interest in their sex lives that they made up the kind of stories that Mead apparently wanted to hear. Freeman argued that Mead's gullibility is not surprising in that she arrived in Samoa without knowing the language, picked up what she could in a six-week course, lived not with the natives but with a U.S. Navy pharmacist, and left Samoa nine months later. Freeman, who conducted more than six years of field work in Samoa, asserted that Mead had proven to be a fool and a liar and that Boas, the famous skeptic, turned out to be naively credulous about the findings of his students that supported his own political biases.[164]

Predictably, Freeman's book caused an uproar in anthropological circles. "Freeman's attack on a leading female scholar . . . cannot fail to have racist implications," protested Eleanor Leacock.[165] Anthropologist Lowell Holmes went into an ethnocentric pout: "I find an element of resentment at a foreigner attacking *our* Margaret. America loved this woman."[166] While conceding Mead's flaws "from the perspective of anthropology today," anthropologist Annette Weiner sought to defend her conclusions by condemning the "old myth that human behavior is grounded in only one kind of truth and one set of values."[167] Colin Turnbull in *The New Republic* termed Freeman's research "a personal attack on a great woman, a great humanitarian and a great anthropologist." Yet his defense of Mead's Samoan findings was tepid. "Mead made no bones about her lack of training." Absurdly, Turnbull states that "the nature-nurture issue was not what Margaret Mead set out to investigate."[168] As even her defenders' rhetoric suggests, Mead's Samoan reporting is now regarded by most scholars as partial and questionable at best. As Bradd Shore put it, "We have sought to explain away her errors."[169] Another sympathetic scholar, Peter Worsley, concluded that Mead produced "creative speculation but poor anthropology."[170]

Mead's Samoan escapade turned out to be simply one of a series of Boasian initiatives, all aimed at providing empirical fortification for the model of cultural relativism. Ruth Benedict made a study of the Pueblo Indians, where she seems to have found in the Pueblos precisely what she may have been looking for: a society where sex was free of guilt, marital fidelity ignored, divorce simply a matter of casual change-of-heart, and homosexuality an "honorable estate."[171] As part of a Carnegie Foundation study commissioned by Gunnar Myrdal, another Boas student, Melville Herskovits, undertook a study of the African heritage of Americans. Through field work in Surinam and Dahomey, Herskovits produced what is now widely regarded as a sanitized portrait of Africa and an exaggerated account of Africanisms in America.[172] Like contemporary Afrocentrists, Herskovits conducted his research with the stated objective of boosting Negro pride and improving white perceptions of blacks:

> Let us suppose it could be shown that the Negro is a man with a past and a reputable past; that in time the concept could be spread that the civilizations of Africa, like those of Europe, have contributed to American culture as we know it today; and that this idea might eventually be taken over into the canons of general thought. Would this not, as a practical measure, tend to undermine the assumptions that bolster prejudice?[173]

Over the years, the Boas school's pattern of discovery became clear. Whether it was Boas among the Eskimo, or Mead in Samoa, or Benedict among the Pueblo Indians, or Herskovits in Africa, the conclusion was always the same: cultures that seem on the surface to be hopelessly primitive are in fact enormously sophisticated and complex, no less worthy of admiration than Western culture. And the moral, never concealed, was that white Europeans have no cause for civilizational arrogance, at the very least they should accept other cultures and peoples on a plane of equality, and as a matter of fact they have a good deal to learn from them.

ARE ALL CULTURES EQUAL?

Many of the assumptions of cultural relativism are so widely accepted today that we should try to step back and examine the contours of the relativist argument as it emerged from the Boasian school. To do so, let us focus on Ruth Benedict and Melville Herkovits, the most vocal advocates of cultural relativism in its strong form. The challenge confronted by Benedict, Herskovits, and the Boasians was cogently articulated in a UNESCO study, published in 1952, by Claude Lévi-Strauss:

> If there are no innate racial aptitudes, how can we explain the fact that the white man's civilization has made the tremendous advances with which we

are all familiar, while the civilizations of the colored peoples have lagged behind, some of them having come only halfway along the road, and others being still thousands or tens of thousands of years behind the times?[174]

This question raises a possible conflict between progress, a product of Western modernity, and the equality of all cultures. Benedict begins by implicitly conceding both progress and European cultural superiority, but denying that either are related to race. "Higher civilization is not a characteristic of all whites but only of certain areas of white civilization." Benedict denies what she terms "biological laws . . . of cultural progress." Benedict illustrates her rejection of the racial basis of civilizational development with a convincing example. American Indians may strike whites as primitive and backward peoples, Benedict argues, but is this because of intrinsic characteristics, such as race, or because of culture? Benedict admits that Indians share racial features, but she denies that this determines their thinking or behavior. Both Plains tribes and Pueblos are Indians, yet the former are rugged and individualistic, while the latter are mild and peaceful; clearly, she suggests, they have developed different cultures in response to different needs and conditions. Benedict also impugns claims of permanent or intrinsic Anglo-Saxon superiority by pointing out that these very people are descended from some of the wildest tribes who were painfully subdued by the Romans and the Normans in the ancient and medieval period. "A Norman in the time of Ivanhoe could have written of the impossibility of civilizing the Saxons," Benedict writes.

Next Benedict proceeds to question both the inevitability and the desirability of the kind of progress made possible by the West's new science of man. She asserts empires such as the Egyptians, the Persians, the Macedonians, the Romans, the Mongols, and the Arabs all rose to great eminence, only to collapse and never recover. "The history of all civilizations, whether they are Caucasian or Malay or Mongol, shows periods of great vigor and also periods of stability and even ossification." Moreover, "Our civilization has invented many things which white intelligence has not shown the ability to handle. Surely this too is a test of intelligence, and one in which Western civilization has not distinguished itself." Benedict then goes on to reject even the possibility of being able to evaluate other cultures in a detached or objective manner. "No man ever looks at the world with pristine eyes. He sees it edited by a definite set of customs and institutions and ways of thinking. He cannot go beyond these stereotypes. His very concepts of true and false will still have reference to his particular traditions."[175] Here Benedict suggests that Europeans can only view other cultures through color-tinted lenses.

Finally, Benedict and Herskovits move from a neutral relativism, which says that we cannot know that which is alien to us, to the advocacy of a specific form of global knowledge: the equality of all cultures. "Every society has worked out a material culture and techniques of exploiting the natural resources of its habitat," Herskovits writes. Consequently, in Herskovits's view, "the characteristics held to distinguish 'primitive' or 'savage' ways of life are open to serious question."[176] Herskovits and Benedict both argue for the parity of cultures based on the premise that every one of them has made an inherently legitimate adaptation to its environment. Benedict writes, "No man can thoroughly participate in any culture unless he has been brought up and has lived according to its forms, but he can grant to other cultures the same significance to their patterns which he recognizes as his own." Benedict even offers a moral justification for eschewing Western cultural superiority and embracing cultural relativism.

> Modern existence has thrown many civilizations into close contact, and at the moment the overwhelming response to this situation is nationalism and racial snobbery. . . . The recognition of the cultural basis of race prejudice is a desperate need in present Western civilization. . . . Those of us who are members of the vaunted races . . . should make it clear that we do not want or claim the kind of superiority that the racists offer us.[177]

In its criticism of the racial basis of civilizational achievement, relativism proved convincing. After all, the racists had presumed, rather than demonstrated, the necessary correlation between the white physical makeup and the achievement of Western civilization. As Boas and later Benedict maintained, the burden of proof was on the racists, and they seemed unable to meet it. Thus the greatest achievement of the Boasians was to detach the idea of race from the idea of culture.

Relativism also appealed to many because it seemed to offer a basis for detached and value-neutral scholarship. For decades the project of investigating non-Western cultures was murky territory, attracting an assorted band of theologians, philosophers, biologists, and naturalists. Much of their theorizing was interdisciplinary and amateurish, presuming an evolutionary model that seemed arbitrary and self-serving in its criteria for social and racial hierarchy. The new relativism professionalized American social science by offering sociology, anthropology and other fields a new method and mission: to study other cultures on their own terms and try to explain why peoples lived as they did. Cultures could now be studied not from distant vantage points but, as the new terminology had it, "from within." Many scholars were attracted by an approach that gave them a sense of being sympathetic insiders rather than judgmental outsiders.

Finally the moral appeal of Boasian relativism also became evident. Instead of being ideological apprentices for ideologies of Western superiority, American scholars could now be cultural ambassadors from other cultures to the West. Indeed they could invoke the seemingly peculiar mores of other cultures as models for the West: they could become apostles of unlimited cultural plasticity and human freedom in the United States. If the natural scientists promised material prosperity based on the "conquest of nature," social scientists could offer social emancipation based on the conquest of human nature. Indeed this claim to the value-neutral study and manipulation of cultural mores within their own society lies behind the term "social scientist." Much of the social engineering of the second half of the twentieth century, aimed at guaranteeing personal self-expression for individuals and social equality for groups, is based on this vision.

But relativism raised problems too, which have become more apparent over the years. By insisting on the adaptiveness or functionality of all norms and practices, it compelled a suspension of critical judgment in assessing other cultures. In a frank statement, Melville Herskovits invoked relativism to justify "the right to be exploited in terms of the patterns of one's own culture."[178] Such an approach sometimes required an averted gaze from practices such as witchcraft, mutilation, torture, female clitoral removal, destructive taboos, foot-binding, bride burning, blood feuds, the sacralization of disease, and horrendous sanitary practices. Instead of trying to rationalize indefensible customs, anthropologist Robert Edgerton protested, Western scholars should consider the possibility of maladaptive or dysfunctional practices.[179] Yet Edgerton's concerns have gone largely unheeded. According to the relativist paradigm, the apparently outrageous customs of other cultures were to be politely overlooked, or explained as ingenious and necessary adaptations to the special needs of a particular environment.

A recent example is Renato Rosaldo's empathetic account of why the Illongot men of the Philippines upon encountering a personal tragedy express their grief by hunting down strangers and cutting off their heads. Rosaldo's answer is that the Illongot are displaying an honest and admirable rage. "Upper middle class Anglo-American culture tends to ignore rage," Rosaldo complains.[180] Of course by this logic there are no moral constraints whatsoever on human behavior. Drawing on the vocabulary of philosophical relativism, American social scientists employed the new vocabulary of "values."[181] There are no enduring truths, only subjective preferences, and there is no rational basis for saying that one option is superior to any other. Just as each culture's customs were regarded as adaptive for them, so each individual's norms of conduct could be considered adaptive for that person. Although many tried to resist this implication, ultimately cultural relativism seemed to legitimize the distinct but related notion of moral relativism as well.

Despite its apparent toleration of the offensive practices of other cultures, the Boasian paradigm promoted a peculiarly harsh condemnation of American customs and mores. This double standard became evident in the way American social scientists insisted that the practices of other cultures were exempt from moral criticism, yet these scholars did not prove reluctant to condemn Western practices that they considered repugnant. Relativism did not seem to protect domestic American cultures, such as the culture of evangelical Christians who condemned homosexuality, or of Southerners who celebrated the antebellum era. Why this moral asymmetry? Were these groups not also adapting to their unique environments and did not their rage, like that of the Illongots, require empathy and understanding? On the contrary: these cultures were held to full moral accountability. Yet in holding them responsible for their actions, American scholars seemed to judge them by a higher standard than that applied to nonwhite peoples, thus granting to white groups a kind of implicit claim to moral superiority.

Cultural relativism seemed convincing as long as it was based on both a vague and a low view of culture. The low view was implicit in the term culture itself: relativists could plausibly argue that the Western habit of eating potatoes was no better than the Asian habit of eating rice. (Even this is not obvious: nutritionists can make a case that the diets of certain cultures are healthier than others.) But it was far more difficult to make the case that Western liberal democracy was not a better system of government than Islamic theocracy, or that cultures that violated human rights and those that respected human rights occupied the same moral plane. Thus while it seemed considerate to proclaim all cultures equal, relativism raised the problem of specificity: Equal in what respect? Obviously some cultures were better than others at doing certain things, such as producing consumer goods or sending rockets into outer space. Taken literally, cultural relativism was compelled to deny the very existence of progress, because in its lexicon, the new culture is no better than the one it replaced. As Ernest Gellner argued, the fact of relativism—that cultures differ in their mores—did not entail an ideology of relativism—that we have no basis for moral judgment about other cultures and should embrace cultural egalitarianism.[182]

Relativism also seemed problematic at the deepest philosophical level. Insisting that Europeans could not understand other cultures except through Western ideological spectacles, Theodosius Dobzhansky reached the approved Boasian conclusion: "No one culture's way of life is better than another; people live differently and that is all."[183] How did Dobzhansky know this? Either he had discovered a universal truth, in which case it was possible for a westerner to objectively understand other cultures and the Boasian premise was false or, alternatively, all knowledge was truly local and relative, and this applied to Boasian relativism as well.

THE RACIST AS BARBARIAN

Whatever the merits of the arguments, the Boas school prevailed, and largely through its influence cultural relativism became an operating assumption in American social science. Boas and his students were effective in rebutting many of the arguments of the scientific racists, and they won important converts such as Howard Odum, a Southern scholar who espoused theories of black inferiority in the early part of the twentieth century, but later converted to the Boasian point of view, became a liberal voice in support of civil rights, and during the 1950s refused to testify in favor of segregation during the *Brown v. Board of Education* case.[184] Other scholars underwent similar metamorphoses.[185] By the early 1930s, Boas's students and followers dominated the major anthropology departments of top universities, as well as the leadership of many professional social science organizations.

But it is a mistake to believe that the Boasians succeeded through reason alone. As Carl Degler writes, "We see essentially the substitution of one unproved assumption by another."[186] The event which guaranteed the intellectual victory of cultural relativism in Western scholarship was

World War II. Western social scientists watched in horror as Adolf Hitler openly championed the cause of racial nationalism—warning in *Mein Kampf* of the prospect of a "bastardized and niggerized world"[187]—and then used it to justify the extermination of millions of Jews and other peoples he held as inferior. "However hard scientists tried to disassociate themselves from Nazi racism by labelling it a ghastly perversion of science for political ends," Nancy Stepan writes, "the fact was that racism had received its sanction from science."[188] Even more embarrassing, eugenic groups in the United States had lent general support to the so-called Aryan science of the Nazis.[189] In one notorious case, Lothrop Stoddard, the author of *Clashing Tides of Color* and other paeans to white supremacy, interviewed Adolf Hitler in 1940 and found many of his political and eugenic theories to be excellent, although he conceded that in Hitler's overzealousness they were being carried too far.[190]

As the United States mobilized for war against Hitler, such views became not only unpersuasive, but bordering on treason. America and much of the world saw that ethnic and racial animus carried with it the prospect of mass destruction and genocide. Suddenly the war against bigotry seemed a crusade relevant to the lives of all Americans. Bigotry seemed not only irrational, as many scholars insisted, but also deeply immoral, as historical events demonstrated. In American intellectual quarters, it became apostasy to argue that one race was superior to another.

The Boasians proceeded to launch an assault on the motives of their opponents, including serious scholars of racial differences who were accused of harboring sympathies for Nazism. Pat Shipman writes in a recent book that "those who meant to strike blows for equality . . . bent the truth to their cause." Even tactics that would otherwise be considered unacceptable proved effective, Shipman argues, because many in the West were terrified of the "risk of providing ammunition to potential racists."[191] The Boasians were able to establish themselves as the only humane alternative to genocide. As a result of lobbying by Boas and his students, the American Anthropological Association in 1938 passed its first resolution proclaiming the equal capacity of all cultures and denouncing racism.[192] At the time such a political gesture was considered highly unusual, but over the next few decades these resolutions became fairly routine.[193]

In 1944 the international group UNESCO appointed a committee to issue a statement on race which was headed up by a prominent Boasian, the cultural anthropologist Ashley Montagu. The draft statement concluded that "biological studies lend support to the ethic of universal brotherhood, for man is born with drives toward cooperation." This radical rejection of Darwinism prompted such unease among scholars that UNESCO assembled a new committee which issued a revised position. Once again, the committee was dominated by Boasians: Montagu, L. C. Dunn, Otto Klineberg, and Theodosius Dobzhansky. They moderated the ideological zeal of the first draft and rephrased their conclusion into language that commanded wider, although by no means unanimous, scientific assent. The UNESCO final statement declared that "available scientific evidence provides no basis for believing that the groups of mankind differ in their innate capacity for intellectual and emotional development."[194] Over the next several years UNESCO issued four antiracist manifestos, which reaffirmed that all groups have equal civilizational ability.

The consequence of the Boasian triumph was the enshrinement of a new conventional wisdom in American scholarship. This can be seen in perhaps the most influential book on race in America published in the twentieth century, *An American Dilemma* by Gunnar Myrdal.[195] A world-renowned Swedish social scientist who went on to win the Nobel Prize in economics, Myrdal was invited to the United States by the Carnegie Foundation to supervise a major study of "the Negro problem." Published in 1944, Myrdal's book changed the entire race debate in the United States. It was instrumental in preparing the ground for the civil rights movement, and for shaping many of its assumptions and arguments.[196] Basing his study on what he termed "relativistic scientific knowledge," Myrdal popularized two crucial terms which continue to frame the American race debate: prejudice and discrimination. For his data, Myrdal interviewed a wide range of sources, but he attached the most credibility to the anthropologists of the Boas school. Kenneth Clark, a young black sociologist and a Boas disciple, worked as a researcher on the Myrdal project. Two Boas students, Otto Klineberg and Ashley Montagu, were specifically commissioned by Myrdal to write monographs and reports, and Myrdal cited Klineberg's work to justify his conclusion that there are no differences in innate intelligence between blacks and whites.

Myrdal took it for granted that race was more a social than a biological category, and that enormous variations within groups made it impossible to speak scientifically about pure races. He dismissed the possibility of natural differences between the races, saying it was "increasingly evident that little, if anything, could be scientifically explained in terms of the peculiarities of the Negroes themselves." Myrdal blamed whites for the false attribution of the inferior social condition of blacks to race, a condition he termed "prejudice." Ignoring the historical circumstances in which racism first arose, Myrdal asserted, contrary to the claims of the old racists, that slavery and segregation were the cause, rather than the consequence, of black inferiority.

In fact, Myrdal said that since the political power of whites conditioned the social circumstances of blacks, there was no Negro problem, only a "white man's problem." Myrdal argued that "white prejudice and discrimination keep the Negro low in standards of living, manners and morals. This, in turn, gives support to white prejudice." Consequently, Myrdal maintained that "if white prejudice could be decreased and discrimination mitigated, this is likely to cause a rise in Negro standards, which may decrease white prejudice still a little more, and so on through mutual interaction." Myrdal proposed an "educational offensive against racial intolerance," and concluded that there was simply no scientific justification for "differential treatment in matters of public policy, such as in education, suffrage, and entrance into various sections of the labor market."[197]

By the 1950s, these premises were the secure and unquestioned underpinning of American intellectual life. Two influential studies, published in 1950, reveal the new orthodoxy, what Pierre Van Den Berghe terms the "genuine party line" on race that persists today.[198] In *The Dynamics of Prejudice,* Bruno Bettelheim and Morris Janowitz shifted the focus from the intellectual abilities of blacks and other minorities to the psychological profile of the racist. Their study of veterans identified irrationality and fear as two of the galvanizing forces behind prejudice.[199] In *The Authoritarian Personality,* T. W. Adorno and his colleagues went further, charging that middle-class Western values were highly conducive to racism, so that those who conformed to these ideals were probable bigots and "potential fascists," suffering from insecurity anxieties, quick to project their own failings onto others, susceptible to demagogic manipulation, highly in need of education in tolerance and group understanding.[200]

According to the relativist paradigm that emerged, there is no justified criticism to be made against any culture or group; any such attempt is prima facie evidence of irrational "prejudice." In his classic work *The Nature of Prejudice,* published in 1954, Harvard psychologist Gordon Allport defines the term as "thinking ill of others without sufficient warrant . . . a feeling prior to, or not based on, actual experience," indeed often "composed wholly of hearsay evidence, emotional projections and fantasy."[201] This definition persists to the present.[202] It dismisses as highly unlikely any suggestion that under circumstances of uncertainty, prejudices may be necessary or prudent. Group generalizations, similarly, are viewed as unchanging "stereotypes," a term derived from printing which Walter Lippmann introduced in the 1920s. Stereotypes are regarded as "over-generalizations of psychological characteristics to large human groups," and thus faulty and unscientific, in the words of a leading textbook.[203] "A stereotype is a preconceived or oversimplified generalization about an entire group of people without regard for individual differences," reports the Anti-Defamation League of B'nai B'rith in a curricular package designed to combat prejudice. "Even when stereotypes are positive the impact of stereotyping is negative."[204] The possibility that stereotypes might be based on accurate statistical generalizations, whether positive or negative, is ignored altogether or rejected out of hand. Prejudice and stereotypes, of course, lead to "discrimination," which is now defined as "the restrictive treatment of a person or group based on prejudiced assumptions of group characteristics, rather than on individual judgment."[205] Yet this definition does not take into account discrimination that may have a rational basis, because in the absence of full information about individuals we may be compelled in limited cases to evaluate them based on discernible group characteristics.

Today the relativist paradigm is not defended, but taken for granted. According to this model, cultural relativism or group equality is natural and inequality or hierarchy is conventional. Other cultures are automatically viewed on the same plane as the West; minority groups are entitled to a presumption of moral and intellectual equality with whites; no group, whether blacks in America or aborigines in Australia, can be considered inferior. Group differences, according to the antiracist model, can safely be attributed to environmental causes, specifically, in the case of American minorities, to past and present discrimination. The remedies seem naturally to suggest themselves: education, desegregation, equality under the law. Moreover, those who do not endorse the new ideology are said to require not persuasion, but diagnosis. "Through particular social attitudes," Thomas Pettigrew writes, "people project their emotional problems onto the external world."[206] Because their critical and hostile views toward other groups violate the presumption of group equality, they are considered suspect, both ignorant and psychologically deficient, products of irrational hatred. The racist who emerges from the Boasian paradigm is the new barbarian. In the relativist view, those who assert

Western civilizational superiority are the true Neanderthals. The racist is deemed unworthy of participation in serious discussion; indeed there is some question about whether he or she is a legitimate member of the liberal community. Racists are regarded as at best unenlightened, at worst malevolent, requiring appropriate legal and educational remedies to combat their alleged ignorance and fear. Upon these assumptions American scholars and activists constructed the rationale and policies of the civil rights movement.

5

A DREAM DEFERRED

Who Betrayed Martin Luther King, Jr.?

I have a dream that my four little children will one day live in a nation where they will not be judged by the color of their skin, but by the content of their character.
—Martin Luther King, Jr.[1]

A generation after the civil rights movement, blacks have made remarkable progress, and Martin Luther King, Jr.'s birthday is a national holiday.[2] Yet along with this progress, and perhaps inseparable from it, African Americans today suffer the seemingly intractable pathologies of the underclass, even the black middle class seems disgruntled, and throughout the country King's vision of a society in which we are judged as individuals on our merits appears more distant than ever. In many ways, America is a less hopeful and more race conscious society in the 1990s than in the 1960s. Derrick Bell offers his bitter assessment of the aftermath of the civil rights era: "We have made progress in everything, yet nothing has changed."[3]

Today Martin Luther King, Jr. is venerated as a national hero and a virtual icon of the civil rights movement. This hagiographic treatment of King is peculiar in that many African Americans, including some who marched with King, now seem to regard his vision as largely misguided. Indeed many people may be surprised to discover that not white racists but black leaders are the strongest opponents of King's principles. David Troutt acknowledges that for many African Americans "the reverend's rap is weak today."[4] Spike Lee argues that contemporary young blacks identify not with King but with Malcolm X. "The whole nonviolent, turn-the-other-cheek business just isn't getting anywhere in America. That is one of the reasons why people aren't walking around with a *K* on their hat."[5]

Some African American leaders have not abandoned color blindness as a goal, but virtually all seem convinced that race-neutral laws and policies are not the desired means. Yet even while repudiating his programs, black activists continue to invoke King's name and benefit from his moral authority. That is why mention of King's insistence that character, rather than color, should be the basis of public decisions inspires embarrassment and anger: Jesse Jackson calls it "intellectual terrorism," and Eleanor Holmes Norton protests, "Stop quoting dead saints."[6] Consider the frankness with which African American scholars repudiate race-neutral laws and policies.

• "There is nothing intrinsically wrong with using race in lawmaking or policy formulation," argues Roy Brooks in *Rethinking the American Race Problem.* Criticisms of race-conscious policies, he argues, are characterized by "the inability to distinguish between policies that engender racial exclusion and those that promote racial inclusion." Individual rights are important, Brooks concedes, but "questions of morality and justice must be decided by considering the individual in relation to the design of society."[7]

• Philosopher Bernard Boxill defends a double standard of justice which denies racial preferences for whites but upholds compensatory preferences for minorities. "Many color conscious policies are wrong," Boxill concedes in his book *Blacks and Social Justice.* "Jim Crow was certainly wrong." On the other hand, "This is not because they are color conscious. . . . Color conscious policies like busing and affirmative action could be correct."[8]

• A race-neutral society, John Hope Franklin writes, "is based on an assumption that flies in the face of the facts. A color-blind society does not exist in the United States and never has existed."[9] Former NAACP executive director Benjamin Hooks says, "The Constitution itself has recognized that there is color in this world. So from time to time we must use those categories to achieve the Constitution's goals."[10]

• "We tried colorblind 30 years ago and that system is naturally and artificially rigged for white males," argues Connie Rice of the NAACP Legal Defense Fund.[11] "The color blindness theory . . . is an incomplete and misleading approach . . . to the constitutional end of assuring substantive, not merely procedural, equality," writes Randall Kennedy.[12]

• Legal scholar Lani Guinier agrees. "A color-blind government . . . happily ratifies a status quo that gives whites a property right in being white, or at least legitimates expectations derived from participating in a plantation economy."[13] Charles Lawrence goes further, urging African Americans to "combat the ideology of equal opportunity."[14]

• "Formal equality has done a lot but misses the heart of the problem," writes legal scholar Patricia Williams. "The rules may be color-blind, but people are not." Williams urges "some measure of enforced equality" to replace "blindly formalized constructions of equal opportunity."[15] Robert Carter, a federal judge who once promoted race-neutral laws on behalf of the NAACP, scorns "arid pronouncements of color-blindness that either leave racial discrimination undisturbed or foster its further retrenchment."[16]

• Writing in the *Harvard Law Review,* Kimberle Crenshaw condemns "the restrictive vision which . . . treats equality as a process," preferring instead "the expansive view stressing equality as a result." She argues that civil rights laws should aim not at race neutrality but at "the eradication of the substantive conditions of black subordination."[17]

• Adolph Reed and Julian Bond argue that the pursuit of race neutrality is both unrealistic and oppressive because "at bottom it stems from an inability to perceive black Americans as legitimate, full members of the polity."[18] And Mary Frances Berry, who chairs the U.S. Commission on Civil Rights, goes so far as to assert that "civil rights laws were *not* passed to give civil rights protection to *all* Americans."[19]

It is no exaggeration to say that a rejection of Martin Luther King, Jr.'s vision of a regime in which we are judged solely based on the content of our character is a virtual job qualification for leadership in the civil rights movement today. Not only is the concept of a race-neutral society repudiated as an ingredient of policy, but some even question whether it should be a national goal. For better or worse, the contemporary civil rights community is wedded to a color-conscious philosophy and race-based policies.[20] "The removal of legal barriers to racial discrimination didn't produce the expected outcomes," sociologist Nathan Glazer says, "so many people have lost faith in this kind of liberalism."

SECOND THOUGHTS ABOUT KING

The historical significance of the rejection of race-neutral policies by many African American leaders is not always recognized. This rejection goes beyond Martin Luther King; it is a departure from the central principle of antiracism, espoused by blacks and progressive whites for more than a century. As early as 1849, Frederick Douglass wrote:

> It is evident that white and black must fall or flourish together. In the light of this great truth, laws ought to be enacted, and institutions established—all distinctions, founded on complexion, and every right, privilege and immunity, now enjoyed by the white man, ought to be as freely granted to the man of color.[21]

During the Reconstruction era, those Republicans who were most strongly committed to the black cause fought to erase racial classification and racial preference from the law. First Thaddeus Stevens and then Wendell Phillips and Charles Sumner supported a constitutional amendment that would prohibit the federal government and the states from using race as the basis for public policy. These proposals were rejected in favor of the weaker and more ambiguous language of "equal protection of the laws," but they remained the aspiration of the most committed antiracists among the abolitionists.[22] Black activists felt the same way. Eric Foner writes that during Reconstruction, the emerging black leadership embraced "an affirmation of Americanism that insisted that blacks were entitled to the same rights and opportunities that white citizens enjoyed."[23] Since the middle of the nineteenth century, black pioneers and activists have fought consistently for inclusion on the same terms as whites in the nation that brought them here as slaves. Leading figures from Douglass to King all worked in different ways to extend to blacks the political and economic rights of the nation, to assure access to the American dream. It is a dream not of success but of opportunity, not of happiness but of the pursuit of happiness, not of entitlements based on birth or color but of rights granted on an equal basis to all citizens.

"The unavoidable fact," writes Andrew Kull in *The Color Blind Constitution,* "is that over a period of some 125 years the American civil rights movement first elaborated, then held as its unvarying political objective, a rule of law requiring the color-blind treatment of individuals."[24] After a long struggle, punctuated with obdurate resistance, blacks finally gained the object of their political crusade. Thanks to the landmark legislation and court decisions of the civil rights era—*Brown v. Board of Education,* the Civil Rights Act of 1964, the Voting Rights Act of 1965, and the Fair Housing legislation of 1968—black Americans had the right to go to their neighborhood schools, to compete for university admissions and jobs on the same basis as whites, and to buy homes and join communities according to their resources and choices. Yet no sooner were these laws enacted, than African American leaders found themselves wracked with deep doubts and second thoughts, epitomized by black novelist James Baldwin's dilemma, "Do I really want to be integrated into a burning house?"[25] Once the struggle for equality under the law had prevailed, many passionate voices clashed over the future direction of the civil rights movement, and the result was a strategy that abandoned race-neutral policies as a means to achieving racial justice. In Kull's words, "The color-blind consensus, so long in forming, was abandoned with surprising rapidity."[26]

The liberal goal of integration, eagerly espoused by King, is now under assault both from the right and the left, and even moderate African American leaders seem ambivalent. The masses of black America "are equally opposed to integration and amalgamation of the races," Afrocentrist Chancellor Williams writes.[27] Molefi Asante adds, "Integration makes us cultural hostages. It threatens our existence as a people." Television host Tony Brown concurs. "Integration dismantled black institutions of empowerment. Its covert objective [was to turn] black people into white people. . . . Choice includes a black neighborhood if that's what you like."[28] Elizabeth Wright, who edits *Issues and Views,* a newsletter that promotes self-help, charges, "King and the other civil rights leaders, so called, are to blame for destroying our schools, our businesses, our communities." These are strong charges, yet even many mainstream civil rights leaders express second thoughts about the movement to which they devoted much of their lives. Margaret Bush Wilson, former chairman of the NAACP, offers an account of her own experience.

> I grew up in a ghetto in Saint Louis, but it was a safe and clean ghetto, if you can imagine that. We had hardworking families living there. We had a doctor, a lawyer, a bricklayer and a drunk on the same street. But now those neighborhoods are gone. Hardworking parents are losing control of their children. The church and the family have deteriorated. There is blood in the street. We have been fighting since the 1950s to remove barriers. But no one predicted this. Will someone please tell me what is going on?

Starting in the late 1960s, African American leaders, supported by many white liberals, began to move away from policies that promote race-neutrality and assimilation. For about two decades, it appeared as if a new agenda of affirmative action combined with an emphasis on black collective identity would prevail. But that approach, too, appears not to have fulfilled expectations. The consequence is confusion and conflict within the black leadership and among white liberals. Sociologist Christopher Jencks says, "Many blacks are angry and many liberals are frustrated. Nobody knows what the hell to do." Derrick Bell has concluded that the civil rights movement was a failure characterized by "weakly worded and poorly enforced legislation, indeterminate judicial decisions, token government position and holidays." Bell alleges that white liberals never really supported black aspirations, that "reform resulting from civil rights invariably promotes the interests of the white majority," and that American racism is ingrained and unalterable. In order to determine whether Bell's widely shared cynicism is justified, we must seek to answer a dilemma he poses: "Those most deeply involved in this struggle are at a loss for a rational explanation of how the promise of racial equality escaped a fulfillment that 30 years ago appeared assured."[29]

Did the color-blind vision so eloquently articulated by Martin Luther King, Jr. unravel so quickly because it was flawed from the outset? The extensive literature on the civil rights movement offers no good answer to this question. The reason is that most of this literature is triumphalist in tone, uncritically embracing the premises which framed the civil rights agenda of the 1950s and 1960s. Simply put, the prevailing message of these works is that the movement represented a triumph of good over evil, of truth over ignorance, of noble suffering over grotesque hatred, of black courage over white racism. Even the titles of leading works reflect their evangelical tone, complete with themes of martyrology and spiritual warfare: Taylor Branch's *Parting the Waters,* David Garrow's *Bearing the Cross,* Ralph Abernathy's *And the Walls Came Tumbling Down,* Stephen Oates's *Let the Trumpet Sound,* Vincent Harding's *There Is a River,* Henry Hampton and Steve Fayer's *Voices of Freedom,* Peter Albert and Ronald Hoffman's *We Shall Overcome,* and Jack Greenberg's *Crusaders in the Courts.*[30]

Few Americans are unfamiliar with the moral narrative generated by this literature. There are the valiant knights, like Thurgood Marshall and Martin Luther King, Jr. The villains are represented by George Wallace ("Segregation now, segregation tomorrow, segregation forever!") and Birmingham police chief Eugene "Bull" Connor. Famous battle sites include Selma and Montgomery. Unlikely heroes and heroines have emerged: Linda Brown, James Meredith, Autherine Lucy. The names of the groups spearheading the civil rights movement provide a forest of acronyms: Southern Christian Leadership Conference (SCLC), Student Nonviolent Coordinating Committee (SNCC), Congress of Racial Equality (CORE), and so on. Outnumbered yet undaunted, civil rights activists are credited with slaying the dragon of Southern segregation. There is much that is admirable and inspiring in these books, yet most of them conveniently end with the apparent triumph of the civil rights revolution. Indeed it would be painful to go further, because the authors would have to confront the possibility that the civil rights movement imploded because of confusions and contradictions within its own basic principles. Heroes appear less heroic when it turns out that they have only a limited understanding of the nature of their struggle. Yet in order for us to understand where the civil rights movement may have gone wrong, it is essential to question its premises, and to ask whether they were misconceived from the start.

History shows that the principles of the civil rights movement developed as a direct outgrowth of cultural relativism. The guiding assumption was that racism is the theory and segregation and discrimination are the practice. As whites came into regular contact with blacks, the theory went, their prejudices and stereotypes would dissipate. As blacks were permitted to vote and compete on equal terms with whites, activists argued, black performance would close much of the large gap of income and power between blacks and whites. The benefit would be twofold: white racism would be undermined even as blacks were successfully integrated into the mainstream institutions of American life.

It didn't work out, we will discover in the next two chapters, because the basic theory was flawed. In this chapter we will see that despite the enthusiasm of its chroniclers, the civil rights movement was not simply an expression of truth, justice, and the American way. The movement emerged out of an intense debate over competing strategies to fight racism. It was right to oppose segregation, but it misconstrued both the purpose and effects of segregation. It correctly targeted discrimination, but wrongly construed private individuals and companies, rather than government, as the primary threat to black prospects. It sought to undermine white racism through a protest strategy that emphasized the recognition of basic rights for blacks, without considering that racism might be fortified if blacks were unable to exercise their rights effectively and responsibly. Finally it harbored, from the outset, an expectation of group equality that would eventually prove destructive to its own cherished principle of nondiscrimination.

RACISM AS A FORM OF HATE

Let us examine the question of whether segregation was an expression of the virulent racism that is said to have pervaded the South since the time of emancipation. In the contorted expressions of Southern sheriffs and howling mobs, after all, one gets the clearest confirmation of the "hate" that the contemporary view of racism predicts and expects. In keeping with this view, Alvin Poussaint blames segregation as an expression of institutionalized hate for "stunting the development" of blacks, even imposing a sense of inferiority that many have internalized. "We are still living with the consequences of that self-hate." Bell Hooks describes segregation as apartheid, and Lerone Bennett compares it to Nazi Germany.[31]

These scholars are right to the extent that blacks were subjected to a vicious racist backlash, which was mainly a reaction to Southern humiliation in the Civil War and black gains during Reconstruction. This heyday of racism, symbolized by the Ku Klux Klan, only began at the end of the nineteenth century, however, and was over by the 1920s. Segregation developed not as an expression of this radical racism but in response to it: it represented a compromise on the part of the Southern ruling elite seeking, in part, to *protect* blacks. Despite the limited world which segregation imposed, blacks maintained intact families, voluntary associations, and cohesive communities. Escaping to Midwestern and Northern cities, many blacks created a rich culture of learning, art, and music, reaching its pinnacle in the Harlem Renaissance.

The racist, in the modern sense of a chronic hater, only emerged in the United States after slavery. Prior to that there is plenty of evidence that slaveowners considered blacks to be inferior and used them as human tools, but very little that they hated or despised them. Racism as a form of animus only developed under Reconstruction, as poor white Southerners, humiliated by their defeat in the Civil War, lashed out against the rising political power of Southern blacks and their Republican supporters in the North. In rhetoric that was not atypical, one Southern newspaper warned that the land of Dixie had been taken over by "louse-eating, devil-wor-

shipping barbarians from the jungles of Dahomey, and peripatetic bucca-
neers from Cape Cod, Memphremagog, Hell and Boston."[32]

Many Southerners were enraged that their presumed inferiors had, as
a consequence of the Thirteenth, Fourteenth, and Fifteenth Amend-
ments, been proclaimed equal as free citizens and voters; in economic
and political terms, some even appeared to be surpassing the white man.
After emancipation, many blacks who had simply picked cotton or
worked in menial tasks were compelled by necessity to become share-
croppers, where they worked long hours under daunting conditions.[33]
But other blacks had learned valuable skills on the plantation while their
masters idled: they became plumbers, carpenters, mechanics, cooks and
masons. Meanwhile, former plantation owners watched in consternation
the embittering sight of their land depreciated, their property destroyed
or emancipated, many of their loved ones dead—indeed a whole way of
life gone forever.

During Reconstruction, blacks made rapid and virtually unbelievable
gains. A former slave named Blanche K. Bruce became a U. S. senator
from Mississippi. Francis Cardozo served as South Carolina's secretary
of state. When Louisiana governor Henry Warmouth stepped down as a
result of impeachment proceedings, P. B. S. Pinchback, lieutenant governor at the time, became the first black governor in American history.
Twenty-two blacks were elected to the House of Representatives from
eight Southern states. Blacks won numerous positions such as mayor,
state supreme court justice, superintendent of education, and state treasurer.[34] Thomas Holt reports that of five hundred men elected to various
federal and state offices in South Carolina between 1867 and 1876, more
than half were black.[35] Altogether, Eric Foner calculates, blacks won
more than 1,400 positions of political authority in the South where they
assessed taxes on the property and passed laws governing the conduct of
their former owners.[36]

Predictably, strong and bitter resistance to black success developed,
and not just in the South. Northern unions mobilized to prevent blacks
from moving to their states and competing with white workers. Most
unions refused to allow blacks to become members, and those who did
segregated them into black locals with lower pay scales. Labor unions,
Herbert Hill writes, "emerged as the institutional expression of working-
class racism."[37] Those blacks who did migrate northward found employment confined to a few fields: laborers, porters, servants, janitors, and

waiters. Most black women worked as cooks and maids.[38] At the same time, the Republican coalition which had successfully prosecuted the war was disintegrating. Suffragists, for example, who were once allied with blacks campaigning for freedom and the right to vote, became frustrated that blacks enjoyed success at the ballot box while women still could not vote. Some who had supported the black cause became hostile. "Think of Sambo and Ung Tung who do not know the difference between a monarchy and a republic," Elizabeth Cady Stanton scoffed, "making laws for Lydia Maria Child, Lucretia Mott or Fanny Kemble."[39]

Exploiting divisions among Northern Republicans, Southern activists began a relentless campaign to restore white supremacy. The earliest effort to do this was enactment of the Black Codes, which were simply drawn from laws governing free blacks during the antebellum period.[40] Blacks were flatly prohibited from entering certain trades, like manufacturing or selling liquor. For others, they required licenses, which sometimes carried prohibitive fees. Sometimes they were given a specified period, say two weeks, to find work or else they must leave the state. Vagrants were vulnerable to arrest and imprisonment, or liable to be put to work without pay on public roads and projects. Finally the codes included myriad punishments for seemingly arbitrary offenses such as owning a firearm or insulting a white man.[41]

But oppressive as these rules were, they paled before the systematic violence directed against the property and persons of blacks, often with the acquiescence, if not approval, of state and local governments. No group epitomizes this terrorism better than the Ku Klux Klan, undoubtedly the most racist organization in American history. The Klan was founded in 1866 by a group of former Confederate soldiers in Pulaski, Tennessee. At first a social club that met in secret and held costume parties, the Klan soon developed a political vendetta against Northern carpetbaggers who were seen as interfering with Southern life. Soon Klan hostility spread to Southern Republicans, who were called "scalawags" and "white niggers" for supposedly betraying the Old South. Taking the law into their own hands, robed Klansmen would ambush these adversaries and flog or tar-and-feather them.[42]

At first the Klan paid little attention to blacks. Early Klan members did find out that by putting on white sheets and claiming to be ghosts from hell they were able to frighten former slaves, many of whom were ignorant and initially gullible. As Negroes started to gain political power during the Reconstruction period, however, the Klan grew more vicious toward

Southern blacks and began to treat them the same way it treated unwelcome Northerners and scalawags.[43] The Klan had already adopted the practice of lynching, although it was not restricted to blacks. In fact, the term lynching goes back to the American revolution, when a patriotic judge named Charles Lynch developed the novel idea of punishing Tory sympathizers in America by hanging them by their thumbs until they yelled "Liberty forever."[44] Eventually lynching became a form of vigilante or mob justice, and many an armed posse would track down suspected criminals and hang them by the neck. Until the 1890s lynching had no specific racial application and the majority of people lynched were white.[45] The Klan, however, found blacks to be an especially vulnerable target for lynching, usually under the pretext of unpunished crime or miscegenation. In only a few years, even for most Southerners, the Klan had completely outlived its pyromaniac charm. Responding to numerous reports of the abuse of law, Congress began hearings on Klan membership and activity. Soon these escalated into an effective campaign of exposure and prosecution. By 1873, less than a decade after it started, the Ku Klux Klan was out of business.[46] Similar organizations like the Knights of the White Camelia, the Pale Faces, the Men of Justice, and the White Brotherhood continued to operate in clandestine and paramilitary fashion.

Symbolic of the persistence of nineteenth century racism into the twentieth century, the Klan soon made a major comeback. It began with the racist propaganda of Thomas Dixon, who came to public attention in 1902 with an anti-Negro exposé, *The Leopard's Spots: A Romance of the White Man's Burden,* and followed it up with *The Clansman: An Historical Romance of the Ku Klux Klan* in 1905.[47] This second book was an instant best-seller which sold more than a hundred thousand copies in a few months. Apparently there were many in the South who felt a keen nostalgia for the now-defunct Ku Klux Klan. The entrepreneurial Dixon soon converted his story into a script which played to full houses across the former confederacy.[48] A few years later Dixon collaborated with D. W. Griffith, a film producer who used Dixon's work as the basis for one of the first full-length motion pictures ever shown in the United States, and one that would transform the genre because of its innovative cinematic technique. *The Birth of a Nation,* released in 1915, was a sensation with its dramatic scenes of crazed Negroes and Northerners preying on the South and its beautiful maidens with impunity, until the climactic restoration of sanity and justice by the galloping horsemen of the Ku Klux Klan. There were strong protests from Northerners like Harvard president Charles Elliot and Jane Addams, and from the Southern black leader Booker T. Washington. The film drew angry demonstrations by whites in Boston and New York. Some Southern leaders and writers were chagrined. But it met with an enthusiastic response from the Chief Justice of the Supreme Court, Edward White, who was a member of the original Klan. And President Woodrow Wilson arranged a private screening for the cabinet in the White House, after which he declared, "It's like writing history with lightning, and my only regret is that it is all so terribly true."[49]

When *Birth of a Nation* opened in Atlanta, one William J. Simmons took out advertisements in the paper announcing a Ku Klux Klan revival. From that beginning, Klan chapters mushroomed all over the South and, when the Klan announced well-publicized campaigns against Catholics and immigrants, it found eager recruits from both cities and rural areas all over the country. According to one of the Klan's recruiting pamphlets:

> Every criminal, every gambler, every thug, every libertine, every girl-runner, every home wrecker, every wife-beater, every dope-peddler, every moonshiner, every crooked politician, every pagan Papist priest, every shyster lawyer, every K of C [Knight of Columbus], every white slaver, every Rome-controlled newspaper, every black spider is fighting the Klan. Think it over, which side are you on?[50]

For a flat ten-dollar fee Americans could join a group which professed to combat dope, bootlegging, immorality, and corruption, which would protect the nation from the threats of Negroes, Catholics, Jews, and Orientals, which would stand up, in the Klan's own words, for "one-hundred-percent Americanism."[51] The benefits of membership included associating with titled men called Grand Dragon, Giant, and Cyclops; a uniform to attend late-night vigils and cross-burnings, Klonciliums and Klonvocations; as well as an institutional license to identify and punish aliens and troublemakers. For many poor whites, the Klan provided a source of theatrical release, what one writer in the 1920s termed "perpetual Halloween."[52] For the frustrated and desperate, it offered an exhilarating sense of power. The popularity of the Klan, in a sense, illustrated the appeal of racism to those at the bottom of society: it served not material but psychological interests. Even if it divides white from black workers and thus undermines collective bargaining strength, racism for poor whites serves the function of establishing a social floor beneath which they cannot fall. However degraded their lives become, at least they will never be black. Richard Wright termed racism of this sort a "religion of the materially dispossessed and culturally disinherited."[53]

Between 1920 and 1925, membership in the Ku Klux Klan was estimated at between two and five million, making it the largest fraternal nativist organization in U.S. history. Its membership included the governors of Texas, Indiana, and Oregon, as well as the mayors of several major cities, and innumerable sheriffs, councilmen and local judges. The Klan was a major force in American politics in at least sixteen states, where senate, house, and local races frequently hinged on Klan support. In fact the Klan sometimes held its own primaries to decide which Klansman or sympathizer should be supported in the general election. In 1925, the Klan electrified Washington when 40,000 of its members marched down Pennsylvania Avenue in one of the largest parades of that era, shouting nativist, racist, and anti-Semitic slogans.[54]

THE RADICAL RACISTS

In the early decades of the twentieth century, the United States was a society where racism flourished, and where those who did not share it were reluctant to say so. In popular magazines like *Scribner's* and *Century* blacks were routinely described with terms such as nigger, coon, darkey, blackamoor, gollywog, pickaninny, buck, shine, mammy, and high yaller.[55] A central theme in American humor consisted of minstrel jokes, in which blacks were portrayed as "irresponsible, happy-go-lucky, wide-grinning, loud-laughing, banjo-playing, singing, dancing sorts of beings."[56] In courts, Leon Higginbotham reports, black defendants were frequently called "black rascal," "mean Negro," and "burr-headed nigger."[57] Both in the media and on the street, adult black men were routinely summoned with the infantilizing epithet, "Boy!" The familiar faces of the period were Uncle Ben and Aunt Jemima in ads for rice and pancakes, and Stepin Fetchit and Amos 'n' Andy in entertainment.

Yet the image of blacks as amiable buffoons and national jesters carried a menacing shadow as well. The presumption among many whites was that at any moment the black man's natural barbarism might surface—that Sambo would be transformed into Nat Turner. These fears were articulated in successful books of the period such as Charles Carroll's *The Negro a Beast* (1900), Charles McCord's *The American Negro as a Dependent, Defective and Delinquent* (1914), and Robert Shufeldt's *The*

Negro, a Menace to American Civilization (1907) and *America's Greatest Problem: The Negro* (1915).[58] Antiblack sentiments carried into the halls of the U.S. Congress. When President Theodore Roosevelt invited the most eminent black statesman of the era, Booker T. Washington, to dinner at the White House in October 1901, Senator James K. Vardaman of Mississippi reacted, "I am just as opposed to Booker Washington with all his Anglo-Saxon reinforcements as I am to the coconut-headed, chocolate-colored typical little coon, Andy Dotson, who blacks my shoes every morning."[59] Senator Benjamin Tillman of South Carolina offered an even more outrageous response: "Now that Roosevelt has eaten with that nigger, we shall have to kill a thousand niggers to get them back to their places."[60]

These were the radical racists. Vardaman and Tillman were notorious, and not representative of the typical American politician of that time, even among Southern politicians. Yet what is striking is the candor with which they bellowed their bigotry on the floor of the U.S. Senate. And their flagrant racism was not mere rhetorical bombast. It served the practical function of keeping blacks, economically, politically, and in every other way "in their place." As Vardaman put it, voicing support for an education system that would keep blacks ignorant, "Educating the black man simply renders him unfit for the work which the white man has prescribed. . . . The only effect is to spoil a good field hand, and to make an insolent cook."[61]

Although no president of the United States shared the agenda of the radical racists, which was basically to deport if possible, destroy if necessary, and subordinate at all times the black population of the South, nevertheless American presidents could not ignore this constituency and were themselves hardly immune to bigotry. At various times Grover Cleveland, Theodore Roosevelt, and Woodrow Wilson expressed openly derogatory attitudes toward blacks, and sometimes made policy based on those views; Wilson, for example, widely extended segregation in the federal government during his administration.[62]

Worst of all, violence against blacks was commonplace in the American South in the early years of the twentieth century. In 1911 a white mob in Kentucky dragged a black man accused of murder to a local theater and hanged him before a large audience which paid admission to see the event. Those in the expensive seats were permitted to fire pistol shots into the Negro's dead body.[63] Lynchings were now increasingly and overwhelmingly targeted against blacks, sometimes for trifling offenses such as insulting white persons. One newspaper gleefully described lynchings as "Negro barbecues."[64] Lynchings reached their high point in the last two decades of the nineteenth century; between two and three thousand blacks were killed in this manner before the outbreak of World War I.[65]

Blacks were also victims of another white American tradition of the early twentieth century: the race riot. Today such riots have an entirely different connotation; then they described assaults by white mobs on black communities. During the first two decades of the twentieth century, white bigots fomented race riots in New York; Springfield, Illinois; East St. Louis, Illinois; Washington D.C.; Omaha, Tulsa, and Chicago. The Chicago riot of 1919 lasted two weeks and left fifteen blacks killed, five hundred injured, and nearly a thousand homeless.[66] "So long as the Negro had been property, worth from five hundred dollars up, he had been taboo—safer from rope and faggot than any common white man," writes W. J. Cash in *The Mind of the South.* "But with the abolition of legal slavery, his immunity vanished."[67]

THE PATERNALIST SOLUTION

The institution of segregation in the South was not established and maintained solely by the radical racists. Rather, it developed starting in the late nineteenth century as part of an ongoing tension between the radical racists and another powerful group, the Southern paternalists. The radicals were dominant in the last decade of the nineteenth century and the first decade of the twentieth. Then, Joel Williamson reports in *The Crucible of Race,* the radicals lost their distinctive strengths, both succumbing to and merging with the paternalists. Liberalism in the South during the period was too minor to have any measurable impact.[68]

Segregation was not widely entrenched in the South until the first decade of the twentieth century. Between emancipation and the end of the nineteenth century, there were proposals for Negro segregation, usually introduced by radical racists, but these were resisted by Southern conservatives like Henry Grady, editor of the *Atlanta Constitution,* who had lived with blacks for a long time and found plans for complete separation bizarre. Like many statesmen, clergy, and professionals who could be counted in the conservative camp, Grady opposed social equality with blacks but supported their right to vote and enjoy basic civil rights.[69] In response to a proposal for railroad segregation one Southern newspaper with a conservative editorial viewpoint in 1898 offered the following *reductio ad absurdum:*

> If there must be Jim Crow cars on the railroad there should be Jim Crow . . . passenger boats. Moreover, there should be Jim Crow waiting saloons at all stations, and Jim Crow eating houses. . . . There should be Jim Crow sections of the jury box, and a separate Jim Crow witness stand in every court. . . . Perhaps the best general plan would be to take the short cut by establishing two or three counties at once, and turning them over to our colored citizens for their special and exclusive accommodation."[70]

Yet soon after the Supreme Court upheld the "separate but equal" doctrine as constitutional in 1896,[71] precisely this tragicomic forecast became a legal reality all over the American South. Ironically, writes C. Vann Woodward in *The Strange Career of Jim Crow,* Southern segregation laws were imported from earlier Northern statutes which applied to free blacks.[72] Some of the radical racists supported segregation in order to limit their interactions with a black population that they could only endure in the slave condition, not as free persons. But others simply preferred to terrorize and kill blacks; they sought to resolve their contemporary problems with medieval tortures and bonfires. To the radical racists, the concept of free blacks was a scandal, like beasts wandering about without owners. Some, like Hinton Helper, lobbied to have blacks deported to Africa: "Already they have outlived their usefulness," Helper wrote soon after emancipation, "if indeed they were ever useful at all."[73]

Most of the radical racists recognized that the African solution was implausible. So they adopted or supported measures to prevent blacks from opening businesses, to burn down their stores and homes, to terrorize them in nightly raids, to hunt them down in mobs, to pitchfork and hang and lynch them in a virtual campaign of extermination. But this was not the majority position in the South. Had it been, there would be few African Americans still alive, whereas in fact only an infinitesimal fraction of the black population was killed. The ruling class in the South was patrician and conservative, a product of the Bourbon tradition. These conservatives united with the radical racists during the Civil War. The two groups shared the position, espoused by George Fitzhugh, that "slavery begets friendly, kind and affectionate relations, just as equality engenders antagonism and hostility on all sides."[74] But after emancipation, while the radical racists sought deportation or terrorization, the Southern paternalists sought a more discreet *modus vivendi* to coexist with blacks. Joel Williamson writes:

> Segregation as executed by conservatives was for a purpose quite different from that of the radicals. Conservatives sought segregation in public accommodations to protect black people and their dignity. For conservatives, segregation meant giving the black person a very special place in which he would be protected. Far from putting down the self-esteem of black people, conservative segregation was designed to preserve and encourage it.[75]

Southern conservatives were hardly apostles for the cause of black equality. Rather, they agreed with the radical racists that blacks were inferior. They disagreed, however, about how whites should respond. The patrician code held that it was unchristian and uncivil for the strong to harass the weak. Inferiority, in other words, did not provide a moral license for murder. While the radicals had no qualms about tormenting and killing blacks, conservatives were appalled by such vulgar displays of bloodthirstiness. For conservatives, the remedy was paternalism: a practical and stable arrangement by which two races perceived to have vastly different capacity and temperament could live in the same region of the country. For them, segregation offered an attractive alternative to lynching. It permitted whites to avoid what they perceived as offensive or contaminating contact with free blacks, and it allowed blacks to develop their allegedly modest talents in peace and among their own kind.[76]

The Southern paternalist position was based on the code of the Christian and the gentleman. It presumed but did not advertise black inferiority. Rather, the presumption remained tacit and unspoken, but it was acted upon in the kinds of institutions that Southerners developed. Segregation was intended to assure that blacks, like the handicapped, would be insulated from the radical racists and—in the paternalist view—permitted to perform to the capacity of their arrested development.

WHY STREETCARS OPPOSED SEGREGATION

By 1910, with the support of an odd coalition of radical racists and Southern paternalists, an elaborate structure of legal segregation was in place throughout the South. As C. Vann Woodward points out, railway cars, steamships, and ferries had separate sections for whites and blacks. So did post offices, prisons, restaurants, theaters, swimming pools, bowling alleys, zoos, and churches. There were separate floors for blacks and whites in mental hospitals, retirement homes, and institutions for poor people and orphans. Schools and hospitals were segregated, and nurses and teachers forbidden from serving students or patients of another race. Negroes and whites used separate public toilets and drinking fountains. Parks and beaches had their clearly marked areas for Negroes. Many companies had two entrances marked "white" and "colored," and job segregation existed throughout the workplace. Courts typically kept separate seating areas and jury boxes for blacks, and a separate Jim Crow Bible on which they would swear to tell the truth. When blacks and whites died, their bodies were preserved in separate funeral homes and they were buried in separate cemeteries.[77]

Who fought segregation? Not the liberals: there were few outspoken liberals in the South and their opinions were irrelevant. Rather, it was the private companies such as streetcar owners who mounted the only significant, albeit unsuccessful, opposition. This private sector resistance is explained by the fact that segregation in the government does not impose a severe burden on public agencies, which are monopolies. If costs of maintaining segregated public institutions rise, they are automatically borne by the taxpayer, and there are no competitors to take advantage. By contrast, private companies found that segregation raised their costs and inconvenience of doing business, and raised the specter of reduced demand for those goods and services.

Economist Jennifer Roback, in her study of streetcar segregation, shows that proposals for such laws were challenged by the streetcar companies, which found them expensive and inconvenient to administer. There was simply no economic logic to providing separate cars for different racial groups. At first, some companies tried to get around segregation ordinances by refusing to enforce them. In Jacksonville and Mobile, blacks were permitted to sit with whites. Eventually the government coerced the streetcar companies into compliance with fines. In an ironic twist of ethics, politicians accused the railroads of putting profits ahead of racist principle.[78] Segregation, therefore, represented a triumph of government regulation over the free market. It served as an instrument of Southern racism by establishing a racial caste system with facilities and opportunities that were theoretically comparable but in fact grossly unequal. Nothing confirmed the racist principle embedded in legal segregation better than its peculiar system of racial classification. Segregation laws applied not just to pure blacks but to all members of mixed races, no matter what their proportion of white or black blood.

Segregation was premised on the "one-drop rule," so called because of its suggestion that as a result of even a single drop of black blood the law regarded you as a black person.[79] In Thomas Dixon's *The Leopard's Spots,* one of his characters vividly articulates the philosophy of the one-drop rule. "One drop of Negro blood makes a Negro. It kinks the hair, flattens the nose, thickens the lips, puts out the light of intellect, and lights the fires of brutal passions."[80] Although the one-drop rule is often traced back to slavery, in fact slave status generally passed through the descent of the mother: mixed-race children of black men and white women were free. Because of the reality of substantial racial intermixture between blacks and whites in the antebellum period, Winthrop Jordan writes, "accommodation had to be made for those persons with so little Negro blood that they appeared to be white, for one simply could not go around calling apparently white persons Negroes."[81] Under slavery, a kind of pragmatic rule of appearance governed the racial perception of free persons. But under segregation, white fears of miscegenation were much stronger, and the law was radicalized so that a single black ancestor bestowed on all his descendants what novelist Charles Chesnutt termed "the mark of the Ethiopian."[82] As Joel Williamson puts it, "In white eyes, all Negroes came to look alike."[83] In 1920, for the first time, the U.S. Census stopped counting mulattoes, separating American citizens into the stark categories of white and black.[84]

In the face of these hardships, blacks as a group showed great endurance and resiliency. From the time black aspirations to full citizenship were betrayed after the Civil War, black leaders and spokesmen emerged who challenged the structure of legal segregation, and demanded justice from all who would listen. Yet the forces in favor of white supremacy were so strong that these were voices in the wilderness. As under slavery, blacks could chafe but had few allies and were not strong enough to challenge the system. Economically and culturally, they had to adapt to it.

The most resourceful blacks realized that in a perverse way segregation created economic opportunity, because it kept whites out of businesses and professions that serviced the black community. "The reluctance of whites to minister to the hair, the bodies, or the souls of blacks created a class of black barbers, physicians, undertakers and religious ministers," Thomas Sowell writes.[85] Black masons, repairmen, jewelers, tailors, and teachers made a modest living in the Jim Crow world. On a larger scale, building on the self-help and fraternal organizations that free blacks set up during the antebellum era, blacks in the early twentieth century developed a flourishing banking, real estate, and insurance industry in several cities, including Chicago, Memphis, Tulsa, and especially Durham, North Carolina. African American scholar John Sibley Butler portrays Durham in the 1930s and 1940s as teeming with black-owned concerns, including cafes, movie houses, grocery stores, funeral parlors, and large businesses such as North Carolina Mutual Life Insurance Company, Banker's Fire Insurance, Mutual Building and Loan Association, Home Modernization and Supply Company, and the Mortgage Company of Durham.[86] Outside the orbit of segregation, a few blacks found that whites were willing to patronize blacks in such areas as entertainment and athletics, which offered a route to fame and affluence.[87]

Despite poor funding and facilities, as a consequence of Northern philanthropy, Southern conservative support, and the efforts of black churches and voluntary institutions, educational opportunities for blacks did improve. In 1880 only 20 percent of blacks were literate; by 1930, a majority could read and write. At the time of the Civil War less than 10 percent of young blacks attended public schools; by 1930, more than 60 percent did.[88] Blacks also stayed in school longer, and an increasing number each year attended the Negro colleges in the South. Educated blacks maintained a small but lively forum for ideas in black-owned newspapers.

Drawing on techniques learned under slavery, many blacks gave ritual obeisance to the racist presumptions of the Southern way of life, while subverting them in subtle ways that did not change the social order but preserved self-respect. One such device was the "mask," an expression of public conformity which concealed inner hostility toward whites. A second practice came to be known as "passing," where light-skinned blacks would, sometimes permanently and sometimes temporarily, enter the white world unnoticed, their successful camouflage opening up valuable opportunities and mocking the one-drop rule which sought to establish an ineradicable demarcation between the races. Finally black culture continued to uphold the archetype of the "bad nigger," who was respected for his complete rejection of sycophancy in the face of white oppression.

Migrating in ever-increasing numbers to cities outside the South, blacks settled into urban life with both its freedom and its possibilities for license. In the 1920s this freedom inspired creativity, and America witnessed an efflorescence of black cultural genius. In New York, blacks sponsored an intellectual and artistic renaissance, where in the midst of poverty and dilapidated buildings, nightclubs blossomed, restaurants flourished, and scholars and playwrights published trenchant writings.[89]

"More than Paris or the Shakespeare country," wrote Langston Hughes, "I wanted to see Harlem, the greatest Negro city in the world."[90] It was the age of Hughes, Countee Cullen, and Claude McKay in literature; of Paul Robeson and Josephine Baker on the stage and the screen; of Alain Locke, George Schuyler, James Weldon Johnson, and E. Franklin Frazier in social analysis and commentary; of Louis Armstrong, Duke Ellington, Ella Fitzgerald, and numerous other great names in the music of jazz and blues and gospel. Many of these men and women were light-skinned blacks, descended not from slaves but from Northern free persons, and part of a cultural and social elite within the black community.[91] Indeed the white-owned Cotton Club, which offered the liveliest nightlife in Harlem, only hired mulattoes to perform in its famous chorus line.[92]

Just as blacks evolved a unique and creative culture to deal with slavery, they developed an equally resilient response to their circumstances in the early twentieth century. Particularly striking was their capacity for pungent criticism on the one hand, combined with a remarkable capacity for music, laughter, and joy even under conditions of extreme economic and social oppression.[93] Segregation imposed a harsh life on American blacks, with freedom inhibited and prospects narrowed through state control. Yet it is wild exaggeration to equate segregation with apartheid or the Holocaust. Many blacks found a way to build fulfilling lives within the circumscribed limits of segregation, whereas it would be cruel and absurd to say this about Holocaust victims. The creativity and moral strength of blacks under segregation is reflected in Countee Cullen, who converted the presumptions of white racism into black humor, as indicated in the poetic epitaph he composed, *For a Lady I Know*.

> She even thinks that up in heaven
> Her class lies late and snores,
> While poor black cherubs rise at seven
> To do celestial chores.[94]

UP FROM DEPENDENCY

What was the best way for blacks to respond to early twentieth century segregation and discrimination? The civil rights movement, in the view of its cheerleading chroniclers, emerged as a spontaneous eruption of freedom-loving activism that overwhelmed the dogs and hoses of white prejudice and forced the racist establishment to capitulate to the sheer moral power of black claims for freedom and basic rights. Actually, the civil rights movement and its agenda arose out of a ferocious debate between W. E. B. Du Bois and Booker T. Washington, two men who represent contrasting black strategies of political protest and self-help. The civil rights movement represented a choice of the path outlined by Du Bois over that of Washington. By revisiting the debate between these two great men, we can discover options exercised and options foregone. Blacks, after all, would be in a different situation today if the civil rights leadership had opted for Washington instead. Washington is respected in two camps today: black conservatives and black nationalists. "I'm not one of those people who is down on Washington," Molefi Asante says. "I remind you that Washington was a hero for Marcus Garvey." Elizabeth Wright goes further.

> Du Bois was a creation of Europe and Harvard, but Booker T. stayed close to the land. He was one of us. Instead of following his example, instead of building ourselves as a people, we have this generation of self-promoting octoroons who are making a good living by playing the white man. Is this how we advance the race: by wailing and crying?

For many mainstream black scholars and civil rights activists, however, Booker T. Washington is an embarrassment. He is ignored altogether or reviled. Alphonso Pinkney views him as a traitor and "collaborator"; for Martin Kilson, he is a "client or puppet figure."[95] Washington's own biographer, Louis Harlan, is sharply critical and condescending toward his subject's philosophy.[96] By contrast, as David Levering Lewis's recent biography makes clear, W. E. B. Du Bois has been elevated to legendary status.[97] One reason for this biased assessment is that the civil rights movement was, in a sense, founded by Du Bois, and continues to reflect his intellectual assumptions, which are at bottom the assumptions of cultural relativism.

At the Atlanta Exposition fair in Georgia in 1895, Booker T. Washington outlined a vision of race relations in America that brought thunderous applause from the audience, and press accolades from across the country. Southern women were said to leap out of their seats. Not since the prose of Frederick Douglass electrified white abolitionist audiences in Boston was a Northern reading public so moved. And never in America over three centuries had a black man attracted the public admiration of the white South. Born a slave, Booker T. Washington overcame an almost unbelievable set of obstacles to become America's leading black educator, orator, and institution builder. Washington transcended his experience of victimization without any trace of psychological debilitation or bitterness toward whites.[98] On the principle that "it is a hard matter to convert an individual by abusing him,"[99] he sought reconciliation and common ground even with Southern segregationists. As Washington said in his famous Atlanta speech:

> The wisest among my race understand that the agitation of questions of social equality is the extremest folly, and that progress in the enjoyment of all the privileges that will come to us must be the result of severe and constant struggle rather than of artificial forcing.[100]

Rather than emphasize political protest and denunciations of white racism, Washington advocated that through industrial education, personal discipline, mutual aid, and racial solidarity, blacks should achieve self-reliance and at the same time contribute to society. This, he believed, would be the best practical strategy to undermine racism.

> The Negro should not be deprived by unfair means of the franchise, but political agitation alone will not save him. Back of the ballot, he must have property, industry, skill, economy, intelligence and character. No race without these elements can permanently succeed. . . . We have a right to enter our complaints, but we shall make a fatal error if we yield to the temptation of believing that mere opposition to our wrongs will take the place of progressive, constructive action. . . . Whether he will or not, a white man respects a Negro who owns a two-story brick house.[101]

W. E. B. Du Bois was born a free man in the North of black, French, Dutch, and American Indian ancestry—"Thank God, no Anglo-Saxon," he liked to add.[102] He attended schools in Europe and the United States, studying with the philosophers George Santayana and William James, and becoming in 1895 the first black to get a postgraduate degree from Harvard.[103] Du Bois represented the generation of light-skinned Northern mulattoes, the offspring of Negro doctors, teachers, and educated clergymen, who had accumulated far more capital and skills than the newly freed slaves, and who keenly felt the limitations that the color line placed on their chances for full acceptance in American society.[104]

To Du Bois and his group, Washington's approach seemed painfully accommodationist. In *The Souls of Black Folk* and other writings and speeches, Du Bois portrayed Washington as the original Uncle Tom, willing to embrace the slights of segregation in return for crumbs from the white man's table. Du Bois repudiated Washington's populist program of basic industrial education which he viewed as menial and degrading.[105] Du Bois's indignation sprang in part from his own background: he was an unabashed elitist who spoke French and German; used words like "yonder," "hark," "anon," and "whence"; and was rarely seen in public without gloves and a cane. Du Bois called for a Talented Tenth of liberally educated blacks who could shepherd what he considered the ignorant masses to the blessings of full citizenship. "The Negro race," he said, "is going to be saved by its exceptional men."[106]

While Washington spoke the older language of duty, Du Bois spoke the more modern language of rights. Rather than making deals with segregationists, whom Du Bois considered the worst enemy of blacks, Du Bois called for a militant campaign of political agitation that would expose, educate, and wrest concessions from the white oppressor. "We claim for ourselves every single right that belongs to a free American, political, civil and social, and until we get these rights we will never cease to protest and assail the ears of America."[107] For Du Bois, blacks confronted a single and obvious enemy: white racism. Washington's view was that blacks faced two obstacles, which reinforced each other: white racism, which inferiorized blacks; and black civilizational backwardness, which strengthened white racism and prevented blacks from making advances that were possible even in the restricted orbit of segregation. Precisely because he held that racism was entrenched, unyielding, and regrettably confirmed by black behavior, Washington argued for an emphasis on black self-help. In blunt language, he criticized black profligacy, promiscuity, and crime.

> A race or an individual which has no fixed habits, no fixed place of abode, no time for going to bed, or getting up in the morning, for going to work; no arrangement, order or system in all the ordinary business of life—such a race and such individuals are lacking in self-control, lacking in some of the fundamentals of civilization.[108]

Such criticism of his own people outraged Du Bois, who saw it as ignoring the basic causes of black disadvantage, and thus a craven surrender to the white racist adversary. He roared:

> If they accuse Negro women of lewdness, what are they doing but advertising to the world the shameless lewdness of those Southern men who brought millions of mulattoes into the world? Suppose today Negroes do steal; who was it that for centuries made stealing a virtue by stealing their labor?[109]

Washington did not deny that black cultural pathologies were the consequence of generations of slavery and oppression. The relevant issue for him was that they existed, and had to be confronted. His argument was that as a result of ignorance, sexual irresponsibility, and crime, many blacks were simply not in a position to take full advantage of the opportunity, and to exercise the responsibility, of free citizens, and thus Du Bois's agenda was sound but premature.

> In spite of all that may be said in palliation, there is too much crime committed by our people in all parts of the country. We should let the world understand that we are not going to hide crime simply because it is committed by black people.[110]

Du Bois did not entirely disagree. He recognized the civilizational deficiencies of the black community, and in a remarkable passage he insisted that "a little less complaint and whining, and a little more dogged work and manly striving, would do us more credit than a thousand civil rights bills."[111] But he argued that Washington's program for economic and civilizational development was utterly unrealistic without confronting Southern racism. Du Bois was not against skills and character, but he argued that blacks needed legal rights and economic opportunities to develop their capacities and realize their cultural potential.

> So to those people who are saying to the black man today, "Do your duties first and then clamor for rights," we have a right to answer and to answer insistently, that the rights we are clamoring for are those that will enable us to do our duties.[112]

For all his pessimism about white racism, Washington was basically a believer in the American dream. "Merit, no matter under what skin found, is in the long run recognized and rewarded," he said. Indeed he argued that racism actually hurt whites just as much as, if not more than, blacks, because it corroded their moral fiber. "No man whose vision is bounded by color can come into contact with what is highest and best in the world."[113] Du Bois rejected Washington's color-blind vision, both as a strategy and as an ideal. Indeed Du Bois was an enemy of racism but a believer in race, as both a crucial biological and a cultural category. Du Bois argued that anyone who ignores the race idea "ignores and overrides the central thought of all history." In a revealing passage, Du Bois wrote:

> The history of the world is the history, not of individuals, but of groups, not of nations, but of races. . . . While race differences have mainly followed

physical lines, the deeper differences are spiritual. . . . The full complete Negro message of the whole Negro race has not yet been given to the world. . . . As a race we must strive by race organization, by race solidarity, by race unity. . . . We believe it is the duty of Americans of Negro descent, as a body, to maintain their race identity until this mission is accomplished.[114]

Here we see that unlike Washington, who attempted to transcend the identification with race, Du Bois embraced it. Du Bois was a racialist and a cultural relativist, views that may have first arisen from his interpretation of the *Volk* philosophy of Johann Gottfried Herder, one of the philosophical advocates of relativism.[115] Du Bois's relativism, moreover, was undoubtedly influenced by his association with Franz Boas, whom he worked with and invited to speak at his university.[116] Du Bois found Boasian relativism to be a useful truncheon with which to hammer away at the racist doctrine of Anglo-Saxon superiority.

Du Bois gave relativism a different cast than Boas, however. While Boas argued that the basic equality between blacks and whites pointed to the possibility of assimilation, Du Bois contended that group equality meant that blacks and whites could, as distinct racial and cultural groups, make separate and equally important contributions to world civilization. In a famous passage Du Bois remarked that American blacks experience a powerful dual identity—"two souls, two thoughts, two unreconciled strivings, two warring ideals in one dark body, whose dogged strength alone keeps it from being torn asunder."[117] In one sense Du Bois deplored this double consciousness as an imposition of white racism, but in another he celebrated it. Appealing to a pan-African identity, Du Bois argued that blacks have a unique spiritual and social "message." This message was not inferior, only different, from the white civilization message.[118] The racialism of Du Bois contains a notion that many blacks would later embrace: that if race is the key to the problems faced by blacks, race would also be the key to their solution.

Booker T. Washington and W. E. B. Du Bois basically differed on the nature of racism and the nature of the white man in America. While they both agreed that blacks were downtrodden as a consequence of environment and not biology—they were both Boasians in this sense—Du Bois emphasized the impediments of white racism while Washington also considered the defects of black culture. Du Bois was fundamentally an idealist. As a consequence of his deep belief in the equality of racial groups, Du Bois assumed that once blacks were given legal rights they would be able to compete effectively with whites. Washington was a realist and a pragmatist. He conceded the civilizational superiority of whites, and sought to use segregation to promote black solidarity and economic development—the first step, he believed, that blacks needed to take to raise cultural standards to the level of whites'. Du Bois believed that racism was a product of irrational antagonism, yet through education and activism whites could be made to appreciate black appeals for rights and justice. Washington insisted that whites would deal with and respect those blacks who lived decently and produced things that whites wanted. Washington argued that, even as victims, blacks should learn to get up, while Du Bois maintained that they must pressure the white oppressor to raise them up.

Booker T. Washington was right, ultimately, that in the early part of the twentieth century blacks had little alternative but to make the best of a bad situation. As Louis Harlan reports, despite his public concessions to legal segregation, Washington clandestinely funded and organized lawsuits challenging the denial of jury privileges to black defendants as well as segregation in public transportation.[119] Recognizing the civilizational disadvantages of Southern blacks, Washington worked hard to develop their social and economic skills. At the same time, W. E. B. Du Bois was right that it would have been disastrous for blacks not to contest directly the depredations of white racism. Some strategy was necessary to begin to build intellectual and political resistance to the legal structures of segregation and discrimination. Already in the social sciences, Du Bois's field, arguments were being pressed against racism and social Darwinism. For Du Bois, it was time for the black community to move into the activist mode. By helping to found the NAACP in 1909, Du Bois put his principles into action, with enduring consequences.

THE NAACP'S EASY VICTORIES

The National Association for the Advancement of Colored People (NAACP) was actually founded by white people, in part as a platform for Du Bois. Several white liberals such as William Walling, Mary Ovington, and Henry Moskowitz wanted a new organization to revive the lost spirit of abolitionism. Significantly, they did not choose to support Booker T. Washington's Southern self-help program. Rather, they teamed up with a Northern contingent of more activist blacks, including Du Bois and his other colleagues, Ida Wells-Barnett and Monroe Trotter, who had founded the Niagara Movement in Buffalo, New York, in 1905. It was Du Bois who insisted on using the term "colored" in the new group's name, thus highlighting the NAACP's Northern and mulatto membership.

In 1909 Du Bois's Niagara Movement was dissolved and the NAACP would go on to become the most powerful civil rights group in America. Du Bois became editor of the NAACP journal, *The Crisis,* a position he would hold for almost a quarter of a century. The organization became an unrivaled forum for Du Bois's program. An early NAACP declaration reveals the Du Boisian touch, insisting that the responsibility for the conditions of blacks "rests chiefly upon the white people of the United States, and it is their duty to change them."[120] Du Bois's Niagara Movement manifesto basically became the NAACP's agenda for the next few decades. It points included:

- Anti-lynching legislation
- Legislation to end peonage and debt slavery
- Enfranchisement of the Negro in the South
- Abolition of racial discrimination in criminal justice procedure
- Equitable access to public education
- Abolition of segregation
- Equality of opportunity to work in all fields
- Abolition of discrimination in union membership[121]

This represented a program strongly influenced by Franz Boas and Boasian assumptions. Indeed Boas himself worked with the NAACP and was invited by Du Bois to address some of its early conferences and sessions.[122] Triumphalist histories show NAACP victories gained against great odds, but the organization was able to prevail against surprisingly weak intellectual opposition. One of its most important goals, a reduction in lynching, was realized beyond realistic expectations. But this reduction was not accomplished through NAACP efforts; rather, it resulted from the unexpected and sharp decline in the membership and influence of the Ku Klux Klan during the mid to late 1920s. There were two reasons for this decline. The first is that Klan leaders began to quarrel with each other about positions and authority, and being dogmatic and dangerous people their fights soon escalated into small-scale guerrilla wars. The effect of these internecine conflicts was to weaken and decentralize Klan authority. The second reason was the Klan's promiscuity in its selection of targets. First it was the blacks, then the Catholics, then the drunks, then the adulterers, then the unions, then the Jews, then the Communists—pretty soon too many Americans began to feel at risk. The Klan's roster of powerful enemies multiplied. Politicians and newspapers amplified Klan outrages and abuses. By the late 1920s it was a political liability to be identified with the Klan. Soon the Invisible Empire began to shrink to only a fraction of its former membership.[123] By the mid 1930s, the number of lynchings per year in America was down to less than ten.[124]

Never did civil rights groups enjoy a public relations victory like World War II.[125] As the eventual leaders of the Allied Forces, Americans became acutely conscious of the hypocrisy inherent in battling racial bigotry abroad while practicing racial segregation and discrimination at home. Black leaders were quick to point out the contradiction,[126] and President Roosevelt agreed, declaring, "Americanism is not, and never was, a matter of race or ancestry."[127] It was the beginning of a new era, as suggested by the following indicators:

• Pressured by A. Phillip Randolph's threat to organize a massive protest march in Washington, Roosevelt in 1941 issued an executive order prohibiting discrimination in government employment and setting up the Fair Employment Practices Committee to investigate and arbitrate charges of bias.[128]

• Toward the end of the war, the military initiated an experiment in which, for the first time, it placed black and white enlisted men in the same fighting units. The purpose of the exercise was to demonstrate the irrationality of segregation, and it proved successful.[129]

• In 1947 the major leagues in baseball were integrated, a process that was under way in all sports. During this period several states passed anti-Klan laws which prohibited the wearing of masks and the burning of crosses.

• In the mid to late 1940s, unions came under strong pressure to accept blacks on the same terms as whites. Blacks were appointed to numerous government posts in the Truman administration. NAACP membership increased tenfold during the war years to reach half a million by the late 1940s.[130]

• The Supreme Court in 1948 outlawed racial discrimination in the private sale of homes, striking down restrictive covenants that sought to exclude blacks and other groups from purchasing certain properties.[131] That same year, President Harry Truman issued an executive order desegregating the armed forces.[132]

• Between 1945 and 1964, many states and cities implemented antidiscrimination provisions in hiring and contracting. During that same period, twenty-six states passed laws outlawing job discrimination and establishing fair employment commissions, some of which had the power to force companies to hire or reinstate workers who had suffered racial discrimination.[133]

Although paltry by contemporary standards, these developments suggest that after World War II, white racism no longer seemed to be the insuperable barrier that it undoubtedly was in the early part of the twentieth century. What this means is that the civil rights movement did not entirely transform American society; it was, in part, created by a prior transformation. Indeed in the period from 1930 to 1950 blacks made dramatic gains in schooling, college enrollment, family income, and life expectancy.[134] The changing political landscape emboldened the NAACP and other groups to launch a direct campaign to achieve the two basic goals of the emerging civil rights movement: desegregation and antidiscrimination.

SEPARATE AND UNEQUAL

No Supreme Court result is more widely endorsed in American scholarship than *Brown v. Board of Education.* It is impossible to be taken seriously in academia, or to receive an appointment to the federal courts, without embracing the desegregation outcome of the *Brown* case. Yet virtually no scholar or public figure has convincingly stated why *Brown* was rightly decided, nor did the Supreme Court itself do so in announcing the decision. Indeed few rulings are more misunderstood: immediately after the decision, the *New York Times* declared that the Supreme Court had finally embraced Justice Harlan's famous color-blind declaration— "Our Constitution is color-blind and neither knows nor tolerates classes among citizens."[135] In fact, the Court, even while embracing a color-blind result, had rejected color blindness as a basis for constitutional reasoning. Indeed, the famous desegregation ruling contained the seeds for its later abandonment.

The desegregation battle spearheaded by the NAACP in the early 1950s illustrates the ambiguity of the constitutional term "equal protection of the laws" and the radicalism of giving this phrase a color-blind interpretation. Today such an interpretation seems obvious to many, which is why it is helpful to take seriously the Court's argument in *Plessy v. Ferguson,* the 1896 ruling which upheld segregation for more than half a century. *Plessy*, the case the NAACP challenged in *Brown*, upheld the constitutionality of "separate but equal." The Fourteenth Amendment guarantees citizens "equal protection of the laws" but what does this mean? Surely it does not mean that all citizens have a right to be treated identically. Public buildings have separate restrooms for men and women—a clear case of state-sponsored segregation—yet such facilities are not considered an egregious constitutional violation. Even though both groups are composed of citizens, the laws regularly distinguish between adults and children: are fifteen-year-olds who are denied driving privileges or prevented from voting being denied "equal protection"?

The point is that the Fourteenth Amendment was not intended to grant and does not grant an unrestricted right to equality. Rather, it seems to offer a procedural guarantee: citizens similarly situated are entitled to be judged identically under the law. But such an interpretation begs the question: are blacks and whites similarly situated? If it is reasonable to segregate men from women, or adults and children, under certain circumstances, why not blacks and whites? Although his view is widely scorned today, Justice Henry Brown's interpretation of "separate but equal" is intellectually consistent. Rejecting the argument that "the enforced separation of the two races stamps the colored race with a badge of inferiority," Justice Brown held, "If this be so, it is not by reason of anything found in the act."[136] Of course in practice "separate" was never "equal." But this discrepancy only provides a justification for insisting that facilities be equalized, not for overturning segregation itself. Is there a case to be made against segregation even when it meets a strict enforcement of "separate but equal"? Justice Harlan's radicalism was to suggest a novel interpretation, resting on unstated premises: blacks and whites are not fundamentally different, they have a right to be treated identically. Consequently, in Harlan's view, the state is color-blind in the sense that it is not permitted to make racial distinctions at all.[137]

This nineteenth century argument was considered so audacious that the NAACP did not dare to advance it in the Supreme Court until the middle of the twentieth century.[138] Prior to that, the NAACP did not challenge segregation frontally but filed numerous suits within the parameters of *Plessy*, alleging that blacks were receiving separate but unequal treatment, which was certainly true.[139] The Supreme Court and lower courts proved sympathetic, and during the 1930s and 1940s compelled states such as Maryland, North Carolina, and Oklahoma to equalize facilities or end segregation. Some Southern states were so eager to preserve segregation that they actually spent a bit more per capita on black teacher salaries than on white teacher salaries to meet the court's requirements.[140] Yet the NAACP was able to prove that even schools of comparable resources did not enjoy the same public reputation, so that black attendees at less prestigious institutions were stigmatized. The NAACP won several such landmark cases.[141]

Encouraged by these victories, NAACP counsel Thurgood Marshall spearheaded a direct attack on segregation, and chose to premise it on the findings of Boasian relativism. "As he sought to convince the Supreme Court to sweep aside Jim Crow law," writes Richard Kluger in *Simple Justice,* his in-depth study of the *Brown* case, "Marshall had the benefit of a half-century evolution in the social sciences that had declared segregation to be both a cause and a result of the victimization of black America."[142] Indeed as a consequence of the Boasian intellectual revolution, more than 90 percent of social scientists surveyed as early as 1948 declared segregation to be wrong and harmful to blacks.[143]

As the *Brown* case made its way through the legal system, many leading anthropologists, psychologists, and educators attested to the destructive effects of segregation as an expression of racism in a statement that the NAACP presented as evidence to the appellate court. The group included Jerome Bruner of Harvard, Robert Redfield of the University of Chicago, Otto Klineberg and Robert Merton of Columbia, Gordon Allport, author of *The Nature of Prejudice,* Arnold Rose of the University of Minnesota, and Allison Davis of the University of Chicago. All of them were liberal and Boasian in their views, and the group included Boas's own students Isidor Chein and Otto Klineberg.[144]

Thurgood Marshall's star witness in the *Brown* case was Kenneth Clark, a protégé of Franz Boas and former researcher for Gunnar Myrdal's *American Dilemma.* Firmly convinced that segregation was racist and had a destructive educational effect, Clark sought to demonstrate this with a study of black dolls and white dolls. Clark's experiment showed that black children who attended segregated schools, when asked to choose between white dolls and black dolls, frequently chose the white doll. Clark concluded from this finding that segregation expressed white prejudice about black inferiority, and black students internalized these prejudices. Clark testified that segregation produces in the black student "basic feelings of inferiority, conflict, confusion, resentment, hostility toward himself, hostility toward whites."[145] Actually, Clark's conclusions were premature. Given the well-documented pancultural preferences for the color white over black, Clark's findings proved little. In fact, a recent study of black-run preschools in Trinidad found that three-fourths of the children there chose white dolls over black dolls, a finding hard to attribute to the influence of white segregationists.[146] Today many social scientists consider Clark's conclusions questionable and an inadequate basis for national policy.

On May 17, 1954, the Supreme Court announced its famous decision rejecting "separate but equal" on the grounds that "separate educational facilities are inherently unequal."[147] Yet the Court's opinion offered no argument to prove this. Rather, it cited Kenneth Clark and other social scientists in order to show that segregation damaged the educational motivation and mental development of black children.[148] Indeed the judges' own reasoning in the unanimous ruling appeared to be lifted directly from the social science appendix drafted by Kenneth Clark. As the court put it:

> To separate Negro children from others of similar age and qualifications solely because of their race generates a feeling of inferiority as to their status in the community that may affect their hearts and minds in a way unlikely ever to be undone.[149]

The fundamental problem with this reasoning in *Brown* is that it seeks to support a constitutional result based on a (dubious) finding of fact. Even if we assume that segregation has precisely the Boasian effect the Court proclaims, would segregation be acceptable if facilities were genuinely equal and if black self-esteem turned out to be unaffected? Andrew Kull writes that *Brown* and *Plessy* do not differ in their constitutional reasoning, only in their social science assumptions about student psychology.[150] The Court's exaltation of the "feeling" of inequality reflected the subjectivity of Boasian relativism: to be unequal is to be perceived as unequal. With this justification the Court avoided making the case that "equal protection" required, on the part of the state, a color-blind approach to laws. By refusing to embrace Harlan's radical nondiscrimination principle, and implying that segregation is right or wrong depending on its effect on people's feelings, the Supreme Court laid the groundwork for arguments in later years that would undermine the color-blind result in *Brown* and support race-conscious assignments of students to public schools.

None of this was obvious in 1954. The Supreme Court had struck down school segregation, one of the bulwarks of Southern racism. Robert

Williams, an NAACP official in North Carolina, compared his elation to "what the Negro slaves felt when they first heard about the Emancipation Proclamation. I was sure that this was the beginning of a new era for American democracy."[151] "Old Man Segregation is on his deathbed," exulted another black activist named Martin Luther King, Jr.[152]

HOW KING PREVAILED

It was Martin Luther King, Jr. who made possible the great victories of the civil rights movement: the Civil Rights Act of 1964, forbidding discrimination in education and employment; the Voting Rights Act of 1965, removing obstacles to the right to vote; and the Fair Housing laws of 1968, granting blacks access to rent and purchase homes. The unifying principle of these laws was nondiscrimination: race was outlawed as a legitimate basis for employment, voting, and the sale of real estate. How did King succeed, almost single-handedly, in winning support for this agenda? Why was his Southern opposition virtually silent in making counterarguments? And why did King's victory ultimately prove so fragile: only a few years later, race-based hiring and voting were back in vogue and receiving legal sanction.

King's myriad chroniclers have emphasized the visceral opposition he met in the South: mobs, fire hoses, police dogs. Such opposition was real enough, yet the civil rights movement was able to prevail against it with only a few lives lost. What often goes unremarked, however, is that King met with little or no *intellectual* resistance in the South. He encountered no cogent argument for a Southern way of life that had prevailed since the late nineteenth century. It is implausible that the South, whose leaders considered themselves the embodiment of the highest values of Western civilization, could offer no justification for segregation. Yet if such a justification existed, why was it not advanced, thus giving King a moral monopoly on the debate?

The answer lies with King himself. King was a remarkable combination of Tuskegee and Boston: he combined Booker T. Washington's emphasis on personal integrity and group solidarity with W. E. B. Du Bois's emphasis on securing basic rights. King's views too represented an odd combination: he was a cultural relativist and a moral universalist. His relativism was directly influenced by Margaret Mead, Ruth Benedict, and Melville Herskovits, whom he cited by name.[153] King's ideology was based on a denial of intrinsic differences and an assumption of group equality. Everything he said and wrote presumed the Boasian proposition that inequality between whites and blacks is not natural but the conventional product of past and continuing discrimination. Once artificial barriers were removed, King's expectation was that equality of rights for individuals would produce equal successes and rewards for blacks and whites in America. What King termed "the principle of equality" embodied for him "equality of opportunity" as the mechanism to produce the outcome "of privilege and property widely distributed."[154]

Yet, for the most part, King's cultural relativism was implicit and rarely stated in public. His argument was framed entirely in the vocabulary of individualism and moral universalism, which he derived from his religious education and background.[155] King's genius was that he attacked racism with religious and political principles that many of the Southern racists themselves professed. These were not black principles but American principles, rooted in the nation's Christian and constitutional tradition. Much of what King said sounded like an elaboration of the Declaration of Independence. King frequently cited the Declaration and did not endorse the view that its author was a hypocrite; on the contrary, King realized that his uncashed "promissory note" was nothing more than the "sublime words" of Thomas Jefferson.[156]

Like Booker T. Washington, King recognized the importance both of political right and of democratic consent. Nonviolence and civil disobedience were his calculated techniques for building that consent. If black activists had sought to overturn or set fire to the buses in Montgomery, the white establishment would have recognized that as a riot. Riots were not unknown to American history. The radical racists would have responded with their own paroxysm of violence, and Southern conservatives were famous advocates of law and order in the face of mayhem in the streets. But when King employed Christian and Gandhian rhetoric and announced his intention to use the power of love to transform the soul of his enemies, the Southern conservatives were perplexed. Here was a man they regarded as their intellectual and civilizational inferior seizing the highest moral ground and appealing to the most elevated religious and political principles of the West.

The conservatives had worked to shape a Southern culture that embraced both Christianity and the American founding, but one that was premised on the tacit assumption of black inferiority. For the paternalists, who lived by the code of the gentleman, it was crucial that this assumption remain unspoken. When King challenged them in the name of their own religion and political values, the Southern conservatives could only defend their way of life by making explicit their premise of intrinsic white superiority and defending it. They proved unable and unwilling to justify this view against King's eloquent campaign of chivalry, Christianity, and equal rights under the law.

When the Southern conservatives fell silent, the leadership of the resistance fell to the radicals, who fit the Boasian stereotype of the ignorant and hateful racist. The radical segregationists unleashed a volley of epithets, dogs, and rocks, but the rougher their tactics, the worse they appeared before a transfixed national audience. Civil rights activists learned to use the excesses of their opposition; as James Farmer admitted, "We planned the Freedom Rides with the specific intention of creating a crisis—we were counting on the bigots in the South to do our work for us."[157] Soon it became obvious to much of the country that the segregationists were morally bankrupt. Unable to answer King's arguments, they had to resort to blows.

Although King often spoke of the pervasiveness of American racism, all his rhetoric was based upon the contrary assumption that Americans were basically opposed to racism. After all, it is useless to accuse someone of a character trait of which they are proud. If Americans were confident in their racism, they would take King's allegations as a compliment. Only because many Americans by this time considered racism to be fundamentally wrong did King succeed in establishing the foundation for landmark changes in law and policy. The tragedy of King's life is that he was never able to pursue the second dimension of his project: a concerted effort to raise the competitiveness and civilizational level of the black population. King recognized the basic truth of Washington's argument that regardless of the cause, blacks as a group were deficient in important skills which required careful cultivation and training. King said:

> We must not let the fact that we are the victims of injustice lull us into abrogating responsibility for our own lives. We must not use our oppression as an excuse for mediocrity and laziness. Our crime rate is far too high. Our level of cleanliness is frequently far too low. We are too often loud and boisterous, and spend far too much on drink. By improving our standards here and now, we will go a long way toward breaking down the arguments of the segregationist. . . . The Negro will only be free when he reaches down to the inner depths of his own being and signs with the pen and ink of assertive manhood his own emancipation proclamation.[158]

Yet King did not live long enough to pursue this path. Indeed it is not clear whether he would have: toward the end of his life, he became embroiled in the antiwar and Third World causes. To his credit, King never abandoned his principled position of color blindness. Precisely for this reason, he has become a millstone for civil rights activists who seek to set aside his principles even as they invoke his moral authority. Yet King's legacy remains ambiguous. Color blindness turned out to be only half the answer. King's agenda, enacted into law by the late 1960s, might have survived more than a few short years if he had pursued with more vigor the neglected agenda of Booker T. Washington.

6

THE RACE MERCHANTS

How Civil Rights Became a Profession

You guys have been practicing discrimination for years. Now it's our turn.
—Justice Thurgood Marshall[1]

Tens of thousands of people gathered on the mall in the nation's capital on August 28, 1993. They were there to celebrate the thirtieth anniversary of Martin Luther King's famous march and "I have a dream" speech. They also came to protest. "We're marching 30 years later," Los Angeles City Treasurer Paul Brownridge said, "because racism is more pervasive, economic despair has spiralled and poverty and homelessness are at record levels."[2] One by one the leading civil rights spokespersons took the podium, gravely invoked the memory of Martin Luther King, Jr. and demanded that Americans do more to vanquish the forces of white racism so that blacks could achieve what one speaker termed "meaningful equality."

Plenty of King posters, books, and other paraphernalia were in evidence, and the speeches included lots of first-name references to "Martin." But I did not hear anyone invoke King's principle of a race-neutral society in which laws and policies are indifferent to color. The reason for this reluctance was implicitly expressed in black activist Benjamin Chavis's rallying cry. "We don't just want equal rights," he said. "We want our fair share of the national economy." Other speakers decried what they termed "institutional racism," although they were not specific about the meaning of this term. The rhetoric suggested the existence of a new civil rights agenda, in important respects different from the one which Martin Luther King, Jr. championed. Among the banners displayed were calls for the defeat of the North American Free Trade Agreement, "Democracy for Ethiopia," and passage of the striker replacement bill. Groups represented at the march included the American Association of Retired Persons, the National Organization for Women, the Environmental Defense Fund, the AFL-CIO, and gay rights organizations.

Perhaps, as black legal scholar Randall Kennedy suggests, "The goals remain the same but the tactics are now different." Certainly the style and tone of the 1993 assembly differed in two important respects from that of King's march three decades earlier. First, many in the audience seemed middle-class, and there were conspicuous signs of prosperity. A number of the speakers arrived in chauffeured cars. I overheard talk of appointments and schedules. "I have to be at the coalition meeting by six." "I hope that they hold my dinner reservation." "I can't wait to meet Maya Angelou and Morgan Freeman at the Kennedy Center tonight." Some activists engaged in minor turf warfare, sparring over whether they had been booked at the Willard or the Madison hotel, over who spoke first at the podium, over who sat where on the dais, and so on. One black professor who felt neglected erupted, "This event replicates the structures of oppression in American society." Despite this distress, it was gratifying to see indications that the lives of many blacks in the United States have improved dramatically. People whose condition is economically and socially desperate do not fret over speaker schedules and hotel bookings.

Notwithstanding the familiar tunes of "We Shall Overcome" and the Lucullan feast of nostalgic recollection, another reality was evident at the conference: there is a second black America living in conditions of poverty, illegitimacy, addiction, and violence. This segment of African Americans was not well represented on the mall. A few such voices surfaced at the People's University held prior to the march. One activist said that blacks should start looking for jobs in Africa because "the American system has said there's no place for us in the job market." Another warned that jobs were being "taken away from us and given to workers out of the country." Indeed at a workshop on racism and violence, teenagers who had been recruited to attend expressed disappointment. Lakia Robinson, a fifteen-year-old from New York, told the *Washington Post* that she kept hearing about violence against women, violence against Arab Americans, and violence against homosexuals, but nothing concrete about what to do about black-on-black violence. "Especially where I'm from, there are a lot of brothers killing brothers. Close to 10 people I know have died. I'm worried about what the next generation is going to be." A sixteen-year-old, Shenek'Qua Clemmons, said that "these workshops have nothing to do with the problems we are dealing with today."[3]

Several activists at the march did acknowledge inner-city travails, attributed them to racism, and angrily demanded public action. One organizer, who bore a name tag and a militant gait, warned the people around him: "The brothers in the 'hood—they are angry. They are very angry. It's gonna be a hot summer. I just hope we get our jobs bill." He received murmurs of assent from his listeners, but I detected a lack of conviction, evident in expressions of confusion and quiet despair. The confusion was suggested by a young man who kept reciting to himself phrases from Jesse Jackson in what I took to be a mild form of dementia. "From the outhouse to the courthouse to the White House." "Just because you were born in the slum does not mean that the slum was born in you." "We must choose the human race over the arms race." "It's not my aptitude but my attitude that determines my altitude, with a little intestinal fortitude." Every time someone paid him a moment's attention he would advise them, "Stay black."

I asked some of the activists gathered on the mall whether the liberal vision of integration and of a race-neutral society had proven to be a failure. "White liberals are now the enemy," one young African American said, drawing me aside in the apparent belief that I was a Third World soul brother. "Those motherfuckers are responsible for our problems." Not white racists, I asked, but liberals? He looked at me fiercely. "What's the motherfuckin' difference, man? We're living in a racist country." Black rage, combined with a more complex conviction of betrayal, was evident in those words.

CLASS DIVISIONS

The march of 1993 illustrated dramatic changes that have overtaken the civil rights movement in the past generation. The first change is that there is now a distinct and thriving black middle class, whose lifestyle is quite different from that of the black underclass. Yet there are some indications of a troubled relationship between the two classes; Henry Louis

Gates, Jr. indignantly asserts, "It's time for the black middle class to stop feeling guilty about its own success while fellow blacks languish in the inner city of despair. Black prosperity does not derive from black poverty."[4] It seems odd that Gates would feel the need to make such a denial. An interesting issue arises: why would middle-class blacks experience guilt or responsibility for the poverty of underclass blacks?

What seems most striking, at first glance, is not the class distinctions within the African American community but the extent of black solidarity. For all its variety the black community nevertheless maintains a distinct and recognizable black culture, exhibited in shared ways of speaking, cultural tastes, and voting habits: across economic lines, approximately 90 percent of blacks vote for the same party, the Democrats, in national elections. Many middle-class and underclass blacks also seem to share an alienation from the mainstream institutions of America, and a smoldering anger at the persistence of racism. Black rage, as Ellis Cose calls it, is not confined to poor blacks living in dire circumstances but is also exhibited by apparently successful blacks. Clearly these persons are incensed not just about their own lives but about the conditions afflicting African Americans as a group. As Carl Upchurch wrote in the *New York Times* after the 1993 march, despite the gains of the civil rights movement blacks continue to endure "the unprecedented number of children living in poverty . . . the filth, stench and genocidal conditions created by the crack scourge in our cities, the slaughter of African American men, the exploding prison population, the deadly HIV problem that plagues all our young, the 800 gang-related deaths in Los Angeles County in 1992 alone."[5] This literature of discontent is notable for how starkly it contradicts the hagiographic literature of the civil rights movement.

Yet for today's black leaders, black solidarity remains a central organizing principle for the battles to come. How can an African American community so divided between a middle class and an underclass expect to preserve a cohesive political identity? Part of the answer comes as a surprise: the one-drop rule. Once devised by slaveowners and segregationists to enforce a racist demarcation and deny any kinship between groups, the one-drop principle continues to define blackness in America and now serves as a unifying force for African Americans. Joel Williamson observes that "millions of Americans who are more European than African in their heritage continue to insist, sometimes defiantly, upon their blackness."[6] Mary Waters writes, "Black Americans are highly socially constrained to identify as blacks, without other options available to them, even if they believe or know that their forebears included many non-blacks."[7] In a recent book on the one-drop rule, F. James Davis notes the irony:

> Blacks are just as anxious as whites to instruct the young and the deviant about how the rule works and how important it is to follow it. The rule is now strongly enforced within the black community. American blacks now feel that they have an important vested interest in a rule that has for centuries been a key instrument in their oppression.[8]

The paradox runs deeper. Not only does the one-drop rule help to maintain cultural cohesiveness, but it also serves as the official instrument of enforcement of civil rights laws. Ever since 1965, when the Equal Employment Opportunity Commission required race-conscious record keeping and reporting on the part of companies, racial classification has an organizing principle for the American work force.[9] All the major civil rights organizations, such as the NAACP, the Urban League, and the Leadership Conference on Civil Rights, now strongly support the one-drop rule and would strongly resist getting rid of it. As activist Julian Bond puts it, "I very much oppose diluting the power and strength of numbers as they affect legal decisions about race in this country."[10] Thus on an essential element of ideological doctrine—the existence of clear lines of demarcation between the races—the contemporary civil rights movement is in basic agreement with the old racists.

We are confronted with a new civil rights program that is substantively different from that of Martin Luther King, Jr. The new agenda involves neither integration nor laws that assess citizens solely according to their merits or character. In some ways, it appears to be a repudiation of King's vision, in that it involves a celebration and affirmation of group identity, combined with a demand for race consciousness in private and public hiring, the drawing of voting districts, public school assignments, and so on. Many liberals seem uncomfortable with this agenda, but some groups promote it; once an advocate of Harlan's color-blind doctrine, the *New York Times* now opines that "the struggle to achieve a healthy race-consciousness in our politics has been an ennobling part of our system."[11]

For the most part this new liberalism, however, sounds distinctly like its predecessor. Curiously a new civil rights program is packaged in the vocabulary of the old one. Thus racial preferences are promoted as a form of "nondiscrimination," the use of government power to assign students to schools on the basis of race is touted as "desegregation," and opposition to race-conscious policies is said to constitute "turning back the clock" and a racist effort to obstruct "civil rights." King's moral language and authority, it seems, are now invoked to promote policies he never endorsed and which, on principle, he opposed.

Over the past generation, we have also seen the rise of a civil rights *establishment,* quite different from the civil rights movement that King led.[12] As Congressman John Lewis puts it, "We civil rights leaders got sidetracked. We lost that sense of moral clarity."[13] But now there is more than ethical confusion: there is also a community of tens of thousands of people whose full-time job it is to promote civil rights. The civil rights establishment includes staffers at the Equal Employment Opportunity Commission, state government affirmative action officers, corporate and university diversity personnel, and the employees of the myriad private and public interest groups, all of whom work in concert to shape and enforce civil rights laws. "Most Americans have no idea what the term civil rights means today and how it is implemented," remarks Evan Kemp, former chairman of the EEOC. "There is so much doublespeak, so many powerful vested interests. I believe in the color-blind ideal, but even I'm not sure I understand how we got to this point."

This chapter seeks to account for the repudiation of King's concept of strict nondiscrimination or color-blindness, the rise of racial preferences in all spheres of American policy, the consolidation of civil rights as a way of life, and the subsequent (and to many, mysterious) phenomenon of black rage. My argument is that there is an unresolved tension between the liberal vision of equal rights for individuals and the civil rights agenda of equal results for groups. Gradually but unmistakably, the former agenda which was advocated by King was displaced by the new agenda which is supported by the civil rights establishment. Although some view this change as a betrayal of Martin Luther King, Jr. in fact it is a logical working out of the principles of cultural relativism which King shared. Cultural relativism posits an inherent equality among groups. Ignoring the Boasian distinction between race and culture, activists who fought for civil rights automatically applied the relativist paradigm to blacks and whites. Their assumption was that blacks and whites were basically equal, and that differences of academic and job success between them were the artificial legacy of segregation and racial discrimination. Many civil rights activists and liberals expected that once the artificial barriers of segregation and legal discrimination were removed, the presumed equality of group capacity would ensure that equality of rights would begin to produce equality of results in a reasonable period of time. "In the 1960s, sure, most of us thought that equal rights would lead to equal performance," remarks Christopher Jencks. "For most liberals, I believe, that was considered self-evident." But equality under the laws did not produce equality of outcomes. Nor did Martin Luther King, Jr.'s principles, enacted into law, show the prospects of producing, within the foreseeable future, the group equality that defined the relativist worldview.

Consequently, many civil rights leaders and sympathetic white liberals drew the obvious conclusion: formal equality is not enough. Moreover, they inferred that despite external signs, racism could not have abated very much, but it must have simply grown more subtle and institutional than once naively believed. Activists began to press for more drastic action to uproot this hidden racism and enable blacks and other minorities to realize substantive group equality. The new measures required an abandonment of desegregation and race-neutral policies. Thus the civil rights establishment exploited contradictions in Martin Luther King's ideology to steer it in a direction he never anticipated, and color-blindness as the basis for American law became history. Moreover, in an ingenious adaption of the principles of relativism, civil rights activists after King's death were successful in redefining the meaning of "progress." Strictly speaking, relativism does not permit social progress, because the new culture is by definition no better than the one it replaced. By defining relativism in terms of group equality, however, activists were able to measure progress as continuing movement toward equality of results for racial groups. Also they proceeded to castigate opposition to the new agenda as regressive and reactionary, as deplorable attempts to "roll back hard-won gains."

The new class divisions within the black community, the institutionalization of the one-drop rule, the techniques of the new civil rights establishment, and black rage are all understandable in the context of these developments. Let us begin by tracing how the concept of America as a racist society became widely popularized, how race-conscious policies replaced race-neutral ones, and how, as a consequence, the liberalism of the early civil rights movement was superseded by a new ideology that took its name.

By Any Means Necessary

Both liberals and civil rights activists who fought alongside King began to abandon the color-blind concept in response to an increasing conviction, established during the mid to late 1960s, that America is a racist society. Prior to this period, the liberal consensus was far more benign: American practices fall short and must be brought into full conformity with national ideals. But to say that America is fundamentally racist is to call those ideals into question, and to legitimize policies that depart from traditional American principles. For blacks, the figure who articulated the new alienation was Malcolm X. For liberals, the document which expressed the belief in a systematic and entrenched racism was the Kerner Commission Report.

Malcolm X seems to have replaced Martin Luther King, Jr. today as the leading inspiration for African Americans, especially among young people. In *Making Malcolm,* African American scholar Michael Eric Dyson celebrates his hero's "cultural renaissance," which he terms a virtual "second coming."[14] As TV producer Orlando Bagwell says, young blacks prefer Malcolm because "they see a person who speaks honestly about a reality that hasn't changed so much."[15] The meteoric rise of Malcolm X during the 1960s can be explained by the fact that he articulated and glamorized the sentiments of many blacks who felt bypassed by the civil rights movement. By contrast with King, who came from a Southern background and spoke most for the aspirations of middle-class blacks, Malcolm X eloquently communicated the bitterness of millions of urban blacks who stood to gain little from desegregation and the right to compete on equal terms for jobs. The problem for these blacks was less discrimination than the lack of job qualifications and civilizational skills, a problem highlighted by Booker T. Washington. Rather than focus on what should be done about this problem, Malcolm X emphasized the historical crimes that brought it about.[16] Malcolm X recognized the humiliation imposed on blacks who were legally permitted to compete for jobs but found themselves unable to do so. He offered an attractive balm: black pride. The pride that Malcolm X invoked was based on two foundations, both easily accessible to the poorest of blacks. The first was pride in blackness. The second was pride based on a posture of stylized rebelliousness against mainstream society. "We want freedom by any means necessary. We want justice by any means necessary. We want equality by any means necessary."[17] Malcolm X was the original apostle of black rage.

Unlike King, Malcolm X regarded whites as incorrigibly racist. Thus he made little effort to convert them or seek to establish the "beloved community" of which King spoke. Nor did Malcolm express much confidence in American ideals. Blacks, he said, were not Americans but "victims of Americanism." Instead of an American dream, he saw an American nightmare.[18] Indeed for most of his life he subscribed to and promulgated Nation of Islam theories about how the white race was created by a satanic apprentice named Yacub in order to deceive black people, their civilizational superiors, and rule the world through ruthless exploitation.[19] Malcolm X urged revolution as the means for overthrowing the American system. "Revolution is bloody, revolution is hostile, revolution knows no compromise, revolution overturns and destroys everything that gets in its way."[20]

Although unrealistic as a practical strategy, Malcolm's ideology was calculated to promote militancy as a form of black authenticity, and to call middle-class moderation into question as a betrayal of blackness. Even among blacks, Malcolm made a distinction between "house negroes" and "field negroes." Malcolm attacked King as a house negro and an Uncle Tom, and termed his March on Washington a "picnic," a "circus," and a "farce on Washington."[21] Malcolm reveled in his image as a fearless leader who spoke the language of truth by speaking the language of power. "You show me a black man who isn't an extremist," he said, "and I'll show you one who needs a psychiatrist."[22]

Yet Malcolm X was not merely a demagogue of discontent. He was clear-minded in exposing an inconsistency or tension in King's civil rights ideology. Like many white liberals, King argued that race constituted a legitimate basis of private identity but should not be the basis for public conduct. This was the liberal compromise of the 1950s and early 1960s: welcome celebrations of racial pride, but then demand nondiscrimination. Yet if race is a source of identity and legitimate group membership, why not discriminate in favor of one's own group and against other groups? As we saw earlier, ethnocentrism or a preference for the home team seems to be virtually a universal basis for human behavior.

So what is wrong, Malcolm demanded to know, with being black and affirming blackness and acting as though that mattered? "Integration would destroy our people," Malcolm warned. "No sane black man really wants integration."[23] Indeed Malcolm X took that logic to its conclusion, advocating that blacks ultimately separate from whites and establish a nation of their own.[24] Martin Luther King, Jr. was visibly perturbed by Malcolm's proposals, but he offered no effective rebuttal to them. He recognized that American blacks constituted a distinct cultural group and it was natural to expect them to unify along those lines. Indeed King said he had no objection to black power, only to the name. He did not oppose black ethnocentrism, but he did oppose, and seek laws to curtail, white ethnocentrism (expressed in the form of discrimination). Because Boasian ideology held ethnocentrism to be an unnatural and irrational expression of prejudice, King found himself unwilling and unable to defend a double standard which would condone black power but reject white power.

Malcolm did not find himself under such constraints. Not only did he promulgate the concept that "black is beautiful," but he celebrated a "bad negro" version of blackness. Thus Malcolm X helped to legitimize the culture of the black underclass in the name of race pride. White racism, for instance, could be invoked by the convict to transform his identity into that of "political prisoner." Eventually, the term "black" replaced "Negro" both among poor and middle-class blacks. After Malcolm, virtually nobody wanted to be a viewed as a "good negro." The Afro hairstyle and the Black Power salute came into vogue, especially among the young, symbolizing blackness as an esthetic and as an ideology. Cornel West probably goes too far in asserting that "King was near death politically and organizationally before he was murdered,"[25] but the momentum was clearly against him.

• As early as 1965, James Farmer, who headed the Congress of Racial Equality (CORE), impatiently wrote: "We have found the cult of color-blindness not only quaintly irrelevant but seriously flawed. America could only become color-blind when we gave up our color. We would have to give up our identities."[26]

• In 1966 another King follower, John Lewis, was outvoted as chairman of the Student Nonviolent Coordinating Committee by a West Indian activist, Stokely Carmichael, who supported Black Power, "a movement that will smash everything Western civilization has created."[27] That same year the Black Panther Party was founded in Oakland, California by Huey Newton and Bobby Seale: its demands included the release of all black prisoners from American jails, regardless of their crimes.[28]

• In 1967 Carmichael and Charles Hamilton published *Black Power,* in which they insisted upon a strengthening of black consciousness and rejected integration as "a subterfuge for the maintenance of white supremacy."[29] Around the same time, James Cone, a leading voice in black theology, published *Black Theology and Black Power:*

In order for the oppressed blacks to regain their identity, they must affirm the very characteristic which the oppressor ridicules—*blackness*. Black people must withdraw and form their own culture, their own way of life.[30]

• In 1968 Julius Lester (who has since radically changed his views) published a manifesto which declared:

> Psychologically, blacks have always found an outlet for their revenge whenever planes have fallen, autos have collided, or just every day when white folks die. It is clearly written that the victim must become the executioner.[31]

• In 1972 several thousand blacks assembled in Gary, Indiana for the National Black Political Convention. The Reverend Jesse Jackson was there, as was Benjamin Chavis, later to be named head of the NAACP. Symbolizing the way in which the future leadership of the civil rights movement was going, Jackson and Chavis defied the integrationist posture of the NAACP and joined the delegates in a Black Power salute. "Everybody raised their fists," Chavis recalls.[32]

An enormous change was taking place in the civil rights movement in the 1960s. As C. Vann Woodward describes, leadership was moving from Southern integrationists toward Northern militants. Religious leaders were being displaced by lawyers, social workers, and full-time activists. Whites who once dominated organizations like the NAACP found themselves increasingly unwelcome in the front ranks. Nonviolence was no longer the operating philosophy. Woodward observes, "Black nationalism assumed many new guises."[33] Eventually this separatism would become institutionalized in law and policy.

PROGRESS AND PESSIMISM

Although many white liberals during the 1960s were confused by Black Power, what seems to have really traumatized them was the outbreak of riots across America. Starting in the Watts area of Los Angeles and spreading to Detroit and elsewhere, the riots seemed to turn previously tranquil areas into cauldrons of violence and mayhem. Altogether between 1965 and 1968 there were more than a hundred riots: eight thousand people were killed or injured, fifty thousand were arrested, and an estimated half a million blacks participated.[34] Anarchy seemed to reign in urban America.

To many, the riots came as a complete surprise. The nation, after all, had just undergone a virtual revolution in its laws, which for the first time were applied not just to whites, but equally to the descendants of slaves. While racial progress in such a short time was bound to be limited, and while many Southern districts truculently resisted school desegregation, many white liberals were encouraged by conspicuous signs of change. Desegregation proceeded rapidly in many areas of American life: buses, railroad cars, airport terminals, drinking fountains, lunch counters, and so on. The Justice Department filed hundreds of suits against hotels, restaurants, and gas stations, but in many cases no judicial rulings were necessary. Americans began to understand that it was no longer legitimate to separate citizens based on race or color. Some were combative, many were reluctant, but under the pressures of law and black activism, institutions and individuals began to conform to a new regime in race relations. Writing in 1968, Gary Orfield noted that even in the Deep South, the schools were changing.

> Counties with well-attended Ku Klux Klan cross burnings have seen the novel and amazing spectacle of Negro teachers instructing white classes. In the red clay counties in rural backwaters, where racial attitudes have not changed much for a century, dozens or even hundreds of black children have recently crossed rigid caste lines to enter white schools. It has been a social transformation more profound and rapid than any in peacetime American history.[35]

No one would argue that discrimination was completely eradicated from jobs in the private and public sector, yet in places where blacks could previously only be hired as menial workers and servants, they started showing up in an increasing array of skilled jobs and in the professions. Thousands of cases of discrimination were filed under the new civil rights laws, and both companies and government began the process of adjustment to a system in which discrimination was not simply considered wrong but also illegal. One example of the practical effect of those changes comes from civil rights activist Julian Bond. "As a boy," he recalls, "I thought that the most I could ever achieve was a teaching or administrative post in a black school." By the mid 1960s, Bond was elected to the Georgia House of Representatives, a post he held for more than twenty years.[36] This example also illustrates the new power of African Americans at the ballot box. Thanks to the sanction of law and the labors of civil rights volunteers, hundreds of thousands who had never cast a ballot were now eligible to vote and registered. Blacks began to appear in

Congress, as well as to win election in a wide range of posts at the state and local level.[37]

One problem, however, was that although there was measurable progress, it was unevenly distributed. The civil rights movement led by King was primarily a southern crusade against the institution of state-sponsored segregation; removing this barrier offered little to northern blacks. This was a rising population: while at the turn of the century almost 90 percent of blacks lived in the rural South, as Nicholas Lemann documents in *The Promised Land,* several million moved to southern cities and then to the North.[38] Moreover, as C. Vann Woodward argues, as blacks arrived in the cities, many whites fled the schools and neighborhoods, so that "the slow retreat of *de jure* segregation in the South was paralleled by a rapid advance of *de facto* segregation in the North . . . and an acceleration of urban decay, crime and delinquency."[39]

The civil rights movement also seemed to disproportionately benefit what Du Bois had called his Talented Tenth: the relatively small proportion of blacks who had the skills and motivation to take advantage of new opportunities in education, employment and political life. The very rapidity of progress for this group raised the expectations of the black population as a whole, especially among a new generation of young blacks for whom the slow accretion of civilizational skills seemed a counsel of interminable and unacceptable delay. One may say that the civil rights revolution generated a kind of Malthusian result: material benefits rose arithmetically, but expectations rose geometrically. Martin Luther King, Jr. recognized this when he observed in 1966, "We raised hope tremendously, but we were not able to produce the results inherent in that hope."[40]

Yet these are the reflections of hindsight. When the Watts riot broke out a few days after the passage of the Voting Rights Act, many liberals expressed bewilderment. Confusion mounted with the spread of looting and the garish symbols of black militancy. Against this scarlet backdrop of violence and black separatism—which seemed both a product of and a contributor to the riots—liberals and black leaders in the late 1960s and early 1970s underwent a profound reevaluation of their views about American racism and the need for strong measures to combat it. A crucial document reflecting the new thinking was the so-called Kerner Commission report, issued in 1968 by President Lyndon Johnson's National Advisory Commission on Civil Disorders. Despite many of its members' reputation for moderation, the Kerner Commission came to be dominated by Roy Wilkins, executive secretary of the NAACP, liberal New York mayor John Lindsay, and Senator Fred Harris, a populist Oklahoma Democrat. Published with an introduction by *New York Times* columnist Tom Wicker, a liberal white Southerner, the findings of the Kerner Commission made a powerful imprint and the report became perhaps the most authoritative and widely cited civil rights document of its time.

The striking conclusion of the Kerner Commission was that society, not the rioters, was primarily to blame for the riots. The commission portrayed the unrest as an expression of social protest by those who had a justified claim on American society. In this view, the riots were a form of political dissent by desperate people who could not express themselves in any other way. While the Kerner Commission did not endorse race-based remedies, and rejected Black Power as a futile retaliation against white power, it basically endorsed the view of Malcolm X that America was at its core a racist society. Indeed the Kerner Commission placed the blame for the plight of blacks as a group on a single source: white racism.

> What white Americans have never fully understood—but what the Negro can never forget—is that white society is deeply implicated in the ghetto. White institutions created it, white institutions maintain it, and white society condones it. . . . White racism is essentially responsible for the explosive mixture which has been accumulating in our cities.[41]

By 1968, there was a growing consensus among liberals and black leaders that white racism was pervasive, that it thwarted black aspirations at virtually every stage, that "the vital element of time" was running out, and that America should take immediate action, as the Kerner Commission put it, "to close the gap between promise and performance."[42] In his last book, Martin Luther King also acknowledged, "The gap between promise and fulfillment is distressingly wide."[43] What promise? Neither the Kerner Commission nor Martin Luther King was specific on this point. Neither could be referring to the promise of legal equality in schooling, jobs, or voting because those rights were already established in the law. Rather, what the Kerner Commission and King seemed to mean was equality of result, actual equality with whites as a group. Whites would have to do more to bridge the chasm between formal equality and the expectation of a fuller and more tangible equality of income, possessions, and power.

These suggestions were made explicit in 1965 by Bayard Rustin, an activist and organizer who worked closely with Martin Luther King. Whatever disagreements may arise, Rustin wrote in *Commentary,* the new concern of the civil rights movement would be "not merely with removing the barriers to full opportunity but with achieving the fact of equality."[44] A similar argument that same year came from Daniel Patrick Moynihan, who was assistant secretary of labor.

> In the new period the expectations of Negro Americans will go beyond civil rights. . . . They will now expect that in the near future equal opportunities for them as a group will produce roughly equal results as compared with other groups.[45]

To achieve equality of result, an expectation generated by the relativist premise that all groups are inherently equal, civil rights activists with the support of many white liberals began to abandon their long-standing commitment to color blindness, and although no doubt with nobler motives, to imitate the racists and segregationists by putting racial classification and racial preferences back into the law.

THE ADVENT OF RACIAL PREFERENCES

In order to get beyond racism, we must first take account of race. In order to treat some persons equally, we must treat them differently.

—Justice Harry Blackmun[46]

The contemporary debate over affirmative action is a kind of idiots' quarrel between those who chant the word "goals" and those who whisper the word "quotas." Liberals and civil rights activists form the first group: we only want goals. Conservatives dominate the second group: you really want quotas. Yet quotas are simply goals reified. Are they wrong because they rigidly enforce goals or because they unfairly discriminate in the first place? Some people argue that goals are flexible while quotas are rigid, but it is entirely possible, as Michael Rosenfeld points out, to have inflexible goals or flexible quotas.[47] In fact, as political philosopher Harvey Mansfield argues, goals and quotas operate on identical principles, differing only in degree, as a push differs from a shove. The real question is the legitimacy of racial preferences themselves.

In a recent column in the *Washington Post,* Richard Cohen reports on the Clinton administration's decision to reject all white male candidates for a senior State Department post and to insist that such a position go to a minority. "It is one thing to seek diversity," Cohen protests, "and quite another to reject a qualified individual on account of race or sex."[48] Here Cohen appears to be endorsing goals but rejecting quotas. Where is the distinction? If it is legitimate to seek diversity, it follows that diversity becomes a job qualification. If the color of one's skin contributes to effectiveness on the job, then racial preferences are justified. Whether they are accomplished by goals, quotas, or some others means becomes an administrative problem. So let us ignore the bureaucratic distinction between goals and quotas and ask the basic question: is discrimination based on race justified? This is a difficult question to answer because leading African American scholars and activists sometimes deny that, under current law and practice, blacks and other minorities are given preference at all.

> An affirmative action program has nothing to do with finding unqualified black men or women. It is about finding qualified black people who are there in abundance but who, either inadvertently or by choice, have been overlooked.
>
> —Clifford Alexander, former EEOC chairman[49]

> Affirmative action is simply any action taken to ensure or affirm equal opportunity for oppressed or previously disadvantaged groups. What's wrong with that?
>
> —Benjamin Hooks, former NAACP head[50]

> Affirmative action has to do with opening up new places that were not open. It makes no compromise with respect to ability.
>
> —John Hope Franklin, historian[51]

As we will soon discover, these assertions are untrue, but neither are they lies; rather, they can be viewed sympathetically as statements of ideals. The credibility of these witnesses can be preserved by reformulating their argument to say that the means of discrimination may be necessary to achieve the ultimate end of a color-blind society. There is no doubt, however, that all three of the distinguished figures quoted above support preferences, yet apparently feel obliged to defend those preferences in race-neutral language. On the question of whether racial discrimination is sometimes justified, the civil rights establishment has learned to publicly answer no, but privately answer yes.

On June 4, 1965, President Johnson delivered the commencement address at Howard University and offered perhaps the earliest and best defense of what came to be called "affirmative action."

You do not take a person who for years has been hobbled by chains and liberate him, bring him up to the starting line of a race and then say, "You are free to compete with all the others," and still justly believe that you have been completely fair. . . . Thus it is not enough just to open the gates of opportunity. All our citizens must have the ability to walk through those gates. We seek not just equality as a right and a theory but equality as a fact and equality as a result.[52]

Johnson's argument was not racial, and could apply to any economically or socially disadvantaged member of society. The logic of the argument was spelled out by Anatole France a long time ago, when he ridiculed "the law which in its majestic equality forbids rich and poor alike to sleep under bridges and to steal bread." According to this view, rights are rendered meaningful not simply by their formal recognition but by providing as well the means by which they can be put into practice. Yet Johnson's speech was clearly intended to apply specifically to the group he was addressing, namely blacks. Undoubtedly a case could be made that since blacks as a group had been disadvantaged and discriminated against, blacks as a group were entitled to some race-specific forms of compensation.[53] Privately, many activists in the civil rights movement seemed to be moving toward this view, but few articulated it publicly, mainly because the movement had just completed a lengthy campaign on behalf of erasing race-based classifications and privileges that had been long engraved in the laws of the South.[54]

Indeed during the debates surrounding the Civil Rights Act of 1964, Southern opponents of the proposed legislation warned that it would lead to racial timetables, preferences, and quotas. Sponsors and supporters of the act emphatically and unequivocally denied this, and agreed to insert language in the law making clear their intention to assure nothing more than equal treatment to equally qualified applicants seeking education and jobs in a competitive market.[55] Senator Hubert Humphrey pledged that if critics of the Civil Rights Act could find any language permitting racial preferences, "I will start eating the pages one after another, because it is not in there."[56] And a fair reading of the legislation, as enacted, confirms the interpretation of its drafters and backers.

It shall be unlawful employment practice for any employer . . . to discriminate against any individual because of such individual's race, color, religion, sex or national origin. . . . Nothing contained in this title shall be interpreted to require any employer to grant preferential treatment to any individual or to any group because of race . . . on account of an imbalance which may exist with respect to the total number or percentage of persons employed . . . in comparison with the available work force.[57]

The language could not be much clearer. The problem, however, was with the results. Over the years, universities and companies that adopted a view of affirmative action consistent with Title VII—publicity of positions and recruitment of qualified applicants so that the very best person could be selected—quickly found that their minority totals did not go up very much, in some cases scarcely at all.

• As McGeorge Bundy wrote: "The gaps in economic, educational and cultural advantage between racial minorities and the white majority are so wide that there is no racially neutral process of choice that will produce more than a handful of minority students in our competitive colleges and professional schools."[58]

• Peter Winograd, a law dean at New York University, went so far as to assert in 1969 that "the fact of the matter is that if you're color-blind, you don't admit minority groups."[59]

• During the 1970s, cabinet official Joseph Califano demanded, "How am I ever going to find first-class black doctors, first-class black lawyers, first-class black scientists, if these people don't have the chance to get into the best schools in the country?"[60]

As Stephen Steinberg points out, "The reason that policy evolved from outreach to preference was that outreach was not working."[61] Consequently, beginning in the late 1960s and continuing through the 1970s and 1980s, private and public institutions began an elaborate process of adjusting scores and lowering standards in order to give racial preference to minorities, particularly blacks, to raise their representation. This process began cautiously, tentatively, and generally in secret. It was driven by the courts, and by the newly established civil rights apparatus of the government—staffed largely with black activists and white liberals. It was not subject to democratic debate, and decisions were for the most part made behind closed doors by judges and bureaucrats. Consequently although good reasons may have existed for racial preference, the American public was not told what they were.

The reason for this reluctance to provide full disclosure is clear. Martin Luther King, Jr. had just led a civil rights revolution based on the moral necessity of erasing race from the entire fabric of American laws and policies. Liberal policymakers and civil rights activists undoubtedly recognized how difficult it would be to attempt to undo the public consensus on color-blindness. It would seem paradoxical, historian Hugh Davis Graham observes, to employ "the means of discrimination to achieve the ends of nondiscrimination."[62] Justice William O. Douglas wrote in 1974, "If discrimination based on race is constitutionally permissible when those who hold the reins can come up with reasons to justify it, then constitutional guarantees acquire an accordion-like quality."[63] The dilemma was clearly posed by the eminent legal scholar Alexander Bickel in the mid 1970s:

> If the Constitution prohibits exclusion of blacks and other minorities on racial grounds, it cannot permit the exclusion of whites on similar grounds, for it must be the exclusion on racial grounds which offends the Constitution, and not the particular skin color of the person excluded.[64]

The arguments for and against racial preferences would rage in the government, the courts, and the universities for decades. Supporters of preferences argued that for most of American history whites benefited from racial preferences. They questioned the relevance and fairness of merit standards, suggesting the possibility of racial bias. They pointed to existing old boy networks and nepotistic arrangements to imply that racial preferences would entail no radical departure from established norms. They argued that such preferences would help to rectify past wrongs and to integrate blacks into the mainstream of American society fairly quickly. They expressed the hope that preferences would produce role models for future generations of blacks. Finally they promised that preferences would promote a diversity of cultures and views that would enrich the academic and work environment.[65]

Criticism of racial preferences also surfaced, among liberals as well as conservatives. Their strongest point seemed to be that it was both immoral and illegal to fight discrimination by practicing it. If legal discrimination against blacks was wrong, they argued, how could such discrimination against whites be right? They also pointed out that preferences mostly helped blacks who already had educational and job skills, and did little or nothing for the most disadvantaged blacks. Moreover, they argued, the cost of these preferences was often borne by white ethnics and Asians who played no part in the historical crimes for which affirmative action was said to be a needed remedy. Finally, they insisted, minorities might gain materially from preferences but they would suffer psychologically, because their achievements would always be considered suspect.[66]

Liberal critics of preferences may have had the better of the argument, but this turned out to be irrelevant. The practical issue was: how to quickly and substantially increase the number of blacks in schools and jobs? Both the ideology of cultural relativism as well as the more immediate prospect of continued social unrest compelled a liberal change of policy. The consequence of this change was that Martin Luther King's vision of a color-blind system of laws and policies was destined to enjoy a very short and precarious life in American law. Gradually but indisputably, affirmative action metamorphosed from a project to recruit the best person for the job into a program to prefer minority applicants with weaker credentials over better qualified white applicants who are turned away. The color-blind path became the road not taken.

PROPORTIONAL REPRESENTATION

How did the government and the courts decide how much racial preference was warranted? From the outset, the standard was proportional representation, which continues to provide the foundation for current civil rights law. Here is how the Supreme Court defined the concept in a 1977 decision:

> It is ordinarily to be expected that nondiscriminatory hiring practices will in time result in a work force more or less representative of the racial and ethnic composition of the population in the community from which employees are hired.[67]

Scholars are unsure where the concept of proportional representation comes from. There are few, if any, explicit elaborations or defenses of this civil rights standard in the literature of the late 1960s and early 1970s.[68] Yet proportional representation became the inevitable and commonsense expression of the underlying ideology of cultural relativism. All groups are considered equal. Therefore, group inequalities are presumed to be the product of discrimination or its consequences. Absent discrimination, the relativist expectation is that each racial group would be distributed in every field at roughly its ratio in the surrounding population. This logic may now seem controversial, but one of the early advocates of racial preferences, Laurence Silberman, argues that "at the time we needed *something* to go on." Silberman, who served as under secretary of the Labor Department in the Nixon administration, recalls that during the 1960s, black and liberal activists rushed to staff the civil rights divisions of the federal government: the Equal Employment Opportunity Commission (EEOC), an independent agency established by the Civil Rights Act of 1964; the Office of Civil Rights both in the Department of Justice and the Department of Education; and the Labor Department's Office of Federal Contract Compliance Programs (OFCCP), which supervises government contracts with private sector companies. As early as 1967, Edward Sylvester, director of the OFCCP, defined the strategy of the activists: "Affirmative action is anything that you have to do to get results."[69]

Silberman points out that although President Johnson first established affirmative action with his famous Executive Order 11246 as early as 1965,[70] preferential policies were first implemented by Richard Nixon. "We knew there was a lot of discrimination in the construction industry, and we wanted to change that," Silberman recalls. In 1968 the Nixon administration announced its Philadelphia Plan, which set "goals and timetables" for hiring in the city's construction industry. "Visible, measurable goals to correct obvious imbalances are essential," declared Arthur Fletcher, assistant secretary at the Labor Department.[71]

In February 1970 the Labor Department issued Revised Order No. 4 which codified the goals and timetables requirement for all government contractors. Drawing on the model of proportional representation, the new rule defined the concept of "underutilization," a situation in which minorities are represented below their available numbers in particular areas of the work force. The government insisted that companies maintain data on racial classification and race-based hiring to ensure compliance and assure future government contracts. "Little did we know the juggernaut we were setting in motion," Silberman recalls. Now a federal judge, Silberman has subsequently regretted his role in initiating racial preferences.[72]

In 1971 the Supreme Court devised an ingenious legalistic mechanism to enforce proportional representation. The Court ruled that companies are liable for illegal discrimination, regardless of their intentions, if the effect of their hiring and promotion standards is to advance a disproportionately small number of racial minorities. *Griggs v. Duke Power* held that merit standards that produced such a "disparate impact" could only be justified if the company could prove that those standards bore a "demonstrable relationship" to performance and were required by "business necessity."[73]

At the outset, it seems unobjectionable to ask employers to administer hiring requirements that ensure good performance on the job in question. Yet the precise relationship between standards and actual performance is often quite difficult to demonstrate. By making this connection very difficult to document, courts have succeeded in making virtually all companies vulnerable to a finding of illegal discrimination. Barbara Lerner, a psychologist and expert on job testing, gives some common examples: A supermarket may demand that its checkers have high school degrees and no criminal records. A city may ask applicants for fire-fighter jobs to take a test to demonstrate basic verbal and reasoning skills and pass an endurance test that involves running a certain distance carrying a heavy weight. A newspaper may base its hiring of new reporters on interview assessments and on the results of a standardized test of grammar and comprehension. "But how can you prove beyond a reasonable doubt that these measures are indispensable to job performance?" Lerner asks. It is certainly possible that former convicts can be rehabilitated and serve perfectly reliably as supermarket clerks. It is arguable whether high school graduation is really necessary to perform largely mechanical tasks at the checkout counter. Lerner points out that undeniably some people who would fail the endurance test may make better fire fighters than others who pass. Finally newspaper editors would have to grant that many of their hiring standards, while intended to measure journalistic potential, are highly intuitive and not demonstrably reliable.

Both the government and the courts, Lerner points out, took advantage of these difficulties. The EEOC insisted, for example, that companies using standardized tests for hiring get those tests "validated," a process which is both costly and time consuming. Government agencies also demanded that companies prove not only that their existing standards were absolutely necessary for job performance, but (a seemingly impossible task) that no alternative measures existed that would get the job done while getting more blacks and other minorities hired. In some cases, the government sued companies that used such hiring standards as requiring employees to have a high school diploma or not to have a criminal record. These standards were impermissible, the government declared, because blacks are less likely to graduate from school and more likely to be convicted of a crime than whites. As EEOC chairman Eleanor Holmes Norton admitted during the late 1970s, the purpose of all this maneuvering was simple: the government sought to force companies to avoid these hassles by engaging in racial preferences in the first place.[74] As EEOC affirmative action guidelines made clear, if companies hired a proportionate number of each racial group, the question of underrepresentation would not arise.[75] Historian Herman Belz describes the subtle intimidation that became the operating technique of the new civil rights establishment.

> The essential element of the strategy was the contention that a *prima facie* charge of discrimination should be based on the absence or scarcity of blacks in the work force. Employers who were uncertain about rebutting the charge, and who wanted to avoid the appearance of discrimination, could then be persuaded to hire a specific number of blacks while not admitting to unlawful practices.[76]

It is not hard to predict the results of such pressure. By the late 1970s, racial preferences were a way of doing business both in government and private sector hiring. Between then and now, the Supreme Court has in a series of divided rulings upheld such preferences under limited and specified conditions.[77] Pressed by the scores of groups comprising the civil rights lobby, Congress enshrined the double standard into law in the Civil Rights Act of 1991, which was signed by President Bush in 1992.[78] The Clinton administration is an aggressive practitioner of preferences in the name of making the government "look like America."[79] Indeed such preferences have proliferated to the point where they benefit women as well as ethnic minorities who have recently arrived in this country, who have suffered no historical injustices at the hands of the U.S. government, and who are no doubt amazed to find themselves entitled to privileges denied to many U.S. citizens. It is not a polemical claim, merely a fact, to state that there are two standards of civil rights today: one for white males, another for women, blacks, and other minorities.

THE ADVENT OF BUSING

Precisely what happened in the workplace happened in schools, and around the same time. Using the model of proportional representation, courts directed public schools to use race as the basis for assignments. As Pierre Van Den Berghe puts it, "The federal government suddenly shifted its enormous weight from a policy of stamping out racial discrimination to one of mandating it. *Brown* was quite literally turned on its head."[80] How could courts transform the prohibitions of discrimination apparently stated by *Brown v. Board of Education* into requirements of discrimination? Here the strategy was to invoke the present effects of past discrimination. By imagining a situation in which discrimination did not exist and in which blacks and whites were distributed proportionally in each school, the court was able to justify race-conscious assignments and eventually forced busing in order to move toward the stipulated end of an integrated system. In a now-familiar gambit, race appeared to make a widely publicized exit from the legal system only to make a rapid reentry through the back door.

When Thurgood Marshall of the NAACP argued the *Brown* case before the Supreme Court he emphasized that he was asking only that legally mandated segregation be outlawed and that black students be allowed to attend their neighborhood schools.[81] As they had done many times before,[82] NAACP attorneys in oral argument repeatedly invoked a vision of color-blind jurisprudence and argued:

> The only thing that we ask for is that the state-imposed racial segregation be taken off, and to leave the county school board to assign children on any reasonable basis they want. If you have some other basis . . . any other basis, we have no objection. But just do not put in race or color as a factor.[83]

But a few years after the Supreme Court granted these petitions, the NAACP reversed its position and began to press for race-based assignments in order to compel integration. One reason for this was pugnacious resistance to enforcing the *Brown* decision in the South, where (as we might expect from the earlier example of streetcar opposition to segregation) private institutions such as restaurants rapidly complied with the law but powerful political forces mobilized against public school desegregation.[84] By 1964, a decade after the landmark ruling, segregation remained largely in place in many southern counties.[85] Now that people were keeping count, it could hardly escape notice that very few blacks and whites went to school together in the northern states either. The reason for this was not segregation laws but that blacks and whites tended to be concentrated in different areas, so that each group attended public schools in its own neighborhood. Yet were these residential patterns not themselves the product of historic discrimination? And were they not being exacerbated as blacks migrated to the northern cities and whites retreated to the suburbs? Impatiently, the courts and government agencies collaborated to ensure not just access to the neighborhood school as a right, but racial integration as a compelled reality.

The courts began the process of reviving racial classification in schools by ignoring the distinction (which Martin Luther King, Jr. understood) between desegregation and integration.[86] Desegregation is a restriction on government power. The state may not use race as the basis for school assignments. Desegregation permits racial separation as long as it is not compelled by government. Integration, by contrast, is a state-mandated result. The government overrides personal and parental choice in order to make sure that different racial groups get the same education and obtain it together. The contrast between desegregation and integration can be illustrated with the example of drinking fountains. Obviously drinking fountains are desegregated if anyone can use them. There is no requirement that whites and blacks drink out of particular water fountains at a predetermined rate, or in specified numbers. Desegregation establishes the principle of choice, whereas integration seeks to compel a particular result.[87] The Civil Rights Act of 1964 clearly endorsed desegregation rather than integration, and clarified the distinction.[88] Yet in the case of schools, unlike drinking fountains, courts came to consider desegregation truly accomplished only if whites and blacks were actually using the facilities in rough proportion to their numbers in society. In other words, courts ignored the distinction, central to a liberal society, between securing a right and guaranteeing its exercise.[89] Invoking proportional representation as the standard of justice, courts navigated around the seemingly clear language of the law to coerce integration in the name of enforcing desegregation, and to use the terms interchangeably to disguise this transition.[90]

In 1968, the same year as the Nixon administration's Philadelphia Plan instituting affirmative action, the Supreme Court embraced the principle of race-conscious school assignment.[91] In 1971, the year of the landmark *Griggs* decision, the Court first mandated school busing. The decision was justified in the name of overcoming the effects of past state-sponsored segregation,[92] yet two years later the Court insisted on busing in a northern case where no *de jure* segregation existed.[93] The Court now required mandatory integration not simply to counter mandatory segregation but because it assumed that all schools would be racially balanced in a world without discrimination, and that students would benefit from laws that helped to bring about this result.

On first examination, the busing decisions seem fundamentally at odds with the principles of *Brown v. Board of Education*. A careful reading of the *Brown* decision, however, shows that this is not so. Indeed the 1896 case of *Plessy v. Ferguson* approving segregation, the 1954 *Brown* case overturning it, and the 1971 *Swann* case mandating busing are all based on the same principle, which is a rejection of color blindness and a justification of government power to manipulate race to achieve an allegedly beneficial public goal.[94] No wonder that Thurgood Marshall, once an apostle of color blindness, became on the Supreme Court an energetic promoter of racial preferences and busing. Without any public acknowledgment of changing sides or adopting a dramatically new approach, Marshall proceeded to mobilize the power of government to achieve race-consious outcomes he deemed favorable under the circumstances. Without irony, in a 1986 decision, Marshall spurned the race-neutral principle articulated by Justice Harlan: "We must remember . . . that the principle that the Constitution is color-blind appeared only in the opinion of the lone dissenter."[95]

The Advent of Racial Redistricting

In addition to busing and affirmative action, racial separatism is evident in the way that public officials draw electoral districts. Once again proportional representation establishes the model: blacks, Hispanics, and other minorities are presumed to be entitled to be elected to office in roughly their ratio in the general population. The consequence of racial gerrymandering is a genuine crisis over the very meaning of democracy. "We ought to question the legitimacy of winner-take-all majority rule," writes Lani Guinier, a leading African American legal scholar. Guinier argues that blacks deserve more than an individual right to vote; as a group, they are entitled to "the equal opportunity to vote for a winning candidate."[96]

The Voting Rights Act of 1965 expressed the classic liberal view of democracy when it sought to guarantee that blacks, as citizens, could vote without hindrance for candidates of their choice in local and national elections. The problem, however, is that blacks are a minority in this country, and majority rule means that black votes do not guarantee black elected officials. Responding to intense lobbying from civil rights activist groups, Congress amended the Voting Rights Act in 1982 to permit the race-based construction of districts to help blacks secure proportional representation. "In the new context of voting rights," Andrew Kull writes, "the ultimate standard of a nondiscriminatory electoral system became the degree to which blacks in a given jurisdiction were elected to office."[97]

Government officials and courts are now engaged in an elaborate process of drawing districts in byzantine and complicated diagrams to guarantee minority representation. In some cases serpentine or Z-shaped districts must be fabricated, to ensure not simply a black majority but an overwhelming black majority of voters, taking into account the fact that blacks vote at a lower rate than whites. As Abigail Thernstrom concluded in a recent study, affirmative action has been brought into the voting booth.[98] Once the right to proportional representation was granted to one minority group, activists from other groups rushed to claim their share of the benefits. Even though Hispanics have historically been classified as white, the Mexican American Legal Defense Fund argued that they, like blacks, were victims of discrimination and should qualify for the benign manipulation of voting districts to assure their representation. As Peter Skerry documents, at first black groups resisted, seeking to protect their exclusive right to special consideration, but soon black activists changed their position and supported Hispanic demands on the grounds that minority representatives could form a coalition to advance collective minority interests.[99]

Oddly enough the problem of low minority representation that has provoked racial gerrymandering is largely a product of blacks living in integrated or mixed-race communities. After all, since blacks overwhelmingly vote for other blacks, when blacks are heavily concentrated in an area they are virtually assured of electing black representatives. In larger or more integrated settings, however, black voting power is dispersed. Ordinarily this should not be a problem, because blacks (like every other organized religious, social, and ethnic group) now have leverage. Such bargaining power, when used collectively, can swing close elections and pressure elected officials not to ignore a substantial voting bloc.

But blacks, Lani Guinier argues, are not like other religious and social groups. If they were, Madison's famous analysis of faction in Book 10 of *The Federalist* would apply, and blacks like other "factions" could move in and out of shifting majority and minority coalitions. Guinier insists, however, that blacks and whites constitute distinct ethnic groups with separate and conflicting interests, and that whites—largely because of racism—simply refuse to vote for black interests. Guinier insists that to dismantle race-based voting districts is to risk "resegregating Congress and disenfranchising African, Latino and Asian Americans."[100] Under a race-neutral one person, one vote system, she warns, white interests will always prevail and blacks will vote but their votes simply will not count. In a novel interpretation of democracy, Guinier argues that "fifty one percent of the people should not get 100 percent of the power."[101]

So what is the alternative to majority rule? Guinier proposes a wide range of possible remedies, some of them worth considering, others quite extreme. Perhaps her most controversial recommendation is that courts could give minority groups veto power over certain forms of legislation passed by the majority. She calls this "taking turns" at governing, yet her proposal is remarkably similar to one advanced in the previous century by pro-slavery advocate John Calhoun to give Southern states a minority veto over antislavery legislation passed by the federal government.[102] Guinier endorses a voting rights agenda, seeking "a distributive agenda premised on equality of condition, and not just freedom from overt discrimination."[103] Guinier's doctrine of group rights would fundamentally transform America's system of government by introducing a radical concept: a race-based division of power among contending ethnic factions.

Guinier's entire argument turns on a factual premise: the white majority simply will not vote for black interests. Abigail Thernstrom counters by pointing to numerous white-majority cities which have elected black mayors. David Dinkins was elected mayor of New York City, Douglas Wilder governor of Virginia. Two African American members of Congress, Gary Franks and J. C. Watts, were elected as Republicans by heavily white districts. As early as 1966 Edward Brooke, an African American, was elected as a Republican senator from Massachusetts, a state with a black population of less than 3 percent. Guinier is not impressed. African Americans who are elected by whites, she alleges, are typically not "authentic," which is to say they are not "politically, psychologically and culturally black."[104] Guinier's argument is that such blacks, like most whites, do not bother to represent black group interests.

But in a recent study *Black Faces, Black Interests,* African American political scientist Carol Swain concludes that Guinier's factual premises are wrong. Reviewing a variety of districts—"historically black, newly black, heterogeneous, and majority white"—Swain finds that "effective representation of black interests is in no danger of being diminished by either demographic changes or sell-out black politicians." Swain challenges the concept of distinct black and white group interests, arguing that black elected officials, like their white counterparts, respond to diverse constituencies through conventional techniques of persuasion, constituency services, and coalition-building. Swain argues that racial gerrymandering may increase minority representation but reduce minority *influence*—a result apparently borne out by the 1994 election in which the Democrats lost many marginal districts in part because minority voters had been gerrymandered out.[105] No wonder that some Republican strategists oppor-

tunistically support racial redistricting, not to enhance minority representation, but to create surrounding districts which end up being largely
white and potentially Republican.[106]

The Supreme Court, the final arbiter on these matters, has adopted an
increasingly hostile view of racially rigged voting districts, concluding in
recent rulings that they (in Justice Sandra Day O'Connor's vivid terms)
resemble an American form of apartheid. Yet in other decisions the
Court has allowed racial gerrymandering under specified circumstances.[107]
Justices Anthony Kennedy, David Souter, and O'Connor appear to be
spearheading the Court's basic approach in racial matters, namely that it
is permissible to subvert liberal procedures such as equality of rights and
majority rule as long as the subversion does not reach the point of public
embarrassment.

CIVIL RIGHTS AND WRONGS

The current trajectory of proportional representation is producing a
racialization of all aspects of public policy, for the simple reason that it
is virtually impossible to implement an initiative that does not disproportionately affect some group. So far courts have attempted to rein in
perceived excesses, but absent a countervailing principle there seem to
be no coherent grounds—apart from judicial whim—for such restraints. Consider the example of racial redistricting, which is a prototypical case of an attempt to preserve liberal procedures even while
securing a preconceived outcome. Yet if the goal is to ensure proportional representation for blacks, why bother to choreograph black districts in the hope that their majority-black populations will deliver a
black congressman; why not dispense with the procedural facade and
simply assign blacks 12 percent of all congressional seats, to be decided
by black-only elections?

We could go further. Each minority group could receive a designated
share of the federal budget, to be spent as its own representatives determine. Racial groups could also be allocated the right to enact a proportional share of the laws in the areas of foreign and social policy. Public
schools could be required to ensure racially balanced honor rolls, and not
to discipline a black student without simultaneously punishing a white
student. State universities could be directed to produce specified ethnic
ratios in their graduation rates. Police departments could be directed to
make sure that arrests conform to the racial breakdown of the population

at large, and juries could be instructed to consider proportional representation in reaching verdicts. Alternatively, each racial group could have its
own police force and independently administered judicial system.

At this stage the reader will probably balk, regarding such speculation
as feverish. But under the model of proportional representation, it seems
difficult to offer rational—as opposed to visceral—grounds for opposing
any of the above projects. After all, if disproportionate job qualifications
and school enrollment patterns are the product of historic patterns of
racism, can a plausible case not be made that low black graduation rates
or high black arrest rates are also the present effect of past discrimination? The logic of proportional representation already influences countless public policy choices such as whether the death penalty which
produces racially disparate execution rates is constitutional; whether the
location of toxic waste dumps in poor communities which are predominantly black constitutes "environmental racism," and whether ads that
do not show the required number of black models constitute illegal discrimination. As a consequence, many Americans are troubled by the ongoing racialization of American life, but seem uncertain about what is
producing it and what can be done about it.

Even African American activists who are promoters of racialization
find it difficult to justify themselves within the rhetorical parameters of
civil rights. Apparently seeking to preserve some semblance of family
continuity, Yolanda King, Martin Luther King, Jr.'s daughter, recently defended separatism on the grounds that "We must focus on differences,
until difference does not make a difference."[108] It is easy to be scornful
of such apparent incoherence, and to raise the prospect of a society in
which we are back to "separate but equal" and George Wallace's famous
chant, "Segregation now, segregation tomorrow, segregation forever."
But here it is helpful to make two distinctions. The first is between the
private and the public sphere: conduct which is voluntary should generally be permitted, while government-imposed racialization should be considered suspect. The second distinction is between race and ethnicity:
the former category is biological, the latter cultural. Let us apply these
distinctions to the case of Afro-American societies and black fraternities
which have proliferated on college campuses. In an earlier book I expressed doubts about such groups, on the grounds that although they are
voluntary they contribute to campus balkanization. But this is only a
problem if minority students spend most of their college lives ensconced
in ethnic enclaves.

Because the one-drop rule identifies blacks as a racial group, it is easy for many Americans to forget that African Americans are also an ethnic group with a shared history and to some degree a common culture. Gerald David Jaynes and Robin Williams write in *A Common Destiny,* "The long history of discrimination and segregation produced among blacks a heightened sense of group consciousness and a stronger orientation toward collective values and behavior than exists generally among Americans."[109] There is nothing wrong with people of like proclivities who share a historical tradition associating with each other on a voluntary basis. There is a counterargument which says, "But why can't they all be Americans?" The answer is that we are not limited to two identities: "individual" and "American." We also belong to other intermediate groups, such as families, churches, clubs, and so on. In this sense the classical liberal concept of the individual is too legalistic; it does not offer a rich enough acknowledgment of the multiple group affiliations that contribute to, indeed make up, our individuality. To criticize African Americans for forming groups is to confuse behavior that is public and racial with behavior that is private and ethnic.

The issue is not the legitimacy of minority organizations: it is what these groups actually do. Consider a sample of black organizations: National Association of Blacks in Criminal Justice, National Association of Black Journalists, National Association of Black-Owned Broadcasters, National Association for Equal Opportunity in Higher Education, Conference of Minority Public Administrators, Black Psychiatrists of America, Black Caucus of the American Library Association, American Association of Blacks in Energy, National Black Media Coalition, National Black Police Association, National Black Staff Network, National Coalition of Black Meeting Planners, National Conference of Black Mayors, National Council of Black Engineers and Scientists, National Forum for Black Public Administrators, and the National Minority Supplier Development Council.[110]

These are, for the most part, affirmative action groups. Even though many of them are private, their purpose is not simply to foster association and camaraderie. An equally important purpose, if not their main purpose, is to act as pressure groups within the private and public sector. They are formed under the aegis of racial preferences, and once established, they become vested interests within larger institutions, aggressively promoting race-based policies. They also act as a check on any efforts to limit racialization and balkanization: such efforts bring heated charges of insensitivity and racism. Very few companies and organizations are comfortable with confronting these pressures from within, which is one reason that racial preferences and race-based programs have become so thoroughly institutionalized and will prove difficult to eradicate. The point is that while voluntary racial association is fine, separatism becomes a problem when it intrudes on the public sphere and when it involves vested interests who form internal coalitions to promote minority objectives. Group separatism becomes a serious threat to liberalism when it is offered as the basis for entitlements, because then there is a direct conflict between individual rights and group claims. The problem becomes clearer when we examine the workings of the civil rights establishment.

THE RIGHTS ESTABLISHMENT

There is a class of colored people who make a business of keeping the troubles, the wrongs, and the hardships of the Negro race before the public. Some of these people do not want the Negro to lose his grievances, because they do not want to lose their jobs.
—Booker T. Washington[111]

Booker T. Washington's criticism, issued three quarters of a century ago, turns out to be severe but prophetic. Once the activists who fought alongside Martin Luther King, Jr. secured the color-blind regime they demanded, they probably should have focused on strict enforcement of nondiscrimination combined with a civic mission to raise the civilizational standards of the black community. They rejected this path, however, and denounced those who raised the issue of black cultural defects as racists and enemies of black progress.

During the mid to late 1960s, several white liberals such as Edward Banfield, Lee Rainwater, and Daniel Patrick Moynihan wrote about cultural dysfunctionalities in the black community. In his famous 1965 report, Moynihan warned that the black family was breaking down at a disturbing rate, and that this would lead to a sharp increase in welfare dependency.[112] Although Moynihan called for strong public policy measures to strengthen the black family, the very fact that he had dared to criticize black culture provoked outrage among many black scholars and white liberals.[113] Employing the rhetoric of cultural relativism, Bayard Rustin said, "What may seem to be a disease to the white middle class may be a healthy adaptation to the Negro lower class." Similarly Floyd

McKissick faulted the report because it "assumes that middle-class American values are the correct ones for everyone in America."[114] This assault on the Moynihan report as a sociological cover-up for racism was one of the early signposts of a liberal schism over the race issue. In subsequent years, several disaffected liberals would become neoconservatives. (Not Moynihan: he remains a maverick.)

The mainstream of the black leadership eschewed cultural reform in favor of racial preferences and race-based programs. One reason for this is an ideological commitment to equality of results, but another reason is that civil rights activists found the color-conscious approach far more profitable for themselves. Many of them became black professionals, in other words, by becoming professional blacks. Consider a recent case study of how the civil rights establishment operates. When Denny's restaurant found itself charged with several cases of racial discrimination against black patrons in 1994, the NAACP entered into behind-the-scenes negotiations with Flagstar, the parent company that owns Denny's. The NAACP's goal was not to secure just compensation for black patrons denied service. Nor was it to ensure future nondiscrimination by Denny's. Rather, NAACP officials threatened national boycotts and further bad publicity unless Denny's agreed to enter into a $1 billion "fair share" agreement. With a political gun to its head, Denny's capitulated.

According to its "fair share" agreement, now in effect, Denny's guarantees an increase in the number of minority franchises by more than fifty by 1997, a minimum of 12 percent of food and supply purchases to black-owned businesses by the year 2000, and preferential hiring for black managers and workers. Denny's also made a $68,000 contribution directly to the NAACP in 1994. The restaurant chain's first payoff went to a black consortium called NDI Incorporated which, as a consequence, promptly doubled its annual revenues from $25 million to $50 million. The NAACP has entered into some forty "fair share" agreements yielding, by the NAACP's own estimate, more than $40 million. NDI President James Holden said, "The past, in our minds, has driven us to this opportunity." Nor was this the end of the matter. Civil rights activists in the Justice Department assisted in filing a class action suit against Denny's, inviting blacks across the country to come forward and allege past discrimination. Some four thousand African Americans obligingly asserted that they had received discriminatory service and were entitled to compensation. In May 1994 Denny's agreed to pay $54 million to settle the cases. The money will be divided among the black plaintiffs, activist law firms handling the case on a contingency basis, and black charities like the United Negro College Fund.[115]

Guy Saperstein, attorney for several plaintiffs suing Denny's, is the model of the contemporary civil rights lawyer. According to a *Wall Street Journal* profile, Saperstein's California firm has made tens of millions of dollars filing class action claims of discrimination against large companies. Among Saperstein's racial trophies are a $132 million damage award against Shoney's and nearly $90 million against State Farm Insurance. A former sixties activist who once defended the Black Panthers, Saperstein now lives in a palatial home in Beverly Hills, with all the accoutrements of affluence including three BMWs and a personal psychic. His wife comments that "he doesn't feel he has to be as poor as his clients to be politically correct."[116]

The Denny's case typifies the Machiavellian scheme that has come to characterize the civil rights establishment. Central to the operation is the threat of public accusations of racism. The original complaints against Denny's—some probably substantive, others seemingly dubious—create the political opening. The various divisions of the civil rights establishment quickly mobilize. The government's enforcement arm supplies the heavy-handed threat of federal intervention. Celebrity attorneys team up with the state to threaten a major lawsuit. The NAACP plays "good cop, bad cop," offering to work with Denny's to help it survive the onslaught. The consequence is that everybody concerned makes a considerable amount of money, while at the same time professing to have helped strike a blow against American racism. From one point of view undoubtedly some good is achieved; from another, it is hard to deny that we have witnessed a well-executed racial shakedown. The Denny's case dramatizes the way that civil rights victories today combine elements of justice with elements of expediency. One may say that although they contribute to the offering, the moneychangers have entered the temple of civil rights. How naive, in this context, seems the headline in the Chicago *Sun-Times:* "Denny's Pact Combats Racism."[117]

As the Denny's episode indicates, civil rights has gone from a specific crusade to a way of life. Many black activists who once came from poor and rural backgrounds have found, upon winning their battles for legal equality, that they do not wish to return to obscurity. In the civil rights establishment, these activists have found a way to turn racial victimization, which was their historical condition, into a successful career. Having come to do good, they have stayed to do well. Recent controversy over the leadership of the NAACP is not merely a dispute about the group's direction but also one over access to the comforts of the civil rights lifestyle. In former NAACP chairman William Gibson's case, that included first-class airfares, stretch limousine travel, lavish hotel and restaurant visits, and hundreds of thousands of dollars in expenses charged to the organization's credit cards.[118] Nor do these high-living activists seem to see any reason to be apologetic: who says that one cannot fight racism and live opulently at the same time?

Although unelected by the minority community at large, the leaders of the civil rights organizations such as the NAACP and the National Council of La Raza have moved quickly to proclaim themselves the legitimate representatives of racial minorities. If politicians refuse to work with the NAACP, the "black community" is said to be outraged. If reporters decline to interview the National Council of La Raza, Hispanics as a group are said to be furious. The same routine has played out with women's rights and homosexual rights groups as well. The risk of incurring charges of bigotry makes it difficult for specious claims of political representation to be challenged by outsiders. External criticism or even internal dissent on the part of minorities is quickly branded as "hostile to black interests," "setting the cause back," "threatening to reverse hard-won gains," "preventing meaningful equality," "sending the wrong message," or simply "opposing civil rights."

What this rhetorical Manicheanism conceals is that civil rights is now, to a large extent, a fund-raising operation. Groups like the NAACP work in coalition with other activist groups such as the National Organization for Women, the National Education Association, and the AFL-CIO to win political and financial benefits through horse-trading. For example, the NAACP might support a feminist bill on comparable worth in exchange for NOW's backing for a racial preference measure. There is nothing unusual about such bartering, of course, except that it converts civil rights from a moral ideal that transcends partisan politics into another special interest cause that may or may not warrant public support. Consider some of the financial benefits that constitute America's racial ransom and go along with the civil rights establishment lifestyle in the 1990s:

Federal Government Benefits. Each year U.S. government awards hundreds of millions of dollars in set-aside programs that are awarded on a quota basis to minority organizations and businesses. Such programs exist at the Department of Energy, the Department of State, the National Aeronautics and Space Agency, the Small Business Administration, the Federal Communications Commission, and virtually every division of the U.S. government. In 1990, the total value of federal set-asides exceeded $8.5 billion.[119]

The Defense Department is required to hand over at least 5 percent of procurement, construction, research, and testing contracts to minority businesses or to historically black colleges. Many Defense Department agencies do not allow nonminorities to bid on selected projects. Approximately $5 billion each year is rationed on the basis of race to credentialed minority contractors.

The Surface Transportation Act, first enacted in 1987, requires the Department of Transportation to spend not less than 10 percent of federal highway and transit funds with disadvantaged minority businesses. Airports, for example, must ensure that 10 percent of concession contracts go to certified minority- and women-owned businesses.

The Public Works Employment Act, passed by Congress in 1977 and subsequently renewed and extended, requires that one-tenth of federal funds used for construction and other projects must go to minority contractors and subcontractors, defined as businesses at least 51 percent owned by U.S. citizens who are "Negroes, Spanish-speaking, Orientals, Indians, Eskimos and Aleuts." Each year about $10 billion of taxpayer money is diverted to subsidize these minority profit-making operations.

The Small Business Administration each year awards between $3 and $5 billion in contracts reserved for disadvantaged businesses, the vast majority of them owned by minority entrepreneurs. Some 4,000 black, Hispanic, Asian, American Indian, and Puerto Rican businesses participate. From 1966 to 1977, of more than 3,500 minority businesses that had collected more than $2 billion in subsidies, only 150 had graduated from the program and only 33 showed a positive net worth by market criteria. Even the term "disadvantaged" is relative: minority entrepreneurs qualify with a net worth of under $250,000, excluding the combined value of their home and their minority business.[120]

The Federal Communications Commission awards minority preferences and set-asides in the purchase and sale of radio and television stations. Recently these race-based allocations have extended to the assignment of thousands of licenses to operate wireless telephone, interactive video and data-service businesses. Once again, minority beneficiaries are scarcely disadvantaged. In 1990, former Senate candidate Harvey Gantt invested less than $1,000 as a minority shareholder in a TV station which was awarded to him and his partners on a preferential basis; Gantt and his partners promptly sold the station, netting Gantt a profit of $450,000. During the 1980s, black millionaire Vernon Jordan applied under the minority category for two Washington area radio stations: another company got them, but only after it paid Jordan's group $765,000 to withdraw its bid. Others who have purchased media properties under race-preference schemes include entertainers Bill Cosby and Quincy Jones, and athletes O.J. Simpson, Julius Erving, and Patrick Ewing.[121]

State and Local Government Benefits. By 1989, at least thirty-six states and 190 local governments had adopted minority set-asides, earmarking a fraction, sometimes as high as 25 to 50 percent, of their expenditures for so-called minority business enterprises and women business enterprises. Although publicized as a measure to fight discrimination, virtually all these set-asides work by circumventing low-bid auction schemes which are designed to award contracts on the basis of efficiency rather than patronage.

Yet when the Supreme Court ruled that states could not continue such programs absent proof of actual discrimination in the relevant sector, civil rights activists both inside and outside the government pressured states and municipalities to assemble statistics that would withstand legal scrutiny. George LaNoue reports that in the last few years jurisdictions have spent or contracted to spend more than $30 million in taxpayer money on such studies. Atlanta's study alone was more than a thousand pages long and cost more than $500,000.

The city of Miami hired the accounting firm of KPMG Peat Marwick to locate discrimination in the city's own practices. When the firm produced what would ordinarily sound like good news—it found no pattern of discrimination—Miami public officials were furious. "The whole purpose of this study was for you to prove that there was a disparity in minority hiring," raged Vice Mayor Miller Dawkins, an African American. Xavier Suarez, the Cuban-born mayor, termed Peat Marwick's findings "a pain" and commented on the study: "We should never have done it." Other firms that fail to produce statistics proving discrimination find themselves in disgrace. "When I'm around people who support set-asides," remarks one scholar, John Lunn, "they'll say: oh, you're the one who couldn't find discrimination."[122]

Private-Sector Benefits. Private companies have also set up special programs for doing business with minority suppliers and contractors. According to *Black Enterprise,* Ameritech's Minority and Women Business Enterprise Program purchased $127 million in goods and services from minority vendors in 1990.[123] Avon's in-house publication *Diversity* boasts that the company spends more than $100 million on contracts with minority- and women-owned businesses.[124] In 1991 AT&T spent more than $500 million on purchases from more than two thousand minority-owned businesses. Chrysler Corporation claims to have parted with $700 million for the same purpose, and General Motors an astounding $1 billion. The National Minority Supplier Development Council, a trade group that brings minority businesses together with large companies, reports that corporate America spends approximately $20 billion in goods and services from minority-owned concerns.[125]

Other private sources also finance the civil rights industry. Philanthropic foundations such as Ford and Rockefeller invest tens of millions of dollars in the civil rights establishment each year. The 1993 annual report of the Ford Foundation listed the following grants: $595,000 to the Puerto Rican Legal Defense and Education Fund, $675,000 to the NAACP, $750,000 to the NAACP Legal Defense Fund, another $775,000 to the NAACP Special Contribution Fund, $850,000 to the Mexican American Legal Defense and Education Fund, and $1.8 million to the National Council of La Raza.[126] These sorts of grants are responsible for sustaining activist organizations like the Mexican American Legal Defense Fund. Although it claims to represent the interests of Hispanics as a group, MALDEF's 1994 annual report shows that nearly 70 percent of its annual budget came from corporate and foundation grants.[127]

Now it should be clear why the civil rights establishment has a vested interest in the continuation of spectacular episodes of racism: these provide an important justification for continuing transfer payments to minority activists. This is not to suggest that charges of racism are always false, only that they are likely to be wildly exaggerated because, as the Denny's case shows, they pay handsome dividends. And where racism does not exist, sometimes it has to be invented. This explains the rhetorical militancy of civil rights activists, even when the occasion does not seem to warrant such excess. At the same time, today's race merchants realize that they should not appear too militant. Theirs is a nuanced business. Tactically, they need to maintain a powerful antiracist stance which requires threats and accusations. Many civil rights activists have perfected the art of moral blackmail. Warnings of underclass violence are a favorite tactic for seasoned veterans like Jesse Jackson and Benjamin Chavis: either the government pays protection money, or Americans should prepare for a "long, hot summer." As Daniel Patrick Moynihan observed many years ago, the image of a restive and violent underclass gives the race merchants "an incomparable weapon with which to threaten white America."[128]

Yet the race merchants recognize that they need to appeal to the good-will of whites for a continuing stream of funds and resources to keep the civil rights industry in business. Thus their political strategy involves an odd combination of intimidation, gaudy tales of woe, and sociological jargon about the virtues of inclusion and diversity. Basically the tactic is one that Jill Nelson terms walking "the thin line between Uncle Tom-ming and Mau Mauing."[129] One black scholar acknowledges the activist dilemma in an article titled, "How Do We Rage Safely?"[130] The race merchants have developed a political technique that alternates between the outstretched hand and the clenched fist.

It should now be apparent why the one-drop rule serves important in-stitutional objectives for black activists today, even as it once served vital interests for white racists. In the contemporary environment, the one-drop rule guarantees that the African American community remains as large as possible: all mixed-race persons with any black heritage continue to be identified as "black." As F. James Davis points out, this classifica-tion increases the political base of the civil rights establishment, as well as providing tangible rewards: more racially designated black districts, more federal funding for race-based programs.[131] Paradoxically the rule that forms the essence of American racism is now the operating principle of the civil rights establishment.

THE NEW BLACK BOURGEOISIE

The effect of affirmative action has been to accelerate the growth of the first sizable middle class in the history of African Americans.[132] This class began to emerge gradually after World War II, as the new economic and political climate provided more opportunities. As Bart Landry points out in *The New Black Middle Class,* the group constituted a distinct social phenomenon by the 1960s, as desegregation and antidiscrimination laws went into effect.[133] Yet although scholars debate their precise effect, racial preferences have undoubtedly helped to solidify the black middle class.

As of 1994 only about one-third of blacks were poor; the rest were middle-class or better off. Approximately 16 percent of black families currently earn more than $50,000, 27 percent earn between $25,000 and $50,000, 30 percent earn between $10,000 and $25,000, and 26 percent earn under $10,000.[134] What this means is that poor blacks are now a minority of African Americans. Yet in important ways, their condition has worsened in recent years. "What happened in black America in the era of affirmative action is this," Stephen Carter writes. "Middle-class black people are better off and lower-class black people are worse off."[135] William Julius Wilson remarks:

> Talented and educated blacks are now entering positions of prestige and influence at a rate comparable to, and in some situations exceeding, that of whites with equivalent qualifications. It is equally clear that the black underclass is in a hopeless state of economic stagnation, falling further and further behind the rest of society.[136]

How did this cleavage come about, and why did it not occur earlier? The reason is that prior to the 1950s, segregation imposed a coercive economic and social homogeneity upon the black community. Bayard Rustin once observed that before the civil rights movement, eminent blacks like diplomat Ralph Bunche were just as likely to be refused service at a restaurant or convenience store as illiterate porters and janitors.[137] More important, segregation compelled blacks from all walks of life to live in the same neighborhood. In a sense, segregation subsidized the ghetto, because it kept black doctors, lawyers, teachers, and businessmen in the same community as black criminals, alcoholics, and delinquents.

But this situation changed dramatically in an era of affirmative action. The most able blacks seized the new openings made available by the civil rights establishment to dramatically improve their circumstances. Racial preference was a special boon because although it modified admissions and job standards for blacks in comparison with whites, it preserved the merit ideal in that it favored the most qualified blacks. Thus the group we may call (adapting William Julius Wilson's phrase) "the truly advantaged" was able to insulate itself from competition with whites, while competing only against poor blacks for a virtually foreordained result. "My children," black columnist William Raspberry wryly acknowledges, "compete with the children of Anacostia, Watts, Hough, Cabrini Green and Overtown. This is a competition that they are likely to win."[138]

As soon as they were financially able, millions of middle-class blacks did what sensible people do in such situations: they moved out of the ghetto. As a result, they removed a crucial layer of social support that kept the inner city generally poor but nevertheless generally safe and habitable. When the group left, to some degree its members took middle-class standards with them. Thus the rapid departure of the black middle class directly contributed to a deterioration of basic civilizational norms in the ghetto.

Black conservatives such as Robert Woodson and black nationalists such as Nathan Hare have criticized the civil rights establishment for abandoning and betraying poor blacks. Woodson accuses civil rights activists of running a "Poverty Pentagon" and sponsoring an "alms race." Hare writes that professional blacks have become "diplomatic couriers" between the African Amerian community and "the white power structure." With one or two exceptions, Hare writes, none of these so-called leaders would be recognized on the streets of Detroit or Harlem. "About the only place anyone will follow the average dignitary is to a banquet hall or ballroom."[139] Woodson and Hare are expressing frustration at the civil rights establishment's neglect of the black underclass. Yet it should not come as a surprise that most civil rights organizations do not serve the basic needs of the underclass; this is not their constituency.

While the underclass cannot rely on the civil rights establishment, however, the civil rights establishment does rely on the black underclass. This is the dirty little secret of the race merchants. As Glenn Loury writes, "The suffering of the poorest blacks creates a fund of political capital upon which all members of the group can draw when pressing racially based claims."[140] Not only this, but as the National Research Council reports, "A large proportion of lower-status blacks receive public assistance and community services from programs that are disproportionately staffed by black professionals."[141] The point is that the civil rights establishment has a vested interest in the continuation of black poverty. What E. Franklin Frazier wrote of the black bourgeoisie in the 1950s is even more true of the civil rights establishment: "The lip service which they give to solidarity with the masses very often disguises their exploitation of the masses."[142]

No one is suggesting that civil rights activists are responsible for creating the ghetto, or that in a human sense they do not wish their less fortunate brethren well. The guild interest of the civil rights establishment, however, is staked on the continuing and conspicuous horrors of the underclass. If the underclass were to start prospering, many Americans would ask why millions of dollars in transfers and set-asides continue to go to the relatively well-off class of professional blacks. Absent the ghetto, would not the political justification for giving Jesse Jackson's children a preference to get into the best universities and obtain the most desirable jobs vanish?

LIBERAL FRUSTRATION, BLACK RAGE

Many liberals witnessed the rise of the black middle class over the past few decades with great relief. "We all said: Thank God for the black middle class," says Christopher Jencks. The liberal hope, although never quite stated this way, was that as blacks entered the middle class, they would start being middle class and stop being black. In other words, many liberals anticipated the interests of the new group being shaped less by race and more by socioeconomic status. But this hope proved to be an illusion because many middle-class blacks seem to realize very well that the reason they are in the middle or upper-middle class is because they are black. Consequently William Julius Wilson seems to be on a quixotic mission when he urges middle-class blacks to support class-based rather than race-based policies.[143] In an era of affirmative action, few blacks are likely to embrace such proposals when they know that it is race that helps to pay the mortgage.

Viewing the emergence of the black middle class in retrospect, we have to qualify our praise of the civil rights establishment. Its victory turns out to be Pyrrhic. On the one hand, it has helped millions of blacks escape the debilitation of poverty. On the other, this very achievement has accelerated the urban decay that now provides the best rationale for the persistence of racial preferences and monetary payoffs to the civil rights establishment. Black flight on the part of the African American middle class seems to have contributed to intense feelings of guilt. There are two reasons for this: first, many middle-class blacks know that they have abandoned their poorer brothers and sisters; and second, many realize that their present circumstances became possible, and many of their contemporary racial privileges persist, solely because of the heart-wrenching sufferings of the underclass. This recognition can be expected to produce, within many in the black middle class, a sense of being trapped. They relish their new circumstances, but are angry about their consequences.

Black rage arises out of the knowledge that although whites are primarily to blame for historical oppression, the black middle class is also sadly complicit in the contemporary agony of poor blacks. Middle-class African

Americans may feel a moral kinship with poor blacks, but studies of black philanthropy show that as a group they do little to provide financial help, which seems to be viewed as a government function.[144] Ordinarily such neglect might seem unremarkable, but other ethnic groups have collectively advanced in this country by setting up ladders of opportunity for their less privileged members. Moreover, blacks, more than any other group, stress the virtues of ethnic unity, denouncing fellow African Americans who dissent from the civil rights agenda as traitors and Uncle Toms. Yet even as whites who oppose preferences for blacks are reviled as racists, it is difficult for intelligent observers of all races to ignore the fact that, for the civil rights establishment, equal opportunity remains a rhetorical weapon although it has become a practical obstacle. Indeed liberal antiracism now sanctions state-sponsored discrimination and embraces the ideological premise of the one-drop rule. By a curious somersault of history, the antiracist has become the mirror image of his enemy.

7

IS AMERICA A RACIST SOCIETY?

The Problem of Rational Discrimination

It is utterly exhausting being black in America—physically, mentally and emotionally. There is no respite or escape from your badge of color.
—Marian Wright Edelman[1]

The contemporary division between whites and blacks in America arises out of the white conviction that the civil rights movement achieved its antiracist objective and recognized the basic rights of blacks, and the black conviction that despite changes in the law, racism remains the central problem.[2] Many whites do not deny the existence of racism, but view it as greatly abated, more a case of "the way we were" rather than "the way we are now." Blacks, by contrast, tend to see racism as different in appearance today but not in reality; for them, racism may have burrowed underground but it remains deeply embedded in the national psyche and in American institutions. This perception gap between blacks and whites on the issue of race—what Richard Wright once termed a conflict over the nature of reality[3]—is politically dangerous because it balkanizes the society into hostile camps that cannot effectively communicate with each other. A breakdown in goodwill can make a negotiated peace difficult, and the possibility of conflict becomes real, with a future event supplying the trigger. Moreover, it is important to figure out whether blacks or whites are right in their assessment of American racism, because no issue of social justice is more important for a multiracial democracy than whether it treats its minority groups fairly. Charges of bigotry against blacks are worth examining because they are the paradigm case of white racism.

Is it possible to resolve this clash of perceptions that has itself become a major obstacle to interracial understanding? I believe that it is, but to do so we must question many of our assumptions about racism. Most of us take for granted that what we call "racism" is based on irrational hostility, that its sources are "prejudices" and "stereotypes," and that their consequence is unwarranted "discrimination." Writing as early as 1966, Michael Sovern expressed the conventional liberal view that racial discrimination is "unfair, inhumane, and utterly without justification of any kind. Assessed in the light of the damage it does to our society, it is costly, wasteful and explosive."[4] America's entire apparatus of civil rights laws and policies is based on this premise.

Yet is the premise true? This chapter challenges the prevailing liberal paradigm, and concludes that only by abandoning it can we understand the way in which the black-white conflict of visions arises out of a radical social transformation: racism and discrimination are fundamentally different now than in the past. My basic conclusion is that whites view racial discrimination today as a rational response to black group traits, while blacks view it as an immoral assessment of individuals who do not conform to group patterns of behavior. Moreover, both the white and black understanding are reasonable and compatible with each other; neither group is "seeing things." If this thesis is correct, then much of our current vocabulary of race is obsolete, and we should modify our educational remedies and antidiscrimination laws to reflect the new situation.

ACCUSATIONS OF RACISM

One of the profoundest ironies of the past few decades is that as laws and policies outlawing racism and discrimination have been instituted and expanded, charges of racism have multiplied. Many scholars and activists assert what most African Americans seem to believe: that America remains a deeply racist society, and racism (although more camouflaged in its expression) may even be on the rise.

- "This is a racist society, and it will be for a long time to come," says civil rights activist Roger Wilkins.[5]

- "Racism is alive and well in America," African American educator Johnnetta Cole writes. "We have a collective sense that we are still not free."[6]
- "What does it take to be successful in America?" asks Coca-Cola executive Charles Morrison. "I'll tell you what it takes—being white, that's what."[7]
- "Racism . . . infects our economic institutions, our cultural and political institutions, and the daily interactions of individuals," legal scholar Richard Delgado writes.[8]
- "Racism has become fashionable once again," charges Henry Louis Gates, Jr.[9]
- Legal scholar Kimberle Crenshaw asserts that "racism is the central ideological underpinning of American society."[10]
- "This society is chronically racist, sexist, and homophobic," remarks African American philosopher Cornel West.[11]

An impressive gallery of incidents—some infamous, others relatively unknown—support these allegations. Rodney King was excessively and sadistically beaten by Los Angeles policemen. Blacks were harassed, brutalized, and killed in Bensonhurst and Howard Beach. Each year Skinheads and white supremacist groups threaten and harm African Americans. Susan Smith blamed a black man for kidnapping her two children and later confessed to drowning them herself. Black families in certain parts of the country have witnessed crosses burning on their front lawns. Based on their interviews with middle-class blacks, Joe Feagin and Melvin Sikes have collected more than a hundred reports of racial discrimination which lead them to conclude:

> Racism shapes our paradigmatic assumptions about life and the social world. A black American's perspective comes to embed a repertoire of responses to hostile and racist acts by whites. No amount of hard work and achievement, no amount of money, resources and success, can protect black people from the persisting ravages of white racism in their everyday lives.[12]

Discrimination so rampant must spring from racism that is deeply ingrained in the white psyche. However unpopular they are to utter, such views occasionally find their way into the public domain.

- A few years ago, the late sportscaster Howard Cosell, in reporting a brilliant play by a black football star, blurted out, "Look at the little monkey go."[13]

- In 1990 CBS commentator Andy Rooney was suspended for a month from *60 Minutes* for allegedly making remarks offensive to blacks and homosexuals.[14]
- In 1991 a North Carolina school teacher was fired for frequently calling American Indian students "wagon burners" and black students "jungle bunnies."[15]
- A New Jersey man raised an uproar when he sent a "gorilla gram" to the township's only elected black councilman, congratulating him on his 1992 election victory.[16]
- In 1993 Cincinnati Reds owner Marge Schott was fined and suspended for a year for using terms like "nigger" and "monkeys" to refer to African American baseball players.[17]
- That same year Senator Ernest Hollings angered many blacks by making jokes about Africans "getting a good meal" at international conferences so they could avoid "eating each other."[18]
- In 1994 a white professor at a historically black college in Florida brought on a complaint of racial harassment for warning African American students against having a "nigger mentality."[19]

Such examples have inspired a campaign of sensitivity education in American institutions. Campuses routinely conduct workshops in racial tolerance. Newspapers bring in counselors to explore bigoted attitudes. Some scholars have even called for outlawing the expression of stereotypical and racially offensive beliefs.[20] Legal scholar Catharine MacKinnon goes so far as to find "expressive value" in minority students' destruction of newspapers that offended their sensitivities.[21] One reason for these draconian measures is the belief, articulated by literary critic Stanley Fish, that racially provocative speech is indistinguishable from, and leads to, racist acts.[22] Indeed there are indications that racist perceptions lead to racial discrimination. In September 1991 the TV show *Prime Time Live* sent two twenty-eight-year-old men, Glen Brewer who is black, and John Kuhnen who is white, to shop in stores, try to rent apartments, and apply for the same job, all in the city of St. Louis. The result:

> At several stores, Mr. Kuhnen gets instant service. Mr. Brewer is ignored except at a record store, where a salesman keeps a close eye on him, without offering any assistance. When they go for a walk, separately on the same street, a police car passes Mr. Kuhnen but slows down to give Mr. Brewer a once-over. At a car dealership, Mr. Kuhnen is offered a lower price and better fi-

nancing terms than Mr. Brewer. Inquiring about a job at a dry cleaner that has advertised for help, Mr. Kuhnen is told jobs are still available, Mr. Brewer is told that the positions are taken. Following up a for-rent sign, Mr. Kuhnen is promptly offered an apartment, which he does not take. Ten minutes later, Mr. Brewer is told it has been rented for hours.[23]

The question is whether these troubling incidents are infrequent or typical. One of the problems with the extensive literature seeking to demonstrate systematic racism is that it conveys an aura of unreality. In Andrew Hacker's *Two Nations,* the author conducted an experiment among his white students at Queens College in New York to find out how racist they were. He asked them how much they would have to be paid to be black, and apparently the average sum demanded was one million dollars per year. Hacker concludes that being white in America is worth one million dollars annually, since "this is the value that white people place on their own skins."[24] Yet Hacker's test might have taken an interesting turn had he posed the same question to his black students. How much would they have to be paid to be white? Many young African Americans today are light enough to pass for white, yet despite the reduced risk of being victims of racism their refusal to do so suggests that they attach a high value to their black identity. If Hacker is right, blacks on average should be willing to pay one million dollars, the present value of whiteness in America. To take the experiment further, how much would Hacker's male students have to be paid to be female, or the other way around? Hacker's experiment proves nothing more than that most people are reluctant to give up their identities.

African American scholar Derrick Bell offers a no less unique technique for demonstrating the pervasiveness of white racism. In his latest book *Faces at the Bottom of the Well,* he devotes a chapter to a story, "The Space Traders," which has been made into a movie. What would happen, Bell asks, if invaders from outer space offered to solve every problem plaguing the country, including the deficit and health and environmental problems, all in exchange for selling black people into slavery? Bell slyly suggests that confronted with the alien bargain, whites would be awfully tempted. He concludes that the probability that whites would accept the alien bargain shows that, underneath their egalitarian rhetoric, whites are incorrigible racists.[25] Although Bell's work reveals a supple imagination, it is hard to see how his hypothetical dilemmas prove much about the real-world existence of racism.

Yet Hacker and Bell are taken very seriously by many blacks and white liberals. Perhaps the reason for this is that they are seen as offering suggestive parables rather than strict proofs. The popularity of their books among African Americans indicates that their ideas do strike a note of metaphorical truth. They fit into the liberal expectation that racism is real, even when it is not apparent. Yet other scholars use a more concrete approach. In a 1992 article, Henry Louis Gates, Jr. brought such theorizing down to earth by identifying what are clearly the most keenly felt charges. Gates cited routine indignities suffered by blacks, such as "the unwillingness of cab drivers to pick us up," and he also alleged systematic racial discrimination: in hiring, in the availability of loans and credit, and in criminal justice.[26]

DRIVE-BY RACISTS

The alleged racism of cabdrivers who refuse to pick up black males is a virtually mandatory entry in the ledger of discrimination maintained by many black scholars and activists. Cornel West gives an embittered account of being passed up by ten taxis in New York.[27] Columnist Clarence Page writes that he must dress well so that he is not confused with a welfare recipient.[28] Andrew Hacker pronounces white cabdrivers "patently racist."[29] To assess the justice of such charges, let us consider an interesting complaint filed by Gregory Wright in June 1993 in the *Washington Post:*

> As an African American, I am fed up with Washington taxicabs, fed up with having to flag down five cabs before finding one that will take me home, fed up with feeling anger, embarrassment and frustration when cabdrivers swear they are off-duty and then pick up a white customer before I can get around the corner. Taxidrivers, many of whom come from Africa, the Caribbean and the Middle East, say they don't want to pick up African American passengers because they are afraid of being robbed, assaulted or murdered. One Nigerian cabdriver told me he only picks up African Americans who are well dressed and look like businessmen. For African Americans, this discrimination can be inconvenient and downright humiliating.[30]

It is easy to sympathize with the indignation expressed at such flagrant acts of racial discrimination. Such experiences when made routine can constitute an unacceptable denial of the right of law-abiding citizens to fair and equal treatment in the daily business of life. In 1993, the Lawyers' Committee for Civil Rights conducted an informal survey which found that one-third of taxidrivers routinely refuse to stop for black customers. "This is a problem of scandalous proportions," remarked Joe Sellers, who directed the study.[31] The law in the District of Columbia and many other cities penalizes taxidrivers who discriminate on the basis of race. The Washington, D.C., human rights department has an official procedure for investigating complaints of drive by discrimination. The district's taxicab commissioner employs a dozen full-time inspectors to patrol the streets hailing cabs and recording the license numbers of those who discriminate in the way they treat passengers. The usual fine is $500 for a first offense; future wrongdoing can lead to a suspended license.[32]

Wright's complaint describes precisely the sort of behavior that could be expected of a racist. Yet according to Wright's account, African, Caribbean, and Middle Eastern cabdrivers also seem reluctant to pick up young African American males. (Indeed most cabdrivers in Washington, D.C., are nonwhite.) Moreover, the refusal of a Nigerian taxidriver is not absolute: he will pick up blacks, but only if they are suitably dressed. His discrimination seems not be to based simply on an automatic reflex conditioned on skin color but is also based on other aspects of appearance— in other words, it may have a rational basis.

To discover the perspective of the accused racists, I took up the issue during my travels with a number of taxidrivers in New York, Washington, Chicago, and other cities. Most of them denied that they refuse to pick up every black male, although some admitted that to do so was an occupational hazard, and all ridiculed the notion that cabdrivers pass up black women. But many groused that African American passengers frequently leave no tip and sometimes beat the fare, and virtually all acknowledged that as a consequence of previous threats, robberies, and assaults they employ a kind of heightened scrutiny before they will stop for young black men. Riddick Bragg is a middle-aged African American who drives a Yellow Cab in the nation's capital. "I don't have a problem picking up anybody, but I have to be careful. I won't pick up three black men at one time. If I pick up two, I sit one up front. There are some places I simply won't go. Listen, I've had a gun pointed at the back of my head. I have to look after myself, because no one else will."

"This racism stuff is all bullshit," one African student who was driving to put himself through school told me. "I'm not going to pass up a fare, which is money in my pocket. But I don't want to get robbed. You know what the black crime rate is in New York? Do you want me to risk a gun to my head, man? What's wrong with you?"

A white driver in Chicago told me, "No exceptions, pal. I never pick up niggers."

"You don't like blacks?" I asked.

"Not blacks. Niggers."

"That sounds like racism to me."

"Hey, that's crap. I pick up older blacks all the time. I have no problem with giving black women a ride. My black buddies won't pick up no niggers. I ain't no more racist than they are."

Similar sentiments surface when the national media report on African American charges of discrimination by cabdrivers. "Drivers have been murdered, wounded and beaten, thousands robbed or defrauded," J. R. Green, a white taxidriver, wrote to the *New York Times*. "The one effective way of protecting against the murderous thieves who prey on us is to exercise experienced discretion in whom we pick up."[33] Gerald Schaeffer, president of the American Cab Association, said simply, "It's fear."[34] An older black driver bluntly told the *Washington Post* he would not pick up young black males because "I'd rather be fined than have my wife a widow."[35]

These fears seem to be borne out by cabdriver muggings and killings. In August 1994 Keith Moore, a thirty-eight-year-old cabdriver and single father, was found with the keys in the ignition and two bullet wounds in his head. His friends told the *Washington Post* that he never worried about picking up passengers in questionable neighborhoods no matter what the time of day. If he had exercised prudence, his colleague Louis Richardson said, echoing the view of many other Yellow Cab drivers and managers, he probably would be alive today.[36] The U.S. Labor Department recently reported that driving a cab is the riskiest job in America, with occupational homicide rates higher than those for bartenders, gas station attendants, and policemen.[37]

These facts suggest how hollow it sounds to accuse cabdrivers of "prejudices" and "stereotypes" when their perceptions seem to be based on empirical reality. While we can be sure that racist taxidrivers would discriminate, it is not clear that all taxidrivers who discriminate are racist. Indeed cabdriver discrimination cannot be viewed as a simple case of irrational and socially destructive behavior that should inspire public outrage and punishment; it turns out that legitimate competing interests are at stake. African American males have a right to be concerned about their convenience and dignity, but cabdrivers too are entitled to care about their property and safety. In these situations, are cabdrivers intolerant, or are young black males intolerable? Whose rights should prevail?

THE CODE LANGUAGE OF RACE

The question of whether whites consider blacks to be inferior and hence deserving of a subordinate place in society must be separated from the question of how whites treat blacks. The first is an issue of racism, the second of discrimination. Let us begin with attitudes. What whites think about blacks has been comprehensively studied for half a century,[38] and the research—summarized by three leading demographers, Howard Schuman, Charlotte Steeh, and Lawrence Bobo, in *Racial Attitudes in America*—shows a revolution of mind unprecedented in American history. Consider some of the surprising beliefs that whites held in the 1930s and 1940s.

- More than half of all whites said that blacks were less intelligent than whites.
- More than 60 percent favored segregated schools, and just over 50 percent preferred to ride in segregated public transportation.
- Some 55 percent declared themselves opposed to proposed legislation to abolish the poll tax and end job discrimination.
- An overwhelming majority opposed intermarriage between blacks and whites.
- A majority said that if a white man and a black man were equally qualified, the white should be given preference (a remarkable case of support for affirmative action—for whites).

In just over a generation, white attitudes have changed dramatically, as recent survey data consistently show.

- Now more than 75 percent of whites assert that both whites and blacks are equal in intellectual capacity.
- More than 80 percent of whites say they are willing to vote for black political candidates.
- At least 90 percent say that blacks and whites should have the same rights to public accommodations and to attend the same schools.
- Virtually 100 percent of whites say that blacks and whites should have an equal chance to compete for jobs.

- Even the final taboo on miscegenation is weakening: 40 percent of Americans now have no problems with it, and more than two out of three Americans oppose laws restricting intermarriage.[39]

But isn't it true that the new generation of young people, untutored by the civil rights experience of the 1960s, display a resurgent bigotry evident in reports of racial tension on campus during the 1980s? Actually, no. In 1992, Charlotte Steeh and Howard Schuman found "no indication of decreasing tolerance among cohorts coming of age in the 1980s": young Americans are just as strongly committed as their parents to equal rights for blacks.[40] These unchallenged data document a largely peaceful social revolution that would seem to be some cause for modest celebration of the American capacity for change and for measured optimism about the future prospects for black equality. Few such hopeful sentiments are evident in the extensive literature on racial attitudes.

- Johnnetta Cole contends that white opposition to affirmative action is a "sophisticated expression of racism."[41]
- Patricia Williams says that terms such as "quotas," "preference," and "reverse discrimination" are "con words" which conceal the "seeds of prejudice."[42]
- Anthony Lewis insists that public resistance to welfare and affirmative action is conducted in "code" which conceals "white hostility to blacks."[43]
- Jennifer Hochschild identifies white opposition to busing as proof that racism remains "deeply embedded" in American society.[44]

What justification do these figures have for the insistence that for blacks, the American dream has been shipwrecked on the shoals of racism? Leading scholars such as David Sears, John McConahay, Joseph Hough, and Donald Kinder seek to offer intellectual support for these sentiments by advancing a theory of "symbolic racism."[45] Sears and his colleagues take as their premise the view the "racism continues to pervade white America" and that it is "deeply ingrained throughout Western culture."[46] At the same time, they argue, whites recognize that openly racist views are now disreputable. Therefore, Sears and McConahay argue, whites hypocritically claim to support equality in principle but oppose all measures like busing and racial preferences which seek to *implement* equality. Advocates of "symbolic racism" argue that contemporary racism comes disguised in the rhetoric of support for quintessential

American principles such as individualism and merit. McConahay and Joseph Hough find racist attitudes to be correlated with, and concealed within, support for political and religious conservatism.[47] If racism is not the culprit, these scholars sarcastically ask, why do whites say they support desegregation but then fight school busing; proclaim they are for equal housing, but practice "white flight" when too many African Americans move into the neighborhood; say they want blacks to enjoy opportunity, but then criticize federal funding and affirmative action programs designed to provide that opportunity? Is it not reasonable to assume that whites who continue stereotypically to associate blacks with welfare and express other prejudiced views have not really changed their spots but are only using color-blind principles to cover up a racism that dares not speak its name? As Donald Kinder sums up the exasperated demand of the symbolic racism school: "Why do so many white Americans continue to resist efforts designed to bring about racial equality?"[48]

These scholars concede one important measure of progress since the civil rights era: openly racist attitudes are thoroughly stigmatized. Not only do Americans not wish to reveal such sentiments to others, they do not like to think of themselves as racist. Precisely for this reason, even in confidential surveys, whites decline to endorse openly racist views even when enticed to do so. Thus, the good news is that most Americans now firmly espouse a moral code that is explicitly antiracist. For Sears and McConahay, however, this is no solace since whites hypocritically persist in frustrating black aspirations to full equality, thus revealing a deeply rooted racism.

Sears and McConahay are certainly right that large numbers of whites continue to resist crucial aspects of the new civil rights activist agenda. Recently the Anti-Defamation League of B'nai B'rith released a poll on racial attitudes which reinforces other studies from the past few years. The results showed that although more than 60 percent of whites support the principle of affirmative action, an overwhelming 79 percent said minorities should not receive "special consideration in college admissions" and 84 percent opposed "hiring preferences to make up for past discrimination."[49] And some studies have shown that whites act on their apparent fears and suspicions about blacks: for example, although few whites seem to mind a black family moving into their neighborhood, many acknowledge that they fear declining property values and higher crime rates, and about 50 percent of whites say they would consider moving if the black population in their area reached a critical mass or majority.[50]

Scholars of the "symbolic racism" school also have good reason to sus-pect the motives of those who publicly deny espousing bigotry. For much of the twentieth century, now that racism has ceased to be respectable, bigots have presented other explanations for their views and conduct. Segregationists, for example, usually made their case not in terms of black inferiority but in the more neutral vocabulary of states' rights and the prerogative of individuals to choose their own associates. Clearly whites now mask their racial sentiments in the way that blacks once did. Yet have Sears and McConahay really proven their case? Although bigots may fairly be suspected of trying to conceal their racism today behind banners of equal opportunity and individual rights, can the opposite be automatically inferred: that those who believe in equal opportunity and individual rights, and resist the agenda of the civil rights establishment on those grounds, are all bigots? Is the philosophical position that the ends don't always justify the means inherently racist?

The main reason that Sears, McConahay, and others who share their general view seem to readily answer yes is that they are operating entirely within the framework of a cultural relativism they show no signs of recog-nizing. Since relativism in this context implies a commitment to group equality, then any white refusal to endorse not simply equal rights but those measures that would produce equality of group outcomes, is impa-tiently branded as racist. White recalcitrance is presumed to emanate not from the authentic American principle of equal opportunity but from the equally long-standing American practice of white supremacy. The argu-ment of the "symbolic racism" school would be convincing if no legiti-mate reasons could be given other than bigotry for white opposition to preferential treatment, busing, and other racial remedies. Yet as Seymour Martin Lipset points out, "White opposition to various forms of special governmental assistance for blacks and other minorities may be a func-tion of a general antagonism to statism and a preference for personal freedom in the American value system."[51] Traditionally this commitment, sincerely held, has been considered liberal. Is it now redefined as big-otry? The "symbolic racism" theorists seem to be saying that whites who agree with Martin Luther King that laws should be based not on skin color but on the content of our character are racists. Yet historically King's view has been associated with resistance to racism. Only in a very strained analysis can it now be declared proof of it.

Similarly many whites who oppose busing may be concerned about the quality of schools, about inconvenience to their children, about levels of parental involvement in schools outside the neighborhood, about safety, and about the waste of money and time. These reasons are also cited by a majority of black parents, who oppose busing.[52] As critics of "symbolic racism" have pointed out, it is not reasonable to assume without independent proof that these parents are therefore bigoted against black children.[53]

IS RACISM HERE TO STAY?

In the last several years, the symbolic racism school has come under empirical challenge. In 1980, Stephen Johnson devised an experiment in which white students were asked to solve a puzzle. They were told that their responses would be judged against that of a competitor, who in fact was nonexistent. Half of the subjects were told that they lost to the competitor because the other person's solution was better. The other half were told that they lost because the competitor received bonus points on account of racial victimization. In each of these groups, half of the subjects were informed that their competitor was black; the other half were told that the competitor was white. Johnson found that whites responded with far less hostility when their losses were due to competitive failure, and far more aggressively when they suffered on account of perceived arbitrary disadvantage. Despite its small sample size and laboratory setting, Johnson's test raises doubts about the symbolic racism view because it seems to show white hostility rooted in a sense of fair play, not simple anti-black sentiment.[54]

Two social scientists, Paul Sniderman and Thomas Piazza, recently devised a set of experiments to test the symbolic racism thesis more systematically.[55] Taking up the issue of government programs that predominantly benefit blacks, they began with the assumption that "there is something unacceptable in insisting that a conservative must be as enthusiastic as a liberal about government spending for social programs or else be a racist."[56] The authors sought to discover whether the reasons for white opposition were rooted in a philosophical commitment to limited government or whether they were a mask for bigotry. Sniderman and his colleagues devised a "laid-off worker" experiment in which people were asked whether the government should provide economic support for a worker who has lost his job. Since some people might be expected to lie, even on an anonymous survey, the researchers performed multiple experiments, varying the race of the potential beneficiary of government assistance. They reasoned: if beneficiaries are alike in all other respects, and if there is less support for government help for blacks, the reason must be racism. Sniderman and his colleagues found that whites who classify themselves as liberals showed no difference in the way they responded to government assistance for whites and blacks. Whites who described themselves as conservatives showed a slight racial preference—for blacks.[57]

In another experiment, Sniderman and his colleagues tested the responses of whites to the proposition, "While equal opportunity for blacks and minorities to succeed is important, it is not the government's job to guarantee it." In another version, they changed "blacks and minorities" to "women." Here the researchers found that liberals and conservatives were equally likely to give a slight preference to women. Sniderman and his colleagues interpret the preference for women over blacks as proof that racism persists. This is perhaps questionable: there are chivalric reasons why some people may extend preferences to women but not to racial minorities. Sniderman and his colleagues do show, however, that documented antiblack sentiments seem to vary inversely with education. Poorly educated people are about three times more likely to discriminate in favor of women and against blacks than well educated people. Sniderman and colleagues contend that it is not the ideology of equal opportunity and individualism, but rather income and social class, which best correlate with residual racism.[58]

The basic problem with any explanation which seeks to infer bad motives such as symbolic racism is that motives are notoriously difficult to ferret out. To say that racism is no longer overt, but is now largely invisible, seems to be just another way of saying that racism has dramatically declined—it is no longer easy to find direct evidence for it. Yet the continued popularity of the "symbolic racism" school shows the deep commitment of relativist ideology to "finding racism under every bed," as Paul Sniderman puts it. Sniderman and Piazza assert that racism "no longer has the power to dominate the political thinking of ordinary Americans."[59]

Yet we cannot conclude that racism is no longer a serious problem in America without investigating the evidence of several opinion surveys which show that whites continue to entertain many hostile prejudices and stereotypes toward blacks, whom they consider to be lazy, parasitic on government, sexually promiscuous, and violent. One survey showed that while the vast majority of whites said they admired blacks for their strong religious faith, warm and friendly nature, and honesty and perseverance, about one-third of whites also acknowledged that they thought blacks are loud and pushy, less ambitious than whites, prefer welfare over work, and are more prone to crime.[60] Other recent surveys have produced similar evidence of derogatory attitudes.[61] Before concluding that these views constitute prima facie evidence of racism, however, it is necessary to investigate what may be termed the cabdriver's rebuttal. In other words, we must inquire whether stereotypes are accurate and whether prejudice has a rational basis.

THE BLACK MALE STEREOTYPE

Michelle Joo, an Asian American shopkeeper in Washington D.C., understands the logic of affirmative action. When deciding whether to let people into her jewelry and cosmetics store, "I look at the face," she tells the *Washington Post*. She won't release the glass door "if he looks ugly, if he's holding a bottle in a paper bag, if he's dirty. . . . If some guy looks kind, I let him in." Young black men are kept out if they seem rowdy, Joo says. Usually they react by banging on her glass windows.[62] One may say that Michelle Joo has no fixed policy of keeping blacks out. Nor does she have a quota about the number she will admit. Rather, she seems to be a prudent statistician. She employs race as one factor, but not the only factor, in her decisionmaking. She seeks to discriminate among blacks, choosing those who pose the least risk. As a means to ensure her security and business survival, Michelle Joo is practicing what may be termed *rational* discrimination.

Thousands of store owners in major cities make similar decisions every day. So do countless young women—black, white, Hispanic, and Asian— who come across black males in circumstances they consider not entirely safe. Regardless of their general attitudes about civil rights, they do what they feel is necessary in each particular case. Shopkeepers scurry to the front of the store where they can monitor the exit. They follow the shopper with a suspicious eye. Female pedestrians walking the street in the evening may clutch their hangbag more tightly, or cross the street if approached by one or more young black men. Sometimes people snap the locks on their car doors as African American youths walk by.

The psychological toll of such reactions is high. If you are black, columnist William Raspberry says, it is unusual to find yourself treated as an individual, and to receive the kind of personal treatment that whites have come to expect.[63] In *The Rage of a Privileged Class*, Ellis Cose describes a typical justification for black rage: "Why am I constantly treated as if I were a drug addict, a thief or a thug?"[64] It is hard not to sympathize with the sentiments of a young African American who wrote to a national newspaper:

> If I'm walking in certain places, I'll notice the lady next to me, and she'll switch her purse to the other side of her. That just shows her ignorance. It hurts, but it's her ignorance. Personally I'm academically inclined. I don't steal car stereos or pick people's pockets, and I don't carry a weapon.[65]

Many who echo these sentiments also question the basis for group judgments about blacks.

• A columnist for the *Los Angeles Sentinel* protests, "The stereotype of young black males as a criminal menace has become a mainstay. The fact is: three out of four young black males are not involved in criminal behavior."[66]

• Legal scholar Charles Ogletree goes further. "Ninety-nine percent of black people don't commit crimes."[67]

• African American scholar Martin Kilson agrees: "The implication that the criminality of a minority of black males can be construed as representing Afro-American behavior generally is outright defamation. . . . It's open season on black folks."[68]

Blacks make up approximately 12 percent of the national population. Yet according to *Uniform Crime Reports,* which are data published annually by the FBI, blacks comprise 39 percent of those arrested for aggravated assault, 42 percent of those arrested for weapons possession, 43 percent of those arrested for rape, 55 percent of those arrested for murder, and 61 percent of those arrested for robbery.[69] Even discounting for the possibility of some racial bias in criminal arrests, it seems clear that the average black person is between three and six times more likely to be arrested for a crime than the average white person. To use the logic of proportional representation, blacks are vastly overrepresented among criminals in America today.

But in evaluating black crime, it is necessary to consider not just average rates but also the distribution. One has to factor in variables such as gender and age. The overwhelming majority of crimes of robbery, mugging, sexual assault, and murder are perpetrated by men.[70] There are very few elderly people arrested for committing those offenses.[71] The data show that young males between the ages of eighteen and thirty-five make up the segment within the African American community that is largely responsible for the black crime rate. "This group," political scientist James Q. Wilson says, "commits a larger fraction of violent crimes than any segment of the national population."

Yet it is not enough to know that a large fraction of crimes are perpetrated by young black males. It is equally important to know what percentage of young black males have been arrested and convicted of committing crimes. *Newsweek* recently estimated that about one-fifth of black males between the ages of fifteen and thirty-four have criminal records.[72] But this figure errs on the conservative side. According to the Sentencing Project, a liberal advocacy group, about 25 percent of young black men in America are in prison, on probation, or on parole on any given day. For whites, the figure is about 6 percent.[73] In major cities, the figures for young black men are even higher.

• In California, 33 percent of black males between the ages of twenty and twenty-nine are either in jail, on probation, or on parole in any given year, compared with 5 percent of whites and 9 percent of Hispanics, according to a study by the National Center on Institutions and Alternatives, a group which promotes alternatives to imprisonment.[74]

• In Washington, D.C., another study shows, some 42 percent of black males between eighteen and thirty-five are either in prison or in trouble with the criminal justice system. The study estimated that the likelihood of a young black man being arrested by the time he turns thirty-five is 70–75 percent.[75]

• A recent study in Baltimore found that, on any given day, more than 50 percent of black males between the ages of eighteen and thirty-five are in prison or under criminal justice supervision. More than 80 percent of young people arrested in the city in 1991 were black. Among drug arrests, more than 1,300 involved black males, compared with 13 arrests of white males.[76]

Most people on the street cannot be expected to be familiar with official data on crime rates. No one goes around with a pocket calculator computing the probabilities of criminal attack. Yet everyone knows that young blacks are convicted of a high percentage of violent crimes, and since most Americans are highly risk-averse to crime, they have good reason to take precautions and exercise prudence. Compounding these alarming statistics is the intimidating ethnic style of many underclass black males, which everyone observes but few writers acknowledge in public. Yet in a candid autobiography, former gang member Sanyika Shakur describes the "attitude" of African American gang members. "It's not how you stare at someone but what you've been through that others can see in your eyes and that tells them you're the wrong one to fuck with."[77] Black anthropologist Elijah Anderson writes in his book *Streetwise* that "black males exercise a peculiar hegemony over the public spaces, particularly at night or when two or more are together." Wearing what Anderson terms their "urban uniform," consisting of sneakers, gold chains, sunglasses, and portable radios, these young men can often be seen laughing loudly, singing, cursing, or discussing their fights, robberies, and sex lives. Not only do they show little concern for others, Anderson notes, but their behavior seems designed to intimidate and terrorize. Anderson observes that law-abiding blacks develop special skill at recognizing and avoiding the dominant criminal element. Whites who are unaccustomed to coping with this "street etiquette," Anderson concludes, are right to feel endangered, because they may well be.[78]

Media Bias?

Despite the statistics on crime rates, many black activists argue that the media exaggerate the threat posed by young blacks. When they are not "maligning black character in print," African American novelist Ishmael Reed writes, "they do the job with pictures and Willie Horton-style layouts." Some TV media, in Reed's view, "cover blacks . . . the way the Nazi press of pre-holocaust Germany covered the Jews."[79] Richard Majors and Jacob Gordon blame the media for racist characterizations of blacks as "punks, troublemakers, dope addicts, gang-bangers, lazy and hostile."[80] Jesse Jackson has announced a Commission on Fairness in the Media which seeks to use "research, education, negotiations and boycotts" to enforce a more positive image of blacks, especially black males.[81]

But the function of the media is to cover the news, not to serve as a public relations agency for blacks or anyone else. It is true that television places a nightly spotlight on violent crime, which is hardly surprising given the degree of public concern. It is understandable but implausible for Reed, Jackson, and others to insist upon prominent media accounts about law-abiding citizens and quotidian virtue; this is a bit like the airline industry complaining that the press does not write stories about airplanes that land safely. Media sensationalism cuts both ways: as Paul Sniderman points out, scholarly studies that find racial discrimination to be prevalent often receive extensive publicity, while studies which find little or no discrimination are ignored. In addition, many newspapers seem to tread extremely cautiously when reporting incidents in which blacks and other minorities are placed in an unfavorable light.[82] Even while reporting such gruesome crimes as rape, the *New York Times* sometimes provides a description of the suspect but omits the crucial detail of race, apparently to avoid reinforcing public suspicions of African Americans.[83] A classic instance of how even trivial episodes become the occasion for liberal soul-searching is a recent item in the *Sacramento Bee* which ran under the headline, "An Apology to Our Readers."

> On page A-1, we ran what was initially seen as a cute, innocent picture of two children dressing up for Halloween. But what was not caught in the editing process was the stereotype enforced in the picture of an African American child dressed in a maid's uniform putting lipstick on a white child dressed in a party outfit. The implication of the images in the picture and the words in the headline should have been recognized and they should not have run. We were wrong, and our sincere apologies are offered. A hard lesson in the area of sensitivity has been learned.[84]

The real question is whether the media, in non-news coverage, portray African Americans as potentially dangerous. Two liberal social scientists, John Dovidio and Samuel Gaertner, found that while blacks were once portrayed as servants or entertainers, since the late 1960s they are increasingly "presented as regulators of society in positions such as teachers and law enforcers." Today television series and films self-consciously depict blacks in counterstereotypical roles: as physicians, scientists, supervisors, purveyors of wisdom, and solvers of impossible movie dilemmas. Dovidio and Gaertner conclude, "Mass media portrayals of blacks have become more frequent and increasingly positive."[85] Similarly when Robert Lichter and Stanley Rothman surveyed more than six hundred programs aired over three decades of prime time, they found that "nine out of 10 murders on TV were committed by whites. Only 3 in 100 murders on TV were committed by blacks. Blacks are about 18 times less likely to commit homicide on TV than in real life."[86]

Perhaps on account of the paucity of evidence, critics who allege media racism typically resort to vagueness or hyperbole. "I would never say that all movies are racist," argues Serita Coffee, author of a report on media bias for the Los Angeles chapter of the NAACP. "However, I have yet to find one that isn't." Among Coffee's examples is the film *The Si-*

lence of the Lambs, which is charged with racism because Hannibal the Cannibal "is historically linked with the legendary African general who rode elephants to Europe across the Alps."[87]

If there was one television series that seemed to portray blacks in an unfailingly flattering light, it was the *Cosby Show.* One of the most popular sitcoms of the 1980s, it depicted the Huxtables as a successful, law-abiding, well-adjusted family headed by an eminent and likable physician. The Huxtables did not seem ashamed of their blackness; rather, they found a way to integrate their ethnic and American identities. The show did not portray pimps, drug dealers, and drive-by shootings. Precisely for this reason, Sut Jhally and Justin Lewis argue in *Enlightened Racism,* the *Cosby Show* catered to white racism.

> The *Cosby Show* strikes a deal with its white audience. It asks for an attitude that welcomes the black family onto TV screens in white homes, and in return it provides a picture of a comfortable, ordered world in which white people and the nation as a whole are absolved of any responsibility for the position of black people. The Huxtables' achievement of the American dream leads them to a world where race no longer matters. This attitude enables white viewers to combine an impeccably liberal attitude toward race with a deep-rooted suspicion of black people.[88]

Faulting the *Cosby Show* for offering "no acknowledgement of the severely constricted social life opportunities that most black people face," Henry Louis Gates, Jr. proceeds to criticize other TV shows for encouraging white stereotypes of African Americans as antisocial.[89] So if *Hill Street Blues* was racist because it portrayed black criminals, and the *Cosby Show* was racist because it did not, is it possible to arrive at agreement on what constitutes nonracist television? None of this is to deny the problems that are characteristic of contemporary media, such as sensationalism and the inundation of the American public with numbingly simplified images. These problems, however, are not specific to race. Frequently the press, when it has the discretion to do so, seems to go out of its way to euphemize disagreeable empirical realities and to present blacks in a benign, socially responsible light.

WHY DID THE WOMAN CROSS THE STREET?

The subject of whether Americans are discriminating rationally in treating young blacks as potential criminals is beginning to surface in general discussion. Among those taking it up in their own ways are liberal cartoonist Garry Trudeau and New York's former Democratic mayor Ed Koch.[90] This question was energetically debated recently in the *Journal of Social Philosophy,* an exchange that participants recognized as a violation of the unspoken academic taboo against discussing such matters in public.

"A black male is ten times more likely than his white counterpart to be a criminal." Thus the first grenade was launched by Michael Levin, a white philosophy professor. Levin, who has also alleged that blacks are on average less intelligent than whites, has been heatedly denounced at his university, City College of New York, as a racist. A racist he may be, yet we still have to account for the statistics on black crime and figure out what constitutes a rational and ethical response. The need for candid debate on a genuine social problem undoubtedly explains why Levin's provocation was taken seriously by his academic colleagues.

Levin argues that the remarkably high crime rate among young black males legitimizes rational avoidance of blacks in a world where people have limited information. If statistics show that one-fourth of young blacks in urban areas have criminal records, Levin argues, then as far as pedestrians are concerned, the young black they encounter on the street or in a store or on the jogging track poses a genuine risk.

> Ideally you would base your expectations about him on . . . complete knowledge of . . . characteristics. But you do not know. Relative to your state of knowledge, he is a typical member of a class one fourth of whose members are felons.[91]

Levin's controversial article naturally invited criticism. Sociologist J. Angelo Corlett scornfully asked, "Does it not matter how the young man walks, is dressed, looks at me as I approach him, or whether or not it is nightfall?"[92] Corlett's point is that Levin seems unwilling to make distinctions between young African American men: all blacks don't look alike, and it cannot be assumed that they all act alike. Yet although useful as a general caution to people not to arrive at hasty judgments, Corlett's refutation fails to consider Levin's premise that, in his hypothetical scenario, other information is scarce and people must base their actions on probability. Levin concedes that all available personal criteria should be considered, but the kernel of his argument is that "race is an information bearing trait" and should be one factor, sometimes a determining factor, in private and public choices.

Corlett is on his strongest ground when he moves from actuarial logic to moral reasoning. Young black males cannot change their physical characteristics and have a moral and legal right to be treated as individuals and "not to be singled out as a member of a certain group and treated adversely."[93] This is simply a restatement of Martin Luther King's doctrine that race should be ignored and we should be judged on our merits as persons. Levin concedes the moral seriousness of an appeal to individual rights, but such an appeal, he insists, cannot be made by those who support the group rights logic of affirmative action. After all, Levin argues, racial preferences in college admissions and job hiring are rationalized on the grounds that the collective interests of African Americans have been injured by whites as a group. Affirmative action subordinates individual rights to group claims and institutional interests such as historical compensation or ethnic diversity. Fair enough, Levin maintains, but advocates of rational discrimination in favor of blacks to promote those goals have no grounds for objecting to identical reasoning aimed at securing the highest goal of citizens and the state: ensuring security for life and property. Just as affirmative action makes race a proxy for disadvantage or victimization, Levin concludes that as far as young African American males are concerned, race is also a proxy for criminal potential.

Philosopher Jonathan Adler, another critic of Levin, admits that discrimination may be rational, but argues that "black crime owes much to a history of discrimination and prejudice." This history, Adler contends, "we do not want to extend . . . yet we may be extending it if we noticeably avoid this young black male."[94] Adler's point is that, as an issue of public policy, we should not blame African Americans—especially law-abiding ones—for historical patterns which they did not cause. However reasonable under the circumstances, discrimination against young blacks in Adler's view perpetuates the legacy of unjust oppression and insult. Levin responds that Americans walking the street cannot be expected to worry about the historical causes of crime. Their primary concern, he argues, is properly aimed at their own security. Levin contends that the right of African Americans not to be insulted is outweighed by the right of Caucasians not to be assaulted. Moreover, Levin concludes that "responsibility for harm to the innocent black is naturally assigned to other black criminals."

What can we make of this grim but unavoidable argument? First, it suggests that some stereotyping is inevitable in a world where citizens do not have full knowledge and must act on probability. Yet, as Judith Lichtenberg writes, generalizations may be necessary and yet morally flawed because they are bound to hurt some of the wrong people: "To generalize is to overgeneralize." Lichtenberg concedes: "The probability of black teenagers being muggers surely is greater than the probability of gray-haired ladies being muggers. The crucial question is: how much more?"[95] Ishmael Reed writes, "Do the 0.1 percent of Italian-Americans engaged in organized crime represent the Italian-American community?"[96]

The answer to these questions is obvious. The percentage of Italian-Americans involved in organized crime is infinitesimal, but as we have seen the percentage of young black males involved in crime is substantial. A young black male is literally thousands of times more likely to be a mugger than a gray-haired lady. Moreover, it is not a matter of whether these felons represent the black community—they are not being invited to serve in Congress—but rather whether the probability of their criminal behavior should be taken into account in situations where people cannot get to know them personally.

Thus whatever our other reservations about Levin, we must concede as plausible his conclusion that when people say "blacks are dangerous" or "blacks are criminals," they don't necessarily mean all blacks. As a social scientist would put it, they are drawing rational conclusions based on probabilistic judgments taking into account their own degree of aversion to risk. In layman's terms, better safe than sorry. Jesse Jackson recently affirmed this view when he said, "There is nothing more painful for me than to walk down the street and hear footsteps and start to think about robbery, and then see it's somebody white and feel relieved."[97] Jackson's statement was, of course, the classic gaffe, which Michael Kinsley defines as a situation when a politician accidentally tells the truth. Jackson hurried to "clarify" his views and deny that he meant what he said.

But several African American scholars have made the same point. Johnnetta Cole writes that among black women "one of the most painful admissions I hear is: I am afraid of my own people."[98] William Oliver remarks in *The Violent Social World of Black Men* that "in response to the prevalence of violence in their communities, many blacks manifest an overt fear of other blacks."[99] Tens of thousands of African Americans have moved out of cities like Washington, D.C., into the suburbs in part to escape high rates of crime in their old neighborhoods.[100] Given the crime rates of young black males, "the stereotype is not a stereotype any more," says Howard University education professor Kenneth Tollett. "A stereotype is an overgeneralization. The statements we have called stereotypes in the past have become true."[101]

There is another side that should not be overlooked. The moral dilemma, which Levin does not really confront, is that the behavior of those who rationally discriminate against blacks is indistinguishable from that of actual racists. Thus whatever the motive, the objective result is the same. Racial screens are forms of dehumanization—a collectivism of mind that imposes real and undeserved suffering. Understandably young black males who do not conform to the statistical pattern are going to blame such discriminatory treatment on racism, and to link it with historical patterns in which their ancestors were treated as subhuman and dangerous predators. Personally I would be angry and upset if, as a law-abiding person, I could not get a taxi. Yet, equally predictably, taxidrivers, storekeepers, and women who clutch their purse or cross the street will attach little significance to such personal and historical sensitivities. They are not historians but amateur statisticians acting on impressionistic but not unreasonable generalizations of the sort that we all make in other contexts every day. Such people are unlikely to be intimidated by accusations of prejudice. For them, the charges are meaningless, because the prejudice is warranted. In this context, a bigot is simply a sociologist without credentials.

Prejudices and Conclusions

Prejudice engages the mind in a steady course of wisdom and
virtue, and does not leave the man hesitating in the moment of
decision. . . . Prejudice renders a man's virtue his habit.
                                    —Edmund Burke[102]

It may now be useful to reconsider the meaning of familiar terms such as prejudice and stereotype, and examine the conventional liberal understanding of racism. This understanding is expressed by Henry Louis Gates, Jr., who writes: "Racism exists when one generalizes about attributes of an individual, and treats him or her accordingly." Gates offers some specific examples: "Skip, sing me one of those old Negro spirituals," "You people sure can dance," and "Black people play basketball so remarkably well." He concludes, "These are racist statements."[103] Why are they viewed as racist? Because contemporary liberalism is constructed on the scaffolding of cultural relativism, which posits that all groups are inherently equal. Since all groups are equal, adverse group judgments are presumed to constitute "prejudices" and "stereotypes" that are almost always regarded as wrongheaded and ignorant. The civil rights laws of the 1950s and 1960s were based on the assumption that as whites and blacks came into closer contact and learned more about each other, the similarity of all groups would become evident and white prejudices and stereotypes would dissipate.

Consider some definitions. The *Encyclopedia Britannica* identifies prejudice as "an attitude, usually emotional, acquired without or prior to adequate evidence or experience."[104] For Thomas Pettigrew, a psychologist who studies race relations, prejudice is "irrationally based . . . an antipathy accompanied by a faulty generalization."[105] Christine Bennett in *Comprehensive Multicultural Education* argues that "prejudice is an erroneous judgment, usually negative, which is based on incomplete or faulty information." Bennett adds that "a prejudice becomes a sterotype when it is used to label all or most members of a group."[106] Another leading textbook defines a stereotype as "an overgeneralization associated with a racial or ethnic category that goes beyond existing evidence."[107] *Webster's New World Dictionary* defines a stereotype as "a fixed or conventional notion or conception, as of a person or group . . . allowing no individuality and critical judgment."[108]

In *The Nature of Prejudice,* Gordon Allport draws on modern social science theories to explicate the paradigm of liberal antiracism. Allport argues that prejudices and stereotypes reveal less about their objects than their subjects. Applying such concepts as displacement and frustration-aggression theory, Allport maintains that when whites feel hostility and anger which they have difficulty coping with or explaining, they project it onto others, who thus become sacrificial victims or "scapegoats." Allport conveys the assumption of many social scientists today: prejudices and stereotypes endure because of the principle of self-selection. From the distorted perspective of the racist, blacks who do not conform to preconceived notions simply do not exist; they are, in Ralph Ellison's term, invisible men. Thus prejudices and stereotypes are presumed to be impervious to correction.[109]

For the better part of a generation, this liberal understanding of racism worked fairly well. The reason was that both whites and blacks had indeed developed many erroneous views about each other as a consequence of Southern segregation. During slavery the races stayed in regular, even intimate, contact, but after emancipation the forced separation of the races created a divided society in which dubious and even absurd generalizations could endure, unchecked by contrary experience. Thus the intellectual assault on prejudice and stereotypes, as well as the experience of desegregation, both helped to topple many preconceived group generalizations that could not withstand empirical examination. In 1920, George Jean Nathan and H. L. Mencken listed a number of such popular prejudices and stereotypes about blacks.

- Negroes who are intelligent are always part white
- Negro parties always end up in bloody brawls
- Negroes who have money head straight for the dentist to have their front teeth filled with gold
- Illiterate Negroes labor hard but educated Negroes lose all interest in work
- Negro prize fighters marry white women and then beat them
- Negroes will sell their votes for a dollar[110]

As the widespread popularity of African Americans such as Colin Powell, Bill Cosby, and Michael Jordan illustrates, none of these beliefs seems to be held today by any measurable segment of the population. We can speculate about the roots of some of these stereotypes. Undoubtedly the white prejudice about black intelligence did not begin with, but was strengthened by, the observed preponderance of light-skinned mulattoes in the black middle class. Perhaps the suspicion of vote-peddling among blacks was a legacy from the Reconstruction era, when many blacks voted and many Southern whites were disenfranchised. The reputation of black boxers probably began with the flamboyant experience of Jack Johnson, who raised controversy in the early part of the century when he married a white woman.

These prejudices, loosely anchored in popular experience, proved easy to refute through the liberal remedy of increased education and exposure. Not only were whites in a more informed position to see what blacks were like, but the black community itself was changing, rendering crude generalizations from the past increasingly obsolete. The positive effect of the assault on prejudices and sterotypes, based on the liberal paradigm, has been a vastly more sophisticated perception of blacks on the part of whites. The problem with the paradigm is its premise that all group perceptions are misperceptions: that every negative generalizations about blacks is automatically false and the product of distorted projections. Paradoxically it is desegregation and integration which have now called the liberal paradigm into question. One of the risks of increased exposure to blacks is that it has also placed whites in a position to discover which of their preconceived views about blacks are true. Education and integration can help to dispel erroneous judgments about groups but they are only likely to reinforce accurate ones.

In fact ethnic groups that have had little history of oppressing each other and in some cases very limited previous contact now seem to be formulating clear and often critical images of other groups. In one of the more remarkable surveys of recent years, the National Conference of Christians and Jews reports that many minority groups harbor much more hostile attitudes toward each other than do whites. For example, 49 percent of blacks and 68 percent of Asians said that Hispanics "tend to have bigger families than they can support." Forty-six percent of Hispanics and 42 percent of blacks agreed that Asian Americans are "unscrupulous, crafty and devious in business." And 53 percent of Asians and 51 percent of Hispanics affirmed that blacks "are more likely to commit crimes and violence."[111]

It is, of course, possible that these minority perceptions reveal that, by a kind of social osmosis, everyone is learning their racism from whites. But if so why would minority perceptions be stronger than those of whites who are the alleged racists *par excellence?* More likely, these intergroup minority perceptions are the product of experience. Most people today have fairly regular contact with others of different races, and have many opportunities to verify their collective judgments about other groups.[112] It is the possibility of accurate generalizations about blacks and other groups that gives rise to the problem of rational discrimination.

ARE STEREOTYPES GENERALLY ACCURATE?

Do blacks as a group have certain distinct characteristics? We read in Andrew Hacker's *Two Nations* that "the erotic abandon displayed in black dancing has no white counterpart."[113] Thomas Kochman in *Black and White: Styles in Conflict* cites an African American source describing the black walk: "Rather than simply walk, we *move* . . . a strong rhythmic mode of walking . . . *Where* the young black male is going is not as important as *how* he gets there." Kochman proceeds with some pretty strong generalizations:

> Where whites use the relatively detached and unemotional *discussion* mode to engage an issue, blacks use the emotionally intense and involving mode of *argument*. Where whites tend to *understate* their exceptional talents and abilities, blacks tend to *boast* about theirs. Where white men, meeting women for

the first time, *defuse* the potency of their sexual messages . . . black men make their sexual interest explicit and hope to *infuse* their presentations with sexual potency.[114]

Although both Hacker and Kochman are white, neither can be accused of racism; indeed, their views are extremely popular in the black community. "My black students," Hacker says, "love what I have to say." During my speaking trips to college campuses, I decided, as a journalistic exercise, to test people's perception of group traits by raising the question of whether stereotypes may be true and prejudices based on them therefore legitimate. Inevitably I encounter strong emotional opposition. As a result of the deeply rooted assumptions of cultural relativism, educated people today have been taught to despise group generalizations. In a sense, we are all Boasians. We have been raised to be prejudiced against prejudice.

Recently on a West Coast campus, I raised the question of whether, as a group, "blacks have rhythm." A professor of Afro-American Studies insisted, "Absolutely not," and a number of white students readily agreed. Instinctively, they raised the familiar defenses, "I know a black man who can't dance," "How can you generalize about a group that is so diverse?" "What about Elvis? He had rhythm, and he wasn't black," and so on. I pointed out that these were poor refutations of a proposition that was being offered as true on average, or compared with the experience of other groups. One cannot rebut the statistically irrefutable statement that men are taller than women by producing a six-foot woman and a four-foot man. Those individuals would merely constitute exceptions to a general pattern that has persisted across cultures for most of recorded history.

Incidentally, the view that blacks tend to be more rhythmic than whites is no whimsical recent invention but is supported by observation and experience in several societies over two millennia. In ancient Greece and Rome, which held no negative view of black skin color, Ethiopians and other blacks were celebrated for a perceived natural inclination to music and dance. This is a central theme of that segment of Greek and Roman art which focuses on blacks.[115] Moreover, the same perception of blacks is evident in many Arab descriptions of African blacks, written in the late Middle Ages. Ibn Butlan, for example, writes that if a black man was dropped from heaven "he would beat time as he goes down."[116] In a ninth century Muslim travel account, blacks are praised for their rhythm and for being able to play music without instruction.[117] As we saw earlier, Ibn Khaldun, the greatest Arab historian of the Middle Ages, speculates that the black propensity for music and rhythmic dancing derives from the relaxing influence of the warm climate.[118]

In a recent book on cultural diversity, Taylor Cox compiled the results of several surveys that sought to identify negative generalizations that many Americans believe about various groups. Here are some stereotypes about males from different backgrounds.

- *Japanese:* Studious, meticulous, workaholics, business-oriented, nationalistic, unemotional, sexist, productive, good at math and science, defer to authority, carry cameras.
- *Jews:* Rich, miserly, support Israel, well-educated, complainers, good at business, take care of their own, not rhythmic or coordinated, sensitive to criticism.
- *Blacks:* Athletes, good dancers, expressive in communication, poor, too concerned about what they wear, uneducated, oversexed, on welfare, funny.
- *French:* Romantic, unfaithful, egotistical, enjoy a drink of wine, dry-humored, do not shower often, dislike Americans, proud of their country.
- *Whites:* Insecure, domineering, wear Dockers, enjoy privileges handed to them, manipulative, insensitive, competitive, opportunistic, enjoy drinking beer.[119]

The liberal paradigm holds that, since racial and ethnic generalizations are irrational, none of them can accurately reflect group differences. On one point the theory is sound: people's perceptions of others are always filtered through the lens of their own prior experience. But the liberal understanding cannot explain how particular traits come to be identified with particular groups. Only because group traits have an empirical basis in shared experience can we invoke them without fear of contradiction. Think of how people would react if someone said that "Koreans are lazy" or that "Hispanics are constantly trying to find ways to make money." Despite the prevalence of anti-Semitism, Jews are rarely accused of stupidity. Blacks are never accused of being tight with a dollar, or of conspiring to take over the world. By reversing stereotypes we can see how their persistence relies, not simply on the assumptions of the viewer, but also on the characteristics of the group being described.

This is no case for group traits having a biological foundation. Probably the vast majority of group traits are entirely cultural, the distilled product of many years of shared experience. Yet prejudices and stereotypes are not intended to explain the origins of group traits, only to take into account their undisputed existence. Nor is this an argument to emphasize negative traits. Stereotypes can be negative or positive. Indeed the same stereotype can be interpreted favorably or unfavorably. One can deplore Roman machismo or admire Roman manliness; deride traditional Spanish superstition or exalt Spanish piety; scorn Jewish avarice or praise Jewish entrepreneurship; ridicule English severity or cherish English self-control. In each of these interpretations, we see a single set of facts, a different set of values.

Not surprisingly, ethnic activists frequently offer a positive interpretation of their group's distinctive characteristics. Richard Gambino's *Blood of My Blood* is almost embarrassing in its corroboration of "Godfather" stereotypes about Italian Americans. Gambino elaborates the code of *la famiglia,* and proceeds to give a rich and sympathetic account of how it shapes something resembling an Italian American worldview.[120] Thomas Sowell's *Ethnic America* and Nathan Glazer and Daniel Patrick Moynihan's *Beyond the Melting Pot* also acknowledge ethnic differences and relate them to group performance in America.[121] Black stereotypes are frequently given a positive spin and celebrated by members of the African American community.

• Paul Robeson identified the "characteristic qualities" of blacks as including "a deep simplicity, a sense of mystery . . . great emotional depth and spiritual intuition."[122]

• In *Shadow and Act* Ralph Ellison exulted in the fact that "Negro music and dances are frenzied and erotic, Negro religious ceremonies violently ecstatic, Negro speech strongly rhythmical and weighted with image and gesture."[123]

• More recently, Ralph Wiley notes that "Creativity is at the root of all forms of music, which is why black people are so adept at it. Creativity is black people's middle name."[124]

• A contemporary book on African culture remarks, "This culture is identified by jazz, blues, gospel and soul music, by modern dance and tap dance, by hip talking, pimp walking, and high-five passing."[125]

William Helmreich in his book *The Things They Say Behind Your Back* takes up the controversial issue of whether there is a rational basis for group stereotypes. Helmreich finds some stereotypes that are clearly false. During the Middle Ages, for example, apparently many Christians took religious polemic literally and came to believe that Jews have horns.[126] Clearly this was not a perception destined to last: one only has to encounter a few Jews to discover that they do not, in fact, possess horns. Helmreich takes up other stereotypes, however, such as the view that many Nobel laureates are Jewish, or that the Mafia is largely made up of Italians, or that the Japanese tend to be xenophobic and nationalistic, or that Latin Americans are typically macho and sexist, or that many Irishmen and American Indians drink enormous quantities of alcohol. Basically Helmreich finds that these perceptions are confirmed by the data. Of all the stereotypes he considers—many of them now outdated and not widely held—Helmreich concludes that "almost half the stereotypes have a strong factual basis."[127] This is a remarkable refutation of the a priori assumption that group generalizations are always erroneous and unwarranted.

It is obvious to most people that groups do differ. Therefore it is possible to make accurate generalizations. As the term suggests, generalizations hold true in general: they work best when, circumstances permitting, they take into account individual exceptions to the rule and overlapping traits between groups. Stated in this form, it is not clear that group generalizations constitute prejudice or stereotypes at all. They do not satisfy one crucial criterion, what Gordon Allport terms making critical judgments "without sufficient warrant." Allport offers as an exception to his theory of prejudice what he calls the "well-deserved reputation theory."[128] It is no prejudice or stereotype to say that Indians eat curry or that Mexicans eat enchiladas: Indians and Mexicans really do these things.

Since groups do possess distinguishing traits, the liberal assumption that greater contact between groups can be expected to eliminate prejudices and stereotypes turns out to be illusory. It is possible to tell a young boy or girl who has never met Puerto Ricans that they have no recognizable group traits, but after that child has lived in New York for a few months, such an argument from a sensitivity counselor will come to sound comical. In fact, studies confirm that greater exposure often has the effect of reinforcing negative perceptions of distinguishing group traits: familiarity sometimes does breed contempt. One study showed that "teachers, nurses and physicians working in Alaska had much more negative stereotypes of Eskimos than those having little contact" and concluded, "Contact does generate prejudice."[129] Another survey found that whites who live in areas with high concentrations of blacks exhibit greater hostility to them and oppose government race-based programs far more strongly than whites who live in areas with few if any blacks.[130] Thus the relativist assumption that groups do not differ and that group generalizations are irrational turns out to be wrong. Indeed it generates a liberal antiracist paradigm which is at variance with most people's direct observation of the real world.[131] Prejudices and stereotypes merely reflect a human tendency to generalize from experience; they can only be refuted by showing that the group in question does not empirically possess the quality attributed to it. Since this is often difficult to show, we would do better to acknowledge the reality of group traits and ask how we should act on them.

DISCRIMINATION IN HIRING

It is impossible to answer the question of how much racism exists in the United States because nobody knows how to measure racism and no unit exists for calibrating such measurements. If we assume that racists are likely to conceal or misrepresent their true beliefs, we are better off not trying to read people's minds but focusing instead on the consequences of their actions. Many African American scholars agree. "We're not looking for white approval," Alvin Poussaint says. "We're looking for protection for our rights." What follows is a critical examination of three studies which seek to prove racial discrimination against blacks in the areas of job hiring, mortgage lending, and criminal justice.

"Racial discrimination in the workplace is as vicious, if less obvious, than it was when employers posted signs: No Nigras Need Apply." Typically, Derrick Bell issues the above proclamation without offering any evidence.[132] Indeed such evidence is not readily available; after an extensive review of job discrimination studies, a distinguished panel of scholars, in their report *A Common Destiny: Blacks and American Society,* concluded, "Direct evidence of systematic discriminatory behavior by whites is difficult to obtain."[133]

But in 1991, the Urban Institute, a group concerned with civil rights issues, attempted such a demonstration. The Institute recruited twenty male college students, ten white and ten black, and matched them in black-white pairs so that each had virtually identical appearances, deportments, and credentials. They then applied for a range of private sector entry level jobs in Chicago and Washington, D.C. The Institute monitored their progress at each stage of the application process, and entered more than four hundred separate application results into its computer.[132] The results were as follows: in 67 percent of cases, neither candidate received a job offer; in 13 percent of cases, both did; in 15 percent of cases, only the white tester received an offer; in 5 percent of cases, only the black tester did. In its report, the Institute publicized these findings as proof that reverse discrimination is negligible and that discrimination against blacks in the American work force is "widespread and entrenched." According to an article on the study in the *Washington Post,* "Young white men seeking entry level jobs receive . . . job offers three times more often than their equally qualified black counterparts."[135]

Upon more careful review, however, these results raise some unanswered questions. The study is not a survey of the job market as a whole, but only a small part of it. The Institute excluded all public sector jobs, where a large number of blacks are employed, as well as a disproportionate number of private sector firms with affirmative action programs. This could be mere oversight, or it could reflect the organization's desire to minimize the possibility of recording preferential treatment for blacks, a result easily achieved through a biased selection of potential employers. Our suspicions are heightened when we recognize that the purpose of the Urban Institute's study was to prove the pervasiveness of discrimination. Indeed it seems unlikely that the Institute would have released the study had it shown that discrimination against blacks was negligible. Although the Institute is a credible organization which no doubt attempted to minimize scholarly bias, its expectations for the result could have been known or communicated to the testers, who might then act toward potential employers in a way that would confirm the Institute's objectives. It would be going too far to compare the results of the study to that of companies seeking to prove the popularity of their products, but undoubtedly the study would be more reliable if there were no political stake in the outcome.

Even when its limitations are taken into account, however, a fair reading of the Institute study shows that racial discrimination does occur. The study does not, however, ask the question of why. One of its crucial findings—that white and black interviewers were equally likely to discriminate—offers a clue. Perhaps such discrimination persists in part because it is rational. It is efficient. It makes economic sense. As Randall Kennedy correctly observes, "The market cannot be counted on to drive out all forms of discrimination." Conventional economic theory holds that arbitrary racial discrimination is economically costly. The reason is pointed out by Nobel laureate Gary Becker: employers who won't hire the best person for the job are going to suffer relative to their competition.[136] Even discrimination based on arbitrary features can be profitable, however, when the cost of discrimination is lower than the transaction cost of evaluating candidates on an individual basis. In such cases, the result is what economists sometimes call "statistical discrimination" or what I have termed rational discrimination.

Consider the case of a chain of stores seeking to hire entry-level workers recruited mainly from high school graduates in the local population. Let us assume, further, that African Americans as a group have a substantially higher crime rates than whites, Hispanics, or Asians. Employers could disregard this fact and carefully scrutinize the individual history and character of each applicant. This would certainly be the ideal course of action. But employers, who are in business to make a profit, may reason that entry-level jobs do not warrant the expenditure of time and effort to investigate personal case histories of each applicant. The employer may save search costs by simply refusing to hire blacks, or keeping the number of blacks hired to a minimum. This may entail some losses in job performance, if particular black applicants would actually to be better at the job and yet are refused. But these losses may be outweighed by the savings in transaction costs.[137]

That the discrimination unearthed by the Urban Institute study was probably rational is suggested by its finding that the race of the interviewer showed no correlation with the likelihood of discriminating. The reason that rational discrimination is likely to be practiced by white and black employers alike is that it does not depend on racist intentions. Rather, it applies the logic of predictive evaluation to racial groups, discriminating against people in high-risk categories. Race is not being singled out here: employers may have similar rational reasons for their reluctance to hire women, who may get pregnant and leave, or the elderly, who are more likely to fall ill, or young people, who may prove less reliable as employees. In Chicago, one of the sites of the Urban Institute study, Joleen Kirschenman and Kathryn Neckerman interviewed employers about their motives for hiring and found support for the rational discrimination hypothesis. Here are some of the candid reasons given by employers to explain their reluctance to hire inner-city black males.

- In general, one construction company owner said, for urban blacks "the quality of education is not as great as white folk from the suburbs, and it shows."
- Another commented, "The minority worker is not as punctual. They're not as wired to the clock in keeping time."

- A third employer remarked, "The Polish immigrants that I know are more highly motivated than the Hispanics."
- Asked whether whites have the best work ethic one employer said, "Not in every case, but as a group, I guess, yes."
- Several employers told the authors that blacks "don't want to work" and that "they've got an attitude problem."
- One manufacturer said, "We are not shutting out any black specifically, but I will say that our experience has been bad."

The authors conclude that blacks are victims of rational discrimination. Employers, they say, use race as a proxy for "aspects of productivity that are relatively expensive or impossible to measure." Many employers do seem to recognize diversity among blacks, often describing a particular individual as a good prospect, "the exception to the rule." Nevertheless, employers do use group generalizations so that in Kirschenman and Neckerman's view, "black job applicants, unlike their white counterparts, must indicate to employers that the stereotypes do not apply to them."[138]

DISCRIMINATION IN MORTGAGE LENDING

"Federal Data Detail Pervasive Racial Gap in Mortgage Lending," proclaimed the *Wall Street Journal* in March 1992.[139] "The Cost of Bank Bias," ran the headline in *Black Enterprise* in July that year.[140] "There's No Whites Only Sign, But . . ." fretted *Business Week* in October 1992.[141] In the last several years, hundreds of such articles alleging lending bias have appeared in the national media. It is now an article of conventional wisdom among many, especially African Americans, that minorities have a more difficult time getting loans than whites.[142] Energized by charges of bias from activist groups such as the Association of Community Organizations for Reform Now (ACORN), the Clinton administration has launched a campaign to force banks and lending institutions to increase their loans, sometimes at below-market rates, to blacks and to poorer communities in which minorities are disproportionately concentrated. "To shun an entire community because of its racial makeup," declared Attorney General Janet Reno, "is just as wrong as to reject an applicant because they are African American." Reluctant to be perceived as racist or to incur federal sanctions, many banks have agreed to invest millions of dollars in loans that they would not otherwise have made.[143]

Although charges of lending discrimination have been around for years, going back to the redlining controversy of the 1960s, discrimination studies until recently have tended to be amateurish and inadequate, propelled to public attention by uncritical news reports. The problem with most of the studies was that they focused mainly on differences in rejection rates between black and white applicants, taking into account their levels of income but without considering other factors such as net worth, existing level of debt, credit history, job stability, and size of down payment. Lenders consider all these factors, not just earnings, in approving credit applications.[144] Consider this startling fact: white households have a median net worth of around $45,000 while black households have a median net worth of only $4,200, less than one tenth that of whites. Since black incomes have risen dramatically only during the last few decades, even blacks and whites who earn roughly the same amount often have vastly different levels of net worth.[145] These gaps in accumulated wealth would obviously influence mortgage lending decisions.

Undoubtedly the most systematic evidence for racial discrimination in mortgage lending was presented in 1993, when the Boston Federal Reserve Board released a detailed study of more than six million 1991 home mortgage applications which showed that, holding constant for income levels, 38 percent of blacks and 27 percent of Hispanics were refused loans, compared with only 17 percent of whites. Directed by Alicia Munnell of the Boston Federal Reserve, analysts then corrected for standard credit criteria, such as net worth, age, education, probability of unemployment, and credit history. These criteria substantially closed the loan gaps among racial groups, but they did not eliminate them. Taking into account all conceivable factors, blacks were still rejected for loans 17 percent of the time, compared with 11 percent for whites. Obviously, concluded Richard Syron, president of the Boston Fed, discrimination was responsible for the balance. Syron was so confident of his conclusion that he pronounced the study definitive, so that "no more studies are needed."[146] Although the Boston Fed study uncovered a relatively small 6 percent differential between whites and blacks, for her success in proving discrimination, research director Alicia Munnell was vaulted to the position of Assistant Secretary of the Treasury in the Clinton administration.

Although critics pointed out some glaring statistical errors by Munnell's team, these were not large enough to entirely discredit the study.[147] The Boston Fed statistics do show a small but significant racial bias against blacks. The question is whether such discrimination is rational or irrational. Two enterprising reporters for *Forbes,* Peter Brimelow and Leslie Spencer, asked Munnell whether she had compared default rates of blacks and whites who were granted loans. Munnell confidently said yes, and those turned out to be the same. But Brimelow and Spencer pointed out that this result entirely undercut her thesis, because if it was harder for blacks to get loans than for whites due to irrational discrimination, then one would expect blacks to have a lower default rate on average. Equal default rates meant that the market was working well and that blacks and whites who received loans posed an equal credit risk to the lenders. Obviously if African Americans failed to make their loan payments at a higher rate than whites, then banks could be expected to be more selective in offering loans to blacks or to charge a higher rate to offset default risks.[148] This would constitute rational discrimination. Lenders could lower the information costs of considering the complex circumstances of borderline applicants. Instead of judging such applicants on their own merits, and giving credit where credit is due, bankers could predict their eligibility for loans by judging the economic circumstances of the racial group to which these applicants belong. This would save them the cost of determining whether and to what degree individuals vary from their group average in the likelihood of full repayment. Thus even identically situated individuals could be treated differently for legitimate economic reasons.

Rational discrimination may be difficult to understand in loan practices to racial groups, yet its economic justification is obvious in other areas. Insurance companies, for example, have no special dislike for teenage boys, but they charge them higher rates than female and older drivers. This is very unfair to an individual teenage boy who is a skilled and cautious driver, because he is penalized on account of the statistical habits of his group, a group he did not voluntarily join. Yet even with reasonably thorough personal information, companies are not in a good position to predict individual behavior. By contrast, group judgments, even when they are based on arbitrary characteristics such as age, can result in relatively accurate statistical predictions of group behavior, in this case accidents, and thus constitute a sound business rationale for decision making. Similarly, there is a sound economic rationale for companies to charge lower automobile and life insurance rates for women, who have a lower risk of accidents on average than men, and who tend to live longer. By the same logic, if there are differences in accident rates and life expectancy between whites and blacks, as there are, that would constitute a valid business criterion for insurance companies to take into account.

In a detailed analysis of Home Mortgage Disclosure Act data, published in the *Federal Reserve Bulletin,* a team of government statisticians provide evidence that supports the existence of rational discrimination. Focusing on a little-discussed aspect of the data, the authors point out that "the rate of denial for home purchase loans generally increases as the proportion of minority residents in a neighborhood increases." The authors bluntly observe that predominantly black neighborhoods "typically have high unemployment rates, lower owner-occupancy rates, higher vacancy rates, more boarded-up properties, older homes."[149] Consider the situation in inner-city Detroit. As outlined in a report in the black magazine *Emerge,* the median home value of a single-family residence in that city fell in constant dollars from $50,000 in 1970 to $36,000 in 1980 to $27,000 in 1990, virtually a 50 percent decline during a period when property values nationwide rose substantially.[150] Many factors conspired to produce this dismal outcome: white flight, black flight, crime, business closures, unemployment, terrible public schools. Can lenders be expected to ignore these economic patterns which are highly correlated with race? Are whites and blacks who can afford to move duty-bound to endure such urban decay? Granted that white flight as well as black flight are likely to accelerate neighborhood deterioration, nevertheless these patterns of behavior can be explained as a largely rational response to the economic and social disadvantages of maintaining a stake in predominantly black neighborhoods.

DISCRIMINATION IN CRIMINAL JUSTICE

Although blacks make up 12 percent of the national population, they comprise almost 50 percent of the prison population.[151] This overrepresentation, read against the background of a history of unequal justice for blacks and recent incidents like the Rodney King beating, convinces many that African Americans are systematically mistreated by policemen and the courts.[152] Bruce Wright, a black judge on the New York State Supreme Court, alleged the presence of a "killer instinct seemingly aroused in so many white police officers by the sight of black skin," and warned that African Americans were living in a virtual "police state."[153] And writing in the *Fordham Urban Law Journal,* one scholar concluded, "The majority of white Americans, deep in their psyches, want the police to act just the way they did in the Rodney King videotape."[154]

Is it true, as African American Congressman John Conyers says, that "government-sanctioned violence against its citizens is still in order"?[155] There have been literally hundreds of studies of judicial bias, and they have probed every aspect of the system. Frustratingly, the studies have left most scholars in the field bitterly divided, not because they are inconclusive, but because they seem to arrive at different conclusions depending on the technique and assumptions of the researcher.[156] How can we make sense of competing scholarly claims? Fortunately, there are some direct means to verify broad assertions of bias. For the past two decades, the Department of Justice has maintained an annual victimization survey in which those who have been robbed, mugged, and raped are asked to provide information about the circumstances surrounding their misfortune. Since victims are unlikely to lie about the race of their offenders, whom they want found and arrested, these victimization surveys can be usefully compared with FBI arrest statistics to see if there are large discrepancies between the racial proportion of victim identifications and the racial proportion of actual arrests. In fact, victimization surveys tend to confirm that blacks commit violent crimes at a much higher rate than whites. This finding is based on reports by victims of all races, including African American victims.[157]

If racism were pervasive in the criminal justice system, we might expect to find the racial gaps between blacks and whites increasing at every stage of the process from arrest to conviction to parole. This turns out not to be the case. Black overrepresentation is overwhelmingly concentrated at the arrest stage, and does not change very much throughout the criminal justice system.[158] A second reasonable expectation is that racial discrepancies between blacks and whites would have decreased over time, since no one argues that the criminal justice system is more racist now than twenty or fifty years ago. In fact, a larger proportion of blacks are in prison today than at virtually any time in the twentieth century.[159] A third plausible forecast is that Southern states where blacks are thought to be at the mercy of bigoted sheriffs and juries would have larger black-white differences in arrests and convictions than Eastern, Midwestern, and West Coast states. In fact no such pattern is evident, and many Southern states show gaps smaller than the national average.[160]

As Alfred Blumstein writes in the *Journal of Criminal Law and Criminology*, whatever discrimination exists in the criminal justice system is most likely concentrated at the front end, and reflected in the differential of arrest rates between whites and blacks.[161] Quite possibly many policemen in high-risk jobs use intuitive criteria such as dress and demeanor in deciding whether someone should be carefully scrutinized. Since police-men know from experience that blacks—especially young African Ameri-can males—are more likely to commit street crimes than whites, they too may practice a kind of rational discrimination. This would not mean, of course, that they arrest young blacks simply for being black, but rather that they are more disposed to see young blacks as potential criminals and thus show some bias in the way that they pursue some criminals and not others.

Perhaps the strongest evidence for arbitrary racial bias in the justice system lies in the area of death penalty convictions. According to a fa-mous study by David Baldus, Charles Pulanski, Jr., and George Wood-worth, which examined more than two thousand murder cases in Georgia in the 1970s, defendants charged with killing whites received the death penalty 11 percent of the time, while defendants charged with killing blacks were sentenced to capital punishment in only 1 percent of cases. Taking 230 variables into account that could account for the dis-parity on nonracial grounds, the so-called Baldus study concludes that defendants who kill white victims are 4.3 times as likely to get a death sentence as defendants who kill blacks.[162]

The Baldus study was offered to the Supreme Court as the basis for a death penalty appeal in *McCleskey v. Kemp,* decided in 1987. Writing for a majority of the court, Justice Lewis Powell rejected the argument that sta-tistical disparities prove very much on the grounds that the circumstances of each death penalty case are unique. He pointed out that juries consider an enormous range of witnesses and circumstances in making their deci-sion, and "discretion is essential to the criminal justice process."[163] Powell noted that the Supreme Court has insisted upon numerous procedural safeguards to ensure fairness in death penalty cases, and within these con-stitutional parameters discretion is permitted. Some states allow the death penalty and others do not: this is discrimination not by race but by geogra-phy, and it is constitutional. Since the 1970s more than two hundred men and only one woman have been sentenced to death; this disproportion is not considered proof of sex discrimination.[164] Powell also pointed to flaws in the Baldus study that were uncovered by the District Court at the lower level. The study relied on questionnaires that did not take into account all the aggravating and mitigating circumstances in the crimes under review. It lacked information on cases involving multiple victims, on whether plea bargain arrangements were considered, and on whether witnesses were credible or not. Taking into account additional variables that Baldus over-looked, the district court found a substantial drop in the racial gap. Finally the court placed the predictive value of the Baldus study at less than 50 percent: in other words, in fewer than half the cases could its statistical model predict the outcome of actual verdicts.[165]

It is true that there are no precise duplicates in death penalty cases. Moreover, death penalty cases are relatively infrequent, so that the statistical sample is necessarily limited. Even taking all of this into account, the Baldus conclusions are striking because they show such a notable racial disparity. In a pungent dissent, Justice Brennan placed the statistics into the context of Georgia's documented history of judicial bigotry to conclude that there was an unacceptable likelihood of racial bias. The findings of the Baldus study, which focuses on Georgia, are replicated in other studies that examine the nation as a whole.[166] The work of Baldus and others goes back to the 1970s, however, and is contradicted by more recent studies by Stephen Klein and others at the Rand Corporation which show no racial discrepancy in death penalty sentences when a full range of variables are considered.[167] Interestingly, even the studies that do find bias allege that the likelihood of a death sentence correlates not with the race of the defendant, but with the race of the victim. What this seems to suggest is not that predominantly white juries are biased against black offenders, but that they are more likely to identify with victims of their own race. Ironically this racial rapport benefits black offenders, be-cause most murderers choose victims of their own race. Discrimination against black victims results in discrimination in favor of black defen-dants. Thus white killers are more likely, on average, to receive a death penalty sentence than black killers. Whites who kill whites are more like-ly to get the death sentence than blacks who kill blacks.[168]

My conclusion is that racial discrimination does exist in the criminal justice system and that most—though not all—of it is rational discrimi-nation. Since justice is not a matter of groups but of individuals, howev-er, strong efforts must be made by legislators, judges, and juries to ensure that accused citizens are treated as persons and examined for what they did, not how their group as a whole behaves. Even if bias were to be wholly eliminated, however, Alfred Blumstein is right to caution, in his study of racial disproportionality in prison populations: "It must be rec-ognized that accomplishing that will not result in dramatic changes in the racial composition of prisons."[169]

THE FUTURE OF RACISM

In 1993, Senator Carol Moseley-Braun waged a histrionic campaign for the government to refuse to renew a design patent for the United Daughters of the Confederacy. Although the group mainly conducts philanthropic and social work, Moseley-Braun rallied a bitterly divided Senate with tearful references to slavery, her ancestors, and the symbolism of bigotry.[170] Similar campaigns to delegitimize Southern symbols like the confederate flag routinely erupt on campuses and in cities.[171] Despite the drama surrounding these confrontations, the evidence suggests, as Paul Sniderman puts it, that "the world has changed over the last half-century. It is very hard for people to recognize that America is a different place now. Yet we continue to fight old battles." This is not to say that the old racism has been completely obliterated from American life, only that discrimination is vastly less prevalent today than in the recent past, although there is evidence for the persistence of rational discrimination.

This rational discrimination is then identified as racism. But such an identification is wrong, because rational discrimination is based on group conduct, not biology. Rational discrimination is not premised upon assumptions of biological inferiority. Its existence compels us to revise the liberal paradigm which holds that racism is the theory and discrimination is the practice. It is possible to be a racist and not discriminate: this would be true of many poor and marginalized whites who might hate blacks and consider them inferior, but not be in a position to enforce their convictions. So too it is possible to discriminate and not be a racist: this would constitute rational discrimination.[172] Rational discrimination explodes the myth that differential group judgments are always based on erroneous prejudices and stereotypes and forces us to accept the reality of group differences which are real.

Just because discrimination is rational, however, does not mean that it is moral. As Christopher Jencks points out, rational discrimination is wrong because it penalizes minorities for physical characteristics that they cannot change.[173] This is also the case with gender and age. In this sense, rational discrimination based on unalterable characteristics is problematic in a way that discrimination against high school dropouts and convicted felons, who are in a position to reform their circumstances, is not. Thus the question of whether rational discrimination should be legal is a real one. The public policy dilemma is that such discrimination forces a choice in which the claims of morality are on one side, and the claims of productivity are on the other. Ideally, perhaps, rational discrimination should be illegal in situations where it is reasonable to impose the information cost of securing individual information on the potential discriminator, rather than allowing the use of race as a proxy. In the case of mortgage companies, such an expense can be spread or socialized over a large number of people, thus minimizing the burden borne by any single party. But obviously these are options not open to the cabdriver, whose security is at stake and who can neither gain personal information nor share the risk with society.

African Americans who suspect that discrimination today is more subtle and elusive are right: they might add that it is also based more on reality than on illusion. Blacks are also correct in their frequent assertion that it is a disadvantage to be a young black male in America today, and that even innocent blacks (especially males) are harmed by the decisions people make based on group characteristics. Rational discrimination against young black men can be fully eradicated only by getting rid of destructive conduct by the group that forms that basis for statistically valid group distinctions. It is difficult to compel people to admire groups many of whose members do not act admirably.

Thus the puzzle of whites and blacks witnessing the same racial landscape and coming up with radically different interpretations of it is finally resolved: whites are correct in their observation that they do not generally engage in irrational discrimination against blacks, and blacks are warranted in their conviction that discrimination against innocent members of their group, whether rational or not, is often painful, dehumanizing, and immoral. Whites are making a rational appeal to group traits, whereas blacks are making an ethical appeal to personal rights. Perhaps the most sensible appraisal of the new and complex face of contemporary racism and discrimination comes from African American historian John Hope Franklin. "There's still racism manifested everywhere in this country," Franklin said in a recent interview. "Not all of it is in our heads. A lot of it is in our heads. But blacks ought to help themselves more and stop crying about what they don't get. There are enormous opportunities that they ought to grasp."[174]

8

INSTITUTIONAL RACISM AND
DOUBLE STANDARDS

Racial Preferences and Their Consequences

Would you fly in an airplane from a company whose motto is, "We Put Diversity First"?
—Arthur Hu, *Asian Week*

With overt forms of racism being relatively scarce, and rational discrimination being attributable to accurate perception of group traits rather than a belief in black inferiority, civil rights activists have radicalized the definition of racism to locate it in the very structures of the American workplace. "Institutional racism" refers to merit standards of hiring and promotion that fail to produce proportional outcomes for minorities. It is a view based on an assumption of concealed or disguised racism. "The nature of discrimination today is such that there is not going to be a lot of documentation of what happened," remarks Franklin Lee of the Minority Business Legal Defense Fund. "There's not going to be a corpse where you can see the crime has been committed."[1] Here are some definitions of institutional racism.

> Institutional racism refers to the complex of institutional arrangements and choices that restrict the life chances and choices of a socially defined racial group in comparison with those of the dominant group.
> —Thomas Pettigrew[2]

289

Institutional racism can be defined as those established laws, customs and practices which systematically reflect and produce racial inequalities in American society.

—James Jones[3]

Racism can mean culturally sanctioned beliefs which, regardless of the intentions involved . . . justify policies and institutional priorities that perpetuate racial inequality.

—David Wellman[4]

Traditionally, racism refers to an ideology of biological superiority. The concept of institutional racism abandons this conventional view, divorcing racism from the concept of intentions or even individuals who are alleged to hold racist views. For the first time, racism is regarded as an impersonal force, an invisible hand, which operates through the structures of society to thwart black aspirations. One may say that the accusation of institutional racism infers the presence of racism from the failure of existing rules and standards to produce equality of results between racial groups. The persistence of inequality generates a conviction of imposed inferiority.

The criterion that civil rights activists use to measure the degree of institutional racism is proportional representation.[5] Both the charge of institutional racism and the expectation of proportional representation arise directly out of cultural relativism. Since all groups are presumed equal, many scholars and activists expect that a non-racist work force will automatically result in each group fanning out into the work force in a manner roughly approximating its ratio in the relevant population.[6] Since contemporary liberalism has a long-standing prejudice against American companies as amoral and rapacious, many liberals have found themselves acquiescing in the charge that corporate standards are inherently racist. Thus, many activists argue in favor of laws and policies that combat institutional racism by imposing race-based hiring and promotion on American industry. As legal scholar David Strauss writes, "The employment discrimination laws should be designed to give employers incentives to hire and promote members of minority groups in proportion to their representation in the general population."[7]

Consequently, a new form of discrimination has become widespread in today's workplace. Like discrimination of the old sort, it employs racial classification to prefer less qualified members of some groups over more qualified members of other groups. The new discrimination is legal, as the old used to be. What differentiates the new discrimination is that it targets whites, specifically white males, and sometimes Asians. Another novel feature of this discrimination is that it is clad not in the robes of a racism that dares not speak its name, but in the full regalia of moral indignation and social justice. The new discrimination is justified as an indispensable instrument for *fighting* racism. As former EEOC chairman Evan Kemp puts it, "Our government is in the business of stopping racial discrimination, and of promoting racial discrimination."

Racial preferences are now widespread in private sector job hiring. Pressured by the government as well as by internal minority constituencies, the vast majority of companies now give preference to black and Hispanic applicants both in hiring and promotion in order to meet affirmative action goals and targets. More than 70 percent of chief executives of Fortune 500 companies said that they engage in race-based hiring, according to a recent survey; only 14 percent said they recruit strictly on merit.[8] Companies such as IBM, Xerox, American Express, and Price Waterhouse have set up aggressive preferential hiring systems for minorities.[9] Marc Pacala, general manager for the Walt Disney Company, pledged that in order to achieve a "diverse team," Disney would establish minority hiring targets "at every level" of the theme park's operations.[10] Kentucky Fried Chicken established a policy of asking head-hunting firms to produce separate lists of white and black candidates, as well as men and women, to facilitate race- and gender-based hiring for its senior executive positions.[11] Theodore Payne, manager of corporate employment at Xerox, explains how racial preferences work. "We have a process that we call Balanced Workforce at Xerox, everybody understands that, and it's measurable, it's goals. Relative numbers. That's the hard business, but we do that all the time."[12]

Thousands of companies are pressured into racial concessions each year as a result of class-action lawsuits or intervention by government antidiscrimination agencies.[13] Northwest Airlines agreed to a settlement that could cost as much as $40 million to end a discrimination suit that was based not on proof of intentional bias but on statistical imbalances in the airline's work force. Northwest consented to accelerated hiring and promotion of black workers, special scholarships for black mechanics and pilot trainees, as well as back pay and possible promotions for existing minority employees.[14] In a blunt instance of racial preferences in action, *Los Angeles Times* Washington bureau chief Jack Nelson announced at a 1993 staff meeting that he would limit his future hiring to women and minorities. He was challenged, "Do you mean it's a rule that no more white males will be in the bureau?"

"That's right," Nelson said.

"Isn't that discrimination?" he was asked.

"No," he replied. "It's affirmative action."

Nelson justified the increasing flagrancy with which private companies, including the media, discriminate based on race. "Everybody knows it's true. I'm just being honest with people."[15]

Racial preferences have multiplied not only in the private sector but also in virtually every government department. As a result of internal pressure from a group called Black Agents Don't Get Equality (BADGE), the FBI recently agreed to establish race-based guidelines not just for hiring but also for merit awards, discipline, and coveted assignments. FBI agent Christopher Kerr terms these programs inexplicable in view of the fact that neither BADGE nor anyone else has presented any evidence that the FBI discriminates on the basis of race. For years the FBI has been rigging the results of its hiring tests, adding bonus points to the scores of minority applicants. Even after that, reports Hugo Rodriguez, who worked as an FBI minority recruiter until 1987, "They would decide they want so many blacks or so many Hispanics. Then they would go down the list until they got that number."[16]

Similarly the State Department, upon discovering that few African Americans speak foreign languages, routinely discards foreign language ability in its efforts to increase minority representation. Not only does it practice racial preferences in hiring, but since 1979 the department has also created a "near pass" category so that blacks who fail the entrance examination can be considered for jobs. Recently several white officials wrote to the *Foreign Service Journal* to protest what they insisted were promotion quotas throughout the department. "Instead of being considered as assets after our long, step-by-step rise through the ranks of a highly competitive Foreign Service," one officer wrote, "we suddenly seem an embarrassment to the department: too male or too white." Officers reported that they had been told not to bother applying for senior positions that were being reserved for a woman or a minority. Yet the State Department's legal adviser Conrad Harper, an African American, defends current hiring practices on the grounds that "it just doesn't do to walk into a bureau and see no one who looks like me."[17]

Public investment and pension funds, which invest the lifetime and retirement savings of millions of government workers, have increasingly gotten into the business of reserving a certain percentage of their capital for black- and minority-owned businesses. For example, the Resolution Trust Corporation and the Government National Mortgage Association both specify that a percentage of their business of issuing mortgage-backed securities must be assigned to minority-owned firms. Cities such as Atlanta allocate fixed ratios of their municipal bond issues to minority and female enterprises. Municipal pension funds such as the California Public Employees Retirement System and the Illinois Investment Board have set-aside programs for managing pension fund assets. "In the past, if you said you tried to do some things with black-owned firms, the pension funds would let you slide," William Cunningham, president of Creative Investment Research, a consulting firm, told the *Wall Street Journal.* "But now they've become inflexible. Now for some funds a certain percentage of investing has to go through minority-owned firms." According to J. D. Nelson, who runs an investment firm in Boston, the new program "clearly offers me an opportunity to get business that I wouldn't get if I wasn't a minority."[18]

Among those who are hardest hit by racial preferences in the work force are the thousands of whites who are denied jobs and promotions as fire fighters and policemen because of affirmative action goals and quotas. Unlike many jobs where hiring is based on fairly subjective and discretionary criteria, positions on the fire-fighting and police forces are typically awarded based on the results of a standardized test that seeks to measure job skills. Whites frequently discover that performance is no guarantee of reward, as positions they earn on merit are denied to them and offered on the basis of skin color to minority candidates who did not perform as well on the test. In 1994 the Chicago police department announced the results of its police sergeant test: out of five hundred officers who scored high enough to win promotion, only forty were African American and twenty-two were Hispanic. Immediately black congressman Bobby Rush declared, "Structurally the test was biased. It wasn't meant to promote African Americans." John Steele, a Chicago alderman, insisted that promotions "are done on who you know and not what you know." But in fact neither Rush nor any of the other activists claiming bias had seen the test, whose questions were not made public. A few years earlier, Chicago had paid more than $5 million to several consulting firms to devise multiple-choice tests that were free of bias. The 1994 test was the product of such a collaboration. Moreover, Asians who took the test scored higher than whites, undermining charges that the test simply measured familiarity with white middle-class amenities. The real problem, it seemed, was that very few minorities were meeting the police sergeant standards in a city that is more than 50 percent black and Hispanic.[19]

"We hire 60 percent Hispanics here, regardless of qualifications," says Freddie Hernandez, a lieutenant in the Miami fire department. Hernandez is an exceptional minority fireman in that he turned down three minority preferences and waited until he had the seniority and test scores to qualify under merit criteria for a promotion himself.[20] In 1992, in what fire chief Robert Osby termed a "national model," San Jose, California, announced the hiring of twenty-two fire fighters, including Hispanics, blacks, Filipinos—the most ethnically diverse mix in the department's history. But when Arthur Hu, a columnist for *Asian Week*, looked closely, he noticed that out of nearly two thousand white male applicants, only one was hired, and many had as good or better qualifications as minority candidates who were accepted. Asked about his hiring policy by the *San Jose Mercury News*, Osby explained, "Mathematically if you're going to include more people of color . . . then it will be at the expense of those people who had been included over the last 200 years."[21]

In a case where racial preferences seem to have come full circle, a county board of supervisors in Jackson, Mississippi, came under criticism in 1994 because since its membership became majority black in 1992, no whites had been hired to head any department. "I think we ought to promote a person from within, and I think that person should be a white," argued Ronnie Chappell, a white supervisor who previously supported the board's minority recruitment program. "We've got good qualified white people too." But Mary Coleman, a Jackson State University political science professor, denounced Chappell's recommendation. "If we have reached a point where race is the determining factor," she exploded, "then we need to renew our own integrity and morals."[22]

MERIT AS A RACIST CONCEPT

As these examples indicate, the enforcement of a norm of proportional representation conflicts with the classical liberal principle of individual merit. Merit poses an obstacle because, like the old racism, it too produces group inequality. As the results of any Olympic sprint quickly demonstrate, a race in which everyone starts at the same line inevitably ends with people hitting the finishing tape at different times. Moreover, as black domination of track events clearly shows, such contests produce not just individual but also group differences. As Daniel Patrick Moynihan wrote in the 1960s, "To the extent that winners imply losers, equality of opportunity almost insures inequality of results."[23] Consequently, many activists blame qualifications and standards of achievement for generating unequal outcomes between racial groups.

• "Though blatant racial discrimination is no longer the means of choice," Derrick Bell writes, "other seemingly race-neutral selection criteria, such as merit hiring, lead to similar results."[24]

• "Institutional arrangements such as efficiency and standards," writes David Wellman in *Portraits of White Racism,* "justify arrangements that in effect, if not in intent, maintain the status quo and thereby keep blacks in subordinate positions."[25]

• Legal scholar Paul Gewirtz argues, "Where an employment practice has a disparate impact on minorities or women, the practical effect is just as harmful whether or not it is caused by intentional discrimination."[26]

• "At the present time," asserts Joel Kovel in *White Racism,* "the main force of racist oppression is being administered impersonally, through the cold savagery of the economy. . . . Racist oppression occurs today through the seemingly automatic laws of the economic system."[27]

• Race-neutral selection procedures, Alfred Blumrosen writes, "preserve the status quo of white male supremacy, while using the rhetoric of equal opportunity."[28]

• Legal scholar Richard Delgado argues that "merit standards . . . reflect what the dominant group does well." Although neutral on their face, Delgado argues, standards of achievement "conceal the operation of racial favoritism." Thus merit, in Delgado's view, "has a special affinity for procedural racism."[29]

• In *Racism and Justice,* Gertrude Ezorsky offers a specific illustration of institutional racism. "To obtain a position, a worker often needs specific training or experience. If blacks tend to lack such qualifications, they are excluded disproportionately from employment. That impact is appropriately called racist."[30]

It should be clear from these remarks that the scholars and activists who allege institutional racism reject as fundamentally unsatisfactory the concept of equality of rights. Equality of rights seeks to mediate the conflict between merit and equality. It is egalitarian, in that it offers all a chance to compete, but it is also meritocratic, in that it permits those who excel to prevail. In a sense, equality of rights morally legitimizes inequality of result. We can endure losing the race because at least we had a chance to compete on the same basis as the other competitors. But equality of rights is only a meaningful concept when applied to individuals. Charges of institutional racism arise out of the conflict between merit and group equality. Most Americans can live with the idea of individual inequality as an outcome dictated by differences of natural ability or competitive effort. But, on relativist grounds, many scholars and civil rights activists reject as unacceptable and racist the idea of group inequality, specifically inequality between racial groups.

Few scholars or civil rights activists are against the idea of merit per se. There is no organized political or intellectual lobby on behalf of incompetence. But many who are committed to a doctrine of the natural equality of groups find it incomprehensible that fair procedures would not produce what they view as the necessary outcome of proportional representation. When this result does not occur, they insist that institutional racism is responsible for the discrepancy, and that traditional standards should be changed or set aside to enable an equitable ration of social rewards between racial groups. Some critics have charged that those scholars and activists who seek to fight racism by implementing a doctrine of proportional representation are enemies of the merit principle. This is only partly true. These scholars and activists seek to preserve merit, but within racial groups. Each group runs, in a sense, within its own racial lane. There is no direct competition between racial groups. Whites can compete with other whites for their racial share, blacks can compete with other blacks, Hispanics can compete with other Hispanics, and so on. Through such a multiple-track system of racial allocation, the civil rights establishment seeks to reconcile the principle of merit with the principle of group equality.

This chapter is an investigation of the charge that merit is a racist concept. It examines the assumptions of proportional representation to see if they make sense. It discusses the debate over whether standardized tests are racially biased against African Americans. It explores the consequences of our civil rights laws which seek to fight discrimination by practicing it. Finally, it analyzes the new concept of "managing diversity," a business technique for improving American competitiveness by transforming the corporate environment to harness the untapped resources of minorities.

THE PROPORTIONAL FALLACY

Let us examine the logic of proportional representation that underlies America's civil rights laws. The assumption is that if blacks or Hispanics are 10 percent of a particular population, the government may reasonably expect that each employer should hire at least 10 percent of blacks or Hispanics. If employers fail to approximate these proportions, then they are presumed guilty of illegal racial discrimination. Upon settling the case or being found guilty, they typically must pay expensive damage awards or establish preferential hiring programs to remedy their statistical imbalances.

A sophisticated advocate of proportional representation, David Strauss, argues that it is a necessary remedy for rational discrimination. At first glance this seems problematic. After all, rational discrimination is morally objectionable because it treats competent individuals as incompetent on account of their involuntary membership in a disfavored group. This is hardly remedied by racial preferences which treat incompetent individuals as competent on account of their membership in a favored group. Far from canceling out the effects of wrongful discrimination, racial preferences appear to exacerbate them. Strauss argues, however, that preferences are justified because rational discrimination "cumulatively disadvantages" blacks who would "not be less qualified as a group were it not for past wrongs."[31] In the similar vein, Michael Perry attributes the contemporary economic shortfall of blacks to "prior government misdeeds."[32] Michael Rosenfeld writes that proportional representation seeks to make victims of past discrimination whole by "increasing their prospects for obtaining competitive positions to the point where their prospects would have been, absent any past discrimination."[33] These scholars are relying on the "stolen goods" argument:

> It is not unreasonable that sons sometimes be deprived of certain benefits that derive from injustices done by their ancestors. A son who has inherited stolen property . . . has no right to the goods and may reasonably be expected to give them up. It seems entirely appropriate that they be transferred to the daughter or son of the thief's deceased victim.[34]

But this argument begs the question: what would be the natural distribution between groups absent historical discrimination? The mathematical logic of proportional representation requires that, absent discrimination, group outcomes be equally distributed. This assumption can be tested with the simple experiment of tossing a coin. On a single toss, it is true that the probability of getting "heads" is 50 percent, and the probability of getting "tails" is also 50 percent. But it is not true that in tossing a coin repeatedly, say 100 times, the guaranteed result is 50 heads and 50 tails. In fact, the statistical likelihood of getting precisely that result is very low— 7.958924 percent, to be exact.

Thomas Sowell performed the coin experiment of a hundred tosses, and came up with 41 heads and 59 tails. He also noticed that when he tabulated his results in increments of ten, he found large disparities. Sometimes he got 3 heads and 7 tails, at other times 6 heads and 4 tails, at still other times 2 heads and 8 tails. In short, he observed what statisticians call variance. The implication of this experiment is that even if in the aggregate we might expect workers of a particular racial group to participate in a sector of the work force in roughly their proportion in the relevant population, it does not follow that every company will be able to produce the expected racial ratio. Instead of being guilty of racial discrimination, companies could simply be guilty of statistical variance. The charge of institutional racism, in this analysis, is nothing more than a mathematical fallacy: blacks are being oppressed by the law of averages.[35]

The Equal Employment Opportunity Commission uses an 80 percent rule to enforce proportional representation: companies whose minority recruits are less than four-fifths of the ratio of each group in the population are automatically presumed to be discriminating based on race.[36] Using this rule, economists Robert Follett and Finis Welch calculate that "if the 0.05 rule were applied to 14 independent practices, the chance is about 50-50 that one or more would fail, even with neutral treatment."[37] In other words, companies entirely innocent of discrimination have a one-in-two chance of being wrongly accused by the government and forced to pay enormous fines and forced to engage in preferential hiring.

Legal scholar Richard Epstein writes that in formulating rules, the government should not merely consider the chance that illegal standards such as tests designed to screen out minorities will go undetected. The government, he argues, should also consider the likelihood that employers will be faulted for discrimination when they have engaged in entirely legal conduct.[38] There seems to be no historical warrant for expecting that absent discrimination, ethnic groups disperse into the various sectors of the work force in roughly their population ratios. In fact it is impossible to know what society would look like "but for" historical injustices such as slavery and segregation. Thomas Sowell writes:

> What would the average Englishman be like today but for the Norman conquest? What would the average Japanese be like but for the enforced isolation of Japan and two and a half centuries under the Tokugawa shoguns? What would the Middle East be like but for the emergence of Islam? In any other context, the presumption of knowing the answers would be regarded as ridiculous.[39]

In a comparative survey called *Preferential Policies: An International Perspective,* Sowell cites numerous studies which conclude that nowhere in the world, regardless of the presence or absence of particular forms of discrimination, do the assumptions of proportional representation hold true. One survey of ethnic groups by Donald Horowitz considered the markedly different characteristics of such groups as the Chinese, Indians, and Malays in Malaysia; the Gujaratis, Parsees, and Jains in India; the Ibos and other groups in Nigeria; the Lebanese, East Indians, West Indians, and Chinese in the Caribbean. Horowitz concluded that "few if any societies" have ever approximated a proportional distribution of jobs and social rewards between groups. Similarly, a study by Myron Weiner found "the universality of ethnic inequality. . . . All multiethnic societies exhibit a tendency for groups to engage in different occupations, have different levels and often types of education, receive different incomes, and occupy a different place in the social hierarchy."[40]

In *A Piece of the Pie,* Stanley Lieberson shows that the Italians, the Irish, the Swedish, the Greeks, and the Jews all entered "ethnic niches" where they built on skills that they brought with them to the New World, and took advantage of distinct market opportunities available at the time. The Irish, for example, were three times more likely than other whites to become policemen or firemen; the Italians were eight times more likely to become barbers; Russian immigrants were seventeen times more likely to become tailors or furriers.[41] Such patterns persist today. In a recent study of foreign-born professionals in the United States, the Center for Immigration Studies found that "whites are predominantly in the teaching field . . . while foreign-born blacks concentrate more in nursing and other health assessment occupations. Asians are more likely to be found in the sciences. Hispanic professionals are found more in teaching as well as among writers, artists and entertainers." Even within these fields, the study found differences in levels of skill, rank, prestige, and income: for the most prestigious occupations, Asians ranked at the top, whites in the middle, and Hispanics and blacks were last.[42]

Christopher Jencks calculates that the top earners in today's work force are the Jews, the Japanese, the Chinese, the Irish, Asian Indians, and Italians. The incomes of white Anglo-Saxon Protestants (WASPs) fall squarely in the middle. Hispanics, American Indians, and blacks are at the bottom.[43] Obviously there is no direct correlation between historical discrimination and success for all groups. Proportional representation fails to consider differences in talents, culture, interests, and preferences that partly explain the current dispersion of groups in the work force. Moreover, the enforcement of a proportional norm generates a paradoxical outcome. It ends up punishing groups, such as Asians, who are themselves in this country a minority, who have themselves suffered legal discrimination, and who have played no part in the historical crimes for which racial preferences are said to be a needed remedy. The reason that Asians and Jews suffer under current policies is that there is no algebraic way to increase the proportion of underrepresented groups without simultaneously reducing the proportion of overrepresented groups. Thus even groups whose success is manifestly due to talent and effort, rather than racism, find their prospects sacrificed at the altar of a questionable vision of social justice.

WHY BLACKS EARN LESS

Let us examine specifically the argument that if African Americans earn less than whites, the income differential can be presumed to be the result of discrimination. Such logic is very familiar: in a similar vein, we hear that women earn fifty-nine cents for every dollar earned by a man, the insinuation being that sexism is responsible for the differential. Andrew Hacker presumes the existence of discrimination because "while black Americans made up 12.1 percent of the tabulated population, they ended up with only 7.8 percent of the monetary pie."[44] Yet as is the case with gender gaps, racial gaps in family earnings between groups cannot be understood without considering relevant variables such as gender, age, geography, family structure, and most important, credentials, experience, and levels of skill. It proves nothing to point out that black college graduates as a group earn less than white college graduates. Only if black students attend the same colleges, take the same courses, and attain the same grade point average, would a group comparison of this sort make sense. Why is it reasonable to expect that black students majoring in education with a C average at a community college should command incomes comparable with white students majoring in business with a B average at the University of Wisconsin or Cornell? Christopher Jencks writes:

> When black and white students take tests that measure vocabulary, reading comprehension, mathematical skill, or scientific information, blacks do much worse than whites. If employers valued educated workers mainly for their skills, whites would almost inevitably earn more than blacks with the same amount of schooling.[45]

Consider that while black men on average earn substantially less than white men, black women at all levels of education earn about the same as white women with comparable credentials. Remarkably, black women with college degrees earn more than white women with college degrees.[46] This result directly contradicts to the theory of discrimination which holds that black women are subject to the "double jeopardy" of both racism and sexism.[47] Moreover, since black women are no less black than black men, their relative earnings parity with white women suggests the possibility that factors other than race might account for the black male earnings deficit.

Consider also that Mexicans, Puerto Ricans, and African Americans are a relatively young population. Mexican Americans and Puerto Ricans have a median age in the United States of under twenty-five, American Indians have a median age of twenty-six, African Americans have a median age of just over twenty-eight, while the American median is thirty-three, the median for many white ethnic groups is around thirty-five, and for American Jews is over forty.[48] Since most people's earnings go up as their careers mature, age differences are clearly part of the reason for average race differences in earnings.

So too wage scales are higher on the East and West Coasts than in other parts of the country, especially the rural South. Asians tend to be concentrated on the West and East Coasts, as do American Jews. Hispanics are concentrated in the American Southwest, and American Indians in a few states: Oklahoma, California, Arizona, Alaska, and New Mexico. Since 50 percent of blacks still live in the South, this regional distribution probably has the effect of depressing mean earnings of the group.[49]

Additionally, statistics that measure family income must take into account the fact that Mexicans have larger families, diminishing the group's per capita income which is distributed over a larger number of children, and many African Americans live in single-parent families which are likely to have much lower average earnings than two-earner families. Asian Americans have a higher rate of intact families than other minority groups, as well as the highest percentage of working members per family.[50]

When these factors are considered, racial gaps in earnings narrow but do not disappear. The remaining gap can be largely accounted for when economists and labor market analysts factor in relevant variables such as level of education, quality of education, field of concentration, skills possessed, regional location, specific character of the labor market, time of entry into that market, amount of work experience, and so on. Correcting for the whole range of criteria that influence earnings, economist June O'Neill, head of the General Accounting Office, concludes:

> Overall black men earned 82.9 percent of the white wage. Adjusting for black-white differences in geographic region, schooling and age raises the ratio to 87.7 percent; adding differences in [standardized] test scores to this list of characteristics raises the ratio to 95.5 percent, and adding differences in years of work experience raises the ratio to 99.1 percent.[51]

THE MERIT GAP

Undoubtedly the main obstacle to the implementation of proportional representation in the work force is the fact of large differences of developed ability and demonstrated performance among various ethnic and racial groups. These merit gaps are significant because companies do not hire people randomly or based on lottery, but generally based upon some test of qualifications or achievement. Consequently, courts, government officials, and civil rights activists who seek racial proportionalism have found themselves compelled to sidestep or confront the reality that on virtually every measure of achievement, some racial groups do better than others.

Scholastic Aptitude Test: According to data from the College Board, which administers the SAT as a measure of verbal and mathematical preparation for entering college students, large racial gaps between the performance of whites and Asians on the one hand, and Hispanics and blacks on the other, are apparent every single year on both sections of the test.

Both the verbal and math sections of the SAT are scored on a scale of 200 to 800.

Consider an SAT cutoff of 700 out of 800, a high score, but one that is close to the mean score of students admitted to the most selective colleges and universities in the country. In 1994, only 493 African Americans in the United States scored above 700 on the math section of the test, and only 148 African Americans scored that high on the verbal section. These figures compare with 11,000 Asians who exceeded 700 on the math section and 1,800 who did so on the verbal section. These figures are especially astonishing considering that only 80,000 Asians compared with more than 100,000 blacks took the test.

Now consider an SAT cutoff of 500 out of 800, which is not a high score, one that falls at or below the average of many private and state colleges. In 1994, 56 percent of whites scored over 500 in math and 30 per cent of whites did so on the verbal section. Sixty-one percent of Asians made the grade in math and 28 percent in verbal. For Mexicans, the percentage who made the cutoff was 26 percent math, 11 percent verbal. And for African Americans, only 15 percent and 8 percent surpassed the 500 mark in math and verbal scores respectively.

For the years 1990–1994, whites and Asians averaged around 945 out of 1600 on the SAT, Mexicans averaged 800, and African Americans averaged around 740. These are average gaps of almost 150 and 200 points separating whites and Asians from Hispanics and blacks respectively.[52]

National Assessment of Educational Progress: In 1992, the NAEP routinely administered tests of basic reading skill and mathematical competence to some 250,000 students in the fourth, eighth, and twelfth grades in schools across the country. Although black scores have risen over the years, they continue to lag substantially behind white scores. Here are some results for the math section in which students were asked to give "constructed response" answers to questions in the areas of numbers, measurement, geometry, basic statistics, and simple algebra. At the fourth grade level, whites answered 47 percent of the questions correctly, Hispanics answered 31 percent correctly, and blacks 24 percent correctly. At the eighth grade level, whites got 59 percent correct, Hispanics 42 percent, blacks 36 percent. At the twelfth grade level, whites scored 44 percent correct, compared with a Hispanic score of 32 percent and a black score of 26 percent. Similar patterns persisted for other "extended response" and "multiple-choice" tests.[53]

These NAEP ethnic gaps have persisted. On the 1987–1988 NAEP test administered to seventeen-year-olds, on the reading section, only 24 percent of blacks compared with 40 percent of whites performed competently; only 2 percent of blacks compared with 6 percent of whites read at an advanced level. For math, 21 percent of blacks compared with 51 percent of whites could demonstrate "moderately complex procedures and reasoning." Only 0.3 percent of blacks compared with 8 percent of whites could do "multi-step problem solving and algebra."[54] Relying on this data, one 1989 report concluded that in reading, mathematics and science "the average proficiency levels of black and Hispanic 17-year-olds are closer to those of white 13-year-olds."[55]

Doctoral Degrees Earned: Each year the National Research Council publishes data on Americans who earn doctoral degrees. While doctoral degrees reflect a serious educational commitment, they are an essential prerequisite for teaching jobs at most colleges and universities, for senior-level research and policy positions in many areas requiring specialized knowledge. In virtually every field they are considered a professional asset.

Yet consider the number of doctorates earned by particular groups in selected fields in 1992. *Mathematics:* whites 423, Asians 51, Hispanics 12, blacks 4, native Americans 2. *Computer Science:* whites 376, Asians 86, Hispanics 8, blacks 5, native Americans 2. *Physics and Astronomy:* whites 733, Asians 92, Hispanics 30, blacks 7, native Americans 6. *Chemistry:* whites 1,211, Asians 132, Hispanics 42, blacks 17, native Americans 6. *Engineering:* whites 1,874, Asians 447, Hispanics 72, blacks 48, native Americans 11. *Biological Sciences:* whites 3,043, Asians 262, Hispanics 101, blacks 61, native Americans 13.

Altogether, whites earned more than 23,000 doctorates in 1992, compared with 1,700 for Asians, nearly 900 for Hispanics, and just under 1,100 for blacks. Remarkably, nearly one-half of all black doctorates were in a single field, education, with most of the rest in fields like social work and sociology. In a long list of specialized areas, such as algebra, geometry, logic, astronomy, atomic physics, geophysics, paleontology, oceanography, biomedical engineering, nuclear engineering, cell biology, endocrinology, genetics, microbiology, geography, statistics, classics, comparative literature, archeology, German language, Italian, Spanish, Russian, accounting, and business economics, in 1992 there were no blacks who earned doctorates in the United States.[56]

National Adult Literacy Survey: In 1993, the U.S. Department of Education reported the results of a national test of what it termed basic adult literacy. The test measured not merely ability to read simple sentences, but also capacity to perform real-world tasks, such as understanding the point of a particular newspaper article, figuring out percentages from a tax table, filling out applications, writing a letter, reading a pay stub, balancing a checkbook, following directions on a map, and using a bus schedule. Tests were scored on a scale of 0 to 500.

On all three sections—Prose, Documents, and Quantitative—approximately 25 percent of whites, compared with less than 5 percent of blacks, scored above 325. Blacks were more than twice as likely as whites to score at the lowest level (below 225). Even when differing levels of education were taken into account, the Education Department found a 40-point gap separating blacks from whites in each testing category.[57]

Armed Forces Qualification Test: Each year the army administers a battery of tests designed to determine enlistment eligibility and qualifications for various military occupations. The AFQT, which is part of a more general test called the Armed Services Vocational Aptitude Battery, measures skills and training in such areas as arithmetic reasoning, mathematical ability, vocabulary and word usage, and comprehension of ideas. AFQT scores, listed on a percentile scale, reflect the applicant's standing relative to the national population of men and women between the ages of eighteen and twenty-three. Based on five levels of achievement, each reflecting a percentile cutoff score, some 45 percent of whites compared with 26 percent of Hispanics and 16 percent of blacks scored in the top two levels. By contrast, only 8 percent of whites compared with 20 percent of Hispanics and 29 percent of blacks scored in the bottom two levels. Seventy percent of whites compared with 50 percent of Hispanics and 37 percent of blacks scored above the level of the 50th percentile.[58]

Teacher Competency Tests: More than thirty-five states have some form of testing for aspiring teachers to try to ensure that they have reasonably good reading and comprehension skills to qualify them to teach in a classroom. Yet on a typical teacher certification test, psychologist Rogers Elliot reports, "About 90 percent of whites pass, and 35 percent of blacks. . . . The disparity in passing rates is universal."[59] Reviewing the results of teacher competency tests administered in ten states in

1982–1983 to determine the basic level of knowledge of reading, writing, and mathematics brought by teachers to the public school classroom, once again we see large racial gaps.

- In California, 76 percent of whites, 50 percent of Asians, 38 percent of Hispanics, and 26 percent of blacks passed the test.
- In Florida, 90 percent of whites, 63 percent of Asians, 51 percent of Hispanics, and 35 percent of blacks passed.
- In Arizona, 73 percent of whites, 50 percent of Asians, 42 percent of Hispanics, and 24 percent of blacks passed.
- In Texas, 62 percent of whites, 47 percent of Asians, 19 percent of Hispanics, and 10 percent of blacks passed.
- Similar white-black gaps were found in Georgia, Virginia, Oklahoma, and elsewhere.[60]

THE ATTACK ON TESTING

Aware of the merit gap, starting around 1980, civil rights agencies within the government carried out a largely covert agenda called "race norming." With the support of outside activist groups, the Labor Department used an "ethnic conversion table" to adjust minority scores on the General Aptitude Test Battery, a standardized test administered by the U.S. Employment Service and used as the basis for employment referrals. More than thirty-eight states relied on the data computed in this way by the U.S. government. As Mark Kelman candidly states, "Race norming simply reflects a substantive commitment to interpreting raw test scores in a fashion that facilitates the hiring of workers from groups that do poorly on the test."[61] An African American who scored in the 15th percentile, or at the very bottom rung of those taking the test, might have his scores raised to the 40th or 50th percentile, if that is how he fared compared to the performance of other African Americans. Ironically a white, an Asian, a Hispanic, a black, and an American Indian who took the test and received identical raw scores would end up with radically different percentile scores, since the results were adjusted to reflect how each person scored against competitors from that particular racial group. The worse the group performance, the more bonus points awarded to individuals from that group.[62]

Race norming reflected an ingenious technique promoted by civil rights activists to achieve proportional representation. By manipulating the scores released to employers, race norming circumvented the inconvenient reality of large differences in the performance distribution among racial groups. Obviously, secrecy was crucial if the system was to work, so employers typically were not clearly told that the percentile scores they received from the government described different levels of performance for each racial group. Yet the deception proved risky: when sociologist Linda Gottfredson publicized the practice of race norming in 1990, she provoked a national scandal.[63] Public officials expressed outrage that racial rigging of test results had been going on for years, without public scrutiny or accountability. Civil rights activists who had long been promoting what they euphemistically termed "within group scoring" now expressed shock at the revelation that the numbers were being rigged in their political casino. Faced with the challenge of defending race norming, these activists fell silent. Virtually without public supporters, race norming was outlawed by Congress in the Civil Rights Act of 1991, which was signed into law by President Bush.[64]

Paradoxically, the civil rights community's abandonment of race norming, as required by law, forced its activists into a more radical posture with respect to performance differences between racial groups as demonstrated in various tests. Previously civil rights activists could ignore the question of group differences because race norming made them irrelevant in terms of reaching the goal of proportional representation. Race norming, in a sense, permitted "separate but equal" race-based selection. But without race norming, scholars and activists committed to the goal of racial proportionalism found themselves compelled to launch a frontal attack on the very idea of merit, and the very possibility that it could be measured without racial bias. Thus the civil rights establishment's original attack on race-based selection has now developed into an attack on competence-based selection.[65]

• Programs to establish national standards of testing for American students are routinely denounced by coalitions including the NAACP, the Mexican-American Legal Defense and Educational Fund, and the National Center for Fair and Open Testing, known as FairTest. "We don't believe there is any evidence that national testing will lead to better education," Monty Neill of FairTest complained in opposition to one such initiative.[66]

• "Any tests that emphasize logical, analytic methods of problem-solving will be biased against minorities," charges Nancy Amuleru-Marshall, the director of research for Atlanta's public schools.[67]

- Standardized tests, according to Richard Seymour of the Lawyers' Committee for Civil Rights, are an "engine for the exclusion of minorities."[68]

- Teacher competency tests, according to African American educator Faustine Jones-Wilson, are "still one more way of reducing the number of minority teachers under the guises of *excellence* and *accountability.*"[69]

- Diversity consultant Ann Morrison argues that "the weight placed on math, science and engineering credentials may be considerably biased."[70]

- In her book *Affirming Diversity,* Sonia Nieto argues that tests should either be challenged for bias or opposed altogether; in their places, teachers should consider such alternatives as "creating class rules with students" so that outcomes can be "stated in positive rather than negative terms."[71]

- Denouncing what she calls "the misconception of sameness of treatment for all students," Geneva Gay alleges in a widely used textbook that "standardized achievement tests, minimum competency tests, teacher-made tests . . . by their nature contribute to the social stratification of students."[72]

- Derrick Bell argues that "Terms like *merit* and *best qualified* are infinitely manipulable" and serve as a mere excuse for "whites to treat one another like family."[73]

- Black scholar Michael Eric Dyson refers derisively to "the myth of meritocracy" which he defines as "the dominant belief that legitimates the central place of achievement in U.S. culture."[74] Civil rights activists are so skeptical of the basic concept of merit that they almost always use the term in quotation marks.[75]

- Yolanda Moses, president of the City College of New York, complains that in American colleges "masculine values like an orientation toward achievement and objectivity are valued over cooperation, connectedness and subjectivity."[76]

- Andrew Hacker expresses a thoroughgoing skepticism that any test measures performance. "I have never seen why a Ph.D. should be a requisite for college-level teaching. . . . There are no known correlations between good grades or high scores and subsequent success with a scalpel. . . . Tests cannot show who has a flair for diagnosing illnesses, salvaging burning buildings, or inspiring youthful minds."[77]

Scholars and civil rights activists propose a range of new approaches. One is to set a relatively low cutoff of "basically qualified applicants" and then treat scores above that merit floor as essentially comparable.[78] A second is to use "diversity-based sliding bands," in which employers do not select the most qualified applicants but establish fairly broad parameters within which test scores would be considered identical.[79] A third is to abolish tests altogether.[80] Other proposals involve forcing companies to provide remedial training to minorities, compelling firms to change their job descriptions so that more blacks can meet the new requirements, as well as pressuring companies to set different goals or sell other kinds of products, once again with a view to producing proportional parity.[81]

PREDICTIVE VALIDITY

Is it true that standardized tests discriminate unfairly against blacks and other minorities? Numerous such tests are in use. The U.S. Employment Service administers the General Aptitude Test Battery to make employment referrals. The military uses the Armed Services Vocational Aptitude Battery. In addition to the Scholastic Aptitude Test (now called the Scholastic Assessment Test), used for undergraduate admission, colleges and universities select students for graduate programs in part based on scores earned on the Law School Admissions Test, Graduate Management Admission Test, and the Graduate Record Exams. The Foreign Service administers the Foreign Service Entrance Exam. Standardized tests are frequently used to license or hire postal clerks, commercial truckdrivers, auto mechanics, real estate agents, travel agents, teachers, police sergeants, fire fighters, civil service personnel, office managers, architects, emergency dispatchers, air traffic controllers, certified public accountants, and practical nurses.

Two essential questions arise: how well do such tests predict performance in school or on the job, and are the tests racially biased against blacks and other minorities? Consider the case of the SAT, used for college entrance, and the GATB, used for job referral. The predictive value of the SAT has been extensively studied both by the College Board, which administers the test, and by outside analysts. Critics have expressed great skepticism that a multiple choice exam which measures vocabulary and basic math skills can provide anything more than a very impressionistic survey of student intellectual capacity. Stanley Fish argues that the SAT tests little more than "accidents of birth, social position, access to libraries, the opportunities to take vacations or tennis lessons."[82]

Yet the general conclusion of psychologists and psychometricians is that the SAT predicts college performance reasonably well.[83] In technical terms, the predictive validity of the SAT is approximately 0.50. (A score of 1 would indicate a perfect correlation between SAT scores and college grades.) Taken in conjunction with high school grades, the SAT is an even better predictor of academic success at the university level. In virtually all studies, the SAT turns out to be a better predictor than any alternate measure: high school grades, interviews, and recommendations. The reason is not difficult to surmise. High school grades depend on where the student went to high school, not only the relative academic strength of students there but also whether grades are assigned leniently or stringently. Interviews and recommendations are both highly subjective, and since references are often hyperbolic and list strengths but not weaknesses, it is not easy to know how to use them as a basis to compare candidates, or even whether they can be trusted.

Some critics have minimized the importance of the SAT's predictive value by insisting that it does not predict the grade point averages of individuals at a particular selective academic institution, say Princeton. But this is because Princeton students have for the most part been drawn from a relatively narrow range of SAT scores. It is possible for a student with 1,250 on the SAT to do better at Princeton than a student with 1,300, just as it is possible for a basketball player who is six feet, six inches tall to shoot better than a player who is six feet, eight inches. But it does not follow that the score is irrelevant to performance, any more than it follows that height is irrelevant to shooting. Like all statistically reliable predictors, what the SAT assures is that the average college performance of students who do well on the test will be far better than that of students who do not do well. Midgets are unlikely to succeed at basketball.

Some of its critics charge that the SAT does not predict success in later life, and this is largely true. But the test is not designed to do that. Indeed it is hard to imagine any test given to seventeen-year-olds that could fulfill that ambitious assignment. Success in life is difficult enough to define, let alone measure. Even if we are only calibrating material success, clearly that does not depend only on academic preparation or even cognitive ability generally, but also on other factors: ability to get along with people, willingness to take risk, good fortune, and so on. But there is no easy way to measure these personality traits and vicissitudes with any degree of comparative accuracy. Nor is there any reason to believe that people who do poorly on standardized tests possess these other qualities in greater measure than those who do well. What the SAT can measure is the ability to understand and use language, the skill to work with numbers, the capacity to make logical deductions. These are not the only skills required for academic success, but they are all important ones.

Like the SAT, the GATB turns out to be a strong predictor of subsequent performance. Studies on the predictive value of the GATB for jobs have been extensively reviewed for the Labor Department by industrial psychologists John Hunter and Frank Schmidt. What the studies attempt to do is to correlate success on the test with success on the job as measured by independent criteria, such as supervisor ratings or on-the-job evaluations. Using a technique known as meta-analysis, which combines the findings from many validation studies, Hunter and Schmidt conclude that the test is highly predictive for complex jobs and usefully predictive even for relatively unskilled jobs. While this may seem counterintuitive for a test that measures general rather than specific skills, Hunter and Schmidt argue that the verbal facility, reasoning ability, and mathematical cogency that the tests measure are all skills that can be applied to a vast array of job challenges. Hunter and Schmidt estimate the validity of standardized tests as predictors of job performance in intellectually demanding jobs at about 0.53. They rate other predictors such as references and interviews at 0.25 and lower. Even comprehensive biographical records and previous educational experience do not predict job results as well as standardized tests such as the GATB taken by all applicants.[84] Hunter and Schmidt's appraisal of the GATB's predictive value is probably the most thorough in the literature, but there have been other authoritative studies. When John Hartigan and Alexandra Wigdor made their own assessment of the GATB for the National Research Council, they significantly lowered Hunter and Schmidt's high estimates. Yet they too found a significant correlation of about 0.3 between test scores and job performance. Their conclusion was that the GATB was a modest but reliable predictor of job performance, and that it predicted better for some jobs than for others.[85]

Those who devise and study tests are well aware of the difficulties of constructing infallible or even highly predictive tests. Andrew Hacker is right that no one can definitely establish that a degree from a law school or medical school is indispensible to successfully practice in those fields. There are eminent teachers at many academic institutions who do not have a Ph.D. But in a world where self-taught geniuses are few and not easily identified, doctoral degrees will probably continue to be valuable prerequisites for the vast majority of senior-level teaching appointments. Imagine the case of a fire-fighter test that asks candidates to perform a series of basic verbal and reasoning tasks, and then to carry a heavy bag and run for 100 meters. The test is vulnerable to scornful challenge. Who is to say that those tasks precisely measure what fire fighters actually do? Certainly it is possible to imagine candidates who fail the test who could be competent fire fighters, and other candidates who pass the test who may not perform so well on the job. But if this criticism is valid, it simply means that critics and the fire department should work together to come up with a test that is more predictive of fire-fighting skills. Perhaps instead of carrying a heavy bag, applicants should be required to maneuver the fire hose while suspended from heights in awkward positions. Perhaps instead of doing basic algebra, candidates should be tested for their ability to read a map. These seem entirely relevant skills to measure: fire fighters, after all, do have to find the fire.

This is the point at which the civil rights critique breaks down. Existing tests are modest and fallible predictors of performance but they are the best that we have. Activists have shown no interest in coming up with tests that have a higher predictive value than the tests now used. The exclusive concern of the activists seems to be with tests that produce higher ratios of minority success. They seem perfectly satisfied with tests that predict little or nothing so long as they produce proportional minority hiring and promotion rates.[86] "Although they fault the tests for not being very good at prediction," concludes Barbara Lerner, a psychologist and test consultant, "it is the most predictive tests that make them unhappiest of all." Albert Shanker, who is head of the American Federation of Teachers, argues that "the better the standards measure performance, the more these activists will oppose them. If groups do not succeed in equal proportion, these ideologues will try and discredit all standards no matter how accurate they prove to be."

RACIAL BIAS

Even predictive tests, however, must survive the charge of being racially biased, which is to say, they must be equally predictive for whites, blacks, and other minorities. There is an intuitive appeal to the accusation that tests like the SAT and the GATB are unfair in this sense. Critics such as David Owen have scoured years of test questions to produce a handful of items which seem manifestly one-sided. Certainly it is hard to deny Owen's suggestion that blacks and those who live in the inner city are less likely to be familiar with terms like "regatta" and "sonata" than whites who grow up in the suburbs.[87] In fact, in recent years the College Board, which administers the SAT, seems to have made strenuous efforts to avoid questions presuming middle-class and suburban experience, and to emphasize passages involving African American and minority authors or subjects. One senior at Georgetown Day School complained that SAT material "tries to reverse every stereotype" by emphasizing black boys who are unrivaled in academics, and Asian girls who win every athletic race.[88]

None of this seems to affect the result. H. D. Hoover, who is director of state testing in Iowa, says that "there is no evidence that on those passages that include a poem by Gwendolyn Brooks that black kids do better than white students. There is no evidence that in passages with a woman as the main character that girls do better than boys."[89] But put aside the verbal section of the test. Concentrate only on the math section. Hardly anyone has seriously maintained that equations are racially biased, or that percentages are rigged against Hispanics. Yet strikingly the racial gaps that are evident on the verbal section of the test are, year after year, equaled and sometimes exceeded on the math section.[90]

The issue of how well tests predict for different racial groups is one of the most extensively studied subjects in psychology. Scholars have performed literally thousands of studies on a wide assortment of tests, including the SAT and the GATB. And the conclusion, hardly contested by a single reputable psychologist in the country, is that the tests are not biased against blacks. Even critics of standardized testing such as James Crouse and Dale Trusheim in *The Case Against the SAT* admit that the tests are slightly biased—in favor of blacks.[91] What this finding means is that tests are about equally valid in predicting the college and job performance of whites and blacks. African Americans do no better, in fact they do marginally worse, than their test scores predict. Moreover, the same test items that show the greatest differences between blacks and whites also discriminate most between high-scoring and low-scoring candidates within each racial group. These results were confirmed for the SAT in 1982 in an exhaustive review of studies by the National Academy of Sciences. The study found that, compared to their predictive value for whites, tests were slightly more likely to overpredict black success. "Ability tests have not been proved to be biased against blacks," the study concluded.[92] In an independent study, African American scholar Jacqueline

Fleming found that for students who attend historically black colleges, standardized tests such as the SAT "predict college grade point average exceptionally well."[93]

Similarly the GATB does not test esoteric knowledge about sonatas and regattas. The main sections of the test include numerical aptitude, spatial aptitude, motor coordination, and manual dexterity. And the GATB has survived extensive scrutiny seeking to prove racial bias. In 1989 John Hartigan and Alexandra Wigdor in their exhaustive study *Fairness in Employment Testing* reviewed seventy-eight studies of the predictive value of the GATB for different ethnic groups. Hartigan and Wigdor found no evidence of bias against blacks and some evidence of bias in favor of blacks "particularly in the higher score ranges."[94]

Tests do not create differences of individual and group ability; they merely measure such differences. "Tests should not be required to do things they cannot do," remarks psychologist Lyle Jones, "such as guarantee that distributions of scores will not differ for different racial or ethnic groups."[95] The tests are, for the most part, pointing to other social problems that should be confronted: problems of poverty, broken families, terrible neighborhoods, and so on. It is simply an evasion to seek to dispense with the test. Such a gesture would not eliminate, only conceal, differences in skill and ability. Precisely such concealment, for the purpose of facilitating race-based selections, seems to be the objective of the activists at the EEOC and the civil rights establishment.

THE REVIVAL OF NEPOTISM

It is now possible to reassess the accusation that merit is racist because achievement standards are merely a cover for the old nepotism. This charge does not contest the existence of valid criteria of measurement but expresses suspicion that they are being justly or neutrally applied. In an article, "The Myth of Meritocracy," Ellis Cose questions whether elaborate requirements imposed on applicants for seemingly straightforward jobs are really necessary; he implies that they may be a kind of racial screen, aimed at discouraging and eliminating minority candidates.[96] A sharper version of this critique, articulated by Stanley Fish, poses a more fundamental question: Whose standards? The logic is that of cultural relativism: standards are in the eye of the observer, neutral standards do not exist, all admissions and hiring criteria reflect power relations, those who are in charge are merely imposing their white male standards on the rest of us, merit is basically a political concept, and therefore society may as well recognize this reality, abandon pretensions to objectivity, and ration power and rewards according to race or some other political criterion.[97]

Undoubtedly some of the concerns expressed about merit and standards are well founded. Many jobs do not have any clear or neutral hiring criteria, and whether you get the job may very much depend upon whom you know. As Cose points out, selective colleges consider nonacademic criteria, such as athletic prowess, in shaping their freshman class, and it doesn't hurt if you are Ted Kennedy's son or the offspring of an alumnus or alumna. Even professional hiring always runs the risk of credentialism: the assumption, sometimes unwarranted, that if candidates have the proper background and résumé they are guaranteed to perform well on the job. Argues William Coleman, an African American who was transportation secretary in the Ford administration, "There are a lot of dumb white people who get breaks, and nobody seems too upset about that."[98]

Credentialism is only a problem when credentials are misused. When credentials become a substitute for demonstrated ability, or when the wrong credentials are demanded, inefficiencies can result. But the solution to this would seem to be a more careful use of qualifications in order to assure that they are relevant to the job at hand. Alumni preferences have no meritocratic justification and can be defended only by crass but realistic appeals to financial expediency. Athletic prowess is a different matter: colleges do not simply measure qualifications through grades and test scores, but also through extracurricular talents. If playing the violin or doing community service counts toward an all-round definition of merit, there is no reason why being a good quarterback should not. Without condoning the excesses of quasi-gladiatorial recruitment of student athletes by some universities that seek to make money through TV contracts, there is nothing wrong in principle with considering athletic ability as part of the comprehensive mix of skills that define merit. What makes being a quarterback different from being Hispanic is that the former is a talent, while the latter is a matter of chance.

To the degree that the civil rights critiques of merit have forced colleges and employers to reconsider the relevance of their recruiting standards to educational performance and business efficiency, they may be, as Randall Kennedy argues, "a salutary antidote to complacency."[99] The irony, however, is that activists who expose examples of the old nepotism at work never seem to want to stop those abuses. William Coleman is not demanding an immediate end to breaks for alumni children and athletes, but an expansion of preferences for minorities. Martin Kilson un-abashedly justifies racial preferences under what he calls the "modified merit paradigm."[100] Far from seeking to defeat the nepotists, Coleman and Kilson seem eager to join them.

Nepotism, which literally means nephew-favoritism, is of course nothing new. Indeed it is common in traditional societies for status, identity, and social obligations to be determined on the basis of membership in tribe, caste, or clan. Modern industrial societies such as America seek to uproot the stratified order of the *ancien régime* by replacing inherited status with talent or achievement. This was the rationale for Thomas Jefferson's "aristocracy of virtue and talent" which he intended to replace the old "aristocracy of wealth." Similarly, John Adams supported a regime based on "capacity, spirit and zeal" to supply the place of "fortune, family and every other consideration which used to have weight with mankind."[101] As Jefferson recognized, talent does not eliminate inequality but rather gives it a more justified or defensible foundation.

Of course merit standards only operate within accepted social parameters; they cannot entirely eliminate nepotism. All societies have elements of ascription and meritocracy. Modern industrial societies, however, seek to move as far as possible in the direction of merit-based selection, so that social rewards are assigned on the basis of achievement, and not simply based on arbitrary criteria such as birth, family, and skin color. At the same time, practices such as union-enforced seniority systems and college-administered tenure persist as the residues of the ascriptive world, as refuges from pure meritocracy. Standardized tests were introduced in the early part of this century for the purpose of separating the competent from the incompetent. As John Gardner writes, "Tests introduced an objectivity into the measurement of human abilities that never before existed."[102] Yet some scholars are appalled by the social consequences of standardized tests, not because they fail to sort people based on achievement, but because they do. Sociologist Jerome Karabel writes:

> A meritocracy is more competitive than an overtly class-based society, and this unrelenting competition exacts a toll both from the losers, whose self-esteem is damaged, and from the winners, who may be more self-righteous about their elite status than is a more traditional ruling group. . . . It is doubtful whether a frenetically competitive inegalitarian society is much of an improvement over an ascriptive society which, at least, does not compel its poor people to internalize their failure.[103]

The civil rights movement of the 1950s and 1960s mobilized opposition to the old racial nepotism. Martin Luther King and other black activists appealed to merit-based hiring, conducted without regard to race, as an effective means to ensure that able and deserving candidates got the job. But today's civil rights establishment has discovered that merit-based selection, like the old nepotism, produces inequality of result, because some groups perform better than others. Thus many civil rights activists are mobilized to fight what Nathan Glazer terms "discrimination against the less competent."[104]

This project is so embarrassing that activists find it necessary to conceal what they are doing. Thus college administrators who admit minority students with weaker credentials than white or Asian applicants who are turned away typically justify their actions as based on "other factors," yet they never supply a list of those factors. Apparently no whites or Asians possess them, because whites and Asians virtually never secure admission with the low scores that prove entirely adequate for the selection of blacks and Hispanics. Now, as before, favoritism disguises the unfairness of its transactions by hiding behind the curtain of subjectivity.

Although it is not easy to measure potential for achievement, which is what tests do, we need some measure, however imperfect, or else we cannot use achievement as a criterion for selection. The only alternative to a society based on achievement is a society based on ascription. This is what the race activists seem to want. In other words, they seek a *revival* of the nepotistic society. Racial preferences are no longer a cure for nepotism but a form of nepotism. The civil rights establishment today simply seeks to rearrange the old system so that there are new "ins" and new "outs." Ironically this campaign of self-promotion and expediency is waged under the moral banners of racial justice.

THE PATRONAGE INDUSTRY

Relativist attacks on merit selection, however dubious, serve an important political purpose: they legitimize a campaign advanced in the courts and in the legislature to allocate social rewards based not on achievement but on race. This campaign is irrelevant to the concept of civil rights as Martin Luther King understood it. Indeed it has little to do with proven cases of unwarranted discrimination. Rather, it is best understood as a patronage system for the civil rights establishment. Such patronage works through dual pressure from outside groups like the Leadership Conference on Civil Rights and the Lawyers' Committee on Civil Rights, and inside groups such as the Equal Employment Opportunity Commission and the Civil Rights Division of the Department of Justice. Instead of identifying and combating discrimination, these organizations are now in the business of manipulating the issue of discrimination in order to secure handsome reparations, payoffs, and jobs for its constituencies. This *modus operandi,* developed in the early 1970s, has now been perfected.

Starting in the late 1960s, civil rights activists in the Office of Federal Contract Compliance Programs (OFCCP) used their leverage over government contractors to force them to adopt "goals and timetables" for minority hiring. These early forms of racial preference had nothing to do with proven cases of discrimination. Rather, they were simply a condition for doing business with the federal government. Since most large companies, universities, hospitals, and many nonprofit groups are government contractors, they were in no position to refuse. Thus the tentacles of government became an instrument for the enforcement of racial discrimination against whites.

In 1972, when it gained legal power to sue private employers, the Equal Employment Opportunity Commission (EEOC) began its aggressive campaign of threats and lawsuits aimed at coercing companies to hire minorities on a merit basis if possible, preferentially if necessary. The EEOC targeted virtually every major company—including AT&T, General Motors, and General Electric—and, using the threat of lawsuits alleging racial discrimination, negotiated consent decrees typically mandating millions of dollars in back pay, settlement costs, as well as the implementation of minority hiring programs.[105] "Once we get the big boys," declared EEOC chairman John Powell, "the others will soon fall in line."[106] During the 1970s and 1980s, despite political vicissitudes, the civil rights bureaucracy in the federal government grew into a well-funded and powerful juggernaut, often operating in conjunction with courts, political committees, and interest groups, virtually unaccountable to the public at large. Former EEOC official Alfred Blumrosen boasts that by 1989 the commission had settled more than a quarter of a million complaints in favor of aggrieved minorities, and nearly 90,000 cases had been filed in federal courts.[107]

The EEOC's technique for enforcing racial preferences against whites and in favor of minorities typically begins with a filed grievance by an individual alleging discrimination. But instead of simply seeking to resolve the particular dispute with the employer, the EEOC uses the complaint to investigate the employer's overall minority hiring data. If it finds evidence of minority underrepresentation, the EEOC applies legal pressure, threatening a class action suit, and seeking to force the employer to agree to a package of compensatory payments as well as enforceable minority hiring targets for the future. "Originally justified in remedial terms," Andrew Kull writes, "these preferences came increasingly to be defended in terms that imply a system of proportional economic entitlements for racial and ethnic groups."[108]

The government's strategy is simple. If an employer has a racial composition that is out of proportion with the ethnic breakdown of the relevant population, then the employer is presumed guilty of illegal discrimination. As Nathan Glazer puts it, the law "assumes that everyone is guilty of discrimination, and then imposes on every employer the remedies which in the Civil Rights Act of 1964 could only be imposed on those guilty of discrimination."[109] In other words, employers who do not engage in proportional hiring have the burden of proving that they are not guilty of illegal discrimination. "We have vetoed the presumption of innocence," remarks Evan Kemp, former EEOC chairman. This is not unlike the criminal procedures in some countries, where defendants who are found in the vicinity of the crime are required to prove that they didn't commit the offense. Since the burden of proof is heavy, even defendants who are not guilty have an incentive to plead no contest or enter into a plea bargain to minimize their risk of severe and sometimes ruinous punishment. As Stuart Taylor puts it, many employers are branded as discriminators "whose only sin is hiring the best employees they can find."[110]

Precisely the same result obtains with employers embroiled in antidiscrimination litigation with the government. The presumption of guilt undoubtedly results in discriminators being penalized at a higher rate. But it also results in many nondiscriminators being coerced into pleading guilty. One may say that the charge of discrimination is so heinous that in many cases innocence itself is not a viable defense. The reason is that the government and the courts have imposed such stringent criteria for establishing the absence of guilt, that rather than risk a damaging verdict, many companies find it less onerous to pay damages and change their hiring practices. As political philosopher Harvey Mansfield puts it, hiring by mutual consent has, to a surprising degree, been replaced with hiring by consent decree.

Tama Starr, who is president of a small New York service company, writes in a trade magazine that it is virtually impossible to avoid the tentacles of the litigious government personnel. "One complainant had been late for work or absent for 70 out of 249 consecutive workdays. When we fired him, I had to provide reams of data comparing lateness and absenteeism by observed skin color for all apprentices within his particular trade over a 52-week period." Starr argues that rather than spend a great deal of money and waste time that could be productively spent, "Why don't we drop this outrageous game before it puts the United States out of business?"[111] The EEOC is unmoved. In recent years, James Bovard reports, it has participated in discrimination lawsuits against a life insurance company which fired a black employee who committed expense account fraud; against an oil company that fired a minority employee who stole company property and falsified expense reports; against a company that fired a secretary for refusing to answer the telephone; against the post office for refusing to hire a mail delivery man whose driver's license had been suspended four times; against a trucking company which declined to hire a job applicant who had served time in prison.[112]

There is now in place a massive bureaucracy to enforce these policies which are mandated by the ideology of proportional representation. Since the early 1960s, the OFCCP has expanded from a small division within the Labor Department to a powerful fiefdom, with around eight hundred employees and an annual budget of approximately $50 million. All companies with more than fifty employees and $50,000 in federal contracts are subject to OFCCP's racial preference rules. The OFCCP monitors about 400,000 companies that do business with the federal government. Each year it conducts thousands of "compliance reviews" and extracts monetary concessions and hiring agreements.[113] Similarly, EEOC has gone from a staff of a few dozen to its current size of nearly three thousand full-time employees, including several hundred attorneys. Meanwhile, its budget has escalated to around $220 million per year. All firms with more than fifteen employees are under its domain. All companies with one hundred employees or more must file annual reports delineating progress in minority recruitment. More than 85 percent of the private sector work force falls under EEOC regulations. Each year thousands of cases are filed in federal court with EEOC clearance, and an equal number are resolved through strong-arm negotiation.[114] Then there are the civil rights divisions in the departments of justice and education, as well as numerous affirmative action sections in virtually every government department and agency.

While the recent *Adarand Constructors v. Pena* decision imposes tougher conditions for their use, the Supreme Court has proved itself to be malleable to the logic of racial preferences. The Court has ruled that such preferences do not violate the seemingly explicit antidiscrimination language of the Fourteenth Amendment to the Constitution or the Civil Rights Act of 1964.[115] In addition, the Court has approved criteria that make it very difficult for whites to prove that they are being discriminated against, and for companies to prove that they are not guilty of discriminating against minorities.[116] Although this may change in the future, so far courts have shown themselves willing to impose on both the private and public sector an imaginative array of remedial regulations including numerical quotas, one-for-one promotion ratios, score adjustments on tests, abandonment of tests, and alternate hiring and promotion procedures.

Ordinarily one might expect racial preferences to proliferate in government, and to be resisted by profit-oriented companies which would pay a price for not hiring the best person for the job. Indeed federal and local governments, never known for imposing the highest competitive standards, have become notorious for engaging in blatant race-based hiring and promotion. Yet private companies too have proved generally invertebrate in resisting government pressures. One reason is that they do not wish to enter into expensive and long-lasting litigation, often with its attendant bad publicity. Moreover, while recognizing that racial preferences impose a cost on doing business, many company officials are willing to bear that cost since they know that their competitors must also engage in minority hiring. Thus if preferences are enforced across the board, they hurt the economy but do not impair the relative competitive position of any particular American company. Finally, senior corporate officials are often willing to enter into racial hiring arrangements because they win plaudits for high conscience even though they do not jeopardize their own jobs; instead they prevent opportunities for other whites, frequently at the entry or junior level. Frederick Lynch, a social scientist who studies affirmative action, observes that no corporate CEO has offered to step down to hand over his job to a minority.

Racial preferences are now a part of the daily routine of American business and government. *Business Week* reports that they are "deeply ingrained in American corporate culture."[117] Preferences are "so much a part of the way industry operates today," Alfred Blumrosen recently told the *New York Times,* that "to try to de-establish them would create enormous difficulties."[118] Company officials too have become habituated to race-based hiring because it is familiar, measurable, and may minimize the threat of both government and private lawsuits. In addition, they have now created restless affirmative action bureaucracies within their own companies which would strongly oppose any attempt to revise or scale back preferences.[119]

ADVERSE IMPACT OF PREFERENCES

Although few scholars study the effects of racial preferences—possibly because, as William Beer alleges, they are reluctant to see their relativist premises exploded[120]—it is not too early to make a preliminary assessment. Ironically one likely effect of racial preferences, which are supposedly in place to combat discrimination against minorities, is that as a legal requirement they provide companies with a rational ground to engage in such discrimination. The reason is that the institutionalization of racial preferences in college admissions, graduate school admissions, and job hiring virtually guarantees that, from a particular university or in a given field, the average black will not be as well qualified as the average white. Consequently, a law firm that treats, for example, white Harvard Law graduates as academically stronger on average than African American Harvard Law graduates would be using the same logic as Harvard admissions officers. Also, as Christopher Jencks points out, companies may be cautious about hiring minorities and women because of the recognition that, when it comes to discrimination lawsuits, they have more legal rights than white males.[121]

Several observers have noticed that many new companies now choose to move to states with few black residents, or to the Southwest where most unskilled workers are Hispanic, or abroad. Japanese companies seem to have a special knack for finding American locations such as Marysville, Ohio, where blacks are scarce.[122] These moves are not motivated simply by irrational stereotypes but by the genuine higher costs that companies face when they are forced to set aside merit-based hiring and recruit sizable proportions of less qualified black employees.[123] Consequently the American work force today is rife with cases of racial discrimination: the old discrimination, lessened but not eradicated; racial preferences seeking to combat the effects of such discrimination; and rational discrimination legitimized by such preferences. Whites as well as minorities are vulnerable to the new cross-currents of discrimination.

The vast majority of whites, survey data show, are strongly opposed to racial preferences in favor of minorities.[124] About half of whites insist that such preferences have hurt them a fair amount or a great deal.[125] In the view of some scholars such as Martin Kilson, white opposition to preferences is nothing more than the latest expression of the old racism.[126] In the liberal lexicon, white backlash is routinely attributed to antiblack sentiment. Yet Paul Sniderman and Thomas Piazza found that racial preferences are resisted on principle by large numbers of Americans who are not otherwise hostile to African Americans. In particular, many whites express opposition to unearned privileges being extended to African Americans who are not economically disadvantaged, and to new immigrants to whom this country owes no moral or political debt. Sniderman and Piazza discovered, however, that raising the issue of racial preferences with whites made them much more likely, in subsequent answers, to describe African Americans as lazy and irresponsible. "A number of whites dislike the idea of affirmative action so much and perceive it to be so unfair," they write, "that they have come to dislike blacks as a consequence."[127] A survey by the Anti-Defamation League of B'nai B'rith supports these findings: "Reverse discrimination victims are more apt to hold anti-black beliefs."[128] William Raspberry finds white resistance to affirmative action understandable: "How could we expect them to buy a product we have spent 400 years trying to have recalled—race-based advantage enshrined in the law?"[129]

Of course it is quite possible that white perceptions of the degree of benefits accruing to minorities as a result of racial preferences are somewhat exaggerated. Reginald Wilson, an African American scholar at the American Council on Education, points out that if one hundred people apply for a job and the one black candidate is chosen from somewhere on the list, ninety-nine whites insist that they were cheated. The African American did not take ninety-nine jobs, only one job. Yet he invites the hostility of all other candidates who see him as unfairly taking their job. Perhaps what is most legitimately frustrating to many whites is the perception that they do not have recourse to sympathetic or fair procedures for their grievances. White complaints of discrimination at the Equal Employment Opportunity Commission have risen sharply to around three thousand a year, but even those who file probably know that most EEOC officials do not treat such complaints very seriously. Not only is the EEOC bureaucracy openly hostile to what civil rights activists term "reverse discrimination," but the law itself offers limited protection to whites under the Constitution and the Civil Rights Act. "Some whites respond in the same way that blacks once responded to preferences," remarks legal scholar Nelson Lund. "Racial disadvantage is accepted as a fact of life." A few whites have taken to the old black technique of "passing" in order to win privileges by being counted as minorities.[130] As these grievances escalate, white political opposition to racial preferences is reaching hurricane levels.

Many senior public and corporate executives are well aware of the morale problem of white workers. Many powerful and bitter accounts of injustice are chronicled in recent books such as Frederick Lynch's *Invisible Victims: White Males and the Crisis of Affirmative Action.*[131] Racial preference policies "are creating a new class of the downtrodden and that's us," Mike Callahan, a Chicago firefighter, told the *Washington Post,* which found few of his colleagues who disagreed with that assessment.[132] Testifying before Congress, John Velde protested that because of minority set-asides his company could not get contracts even though they submitted the lowest bids for government work. "We learned we could no longer compete equally. We had the best prices for reputable service. Yet we could not work."[133] John Apel, a white police officer repeatedly passed over for promotion to sergeant despite his strong evaluations and test scores, complains that affirmative action has destroyed his career. "Time has run out for me now," he says, "I'm ruined."[134]

White disenchantment is strong, yet it seems to be exceeded by black frustration or, as African American scholars term it, "black rage." Initially it seems puzzling that a group that is the unquestioned beneficiary of systematized preferences should be doing anything other than celebrating its racial good fortune. And indeed most African Americans do seem to support preferences, which is hardly surprising. Few people have been known to turn down direct subsidies. Yet scholars who study the business world have reported their astonishment at the high volume of black anguish, even among workers making decent salaries. Writing in the *Harvard Business Review,* Edward Jones describes "expressions of disappointment, dismay, frustration and anger" which are the consequence of "careers stymied . . . they feel at best tolerated, they often feel ignored." African American managers feel treated as outsiders, as irrelevant to the success of the company, as inhabitants of a "velvet ghetto." Moreover, those who are hired in part on account of being black are subsequently treated as experts on blackness and civil rights. Black managers are exasperated at being packed off to "The Relations": community relations, industrial relations, public relations, personnel relations. Virtually all of them experience the stigma of being considered unqualified, and none of them like it.[135]

As these remarks suggest, black angst appears to derive in part from the widespread perception of incompetence that racial preferences inspire. "Mobility by means of affirmative action," admits Cornel West in *Race Matters,* "breeds tenuous self-respect and questionable peer acceptance for middle-class blacks."[136] Stephen Carter in *Reflections of an Affirmative Action Baby* poignantly describes the "best black syndrome," according to which black accomplishment is only evaluated on a race-normed scale.[137] Many beneficiaries of affirmative action describe feelings of ambivalence about tangible benefits that seem to bring with them intangible costs.[138]

African American rage comes not simply from white perceptions of black underachievement, but also from the real obstacles that employees hired on racial preferences experience in trying to rise within the corporate structure. Many minority workers and managers are convinced that they are in dead-end jobs. Companies that are legally or politically compelled to hire minorities are unlikely to place them in positions of serious responsibility: consequently racial preferences have inspired countless shop-window positions such as assistant director for human relations, liaison for minority development, coordinator for community affairs, consultant for interpersonal services, diversity officer, and so on. Sometimes these are well-paying jobs, but they rarely involve the substantial business of the company, and while they might lead to a position as vice president for diversity, they almost never lead to the job of chief executive. The reason is that, as a consequence of racial preferences, the Peter Principle, which says that people are promoted to their level of incompetence, sometimes applies to minorities at the time they are hired.

While middle-class blacks are understandably frustrated at occupying such comfortable but usually unimportant perches in the private and public sector, they also recognize that this is part of the Faustian bargain of racial preferences which they have seized upon as a quick route to success. When companies reorganize or downsize, executives are under economic pressure to cut back on generally unproductive divisions which have been created to preserve and display affirmative action employees.[139] Thus black irrelevance in the American work force is in part self-imposed. And black rage is largely a response not to white racism but to black failure.

Finally, there are growing signs of Hispanic discontent. Recently Tirso Del Junco, a Latino who is vice chairman of the Postal Board, complained that African Americans are overrepresented in postal jobs while whites and Hispanics are underrepresented. "They think it is a right to have this overrepresentation," Del Junco said. In Los Angeles, for example, blacks make up 63 percent of postal workers while Hispanics make up only 15 percent. In Washington, D.C., blacks make up 86 percent of the postal work force; Hispanics account for just over 1 percent. While black activists defend the current system, Del Junco concluded, "The black leadership in the major cities who are driving the system must accept responsibility for bringing equality into the system."[140]

MANAGING DIVERSITY

A new ideological movement called "managing diversity" has arisen to cope with the fallout from racial preferences. Promoted by academics and activists on the outside, and affirmative action bureaucracies on the inside, "managing diversity" builds on the logic of cultural relativism in an effort to transform the American workplace. "Managing diversity" is based on the recognition that companies that relativize hiring standards through racial preferences but then insist upon a shared set of standards for corporate performance are going to experience tensions. Thus advocates of "managing diversity" contend that blacks and other minorities experience difficulties on the job not because many of them are not fully qualified, but because corporations are patterned on a white male culture. Consequently, advocates of managing diversity propose a simple solution: relativize standards throughout the work force. They urge a dismantling of the existing corporate culture and its replacement with a set of standards that grants equal legitimacy to all ethnic cultures. By treating "diversity" and "standards" as synonymous, activists argue that companies will be able to harness the equal potential of all ethnic cultures. Specifically, activists call for racial preferences to be made permanent under the rubric of diversity, for such preferences to apply not just to hiring but to all levels of management, and in some cases for companies to go beyond proportional representation to give each ethnic group an equal share in decision making.[141]

Given these remarkable proposals, it may seem odd that "managing diversity" is finding a receptive audience in corporate America. One reason is the legitimate frustration of many executives over the lowered morale produced by affirmative action, which the new program promises to restore. Additionally, managing diversity advocates insist that theirs is not a formula for social justice but a hard-headed means to boost profits. In any event, many company executives seem impressed. "We've got to get right with the future," asserts David Lawrence, publisher of the *Miami Herald.* "Diversity is the soul of what we are all about."[142] Adds Goodyear CEO Stanley Gault, "We must learn to manage diversity effectively."[143] And James Preston, head of Avon, warns that "companies that do not adjust to cultural changes involving diversity are asking for trouble."[144]

According to Barbara Deane, publisher of the newsletter *Cultural Diversity at Work,* there are currently between three thousand and five thousand consultants who are helping import managing diversity to American corporations. For fees typically ranging from $2,000 to $10,000 a day, these diversity experts conduct workshops, seminars, opinion surveys, cultural audits, and in general help to shape the ways companies deal with racial diversity on the job. "Long-term organizational makeovers," reports Frederick Lynch, a political scientist who is studying the movement, "can cost from $100,000 to a million bucks." One consulting company, Elsie Cross Associates, offers a five-year plan costing more than $2.5 million.[145] A 1990 survey of 645 organizations by the Hudson Institute showed that more than 50 percent of them either had in place or were setting up managing diversity type mentorship, training, and promotion programs. Towers-Perrin, a consulting firm based in Atlanta, recently conducted a follow-up survey which shows that diversity-related initiatives have expanded in the past few years into a billion-dollar industry covering nearly 75 percent of the American work force. "The demand curve," says Robert Lattimer of Towers-Perrin, "is very strong."[146] Managing diversity programs and techniques seem to have infiltrated many major companies, including Apple Computer, AT&T, Avon, Coca-Cola, Corning, Gannett, General Motors, Goodyear, IBM, Xerox, Digital Equipment Corporation, Dupont, Hughes, Motorola, and Procter & Gamble. As the following items suggest, companies seem willing to lend not only their ears but also the pocketbooks of their owners and shareholders.

• Roberto Goizueta, chairman and CEO of Coca-Cola, recently pledged to buy over the next five years more than $1 billion worth of products and services from minority-owned and women-owned businesses, much of that specifically from Hispanic companies.[147]

• Kellogg, the world's largest cereal maker, not only conducts diversity training courses for employees, but has announced that vice presidents of the company will be evaluated in part on their progress in minority hiring and promotion.[148] Xerox too links manager compensation to achievement of specified "diversity goals."[149]

• The beer company Anheuser-Busch has a special minority purchasing program in which it purchases products and services from black and Hispanic business. The company has also commissioned several paintings of "the great kings and queens of Africa," each of them, according to Anheuser-Bush, "the proud work of an accomplished African-American artist."[150]

• The Pfizer health care company is committed to hiring a sales force that, by the year 2000, mirrors the racial breakdown of society at that time. Thanks to a special minority recruiting effort, Pfizer recently announced the recent addition of five hundred new salespersons out of which 20 percent were minorities and 40 percent were women.[151]

• Prudential Insurance has in the past few years sent more than seven thousand of its middle and executive level managers to diversity training programs which teach them, among other things, "increased awareness of the negative effects of joke-telling."[152] Similarly, at the New York law firm of Weil, Gotshal and Manges, diversity policy forbids attorneys from observing that minorities "are less qualified or only in the firm because of affirmative action."[153]

"Managing diversity" is presented as a paradigm for the twenty-first century, an adaptation to "the realities of the 1990s and beyond," according to Roosevelt Thomas, founder of the Institute for Managing Diversity. Thomas, an African American consultant whose expertise costs $10,000 a day, invokes the Hudson Institute's *Workforce 2000,* which predicts that women and minorities will make up approximately 75 percent of new entrants to the work force by the turn of the century. Yet Thomas insists that companies are still operating by archaic rules and standards. Protesting that employers practice affirmative action and then expect minorities to survive in a predominantly white male corporate milieu, Thomas argues that companies must undergo a basic transformation of their "core culture" in order to improve productivity and competitiveness.[154] Managing diversity advocates maintain that implicit in the culture of American corporations is a white male heterosexual norm which distorts the personality and stifles the creativity of minority workers. Roosevelt Thomas calls it the "melting pot mythology" which insists that minorities conform to a single standard. Taylor Cox contends that "minority group members . . . feel a part of their identity is sacrificed in order to succeed at their jobs."[155] Diversity consultant John Fernandez asserts that "manufacturing minority clones of white males is not the efficient, productive way to go."[156]

Existing work force standards, in the view of diversity consultants, merely reinforce racism. "Being a white male is like being born on third base and imagining you've hit a triple," argues author and consultant Anita Rowe.[157] Managing diversity activists emphasize that their sessions are designed to fight white hubris. Sometimes this is done in a heavy-handed way, through "shame and blame" sessions focused on white men. "*White male* is what I call the newest swear word in America," consultant Harris Sussman acknowledges.[158] "White people do not see themselves as white," says Judith Katz, author of *White Awareness.* "That's a way of denying responsibility for perpetuating the racist system and being part of the problem." Katz's solution? "Whites need to be reeducated."[159] Another consultant, Jacqueline Dickens, argues, "Whites have got to be willing to be uncomfortable until they learn what they may be doing that's offensive, and black people have got to be willing to take on the role of teacher.[160]

The main goal of managing diversity advocates, however, is not white enlightenment but a critique of existing corporate standards which are identified through so-called "culture audits." John Fernandez writes: "What signals are we getting when someone from a different culture moves their arms, hands or head? We must recognize that a culture may have a more laid-back style, but that doesn't necessarily mean that members of that culture are lazy."[161] Taylor Cox remarks, "There are certain cultural ways of putting together a proposal. If you think in a Western linear fashion, you go a-b-c. When you're from another background, the arguments are made in a different way, following a different kind of logic."[162] Managing diversity activists seek to transform the American corporate culture by giving equal importance to all ethnic cultures including, Roosevelt Thomas generously concedes, the culture of white males. In *Diversity in the Workplace,* Susan Jackson employs the language of cultural relativism: "*Different* is not equivalent to *deficient.*"[163] Jackson and others argue that each culture has a unique way of thinking and acting, and thus a distinct contribution to make to the American work force. Consultant Charles Jamison maintains that "racial diversity generates a mix of voices, and helps you get the best overall product." Taylor Cox argues that ethnically homogeneous workers generate "groupthink" while the most successful companies use heterogenous teams to improve productivity. Cox writes:

Diverse groups have a broader and richer base of experience from which to approach a problem. If persons from different sociocultural identity groups tend to hold different attitudes and perspectives on issues, then cultural diversity should increase team creativity and innovation.[164]

Diversity consultants propose a blizzard of solutions which go far beyond a requirement that workers abstain from insensitive remarks, or that advertising departments exhibit black and Hispanic models, or that companies participate in Hispanic Heritage Week or the United Negro College Fund annual appeal.

• Companies should work to establish and permanently retain a Balanced Work Force (BWF) which "means achieving and maintaining equitable representation of all employee groups at all grade bands in all functions and in all organizations."

• Managers should be given promotions in part based on their commitment to proportional representation. Sometimes they should be instructed: "You *will* have a certain number of minority managers and a certain number of women managers by next year."

• Companies should "require all employees to attend workshops that deal with all forms of *isms*," conduct courses "that teach about different cultures" and make attendance a "requirement for promotion," and sponsor "accent listening courses" to familiarize whites with ethnic pronunciation styles.

• All hiring and operating techniques that reflect the norms of the "dominant culture" should be modified: for example, companies may give up performance evaluations, a European tradition, and abandon "brainstorming" which is said to be a white male way of making decisions.

• Finally, companies should develop strategies for dealing with white male "resistance" which is characterized as "the normal reaction of people who are being displaced from a privileged power position"; one suggestion is that "companies must punish to the extent of firing those who do not appreciate, value and respect differences."[165]

DIVERSITY INC.

In order to see for myself how these managing diversity concepts are communicated to companies, I attended a two-day seminar sponsored by Roosevelt Thomas's Institute for Managing Diversity in Atlanta in March

1994. The Institute sponsors several such seminars throughout the year, with titles such as "Diversity and Cultural Audits," "Launching Managing Diversity" and "A Simulation in Managing Diversity." Most of these cost between $1,000 and $1,500 to attend, and supplementary videos can be rented for $350 to $500 or purchased for around $1,500.[166] Since I work for a nonprofit foundation and was attending the seminar for the purpose of research, the Institute permitted me to attend at the reduced price of $650, which is extended to scholars and students.

Taught by Brad Wilkinson and Kathy Lee, two self-described "change agents," our seminar was attended by a roomful of human resource managers, diversity officers, affirmative action directors, and other mid-level corporate personnel representing General Motors, AT&T, Travelers Insurance, and the Ohio Department of Transportation. The atmosphere was one of a revival meeting. Wilkinson spoke of race neutrality and the melting pot as attractive temptations to be avoided. "It requires a mind-set change, a new corporate lifestyle, a long-term commitment." He added, "Today color blindness is an affront. It used to be a virtue. We need to move beyond cookie-cutter models." Kathy Lee moved her fingers animatedly to place in invisible quotation marks such concepts as "merit," "qualifications," and the "dominant culture."

There was plenty of talk about how new standards would have to be devised to meet the changing needs of a diverse work force. "One size does not fit all," one diversity consultant insisted. Another participant added that "we have to learn that different does not mean inferior." Someone invoked the need to "move away from traditional either-or thinking" and replace it with "both-and thinking." An affirmative action officer stressed the importance of "mindset shifts within the dominant culture." Change agent Kathy Lee summed up the sentiment among those present. Under the new regime of managing diversity, she said, "Standards will not fall, but they will be different."

Accompanied by groans of empathy, participants voiced their complaints. In the plaintive words of Jana Bass of the Travelers Companies: "Nobody cares about race anymore. But race is our source of strength now." Another complained that the senior executives at her company were unsympathetic to her demand for "diversity councils" which would set and enforce "diversity standards." A third insisted that she had received consistently poor evaluations at the various jobs she had held on account of "patterns of prejudice." The lone dissenter in the room was a sardonic white woman, who was sympathetic to some of the diversity issues raised, such as flexible hours and maternity leave for women, but skeptical of the commitment to race-based policies and multiple standards. Minorities, she told me, have gone from accusing whites of treating them differently when they are the same, to now accusing whites of treating them the same when they are different.

Perhaps the challenge that the change agents and participants found most daunting was to supply a business rationale for transforming the company's standards, including hiring and promotion criteria, in the name of diversity. "We have to be able to create an aura of business necessity," Kathy Lee insisted. Brad Wilkinson spoke of the need to build political alliances within companies to overcome opposition. There was plenty of discussion of how to use benign terms. "If the words managing diversity don't work, get rid of them," Kathy Lee recommended. "Try the phrase: full utilization. Try to link that to total quality and see if that does the trick."

One affirmative action officer said, "I don't like the term culture audit. It sounds too social science. We should use the term career development audit. I think the company might go for that." She emphasized the need to neutralize opposition from what she acknowledged would be "real change that would really hurt some people." Brad Wilkinson cautioned, "When you talk to your superiors, don't appear to be on one side. Try to sound neutral. The goal is to educate, to get results, not to come across like an angry person." Kathy Lee added, "If you are perceived to have a political agenda, you are dead in the water."

DIVERSITY AND PRODUCTIVITY

"Managing diversity" has become controversial in the last couple of years mainly in response to excesses and blunders by consultants.[167] Critics such as Heather MacDonald and Thomas Sowell have pointed to the whopping fees and outlandish rhetoric on the part of activists such as "the best I'll ever be is a recovering racist."[168] Sowell may be right that some consultants are "secular versions of Elmer Gantry . . . great at laying on guilt trips."[169] In one serious incident, consultants holding a diversity workshop for the California-based Lucky Stores asked workers to write down lists of minority stereotypes. When some minority employees then proceeded to sue the company for discrimination, a judge allowed notes taken during the diversity workshop to be used in evidence. Lucky Stores was found guilty, and ordered to pay $90 million. The lawyer for the plaintiffs called the workshop notes "direct evidence of discriminatory attitudes. This was the proverbial smoking gun."[170] Yet these missteps and examples of chicanery do not invalidate legitimate new challenges to which the diversity movement is responding.

Undoubtedly many companies do establish rules and codes, explicit and implicit, that run the risk of being ossified. To the extent that those norms are reconsidered to assess their current utility, companies may be better off. Arbitrary rules can be modified or suspended, and only those necessary to job performance can be kept. At the conference I attended, consultant Kathy Lee gave an example: suppose a company refuses to permit its male employees to dress casually or to wear an earring. "That's a Eurocentric dress code," she says. "What bearing does that have on performance?" The answer is: it depends on the job. For someone working in the back of the office or in the mailroom, it might make no difference. For someone who deals with clients or works in the reception area, appearance is part of the image that the company wishes to convey, and thus a dress code may be a job-related standard.

Managing diversity activists are also probably right that in certain situations an ethnically diverse team can be good for business. Large companies and specialized firms are eager to take advantage of ethnic markets which are getting larger: blacks, Hispanics, and Asians reportedly spend $600 billion each year on products ranging from automobiles to perfume to designer jeans.[171] Companies that seek to market perfume, clothing, food, or cars to a black or Hispanic clientele may find it profitable to use minority staff within the company, or a minority advertising agency, in order to reach that specific audience. "We make sure companies like Budweiser don't use Spuds Mackenzie to sell beer to Koreans and Chinese," remarks Eliot Kang, who heads a Korean advertising agency.[172] Charles Jamison remarks, "Many companies wrongly assume that blacks won't buy expensive products, but that's not the case. As a matter of pride, many blacks do engage in conspicuous consumption." Such choices are not crude stereotyping; rather, they reflect a simple and practical understanding that, whatever their origin, there are aesthetic, stylistic, and cultural differences between groups.[173]

Yet the central assumption of "managing diversity"—that a variety of ethnic cultures automatically contributes to better productivity and better morale—remains questionable. Suppose that a company, in recognition of its diverse work force, decides to pipe in rap music instead of classical music, or replace the traditional handshake with the more exuberant "high five." Such changes may improve the morale of one group, but at the cost of lowering the morale of other groups. Michael Porter argues in *Competitive Advantage* that when employee cultures conflict, institutional performance is retarded.[174] Management expert Bradford Cornell argues that homogeneous groups organize more efficiently because they can relate to each other better and minimize confused signals which are the product of different languages or cultures.[175] Thus the potential tensions generated by diversity lead to a surprising conclusion: companies may realize important gains by maintaining an ethnically homogeneous work force. In many cases, smaller companies may find diversity to be undesirable, and large companies may have to pinpoint the optimum degree of diversity that produces the best morale and the higest productivity. Even Taylor Cox, a strong advocate of managing diversity, admits that "highly cohesive groups have higher member morale and better communication than less cohesive groups," and "too much diversity in problem-solving groups can be dysfunctional."[176]

Moreover, advocates of "managing diversity" never seem to consider the possibility that many ethnic traits may be liabilities for the effective functioning of most organizations. Some diversity consultants have identified some of the distinctive elements of black culture: Charles Jamison speaks of "masking," a concept of "elastic" or "colored people's time," an emphasis on emotion over detached logic, "playing" the white man, and exalting the trickster and "bad negro." Are there any companies whose performance in the market is sorely dependent on these qualities? Black cultural traits may well be the product of centuries of oppression. The effect of this discrimination, civil rights activists have argued for a generation, is to disadvantage blacks and entitle them to special programs of remediation. It seems peculiar for diversity consultants to maintain now that the heritage of past oppression has mysteriously transformed itself into a business asset. "Managing diversity" activists seem to want to give a positive spin to ethnic stereotypes, but without recognizing that some group traits may be harmful.

Finally, since ethnic traits are broad generalizations which do not hold true in every case, most companies will probably find that the best way for them to succeed is to define a single set of standards, closely tailored to productivity, and a uniform (though adaptable) culture that will provide the index of performance and the shared ground for employees of different background to relate to each other. A computer software company, for example, has nothing to gain by recruiting programmers with varied ethnic styles. The way for firms to maximize productivity is to specify the discrete skills that are required by the field, and to hire the workers who best meet those standards, regardless of background. If most of those employees turn out to be Asian, so be it. There is no "Hispanic perspective" on computer programming.

My conclusion is that "managing diversity" is an ideological movement masquerading as a booster of corporate performance. While its advocates are right to point to the need for companies to adapt their rules to changing conditions, many of the recommendations of the diversity activists are illogical and counterproductive. Many companies which uncritically embrace these precepts are likely to experience more conflict between employees and weaker performance. Diversity should be pursued pragmatically, not dogmatically.

FAIR RULES

The American work force is being corrupted by the new ideology of racial preferences, which are imposing incalculable costs on productivity. These costs cannot be computed simply by reference to the $30 billion that companies spend annually on remedial training, or the additional billions that companies lose annually due to worker incapacity.[177] Nor can they be limited to the approximately $100 billion that *Forbes* magazine estimates that federal, state, and private race-based policies cost.[178] Rather, the cost of diversity is the cost of lowered standards across the board, so that companies end up with less able employees, poor teamwork, and reduced productivity. More diversity, of course, is usually recommended as the solution to these grievances when in many cases foolish diversity policies are the cause of the problems in the first place. It is difficult to see how a work force oriented to the politics of employee diversity, rather than the economics of product quality, can perform successfully in the global market, which establishes an inflexible standard against which American companies have to compete.[179]

Moreover, what standard of social justice is served by the notion that racism is institutional and that, in some sense, everyone is a racist? If everyone is a racist, then no one is a racist. The term "institutional racism" becomes so broad that it loses clear meaning. Logical extrapolations of racism become increasingly far-reaching to the point that they make perfect sense to activists yet are utterly remote from common sense. Since racism is an ideology of biological superiority, "institutional racism" is a nonsense phrase that avoids the real problem, which is that even under the same rules, all groups do not compete equally well. Liberals seem to be hopelessly divided between a commitment to procedural justice—which is the essence of liberalism—and a desire to rig the rules in order to foreordain the results. The consequence is to weaken the moral foundation of liberalism itself, which ceases to be a just arbiter of competing claims and becomes one redistributionist vision among many. It is time for genuine liberals to abandon the destructive ideology of "institutional racism" and to rediscover the virtues of merit and standards evenly applied.

9

IS EUROCENTRISM A RACIST CONCEPT?

The Search for an African Shakespeare

> Travelers with closed minds can tell us little except about themselves.
> —Chinua Achebe[1]

Just as "institutional racism" is held responsible for the failure of African Americans to meet hiring standards, activists have come up with an equally bold and ingenious theory to explain why blacks do not compete effectively in schools and colleges. This explanation is Eurocentrism, which is said to be an expression of racism. The curriculum in higher education is alleged to be Eurocentric because it conveys the predominance and superiority of a culture that Americans inherited directly from Western Europe.[2] Multiculturalism and Afrocentrism are two systems of antiracist education which are sweeping American schools and universities.

The mission of American education is twofold: to produce good workers and good citizens who will live in a productive and self-governing society. Historically public schools have also served as instruments of egalitarianism and assimilation: for generations of immigrants, they were the "great equalizer" and the "melting pot." Yet since the 1960s, public school spending has risen dramatically but the overall quality of education has, by all reliable measures, declined dramatically.[3] Both in the schools and in the universities, the racial gap in performance between white and black students remains large and embarrassing. Afrocentrism and multiculturalism are championed by their advocates as solutions for these deficiencies. Together they promise what Edward Said terms "an almost Copernican change in the general intellectual consciousness."[4]

Many observers have been frustrated and bewildered by the controversy generated by Afrocentrism and multiculturalism. Critics including myself have charged activists with sponsoring distortions and excesses. Advocates insist that they seek nothing more than to correct historical biases and open doors and windows to the world beyond the West. For liberals, who recognize that more is at stake than a mere outbreak of global curiosity, multiculturalism and Afrocentrism have proved problematic yet impossible to completely jettison. The reason is that, whatever their abuses, multiculturalism and Afrocentrism are logical outgrowths of the Boasian ideology of relativism. Cultural relativism dictates that since all cultures are equal, the relatively poor performance of some groups must be due to the fact that they are being unfairly judged by another group's cultural standards. Relativism also requires that differences of wealth and civilizational achievement cannot be explained by cultural superiority; rather, such differences must be due to the fact that the more powerful culture is oppressing others. Eurocentrism, in this view, is the racist system which explains why whites score higher than blacks on tests, and why Western civilization is richer and more powerful than the Third World.

How can the relatively poor academic performance of blacks be accounted for by the fact that they are asked to write papers about Shakespeare and the French Revolution? The reason was given by James Baldwin several decades ago. Traveling in a Swiss village, Baldwin was struck by the rusticity of the peasant population, yet he resentfully observed:

> The most illiterate among them is related, in a way that I am not, to Dante, Shakespeare, Michelangelo, Aeschylus, Da Vinci, Rembrandt and Racine; the cathedral at Chartres says something to them which it cannot say to me. Out of their hymns and dances come Beethoven and Bach. Go back a few centuries and they are in their full glory—but I am in Africa, watching the conquerors arrive.[5]

As Baldwin's remarks suggest, Eurocentrism is held responsible for injuring the self-esteem of minorities. Since in the liberal view self-esteem is an essential part of identity, a wounded self-esteem is blamed for preventing minority and particularly black students from reaching their full potential.[6]

• "It's because of Eurocentric control of the public school curriculum," Ishmael Reed writes, "that the United States produces generation after generation of white bigots."[7]

• "As a black person," Alice Walker claims, "one cannot completely identify with a Jane Eyre or with her creator, no matter how much one admires them."[8]

• June Jordan concurs. "If you're not an American white man and you travel through the traditional twistings and distortions of the white Western canon, you stand an excellent chance of ending up *nuts.*"[9]

• Andrew Hacker argues that one of the reasons for black academic failure is that "historically white" colleges use curricula that "are white . . . in logic and learning, in their conceptions of scholarly knowledge and demeanor."[10]

• Toni Morrison contends that what distinguishes Western civilization is oppression and therefore a Eurocentric curriculum perpetuates racism. "Canon building is empire building."[11]

• "The traditional monoethnic curriculum in most schools," Christine Bennett writes in *Comprehensive Multicultural Education,* "has presented one way of perceiving, behaving and evaluating: the Anglo-Western European way. . . . It is a classic example of institutional and cultural racism."[12]

• As a result of Eurocentric education, Bell Hooks writes, "Masses of black people continue to be socialized to internalize white supremacist thoughts and values."[13]

• Afrocentric scholar Molefi Kete Asante argues for the necessity of "dismantling the educational kingdom built to accompany the era of white supremacy. No longer can the structure of knowledge which supported white hegemony be defended."[14]

• Another leading Afrocentrist, Asa Hilliard, explains:

> Because the U.S. educational system is built on a monocultural Euro-American worldview, it tends to benefit white students, whose cultural patterns and styles are attuned to this worldview. . . . Students of color, by contrast, experience conceptual separation from their roots. They are compelled to examine their own experiences and history through the assumptions, paradigms, constructs and language of other people. They lose their cultural identity.[15]

Multiculturalism and Afrocentrism represent initiatives in liberal antiracist pedagogy. What unites them is a thoroughgoing rejection of Western cultural superiority. Thus they seek, as Martin Bernal puts it, to "lessen European cultural arrogance."[16] Yet they differ in their intended audience and the positive remedies they propose. Multiculturalism is aimed at boosting the self-esteem and achievement of all students, while Afrocentrism caters mainly to inner-city African American students. Multiculturalism is applied relativism: it seeks an equitable distribution of power and respect between cultures. Afrocentrism tactically draws on the relativist denial of Western standards to invert the racist hierarchy and assert black civilizational superiority. It is worth exploring the impact of these radical pedagogies on America's students.

The Politics of Self-Esteem

The issue of minority self-esteem arises in the wake of the failure of school integration to substantially raise the academic performance of minority students. In 1971, the Supreme Court justified busing on the grounds that as blacks were transported to predominantly white schools, they would benefit from superior facilities and lose the "feeling of inferiority" imposed by segregation, resulting in both enhanced self-image and improved educational achievement. A generation later, millions of blacks are attending schools with white students and yet—as longtime busing advocate Gary Orfield admits—a large gap continues to separate the academic performance of whites and blacks.[17] Writes John Murphy, the current school superintendent of Mecklenburg County, South Carolina, the original site of the Supreme Court busing decision, "Two decades and millions of bus trips later, the promise of court-ordered busing has fallen short where it matters most, in improving learning for African American students."[18]

Moreover, studies show that the self-esteem of blacks attending predominantly black schools is just as high, if not higher, as that of blacks attending integrated schools.[19] Jacqueline Fleming reports in *Blacks in College* that African American men on largely white campuses experience "feelings of competitive rejection that have consequences for their capacity to muster intellectual motivation."[20] Neal Krause argues that one of the reasons for this is that "when blacks in white-dominated schools compare their academic performance with that of their white counterparts, their relatively low academic standing results in a loss of self-esteem."[21] Consequently many black mayors oppose busing in their cities, and in Prince George's County, Maryland, black and white legislators jointly announced a plan to end busing and replace it with a system of enhanced neighborhood schools.[22]

Now some African American activists contend that removing legal, geographic, and even material obstacles to the education of young blacks obviously did not confront the real problem, and may have contributed to it. Asa Hilliard argues that integration "may actually result in cultural disintegration that is borne disproportionately by an oppressed group, with privileged cultural groups being permitted to maintain themselves more or less intact."[23] Hilliard and others argue for the establishment of special public schools for black boys in order to enhance their self-image and thus their academic performance.

Self-esteem is a very American concept and Americans, probably more than anyone else in the world, tend to believe that feeling good about yourself is an essential prerequisite to performing to the best of your ability. Programs such as Outcomes Based Education seek to boost student self-esteem on the grounds that feeling good will help them to do well.[24] Self-esteem is also a democratic idea. In an ascriptive or hierarchical society, one's self-concept is provided by one's designated role: as brahmin, as elder, as patriarch, as peasant, and so on. Aristocratic societies do not speak of self-esteem but of honor. In a democratic society, self-esteem is claimed as an entitlement. Unlike honor, it does not have to be earned. "Feeling good is now an inalienable right," observes Steven Muller, former president of Johns Hopkins University. "Negative characterizations such as stupid, lazy or dumb are offensive violations of the newly defined American right to individual self-esteem."[25] Self-esteem in the West is largely a product of the romantic movement, which exalts feelings above reason, the subjective over the objective, the original being within. Self-esteem is based on the wisdom that Polonius imparted to Laertes: to thine own self be true. The philosophical roots of self-esteem are in Rousseau, who reversed the hierarchical distinction between the civilized man and the savage in favor of the latter. For Rousseau, civil society, however necessary to fulfill modern needs, nevertheless stifles human personality. Self-esteem reflects a quest for authenticity, for the true self under the layers of social convention. Yet as Charles Taylor has written— and as Hegel realized much earlier, in his famous master-slave discussion—self-esteem is part of a broader politics of recognition.[26] Our self-regard as persons and as groups depends in part on others recognizing and affirming us. If recognized as a right, self-esteem imposes on others the responsibility to make us feel good about ourselves. A failure to oblige can be interpreted as a serious social deprivation.

Actually, it is hardly proven that self-esteem promotes achievement. Long-standing organizations such as the Jesuits and the Marines have for generations produced impressive intellectual and motivational results by *undermining* the self-esteem of recruits. One of my Jesuit teachers said that "be yourself" is absolutely the worst advice you can give some people. Both the Jesuits and the Marines are famous for first degrading the pride and self-image of youngsters, then seeking to reconstruct it on a foundation of spiritual, mental, and physical performance.

Undoubtedly unimpressed by these authoritarian examples, the state of California a few years ago set up a Task Force to Promote Self-Esteem. Its mission was to boost the egos of students and thus enhance their educational skills. The state also asked a panel of educators from local universities to publish research on the relationship between self-esteem and other variables such as academic performance, truancy, drug use, and delinquency. In 1989 the panel published *The Social Importance of Self-Esteem.* The title said it all. "One of the disappointing aspects" of the study, concluded sociologist Neil Smelser, "is how low the associations between self-esteem and its consequences are in research to date." Several independent studies found correlations that were "mixed, insignificant or absent." The study found, to its own evident chagrin, that higher self-esteem does not produce better intellectual performance, lower teenage pregnancy, or reduced delinquency.[27]

These findings have been corroborated by studies comparing the self-image and academic performance of American students with that of students from other industrialized countries. Consistently, American students test higher in self-esteem: confident that their own abilities are superior to those of other students, they place themselves first among the developed countries. Yet actual reading and mathematics results show that American students score near the bottom of the list, behind countries such as the United Kingdom, Spain, Ireland, and Korea.[28] Similarly within the United States, students from Washington, D.C., ranked first in the nation in their own estimation of their math ability, but in achievement tests these same students ranked virtually last in the nation, ahead only of students from the Virgin Islands. By contrast, students from top-scoring states such as North Dakota proved more modest about their relative mathematical abilities.[29] American self-esteem, in other words, is unsubstantiated by intellectual achievement.

In an article in the *Review of Educational Research,* Mary Ann Scheirer and Robert Kraut showed that there is a causal relationship between self-esteem and academic performance, but it proceeds in the opposite direction. It is not self-esteem that boosts performance, it is performance that boosts self-esteem. In other words, as students see that they can find the amoeba in the microscope, that they are able to see their way through the logical dilemma, that they can find their way through the educational maze, then students feel empowered and more confident in their abilities. The authors conclude that educators should be cautious about assuming "that enhancing a person's feelings about himself will lead to academic achievement."[30] In layman's terms, it is possible to have a healthy ego and be ignorant at the same time.

MULTICULTURALISM 101

Multiculturalism is more than a self-esteem program. Its advocates present it as a broad alternative to "monoculturalism." Historian Peter Stearns insists that the multicultural debate "is between those who think there are special marvelous features about the Western tradition that students should be exposed to, and others who feel it's much more important for students to have a sense of the way the larger world has developed."[31] This is the unmistakable appeal of multiculturalism: it is obviously better to study many cultures than a single culture, to employ diverse points of view rather than a uniform lens. Yet if multiculturalism represented nothing more than an upsurge of interest in other cultures, it would be uncontroversial. Who can possibly be against hundreds of thousands of American students studying the *Analects* of Confucius or the philosophical writings of Al-Farabi and Ibn Sinha? The debate about multiculturalism is not over whether to study other cultures but over how to study the West and other cultures. Multiculturalism is better understood as a civil conflict within the Western academy over contrasting approaches to learning about the world.

Critics of multiculturalism such as Allan Bloom, Arthur Schlesinger, Jr., and E. D. Hirsch have argued for an emphasis on Western civilization. Bloom asserted in *The Closing of the American Mind* that American students are aliens in their own culture: they are abysmally ignorant of the philosophical, historical, and economic foundations of the West.[32] Hirsch in *Cultural Literacy* listed numerous literary references, historical facts, and scientific concepts that American students should know but apparently don't.[33] Schlesinger argues in *The Disuniting of America* that students should study Western civilization because it is their own. "We don't have to believe that our values are absolutely better than the next fellow's. People with a different history will have differing values. But we believe that our own are better for us."[34] Schlesinger's relativist argument for a Western canon is open to the following objection: what do you mean *we*, white man? Gerald Graff argues that in an ethnically diverse society, "who gets to determine which values are common and which merely special?"[35] Barbara Herrnstein-Smith contends that different groups share "different sets of beliefs, interests, assumptions, attitudes and practices. . . . There is no single comprehensive culture that transcends any or all other cultures."[36]

At its deepest level, multiculturalism represents a denial of all Western claims to truth. Stanley Fish denies the very possibility of transcultural standards of evaluation. "What are these truths and by whom are they to be identified?" In Fish's view, "The truths any of us find compelling will all be partial, which is to say they will all be political."[37] Barbara Johnson identifies the multicultural project with "the deconstruction of the foundational ideals of Western civilization."[38] Renato Rosaldo urges the rejection of "timeless universals" and Richard Rorty declares the following mission: "to abandon traditional notions of rationality, objectivity, method and truth."[39] The multicultural challenge is cogently summarized by philosopher John Searle:

> Religion, history, tradition, and morality have always been subjected to searching criticism in the name of rationality, truth, evidence, reason and logic. Now reason, truth, rationality and logic are themselves subject to these criticisms. The idea is that they're as much a part of the dogmatic, superstitious, mystical, power-laden tradition as anything that they were used to attack.[40]

As these remarks suggest, multiculturalism is based on a rejection of Matthew Arnold's conception of culture and an embrace of the Boasian conception of culture. Arnold advocated education that focused on the deployment of universal standards of reason to identify "the best which has been thought and said in the world."[41] By contrast, multiculturalism reflects the Boasian proposition that there are many cultures, Western standards are invalid for understanding non-Western cultures, all truths are ideological, and cultures should be placed on a roughly equal plane. These assumptions emerge from the reaction to a remark attributed to Saul Bellow: "Show me the Proust of the Papuans and I'll read him." Reflecting a widely held view, literary scholar Mary Louise Pratt termed that statement "astoundingly racist."[42] Why? Not because Bellow said the Papuans do not have the capacity to produce their own Proust; he simply suggested that, as far as he was aware, they had not. Yet Bellow's remarks, by hinting at the possibility of Western cultural superiority, deny to other cultures what Charles Taylor terms "the politics of equal recognition."[43] As Taylor correctly describes it, the multicultural paradigm holds that "true judgments of value of different works would place all cultures more or less on the same footing."[44] Renato Rosaldo argues that minority students have a right not simply to "political citizenship" but also to "cultural citizenship."[45]

Yet in the world and in the traditional curriculum, all cultures are not on the same footing. Consequently multiculturalism in practice is distinguished by an effort to establish cultural parity by attacking the historical and contemporary hegemony of Western civilization. To do it, activists draw heavily on leftist movements such as Marxism, deconstructionism, and anticolonial or Third World scholarship. Noting the spread of Western political and cultural institutions around the world, Gayatri Chakravorty Spivak deplores "the continuing success of the imperialist project."[46] Edward Said blames Western imperialism for the sufferings of "ravaged colonial peoples who for centuries endured summary justice, unending economic oppression, distortion of their social and intimate lives, and a recourseless submission that was the function of unchanging European superiority."[47] Expressing a widely held conviction, Michael Omi and Howard Winant write:

> The broad sweep of U.S. history is characterized not by racial democracy but by racial despotism, not by trajectories of reform but by implacable denial of political rights, dehumanization, extreme exploitation and policies of minority extirpation.[48]

Multiculturalism is based on the relativist assumption that since all cultures are inherently equal, therefore differences of power, wealth, and achievement between cultures are most likely due to oppression. Robert Blauner argues that these global disparities are replicated within the United States, so that blacks, American Indians, and nonwhite immigrants constitute a kind of Third World within the United States.[49] Additionally, Henry Louis Gates contends that a curriculum focused on the great works of Western civilization "represents the return of an order in which my people were the subjugated, the voiceless, the invisible, the unrepresented."[50] In order to compensate for these historical and curricular injuries, and restore cultural parity between ethnic groups, advocates of multiculturalism seek to reinforce the self-esteem of minority students by presenting non-Western cultures in a favorable light. James Banks argues that multicultural education should fight racism and Western "cultural imperialism" by showing students "that other ethnic cultures are just as meaningful and valid as their own."[51] Deborah Batiste and Pamela Harris urge in a multicultural manual for teachers, "Avoid dwelling on the negatives which may be associated with a cultural or ethnic group. Every culture has positive characteristics which should be accentuated."[52] Historian Ronald Takaki argues that blacks, Hispanics, and American Indians were no less responsible than whites for shaping the ideas and institutions of the United States:

> What we need is a new conceptualization of American history, where there's no center, and there's no margin, but we have all these groups engaging in discourse . . . unlearning much of what we have been told . . . in the creation of a new society.[53]

As Takaki's remarks suggest, the multicultural goal is not simply intellectual but also practical: claims of victimization provide the basis for demands for economic and political redress. James Banks contends that multiculturalism will promote power sharing by encouraging students to "participate in social change so that victimized and excluded ethnic and racial groups can become full participants in society."[54] Renato Rosaldo argues, "We are all equal partners in a shared project of renegotiating the sense of belonging, inclusion and full enfranchisement in our major institutions."[55]

DID COLUMBUS GO TOO FAR?

In order to see the multicultural paradigm at work, we would do well to consider the passionate debate that has raged in the academy over the legacy of Christopher Columbus.[56] Provoked by the five hundredth anniversary of the Columbus landing, virtually every leading advocate of multiculturalism—Edward Said, Stephen Greenblatt, Kirkpatrick Sale,

Gary Nash, Ronald Takaki, Patricia Limerick, and Garry Wills—have lashed out against Columbus. Yet it is not Columbus the man who is being indicted but what he represents: the first tentative step toward the European settlement of the Americas. Consequently, the debate over Columbus and his successors is a debate over whether Western civilization was a good idea, and whether it should continue to shape the United States. Multiculturalists typically answer in the negative.

• "Columbus makes Hitler look like a juvenile delinquent," asserts American Indian activist Russell Means.[57]

• Winona LaDuke deplores "the biological, technological, and ecological invasion that began with Columbus's ill-fated voyage 500 years ago."[58]

• The National Council of Churches has declared the anniversary of Columbus "not a time for celebration" but for "reflection and repentance" in which whites must acknowledge a continuing history of "oppression, degradation and genocide."[59]

• Historian Glenn Morris accuses Columbus of being "a murderer, a rapist, the architect of a policy of genocide that continues today."[60]

• Stephen Greenblatt alleges that Columbus "inaugurated the greatest experiment in political, economic and cultural cannibalism in the history of the Western world."[61]

• "Could it be that the human calamity caused by the arrival of Columbus," Ishmael Reed asks, "was a sort of dress rehearsal of what is to come, as the ozone becomes more depleted, the earth warms, and the rain forests are destroyed?"[62]

• "All of us have been socialized to be racists and benefit from racism constantly," Christine Slater laments in the journal *Multicultural Education.* "The very locations on which our homes rest should rightfully belong to Indian nations."[63]

• African American scholar Bell Hooks charges that "Columbus's legacy . . . has provided the cultural capital that underlies and sustains modern-day white supremacist capitalist patriarchy."[64]

Let us examine the consistent portrait that emerges in multicultural literature about the Columbian legacy. First, advocates of multiculturalism are unanimous: Columbus did not discover America. As Francis Jennings writes in *The Invasion of America,* "The Europeans did not settle a virgin land. They invaded and displaced a native population."[65] American Indian activist Mike Anderson says, "There was a culture here and there were people here and there were governments here prior to the arrival of

Columbus."[66] Kirkpatrick Sale contends, "We can say with assurance that no such event as 'discovery' took place."[67] Novelist Homer Aridjis contends that Europeans and native Indians "mutually discovered each other.[68] Garry Wills, Gary Nash, Ronald Takaki, and other scholars typically speak not of a "discovery" but of an "encounter."[69]

As is well known, Columbus was not the first European to reach American shores. Several centuries earlier, Viking boats without chart or compass landed at the northern tip of the Americas. Leif Erikson might have made the first Norse landing at Newfoundland in the eleventh century. Yet although the Vikings were probably the first white settlers, Daniel Boorstin writes that "what is most remarkable is not that the Vikings reached America, but that they settled here for a while without discovering America." By 1020 the last settlements had vanished, and the Americas remained as if the Vikings had never come.[70] The significance of Columbus, therefore, is not that he was the first European to land in America, but that he was the pioneer who, for better or worse, began the importation of Western civilization to the new world. Scholars have devoted plenty of attention to the linguistic implications of the word "discovery": for example, how can Columbus be credited with discovering a continent that he never knew existed, one that was previously inhabited by other human beings?[71] All of this is wordplay. True, Columbus went searching not for native Americans but for my ancestors in the Indies, and admittedly, his discovery of the new world was a revelation not from the Martian but from the European point of view. The real issue, however, as Leszek Kolakowski points out, is that "the impulse to explore has never been evenly distributed among the world's civilizations."[72] It is no coincidence that it was Columbus who reached the Americas and not American Indians who arrived on the shores of Europe. The term "encounter" conceals this difference by implying civilizational contact on an equal plane between the Europeans and the Indians.

A second accusation against Columbus is that, as the prototypical Western white male, he carried across the Atlantic racist prejudices against the native peoples. Gary Nash charges that Columbus embodied a peculiar "European quality of arrogance" rooted in irrational hostility to Indians.[73] In a similar vein, Kirkpatrick Sale in *The Conquest of Paradise* argues that Columbus "presumed the inferiority of the natives," thus embodying the basic ingredients of the Western racist imagination which was bred to "fear what it did not comprehend, and hate what it knew as fearful." For Sale, Europeans are especially predisposed to violence, while the native cultures live in a "prelapsarian Eden." Sale concludes, "It is not fanciful to see warring against species as Europe's preoccupation as a culture."[74]

It is true that Columbus harbored strong prejudices about the peaceful islanders whom he misnamed "Indians"—he was prejudiced in their favor. For Columbus, they were "the handsomest men and the most beautiful women" he had encountered. He praised the generosity and lack of guile among the Tainos, contrasting their virtues with Spanish vices. He insisted that although they were without religion they were not idolaters; he was confident that their conversion would come through gentle persuasion and not through force. The reason, he noted, is that Indians possess a high natural intelligence.[75] There is no evidence that Columbus thought that Indians were naturally or racially inferior to Europeans. Other explorers such as Pedro Alvares Cabral, Amerigo Vespucci, Ferdinand Magellan, and Walter Raleigh registered similar positive impressions about the new world they found.[76]

So why did European attitudes toward the Indian, initially so favorable, subsequently change? Kirkpatrick Sale, Stephen Greenblatt, and others offer no explanation for the altered European perception. But the reason given by the explorers themselves is that Columbus and those who followed him came into sudden, unexpected, and gruesome contact with some of the customary practices of Indian tribes. While the first Indians that Columbus encountered were hospitable and friendly, other tribes enjoyed fully justified reputations for brutality and inhumanity. On his second voyage Columbus was horrified to discover that a number of the sailors he left behind had been killed and possibly eaten by the cannibalistic Arawaks. Similarly when Bernal Díaz arrived in Mexico with the swashbuckling army of Hernán Cortés, he and his fellow Spaniards were not shocked to witness slavery, the subjugation of women, or brutal treatment of war captives; these were familiar enough practices among the conquistadores. But they were appalled at the magnitude of cannibalism and human sacrifice. As Díaz describes it, in an account generally corroborated by modern scholars:

> They strike open the wretched Indian's chest with flint knives and hastily tear out the palpitating heart which, with the blood, they present to the idols in whose name they have performed the sacrifice. Then they cut off the arms, thighs and head, eating the arms and thighs at their ceremonial banquets. The head they hang up on a beam, and the body of the sacrificed man is not eaten but given to the beasts of prey.[77]

When Cortés captured the Aztec emperor Montezuma and his attendants, he would only permit them temporary release on the condition that they stop their traditional practices of cannibalism and human sacrifice, but he found that "as soon as we turned our heads they would resume their old cruelties."[78] Aztec cannibalism, writes anthropologist Marvin Harris, "was not a perfunctory tasting of ceremonial tidbits."[79] Indeed the Aztecs on a regular basis consumed human flesh in a stew with peppers and tomatoes, and children were regarded as a particular delicacy.[80] Cannibalism was prevalent among the Guarani, Iroquois, Caribs, and several other tribes. Moreover, the Aztecs of Mexico and the Incas of South America performed elaborate rites of human sacrifice, in which thousands of captive Indians were ritually murdered, so that their altars were drenched in blood, bones were strewn everywhere, and priests collapsed with exhaustion from stabbing their victims. The law of the Incas provided for punishment for parents and others who displayed grief during human sacrifices.[81] When men of noble birth died, wives and concubines were often strangled and buried with their husbands and masters.[82] Europeans who traveled to other parts of the world expressed similar stupefaction at native habits. George Stocking writes:

> They witnessed modes of behavior which even the staunchest modern relativist might have trouble coping with—cannibalism, patricide, widow-strangling, wife-spearing and infanticide. The sheer vision impact could lead otherwise humane men to question human brotherhood.[83]

These gross realities were especially difficult to reconcile with the Western image, originally shared by Columbus and other explorers, of the pastoral Indian living in harmony with nature and his fellow man, basking in spiritual wisdom and uncontaminated by base human motives of ruthlessness and cruelty. Consequently European hostility toward Indians cannot be simply attributed to irrational prejudice: there was plenty of misunderstanding and confusion, to be sure, but Europeans also encountered practices that produced an entirely justified revulsion at the native cultures.

Multicultural textbooks, which are committed to a contemporary version of the noble savage portrait, typically find it difficult to acknowledge historical facts that would embarrass the morality tale of white invaders despoiling the elysian harmony of the Americas. Kirkpatrick Sale dismisses all European accounts of Indian atrocities as fanciful. "Organized violence was not an attribute of traditional Indian societies," Sale writes.

Seeking to explain away the evidence, Sale adds, "It is hard to think that European seamen would be able to distinguish a disembodied neck or arm as distinctly human, and not from a monkey or a dog, and in any case there is no evidence that they were to be eaten."[84] Stephen Greenblatt acknowledges the existence of human sacrifice but faults the Europeans for not recognizing its "deepest resemblance" to one of their own cultural practices: after all, Greenblatt says, the Spanish themselves symbolically consumed the body and blood of Christ in the eucharist, and mass murder is merely a "weirdly literal Aztec equivalent."[85]

Consider a recent analysis of two recent books on the Aztecs, published as a guide for teachers in the magazine *Multicultural Review.* The first book, Francisco Alarcon's *Snake Poems: An Aztec Invocation* receives high praise as "a wonderful celebration of Aztec religion, beliefs and customs, intermingled with the thoughts and feelings of today's Mexican Americans." The second book, Tim Wood's *The Aztecs,* is denounced for its "sensationalistic and lurid manner . . . the Aztec practice of human sacrifice is described in gory detail. This book is a distortion of the Aztecs."[86] This review illustrates the way in which the relativist ideology shapes the predispositions of the advocates of multiculturalism. Students are exposed to the positive features of Aztec life, which are placed on a dubious continuum with contemporary Mexican-American experience, whereas central Aztec practices such as human sacrifice are suppressed. As Pascal Bruckner puts it, "Exoticism has to stay within the bounds of good taste."[87]

Next Columbus—and by extension the West—is accused of perpetrating a campaign of genocidal extermination, a virtual holocaust against native Americans. Kirkpatrick Sale charges the successors of Columbus with promoting, within a single generation, "something we must call genocide."[88] Claude Lévi-Strauss charges that millions of Indians "died of horror and disgust at European civilization."[89] Tzvetan Todorov in *The Conquest of America* accuses his fellow Europeans of producing "the greatest genocide in human history."[90] The charge of mass murder is largely sustained by figures showing the precipitous decline of the Indian population. Although scholars debate the exact numbers, in Alvin Josephy's estimate, the Indian population fell from fifteen million when the white man first arrived to a fraction of that over the next 150 years.[91] Undoubtedly the Indians perished in great numbers. Yet although European enslavement of Indians and the Spanish forced labor system extracted a heavy toll in lives, the vast majority of Indian casualties occurred not as a result of hard labor or deliberate destruction but because of contagious diseases that the Europeans transmitted to the Indians.[92]

Actually, the spread of infection and unhealthy patterns of behavior was reciprocal. From the Indians the Europeans probably contracted syphilis. The Indians also taught the white man about tobacco and cocaine, which would extract an incalculable human toll over the next several centuries. The Europeans, for their part, gave the Indians measles and smallpox, although recent research has shown that tuberculosis predated the European arrival in the New World. Since the Indians had not developed any resistance or immunity to these unfamiliar ailments, they perished in catastrophic numbers.[93] This was a tragedy of great magnitude, but undoubtedly the term "genocide" is both anachronistic and wrongly applied in that, with a few gruesome exceptions, the European transmission of disease was not deliberate. As William McNeill points out in *Plagues and Peoples,* Europeans themselves probably contracted the bubonic plague in the fourteenth century as a result of contagion from the Mongols of Central Asia—some twenty-five million or one third of the population died, and the plague recurred on the continent for the next three hundred years.[94] Multicultural advocates do not call this "genocide."

WESTERN CULTURAL SUPERIORITY

The reason advocates of multiculturalism charge Columbus with genocide is because they need to explain why small groups of Europeans were able to defeat overwhelming numbers of Indians, capsize their mighty native empires, and seize their land. Hernán Cortés rode into Mexico with around five hundred men, sixteen horses, and a few dozen long-barrel guns. The Aztec force that he faced numbered more than a million men. When Gonzalo Pizarro confronted the Inca he had three ships, 150 men, one cannon, and thirty horses. The Incas had several hundred thousand troops which had ruled over a population of several million.[95] Yet the Aztecs and the Incas were routed. How did the Spanish prevail? The triumph of the Spanish over the Indians is an interesting dilemma because no army, however well-trained, can overcome such numerical odds. Nor did the slow-loading European rifles provide a decisive advantage. It is true that many Indians were astonished at the mobility of European troops on horseback—the Indians had no horses before the Spanish imported them to the Americas—but the novelty of Spanish cavalry could only have caused temporary confusion in the ranks of the enemy. Undoubtedly one factor that contributed to European victory was the defection to the Spanish side of a sizable number of Indians who came from tribes that had long been colonized and persecuted by the Aztecs and the Incas. Yet these are only partial explanations.

Mario Vargas Llosa, the Peruvian writer and statesman, offers an arresting theory. However small their numbers, however crude their representatives, Europeans came to the Americas with a civilizational ideology that was unquestionably modern, even if embryonically so. Among the ingredients of this modernity were a rational understanding of the universe, as well as a new understanding of individual initiative. By contrast, the Indians still lived in the world of the spirits—the enchanted universe. They could not adapt to changing circumstances. They confused the Europeans with gods. They sought to reverse casualties by sacrificing their own soldiers to the totems. When Montezuma's military advisers and soothsayers warned him of ill omens, he ordered them imprisoned and their wives and children killed. The Indians were held in paralyzing obedience to the emperor. They were accustomed to exterminating their inferiors but were unfamiliar with the challenges of combat against well-armed peers.

In short, Vargas Llosa argues, the Indians were defeated and massacred because, by a cruel juxtaposition of history, they encountered, even in the persons of "semiliterate, implacable, and greedy swordsmen," a Spanish civilization that was superior both in the sophistication of its arms and in its ideas. Even today, Vargas Llosa writes, the principles of the West continue to shape the modern world and "the nations that reject those values are anachronisms condemned to various versions of despotism."[96] On account of his defense of the West, Vargas Llosa has been critized for advancing a reactionary position. Yet in a similar vein the left-wing Mexican novelist and diplomat Carlos Fuentes argues that the Europeans prevailed over the Indians because their empirical approach to knowledge gave them enormous civilizational confidence. By contrast, the Indians relied on a combination of direct perception, dreams, hallucination, and appeals to the spirits. Fuentes writes in *The Buried Mirror,* "The so-called discovery of America, whatever one might ideologically think about it, was a great triumph of scientific hypothesis over physical perception."[97]

The West even supplied the Americas with a doctrine of human rights which would provide the basis for a sustained critique of Western colonialism. Today we may join Kirkpatrick Sale, Stephen Greenblatt, and others in expressing outrage at wanton Western seizure of Indian lands and abuses of basic rights. But upon reflection we would have to admit that these criticisms depend upon concepts of property rights and human rights that are entirely Western. Long before Columbus, Indian tribes raided each other's land and preyed on the possessions and persons of more vulnerable groups. What distinguished Western colonialism was neither occupation nor brutality but a countervailing philosophy of rights that is unique in human history.

Shortly after the Spanish established their settlements in the Americas, the king of Spain in the mid-sixteenth century called a halt to colonization pending the resolution of a famous debate over the question of whether Spanish conquest violated the natural and moral law. Never before or since, writes historian Lewis Hanke, has a powerful emperor "ordered his conquests to cease until it was decided if they were just."[98] The main reason for the king's action was the relentless exposure of colonial abuses by a Spanish bishop, Bartolome de las Casas. A former slave owner, Las Casas underwent a crisis of conscience which convinced him that the New World should be peacefully Christianized, that Indians should not be exploited, and that those who were had every right to rebel.[99] Las Casas wrote his *Account of the Destruction of the Indies,* he said, "so that if God determines to destroy Spain, it may be seen that it is because of the destruction that we have wrought in the Indies."[100] Las Casas gave such a flagrant account of Spanish abuse that he created a theological scandal in Europe. An Aristotelian scholar, Juan Sepulveda, engaged Las Casas in a passionate debate at Valladolid in Spain. Although he had never visited the Americas, Sepulveda confidently asserted that Indians were inferior and deserved to be "natural slaves." But Las Casas countered, based on his long experience with the Indians, that they were far superior in intellectual and spiritual potential even to the ancient Greeks, whom he condemned as pagans. Moreover, Las Casas maintained that Indian practices such as human sacrifice, although horrifying at first glance, nevertheless signified a deep spiritual nature that would be well disposed to the voluntary embrace of the truth of Christianity.[101] Although Las Casas is sometimes portrayed as a heroic eccentric, in fact his basic position in favor of Indian rights was directly adopted by Pope Paul III, who proclaimed in 1537 in his bull *Sublimis Deus:*

> Indians and all other people who may later be discovered by the Christians are by no means to be deprived of their liberty or the possession of their

property, even though they be outside the faith of Jesus Christ; nor should they be in any way enslaved; should the contrary happen it shall be null and of no effect. Indians and other peoples should be converted to the faith of Jesus Christ by preaching the word of God and by the example of good and holy living.[102]

Moreover, leading Jesuit theologians such as Francisco de Vitoria and Francisco Suarez interpreted the Bible and the Catholic tradition to require that the natural rights of Indians be respected, that their conversions be obtained through persuasion and not force, that their land and property be secure from arbitrary confiscation, and that their right to resist Spanish incursions in a "just war" be upheld.[103] More than a century before Locke, and two centuries before the French and American revolutions, theologians at the University of Salamanca developed the first outlines of the modern doctrine of inviolable human rights. Although these rights were often abused in practice, largely because there was no effective mechanism for enforcement,[104] they provided a moral foundation for the eventual enfranchisement of the native Indian. Multicultural textbooks are windy in their chronicle of abuses against the Indians, but they are typically sparse in their acknowledgment of the liberal tradition of the West associated with Las Casas. The reason for this reticence is that liberalism is uniquely a Western achievement, and hence could provide the basis for a claim to Western cultural superiority.

In order to undermine this claim, advocates of multiculturalism insist that America is a product not simply of the West but also of minority groups such as American Indians. There is little doubt that American Indians taught the white man a great deal: about canoes, snowshoes, moccasins, and kayaks. The hammock is an Indian invention. Indians also introduced Europeans to new crops: corn, potatoes, peanuts, squash, avocados, and other vegetables and fruits.[105] Ronald Takaki informs us that "the term *okay* was derived from the Choctaw word *oke,* meaning: it is so."[106] Yet even when you add the heroic exploits of Crazy Horse, Sitting Bull, Chief Joseph and Geronimo, the contribution of the native Indians to American civilization still seems fairly modest.

Consequently, advocates of multiculturalism frequently proceed to make a strong claim: that the fundamental institutions for the recognition of liberal rights, such as the U.S. Constitution, were not Western in origin but rather were borrowed or derived from minority groups. One claim taught as fact in many schools is that the Iroquois Indians were the true inspiration for the American founding. Anthropologist Thomas Riley asserts that the League of the Iroquois served "as a model for the confederation that would make up the United States."[107] Alvin Josephy credits the Iroquois with being "particularly influential" on the thinking of the framers in Philadelphia.[108] Jack Weatherford observes that the Iroquois provided a blueprint "by which the settler might be able to fashion a new government."[109]

If these claims are true, then surely the past refusal of teachers to credit the Iroquois for the Bill of Rights and other vital instruments of liberal freedom provides a classic example of the kind of bias that multicultural advocates have insisted pervades the traditional curriculum. Historian Elisabeth Tooker investigated the issue and discovered that the main evidence linking the Iroquois to the American founding is a letter written by Benjamin Franklin in 1754:

> It would be a strange thing if six nations of ignorant savages should be capable of forming a scheme for such a union, and be able to execute it in such a manner as that it has subsisted ages and appears indissoluble, and yet that a like union should be impracticable for ten or a dozen English colonies, to whom it is more necessary and must be more advantageous, and who cannot be supposed to want an equal understanding of their interests.[110]

The Iroquois League, which consisted of Mohawks, Oneidas, Onondagas, Cayugas, and Senecas (with the Tuscaroras joining later), was modestly successful in moderating bloody tribal wars that continually erupted between various Indian groups. The basic theme of Franklin's letter is this: if the barbarians can work out their problems, surely we civilized men can agree on a union. Surely this is an absurd basis for declaring that the American founders relied heavily on Iroquois wisdom. In her inquiry, Tooker proceeded to explore the similarities between the Iroquois League and the American Constitution and found that they were virtually nonexistent. The League consisted of tribal chiefs whose title was partly hereditary. Only one tribe, the Onondagas, were permitted as "firekeepers" to present topics for consideration, and to ratify final decisions. All rulings by the League required unanimous consent. Tooker concluded that the Iroquois claim to be the secret force behind the American Constitution is a myth, sustained only by ideology.[111]

From this case study we see that while advocates of multiculturalism are right to criticize many of the old texts[112]—in which Columbus is presented as a valiant adventurer and American Indians are scarcely to be seen—contemporary activists merely replace the old biases with new ones. Columbus has metamorphosed from a grand crusader into something resembling a genocidal maniac, a European precursor to Hitler. American Indians are now beyond reproach, canonized as moral and ecological saints. It is hardly a curricular secret that white people practiced slavery, yet few students probably know that American Indians practiced slavery long before Columbus arrived. Yet many teachers today seem reluctant to emphasize such facts in order to avoid being spoilers at the multicultural picnic.

BOGUS MULTICULTURALISM

Multicultural demands in American schools and universities do not arise in a vacuum. They arise from the conviction that Western culture is constitutively defined by a virtually uninterrupted series of crimes visited upon other groups: blacks, women, homosexuals, natives of the Third World. Since the West is perceived to be historically defined by racism, sexism, heterosexism, colonialism, and imperialism, multicultural advocates look to other cultures to find some alternative to the oppressive institutions of the white man. Thus begins the search in non-Western cultures for what Marianna Torgovnick terms "alternative value systems."[113] Yet when scholars seriously examine the cultures of Asia, Africa, and Latin America, they cannot help but notice that these cultures are rudely inhospitable to the moral and political hopes of their Western admirers. As Conor Cruise O'Brien points out, the "vague theoretical enthusiasm" of American multiculturalists for other cultures often runs headlong into the actual institutions and practices of those cultures.[114] Indeed non-Western cultures appear perversely designed to frustrate the multicultural ideological quest.

Non-Western cultures have virtually no indigenous tradition of equality. Tribalism and social hierarchy are not only widespread but widely considered legitimate in many Third World countries. In India, for example, there is the long-standing legacy of the caste system which enjoyed the full blessing of Hinduism. Slavery, as we have seen, was practiced in most societies for thousands of years without any hint of principled local opposition. Women are treated very badly in many non-Western cultures. Anthropologist Robert Edgerton points out that "men have approved wife-beating in virtually every folk society." The Chinese practiced female foot-binding for hundreds of years. According to an old Indian practice called *sati,* brides were urged to ascend the burning pyre of their dead husbands. Polygamy is still prevalent in many parts of the world. In Islamic societies today, women are denied the rights of men. Genital mutilation of women is commonplace in parts of Africa and in the Arab world.[115] Also, homosexuality is a crime or an illness, so defined in the legal and medical literature of some Third World countries.

The point is that the Western attitude of tolerance finds itself confronted with the cultural reality of non-Western intolerance, raising the classic dilemma of whether liberals should be tolerant of intolerance. This conundrum is compounded when we consider many of the classic texts of non-Western cultures. These great works can and should be studied, but many of them reflect the temperament and even the prejudices of Third World cultures. The Koran is the sacred text of a great religion and for millions of people it is a rich and spiritually emancipating book. Yet it is impossible to read the Koran without finding in it a clear vision of hierarchy, servitude, and male superiority. The *Tale of Genji,* the Japanese classic of the eleventh century, is a celebration of ritual, of life at court, of the aristocratic virtues; it is oblivious to Western egalitarianism. The Indian classics, such as the *Bhagavad Gita* and Tagore's *Gitanjali,* are spiritual texts which imply a repudiation of Western-style materialism, secularism, atheism, perhaps even of separation of church and state.

American teachers and activists could closely examine non-Western cultures and their greatest works and denounce them for being even more bigoted and retrograde than those of the West. In this approach other cultures would be worth studying, if only as horrible examples. But such an approach is, within the multicultural paradigm, politically impossible. Cultural relativism dictates that non-Western cultures be considered to be victims of Western oppression: of colonialism, imperialism, racism, and so on. In the multicultural view, these cultures need to be vaunted and affirmed, not harshly criticized. Consequently multiculturalism in practice tends to ignore the indigenous institutions of non-Western cultures, avert its gaze from their most important works, and instead project domestic ideological concerns onto the Third World.

Issues such as feminism and sexual identity are *Western* political obsessions. There is no evidence that these issues are of any concern or relevance to the typical peasant in Bihar or factory worker in Addis Ababa. Yet contemporary American ideology is often presented in the classroom as the authentic voice of the Third World proletariat. American students are less likely to read Mencius or Al-Farabi or Sor Juana Ines de la Cruz because their work does not corroborate modern Western presuppositions. Students are more likely to be assigned, say, the journals of a Marxist lesbian from Peru, not because she is representative of Latin American practice or because her work is, in the eyes of Hispanic scholars, "the best that has been thought and said" south of the border, but simply because she confirms what scholars and activists in the United States want to believe about the world and, even more, what they want to believe about themselves. Multiculturalism becomes not an antidote to, but an expression of, American ethnocentrism.

Just as multiculturalism of this sort misrepresents other peoples, so too, within the West, the emphasis on the equality of all cultures results in imbalance and distortion. Manning Marable contends, without offering any evidence, that "the development of what was to become the United States was accomplished largely, if not primarily, by African slaves,"[116] a claim that ignores the fact that much of what the slaves built in the South was destroyed during the Civil War. Yet claims like this are uncritically transmitted to students, some of whom are too young to evaluate them critically. Even at the college level, students who have never read *Huckleberry Finn,* who cannot say whether the Renaissance came before the Reformation, and who are ignorant of the arguments of the Federalists and the Anti-Federalists are in the name of ethnic parity exposed to claims that the term "real McCoy" refers to an African American, and it was a black man who invented the traffic light. Such "compensatory exaggeration" results in the elevation of what C. Vann Woodward terms "ever more obscure and deservedly neglected figures of the past."[117] Even people who should be studied are frequently distorted. Thus many texts credit Benjamin Banneker with surveying the site for the U.S. capital in Washington, D.C., and for writing the proposal to establish a U.S. Department of Peace. In fact, Thomas Jefferson appointed Andrew Ellicot to conduct the survey; Banneker was his assistant for about three months in 1791. The proposal for the Department of Peace was authored by Benjamin Rush.

Thus multiculturalism in practice frequently misrepresents both American history and world history. A relativist framework makes it virtually impossible for advocates of multiculturalism to concede the obvious truth that all cultures have not contributed equally to America. "Our diversity has been at the center of the making of America," Ronald Takaki insists.[118] Yet while many groups in the form of slaves, indentured servants, and migrant workers have helped in the building of the railroads and the cultivation of crops, the distinctive political and economic institutions of this country are the product of a single culture. America's *novus ordo seclorum,* a new order for the ages, was and remains a distinctive product of the philosophical and religious soil of Western civilization.

Similarly the emphasis on the crimes of the West and the victimization of non-Western cultures—what Takaki promotes as a shared narrative of minority oppression—results in multicultural suppression of the illiberal traditions of other cultures and also of the liberal tradition that is a unique product of the West. Thus multiculturalism becomes what Edward Said might call the new Orientalism. It manipulates and distorts other cultures for Western ideological ends. The politics today may be different, but the intellectual transaction is an old one. The consequence is that multiculturalism becomes an obstacle to true cultural understanding, and implants in students an unjustified hatred of the liberal institutions of their society. Both truth and justice suffer as a consequence.

SWAHILI MATH AND OTHER REMEDIES

Can Afrocentrism do better? It represents a radicalization of multiculturalism: a complete repudiation of European institutions, including Western scholarly norms, and an embrace of an alternative "black reality." As Molefi Kete Asante puts it, Afrocentrism implies a total "rejection of white values. . . . Afrocentrists study every thought, action, behavior, and value, and if it cannot be found in our culture, it is dispensed with quickly."[119] Walk into an Afrocentric classroom and you will see people shouting "Hotep" and "Harambee" and chanting the principles of the *Nguzo Saba.*[120] Afrocentrism is not limited to schools: it is increasingly becoming the official ideology of rap musicians, community activists, and black prisoners. Afrocentric claims routinely make their way into mainstream black literature.[121] Afrocentrism has also been embraced as quasi-official ideology by the Nation of Islam.

Yet Afrocentrism fundamentally remains a pedagogy: an initiation into a new form of black consciousness and also into manhood. Many Afrocentrists have proposed that the government fund special public schools for black boys. So far these efforts have been rejected as contrary to antidiscrimination laws. Yet the Afrocentric approach is pervasive in inner-city schools with predominantly African American populations and names like Afrikan People's School, Malcolm X Academy, Nyerere Education Institute, and Timbucktu Academy.[122] Despite public criticism from Arthur Schlesinger, Jr., Robert Hughes, and others,[123] many cities such as Milwaukee, Indianapolis, Pittsburgh, Richmond, Atlanta, Portland, Washington, D.C., Philadelphia, Detroit, and Baltimore have adopted Afrocentric approaches and some 80 percent of black parents are hopeful that Afrocentrism will "improve black student self-esteem and performance."[124] Consider a few examples of Afrocentric principles in operation.

At Dobbs Elementary School in Atlanta, Georgia, teacher Brenda Brown teaches her students numbers in Swahili. One is *moja*. Two is *mbili*. Three is *tatu*. In teaching what she terms "Kiswahili math," Brown gives her students time to finish arithmetic problems. One problem is "moja plus tatu." The teacher instructs, "You must write the answers in Kiswahili." Such African language techniques are used not just in Dobbs Elementary but in many Atlanta public schools, the majority of which have embraced an Afrocentric or Africa-centered approach to their curriculum.

At Bunche Middle School in southwest Atlanta, for example, teacher Carolyn Huff argues that the mathematical wisdom of ancient Egypt can help young people today resolve algebra problems. Huff argues that the standard algebra textbook misleads students in that it does not credit Egypt with discovering ways to represent unknown variables. Long before the Greeks used the x and the y, Huff says, Egyptians around the year 4,500 B.C. thought of representing variables with the word "aha." Yet when Huff proceeds to write a series of fractions on the board, the students are stumped. Huff argues that their ignorance is beside the point. It is important, she says, for students to acknowledge the racial heritage of what she calls "aha calculus." As for simple algebra, Huff acknowledges, "I know they don't really understand fractions."[125]

Atlanta schools are not unique. In several cities, it is not unusual to see predominantly African American students receiving curricular instruction in Swahili. One manual for an elementary school in Milwaukee, Wisconsin provides children with a list of Swahili words that they are expected to memorize with their English translations. Elephant, *tembo*. Water lily, *yungiyungi*. Wedding, *arusi*. Medicine, *dawa*. Mango, *embe*. Broom, *fagio*. Clay jar, *gudulia*. Drum and dance, *ngoma*. Friend, *rafiki*. String instrument, *zeze*. Utensils, *vyombo*. Worship, *ibada*. Donkey, *punda*. Respect, *heshima*. Ambush, *oteo*. The list goes on.[126]

Afrocentric curricula in inner-city schools sometimes includes Egyptian hieroglyphics. Manuals of instruction supply Egyptian picture symbols. Zig-zag lines in three rows: that means water. A rectangle: that refers to the sky. A rectangle filled with zig-zag lines: that's a lake. Students are presented with sequences of drawings like this and asked to make sentences, such as "Water came down from the sky and fell into the lake." Or they are given sentences in pictures and asked to "decode the hieroglyphic message." This knowledge, some African American educators argue, will help prepare African American students for the challenges of the twenty-first century.[127]

When the Washington, D.C., school system decided to adopt an Afrocentric curriculum for its predominantly black student body, superintendent Franklin Smith hired a consultant, Abena Walker, for approximately $250,000 to develop a pilot program. Walker's outline, implemented on a pilot basis at Ruth K. Webb Elementary School, calls for harnessing the power of *Nommo,* "the African concept of the magic power of the word in all subjects." *Nommo,* Walker argues, "is word magic: to control *Nommo* is to control the generation and transformation of sound, energy, thoughts and action." *Nommo,* she adds, is a mysterious African technique for "acquiring power in a social setting that is perceived as hostile."

Yet in August 1993 the *Washington Post* reported on plans for Afrocentric teacher training at an unlicensed and unaccredited institution called Pan-African University founded by Abena Walker herself. Moreover, Walker's master's degree had been awarded by her own university. Despite requests from the media, Walker would not name any of the courses offered by Pan-African University. Despite her dubious credentials, Walker praised her program, claiming that criticism was part of a "racist attack" being directed against her by "white supremacists." Pan-African University does not need accreditation because it is a "community-based organization," she argued, "accredited to our race." Walker acknowledged that her approach did not emphasize academics. "We feel that academics, that's the easy part, because our children are just brilliant."

Among those who spoke out against her unique brand of Afrocentrism was Russell Adams, chairman of the Afro-American Studies department at Howard, the capital's historically black university, who accused "neophytes" and "dilettantes" of jeopardizing the education of young people with claims that failed to "sort out historic fact from fiction." Yet in 1994, school superintendent Franklin Smith said that although evaluations of the pilot effort had not been done, the Afrocentric curriculum had already expanded to six other elementary schools and would be introduced to Spingarn Senior High School before being generally adopted through the public education system.[128]

In 1992 the National Alliance of Black School Educators sponsored a conference in Prince George's County, Maryland. What is significant about Prince George's County is that it is one of the largest black suburbs in the country, with a middle-class African American population and a racially mixed student body. Yet Afrocentrism seems influential even in this relatively prosperous and ethnically diverse community, as indicated by the infusion of the new pedagogy into its public schools. Among the advocates for this change was a keynote speaker at the conference, Nsenga Warfield-Coppock, an African American author and activist who conducts workshops on Afrocentrism around the country. She spoke on African "Rites of Passage."

Warfield-Coppock's main theme was that melanin, the coloring agent in the skin, carries incredible spiritual and physical powers that give African Americans their unique talents. "Melanin can help them glide in the air like a Magic Johnson or hit top speeds like Florence Joyner." Melanin, she added, also helps blacks to "speak and read faster, because they are pulling the basic patterns of how to do that out of their unconscious. Accessing the unconscious is easier for persons who have high levels of melanin." According to Warfield-Coppock, the pineal gland "is known to calcify" at higher rates for whites than for blacks, and this results in horrible sexual perversions. "The prison population of gruesome sexual crime is approximately 97 percent white, with sometimes as many as a third of incarcerated white American men in any given prison being there for sexual offenses."[129]

The persuasive power of Afrocentrism outside the classroom is illustrated by the transforming effect it had on Monster Kody, a Los Angeles gang member, who encountered Afrocentrism in prison. Monster, who has subsequently become a Muslim and changed his name from Kody Scott to Sanyika Shakur, describes the intellectual process by which he was converted by an advocate of Afrocentrism.

"The cradle of civilization is Afrika. Afrika is the motherland. Therefore, Afrika is central to all humanity.

"But . . .

"Those whom we know today as Europeans are actually mutants who left the safe confines of the motherland. . . . The side effects of their development outside of the natural womb have been albinism, aggression and universal weakness predicated on their minority status in the world.

"Well, if that's the case, why don't we just tell everybody what's really going on?

"I wish it were that simple. Hey, ever hear the words mankind and human?

"Yeah, I've heard 'em.

"Do you know what hue is?

"Hue? No, don't know what it means.

"Color, it means color.

"And?

"Bro, can't you see? Look . . . human . . . *hue-man*.

"Oh. Color-man, man of color, right?

"Right. Now that means humans are people of color. And melanin is the ingredient that produces skin color. These . . . [European] mutants don't have any melanin, therefore they are colorless.

"White.

"And to be without color is to be abnormal.

"Damn, that's *heavy*."[130]

PRIDE AND PREJUDICE

Who are the Afrocentrists? Many of them are American black national-ists from the 1960s who have given themselves new names and African accents in order to promulgate what they consider to be a distinctive African worldview. Leading Afrocentrists include Molefi Asante, Ivan Van Sertima, Asa Hilliard, Leonard Jeffries, Maulana Karenga, Tony Martin, Wade Nobles, Marimba Ani, John Henrik Clarke, Yosef Ben-Jochanan, John Jackson, and Chancellor Williams. Molefi Asante is probably the leading Afrocentrist in America. Head of the African Studies Depart-ment at Temple University, he is also an architect of several school pro-grams to transform the traditional curriculum in an Afrocentric direction. In several books, such as *The Afrocentric Idea, Afrocentricity,* and *Kemet, Afrocentricity and Knowledge,* he outlines his critique of the mainstream curriculum and his plan for an Afrocentric replacement. "All around the globe the exclusive Eurocentric view is called into question by those who have finally gained their own footing," Asante writes. He proposes a new approach which "puts African ideals and values at the center of inquiry." What values? Asante makes it clear that he is not referring to American values. He writes contemptuously of "made-in-America Negroes" who have internalized Western norms: "Their rejection of Afrocentricity is tied to their rejection of themselves." Afrocentricity, Asante notes, "is not a matter of color but of perspective." Thus even Africans who have adopted European values are not authentically Afrocentric. Rather, their skepticism of Afrocentrism identifies them as "Africans who seek to be appointed overseers on the plantation."

Asante's goal is to recover ancient African ideals and habits which he regards as unpolluted by European racism, and relevant to the challenges faced by young blacks in America today. "Deify your ancestors," he recommends. Those who are exposed to Afrocentrism, he promises, "walk the way of the world in the *agbadas* of our ancestors' spirits." He urges a recovery of the ancient African "warrior mentality." He scorns homosexuality as a form of "European decadence" and urges black homosexuals to "submerge their own wills into the collective will of our people." He proposes a new canon of heroes, among them Thuthmosis III, Ptahhotep, Shango, Obatala, Legba, Oduduwa, Amenomope, Ogotommeli, Piankhy, Nzingha, Tinubu, Hatshepsut, Asantewaa, Menes, and Zumbi. Employing the vocabulary of relativism, Asante calls for blacks to embrace an Afrocentric reality as an alternative to the parochial reality of Eurocentrism:

> All analysis is culturally centered and flows from ideological assumptions. . . . A total rewrite of the major events and developments in the world is long overdue. Our facts are in our history; use them. Their facts are in their history; and they have certainly used theirs. All truth resides in our own experiences. Your Afrocentricity . . . is a truth, even though it may not be their truth. With an Afrocentric spirit, all things can be made to happen. It is the source of genuine revolutionary commitment.[131]

Afrocentrists take the concept of a unique black reality seriously because they are convinced that black students and white students are so unlike each other that they even think in entirely different terms. Scholars such as Asa Hilliard and Janice Hale-Benson specify certain personality characteristics and intellectual habits that are said to be unique to African American students.

- Black children respond to things in terms of the whole rather than in terms of division into parts.
- Blacks practice intuitive and spiral reasoning while whites and others practice deductive or inductive reasoning.
- Blacks approximate space and time rather than seek punctuality and accuracy.
- Blacks prefer to focus on people and personality, rather than inanimate concepts or objects.

- Blacks have a uniquely developed sense of justice and easily detect unfairness and discrimination.
- Blacks tend to be nonliterate, drawing on oral rather than written traditions.[132]

Similarly, Asante identifies what he calls an "African aesthetic" based upon distinctively black values such as polyrhythm, polycentrism, dimensionality, curvilinearity, and holism.[133] If some of these terms are unclear, Afrocentric activist Jawanza Kunjufu is more specific. He contrasts traditional learning styles, which he considers white, with relational learnings, which he maintains are black. In Kunjufu's terminology, whites favor rules, blacks favor freedom; whites prefer standardization, blacks prefer variation; whites seek regularity, blacks seek novelty; whites are orderly, blacks are flexible; whites would rather be normal, blacks would rather be unique; whites are precise, blacks approximate; whites are logical, blacks psychological; whites are cognitive, blacks are indirect; whites are linear, blacks are affective or emotional.[134] Na'im Akbar in *Visions for Black Men* writes that Afrocentrism "must break away from the traditional social science conceptions of linear time" and from "Western scientific reality" toward "metaphysical causation" and the authority of "the folk traditions."[135]

As a consequence of this view, Afrocentrists seem unabashed about teaching young black students information that is considered dubious, even preposterous, by most mainstream scholars. Nor are Afrocentrists noticeably chagrined by an absence of professional training in the specialized fields from which their confident claims are drawn. While a few leading Afrocentrists are recognized scholars, many of them are political activists, ministers in the Nation of Islam, laboratory technicians, musicians, political organizers, social workers, and self-taught former convicts. As early as 1958, Malcolm X set a precedent for Afrocentric reasoning when he tried to convince Alex Haley that Homer was black based on a chain of verbal similarities. "Homer and Omar and Moor, you see, are related terms."[136] John Jackson, a contemporary Afrocentrist, shows himself no less susceptible to eccentricity as suggested by the titles of his books: *Pagan Origins of the Christ Myth* and *Christianity Before Christ.* Another prominent Afrocentrist, Chancellor Williams, relies on "field work" consisting mainly of customary beliefs that he calls "oral history." Williams is a conspiracy theorist who refuses to credit any theory supported by what he terms the "grand Caucasian consensus," a group in which he includes

"Negro scholars whose skewed vision of reality is through eyes of blue."[137] Even Molefi Asante displays his level of scientific understanding by rejecting the theory of evolution as an "oxymoron" and calling for "some other, more humane view of the evolutionary process."[138]

One of the most widely used Afrocentric texts is the *African American Baseline Essays,* a pedagogical manual which forms the basis for teaching several subjects in public school classrooms in Portland, Atlanta, Detroit, and elsewhere. The scientific sections of the *African-American Baseline Essays* were authored by Hunter Adams who listed himself as a "research scientist at Argonne National Laboratory in Chicago." But according to the information office of Argonne, Adams in fact was an industrial hygiene technician at the time whose job was to collect environmental samples. Although identified as "Dr. Hunter Adams" in the baseline essays, Argonne's spokesman pointed out that he has only a high school degree and "does no research at Argonne on any topic."[139]

A BLACK THING: YOU WOULDN'T UNDERSTAND

Consider the dramatic contrast between the central claims of Afrocentric scholars on the one hand, and mainstream scholars, black and white, on the other.

• Afrocentrists argue that Egypt, one of the earliest human civilizations, was a Negroid civilization, so that African Americans who are descended from Egyptians should be credited as the founders of civilization.[140] The *African-American Baseline Essays* asserts without qualification that "ancient Egypt was a black nation."[141] Chiekh Anta Diop concurs, offering some of his own melanin experiments to prove the point.[142] Egypt was "not only all-black, but the very name of Egypt (Kemet) was derived from the blacks," writes Chancellor Williams in *The Destruction of Black Civilization.*[143] The concept of black Egyptians, specifically black Pharaohs, is at the heart of Yosef Ben-Jochanan's *Africa, Mother of Western Civilization* and Martin Bernal's *Black Athena: The Afroasiatic Roots of Western Civilization.*

In fact, Egyptologists have known for a long time that ancient Egypt was a multiracial civilization. Anthropologist Frank Yurco argues that the ancient Egyptians, like their modern descendants, "varied in complexion from the light Mediterranean hue to the darker brown of upper Egypt, to the darkest shade around Aswan where, even today, the population shifts to Nubian." For a brief period, Egypt was ruled by Nubians who derived from the region now known as Ethiopia, yet this was after its era of greatest architectural and mathematical achievement. During its civilizational zenith, Egypt maintained cultural contacts both to the north and the south. The consequence, Yurco argues, is a genuinely diverse society in which no importance was attached to race.[144]

African American scholar Frank Snowden points out that although Herodotus once described Egyptians as "dark-skinned and woolly-haired" his next phrase reads "though that indeed goes for nothing, seeing that other peoples too are such." Snowden argues that the term Kemet has nothing to do with skin color: it actually means the "black land," a reference to the fertile soil watered by the Nile, in contrast to the red land of the desert.[145] Similarly archeologist Kathryn Bard maintains that it was conventional in Egyptian art to paint men in a dark-red ochre and women in a light-yellow ochre, both for purposes of distinguishing them and because men traditionally worked in the sun.[146] This artistic convention is mistaken by Afrocentrists who use it to claim that Egyptians were Negroid.

• Even before Egypt, Afrocentrists maintain, black Africans invented writing and produced an extensive literature, now sadly disappeared. "Africans themselves invented writing," insists Chancellor Williams. "The African system was very different from the Egyptian. It was simpler and had vowels. Clarity and easy reading were assured by measured spacing between words." Unfortunately, Williams says, virtually all evidence of this literary accomplishment is lost.[147] Moreover, Afrocentrists maintain that ancient African philosophy was advanced even by modern standards. "It reads like if you're reading Jean Paul Sartre or Heidegger or Kierkegaard," Ivan Van Sertima maintains. "It is very complex."[148] Since there is no remaining evidence for early African writing and literature, this claim is impossible to prove, and must be considered entirely speculative. Moreover, Afrocentrists have produced no samples of ancient African theoretical reflection. Indeed Kwasi Wiredu, a leading contemporary African philosopher, writes in *Philosophy and African Culture:*

> The African philospher has no choice but to conduct his philosophical inquiries in relation to the philosophical writings of other peoples, for his own ancestors left him no heritage of philosophical writings. . . . Our traditional society was deeply authoritarian. Hardly any premium was placed on curiosity or independence of thought. Our traditional culture is famous for

an abundance of proverbs . . . generally consisting of what elders said or are said to have said. . . . At the base of them all is the unanalytical, unscientific cast of mind, probably the most basic and pervasive anachronism afflicting our society.[149]

• Afrocentrists claim that in addition to the architectural achievements of ancient Egypt, black Africans developed a virtually modern infrastructure unrivaled in the ancient world. "The Africans constructed a national system of reservoirs," remarks Chancellor Williams, some of them "doubtless at sites not yet excavated." Moreover, they produced "magnificent stone and brick palaces, temples, churches, cathedrals, wide avenues lined with palm trees, government buildings, public baths, water supply systems. The Arab scholars were properly amazed at a way of life so superior to that of their own homeland."[150]

The Arab travel literature on southern Africa is highly mixed.[151] It contains some respectful observations about the character of the people. It reports none of the architectural wonders outlined by the Afrocentrists. And it is replete with scornful references to many practices of the sub-Saharan Africans which Arab writers found disgusting and primitive. As we have seen earlier, the Arabs did not refrain from comparing dark-skinned Africans to animals. These references are edited out of Afrocentric literature.

• Afrocentrists argue that the ancient Egyptian Negroes produced innumerable inventions and insights that are mistakenly attributed to the modern era. Ancient Egyptian myths about the origin of the universe were "very close to modern physics," writes Ivan Van Sertima. "They saw the world as beginning in a kind of plasma, something in an aqueous state." Van Sertima adds, "Africans had built an astronomical observatory in Kenya 300 years before Christ. On the basis of the alignment of stars and constellations, they built the most accurate of prehistoric calendars. . . . They had actually worked out the speed of light. We only learned about that in the twentieth century."

The Dogon people of Mali, according to Van Sertima, had a tribal dance called Bado which exactly paralleled the orbit of the star Sirius B. "This star is impossible to see with the naked eye." Dogon discoveries about the characteristics of Sirius, Van Sertima insists, "NASA discovered five years ago. The Dogon knew about this at least 500 years ago."[152] According to Na'im Akbar, ancient black Africans "understood the structure of the planetary system thousands of years before there was any such thing as a telescope."[153] Writes John Jackson in *Introduction to African Civilizations,* "Today's cannon, long-range missiles, ship propellers, automatic hammers, gas engines . . . have the roots of their development in early African uses of power."[154] The *African American Baseline Essays* claims that black Egyptians developed electricity and built power-driven gliders some four thousand years ago and "used their early planes for travel expeditions and recreation."[155]

Except for a few references to bird effigies which are mistaken for gliders, Afrocentrists have produced no evidence for these claims. Certainly they are irreconcilable with the relatively primitive state of Africa as observed by the Chinese, the Arabs, and the Europeans on a continuous basis since the late Middle Ages. Philip Curtin, a leading African scholar, remarks, "Without scientific instruments and the modern scientific method, it is hard to see how ancient Africans could have made the advances attributed to them."

• In the view of Afrocentrists, Africans around the fifth century B.C. were far more advanced than the Greeks, who are traditionally considered the founders of Western civilization. Writes Ivan Van Sertima, "The African had reached levels that startled the Greeks in astronomy, in mathematics, in literature, in philosophy." He adds, "They are finding technological innovation by Africans far in advance of Europe. They found steel smelting machines in Tanzania that were used 1,500 to 2,000 years ago in an industrial site."[156]

Here Van Sertima exaggerates the presence of iron ore, turning simple hand tools into "smelting machines" (which are entirely undocumented). Scholars point out that the Greeks admired the civilizational accomplishments of the Egyptians and praised the character of the Ethiopians, but many of their spectacular advances in self-government, philosophy, and literature the Greeks made themselves. Consequently, it is a mistake to derive Greek philosophy, politics, and literature from Egypt when the two societies were radically different. Orlando Patterson argues that while "ancient Egyptian society had an incredibly uniform culture" with a "single highly centralized state" ruled by Pharaohs who were "god incarnate" and encouraged such practices as "ancestor worship," the Greeks emphasized democracy, decentralization, and individuality.[157] Classicist Mary Lefkowitz argues that there is nothing in Egypt to compare with the tragedies of Sophocles, the comedy of Aristophanes, the political dissent of Socrates, and the Aristotelian attempt to comprehend the universe as a rational entity which operates according to physical laws.

• Afrocentrists claim to have discovered historical piracy on a grand scale: the Greeks stole most of their philosophy and medicine from Egypt. Wade Nobles writes in *African Psychology,* "Aristotle's doctrines of immortality, salvation of the soul and the summum bonum are examples of the ancient African theory of salvation."[158] Molefi Asante writes, "Of course Plato himself was taught in Africa by Seknoufis and Kounoufis," offering no evidence for an assertion he regards as obvious.[159] George James argues that "all false praise of the Greeks must be removed from the textbooks of our schools and colleges," and students must undergo a "reeducation consisting of a thorough study of the ideas and arguments contained in my book *Stolen Legacy.*"[160]

Classical scholars such as Mary Lefkowitz and Frank Snowden have painstakingly investigated these claims and concluded, in Lefkowitz's words, that they are "one part fact, two parts speculation, and three parts outright falsehoods."[161] Contrary to Afrocentric assertions, Lefkowitz maintains that there is no evidence that Socrates and Aristotle went to Egypt or studied there. "The Egyptian *Book of the Dead* is cited as a source for Aristotle," Lefkowitz says, "but the *Book of the Dead* is a set of ritual prescriptions about the soul's journey to the next world. It could hardly be further apart from Aristotle's philosophical discussions about human nature." Pointing out that the Greeks mainly encountered blacks as mercenaries and soldiers and enjoyed amicable relations with them that did not remotely resemble theft, Snowden writes, "The time has come for Afrocentrists to cease mythologizing and falsifying the past."[162]

• Afrocentrists specifically charge that Greek and Roman armies burned down the library of Alexandria in an effort to appropriate African knowledge and prevent Africans from getting credit. Na'im Akbar embroiders the usual Afrocentric account with his own twist: apparently in order to conceal black influence, Europeans such as Napoleon, apparently with nothing better to do, "shot the noses off the great Egyptian statues that showed that these ancient people were black men with big lips and big noses and kinky hair."[163]

Afrocentric accounts of the alleged Alexandrian theft conflict. In *Stolen Legacy,* George James maintains that Alexander the Great ransacked and looted the library in 333 B.C. and "carried off a booty of scientific, philosophic and religious books."[164] Wade Nobles alleges that

Alexander and Aristotle entered into a conspiracy to "falsify the roots of Greek thought and to fabricate Greek authorship."[165] Na'im Akbar asserts, "Aristotle received credit although he stole the books from African people and put his name on them."[166] On the other hand, John Jackson in *Introduction to African Civilizations* maintains that the library was burned in 48 B.C., almost three centuries later, by invading Romans.[167]

It turns out that all of these accounts are wrong. Frank Snowden points out that "most ancient sources suggest that Ptolemy II founded the library long after Aristotle's death in 322 B.C." Snowden adds that there is no evidence that Aristotle ever visited Egypt, and even if the library was built earlier it is unlikely that it would have contained much of a collection at such an early date.[168]

• Even Judaism and Christianity are largely plagiarized from African blacks, according to Afrocentrists, who add that Jesus Christ was a Negro. "Practically all of the Ten Commandments were embedded in the African Constitution," writes Chancellor Williams. "A major reason why so many later Christian missionaries failed was because they were bringing refurbished religious doctrines that came from Africa in the first place."[169] "One needs only to meditate on Osiris," Chiekh Anta Diop writes, to recognize that he is "a figure essentially identifiable with Christ."[170] Cain Hope Felder, editor of the *African Heritage Study Bible,* asserts that Christ was an "Afro-Asiatic Jew" who "probably looked like a typical Yemenite, Trinidadian or African American of today. . . . If he lived today, he would be a soul brother."

Yet the Bible makes no reference to Christ's skin color or racial features and Jon Levenson, a leading biblical scholar, told the *Chronicle of Higher Education* that "the average Galilean was not black. I don't know of any Jewish groups that were black in the first century." Robert Funk, a New Testament scholar, says that the origins of Jesus were Semitic, which means that he was probably "swarthy in complexion" but hardly black or Negroid. Asked by the *Washington Post* about Felder's theory, Funk exploded, "That's just funny. I suppose we'll be claiming next that he was a woman. Or that he was native American. The possibilities are unlimited."[171] Jewish and Christian biblical scholars also point out that many ancient societies developed ethical precepts with some similarities and notable differences. It is a mistake, they say, to confuse vague and general resemblances between the ethical precepts of all ancient communities with a specific connection between the Bible and ancient Egyptian or African sources.

• At this point, it should come as no surprise that Afrocentrists maintain that Africans also invented democracy and the modern judicial system. "Among the blacks," writes Chancellor Williams, "Democratic institutions evolved. Democracy reached its highest development where the people actually governed themselves without chiefs, where self-government was a way of life, and law and order were taken for granted." Monarchy in Africa, Williams insists, was an aberration and even then, "when they say the king is supreme or has absolute power, they mean that he has absolute power to carry out the will of the people."[172]

Most tribal peoples around the world have lived under systems of monarchy and chieftainship, and scholars point out that Africa was no different. Certainly these systems had to be at least moderately responsive in order to endure for so long, but there is little question that they also relied heavily on arbitrary and autocratic rule. They were certainly not democratic in the modern sense of a government based on popular elections, and rulers typically served until they died or were put to death.

• Afrocentrists teach that Africans enjoyed fundamental legal rights long before they were formulated in the West. Among the rights listed in an Afrocentric document called the Fundamental Rights of the African People: the right to equal protection of the law, the right to a fair trial, the right to indemnity for injuries or losses, the right to health care in the event of sickness or accident, the right to a general education, the right to job training, the right to rise to the limits of one's ability, the right to an equal share in the benefits of society. Even slaves are said to have enjoyed many of these rights.[173] Alas, no such document existed in ancient Africa; all we have is twentieth-century Afrocentric fancy. Scholars point out that such claims project modern conceptions of rights onto ancient peoples who simply did not organize their societies in this way.

• Afrocentrists insist that Africans discovered many of the central remedies of modern medicine. "We found vaccines among them that occured before Jenner, who is supposed to be the discoverer of vaccines," Van Sertima writes. "Africans were using tetracycline long before us here. Tetracycline is an antibiotic that we began using in the 1950s. They found it in Nubia fourteen centuries ago." Not only this, but while European doctors were bleeding their patients to death, East Africans were allegedly performing Caesarean section operations "with one hundred percent success."[174] Adds Na'im Akbar, Africans during the fifteenth century had learned to perform "cornea transplants."[175] Don't be fooled by the reputation of so-called "witch doctors," Chancellor Williams warns. "A long chapter could be devoted to the training of the native doctors and their practice of medicine." Such techniques as "wild dances and mystical speech," according to Williams, were only intended "to impress the people. After all of this, the native physician still had to produce satisfactory results."[176] Scholars are perplexed by such claims, which rely not on evidence but merely on the zeal of Afrocentric teachers and the credulity of their audiences.

• Afrocentrists argue that all the civilizations of the ancient world were either black or owe their achievements to the theft of African ideas. In *They Came Before Columbus,* Ivan Van Sertima argues that it was Africans, rather than Columbus, who discovered America. Van Sertima scrutinizes artifacts of Olmec civilization to find Negro features, thick lips and tousled hair. He also appeals to native American oral tradition, which supposedly confirms the existence of "Negroes and giants." Van Sertima argues that using their impressive navigational technology, Africans produced the mathematical and architectural wonders wrongly attributed to the Mayas, Incas, and Aztecs. Indeed, Afrocentrists maintain that the Indians worshiped black people as gods.[177]

India and China are, in the Afrocentric model, similarly indebted to black ingenuity. "The early inhabitants of India were black," writes John Jackson. "They have Negroid features, dark skin and woolly hair." Indeed those who built the Mohenjo-Daro and Harappa civilizations in India were not Indians at all; rather, they were "Asiatic Ethiopians." Similarly the great philosophy and art that emerged in China during the Shang dynasty really derives from black Africans. Additionally, Olmec, Aztec, and Inca civilizations of the Americas were really inspired by ancient Ethiopia. Indeed, "All the early civilizations were of African Ethiopian origin."[178]

Reputable meso-American scholars generally disagree with these claims, and scholars who are familiar with the archeological evidence say that the Afrocentrists are incompetent in the science of tracing the influence of one society on another. David Grove, an expert on Olmec civilization, says that Afrocentric claims for the black origin of Olmec culture are absurd because "the Olmecs did not have a selection of skin tones to choose from in making their monuments. The only stone available to them was black stone. The source of the stone is the Tuxtlas mountains, of volcanic origin." Additionally, Grove points out, "Monuments get darker by thousands of years of exposure to the elements." He concludes, "What these people have done is go through literally thousands of pictures from all time periods, and have very selectively chosen figures which look foreign. Anything can be subjectively advocated by this methodology." Moreover, Grove says, he has seen instances of pictures which were apparently doctored by Afrocentrists in order to demonstrate negroid features.[179]

Philip Curtin argues that given contemporary knowledge of winds and currents, it would be possible for a few people to make a one-way journey from Africa to the American continent, but virtually impossible for a sailing ship of the kind then available to make the return trip. "From the African side," Curtin writes, "there is absolutely no evidence that voyages reached the Americas and returned."[180] Typical of the scholarly response to books like *They Came Before Columbus* is a classical scholar's *New York Times* review of the book which described Van Sertima as a "deluded scholar" promoting "ignorant rubbish" whose knowledge of historical techniques is "abysmal."[181]

• Afrocentrists do not restrict their claims to the ancient world. They also maintain that African kingdoms during the fifteenth century had university systems that were the most advanced in the world. According to one account, the typical university system consisted of faculties of law, medicine, surgery, letters, grammar, geography, manufacturing, art and craft. Universities were filled with "thousands of students from all parts of Africa" not to mention "the large number of scientists, doctors, lawyers and other scholars." One great African named Babo authored a comprehensive dictionary and forty other works, none of them, regrettably, having survived.[182] In fact, virtually all evidence of literacy in sub-Saharan Africa comes from two sources: Christianity which established a foothold in Ethiopia a few centuries after Christ, and Islam which spread its influence mainly along the east coast of Africa. Apart from these small enclaves, the rest of Africa was basically illiterate.

• Despite the long record of tribal warfare in Africa, which persists to the present, Afrocentrists insist that blacks on the continent did not fight wars to kill each other, but rather as a form of relatively harmless recreation. Chancellor Williams is impressed by "the highly humane aspect of African warfare. . . . In much of the heralded tribal wars, the main objective was to overcome or frighten away the adversary, not to kill at all. . . . Even when the enemy was defeated or completely surrounded, escape routes were provided, the victors pretending not to be aware of them. . . .

Warriors on both sides might meet at the nearest stream to refresh themselves, kid each other, and laugh at each other's jokes. It is clear that it was not much more than a frightful game. This was traditional Africa."[183]

• Finally, Afrocentrists even credit Africans with supernatural powers. The *African-American Baseline Essays* refers to "the extra-terrestrial origin of the Nile" as well as "water-laden micro-comets" which are supposedly the source of the earth's oceans. The document also refers to the paranormal and mystical powers of the pyramids, treats Egyptian astrology as valid science, and credits its black population with expertise "as masters of psi, pre-cognition, psychokinesis, remote viewing and other undeveloped human capabilities." The *Baseline Essays* maintain that ancient Egyptians perfected aeronautics, enabling them to build and use flying gliders for transport and recreation.[184]

Bernard Ortiz De Montellano, a Hispanic anthropologist, argues that these Afrocentric claims are classic instances of "scientific illiteracy" and "pseudoscience." He writes that they confuse religious, mythical, and astrological claims, on the one hand, with science on the other. Montellano argues that universities should resist pressure to teach Afrocentric claims, which like those of astrologers, New Age cults, and creationists, rely not on scientific evidence but on appeals to political representation. "Minorities are already greatly underrepresented in science and engineering," Montellano writes. "Teaching them pseudoscience will make it much more difficult for these young people to pursue scientific curricula."[185]

Afrocentrists typically dismiss these criticisms on the ground that they come from white scholars who cannot be trusted, or from black and Hispanic scholars who have internalized the racism of the Eurocentric model. Thus Afrocentrists are undeterred in claims for their own ancestral greatness. Na'im Akbar concludes, "If there is a people who must be identified as the Fathers of Civilization, the Fathers of Conceptualization, the Fathers of Science, the Originators of Humanity and the Patriarchs of the Human Race, we are it."[186] And Nathan Hare recommends the following anthem for young African American males:

I, the Black Man, am the original man, the first man to walk this vast and imponderable earth. I, the Black Man, am an African, the exotic single quintessence of a universal blackness. . . . I will crush the corners of the earth and this world will surely tremble until I, the Black Man, the first and original man, can with my woman, erect among the peoples of the universe a new society, humane to its cultural core, out of which will at long last emerge, as night moves into day, the first truly human being that the world has ever known.[187]

RACIAL PRIDE, RACIAL CHAUVINISM

Because Afrocentrism abounds in ironies, it is tempting not to take it seriously. Henry Louis Gates, Jr. muses that Afrocentrists simultaneously denounce Western civilization while claiming to be its original founders.[188] "If blacks are the ones who discovered America," one scholar quips, "let them take responsibility for wiping out the Indians." Anthony Appiah remarks that "Molefi Asante has written books about Akan culture without referring to the major works of Akan philosophers such as J. B. Danquah, William Abrahams, Kwasi Wiredu and Kwame Gyekye" and recalls the case of an eminent philospher from Zaire who was firmly told by American Afrocentrists, "We do not need you educated Africans coming here to tell us about African culture."[189] Commenting on the Afrocentric penchant for speaking Swahili and taking North African Muslim names, Bernard Lewis remarks, "We can understand why many blacks would give up the name and language of the white men who bought them as slaves, but why on earth would they want to adopt the name and language of the Arabs who sold them into slavery?" Nicholas Lemann treats Afrocentrism as a harmless assertion of black nationalism with an ancestral twist. "I asked Molefi Asante if you could be an Afrocentrist and work for IBM and live in the suburbs and he unhesitatingly said yes."[190]

This critique misses the central thrust of Afrocentrism, which is an attack on the two central institutions identified with the West, science and modernity. Liberals are frequently blind to this assault because the way for it has been paved by relativist ideology. Science is based on the distinction between "facts" and "values." Perhaps values are subjective, but we can know the facts of the natural world. Drawing on relativism, Afrocentrists radicalize the critique of Eurocentrism, so that the relativism of values clears the ground for an assertion of the relativism of facts. "Black facts" are advanced as the basis for a new set of distinctively African values. These black values, Maulana Karenga emphasizes, may or may not be true for whites "but they constitute the reality of black people." Na'im Akbar writes, "Men don't want to identify with somebody else's knowledge. They want their own knowledge."[191]

The attack on science and modernity is very explicit in Marimba Ali's book *Yurugu: An African-Centered Critique of European Cultural Thought and Behavior.* Ani argues that modernity should be rejected as a product of European ideology, and that logic and science are "the monster" that Western culture has created. "Our task is to throw into question European . . . scientific epistemology. The European conception of science is secular and rests on alienating, rationalistic, linear concepts. What is contradictory in Euro-American logic is not contradictory in African thought."[192] Thus it should come as no surprise that Afrocentrists openly reject scholarly and scientific techniques as a form of Western "tricknology"[193] and use "legends" and "religious cults" as sources of evidence, arguing as Martin Bernal does that "evidence from them is not categorically less valid than that from archaeology."[194] Molefi Asante rejects much of Western science on the grounds that it is "not deep enough for our humanistic and spiritual viewpoint." For Afrocentrists, in Asante's words, "the trees and the mountains have always possessed essences. Thus we rise above the decadence of Western science to the *orisha* of Afrocentricity." Accuse Asante of promulgating myths and he responds, "We act mythically," "All people have a mythology," and black Americans need to "reconstruct our mythology."[195] Wade Nobles writes:

> The importance of mythology is that it is a form of documentation which transcends the human record inasmuch as it states truth rather than fact. Myth can be considered a form of reasoning and record-keeping by providing an implicit guide for bringing about the fulfillment of the truth it proclaims. It connects the invisible order with the visible order.[196]

The tragedy of Afrocentrism for blacks is that, in the name of fighting racism and promoting group pride, it provides young people with falsehoods that can hardly be a source of lasting knowledge or self-esteem. Anthony Appiah points out that instead of preparing black students for the challenges of living in a modern civilization, Afrocentrists teach them languages that are hardly spoken anywhere on the planet and concepts that are "a composite of truth and error, insight and illusion, moral generosity and meanness."[197] Black scholar Wilson Moses argues that like creationism, Afrocentrism is an "evangelical utopian" movement which asserts that "claims of representation override claims of verifiable evidence" and which represents not preparation for but resistance to life in modern industrial society.[198]

The danger of Afrocentrism for society is that its "black reality" and racial chauvinism are producing a deep and unbridgeable mental chasm between blacks and whites in America. If Afrocentrists maintain that blacks invented virtually everything in the period before 500 B.C., what happened after that? How did Africa go from being ahead of the rest of the world to being so primitive? Afrocentrists have to account for why Europeans were able to so easily subdue Africa with only token or sporadic opposition. It is not enough to say that Europeans pirated African knowledge, because even if whites learned much of what they know from Africans, it does not follow that Africans, as a consequence, would immediately forget how to organize universities and perform cornea transplants. Puzzled by this dilemma, Afrocentrists have come up with the obvious answer: European whites are intrinsically evil and oppressive "ice people" who, as Leonard Jeffries puts it, have entered into a continuing global conspiracy to conceal African achievement and control the minds and bodies of blacks. John Jackson argues that "the Europeans, being warlike, had a distinct advantage over the peaceful Africans."[199] The canonical Afrocentric work in this area is Michael Bradley's *The Iceman Inheritance,* endorsed by John Henrik Clarke, who says that it provides "an important message for our times and all times." Subtitled "Prehistoric Source of Western Man's Racism, Sexism and Aggression," *The Iceman Inheritance* argues that having evolved in a glacial environment, whites mated with Neanderthals and earlier forms to produce a particularly vicious mongrel breed of *homo sapiens:*

> These special adaptations had incidental side-effects which resulted in an exceptionally aggressive psychology . . . and a higher level of psychosexual conflict compared to all other races. Not intelligence, nor morality, nor spirit, but aggression is responsible for the expansion of Caucasoids . . . at the expense of other races.[200]

No one should be surprised that Afrocentrism so closely parallels white racism in its historical claims to biological superiority. Despite its fervent denunciations of white racism, Afrocentrists are on most points in basic agreement with the racists. They too believe in the importance of race, and in the role of race in shaping intellect, character, and culture. This is clear in the Afrocentric reliance on the one-drop rule, which is unique to America and was devised by slaveowners and segregationists for the specific purpose of ensuring black subjugation. By what criterion do Afrocentrists claim that Cleopatra, Hannibal, Jesus Christ, Augustine of Hippo, Beethoven, and other well-known historical figures were really black? Not even the least educated Afrocentrist maintains that these people were entirely Negroid. What they mean, rather, is that there is some evidence of mixed blood.

In a revealing admission in the literary journal *Arethusa,* Martin Bernal writes, "I make no claim that the Egyptians were black." Yet in *Black Athena* he argued that the most powerful Egyptian dynasties were made up of pharaoahs "whom one can usefully call black." Bernal explains that these Egyptians were black in the sense that they would not be served coffee in the restaurant in the segregated South.[201] Molefi Asante concurs that "the ancient Egyptians looked no different from present-day African Americans."[202] This is an endorsement, rather than a refutation, of the one-drop rule: any trace of African or nonwhite heritage defines you racially as black. Chiekh Anta Diop takes this reasoning to its logical conclusion: the French, the Spanish, the Italians, and the Greeks, he argues, may all be considered black.[203]

Racialist ideology is also evident in the basic premise of Afrocentrism. What, after all, do the various tribal peoples in Africa, who have historically identified themselves as Wolof, Ibo, and so on, have in common? The color of their skin. What do African American children from Chicago share with contemporary or ancient Africans? The color of their skin. Thus a central principle of Afrocentrism is that biology is destiny, and that the color of your skin determines the content of your character. "Afrocentrism," argues African scholar Anthony Appiah, "shares the presuppositions of Victorian racial ideology against which it is reacting. Basically, knowledge is viewed as a racial possession."

Despite their interest in the ancient world, Afrocentrists appear to have missed one of the most important lessons that we can learn from the ancients, which is their acknowledgment of civilizational differences combined with their refusal to reduce these to biological characteristics. "The ancient Egyptian lack of color prejudice should serve as a salutary lesson for us today," Frank Yurco says. "They would have considered this Afrocentric argument absurd, and this is something we could really learn from."[204] Instead Afrocentrists insist upon projecting their own racial nomenclature and obsession onto the ancient Egyptians, invoking them to justify contemporary assertions of black militancy. This strategy was evident in a public appeal by a black student at Pennsylvania State University for African Americans to "bear arms" and "form a militia" to confront and destroy "white devils."[205]

What Afrocentrists have discovered, like the Afrikaners and the Nazis before them, is that racial grievance can be a source of power. The power does not simply come from assuring young blacks that their ancestors did unbelievable things. This would not mean very much, and it would only highlight the enormous distance between the heroic status of ancient Africans and the despondent position of inner-city African Americans. Afrocentric power derives from its demonization of whites as unscrupulous, homicidal thieves of the black civilizational birthright. Those who endorse this paradigm should not be surprised when the Nation of Islam draws the logical conclusion: whites are the primary source of evil in the world and eternal vigilance, armed if necessary, is the posture that enlightened blacks should adopt in order to counter ongoing white assaults on their most precious possessions.

Afrocentrism is thus both pathetic and formidable: pathetic because it offers young blacks nothing in the way of knowledge and skills that are required by the modern environment; formidable, because it offers them racial dynamite instead: a fortified chauvinism, a hardened conspiratorial mindset, and a robotic dedication to ideologies of blackness. The "revolutionary commitment" to which Molefi Asante refers is evident in the hardened gleam in many Afrocentric eyes. Afrocentrists exhibit a virtually cultic pattern of lockstep behavior: everyone dresses alike, and when the leader laughs, everyone laughs. Gradually but unmistakably Afrocentrists are severing the bonds of empathy and understanding that are the basis for coexistence and cooperation in a multiracial society. The Afrocentric message is basically the one that Hitler delivered in the 1930s: we were great once, we have been humiliated, let us recognize the evil ones who have stolen our birthright, let us confront them and recover our inheritance, by any means necessary.

Doubts About Relativism

If liberals are wondering about how all this dangerous excess came to be identified with liberalism, the answer is simple: both multiculturalism and Afrocentrism are constructed on the logic of relativism, sometimes pushing that logic to its furthest point, sometimes exploiting openings made possible by relativism. Liberals have found it difficult to criticize multiculturalism and Afrocentrism because of their affinities with liberal ideology. Consequently it is the first principle of relativism itself that becomes the issue: one that liberals should confront, and one that students exposed to Afrocentrism and multiculturalism should learn to evaluate critically. Let us follow the relativist logic from its Boasian premise that most Americans cannot objectively study minority and non-Western cultures because they will necessarily view them through the prism of Eurocentric assumptions. As Ramon Saldivar puts it in *Chicano Narrative,* we must free ourselves from "the enslaving myth of absolute and universal truths."[206] This rejection of truths which transcend space and time is now promoted by influential thinkers such as Richard Rorty and Stanley Fish, who argue that truth is an illusion and knowledge is political.[207]

While they are right that none of us approach other societies in a culturally nude state, so that our perspective is necessarily shaped and perhaps clouded by our prior beliefs, does this mean that we have no way to transcend those biases and approach the ideal of objectivity? If so, then multiculturalism itself is an illusion because other cultures constitute inaccessible and incommensurable worlds, and Westerners can do no better than project their own values onto the cultures they appear to be studying. This, as we have seen, is what many multicultural activists do. Ironically the assumption that other cultures are self-contained and untranslatable systems leads to the conclusion that it is a waste of time for outsiders to attempt the inherently impossible project of understanding other cultures. If we simply cannot know the Other, perhaps it makes sense to content ourselves with the ethnocentric dictum: Know Thyself. Richard Rorty has reached precisely this conclusion, arguing that Westerners should be unabashedly ethnocentric because they cannot be anything else.[208]

The vast majority of multicultural advocates reject Rorty's position, because it exposes multiculturalism as Eurocentric, whereas activists like to think of themselves as fighting Eurocentrism. The question then becomes: how can American students transcend Eurocentrism and study other cultures "from within" when such an effort seems doomed at the outset? Multicultural advocates such as Renato Rosaldo, Richard Delgado, and Ian Haney-Lopez typically answer that schools should recruit minority and Third World representatives who can provide much-needed black, Hispanic, Asian, and American Indian perspectives.[209] In some cases, activists insist that it is inadequate for minority recruits to have the right skin color: they must also espouse progressive and left-wing views.[210] But how do we know that these individuals who have necessarily been hired by American criteria (university degrees, publishing records, even radical credentials) are truly representative of the indigenous systems of thought and belief in a particular culture? There is a good chance that they could represent marginal or unrepresentative factions within other cultures, or else they could be Eurocentric impostors.

Multicultural advocates typically avoid this problem by asserting that education does provide a bridge between cultures, and with proper training students can be taught to appreciate the equal worth of all cultures. "If we develop cultural consciousness and intercultural competence," Christine Bennett writes, "we may be able to understand that we might very well accept and even participate in such behaviors had we been born and raised in that society."[211] But this conclusion does not follow from its premises. If all criteria of judgment derive from within cultures, how can we arrive at an external standard of evaluation that permits us to place all cultures on an equal plane? How can we know that the moral codes of other cultures are valid for the people who live under them? Multicultural activists rely on the sleight-of-hand in which "I cannot know" becomes "I cannot judge" which becomes "I know that we are all equal." A skeptical confession of ignorance mysteriously becomes a dogmatic assertion of cultural egalitarianism.

This is not to condone approaching other cultures with a presumption of inferiority. As Charles Taylor argues, "It makes sense to demand as a matter of right that we approach the study of other cultures with a presumption of their value." Thus cultural relativism may provide a valuable methodological starting point of humility and intellectual openness. Yet as Taylor points out, in evaluating other cultures "it can't make sense to demand as a matter of right that we come up with a final concluding judgment that their value is great or equal to others."[212] Perhaps a careful examination of other cultures will reveal good reasons to be critical of other cultures, just as we are often critical of our own culture.

Indeed the first thing we notice when we study other cultures is that without exception they reject cultural relativism. Cultural relativism is a uniquely Western ideology. Thus it should come as no surprise that relativism provokes sharp resistance from people in other cultures. Imagine the legitimate anger of a Muslim who is cheerfully informed by a Western academic that Allah's teachings are true for him, when he deeply believes that they are universal principles. A relativist analysis of Islam as nothing more than a social adaptation reveals, in a new form, the old and perverse Western tendency not to take other cultures seriously as offering fundamental alternatives to Western notions of goodness and truth.

Moreover, as Leszek Kolakowski points out, it seems paternalistic to say that Islamic practices such as punishing thieves by cutting off their limbs represent legitimate judicial options—for those people.[213] Such arguments, which imply that our kind of people deserve democracy and human rights but their kind of people do not, seem self-serving and may be destructive to the contemporary aspirations of millions of Third World peoples. As Claude Lévi-Strauss recognized, many Third World residents are happy to acknowledge the temporary backwardness of their cultures as the basis for gaining access to Western ideas and Western technology and making a transition to modernity which they correctly identify with the West. In a stunning admission, Lévi-Strauss writes:

> The dogma of cultural relativism is challenged by the very people for whose moral benefit the anthropologists established it in the first place. The complaint the underdeveloped countries advance is not that they are being Westernized, but that there is too much delay in giving them the means to Westernize themselves. It is of no use to defend the individuality of human cultures against those cultures themselves.[214]

Consequently a sincere effort to study other cultures "from within" requires a rejection of the Western lens of cultural relativism. Indeed an examination of great Islamic philosophers such as Al-Farabi and Ibn Sinha reveals that they believed in reason and revelation as the two mechanisms for discovering universal truths. Indeed these Muslim scholars studied the Greeks not because they were interested in diversity, but because they were interested in truths which they believed extended across cultural boundaries. Consequently, multiculturalists who wish to take non-Western cultures seriously must take seriously their rejection of relativism. Otherwise a humble openness to other cultures becomes an arrogant dismissal of their highest claims to truth.

Students do need to be exposed to the great accomplishments of other cultures, as well as their influence on the West. Cultural relativism goes beyond this to insist that we should understand cultural differences without applying (inherently biased) standards of critical evaluation. Thus multiculturalism becomes a technique for celebrating differences without making distinctions. Specifically, it forbids at the outset the possibility that one culture may be in crucial respects superior to another. An initial openness to the truths of other cultures degenerates into a closed-minded denial of all transcultural standards. Seeking to avoid an acknowledgment of Western cultural superiority, relativism ends up denying the possibility of truth.

The claim of Western cultural superiority has, for the past several centuries, decisively rested on science and technology, which seem to offer an unrivaled access both to the laws of nature and to the material benefits of harnessing nature's power. Science is a major embarrassment to cultural relativism because it seems ridiculous to claim that each culture has its own equally valid claim to understanding physical laws. Whatever its social benefits in promoting group solidarity, either rain-dancing does or does not cause rain.[215] Does it make sense to say that the earth is round for us, but other cultures may with equal legitimacy insist that the earth is flat? At first glance this seems preposterous, yet some radical multiculturalists draw on Thomas Kuhn's *The Structure of Scientific Revolutions* to contend that even scientific principles only hold within cognitive paradigms and thus have no claim to accurately represent nature.[216] African American anthropologist Johnnetta Cole argues for a "new definition" of science which is "based on the multiplicity of equally valuable truths."[217] Kuhn himself has repudiated concepts such as "ethnoscience," as well as the extreme relativist reading of his work, insisting that he was merely describing how scientific revolutions happen, and not questioning the capacity of scientists to increase knowledge and predict and control external phenomena.[218] And it strains credulity to insist that the law of gravity and the law of non-contradiction are culture-bound.

If we grant, however, that Newton's theory of gravity is universally true, we must then consider the possibility of truths that are Western in origin but universal in their application. To this the thoughtful relativist usually responds by invoking the famous distinction between facts and values. According to this view—first advanced by positivists and made famous in this country by Max Weber—we can through scientific techniques know facts, but we have no rational basis for preferring the values of one culture (or individual) to those of another.[219] Yet the fact-value distinction also contains serious problems. Is the distinction itself a fact or a value? If it is a value, then we must conclude that it is arbitrary and there is no scientific basis for believing it. So how do we know that the values of different cultures cannot be meaningfully compared? Here relativists typically appeal to the diverse moral opinions of various cultures to demonstrate the relativity of values. Yet such surveys prove nothing, because undoubtedly similar surveys in various cultures would produce an equal diversity of opinions on such factual issues as $E = mc^2$ or whether human beings evolved from lower forms.

Advocates of relativism such as Stanley Fish usually win popular support for their case by attacking the straw man of "absolute truth." But not even science claims to have access to absolute truth. Indeed the entire system of scientific hypothesis and verification is based on the assumption that truths are provisional and subject to future revision. We cannot say that evolution is absolutely true, but we can say that there is stronger evidence for Darwin than for Bishop Ussher. Similarly there is more evidence for Einstein than for Newton, just as there is more evidence for Newton than for Ptolemy. The absence of final knowledge does not mean that some claims are not better supported than others. Stanley Fish is wrong to assert that there is no basis for distinguishing between reason and belief.[220]

If some scientific truths are considered valid on the grounds that they are more true than competing theories, why by the same token must we dismiss the possibility that political or moral propositions may be considered as permanent and universal (although not necessarily absolute) truths? Consider the central proposition of the Declaration of Independence—all men are created equal—which Abraham Lincoln declared "an abstract truth, applicable to all men and all times."[221] A good case can be made that, based on what we know about human nature and various forms of government, we can be just as certain as we are of scientific propositions that government by popular consent is a better system than religious theocracy or political totalitarianism. Of course some Islamic fundamentalists might disagree, but they are also likely to disagree about the theory of evolution. In short, they could be wrong on both counts, so American students can be confident that truth both about the natural and the social world is possible.

Cardinal Newman defined the purpose of a liberal education as one to "educate the intellect to reason well in all matters, to reach out towards truth, and to grasp it."[222] Schools and colleges should provide young people with an authentic multicultural curriculum that begins at home but is nevertheless open to the world beyond. Such a cosmopolitan canon would expose students to "the best that has been thought and said" not simply in the West but in other cultures as well. The object is not diversity but knowledge: students should learn ways to seek to distinguish truth from falsehood, beauty from vulgarity, right from wrong. Knowledge is a matter of ascertaining facts, as well as developing the tools to formulate "right opinion." To use Plato's famous image, we live our lives in a cave, distracted by the shadows of perspective and opinion, but it is the aspiration of an authentic multicultural education to help us move from opinion to knowledge, to climb out of the darkness into the illuminating radiance of the sun.

10

BIGOTRY IN BLACK AND WHITE

Can African Americans Be Racist?

Don't you think that the white neo-Nazis and some of these black nationalists ought to get together, to unite so as to save on overhead costs?
—Ishmael Reed[1]

The group of around two hundred whites gathered at the Hilton hotel in Atlanta in late May 1994 seemed to resemble an academic conference. Yet this was a meeting, the first of its kind in recent years, organized by activists seeking to articulate a politics of white power (or, as they term it, "white preservation"). The conference was organized by Jared Taylor, author of *Paved with Good Intentions,* an account of race relations and the follies of multiculturalism. Taylor is a gaunt Southern man whose book purports to criticize the excesses of racial preferences. In a newsletter called *American Renaissance* that he edits under the name Samuel Taylor, Jared Taylor's agenda is more explicitly set forth. Here are a few items—some by Taylor, some appearing unsigned or by others—that I read in the publication before attending the conference.

- "[A]n acceptance of racial differences might be *good* for blacks. . . . [In the nineteenth century] the assumption of inferiority made it easier to accept meager circumstances."[2]

387

- "As long as whites are browbeaten into believing that race does not matter, they will continue to cooperate in their own marginalization."[3]
- "When West African slaves came to America they brought with them their habit of eating dirt. In the southern United States, dirt eating is still surprisingly common."[4]
- "In June, the Chicago Bulls won its third straight professional basketball championship, and blacks celebrated in what has come to be their usual style—they looted and rioted. . . ."[5]
- "More and more whites are rediscovering what their ancestors took for granted: a natural preference for and loyalty to their own race."[6]
- "American slaves had surprisingly positive things to say about slavery."[7]
- "In some cases would slavery not be better than the squalor and barbarism that so many blacks have brought upon themselves?"[8]
- "There are no . . . mantras to numb the brain like: All men are created equal. . ."[9]
- ". . . I can find no cause that is greater, harder or more heroic than that of racialism."[10]
- "Nelson Mandela is now president of South Africa. . . [T]he grisly gods of 'democracy' have now been satisfied."[11]

These themes were elaborated at the Atlanta conference. As I made my way to the first session, notebook in hand, I was startled to see David Duke in the elevator. He looked tan and sporty and was accompanied by a burly man who could have been a bodyguard. I asked him if he planned to attend the conference. No, he said, the organizers asked him not to show up because it might undermine their credibility. But Duke planned to have associates at the meetings, and I spotted him several times in the hotel that weekend, chatting with Jared Taylor.

Taylor's introductory lecture emphasized the dangers to whites posed by blacks and immigrants. "As our population changes, our health standards will change, and it makes one wonder which will be the first American city in which we cannot drink the water." Suburbs are "shrinking enclaves where Anglo-American civility prevails." Other groups may be well-behaved but "[it] is our right, it is our duty not to let our country become full of people who are utterly unlike ourselves." Taylor reserved his greatest contempt, however, for whites who refuse to embrace their whiteness and fight back. Taylor invoked the memory of his Confederate ancestors. "I'm sorry to say that they lost." It is true that blacks and immigrants despise whites, Taylor claimed. "And we *are* despicable. Unless we defend our racial interests and put them first, we will disappear." In a subsequent conversation, Taylor said that while he did not approve of slavery, many slaveholders held that the alternative was "Negro pandemonium." Their fear, Taylor said, may have been borne out. About integration: "The black separatists are right." About whites who are uncivilized and disposed to crime: "They may be boobs, but they're *our* boobs." About violence, Taylor said that whites cannot afford to reject the option of violence in self-defense, and warned of the possibility of a race war. "When it happens," he predicted, "the divisions will be along racial lines." Taylor appears to be a tribalist, who champions group historical consciousness and white racial preservation.

One of the star speakers at the conference was philosopher Michael Levin, whose views on rational discrimination we have encountered earlier. A bespectacled academic with a nasal voice, Levin proceeded to explain why blacks are less intelligent and less motivated than whites. Black inferiority, he argued, is "overwhelmingly likely to be genetic. It is not the result of racism. Are white children taught to metabolize glucose differently than black children?" Laughter. Since blacks are naturally more criminally oriented than whites, Levin suggested the desirability of race conscious policies for African Americans. Perhaps blacks could be treated as adults by the criminal system at an earlier age "given that blacks mature more quickly than whites." He suggested expedited trials for African American defendants "since they have a shorter time horizon." He said the police should be permitted to stop young black males driving expensive cars, since there was probable cause to believe that they were felons.

Another popular speaker was Samuel Francis, a Southern conservative who is also a columnist for the *Washington Times*. A lively controversialist, Francis began with some largely valid complaints about how the Southern heritage is demonized in mainstream culture. At one point he described singer Garth Brooks as "repulsive" because "he has that stupid universalist song, in which we all intermarry." Francis attacked the liberal principles of humanism and universalism for facilitating "the war against the white race." He called for a revival of the *conquistador* spirit among whites:

> Instead of invoking a suicidal liberalism and regurgitating the very universalism that has subverted our identity and our sense of solidarity, what we as whites must do is reassert our identity and our solidarity, and we must do so in explicitly racial terms through the articulation of a racial consciousness as whites. . . . The civilization that we as whites created in Europe and America could not have developed apart from the genetic endowments of the creating

people, nor is there any reason to believe that the civilization can be success-fully transmitted to a different people.[12]

Francis was followed by Lawrence Auster, author of *The Path to Nation-al Suicide: An Essay on Immigration and Multiculturalism*. Auster began conventionally enough, with attacks on affirmative action, but then he proceeded to a gruesome portrait of immigrants epitomized by animal sacrifice cults, Dominican drug dealers, and Muslim extremists and ter-rorists. Auster argued that "white America can survive demographically and culturally only if it recognizes itself as a threatened ethnoculture." Auster contended that advocates of intermarriage were proposing and cel-ebrating "not just the dilution of white America, but its complete elimina-tion." He added, "This is the insanity that results from uncritically accepting the idea that race doesn't matter. . . . It's the current race-blind ideology that is insane." Auster also stated that the "large and enduring differences in average intelligence between blacks and whites" mean that "blacks *on their own* can never be expected to maintain a modern, democ-ratic, civilized society" or "achieve collective economic equality and other kinds of parity with whites."

Perhaps the lecture that generated the most amusement was given by Eugene Valberg, a white man who lived in Africa. Valberg regaled the au-dience with tales of black incompetence, corruption, and stupidity. Most Africans, Valberg said, know that the white man is smarter than the black man. Not only do Africans recognize their intrinsic inferiority but "they are not in the slightest bit upset by this." American black protest, Valberg suggested, is a kind of political pose. "They learn to act angry and show rage. They know it is to their advantage." In Africa, Valberg said, blacks live in a kind of absurdist culture. "The belief in witchcraft is absolutely universal." Most blacks, he said, "view science as a kind of magic." Blacks are absolutely flummoxed by technology, including how to turn a TV set on and off. And there is no concept of obligation. "When a black man makes a promise he means maybe he'll do it, maybe he won't." Valberg told of an African town where blacks seemingly got into car crashes on every street. Apparently most blacks believed that they would be absolute-ly immune from personal harm if they wore a special amulet on their arm. Yet when Valberg asked one injury victim why, despite an amulet, he had still gotten into a crash, the man reportedly replied that this was because the person who slammed into him was probably not wearing *his* amulet.

For me, the only nonwhite there, the conference provided a revealing spectacle. Here were two hundred amateur biologists conversing with great assurance about intelligence quotient, validity coefficients, and the latest findings by Arthur Jensen and Richard Herrnstein. Here were people who were urbane and educated, yet they did not flinch from terms like "chink" and "nigger." Indeed more than once I heard someone say that it was highly significant that he was not socially permitted to call blacks "nigger" when blacks themselves used the term with each other. One man knowingly observed that the physical nature of blacks and the intellectual nature of whites is perfectly captured in the white tendency to refer to "our minds" while blacks refer to "our heads." Several participants cited affirmative action as proof of the basic uncompetitiveness of blacks in American society.

I attempted to argue with some of the participants there, pointing out to one activist the evidence that showed how productive Cubans, West Indians, and many Asian groups were; his lack of interest confirmed my suspicion that he feared increased influx from these groups *because* they were productive—immigrant competition threatened him, just as immigrant dependency appalled him. With another man I raised questions about the claim that the historical record of blacks proved natural inferiority. "Look," he told me. "If the blacks are right that they had the earliest civilization in Africa, then they should be far ahead of other people in development." Another added, "If blacks can run a civilization on their own, how come they have messed up every single time? Look at Haiti. That place belongs in Africa, because blacks have ruined it. South Africa is going down the tubes next." A college student joked, "If blacks are not an inferior race, they do the best imitation of one that I have witnessed." An elderly man who looked like a professor said, "My research proves that it is blacks who should pay us reparations, since their wages in America are far higher than they would be if blacks stayed in Africa." Racial nomenclature came up again: "First it was Negro. Then colored. Then black. Now African American. Why don't they just call themselves skunks?" A publisher of racist tracts offered to put together a book called "101 Excuses for Black Failure," which would give African Americans "lots of reasons for constantly screwing up and blaming others for it." Finally there were the ones who did not openly praise the Skinheads but implied that at least they had convictions and were doing something: Better to light a cross than to curse the darkness!

KKK, RIP

At first glance, we seem to be witnessing a revival of the old racism, of which there is no more powerful symbol in America than the Ku Klux Klan. Scholars show an avid interest in the Klan and related groups: recent books on the subject include *Skinheads Shaved for Battle, Religion and the Racist Right, The Silent Brotherhood,* and *The Rise of David Duke.*[13] Some newspapers publish articles on the Klan every few months or so, and the organization is described perennially as "resurgent."[14] Many scholars also warn of a growing Klan. Alphonso Pinkney in *The Myth of Black Progress* refers to "the revival of the Klan throughout the country" and asserts, "No one knows exactly what the Klan membership is but it is clear that it is growing in the South and elsewhere."[15] Joe Feagin and Hernan Vera insist in *White Racism* that "the white supremacy movement is growing."[16] Organizations that raise money for the purpose of combating hate groups also convey in their literature the specter of a national army of Klansmen and skinheads posing a grave danger to the basic rights of blacks. Perhaps the Atlanta conference will suggest to many that the Klan is making a comeback in the 1990s.

Yet contrary to the expectation of many liberal activists, the Ku Klux Klan is a virtually defunct organization. The Klan today is close to bankruptcy, its membership has been precipitously on the decline for years, its activities are intensely monitored by law enforcement and civil rights groups, and it would not be very surprising if the organization ceased to exist by the end of the century. For a group that once boasted millions of members and wielded considerable political power, especially in the South, the contemporary Klan is a pale image of its former self. Even groups professionally devoted to fighting the Klan, which have a stake in inflating its membership, confirm the massive hemorrhaging of the group's numbers and strength. The Anti-Defamation League of B'nai B'rith and the Southern Poverty Law Center, both of which monitor white hate groups, report that total combined membership in the Ku Klux Klan and the Skinheads in the United States is approximately 7,500 persons. The Anti-Defamation League's 1991 survey of Klan membership estimated 4,000 Klan members, but since then the Klan has split into two rival factions, and membership seems to have declined substantially. The Skinheads reportedly have a wider geographical base than the Klan with chapters in forty states, but the Anti-Defamation League's June 1993 survey found only 3,000 to 3,500 Skinhead members nationwide.[17] Remarks

Stuart Lowengrub, head of the ADL's Atlanta office, "The Klan today has nothing left, no influence at all, political or economic. What's left of the Klan is no more than a nuisance."[18]

One might expect the Klan's collapse to be cause for celebration, particularly among African Americans. Oddly, many scholars and writers are extremely reluctant to acknowledge the end of an era. Rather, they are incredulous and even angry when informed of eroding Klan membership and influence. Yet in fact, the Ku Klux Klan was on the decline throughout the 1980s and early 1990s. Nothing accelerated its political demise more than a lawsuit filed against the organization by Morris Dees, a white liberal activist who heads the Southern Poverty Law Center in Montgomery, Alabama. Representing Beulah Mae Donald, the mother of a teenage boy lynched by Klan members, Dees convinced an all-white jury in 1987 to award a $7 million verdict against the grand wizard of the Klan and his United Klans of America. Already losing members and in financial straits, the Klan was forced to sell many of its meager assets, including its national headquarters. As a final humiliation, several Klansmen were compelled, as part of a civil settlement, to attend a class on racial sensitivity administered in May 1990 by black minister Joseph Lowery.[19] A similar fate befell the Skinheads, a neo-Nazi group primarily composed of teenagers with shaven heads which surpassed the Klan in membership and violence against blacks and immigrants during the early 1980s. Undoubtedly the most powerful and vicious of the Skinhead groups was the White Aryan Resistance, led by a television repairman named Tom Metzger. In 1991 Morris Dees and his Southern Poverty Law Center represented an Ethiopian student clubbed to death by Skinheads, and won a $12.5 million award against Metzger's Aryan group. Metzger's house was auctioned, and court representatives monitor his group's contributions which are siphoned off to pay damages.[20]

Neither the Klan nor the Skinheads have ceased to operate. Some Klan leaders such as Oklahoma's Dennis Mahon have traveled to Germany where they are trying to hitch up with racist and xenophobic groups abroad.[21] In the United States, small renegade outfits continue to operate in a survivalist mode, usually in rural parts of the country. Every now and then the Klan will stage a rally in a city in which small numbers of marchers are inevitably outnumbered by large numbers of protesters against the Klan.[22] Robert Branch, an African American writer, describes a 1992 Klan rally in Ocean City, Maryland, in which "about two dozen" Klansmen were greeted by boos, hisses, and slurs from hundreds of black and white opponents. Scores of police were on the scene, not to protect blacks, but to protect the Klansmen.[23] It is not uncommon these days to see Skinheads appearing on talk shows such as Geraldo Rivera's, where they supply predictable histrionics and offer many opportunities for audience moralism. Television game shows sometimes even feature a slot labeled "KKK Guy," converting the incoherent ravings of a bigot into an occasion for pathetic humor. Media personality Howard Stern urges his listeners to call Ku Klux Klan phone numbers to laugh at the absurd recorded messages about white supremacy. One TV documentary quoted a local Skinhead leader expressing his fondest wish: to stand at the gateway to hell with a pitchfork, spearing Jews and blacks as they entered.

As the April 1995 bombing of an Oklahoma federal building showed, it would be foolish to underestimate the potential of even a small group of racial terrorists for violence and mayhem. Weak and dying organizations sometimes show a dangerous proclivity for striking out in kamikaze fashion. Activist groups and the police are right to be vigilant. Recently in California the authorities thwarted a Skinhead plan to blow up a black church in order to foment continuing race riots in the aftermath of the Rodney King incident.[24] A 1994 report in *Klanwatch,* published by the Southern Poverty Law Center, lists the following incidents: A Skinhead was arrested for beating a black man to death in St. Louis, Missouri. In South Bend, Indiana, three white supremacists belonging to a group called the White Brotherhood were accused of killing a black woman. In Wilmette, Illinois, a white plastic surgeon was reportedly killed because a white racist group believed he was giving minorities a lighter skin and more Aryan features.[25] Yet David Chalmers in his book *Hooded Americanism: The History of the Ku Klux Klan* writes that when reporters constantly press him to describe the resurgence or revival of the Klan, he routinely informs them that *they* are the Klan revival. In other words, an ailing Klan is often magnified into a vast and potent national juggernaut by a media prone to sensationalism and by activist groups whose fund-raising depends on apocalyptic forecasts of a never-ending epidemic of racial terrorism. Chalmers notes that when the Klan announced its plan to patrol the Mexican border against illegal aliens, only eight Klansmen—but a large squad of reporters—showed up. Chalmers even recounts an episode where at a Klan rally in Florida in the late 1980s, the cross-burning was delayed for twenty minutes until the local TV news crew arrived.[26] The contemporary marginality of the Klan is conveyed in a Klan song.

You have to be black to get a welfare check and I'm broke.
No joke.
I ain't got a nickel for a coke.
I ain't black you see,
So Uncle Sam won't help poor nigger-hating me.[27]

Members of white extremist organizations today can subscribe to journals and newsletters with names like *Thunderbolt, Crusader,* and the *Fiery Cross.* They can sport tattoos or bumper stickers saying "White Power," "Thank God for AIDS," and "Nigger Hunting License." They can learn songs about how blacks are "mud people" whom God erroneously created on the third day, or hymns to the ancient Nordic gods.[28] They can purchase ceramic statues of a hooded Klansman whose eyes glow when he is plugged into an electrical outlet.[29] They can order from the Liberty Lobby such pamphlets as "Proud to Be a Racist," "Six Million Did Not Die," "Kosher Food Racket Exposed," "White Man, Think Again," and "The Hitler We Loved and Why."[30]

The fact is that these racial fanatics are few in number and they come from the very dregs of society. Paul Sniderman's studies show that racist attitudes are most likely to be held by whites who are poorest, least educated, and virtually marginalized in society.[31] Fortunately these racists are not in much of a position to deny blacks education and jobs, which they often don't have access to themselves. The Klan, however, continues to recruit from this group whose racism is less a function of its power than of its powerlessness. Indeed it is marginality itself which gives racism its appeal. Today's Klansmen and white supremacists have no plausible justification for asserting civilizational superiority against blacks, Jews, or anyone else. They occupy the lowest rungs on the economic and social ladder. Bigotry seems to be a last line of defense for "poor white trash" against the degrading temptation of barbarism. One may fear these people and yet feel sorry for them at the same time. Like the indigent Southern white man in the movie *Resurgence,* one of their few consolations is to assure themselves, "Every morning, I wake up and thank God I'm white."[32]

So why do we keep hearing about a Klan revival? The reason is the widespread conviction, articulated by Bill Stanton in *Klanwatch,* that "extremist groups are merely manifestations of a powerful current of racism that suffuses American life."[33] Kenneth Jackson concludes his study *The Ku Klux Klan in the City* with the ominous declaration, "Although the Klan is no longer effective, the Klan mentality remains."[34] Elaine Jones of the

NAACP Legal Defense Fund warns that the Klan's views "are shared quietly by many others."[35] Joe Feagin and Hernan Vera charge that "white supremacists are the officiants in extreme racist rites, but many other whites silently sympathize with aspects of their mythology."[36] The Klan also serves as a catalyst for anti-racist unity among African Americans; as Robert Branch writes, "One key to solidarity is to recall and relive our collective history."[37] Another activist recalls, "My dad used to often tell us about when he was a boy, how the crosses would be burned up on the hills. . . . I'm seeing the same thing."[38]

Thus if the Klan were to disappear, this might suggest that white bigotry in America had vastly abated, and blacks and other minorities could move on to other issues. This prospect is unbelievable and alarming to many white liberals and civil rights activists. Black activist groups have a financial interest in using racism to justify preferences and set-asides, and many white liberals have an ideological stake, derived from relativism, in blaming racism for group inequality. White racism scares these persons, but the prospect of the elimination of the specter of white racism seems to scare them even more.

REBIRTH OF A NATION

White racism is not dead, but (as many blacks suspect) it now wears a different face. The Atlanta conference and the literature of racist groups today convey the new spirit of white bigotry. No longer does it seek to establish a global or American hierarchy of races premised on civilizational superiority. Far from being opposed to relativism, the new white racism is based on it: it invokes relativism to demand equal respect for its distinct and inviolable culture. Indeed, the two main themes of white racists today are cultural separatism and white survivalism. It is a new ideology of white power, seemingly formulated on the model of black power. Nor do the new racists seek to destroy every last vestige of Afrocentrism and black separatism. Rather, they are supporters of many aspects of those ideologies, and often work closely with African American extremists to achieve joint objectives. Whether or not Jared Taylor would acknowledge any agreement with black activists, Taylor is in the same camp as many of them in his rejection of the principles of the American founding and specifically the Declaration of Independence. He argues, as they do, that formal equality is a sham and the primary relevant consideration is racial unity and preservation. Taylor's *American Renaissance* also echoes many of the main propositions of the Afrocentrists: Western civilization is inherently white, America was founded on white norms, immigrants are perennial outsiders, blacks are "Africans in America," they are in America but not of America, race determines culture, miscegenation and intermarriage are an abomination, and racial separatism, preferably separate black and white nations, is the answer.

The liberal ideology of relativism, we saw earlier, was developed by the Boasians to destroy the old racist concept of a natural hierarchy of cultures. It sought to do this by questioning the standards by which one culture judges another: no culture, relativists insist, has the right to term another inadequate or inferior. All cultures adapt to their own unique conditions. But if this is true, then it applies to white racist culture as well. It too is adaptive; it too can rationalize its extremism by citing sociological deprivations, it too has a right to promote ethnic self-esteem, it too can claim the right to preserve itself by any means necessary. Today even Ku Klux Klansmen defend their fanatical ethnocentrism and hatred of other groups in terms of upholding their culture which is no less entitled to respect than any other. Reflecting the new relativist thinking, Thom Robb, national director of the Klan, said in 1991, "We don't hate anybody. We just love the white race."[39]

Consider William Gayley Simpson's racist tract *Which Way, Western Man?* Simpson attacks liberal individualism on the grounds that it has promoted rootlessness and undermined ethnic community among whites. He attacks reason, morality, and universalism on the grounds that they deny appeals to affinities of blood and sentiment.[40] Similarly Wilmot Robertson in *The Dispossessed Majority,* published in 1981, argues in favor of separatism for the purpose of preserving both black and white ethnic cultures. Condemning the "numbing ideology" of individualism and assimilation, Robertson praises Afrocentrists and black separatists for advocating all-black schools for boys.[41] In his 1992 book *The Ethnostate,* Robertson argues that since each culture has its own inner essence, it is foolish to expect different cultures to understand each other, and therefore America should be broken up into separate "ethnostates" in which blacks and whites can separately assert their own cultural traditions.[42]

David Duke seems to have traveled in the same direction. According to the Louisiana Coalition Against Racism and Nazism, by the 1980s Duke's kinder, gentler Nazism, marketed under the banner of his National Association for the Advancement of White People (NAAWP), emphasized the "division of North America into separate racial nations." In Duke's own words from a 1989 interview, "There's only one country anymore that's all-white and that's Iceland. And Iceland is not enough." Duke is not concerned about black nationalism; he endorses it. Indeed in the 1970s he authored a pamphlet called "African Atto," written under the pseudonym Mohammed X, in which he instructs blacks on street-fighting techniques to defeat "whitey."[43]

The common themes of ethnic survivalism and separatism are now increasingly evident in white groups, as they have been for some time in black groups. At a recent demonstration in Myrtle Beach, South Carolina, to promote use of the Confederate flag, whites carried banners and wore T-shirts with the messages, "You Wear Your X and I'll Wear Mine," "It's A White Thing," and "The Original Boyz in the Hood."[44] Just as some blacks in the late 1960s rejected Martin Luther King's approach, arguing that they needed Black Power to combat White Power, so too white groups in the 1990s insist that Black Power cannot be resisted with appeals to universalism but only with a reinvigoration of the ideology of White Power. Yet it would be a grave mistake to consider white supremacists and black nationalists to be mere adversaries. Indeed, on several occasions going back to the 1920s, white supremacists have met with black nationalists in order to realize shared visions of separate black and white nations.

In 1922, Marcus Garvey, the prominent black nationalist and leader of the "back to Africa" movement, arranged a secret meeting with the Grand Cyclops of the Invisible Empire of the Ku Klux Klan. Garvey was apparently seeking Klan financing for his Black Star shipping line, which would transport blacks to Africa. Garvey met with Klan leaders in Atlanta and even invited them to speak at his black nationalist convention. When news of this bizarre alliance surfaced, Garvey was embarrassed and forced to break off ties. Yet he protested that the Klan only sought "to preserve their race from suicide through miscegenation and to keep it pure, which to me is not a crime but a commendable desire." And the Klan sent out pamphlets defending Garvey, and blaming opposition to him on a Catholic plot! Later Garvey lived in Britain where he expressed his profound admiration for white racialists like Mussolini. In a tactic familiar by now, Garvey even claimed authorship of Mussolini's philosophy. "We were the first fascists." Without denying the Klan connection, Afrocentric historians such as John Henrik Clarke now insist that Garvey's motives for the alliance have been "seriously misinterpreted."[45]

On January 28, 1961, Malcolm X held a secret meeting with the Ku Klux Klan. He sought the Klan's assistance in getting land for the Nation of Islam to carry out its separatist program. Malcolm X assured Klan leaders, who were understandably suspicious of him, that the Muslims firmly believed in segregation and that "the Jew is behind the integration movement, using the Negro as a tool." Malcolm X also told an increasingly enthusiastic Klan group that Elijah Muhammad had invited American Nazi leader George Lincoln Rockwell, who also hated Jews and advocated racial separation, to speak to the Nation of Islam's 1962 annual convention.[46] Today black nationalists downplay these documented connections. Spike Lee, for example, carefully omitted any reference to Malcolm X's dealings with the Ku Klux Klan in his hagiographic film.

Recently the working relationship between white and black extremists seems to have intensified. Michael Bradley is a white anti-Semite who is author of the book *Chosen People from the Caucasus,* subtitled, "Jewish Origins, Delusions, Deceptions, and Historical Role in the Slave Trade, Genocide and Cultural Colonization." Among Bradley's points:

- Egyptians probably had good reason to persecute Jews because they were "continually worshipping their God instead of working."
- Jews were "major participants in the genocide of American Indians."
- Jews are not really Semitic peoples at all, but impostors descended from vicious tribes "noted for their stench" and "usually regarded as being some kind of beast-men."
- Jewish victimization is part of a "great Hebrew hoax" that partly explains why Jews "have somehow come to influence Western civilization to a degree out of all proportion to their small numbers."
- "Jews today virtually control what Americans see on TV and at the movies."
- A "Jewish mafia" exists to destroy all who seek to expose it like Leonard Jeffries, who is guilty of nothing more than "complaining about the obvious."
- "The current nuclear age was initiated with the help of a Jewish scientist, Albert Einstein, but only when Jews in Germany were threatened. Then, nuclear weapons were tested on a non-Caucasian population outside Europe—where no Caucasians or Jews could be threatened."[47]

Interestingly, Michael Bradley's book is not published by a white racist or anti-Semitic group, but by Third World Press, which is run by black nationalist Haki Madhubuti. Third World Press almost never publishes white authors. Yet Madhubuti also included an essay by Bradley in an anthology he edited on the Los Angeles riots, *Why L.A. Happened.*[48] And the introduction to Bradley's *Chosen People from the Caucasus* is by Afrocentric historian John Henrik Clarke. Moreover, Bradley is cited respectfully in publications such as the *Journal of Black Studies.*[49]

Black nationalists and activists have attended meetings devoted to Holocaust denial sponsored by a group called the Institute for Historical Review. Leonard Jeffries, for example, has been invited by white racists and anti-Semites to join them at conferences convened to expose the Holocaust as a Jewish fabrication. In May 1993, former Milwaukee alderman Michael McGee, an African American, was joined by the head of the White Aryan Resistance, Tom Metzger, at a Dallas rally to call for the overthrow of the U.S. government.[50] The Anti-Defamation League reports that white supremacists such as Robert Miles are seeking to unite hate groups in part by endorsing the racial separatism of black groups such as the Nation of Islam which they "apparently consider their like-minded counterpart."[51]

THE UNBEARABLE WHITENESS OF BEING

White liberals have a difficult time acknowledging the common themes of white racism and black racism—indeed, many express doubts that persons of color are even capable of being racist. Yet in this increasingly diverse society, we are confronted on a regular basis with examples of internecine hostility between minority groups.[52] Sometimes expressions of one minority group's hostility toward another are far more vocal and visible than expressions of white racism. Consider some examples that compel us to take seriously a phenomenon that looks and sounds like black racism.

• When anti-apartheid activist Mark Mathabane, author of *Kaffir Boy,* migrated from South Africa to the United States he was surprised to hear American blacks saying things about whites that he had heard whites say about blacks in his homeland. African American students informed Mathabane that they hated whites because hatred gave them "satisfaction," and they regarded the white man as intrinsically evil: "a murdering, exploiting, cheating, and racist son of a bitch by nature." When Mathabane fell in love and married a white woman, he found himself getting death threats including one photograph of a lynched man with the caption, "This is what happens to traitors of the black race." Mathabane writes, "Militant blacks wanted me to prove my solidarity with their cause by disassociating myself from whites. . . . It pained me to think that there were blacks in America who used the same tactics as the Ku Klux Klan."[53]

• In 1992, a member of a White Student Union at the University of Florida read what he claimed to be a manifesto of his organization, as submitted to the Student Government Association. The apparent bigotry of the publication provoked anger and outrage among many student senators, who began to hiss and make pig noises and shout "racism." After he finished reading, the student revealed that he had simply taken the official publication of the Black Student Union, and changed the term "black" to "white" each time it appeared.[54]

• In his famous Kean College address in November 1993, activist Khalid Abdul Muhammad of the Nation of Islam told a cheering audience what he found objectionable about whites and Jews:

> If the white man won't get out of town by sundown, we kill everything white in South Africa. We kill the women, we kill the children, we kill the babies. We kill the faggot, we kill the lesbian, we kill them all. Kill the old ones too . . . push them off a cliff in Cape Town. Kill the blind, kill the crippled, and when you get through killing them all, go to the graveyard, dig up the grave, and kill them again. . . . The so-called Jew is a European strain of people who crawled around on all fours in the caves and hills of Europe, eating juniper roots and eating each other. You [Jews] slept with your dead for 2,000 years, smelling the stench coming up from the decomposing body. You slept in your urination and your defecation. . . . The so-called Jews are the bloodsuckers of the black nation. . . . That's why you call yourself Rubenstein, Goldstein and Silverstein, because you've been stealing rubies and gold and silver all over the earth. . . . Everybody talks about Hitler exterminating six million Jews. That's right. But don't nobody ask what did they do to Hitler! They supplanted, they usurped, they . . . undermined the very fabric of society.[55]

• Rap activist Sister Souljah, who is described by Jesse Jackson as a voice "representing the feelings and hopes of a whole generation" of young blacks, has suggested in her music that whites are intrinsically evil and that African Americans are justified in harming or killing them. "If black people kill black people every day, why not have a week and kill white people?" Souljah asked in 1992, provoking criticism from Bill Clinton. Oddly, it was Clinton rather than Souljah whose words came in for denunciation by Jesse Jackson.[56] As the lyrics of her album *360 Degrees of Power* suggest, Souljah aggressively promotes what she terms the "total destruction" of the white race in the name of black survival and retaliation for the crimes of slavery and segregation:

They say two wrongs don't make it right,
But it damn sure makes it even.[57]

• In 1993, radio station KPFK in Los Angeles aired its annual "Afrikan Mental Liberation Weekend" which turned into a festival of denunciation and antagonism directed against whites and Jews. Among the statements broadcast by black nationalists and commentators on this publicly funded network:

> White people are genetic mutations of blacks. Only black women can claim all the genetic material necessary to create the other races. Don't call me racist. I can't be racist. I ain't got no power.

> I would not say that the white man is a descendant of Satan, because that would be wrong. We didn't have a Satan before the white man. So the white man is Satan himself.

> Black people can produce white people. White people can only produce white people. They are the mutants from black people. Black has the greatest genetic potential to annihilate white.[58]

• Although they are classified as minorities, Hispanics and Asians are not immune from such black hostility. Recently a Hispanic worker at the Martin Luther King Hospital in Los Angeles received the following letter from a black antagonist.

> We Heard Yours The Ones Whos Been Starting All These Wet Backs To Uprise Against All of Us Who Have Been Here At King For A Long Time. If You Continue To Try And Take Our Jobs Away, Were Just Going To Have To Stop You. If We Have To, We Will Make An Example By Blowing Your Head Off.[59]

• Black hostility to Asians is reflected in remarks by Anderson Thompson, an African Studies professor at Northeastern Illinois University, who condemns "the miserable Asiatic . . . selling wigs, hats, handbags, basketball shoes. He has levied a full-scale economic penetration of the entire African world. Like a parasite, he attacks the African consumer, boring from within." Among Thompson's recommendations are the formation of a black "ministry of defense" to stop and get rid of such parasites.[60] In a similar manner, rap singer Ice Cube justifies arson against Korean stores on the grounds that Koreans are "Oriental one-penny-counting motherfuckers" who "know how they have treated black people over the years and know that they are guilty."[61]

• Perhaps not surprising, some black activists add injury to insult and convert anti-white animosity into violence. In October 1989 a group of young black men in Wisconsin saw the movie *Mississippi Burning,* after which one of them, Todd Mitchell, chased down a fourteen-year-old white youth named Gregory Riddick. "Do you all feel hyped up to move on some white people?" Mitchell asked his friends. "There goes a white boy. Go get him." The gang beat up Riddick so badly that he suffered permanent brain damage.[62]

• During the Los Angeles riots, black hoodlums frequently targeted whites and Koreans for assault. Alicia Maldonado, whose car was attacked, testified in court that blacks pointed at her and said, "Get her. She's not a sister." She also stated that "the persons who were allowed to pass were all black." On the ABC television show *Nightline,* one gang member told Ted Koppel that "everybody that came through here that was not black was in trouble." According to the *Los Angeles Times,* "White people across post-riot Los Angeles are suddenly afraid of being judged by the color of their skin." And Korean entrepreneurs said that during the riots hundreds of their stores were specifically singled out for looting and violence.[63]

• In his book *Makes Me Wanna Holler,* *Washington Post* writer Nathan McCall recalls an incident some years ago where he and a group of African American youths ambushed a white boy on a bicycle. "He was definitely in the wrong place to be doing the tourist bit," McCall observes. "We all took off after him. We caught him and knocked him off the bike. He fell to the ground and it was all over. We were on him. We stomped and kicked him. My partners kicked him in the head and face and watched the blood gush from his mouth. I kicked him in the stomach and nuts." With each blow, McCall remembers, "I felt better." McCall believed he was getting revenge: "This is for all the times you followed me round in stores. And this is for the times you treated me like a nigger. And this is for general principle—just 'cause you white."[64]

• In December 1993 black immigrant Colin Ferguson opened fire in a Long Island Railroad car, killing five people and injuring more than twenty. Three of Ferguson's victims were Asian or Pacific Islander: Mi Kyung Kim, Maria Magtoto, and Minoru Sihto. Two of them were killed. Police found papers in his pocket venting his rage at whites and Asians. Ferguson wrote, "Reasons for this: Adelphi University's racism, the EEOC's racism, workers compensation's racism, the racism of Governor Cuomo's staff, the racism of the lieutenant governor's staff." He also denounced "racism by Caucasians," including one "filthy Caucasian racist female," and "that Chinese racist Mr Sue."

Lillian Kimura, national president of the Japanese American Citizen's League, said that Ferguson's rampage "clearly was a hate crime. He hated all these groups." Yet during his trial Ferguson presented himself as a victim of racist stereotyping on the part of witnesses who identified him as the man who shot them.[65]

• In 1991, after a Hasidic Jewish driver lost control of his car and accidentally killed a black child, African American demonstrators surged through the Crown Heights neighborhood in New York shouting "Heil Hitler" and "Zionazi," accosting orthodox Jews, and smashing cars and other property. In Brooklyn, one black gang located Yankel Rosenbaum, an orthodox Jew from Australia who was visiting the United States, and jumped him, shouting "Get the Jew." Rosenbaum was stabbed to death. The case against gang member Lemrick Nelson seemed airtight: he was seized by police near the stabbing with a bloody knife, DNA evidence established that the knife contained Rosenbaum's blood, Nelson was identified by a dying Rosenbaum as his attacker, and Nelson initially even confessed to the act. Yet a jury primarily composed of African Americans acquitted Nelson, and then proceeded to a celebration dinner hosted by the defendant's attorney. "For Hasidic Jews," Eric Breindel wrote, "New York City today is a lot like the Jim Crow South was for blacks themselves 30 years ago. Justice is all but unattainable."[66]

• In 1994 the Southern Poverty Law Center released a list of racially motivated murders for the previous year. The group reported that nearly 50 percent of all such killings were committed by blacks on victims who were white, Hispanic, or Asian. Among them: a white youth was fatally beaten to death by two black juveniles in Hendersonville, North Carolina; a Hispanic teenager was shot to death by an African American in a racially motivated assault in Pomona, California; a white youth was killed because of his race by a black man in Anniston, Alabama. The previous year, in 1992, black on white crime again exceeded racially motivated crimes perpetrated by whites against blacks. Forty-one racially inspired murders were monitored by the Southern Poverty Law Center that year: seventeen were black on white and thirteen were white on black. "Racism can be found in all groups," commented Reuben Greenberg, Charleston's chief of police, who is Jewish and black. "We've got our racists just like whites have their racists." Morris Dees, who helped to bankrupt the Ku Klux Klan in court, says the new trend of racially motivated violence by blacks is a "shocking reversal" of the past, in which hate crimes were overwhelmingly white on black. "I think there's a rising sense of frustration among blacks that the promises of the civil rights movement are not coming to pass," Dees said. He called for uniform enforcement of hate-crimes legislation against all offenders, concluding, "Today intolerance and racism have no racial or geographic boundaries."[67]

BIGOTRY AND DOUBLE STANDARDS

Some civil rights activists, such as Barbara Jordan, Vernon Jordan and Jack Greenberg, have condemned black racism.[68] Yet many African American and white liberals argue that the similarities between the rhetoric and agenda of black separatists and white separatists is purely coincidental; in their view, black racism is an oxymoron, a contradiction in terms. It poses no threat to society because it does not exist.

• Anna Quindlen, a white liberal columnist, wrote in the *New York Times,* "Hatred by the powerful, the majority, has a different weight and often very different effects than hatred by the powerless, the minority. . . . Being called a honky is not in the same league as being called a nigger."[69]

• "A distinction must surely be made between the ideological hostility of the oppressors and the experience-based hostility of those who have been oppressed," Stanley Fish argues. "Symmetry would require us to pretend that epithets hurled at whites have as much capacity to inflict psychological and material harm as epithets hurled at blacks, and that is simply not so."[70]

• "Black people can't be racist," Spike Lee asserts. "Black people don't have the power to keep whites from getting jobs or the vote. To me, racism is the institution. You got to have power to do that."[71]

• Author Joel Kovel agrees. "There can be no black racism as long as the dominant institutions of Western society are shaped according to white interests."[72]

• "Racism connotes power," black scholar Coramae Richey Mann explains, "and in only a few instances can a minority person have a quantum of power; since they lack institutional power, it is definitionally impossible for American minorities to be identified as racist."[73]

• In her textbook *Racism and Sexism,* liberal activist Paula Rothenberg asserts that "while an individual person of color may discriminate against white people or even hate them, his or her behavior cannot be called racist. Racism requires prejudice plus power."[74]

• According to black activist Al Sharpton, the impossibility of black racism means that whites should understand retaliatory violence against innocent victims like Yankel Rosenbaum. "We must not reprimand our children for outrage when it is the outrage that was put in them by an oppressive system."[75]

• "You can't call me or any black person anywhere in the world a racist," declares Sister Souljah. "We don't have the power to do to white people what white people have done to us. And even if we did, we don't have that low-down dirty nature."[76]

• Harry Allen, minister of information for the rap group Public Enemy, justifies his remarks denouncing whites and Jews by claiming immunity from racism. "It's impossible," he protests. "Only white people can be racist, and I am not white."[77]

Despite clear parallels between black rhetoric and action, and the rhetoric and action of white racists, the notion that blacks cannot be racist relies heavily on the remembrance of history. In the past, it was whites who inferiorized blacks. Stokely Carmichael and Charles Hamilton write in *Black Power,* "The black people of this country have not lynched whites, bombed their churches, murdered their children, and manipulated laws and institutions to maintain oppression. White racists have."[78] Kenneth Clark maintains in *Black Ghetto* that black hostility and discrimination against whites is somewhat understandable because "to a Negro, every white person is, in a sense, a symbol of his own oppression."[79] Similarly Whitney Young of the National Urban League argues in his book *Beyond Racism* that although "antiwhite feelings exist," they cannot be equated with white racism because that would be "to equate the bitterness of the victim with the evil that oppresses him."[80] Malcolm X himself dismissed questions about black racism by saying that "the white man is in no moral position to accuse anyone else of hate."[81] Eldridge Cleaver expressed the extreme version of this view. In his autobiography *Soul on Ice,* Cleaver confessed to numerous rapes of white women but justified them on the grounds that a history of white racism had planted in him an irresistible attraction-repulsion complex toward fair-skinned women. Cleaver triumphantly concluded that rape was, for him, a form of social protest, indeed "an insurrectionary act."[82]

Why do many white liberals acquiesce in such sentiments? Because their ideology of relativism compels them to see black racism as nothing more than a reaction to white racism. Black racism is "the hate that hate produced," as a famous Mike Wallace documentary on the Nation of

Islam put it.[83] In this view blacks are historical victims and whites are historical victimizers. Obviously victimizers do not deserve to be treated with respect: therefore so-called black racism is an understandable and partly legitimate response to the injuries of white racism. Thus, the argument goes, "white racism" is really a redundancy and black racism, if it exists, is nothing more than an epiphenomenon of white racism. These assumptions in varying degrees are embedded in our public thought and discussion about race. They are reflected in countless news articles, essays and books about the relations between blacks and whites, and they are the foundation for many laws and policies, such as hate speech codes and antidiscrimination statutes which may be neutrally worded but in practice often focus on white offenders.

Consider some ways in which the existence of black racism is systematically downplayed or denied in public discourse. Imagine the case of a high school club or college fraternity that announced: we are a white pride organization, we limit our membership to whites, we promote white culture. Such an act would undoubtedly provoke outrage among the authorities who would do what they could to dismantle such a group—threaten and perhaps punish the students involved, probably withdraw school funding. Yet there are literally thousands of black and minority race-based organizations at schools and universities throughout the country, and they receive not simply administrative approval but financial subsidy. For example, many colleges have black fraternities and Hispanic sororities, whereas it would be virtually unthinkable to have *de jure* white fraternities. Apparently when whites cluster together it's segregation; when blacks do, it's a support group.

Derrick Bell and others have impugned "racial bonding by whites" in matters such as voting.[84] Yet whites have proved quite willing to vote for African American candidates who were running against white opponents. Indeed when Jesse Jackson ran for president in 1988 he got his highest percentage of votes in states with a relatively small black population.[85] Many cities such as Seattle, Denver, Kansas City, Charlotte, and New Haven where whites are the majority have nevertheless elected black mayors.[86] Yet it is extremely rare for a city in which blacks are the majority to elect a white candidate who is running against an African American. Although white candidates such as New York mayor Rudolph Giuliani, who receive heavy white support, are criticized for pandering to white bigotry, black candidates such as former New York mayor David Dinkins and former Virginia governor Douglas Wilder are expected to attract overwhelming and nearly unanimous African American approval. One group is permitted its racial bonding, the other is not. When Giuliani, with about two-thirds of the white vote, prevailed over Dinkins, who got almost 90 percent of the black vote, Jesse Jackson bitterly observed that "there is no question that race prevailed over reason." This quotation appears in a *Washington Post* article titled "Conflicting Trends Seen in Whites' Willingness to Vote for Blacks."[87] The reciprocal racial clannishness of blacks at the ballot box apparently raises no eyebrows. In other words when whites vote for whites they are practicing racism; when blacks vote for blacks, that's representative democracy.

The same double standard is evident in the literature on interracial violence. After the unjustified beating of Rodney King and the Los Angeles riots, Anthony Lewis of the *New York Times* predictably observed, "The acquittal of the policemen who clubbed Rodney King and the violent reaction in black communities showed us an American society that has lost its way."[88] This capacity to generalize from particular episodes did not, however, carry over to the far more savage beating of white truckdriver Reginald Denny. The Denny beating, the rape of the Central Park jogger, and other black-on-white assaults are seldom taken as symbolic of an African American community that has lost its way.

While it is true that most violent crime is intraracial, involving blacks preying on other blacks and whites preying on other whites, it is also true that black criminals are much more likely to choose white victims than white criminals are to choose black victims. The probability of a white offender choosing to rob, mug, or attack a black victim is about 3 percent. The probability of a black offender selecting a white victim is more than 50 percent, far in excess of random selection even taking into account the larger white pool of potential victims.[89] "It is not surprising that black offenders choose white victims in robberies, since whites are more likely to have money," criminologist William Wilbanks writes. But as Wilbanks points out, economic avarice would not explain why in 1991 there were 100 cases of white rapists assaulting black victims compared with more than 20,000 cases of black rapists attacking white victims—a result that is especially remarkable considering that rapes are usually perpetrated not just for sex but in order to control, dominate, and humiliate women.[90]

These crime statistics are virtually unknown, for the simple reason that most news reports ignore the possibility that black-on-white crime may have a racial motivation. If there is an argument, and a white person beats up an African American, that is typically christened a racial incident. In the same argument, if the African American beats up the white person, that is nothing more than a dispute that got out of hand. Most of the time, even as far as the police are concerned, racial motives are not probed at all. Similarly, when a white police officer kills a black youth, the officer is immediately vulnerable to charges of racism, whereas black policemen who kill white suspects are simply presumed to be doing their job. When mobs of whites attack blacks, that is advertised as further evidence of white bigotry, and a metaphor for societal racism; when mobs of blacks attack whites, that is downplayed as a natural reaction to decades of white racist exploitation. In this way, both white violence and black violence are traced to the same source: white racism. Given this dual standard, it should hardly be surprising that race riots with white perpetrators have virtually disappeared and are universally condemned, whereas race riots with black perpetrators are increasingly common and frequently rationalized.

Let us consider the validity of this one-sided approach to understanding race relations. It is certainly true that calling a white a "honky" or a "cracker" is less emotionally damaging than calling a black a "nigger." It is also true, however, that whites can be insulted with relative impunity in contemporary society, whereas there are serious ramifications for the person who dares to call blacks "niggers," especially in public. How many blacks would be in serious danger of losing their jobs if they called a white colleague a "honky"? Would public figures who used such a term be forced to resign? "Nigger" today is virtually a boomerang epithet, guaranteed to come back and destroy the accuser.

It is hardly unique in modern history for the persecuted to transform themselves into persecutors, nor in most cases does anyone argue that the original persecution justifies their subsequent behavior. The early colonists in America, for example, came to escape religious persecution, but shortly upon gaining power, many of them promptly proceeded to harass other denominations, not limiting themselves to a short list of their former persecutors. Some immigrant groups such as the Irish and the Italians arrived in America and experienced sharp antagonism and discrimination; in short order, however, many Irishmen and Italians came to develop their own ethnic hostilities and to practice discrimination against blacks and other minorities. Black racism seems to be part of a familiar pattern of the victim adopting the strategies of the former persecutor. As Frantz Fanon suggests, "The native is an oppressed person whose permanent dream is to become the persecutor."[91] Yet these "hideous paroxysms of hate," as Albert Memmi calls them,[92] do not focus exclusively on extracting justice long denied. Black antagonism is not narrowly directed against the sons and daughters of former planters, or even against WASPs; rather, it seems broadly aimed in shotgun fashion at groups such as Jews, Hispanics, and Koreans who seem to have played no significant role in enslaving or segregating African Americans. What these hostilities seem to suggest is that black racism cannot be understood simply as a reaction to white racism; rather, it may have an independent ideological foundation.

PREJUDICE AND POWER

The most common argument that denies the possibility of black racism is that racism requires not only prejudice but also power; blacks may possess the former but they do not possess the latter. Very well: if this is so, then it follows that the Ku Klux Klan and the Skinheads are not racist organizations. The Klan and the Skinheads do not sit in the legislature, there are no Klan or Skinhead mayors, they are absent among directors of major corporations, they cannot be found among foundation heads, university faculty, school principals, and the like. Indeed white racist groups like the Klan and Skinheads enjoy less actual power in America today than black organizations such as the Nation of Islam, the NAACP, and the Congressional Black Caucus.

One African American magazine lists the membership of the Nation of Islam at around two hundred thousand, a figure that seems somewhat exaggerated.[93] Yet all the white racist groups in the country, taken together, do not come close to that number. David Duke would be unlikely today to attract the kind of enthusiastic audiences of between ten and twenty-five thousand that Louis Farrakhan routinely does. In 1992 in Atlanta, Farrakhan outdrew the audience for the World Series game that night. In Los Angeles he filled a sports arena that holds more than fifteen thousand. In New York in 1993, Farrakhan brought more than twenty-five thousand to the Jacob Javits Convention Center.[94] Remarks Randall Kennedy, "Farrakhan may be the biggest draw in the black community in America today."

Some liberal activists concede these points, but argue that since whites have a monopoly on control of major institutions, black antagonism is unlikely to inflict serious harm on the life chances of most whites. In *Words That Wound,* Mari Matsuda argues that hate speech codes should not protect members of the majority because a white person subject to minority denunciations has "access to a safe harbor of exclusive dominant-group interactions."[95] This is a subtler and more persuasive claim, which relies on a crucial distinction between the power of minorities and majorities in a democratic society. Minorities, in this view, are simply not in a collective position to threaten the majority, whereas majorities can bend the destiny of minorities to their will. By analogy, consider the social consequences if most left-handed people developed a pathological hatred for right-handed people. This would be a problem, but not a very serious one, because most people are right-handed and they could easily avoid interactions with left-handed maniacs. If right-handed people as a group sought to deprive left-handed people of basic rights, however, this would be a serious problem.

As this analogy suggests, white racism is potentially a more serious problem than black racism. Yet just as whites are dominant in many rural and suburban parts of the country, blacks control the reins of power in many urban areas. Consequently we must take seriously the possibility of black racism in cities where blacks are quite capable of converting their prejudices into practice. As for the greater threat posed by white racism, it remains theoretical unless one can offer independent evidence that whites express their racial antagonism collectively as a group. Yet there is little evidence of an explicit or implicit alliance between, say, tattooed gangsters in the Ozarks and the chairman of General Motors. Historically white planters have been successful in appealing to racial solidarity with the white poor, but this unanimity across class lines seems to have broken down in the age of affirmative action. Suggestions of a *de facto* alliance of whites ignore the political and economic alliance between affluent whites and middle-class blacks to preserve such nepotistic arrangements as alumni preferences and racial preferences while whites who qualify on their merits are turned away. As we have seen, whites at the top rungs of society have repeatedly shown themselves willing to limit opportunities for whites at the entry level, in order to allocate positions for less qualified blacks.

Indeed in America today, blacks are more likely than whites to show solidarity with the precepts of extremist groups. According to a recent poll by CNN and *Time* magazine, 70 percent of American blacks believe that Farrakhan "says things the country should hear," more than 60 percent believe he "speaks the truth," and only 30 percent consider him "a bigot and a racist."[96] A University of Chicago survey of blacks by Michael Dawson and Ronald Brown found about 50 percent of blacks embracing Farrakhan-style militancy, including Nation of Islam demands for separate black institutions.[97] Many mainstream black figures are evidently reluctant to condemn Farrakhan: as Spike Lee puts it, "I don't agree with everything he says, but I would never say anything in public."[98] Also, there is a dangerous liaison between the Nation of Islam and traditional civil rights groups, including the Congressional Black Caucus. Signing what he called a "sacred covenant" to work together, Kweisi Mfume of the Black Caucus insisted, "No longer will we allow people to divide us."[99]

The national Republican party and conservative organizations have completely repudiated David Duke, while Louis Farrakhan remains a part of the coalition of black organizations, several of whose leaders (despite some ambivalence) invoke the need for racial solidarity. Farrakhan and Leonard Jeffries inhabit political communities that practice "constructive engagement" with their brand of extremism, and refuse to divest themselves completely of it. The point is that white racism has been largely marginalized in American society, whereas black racism enjoys a far greater scholarly and institutional respectability. Thus although if whites acted in concert as a group, white racism would be more of a social threat than black racism, in fact blacks are more likely to demonstrate group solidarity, and therefore—particularly in urban areas where blacks control power—black racism may be more dangerous than white racism.

JEWS AND KOREANS

Two groups who seem to be especially vulnerable to the venom and violence of black racists are Jews and Koreans.

"Jewish people have an influence in our lives far out of proportion to their numbers in the population," alleges the Afrocentric historian John Henrik Clarke. Clarke maintains that "if we are honest about historical information, we would know that what is referred to as the Holocaust was a small event in comparison to other mass-murder events in history." Instead of mourning the Holocaust, Clarke suggests that Jews take responsibility for the slave trade. "Jews who didn't have a whole lot of money would go to the auction block and buy up the sick, the lame and the broken-legged slaves and take them away and fatten them up, straighten out their health, bring them back and sell them for top dollar." Even the term multicultural education, Clarke alleges, "is strictly a Jewish term. The Jewish educational mafia coined it. You've got a Holocaust Curriculum. The Jews have mastered the art of victimization."[100]

Speaking at Howard University, Khalid Muhammad of the Nation of Islam said that slavery was "one hundred times worse" than the Jewish Holocaust. He denied that six million Jews were killed by the Nazis.

Muhammad accused Jews of playing a leading role in the African slave trade, which he said was the real holocaust. As Jewish protesters carried signs outside, groups of African Americans yelled at them, "The only good Zionist is a dead Zionist." Such views have been brewing in the larger Howard community for some time. A few months earlier, more than a thousand people, some students and many local residents, were led in a popular chant by Howard University law student named Malik Shabazz.

"Who caught and killed Nat Turner?"

"Jews," a majority in the audience yelled.

"Who controls the Federal Reserve?"

"Jews."

"Who controls the media and Hollywood?"

"Jews."[101]

"Jewish people control all the money in the United States," Almuydillah Shabazz, an eighteen-year-old Kean College freshman, told the *New York Times* after Khalid Muhammad spoke there. She added, "That's true—that's not being prejudiced." According to historian Jay Spaulding, who was present for the anti-Jewish rally, "the leading Kean College faculty and student exponents of Afrocentricity sat in the front row cheering." Henry Kaplowitz, president of the Jewish faculty association, said, "These faculty members were brought in for diversity, and once here they have eschewed diversity. In their eyes everything is predicated on race and racism, but they deny they are racists because they say an oppressed minority cannot be racist."[102]

Two of the main sources for popular black anti-Semitism are the Nation of Islam and the black intellectual community. The Nation of Islam has published *The Secret Relationship Between Blacks and Jews,* a widely distributed study which purports to expose Jews as historical enemies of black people. The book argues that even as they complain about their own Holocaust, Jews were complicit and active in "the greatest criminal endeavor ever undertaken against an entire race, a crime against humanity, the Black African Holocaust." The study purports to offer "irrefutable evidence" that Jews "more than any other ethnic or religious group" participated in and controlled major aspects of the slave trade. Jews are rich today, the Nation of Islam claims, because of the accumulated profits of black slavery. It goes on to claim that Jews in America "owned slaves in higher proportions than other Southern families" and that Jews played a prominent role crushing slave uprisings, serving in the Confederate army or fighting emancipation.[103]

Two black professors who are public admirers of *The Secret Relationship Between Blacks and Jews* are Leonard Jeffries of City College of New York and Tony Martin of Wellesley. Jeffries is well known for his tirades against Jewish influence in Hollywood; Martin has recently published a book called *The Jewish Onslaught* which details "the Jewish attack on black progress" and alleged Jewish attempts to undermine his career. Martin offers a possible motive for Jewish hostility to blacks: "It may be that the Jewish establishment has concluded that a prostrate African American population, to be oppressed or paternalized as the times warrant, will continue to be its insurance against a Euro-American reversion to anti-Jewish activity."[104]

Contrary to Andrew Hacker's contention that "no one really knows if blacks and whites differ markedly in their feelings about Jews,"[105] survey data show that African Americans are much more likely to espouse anti-Semitic views than whites. One survey showed that 20 percent of whites and 38 percent of blacks hold anti-Semitic beliefs. Another study claimed that 35 percent of whites and 47 percent of blacks qualify as anti-Semitic. A 1992 survey by the Anti-Defamation League showed that 17 percent of whites, compared with 37 percent of blacks, fall into the category of people espousing strong anti-Semitic beliefs. While white anti-Semitism seems to be gradually declining, a consistent finding of surveys in recent years is that black anti-Semitism is increasing. Younger whites are less likely to be anti-Semitic than older whites; this is not the case for blacks. Additionally, while white anti-Semitism tends to decrease with income and education, blacks with some college education or college degrees are much likelier to be anti-Semitic than whites of comparable educational background. One survey found that middle-class and educated blacks tend to be more anti-Semitic than poor blacks.[106]

Although black anti-Semitism persists, black racists seem to have found in Asian Americans and specifically Koreans, who are sometimes called the "new Jews," another ethnic group to demonize. In 1991 the rap musician Ice Cube, in his best-selling album *Death Certificate,* warned Koreans not to "follow me up and down the market, or your little chop-suey ass will be a target." Ice Cube concluded with a chilling warning:

So pay your respects to the black fist
Or we'll burn your store right down to a crisp.[107]

In 1988, black activists led a boycott of Korean stores in the Bedford-Stuyvesant section of Brooklyn. Protesters chanted, "Pass them by, let them die. Koreans out of Bed-Stuy." One activist accused the Koreans of racism. "It's racist that we don't own any businesses. This is a conspiracy against the black community." Such pressure tactics and intimidation have been endured by Koreans for years, and they go downplayed or unreported in the media. Having ignored black terrorist tactics against Koreans, it was only when Korean entrepreneurs succumbed to black duress that the *New York Times* entered the fray to declare a happy outcome to unpleasant ethnic infighting: "Brooklyn Blacks and Koreans Forge Pact."[108]

In 1990, African American activists spearheaded a boycott of Korean stores in the Flatbush section of Brooklyn. Black activists led by an attorney named Sonny Carson distributed pamphlets urging blacks not to buy from "people who don't look like us." African American protesters shouted epithets at Koreans such as "yellow monkey" and "fortune cookie" and some carried signs that said, "God is love, Koreans are the devil." Apparently taking the view that black racism against Koreans did not fit the paradigm of "all the news that's fit to print," the *New York Times* did not report the black boycott for more than three months. Yet its abstinence did not make the incident go away; rather, tensions escalated in Flatbush. A group of African Americans seized a Vietnamese man, mistaking him for a Korean, and fractured his skull with a hammer. Black activists issued threats and manifestos. Sonny Carson pledged, "In the future, there'll be funerals, not boycotts." It was several months before a judge's ruling cleared the black barricades and Korean entrepreneurs could get back to business.[109] Similar black boycotts of Korean stores have been organized in a number of places, such as Washington, D.C., Philadelphia, Chicago, and Los Angeles.

Perhaps the most gruesome targeting of Koreans occurred during the Los Angeles riots. Blacks were not the only rioters, of course, but black activists specifically descended on the Koreatown area, where more than three out of four Korean businesses were looted or burned. Koreans lost some two thousand establishments as the Los Angeles police offered virtually no protection. Even the Korean consulate was attacked. After the incident, one Asian American storekeeper announced the political lesson she had learned. "What we need is a Korean Al Sharpton."[110]

THE POLITICS OF ENVY

What explanation could there be for this documented hostility between blacks on the one hand, and Jews and Koreans on the other? Black animus cannot be put down to "the hate that hate produced," because there is no evidence that Jews and Koreans are particularly disposed to hate blacks. On the contrary, Jews have the most liberal voting record among white ethnic groups in America, as well as the strongest history of supporting black educational and political initiatives. Koreans, who are relative newcomers to the country, are themselves a minority who have suffered discrimination and have not abetted any of the historical offenses visited on blacks. "There is no real justification," Ronald Takaki asserts, "for the hostility that exists."

One Korean businessman in Los Angeles offered his blunt assessment of the reason for the black antagonism. "I think the black people are jealous of the Koreans. They're lazy. We are working hard. They're not making money. We are making money."[111] This evaluation is not new. As early as the 1940s, Kenneth Clark diagnosed strong anti-Semitism among the black poor, which he attributed to the mobilization of political envy against a group that was white in complexion and in direct contact with poor blacks in the form of landlords, pawnbrokers, grocers, and welfare workers. Similarly, James Baldwin in the 1960s analyzed black anti-Semitism as a particular variant of anti-white baiting: "Just as a society must have a scapegoat, so hatred must have a symbol. Georgia has the Negro, and Harlem has the Jew."[112]

Clark's and Baldwin's analyses are supported by scholars like Edna Bonacich, who studies ethnic enterprise. Bonacich argues that Koreans, like Jews, are ethnic middlemen who stand between African Americans and a perceived white power structure. Jews and Koreans become the focus of black antagonism because they are seen as "foot soldiers of internal colonialism."[113] A similar argument, stripped of its disparaging rhetoric about colonialism, is advanced by Thomas Sowell, who argues that all over the world, middleman minorities such as the Tamils in Sri Lanka, the Germans in Russia, the Japanese in Peru, the Ibos in many parts of Africa, the Chinese in Indonesia, the Jews in several European countries, and the Armenians in Turkey have been subject to ethnic vilification and ostracism, not on account of their failure, but on account of their economic success. Sowell writes that the reason middleman minorities succeed is that they have a more productive set of values than native ethnic groups, which inspires envy and rage. "While racial hostility strikes many groups, it seems most virulent against groups who make others feel inferior, rather than groups to whom the racists feel superior." As a result of "wounded egos," Sowell adds, "Middleman minorities are most hated where they are most needed."[114]

In addition to envy and *ressentiment* over the economic role played by Koreans and Jews, blacks also use cultural differences as a pretext for bigoted outbursts and violence. Certainly black and Korean ethnic styles differ. Blacks as a group are expressive and engaging; Koreans as a group are reserved and taciturn: female merchants, for example, sometimes drop change on the counter to avoid physical contact with customers. This Asian reticence is compounded by difficulties with the English language.[115] Moreover, many Koreans who live in ethnic enclaves characterized by intact families, high saving rates, and children who study hard to get into selective colleges view with barely concealed distaste, weird fascination, and fear an African American inner-city culture seemingly dominated by illegitimacy, profligacy, and violence. African American activists seize on these social characteristics to argue that Koreans refuse to offer them respect. There seems to be a strong revival of yellow-peril rhetoric among inner-city African Americans.

The relationship between blacks and Jews is a long-standing one. Of all white ethnic groups, Jews were disproportionately involved in the civil rights movement. Franz Boas, the founder of American antiracism, was Jewish. So was Joel Spingarn, chairman of the NAACP for many years, and Jack Greenberg, head of the NAACP Legal Defense Fund, who argued for desegregation and busing. Many Jews and Jewish groups strengthened the NAACP in its early years with financial and legal assistance.[116] "Jews tended to view blacks as comrades because both were potential victims of arbitrary prejudice," argues Murray Friedman, author of a recent book on the frayed relationship between the two groups. Despite current tensions, Jews continue to view blacks more sympathetically than does any other white, Hispanic, or Asian group.[117]

Yet Jews like Koreans have proven their entrepreneurial capacity in the inner cities in which many poor blacks live. Many Jews who supported civil rights expected that blacks would seize new opportunities and emulate their own group's success. This has not happened, and mutual frustration is the result. Many African Americans find it impossible to acknowledge that they are being outperformed by another ethnic group. They complain that Jews misled them about the benefits of integration; as Harold Cruse puts it, Zionists who did not believe in assimilation or integration for themselves cynically promoted such social objectives for blacks.[118] Moreover, since many blacks have become accustomed to thinking in the language of proportional representation, in which each ethnic group deserves its ration of social goods, they cannot help but notice that Jews are overrepresented in virtually all the desirable schools and professions.[119] Black activists recognize that in order to raise the level of underrepresented groups, it is necessary to diminish the level of overrepresented groups. Consequently, they view Jewish success as disproportionate, undeserved, and extracted at the expense of African Americans. Jews, Leonard Jeffries insists, are "largely responsible" in America for the "institutionalization of racism."[120]

Finally there is the Jewish Holocaust, a potent symbol of ethnic oppression. Many blacks have come to recognize that the large social transfers of resources that they want in the form of government programs or reparations depend on their virtually unique claim to victim status. Thus they are upset and embarrassed that the Holocaust is viewed as the greatest crime of modern history. In an exercise of what Glenn Loury calls "comparative victimology,"[121] some blacks seek to delegitimize the Holocaust directly, by questioning whether it really happened or how many really died, and indirectly, by accusing Jews of being complicit and indeed largely responsible for the greater holocaust of black slavery. Apparently black activists seek ultimate martyr status, an ethnic monopoly on victimhood. In Leonard Jeffries' words, "The chosen people are people of color."[122]

There is some truth to black allegations of Jewish complicity in the institution of slavery. Some Jews such as Judah Benjamin became Southern partisans and statesmen, although others, like Rabbi David Einhorn of Baltimore, campaigned actively for emancipation. "Jews in the North supported the Union," Eugene Genovese says, "and Jews in the South supported the Confederacy." Sephardic Jews were middlemen in the transatlantic slave trade, yet their numbers were too few to dominate the institution as a whole. According to David Brion Davis, there were very few Jews in the South before the Civil War, and many of them were townspeople and small merchants. Thus although many Southern Jews owned one or two slaves, only a tiny fraction owned plantations with more than twenty slaves. Indeed between 1830 and 1860 Jews probably owned fewer slaves than did free blacks.[123]

It is all the more important that black activists deny Jewish claims to earned success and historical victimization because most Jews in the United States are white. "Attacking Jews is an easy way for some blacks to attack whites and get away with it," remarks Abraham Foxman, head of the Anti-Defamation League. Otherwise the inference remains that some whites may not have won their social rewards by oppressing blacks and may have their own historical grievances to parade for educational and political attention. An awareness of the need to counter all such claims by whites explains what New York black activist Sonny Carson said when he was accused of anti-Semitism. "I am not anti-Semitic," Carson said, "I am anti-white."[124]

THE MAN FARTHEST DOWN

Ethnic conflicts between blacks and other groups do not, by themselves, constitute racism. Recall that racism requires biological inferiorization, and Jews and Koreans are not distinctive races but rather groups defined by nationality, religion, and a shared culture. Even black boycotts that are aimed at establishing African American business networks can be explained as a form of tribalism or ethnocentrism. Asians and Jews can themselves prove ethnocentric in this manner. Black hostility toward these groups assumes a new meaning, however, when it is racialized into anti-white and anti-Asian sentiment, and when it invokes the natural or biological inferiority of those groups. Racism comes in when whites and Asians are objectified and dehumanized on account of their race.

Historically racism has expressed itself in the form of groups on the top of the social ladder looking down on and demeaning those at the bottom. Whites have traditionally considered blacks intrinsically deficient on account of intellectual and civilizational inferiority. Black racism is different in that it stakes no claim to intellectual superiority over Jews and Koreans. On the contrary, African American activists implicitly acknowledge that, at least in entrepreneurial terms, their group appears to be uncompetitive with Jews and Koreans.

This is where the argument takes a new turn, however. Black racists argue that while Jews and Koreans may be successful in business, this is due to their moral inferiority. The reason that Jews and Koreans outperform blacks in the inner city is not because they have better skills and work harder, but rather, because they are willing to adopt vicious and underhanded practices that are simply beneath African American ethical standards. Claims of morality are thus invoked in order to deny moral capacity to Jews and Koreans. Charges of inhumanity are raised in order to dehumanize people from these groups. Jews and Koreans are held to account for charging "unconscionable" rates. They are faulted for "sleazy" and "unfair" business tactics. They are charged with "overpricing" goods and "undercutting" the competition. They make "outrageous" and "unearned" profits. They are "cutthroat" people. They are "exploiters" who "take advantage" of customers and refuse to show them basic "respect." In other words, their relative success is explained by the fact that they are natural criminals and degenerates, and blacks are fully justified in treating them that way.

If white racism served the purpose of rationalizing historical oppression, what purpose is served by black racism? In an ascriptive society, in which social rewards are assigned based on birth or tribal status, those who enjoy unearned privileges are likely to justify them by appealing to the natural inferiority of those who have been denied those privileges. In other words, whites deserve preference in terms of jobs and status because blacks were born to be slaves and menial servants. In a more meritocratic society, however, those who win social rewards do not need to justify them because they have been earned. In a fair race, it is the losers who now need to rationalize their defeat. Consequently, in a society with free markets and open competition, it is those who have been outperformed who are likely to develop theories of institutional bias and moral deformity in order to explain their consistent embarrassment at the hands of more able competitors.

This point was made by the English sociologist Michael Young in his novel *The Rise of the Meritocracy*. Young envisioned a strictly meritocratic system which turned out to have the unanticipated effect of widening social divisions between the successful and the unsuccessful. Young's imaginative work ended with the incensed proletariat forcefully overthrowing the meritocracy and restoring nepotistic arrangements that allow winners and losers to coexist without too much tension.[125] In Young's view, however, the merit principle divides groups by class; in America, one sees similar divisions along racial lines. Just as white racism can be understood as a rationalization for white oppression, black racism, in this analysis, can be explained as a rationalization for black failure. Such rationalizations are necessary because of the expectations of group equality generated by cultural relativism. In this framework, where group equality does not exist, the reason for the discrepancy is not natural but conventional. Specifically, groups doing well are blamed for taking advantage of groups not doing as well.

What this means is that meritocracy does not eliminate racism, as many civil rights activists of the 1960s predicted and expected. Rather, meritocracy tends to minimize the reasons for racism "from above" and to maximize the reasons for racism "from below." In a society that tries to implement the merit principle within a relativist framework, those who succeed view themselves as winners but those who fail do not view themselves as losers; rather, they view themselves as victims. Racial victimization supplies a license for bigotry which is disguised as a campaign for equality and social justice. It is no surprise, therefore, that white racism seems less overt and less threatening to the life chances of other groups, while black racism is more explicitly menacing.

The rise of black racism is a new twist on historical racism, but it is entirely consistent with the career of bigotry in the United States. One of the many reasons that whites who did not own slaves fought on the Southern side of the Civil War was that they were convinced by the plantation owners of the social prestige attached to a white skin. Similarly poor whites supported segregation, even when it undermined their class interests, because this enabled the most degraded and ignorant Alabama farmer to place himself above W. E. B. Du Bois. Racism, in other words, embodies what the novelist Shiva Naipaul terms a "bogus aristocracy of color."[126] Those who cannot achieve much in life on their own merits find solace and encouragement in the notion that their very biology provides them with social entitlements. If your station in life is determined by genealogy, then you enjoy the same natural birthright as the old tribal chieftains or the aristocrats of Europe. You can never lose your social privileges, because they are hereditary.

Racism is a program of self-esteem for those who have little to celebrate. It is no surprise that Afrocentric, multicultural, and other self-esteem programs in the schools have chosen to boost the egos of young African Americans through the device of ethnic chauvinism, through delusions of historic grandeur. Black people are born noblemen. Their ancestors invented and discovered everything of importance. Without them the universe would not exist; as a leading Nation of Islam activist puts it, "The black man *is* God."[127] What they rightfully deserve in society has been stolen from them by other groups who do not exceed them in talent, but who do exceed them in wickedness and rapacity. Black racism replaces self-doubt by projecting that doubt onto other racial groups. Of course it is partly a response to white racism, but it is also a response to white and Asian educational and entrepreneurial *achievement.* Whites and Asians are not simply envied for what they have, but they are hated for the human qualities that enable them to earn what they have. Black racism is a worldview built on frustration and jealousy. As Iago says of Cassio in Shakespeare's *Othello,* "He hath a daily beauty in his life that makes me ugly."

It seems unconvincing to excuse or define out of existence any kind of bigotry on the grounds that it stems from a perception of victimization or black rage. "There is a lot of anger in the black community," Alvin Poussaint says, "but we should try to understand the rage." Yet virtually all racial abuse arises out of some perception of anger, and the anger is often both understandable and warranted. The racism of the Boer and the Afrikaner arose out of deep wellsprings of discontent, long memories of the great trek away from regions of British control. Hitler's Nazism too developed out of the siege mentality that Germans felt after the humiliations of the First World War. And these frustrations were for the most part genuine. Racism is frequently a response to such bitter recollections and failures, which far from excusing racism, give it a more paranoid, delusional, and violent cast. Its hatred and viciousness are all the more dangerous because they are accompanied by a sense of moral indignation and entitlement. For those who succumb to its temptations, racism provides a right to abuse others. Social dislocation and a martyrdom complex are characteristic of racism, and we should not be surprised to find such characteristics in black racism as well.

All About Melanin

No doctrine of racism is complete without a theory of biological superiority. Predictably, black racists have concocted their own, and it attributes intrinsic black superiority to that colorizing agent in the human anatomy, melanin. Drawing on the allegedly transforming and even supernatural properties of melanin, blacks who share this view are poised for a new understanding of human history and a newly dominant global role in the future. Melanin theory is standard doctrine at the Nation of Islam, which weaves it into its literature and teachings. It is also burrowing into the Afrocentric and multicultural curriculum.[128] Molefi Kete Asante, perhaps the leading Afrocentrist in the country, himself draws on the melanin theorists while eschewing their overt racism. According to Asante, "Pressures of human survival, xenophobia and reliance on hunting combined to create the philosophical outlook of the European." In his view, Europeans suffer from a bloodthirsty "caveman mentality" while Africans are blessed with a humane "palm tree mentality."[129]

One of the leading melanin theorists in the country is author Frances Cress Welsing, a former professor of social work at Howard University. Welsing came to national attention in 1989 when, at an ABC *Nightline* town meeting, she generated sustained applause for her claim that the black male "is profoundly attacked in this society" because he is "a threat to white genetic annihilation."[130] In her book *The Isis Papers: The Keys to the Colors,* an Afrocentric best-seller that has sold more than forty thousand copies, Welsing elaborates on her thesis that black suffering and pathologies "are the direct and indirect byproducts of a behavioral power system fundamentally structured for white genetic survival." Melanin, Welsing maintains, is the "superior absorber of all energy." In fact, it is of divine origin because God is in fact the source of all energy. "The color black is essential to be in touch with the God force." Since whites lack melanin in their skin, Welsing argues, no one should be surprised at their lack of spirituality. "Because they lack the melanin sensory system, they cannot intuit that all is one." According to Welsing, whites have been driven into a psychotic and terroristic rage "primarily from their own colorlessness." In her view, whites recognize that if they mix with people of color they will lose their whiteness. Yet she reports that whites have a secret desire to acquire melanin and be black, as evidenced by the efforts of many to get a tan. Even hippies who grow long hair and cover their bodies with dirt, Welsing suggests, are in their own perverse way "adding color" to themselves.

Summer tans, however, are not enough. Welsing suggests that whites need "mass psychotherapy" to cure themselves of their melanin envy. Yet she is pessimistic: whites, she is convinced, do not wish to acknowledge their genetic deficiency. After all, it has deep roots: "White-skinned peoples came into existence thousands of years ago as the albino mutant offsprings of black-skinned mothers and fathers in Africa." Even homosexuality, which Welsing regards as a white invention to prevent more mutant albinos from coming into the world, is in Welsing's view only a short-term solution. Therefore, Welsing concludes, these Caucasian "genetic defectives" have launched a "major act of genocide" against other people of color, specifically blacks, "including chemical and biological warfare." Welsing maintains that blacks have to be physically, intellectually, and even militarily willing to resist this white expression of melanin envy. "Black manhood means being a warrior or soldier against white supremacy, embracing everything that the words warrior or soldier imply."[131]

Another leading melaninist is Afrocentrist and black psychologist Wade Nobles, whose book *African Psychology* is a study of the "biogenetic origins of the black personality." According to Nobles, "African psychology is based on the assumption that the African race is evolutionarily more advanced than the Caucasian." Deploring the unhappy results of the usual measures of performance, Nobles argues, "Intelligence must be redefined so it is directly related to the presence of melanin." The mystery of melanin, Nobles writes, transcends the mere provision of color to the skin. "It is an integral part of the psychosomatic system." Drawing on "brain geography and the genetic substance melanin," Nobles concludes that "rhythm is the basis of soul." Moreover, in Nobles's view, melanin provides a unique form of reasoning that transcends "inadequate . . . Western concepts of causality." All logic, Nobles insists, should correspond with black "spiritual reality."[132]

Melanin theories can also be found in works like Richard King's *African Origin of Biological Psychiatry* and a self-published monograph by Carol Barnes titled *Melanin: The Chemical Key to Black Greatness.*[133] King and Barnes have been the organizing force behind a series of "Melanin Conferences," held annually since 1987 in New York, Washington, D.C., Los Angeles, San Francisco, and Dallas. Each conference has drawn more than five hundred participants, including scholars, activists, and members of the black community.[134] Undoubtedly the most famous popularizer of melanin theory is black studies professor and activist Leonard Jeffries. Melanin, Jeffries maintains, is like RNA and DNA one of the building blocks of a full human being. "It allows us," he argues, "to negotiate the vibrations of the universe."[135]

Another classroom melaninist is Clarence Glover, who is director of multicultural education at Southern Methodist University. He informs his students, according to *Time,* that "melanin is the strongest chemical in the human body." He argues that lack of melanin deprives whites of communication skills and melanin gives blacks a unique ability to relate to human beings. Gladys Twyman, who coordinates the African American infusion program for public schools in Atlanta, concedes that melanin is a central part of the Afrocentric curriculum. "It is the thread, the core of the project." And Patricia Newton, a psychiatrist associated with Johns Hopkins University, teaches her students that melanin is "one of the strongest electromagnetic field forces in the universe" and also gives blacks mysterious healing powers.[136] Melanin advocates contend that melanin operates like chlorophyll in plants: it absorbs the sun's heat and converts it into useful energy for the body. While melanin enables blacks to reach "higher states of consciousness," Afrocentrist Marimba Ani writes, melanin-deprived whites suffer an "overall lower level of nervous system integration" resulting in an inability "to comprehend spiritual truths" and a mentality that produces "intensely destructive behaviors."[137]

Scholars who have investigated the claims of the melanin theorists argue that there is no scientific evidence whatsoever for claims that melanin is a superconductor, that it absorbs electromagnetic frequencies, that it converts sound energy into light, that it helps to process information, that it is a spiritual catalyst, and so on.[138] "Lectures about melanin," one anthropologist writes, "are replete with scientific sounding terminology: substantia nigra, solitions, phonons, electromagnetic radiation, melanocyte, extrapyramidal tract, pineal gland, hypothalamus, and so on." Behind all this terminological pomposity, however, melanin theory is a case of "pseudoscience traveling under a guise of multiculturalism."[139]

But what is the point of all this abstruse theory? Marimba Ani spells it out: "White nationalism and aggression, both cultural and economic, are endemic to European culture. . . . Violence and emotional brutality are part of the Western way of life. . . . The pattern of European behavior toward others cannot change because of the nature of the European himself."[140] Afrocentric theories of melanin provides support for the claim that black antagonism toward whites has not merely an historical but also a biological foundation. Thus they legitimize a mental separation between the races, diminishing the chances for improved understanding and increasing the prospects for future conflict.

BLACK ARYAN NATION

The institutional expression of black racism in the United States is the Nation of Islam. This group is a problem for white liberals, some of whom seek to rationalize its extremism as a strong reaction to white racism, and many of whom point to social work that the organization carries out as a way of saying that not everything the black Muslims do is bad. This is obviously true, but it was also true of the fascists in Germany and Italy, and of white supremacist groups, some of which functioned partly as a kind of civic organization. In his study *The Ku Klux Klan in the City*, Kenneth Jackson describes the activity of Dallas Klan No. 66, "which established and operated for several years a $75,000 institution for homeless children." In addition, that chapter lent money to the needy, conducted a program of support for widows, and distributed food and gifts at Christmas.[141] White racist scholars in the early part of the century cited Klan philanthropy to cover up the group's most indefensible practices. Thus black and white racist organizations are joined even in the historical apologies given for their conduct.

Even the Nation of Islam's much-touted reforms are a mixed blessing.

The Nation of Islam attempts, with modest success, to convert gangsters, addicts, and sexual deviants into dignified and bow-tied individuals who could in some respects be described as Puritans if they were not Muslims. Yet as the *Chicago Tribune* reported in March 1995, there is also plenty of evidence of chicanery. Frequently the Nation of Islam offers dubious services—such as hiring convicted criminals to patrol housing projects, which can hardly contribute to overall safety. Despite its rhetoric of economic independence, much of the group's annual revenues come from government contracts. And Louis Farrakhan reportedly uses the profits to subsidize a lavish lifestyle which includes expensive silk suits and a stretch limousine.[142] Yet the larger difficulty with the Nation of Islam, as with the Afrocentrists, is that they identify acceptance of the standards of the white world as the main obstacle facing blacks. "Our major problem," Na'im Akbar writes, "is that we've started imitating Euro-Americans too much."[143] Thus commitments to Afrocentric ideology and the Nation of Islam can have the effect of distancing young African Americans from the civilizational resources that they need to succeed in mainstream society. How many jobs can Farrakhan provide in the restricted areas of rap musician, self-taught black social critic, and Fruit of Islam security guard? *U.S. News and World Report* points out that the Nation's security services experience peculiar obstacles to getting things done ("The Jews put a virus in our computer").[144] It is not easy to envision black militants, energized in a posture of readiness to combat every institutional arrangement of Western culture, functioning very well in working relationships at Exxon or General Motors.

Afrocentrists and the Nation of Islam are committed to finding a distinctively African solution to African American problems. Thus Haki Madhubuti follows a sound diagnosis of problems of illegitimacy and violence in black communities with a package of outlandish remedies: an agrarian vision of collectively owned land cooperatives; a rejection of black-on-black crime combined with a revolutionary defense of black-on-white confrontation; a call for "Afrikan boot camps" to indoctrinate black males in the ideology of blackness; a proposal to address the problem of single-parent families by introducing African family structures such as polygamy, and a conspiratorial mindset that raises such questions as "Was Jonestown a CIA Medical Experiment?" and arrives at such epiphanies as "AIDS was introduced into Africa by the World Health Organization" and white doctors created AIDS "in a laboratory at Fort Derrick, Maryland."[145] These activists are trying to sever blacks from American culture; if they succeed, blacks as a group will be left with nothing but myths and resentment.

Basically, it is antiwhite hatred that unifies and directs the activities of the Nation of Islam. To understand this, it is necessary to go back to the group's founding and understand its original ideology which continues to be preached and disseminated today.[146] A man named Wali Fard Muhammad, who was half white and half black and whose given name was Wallace Ford, surfaced in the early 1930s in the black ghettos of Detroit. A convicted drug dealer and door-to-door raincoat salesman, he called himself "the Prophet," and claimed to have come from Mecca to America to find the Lost Tribe of Shabazz, consisting of black Muslims who wrongly thought of themselves as Negroes. Muhammad set up the first Nation of Islam temple in Detroit. For a fee, Master Fard agreed to change the "slave names" of American blacks to their ancestral names; temporarily, each person was asked to use "X" to symbolize his or her true and unknown family name.

Influenced by the rhetoric of Marcus Garvey, Master Fard informed credulous poor blacks suffering under the Depression that being of mixed race he was able to move undetected among whites and discover their true nature. What he had found, it turned out, was that the white man was "a devil by nature," and that all blacks should prepare for Armageddon, the great race war between black and white. One of Fard's chief lieutenants was Elijah Poole. Fard convinced him to drop his "slave name" and take up the name "Muhammad." Fard and Muhammad jointly set up the Nation of Islam's second temple and current headquarters in Chicago. It was Muhammad who took over the Nation of Islam in the mid 1930s, when Fard mysteriously vanished. Then Muhammad elaborated Fard's teaching into a kind of full-length theological and political doctrine. As Muhammad sums up his doctrine in *Message to the Blackman in America:*

> The original man, Allah, is none other than the black man. The black man is the first and last, maker and owner of the universe. From him came all brown, yellow, red and white people. Allah is proving to the world of black men that the white race actually does not own any part of our planet. The white race is not, and never will be, the chosen people of God. They are the chosen people of their father Yacub, the devil.[147]

Muhammad's racial theology is still taught as scripture in the Nation of Islam. According to Muhammad, Allah is God and Allah is black. The black-skinned Allah created the original human beings, naturally black like himself. One of Allah's scientists conducted special experiments which produced an especially powerful and brilliant tribe of Shabazz, from which American blacks are descended. Unfortunately an evil mad scientist named Yacub rebelled against Allah's authority in Mecca, and was exiled by the holy black people of the city to the island of Patmos. There, as part of his revenge against God, Yacub began to perform genetic experiments to dilute the strength of the black race.

First, Yacub weakened the black genetic strain to produce brown people, which took two hundred years. Then he concocted the "red race" and the "yellow race" which took another four hundred years. Within eight hundred years, Yacub achieved his nefarious objective: a race of white people who walked on all fours and lived in trees. Because of the filthy and disgusting habits of these white savages, the original black people rounded them up and dispatched them across the Arabian desert to the caves of Europe. In the frigid climates of the north, white people mated with animals and produced ever more repulsive offspring, colorless and hairy. Among the craftiest and most dangerous of the white race, this view held, were the Jews.

Since Yacub bred whites to be especially greedy and vicious, these monsters were bound to attack and seek to rule over other peoples. In Elijah Muhammad's view, Allah permitted this for a period of six thousand years. But he arranged for the people of Shabazz to come as slaves to North America where they could get inside information about the wiles of the white man, so as to ultimately spearhead his destruction. Allah also endowed one member of the tribe of Shabazz with virtually supernatural wisdom, so that he would awaken the slumbering members to their true political and spiritual destiny. That man, of course, was Elijah Muhammad.

Today, Louis Farrakhan continues Elijah Muhammad's tradition of urging blacks in America to awaken to the satanic nature of whites, recognize their true pedigree, reclaim their racial heritage, and work with singular purpose to expel the white impostor from his unearned position as master of the universe.[148] The man who once said that Malcolm X deserved to die on account of Malcolm's disloyalty to Elijah Muhammad now directs his rage toward whites, whom he calls the "mortal enemy." Farrakhan has said, "I will fight to see that vicious beast go down into the lake of fire prepared for him in the beginning." To followers who profess affection for his message Farrakhan counsels, "Disorganized love is not as effective as organized hate."[149] The Nation's newspaper, *The Final Call,* continues to indoctrinate members about the intrinsic evil of whites and the coming racial conflagration. The Nation of Islam recruits actively in the inner cities. It has established beachheads on several campuses, especially historically black ones. It is perhaps the most powerful black movement in the prisons, where black racists and white racists abound. Indeed the racial gangs that roam prison compounds serve as a kind of warning symbol of where the country may be headed.

Many liberals have been peculiarly blind about black racism, because of their commitment to cultural relativism. In the relativist paradigm, it is white racism that is to blame for the problems faced by blacks. If blacks act in a manner that resembles racism, they have been compelled to do so by the legacy of white racism. Yet, as we have just seen, black racism cannot be understood as merely reactive. Rather, powered by Afrocentrist ideology and institutionalized in the Nation of Islam, African American racism is a comprehensive ideology of black supremacy. Moreover, this sort of racism "from below" is likely to increase because it provides a convenient rationalization for black failure. White racism and black racism are now mirror ideologies, both anchored in relativism and mutually reinforcing. If unopposed, they will surely draw whites and blacks further apart, until peace between the races becomes impossible.

11

THE CONTENT OF OUR CHROMOSOMES

Race and the IQ Debate

Nothing frightens the liberal mind more than the prospect of inherited differences in intelligence between the races.

    —Sociologist Linda Gottfredson

If black racism is largely a rationalization for black failure, what causes such failure? The conventional liberal explanation is discrimination and the resulting social disadvantage, but this is not the only conceivable explanation. In *The Bell Curve,* Richard Herrnstein and Charles Murray argue that racial groups differ in average intelligence, that these differences may be partly hereditary, and that IQ gaps largely account for ethnic variations in educational and economic performance.[1] The reaction to their argument was one of immediate and unrestrained revulsion. Despite its claim to be based on scientific research, Herrnstein and Murray's work inspired an avalanche of invective, some of it preceding the book's publication, much of it ignoring the evidence presented and focusing on Herrnstein and Murray's motives. In liberal circles, *The Bell Curve* was viewed as a dangerous revival of scientific hereditarianism in a neoracist form, a potential manifesto for white racist backlash. Ignoring Herrnstein and Murray's insistence that their book dealt only peripherally with race, many normally unflappable pundits produced a stampede of epithets.

- "Dishonest pseudo-science," fumed Jesse Jackson. "The last time such racist tripe received celebrity was in Nazi Germany."[2]
- "Racial pornography," declared Bob Herbert in the *New York Times*. For Herbert *The Bell Curve* was nothing more than "a genteel way of calling somebody a nigger."[3]
- Adolph Reed accused Murray and Herrnstein of being "intellectual brownshirts," a "demonic duo" engaged in a "diabolical collaboration" with a "viper's nest" of scholars to promote "reactionary prejudices."[4]
- "Grist for racism of every variety," wrote Jacob Weisberg in *New York*. "You can hear a thousand David Dukes in the background saying: I told you so."[5]
- "A profoundly racist message in academic robes," growled an editorial in the *Atlanta Constitution*.[6]
- "Dreary," "scary," and "apocalyptic," raged Stephen Jay Gould, as he proclaimed *The Bell Curve* a brief for a vicious and dangerous "social Darwinism."[7]
- Leon Kamin added to this typhoon of adjectives: "crude," "pathetic," "troubling," "venomous," "shameful."[8]

In other countries, people talk freely about racial differences.[9] But question the assumption of the inherent equality of the races in America and you are challenging the most powerful twentieth-century taboo of the Western world. Herrnstein and Murray must have known this. Before them, other scholars found themselves accused of being brownshirts and Nazis for wandering into this intellectual minefield, and even today many researchers are cognizant of the dangers of challenging the regnant dogma of equality among groups.[10]

- In 1969, Arthur Jensen published an article in the *Harvard Educational Review* arguing that remedial education was failing in large part because black children were not intelligent enough to take advantage of it; instantly Jensen went from being a renowned educational psychologist to a virtual pariah, protesters disrupted his classes, and there were threats to his life.[11]
- One Jensen convert was Nobel laureate William Shockley, who invited a torrent of abuse and scorn (partly generated by his own provocative style) when he endorsed Jensen's thesis and proposed eugenic remedies such as paying people with low IQs to abstain from having children.[12]
- In 1971, psychologist Richard Herrnstein published an article in *The Atlantic Monthly* reviving the issue of hereditary differences in intelli-

gence. His reward came in the magazine's letters page: "Hitler's propa-gandists used the same tactics in the thirties while his metal workers put the finishing touches on the gas ovens."[13]

• When in the mid 1970s biologist E. O. Wilson published *Sociobiology,* suggesting a Darwinian foundation for racial and gender differences, a group called Science for the People issued *ad hominem* denunciations of Wilson, and during a 1978 lecture to an audience of biologists, demon-strators rushed the podium shouting "Nazi," "fascist," and "racist," and dumped a pitcher of water on Wilson's head.[14]

• In 1985 when James Q. Wilson and Richard Herrnstein attempted to lecture on their book *Crime and Human Nature,* which includes an ex-ploration of the relationship between genes and criminal orientation, they were drowned out by students shouting "Wilson, Herrnstein, you can't hide. You believe in genocide."[15]

• In 1992, when the University of Maryland announced a conference to explore the latest research on the influence of genes on crime, black ac-tivists were immediately activated by the aroma of racial conspiracy. Samuel Yette, a Howard University professor, declared the project "clear-ly racist . . . an effort to use public money for a genocidal effort against African Americans. Hitler and Goebbels were very good at this." A black newspaper ran the headline, "Plot to Sedate Black Youth: Government Program Would Make Zombies of Inner-City Kids." Without examining these allegations, the National Institutes for Health withdrew federal funding and the university canceled the conference.[16]

• Leading scientists from around the world are participating in a project to map the genetic diversity of human populations. Yet the project, pro-posed by prominent geneticists such as Luigi Cavalli-Sforza and Mary-Claire King, has found itself immersed in racial controversy, as activists charge that the Human Genome Project is a bigoted prelude to proclaim-ing minorities to be intrinsically inferior. "Any sensible person can see this is important research," Cavalli-Sforza says, "but I must tell you, I was com-pletely unprepared for the negative reactions we have encountered."[17]

Clearly something very interesting is going on here. The reaction to *The Bell Curve,* as to its predecessors, becomes a revealing snapshot of a pained and apoplectic liberalism. Surely this venom and fury could not be explained by psychologist Robert Sternberg's contention that Herrnstein and Murray's book regurgitates "old stuff," or Stephen Ceci's assurance that scholars have said the same thing "for the last 15 years."[18] Never has old news proved to be so inflammatory. Nor can the outrage be explained on the grounds that *The Bell Curve* contravenes the Declaration of Independence, that "it goes against our entire history," as President Clinton pronounced, or that it "violates a basic tenet of democracy," as the *Boston Globe* asserted.[19] Surely, as history bears out, the Declaration and the Constitution are not premised on the notion that all persons are equal in their intellectual potential, only that they are equal in their possession of certain basic rights.

What makes Herrnstein and Murray and their predecessors controversial is not that they claim individuals differ in intelligence—this is obvious and uncontested—but that *groups* do. This is threatening because it challenges the liberal assumption that racial differences are, as Stephen Jay Gould puts it, merely "skin deep."[20] Thus the fear is that Herrnstein and Murray will restore the concept of group hierarchy and make racism respectable once again. No less scary, as Jacob Weisberg remarks, the existence of racial differences implies that the old Southern segregationists may have been wrong in what they did, but perhaps they were "not altogether wrong in what they thought."[21] Herrnstein and Murray are reviled because they are questioning the foundation of twentieth century liberalism: the denial of natural differences and the premise of the inherent equality of groups.

Much of America's social policy is based on this central assumption of liberal antiracism. The heyday of liberalism was San Francisco judge Robert Peckham's decision in 1979 that IQ tests could not be used to classify blacks as educationally deficient if a disproportionate number of blacks compared to whites fell into that category.[22] The Supreme Court's *Griggs* decision of 1971, as we have seen, permitted the disparate results of general ability tests to be used to establish a presumption of illegal discrimination. Attempting to preserve this intellectual edifice, the *Boston Globe* recently editorialized that public policy cannot afford to view groups as chronically deficient but must view them as victims who have come upon "hard times for a variety of reasons" and "need help getting back on their feet. . . . The danger here is that [Herrnstein and Murray's] theory could be used to justify regressive public policy."[23] Similarly, Labor Secretary Robert Reich warned that *The Bell Curve* provides ammunition for an argument "to do less and less for those who are less fortunate."[24]

The notion that groups who fail are not failing on their own account but because they are *less fortunate* is the unquestioned assumption of liberal social policy. This assumption is generated by Boasian relativism, which arose in opposition to nineteenth century cultural evolutionism and scientific racism. In order to reject "nature red in tooth and claw," in Tennyson's phrase, advocates of cultural relativism denied intrinsic differences and attributed the fact that some groups do better than others in educational and economic performance to a host of environmental factors, specifically an ongoing history of racial discrimination. Consequently, in the liberal mind, there are no rational grounds for believing in natural group differences, which is why all discussions of racial differences inevitably become discussions about racism.

But what if group differences turned out not to be entirely generated by discrimination? This is the heart of Herrnstein and Murray's heresy, and the core of the unspoken liberal fear, which is not about the repudiation of the American founding but the prospect of a racial caste society. After all, if races differ genetically, rather than in their externally imposed fortunes, then the free competition of a multiracial society is likely to produce a natural hierarchy of groups. Moreover, if blacks as a group are less intelligent than whites, less susceptible to education and productive work, more inclined toward crime, then arguments can be made to justify certain forms of segregation and racial discrimination. Byron Roth points out that at one time liberals viewed some ideas as dangerous because they were untrue; now some view these ideas as untrue because they are dangerous.[25] Writing in the *New Republic,* Nathan Glazer candidly articulates the liberal taboo: "Why should we be talking about this at all? For this kind of truth one can ask, what good will come of it?"[26] The liberal position on the possibility of racial differences in inherited capacity has been that of the British lady who responded thus to Darwin's theory of evolution: "Let us hope it is not true, but if it is, let us pray that it does not become generally known."[27]

Yet whatever the virtues of keeping the subject of IQ out of the public square, all such efforts are futile in the aftermath of *The Bell Curve.* Its argument, condemned but so far unrefuted, lies like a corpse on the tennis court. It is difficult to pretend to ignore it and keep playing. Moreover, the *de facto* censorship of public discussion seems to have had the effect of strengthening private convictions that innate differences do exist and are socially important. In a democratic society, where public opinion is the basis for self-government, private speculations cannot be discounted when they are likely to become the basis for public rule. An enlightened polity depends on closing the gap between private suspicion and public knowledge. Three developments of recent years have forced the issue of natural differences out of the closet.

The first is the persistent failure of blacks as a group to compete effectively in American society, and the concomitant demand for racial preferences at every stage to assure black inclusion. "It is a lot easier to think that people are inferior when they are not making it despite relatively free competition," remarks Robert George of the U.S. Civil Rights Commission. Psychologist James Sidanius, who studies racial attitudes, says that even young African Americans are beginning to internalize doubts about their own competitive capacity. "This, to me, is the real self-esteem problem." The problem is exacerbated by the unremitting attack by many African American scholars and activists on all forms of testing and merit evaluation. Conceivably one particular test or another is unfair to blacks, but it seems implausible that every single test—whether measuring reading skills of first graders or mathematical aptitude of college applicants, whether the fire fighter's test or the Foreign Service Examination—are all systematically biased against African Americans (and apparently no other group). It seems hard for some people to avoid the speculation: does the problem lie not with tests but with blacks?

Another factor contributing to intimations of inferiority is the embarrassing fact of Asian American success which has become evident to most people in recent decades. The incredible economic and intellectual achievements within a single generation not just of middle-class and professional Japanese and East Indians, but also of poor immigrants from Vietnam, Cambodia, Thailand, and Korea have called into question the claim that in America one has to be white and preferably male in order to succeed. By proving that upward mobility and social acceptance do not depend on the absence of racially distinguishing features, Asians have unwittingly yet powerfully challenged the attribution of minority failure to discrimination by the majority. Many liberals are having trouble providing a full answer to the awkward question: "Why can't an African American be more like an Asian?"

Finally there is a revival of scientific and scholarly interest in Darwinism, nourished by recent advances in genetics, evolutionary theory, and sociobiology.[28] Scholars have found increasing evidence for the influence of genes on human behavior and personality.[29] In recent years, there have been media reports of a genetic basis for alcoholism, obesity, and homosexuality.[30] Medical researchers have found that racial groups do not merely differ in skin color, but in numerous other traits, such as head shape, body size, blood types, bone density, body temperature, rates of maturation, frequency of twin births, susceptibility to certain diseases, and so on.[31] Two leading African American scholars, James Comer and Alvin Poussaint, admit that "motor development takes place faster during the first year among many African babies than among many European babies" and even suggest that "there may be some physical reason" why blacks are better dancers and singers than whites.[32] As we will see, scholars continue to debate whether there is an evolutionary basis for racial differences.

If biological differences do exist, they cannot be wished away. However unpopular the investigation, we have to take the possibility of natural differences seriously. What is at stake is nothing less than the foundation of contemporary liberalism. Substantial innate differences raise the prospect of a multicultural society characterized not by a benign equality, but rather by a natural hierarchy of groups: whites or Asians concentrated at the top, Hispanics in the middle, and blacks at the bottom.

WHITE MEN CAN'T RUN

In the 1992 Olympics in Barcelona, observers could hardly fail to notice a result that was so improbable that it bordered on the fantastic. West African blacks and African Americans won every gold medal at all men's distances up to the 400 meter hurdles. And East African and North African black males won all gold medals from the 800 meters through the marathon. The same outcome occurred at the 1993 World Track and Field Championships in Germany: black men won every single sprint and long distance event.[33] These results were predicted by Amby Burfoot, executive editor of *Runner's World,* in an article published shortly before the games called "White Men Can't Run."[34] Burfoot noticed that since 1932, blacks have been building a virtual hegemony on the highest honors at Olympic and world championship track races. In 1983, blacks won about half of thirty-three available medals for world championship running. In 1987, they won nineteen. In 1991, they won twenty-nine. In those three years, Burfoot computed, Asians won only one medal. "On the all-time list for the 100 meters," Burfoot writes, "44 of the top 50 performers are sprinters of West African origin. The highest ranking white stands in 16th place."

Sociologist Steven Goldberg estimates that of the fifty fastest runners in the 100 meters in the United States, virtually all are black. Moreover, nearly every record holder in the long jump has been black for the past half-century.[35] The *Sociology of Sport Journal* reports that since the 1930s "there has been no American white woman who was world-class in the 100, 200, or 400 meter dashes. All of the outstanding women sprinters from the 1940s into the 1990s have been black."[36] Similar results obtain in many other sports. What algebraic coincidence could explain the incredible overrepresentation of African Americans in boxing, in football, and especially in basketball? According to a study for the National Research Council, more than half of all the players in the National Football League and approximately 80 percent of all the players in the National Basketball Association are black.[37]

Certainly environmental factors, such as the spur of poverty, are important. In a 1989 article in the *Journal of Sport History,* David Wiggins points out that many poor Jews tried with modest success to make a living at basketball in the early part of the twentieth century just as many poor Irishmen went into prizefighting in the nineteenth century. Without dismissing genetic factors completely, Wiggins concludes, "The weight of the evidence indicates that the differences between participation patterns of black and white athletes are primarily a consequence of different historical experiences."[38] Yet it stands to reason that blacks who strain to "jump their way out of the ghetto," as civil rights activists put it, could expect to face strong competition from whites with better access to technology, professional coaches, and the other benefits that come with socioeconomic advantage. Since countries like China and Japan invest heavily in the quest for Olympic prestige, the relatively poor performance of Asian athletes in sports such as running and jumping cannot be attributed to lack of motivation or resources. In the 1970s, the organizers of the Mexico City Olympic Games approved a study of more than a thousand athletes from nearly a hundred countries which showed substantial physical differences between athletes from different racial groups in a number of sports, including track and field, swimming, basketball, and gymnastics.[39]

Burfoot argues that scientists who seek to explore racial differences in sports cannot find a better case study than running, because unlike sports like tennis which only some countries play and which require access to courts and racquets, running is a worldwide sport that needs very little in the way of special coaching and facilities. "Given the universality of running, it is reasonable to expect that the best runners should come from a wide range of countries and racial groups." Yet the reality is that one group, blacks, win nearly everything; a second group, whites, win a little; and a third group, Asians, win virtually nothing. And Burfoot's argument is strengthened by the fact that successful black sprinters come from various parts of the world— the United States, Canada, the Caribbean, West African nations—with varying cultural patterns and access to training facilities.

Burfoot contacted two of the leading experts on physical performance differences between groups, anthropologist Robert Malina and geneticist Claude Bouchard. Reviewing several studies, Malina and Bouchard pointed out that blacks have less body fat, narrower hips, thicker thighs, lighter calves, and longer legs, all of which generate more powerful speed with less resistance. Blacks seem to have faster reflex time which would assist in sports like sprinting and boxing, yet they also seem to have denser bones, which are a liability in sports such as swimming.[40] (Burfoot points out that no black swimmer has ever qualified for the U.S. Olympic team.) Malina says that there are even important average differences in physique between West African and East African blacks, with the bodies of the latter not as well suited to reflex actions such as sprints, and better suited to endurance tests such as the marathon. As Burfoot writes, at the Seoul Olympics, East Africans from one country, Kenya, won the 800 meters, the 1,500 meters, the 3,000 meter steeplechase, and the 5,000 meters. Similarly, studies show what is evident to the naked eye: Asians are, on average, smaller and shorter than whites and blacks. Thus relatively few Asians meet the minimum requirements to compete in those sports which require size, speed, and physical strength. Not surprisingly, Asians tend to excel in sports like ice-skating and gymnastics rather than at basketball. It is certainly possible to imagine great Asian heavyweight boxers and sprinters, but the physical odds seem to be against it. Bouchard concedes the role of training in preparing athletes for outstanding performance, yet his studies show that racial groups, like individuals, respond differently to the same level of training. Bouchard maintains that even the capacity for training is about 75 percent inherited. Thus, he concludes, there is scientific logic behind the slogan of sports coaches and physiologists who say that the way to win is to "choose your parents carefully."

Many black athletes such as Joe Morgan of the Cincinnati Reds and Calvin Hill of the Dallas Cowboys have said candidly that they think blacks are physically better equipped than whites for certain sports.[41] Yet although the superior performance of many black athletes would seem to provide a good reason for whites to admire blacks and for blacks to feel proud of their abilities, Burfoot remarks on the irony that black athletic superiority cannot be acknowledged in public. Thus many experts in the sports world experience strong political pressure to deny both empirical data as well as the evidence of their senses. Burfoot remarks, "Fear rules."

Fear seems to have been largely responsible for the 1982 firing of Al Campanis, vice president of the Los Angeles Dodgers. Campanis suggested on ABC *Nightline* that blacks had a natural ability to be athletes but not to be managers in major league baseball. Campanis apologized for his gaffe, but was forced to quit. In 1988, CBS commentator Jimmy "the Greek" Snyder told a TV interviewer that blacks make better athletes than whites because they are "bred to be that way." CBS dismissed Snyder the next day.[42] In 1993, Dale Lick, president of Florida State University in Tallahassee, who was a finalist for the presidency of Michigan State University, said publicly what many consider obvious. "As blacks begin to get into sports, their natural abilities come through. A black athlete can actually outjump a white athlete on the average." Lick was promptly accused of racism, forced to apologize, and compelled to withdraw his name from consideration.[43]

The political sensitivity surrounding such speculations goes back at least to 1971, when African American sociologist Harry Edwards angrily denounced an article in *Sports Illustrated* which asserted that "physical differences in the races might well have enhanced the athletic potential of the Negro in certain sports."[44] Edwards, who recently surfaced again to deplore Tom Brokaw's suggestion that blacks may have a natural proclivity for certain sports, insists that "racism throughout the larger society accounts for the disproportionately high presence of black athletes." Studies showing black athletic prowess are part of a "racist ideology," in Edwards's view, because they reinforce stereotypes of blacks as "little removed from the apes in their evolutionary development."[45]

The deeper grounds for such charges are suggested by columnist Richard Cohen, who writes in the *Washington Post* that if civil rights activists concede that populations differ in physical respects, then public suspicions might be raised that they may differ in intellectual and psychological traits as well.[46] It stands to reason that groups that are unlike each other in some respects may also differ in other respects. Why should groups with different skin color, head shape, and other visible characteristics prove identical in reasoning ability or the ability to construct an advanced civilization? If blacks have certain inherited abilities, such as improvisational decision making, that could explain why they predominate in certain fields such as jazz, rap, and basketball, and not in other fields, such as classical music, chess, and astronomy. To see whether this is true, let us investigate whether there are durable racial differences in intelligence between the races, and whether those differences have a genetic basis.

RUMORS OF INFERIORITY

Compared to the vast majority of whites half a century ago, today only about 13 percent of whites profess to believe that blacks are less intelligent than people of other races.[47] Yet even as popular opinion in America has shifted decisively over the past quarter century toward an assumption of inherent intellectual parity between the races, scholarly opinion seems to have shifted in the opposite direction. Within the community of social scientists, mainly psychologists, who study racial differences, there is now a virtual consensus about the existence of substantial IQ differences between Asians, whites, Hispanics and blacks. These differences, psychologist Rogers Elliott writes, "are large, early to develop, slow to change, and validly reflect real differences in performance in education and employment."[48]

Before examining these differences further, let us try to understand what IQ means. The term refers to intelligence quotient. IQ tests seek to measure not specific skills but rather general intelligence, defined as the ability to learn, reasoning capacity, or the mental ability to excel at academic challenges and solve practical problems.[49] Intelligence is measured as a weighted average of performance on various tasks of verbal, spatial, mathematical, and logical ability. IQ can be determined from a wide range of available tests, such as the Wechsler Adult Intelligence Scale (WAIS), the Wechsler Intelligence Scale for Children (WISC), the Stanford-Binet test, Ravens Progressive Matrices, Cattell Culture Fair Test, and the Wonderlic Personnel Test. Even the SAT and the GATB, administered for college admission and prospective employment purposes, are *de facto* IQ tests in that they seek to measure general cognitive ability.

Intelligence testing as a form of social science was founded in the early part of this century by Alfred Binet, director of the psychology laboratory at the Sorbonne.[50] Early intelligence tests were quite varied in the intellectual tasks they demanded, and relatively primitive in their techniques of administration. Yet a British psychologist, Charles Spearman, noticed that regardless of their specific content, the results of all tests that measured complex mental tasks correlated substantially with each other. Spearman advanced the hypothesis that in varying degrees the tests measured a single factor which he called "general intelligence," or simply *g*.[51] Psychologists have made *g* a central part of their lexicon, and Arthur Jensen calls *g* an "operational definition of intelligence."[52]

Today IQ is statistically normed on a scale of cognitive performance, with a score of 100 reflecting the mean or average score. Experts say that an IQ of 130 or higher reflects outstanding mental capacity, an IQ of 115 signals high intelligence, an IQ of 85 or below reveals poor intelligence, an IQ of 70 or lower suggests mental retardation. On literally thousands of tests, administered over the better part of a century, a consistent pattern emerges. While the full range of intellectual capacity is evident in all racial groups, nevertheless there are large differences in the average cognitive level of various races.[53] Specifically, while the IQ mean for whites is 100, that for American blacks is only 85—a difference of one standard deviation. Hispanics and American Indians fall in between, averaging scores in the range of 90 to 95. While the data for American Indians typically relies on small samples and the data for Hispanics breaks down into different scores for Cubans, Mexicans, and Puerto Ricans, the existence of the black-white IQ gap has been so thoroughly and regularly demonstrated over several decades that the best-known critics of IQ testing such as Stephen Jay Gould, Leon Kamin, Robert Sternberg, and Richard Lewontin acknowledge it. Indeed Gould calls the 15-point black-white IQ differential "an undisputed fact."[54]

In 1988 two social scientists, Mark Snyderman and Stanley Rothman, polled over six hundred psychologists and educators anonymously to find out what they believed about IQ tests. They discovered that most experts are convinced that such tests do measure intelligence and not simply the ability to succeed at taking tests. Moreover, 45 percent said that IQ differences between blacks and whites were partly hereditary; only 15 percent insisted that such differences were entirely due to environmental factors; others refused to answer or said the data were insufficient to arrive at a reasoned conclusion.[55] "There has been a real shift in the scholarly community," Christopher Jencks says. "The hereditarian position enjoys much wider support than it did twenty years ago, and the extreme environmental position is now considered dubious."

Because IQ is plotted on a bell curve with fairly sharp tails at both ends, the consequences of the race gap in IQ are startling. The average white is in the 85th percentile of black scores, whereas the average black is only in the 15th percentile of white scores. Blacks are about six times more likely than whites to fall in the IQ range of 70 or below, which educators consider a signal of mental deficiency. Equally disturbing, blacks are scarce at relatively high IQ levels of 110–120: only 2 percent of blacks, compared with 18 percent of whites, score in this range. At very high thresholds of 120 and higher, whites continue to be represented while blacks are virtually nonexistent: about 13 percent of whites, compared with 0.32 percent of blacks, achieve in this outstanding bracket.[56]

In a society in which resources are assigned to a considerable degree on merit, this intelligence mismatch has consequences for social rewards like college admissions and job selection. An IQ score of 75 or above is generally considered necessary to perform the minimum requirements for a high school diploma, an IQ above 100 to graduate from college, and an IQ of 115 or above for admission to graduate school or for holding jobs like scientist, engineer, trial lawyer, and professor. Since tests such as the SAT, LSAT, MCAT, and GRE are to a large degree measures of IQ, they can be expected to show disproportionate levels of performance between blacks and whites, as indeed they do. About 15 percent of whites, but less than 1 percent of blacks, have IQs above 115, which may be taken as a general index of qualification for success at the most selective universities and many prestigious jobs.

Sociologist Linda Gottfredson has used Labor Department data to compute the expected level of representation of blacks and whites in various fields taking into account the level of intelligence required by the job and the differences of cognitive ability between the races. Assuming that doctors and engineers require IQs around 115, or that firemen and policemen require IQs above 90, or that truckdrivers and meat-cutters require IQs above 85, Gottfredson calculates that when cognitive ability is taken into account, American blacks are *overrepresented* in most well-paying and prestigious positions.[57] Gottfredson takes note of the complaints of civil rights activists that blacks today are only 5 percent of university faculty, 3 percent of financial managers, 3 percent of physicians, 2 percent of lawyers and judges, and 1 percent of architects.[58] Recently the *Wall Street Journal* reported that blacks hold only 2.3 percent of the almost 10,000 seats on corporate boards of large companies.[59] Although these percentages seem low, Gottfredson argues that based on black intellectual ability as measured by IQ tests, less than 1 percent of African Americans (compared with around 20 percent of whites) qualify for success in these cognitively demanding fields.[60] Gottfredson's research suggests that the entire ideology of proportional representation is fatally flawed because it insists upon racial parity when groups in fact show widely differing levels of measured ability. Her findings imply that in a meritocratic society we should expect to find whites occupying most high-paying and relatively prestigious jobs such as physician, professor, and engineer, and blacks concentrated in low-paying and less cognitively demanding jobs such as truck driver, meat-cutter, and mail carrier.

Contrary to the Supreme Court's finding in *Griggs v. Duke Power* that standardized tests producing racially disparate results offer presumptive proof of discrimination, Richard Herrnstein and Charles Murray argue that such tests merely measure real differences of cognitive ability. Additionally, *The Bell Curve* summarizes a body of research to show that general ability tests are better predictors of success on the job than tests which seek to measure the particular features of each task. The reason for this, they argue, is that specific skills can be memorized and routinized, but more intelligent workers adapt to the changing needs of a work environment. Herrnstein and Murray present evidence that IQ differences even affect performance, although more weakly, on such relatively low-grade jobs as auto mechanic and restaurant busboy.[61]

The appeal of the new IQ research is its explanatory power: it seems to account for why there is a two-to-four-year gap in academic performance as measured by the National Assessment of Educational Progress between black and white students of the same age. It appears to explain why blacks are underrepresented at selective universities (for example, there are only five black mathematicians at America's twenty-five top-ranked universities) and in intellectually demanding jobs (less than 2 percent of the nation's scientists are black) and overrepresented in classes for the mentally retarded.[62] Also, since Jews and Asians consistently produce average scores above 100, their higher cognitive ability seems to account for why these two groups demonstrate impressive results in the academic and the economic sectors, as well as in prizes and awards for science and scholarship.[63] Some scholars even invoke IQ data to explain the high level of prosperity in Europe, the rising tide of economic achievement in Asia, the moderate standard of living in South and Central America, and the extreme underdevelopment of most of the continent of Africa. John Baker in his book *Race* argues that a low IQ accounts for the civilizational achievements of blacks which "have on the whole been disappointing, despite all the improvements in facilities for their education."[64]

The recent IQ data carry unquestionable political implications in the United States as well, because they suggest that racial preferences are futile and a virtual guarantee of economic inefficiency for private companies and the government. Moreover, IQ differences suggest the circumstances of poverty and deprivation in which blacks find themselves in America today are not the cause, but the result, of low intelligence. It is hard not to hear the triumphant roar of the white supremacist: "Forget about the legacy of racism and discrimination: these people are naturally stupid."

NOT IN OUR GENES

The science of IQ testing has come under severe criticism from its very inception in the early part of this century.[65] The academic critics are few in number but formidable in polemical skill, with many allies in the media. Most of the criticism has focused on five themes: intelligence is a vague and undefined concept; racial differences in test scores are meaningless because the concept of race is meaningless and races have more in common than divides them; tests reflect environmental rather than hereditary qualities; IQ tests are racially and culturally biased against minorities and specifically blacks; and finally, the motives of the testers are racist and their conclusions can be used to justify discrimination. Let us examine each of these claims.

The first argument, which is perhaps the oldest, is that IQ testing is a kind of meaningless numerology because it measures something that eludes clear definition. Intelligence, in this view, is a kind of phantom concept that cannot be captured in tests of verbal, spatial, and reasoning skill. "No one really knows what intelligence is," Ashley Montagu writes in *Race and IQ.* "Intelligence is what the intelligence tests test."[66] Writing in the *Journal of Black Studies,* African American psychologist Robert Williams argues that IQ simply cannot pretend to measure "the ambiguity and senselessness of the nature of intelligence."[67] The partial validity of this argument is conceded by most psychologists, including the controversial Arthur Jensen. "Intelligence, like electricity, is easier to measure than to define," Jensen admits.[68] Psychologist Louis Thurstone distinguishes between several kinds of intelligence: primary mental abilities such as verbal facility and comprehension; numerical abilities such as computational and math skills, and reasoning ability such as skill at classification and logical deduction.[69] Raymond Cattell wrote about fluid intelligence and crystallized intelligence, the one measuring adaptive mental skills, the other accumulated knowledge and capacity.[70]

The concept of intelligence, like that of health, is hard to define except in general terms, yet the entire medical field relies on the distinction between health and sickness. Despite disagreement about how precisely to describe intelligence, few people doubt that human beings differ in the degree to which they demonstrate intelligent thought or behavior. The concept of general intelligence or g is like general athletic ability: it doesn't deny specific skills but implies some underlying capacity that athletes in different sports share. Even if intelligence is simply defined as that which IQ tests test, the capacity being measured is clearly crucial if it can be shown to correlate with and perhaps to produce results in terms of creativity, scholarship, inventions, and other forms of achievement. Psychologists in the field argue that, definitional quibbles aside, there is no reason that carefully devised tests cannot measure the ability of individuals as well as groups to produce specifically enumerated and socially relevant outcomes.

This is not to say that intelligence is the only important social value, or even the most important one. IQ should not be confused with morality: psychopaths and murderers and Nazis often demonstrate above-average intelligence.[71] In his book *Excellence,* John Gardner correctly observes that "there are those whose excellence involves doing something well, and those whose excellence lies in being the kind of people they are."[72] Advocates of IQ testing such as Jensen, Herrnstein, and Murray admit this and deny that they are trying to measure human moral worth. Moreover, there are different kinds of ability and talent, and IQ tests only measure verbal, logistical, and visuospatial abilities. These are crucial for productivity and material growth in modern society, but as Howard Gardner argues in *Multiple Intelligences,* there are other extracurricular talents that matter, and they are not the same talents on display when we take the WAIS or the SAT: musical intelligence of the kind found in Mozart and Louis Armstrong; kinetic or bodily facility which we see in dancers and athletes; interpersonal intelligence, which refers to our ability to relate to others; and intrapersonal intelligence, which describes our ability to understand ourselves. Gardner does not deny the importance of g or general intelligence, but argues that "outside of school tasks" other kinds of smarts matter too.[73]

Even when it comes to material success, in a capitalist society it is not cognitive capacity of the kind measured by IQ tests that alone determines achievement. To succeed in a business venture, perhaps to enter one at all, one must be willing to take prudent risk. To be a good salesperson, one must be able to put customers at ease. For some jobs, it helps to be good-looking or at least skilled in making oneself presentable. As the archetype of the absent-minded professor suggests, intellectually gifted people often lack what Robert Sternberg calls "practical intelligence," which is the ability to work out problems in the real world—very different from solving them on a multiple-choice test.[74] None of this is very controversial; advocates of IQ testing do not contend that *g* measures all capacities, only that it measures basic reasoning ability which is a crucial index of performance and success.

THE MEANING OF RACE

The second argument contesting the validity of racial differences in intelligence derives from the legacy of Boasian relativism. It holds that the concept of race is dubious because racism is a human invention or (in academic jargon) a "social construct." Henry Louis Gates, Jr. argues that the concept of race is a biological "misnomer," a mere "metaphor," because "who has seen a black or red person, a white, yellow or brown person? These terms are arbitrary constructs, not reports of reality."[75] Similarly Christopher Hitchens contends that "scientific advance confirms that there is only one human race," and Steven Holmes writes in the *New York Times* that when the concept of race is "applied to biology, things get murky."[76] A recent cover story in *Newsweek* endorsed the notion that races are social and not biological categories.[77]

In one sense this argument is absolutely convincing: racial categories as employed by the U.S. government have no scientific basis. African Americans are regarded as a distinct race even though the group includes millions of mixed-race individuals, such as Whitney Houston and Lani Guinier, some of whom are so light skinned that they could pass for white.[78] Hispanics cannot be considered a race because there are white, brown, and black Hispanics; at best, Hispanics are a mestizo people who make up a cultural or linguistic group. As for Asians, the classification is geographic rather than racial: such groups as the Chinese and East Indians are biologically distinct and do not even share a common history. And other groups—the Polynesians, for example—are so mixed racially that they defy classification.[79]

Yet these facts produce an anomaly: If the concept of race is entirely fictional, shouldn't all civil rights laws which rely on racial classification be struck down by the Supreme Court as meaningless and unconstitutionally vague? Steven Holmes moves quickly to prevent such a conclusion, insist-

ing that despite their apparent uselessness, racial classifications nevertheless provide "a fine standard for measuring disparities in housing, income,
or employment."[80] Christopher Hitchens explains the apparent contradiction: while race does not exist, "what we still do seem to have are all these
racists."[81] Apparently race is a dubious concept while racism is real enough.

Does this really make any sense? Race may indeed be a social construct
as Henry Louis Gates, Jr. suggests, yet such constructs often provide reliable transcripts of reality. The theories of gravity and relativity were constructed by human beings, yet they are also accurate descriptions of the
laws and workings of the physical universe. "Height" is a social construct,
yet tall and short people do exist. "Racism" is a social construct, yet presumably the term does refer to real people and real-world phenomena.
The concepts of "male" and "female" are social constructs in that they are
definitional contrivances. But it does not follow that the gender distinction between men and women is the product of social fantasy, or that men
and women would cease to be different if only society stopped labeling
them differently.

As Christopher Hitchens suggests, there are common features possessed by human beings of all races. All blood is red when exposed to the
elements, and the four blood types A, B, AB, and O are found in all
human populations. Human beings can also produce children with members of other races, without the offspring being biologically deficient in
any way. It is also a fact that there are no distinct or undiluted races.[82]
Louis Snyder writes, "The peoples of the world have become so intermingled biologically that there is no possibility of the existence of an absolutely pure race anywhere."[83] Yet racial groups also differ in the prevalence or
scarcity of certain features and qualities, usually produced by inbreeding
over time, and measured in terms of blood groups and gene frequencies.
As L. C. Dunn puts it with scientific precision, "A race is a population of
related intermarrying individuals which differs from other populations in
the relative commonness of certain hereditary traits."[84]

The dispute, therefore, is not over whether groups exhibit real differences, but only about where to draw lines of demarcation. Admittedly, scientists and scholars disagree on the best system of classification for
human beings, or on how many races there are. Giuseppe Sergi argued
that there are only two races: people with long heads and people with
round heads, whom he termed Euro-Africans and Euro-Asiatics. William
Boyd agreed with Johann Blumenbach: there are five races. Louis Agassiz
was willing to settle for eight. Carleton Coon maintained that there are

nine. Thomas Henry Huxley proposed eleven races, later changing his count to nineteen. Joseph Birdsell insisted on thirty-two, including "Hindus," "Turkics," "Tibetans," "Guegians," "Neo-Hawaiians," and "Negritos."[85] Critics of IQ testing exploit this taxonomic variety to suggest that racial classification is both arbitrary and meaningless. Anthropologist Jared Diamond argues that "depending on whether we classified ourselves by antimalarial genes, lactase, fingerprints or skin color, we could place Swedes in the same race as either Xhosas, Fulani, the Ainu of Japan, or Italians."[86]

Of course racial classifications are variable in that they involve a human decision to categorize in this way rather than that, but it does not follow that these classifications do not describe real differences in genetic composition (genotype) or its manifestations (phenotype). Clearly human beings do differ biologically and it is difficult for scholars to avoid some system of classification. Categorization is the link between sense perception and cognition. And the presence of intermediate shades does not eliminate the possibility of valid racial classifications any more than the existence of twilight eliminates the division between day and night. As anthropologist Alice Brues puts it, "The visible differences between different populations of the world tell everyone that there is *something* there."[87] Races differ in degree rather than kind—as we make our way from Southern to Northern Europe, the population of blue-eyed people keeps increasing—but along this continuum it is possible to make distinctions. Most anthropologists and biologists agree on the existence of three broad racial groups: the Caucasoid, the Negroid, and the Mongoloid. These groups are conventionally described as whites, blacks, and Asians.[88] Critics have gone to great lengths to prove that these groupings are too vague; for example, there are blacks who have blue eyes and Caucasians who have curly hair. Yet there are hardly any Caucasians who have all the physical elements that are identified with Negroes, and hardly any Negroes who are not mixed-race and yet are confused with whites because they are phenotypically Caucasian. "If I took a hundred people from sub-Saharan Africa, a hundred from Europe, a hundred from Southeast Asia, took away their clothing and other cultural indicators, and asked somebody at random to sort them out, I don't think they'd have any trouble at all," remarks anthropologist Vincent Sarich. "Race is a natural and not an arbitrary category."

The real issue, Sarich and others argue, is whether observed variations of physical appearance are outward manifestations of differences of intellect and temperament. In other words, is race a reliable marker for deeper qualities that are highly valued? This question is not answered by pointing out, as Farai Chideya does, that racial groups have more in common than they have differences.[89] Undoubtedly the full range of physical, intellectual, and temperamental qualities may be found within all groups, and moreover average differences between groups are not so great that they exceed variation within each particular group. This fact, however, only serves to refute those who argue that *all* members of one group outscore or outperform *all* members of another group. But since virtually no one holds this position, the existence of variation within groups does not invalidate the importance of measurable differences between groups. An example may help to clarify the point. Biologically, men and women have more shared traits than differences. It is also a fact that, in genetic terms, human beings and chimpanzees have more in common than separates them.[90] But none of this means that the differences between men and women, or between human beings and animals, are insignificant. Just as variation among individuals explains why some individuals perform better than others, so variation between groups could explain why some groups do better than others.

HEREDITY VS. ENVIRONMENT

Is intelligence inborn or is it the product of environment? Although the popular definition of intelligence as a kind of native ability suggests its inborn quality, psychologists are virtually unanimous in declaring IQ to be a product both of genes and the environment, each interacting with the other.[91] It is not very helpful to pose the question as one of whether IQ is a product of genes or environment, since genetic tendencies are expressed through the medium of environment, just as athletic potential is demonstrated through running fast, jumping high, and so on. Consequently, the sensible question to ask is: to what degree are variations in IQ shaped by nature as opposed to nurture?

The reluctance to address this question seems to spring from the assumption that if intelligence is hereditary to a considerable degree, it cannot be changed or raised. But this assumption, which arises out of a relativist fear that nature might provide an unalterable ground for social inequality, is false. Traits that are biological can be altered not just medically, as in the case of surgery to eliminate inherited maladies, but also through changes in environment and culture. Myopia is largely hereditary, yet this natural defect can be corrected through eyeglasses or contact lenses. By contrast, some environmentally acquired traits like Henry Kissinger's foreign accent are very hard to change.

IQ critics such as Leon Kamin and Richard Lewontin have for years insisted that there is no basis for regarding variations in IQ to be hereditary. In 1974, Leon Kamin argued that "there is no reason to reject the hypothesis that IQ is simply not heritable." Elsewhere Kamin took an agnostic position. "We can make no statement at all about how heritable intelligence might be. We cannot measure such capacities and abilities."[92] In 1993 Richard Lewontin wrote, "We know nothing about the heritability of human temperamental and intellectual traits."[93] Kamin's and Lewontin's argument has collapsed in recent years as a result of a number of reliable studies which show that the hereditary contribution to individual variations in IQ can be measured. The most interesting and compelling way scholars do this is through the study of identical and fraternal twins. Identical twins have the same genes, whereas fraternal or nonidentical twins have about half their genes in common. By comparing the IQs of monozygotic or identical twins raised separately and dizygotic or fraternal twins raised together, psychologists can try to isolate the relative contributions of genes and environment to human intelligence.

After extensive research since 1979 on more than a thousand pairs of monozygotic and dizygotic twins, of whom 128 pairs were reared in different homes, Thomas Bouchard and his colleagues at the University of Minnesota's Center for Twin and Adoption Research found that identical twins, even when raised in different environments from a very early age, remain extremely close to each other in IQ. Meanwhile fraternal twins, even when raised together, maintain IQ gaps that do not automatically close as a consequence of their shared environment. Based on the twin studies, Bouchard calculates the heritability of IQ at approximately 0.7 or 70 percent.[94] Similar findings have been published by geneticist Robert Plomin. Long a proponent of the importance of environment in shaping intelligence and personality, Plomin's recent research has convinced him and many of his colleagues that genes and inheritance play an important role not just in IQ but also in shaping "parenting, childhood actions, television viewing, peer groups, work environments, education and socioeconomic status." These are clearly environmental outcomes, but Plomin insists on what he terms "the nature of nurture," which means that genes seek out propitious environments: "to some extent individuals create their own experiences for genetic reasons."[95]

In the face of mounting evidence against the zero heritability hypothesis, Stephen Jay Gould has grudgingly admitted that it is "trivially true" that IQ has a genetic basis and that "it is hard to find any broad aspect of human performance that has no heritable component."[96] Leon Kamin has also recanted, conceding in a book coauthored with Richard Lewontin that a human being is not a *tabula rasa* at birth and that both genes and environment shape human intelligence and behavior.[97] As these concessions suggest, there is now widespread agreement among scholars that intelligence is to a significant degree inherited and claims about the infinite plasticity of human nature, which trace back to the Boasian school, should be regarded as refuted. Although he has been attacked in the popular media as biased and bigoted, Arthur Jensen's conclusion turns out to be true: "The small handful of dissenters who argue that genetic factors play no part in IQ differences are not unlike the few persons living today who claim that the earth is flat."[98]

TRANSRACIAL ADOPTION

IQ critics such as Richard Lewontin and Stephen Jay Gould have retreated to a fallback argument which they claim is decisive. They have repeatedly deplored what they take to be the fallacy of using within-group heredity to prove between-group heredity. Lewontin writes, "The fundamental error of Jensen's argument is to confuse heritability of a character within a population with heritability of the difference between two populations."[99] Stephen Jay Gould offers an example to prove this point: height is largely hereditary within groups, yet there may be substantial differences in height between two genetically similar American Indian populations one of which is raised in utterly deprived circumstances.[100]

Logically this is unassailable, although Lewontin and Gould are attacking a position that none of the leading hereditarians hold.[101] Moreover, for Lewontin's and Gould's point to have any relevance to the black-white IQ gap one would have to show an enormous difference in the environmental circumstances between blacks and whites as a group. Historically, it is not hard to show a huge chasm between opportunities available to whites and those available to blacks.[102] Blacks in the rural South even had far fewer opportunities than blacks elsewhere: in a little-known study conducted in the 1970s, Arthur Jensen attributed IQ differences between blacks in rural Georgia and blacks in California wholly to differences in environment, specifically to racism and lack of opportunities.[103] Today, however, it seems implausible to believe that external environmental factors such as racism and lack of opportunity are wholly responsible for the IQ gap. The reason is that if a trait is heritable to a considerable degree, there has to be a huge environmental gap in order for average discrepancies in observed performance to be completely attributable to external circumstances. "For the racial differences to be entirely environmental," Herrnstein and Murray write, "the average environment of blacks would have to be at the 6th percentile of the distribution of environments among whites."[104] That such a gap exists they consider unlikely.

The best way to analyze the effect of environment on the intelligence of blacks is to study the children of transracial adoption.[105] Stephen Jay Gould points to evidence of "impressive IQ scores for poor black children adopted into affluent and intellectual homes."[106] Gould's argument is supported by the results of a 1961 study, in which researchers tracked down 264 of the 4,000 or so illegitimate offspring produced during the Allied occupation of Germany between black American soldiers and white German women and raised by their mothers. The researchers compared the IQ of these postwar children to those of 83 illegitimate offspring of white American troops and found no significant difference. One problem with the study is that the IQ of the fathers was unknown—if military selection procedures assured that black and white soldiers had roughly equal intelligence, then the results of the study could not be taken as representative of the black and white population. Despite this caveat, the study is rightly invoked to support environment as the primary basis for intelligence differences.[107]

What Gould fails to discuss is the fact that the results of the German study have been largely overwhelmed by the findings of perhaps the most famous examination of transracial adoption conducted in America. Sandra Scarr, Richard Weinberg, and Irwin Waldman administered IQ tests to more than four hundred adopted children, virtually all from poor or disadvantaged backgrounds. Since all the children, white, black, and mixed-race, were adopted by relatively affluent and well-educated families, Scarr and her colleagues hypothesized that an improved environment would considerably raise measured intelligence across racial lines, producing a rough parity between racial groups. The children were tested for improvements over several years, and their IQs at age seven and seventeen were recorded for comparison.

Scarr, Weinberg, and Waldman first reported their results in 1976 and they were encouraging: by that time, IQ levels for all groups escalated, with the white average reaching 112, the mixed-race average reaching 109, and the black average reaching 97. These figures were consistently lower than the IQs of the adoptive parents as well as their biological offspring, and they continued to show indications of racial gaps, yet they suggested the optimistic result that being in a richer ambiance undoubtedly boosts IQ for all racial groups. But when Scarr and her colleagues did follow-up tests in 1986, they found that IQ levels for all racial groups had plummeted. Now the white average was down to 106, the mixed-race average down to 99, and the black average down to 89. In other words, blacks scored only four points above the nationwide black average of 85 after more than a decade of being placed in a relatively favorable environment.

Scarr, Weinberg, and Waldman emphasize that there is no way to prove that IQ differences between groups are hereditary without exposing representative cohorts of each group to identical social environments, which is virtually impossible to do. And Scarr and her colleagues highlight the hopeful result that "being reared in the culture of the tests and the culture of the schools benefits all children's IQ scores."[108] Yet their results also show that even when black children are subjected to the most radical environmental change, the ameliorative effects seem transient and quite small. "If our studies showed that at age 18, blacks and whites had identical IQs, then we would have refuted the notion that there are hereditary differences between the two groups," Scarr says. "But our data do not permit us to reject that hypothesis. And our results show that changing socioeconomic opportunities will not by itself close the IQ gap."

THE SOCIOECONOMIC FALLACY

Whatever their source, group differences in intelligence and achievement are proving very difficult to eliminate, as many liberal scholars and activists have discovered in recent years. The record of remedial education in the United States over the past generation illustrates this failure. Remedial education was based on the premise that the primary reason for racial differences in test scores was lack of opportunity, generated by a long history of discrimination. In this view, blacks who were disproportionately poor may have developed a "culture of poverty" which contributed to an ethic of underachievement. Popularized by Oscar Lewis, the "culture of poverty" thesis held that poor people who frequently belong to minority groups develop attitudes and behaviors that are an adaptation to chronic joblessness and social immobility. The effect of these cultural patterns, however, is to exacerbate these conditions. Thus begins a vicious cycle of poverty and underachievement.[109] Since the 1960s, thoughtful liberals have been forced to acknowledge two major disappointments. The first is that despite hundreds of millions of dollars of funding and a wide range of experimental approaches over the past three decades, remedial programs to raise performance have proved disappointing, showing minimal or no effects. "What we have learned," says psychologist Rogers Elliott, "is that we have to be cautious about ambitious claims to raise IQ scores, which are to a large degree media hype."

In the 1980s high hopes were attached to the Milwaukee Project, which at the cost of millions of dollars subjected preschool African American children to a six-year program of intensive stimulation. At first the press reported sizable improvements in IQ and performance, but three years later the children's scores had reverted to the below-normal range, only slightly above the low level at which they started.[110] Reviewing other similar initiatives, John Ogbu writes, "Even the most ardent advocates of early intervention programs now admit that the projects have not thus far succeeded . . . in enabling poor and black children to perform at the same rate as their white middle-class peers."[111]

Similarly Head Start programs targeted at preschool children in poor families have spent billions of dollars annually on hundreds of thousands of young people, seeking to raise their intellectual capacity and performance. Head Start is a comprehensive socioeconomic and remedial program which includes parental involvement in education, better nutrition, as well as medical and psychological services. Yet contrary to periodic good-news reports in the media, scholarly reviews of the effect of Head Start are consistent: children report initial improvement, but gains in the first grade are typically reduced by the third grade and disappear by the sixth grade.[112]

Despite funding levels in excess of $5 billion a year, Chapter I of the Elementary and Secondary Education Act, the government's most ambitious program for educationally deprived children, reports equally modest results.[113] Consequently the liberal rationale for continuing and even expanding these programs has generally shifted from the intellectual to the social. And undoubtedly such social effects as providing poor children with dental services and involving their parents in education are desirable. A case can even be made for environments that provide disadvantaged children with a kind of vacation from the trauma of their harsh worlds.

Many liberals have been frustrated, however, in their initial and main expectation for such programs: to improve cognitive skills and educational performance.

Liberal faith in the "culture of poverty" diagnosis and in remedial programs as a solution has been further shaken by the discovery that IQ and performance gaps between groups do not appear to be socioeconomic but rather ethnic. For years, textbooks and media reports exhaustively documented the correlation between socioeconomic class and test scores, the implication being that coming from a wealthy family helps you do better on the test. The conventional wisdom is expressed in a recent article in the *Journal of Blacks in Higher Education:* "As family income levels rise, SAT scores also rise. Since black median family income in the U.S. is less than . . . white family income, black income differentials may explain much of the SAT score shortfall."[114] But this claim is refuted by data showing that even controlling for socioeconomic status, blacks still do far worse on tests than whites and Asians.

Consider the results of the Scholastic Aptitude Test for 1994. According to data provided by the College Board, at every socioeconomic level, beginning with children coming from families earning less than $10,000 a year and ending with children coming from families earning more than $60,000 a year, whites and Asians routinely outperformed blacks. Moreover, the racial gap consistently increased at higher levels of socioeconomic status. Blacks who came from families earning less than $10,000 a year scored about 150 points lower than whites and Asians of the same socioeconomic background. Blacks who came from families earning more than $60,000 a year scored approximately 200 points lower than whites and Asians of the same background. Stunningly, blacks who came from families earning more than $60,000 a year scored lower in the aggregate math and verbal score than whites and Asians who came from families earning less than $10,000 a year.[115]

On the assumption that income provides only a partial clue to socioeconomic status, in 1994 the College Board released data correlating SAT scores with the level of parental education of the students taking the test. Once again, the results were startling. Blacks whose parents had only a high school diploma scored more than 150 points lower than whites and Asians whose parents had the same level of education. Blacks from college educated families were nearly 200 points below whites and Asians of similar family educational background. Indeed blacks whose parents had graduate degrees scored lower on the verbal and math section of the test than whites and Asians whose parents only had high school diplomas.[116] The real problem, Dana Takagi observes in her book *The Retreat from Race,* is not class but "racial differences in academic achievement."[117]

Even taking into account socioeconomic class differences, the racial IQ gap between blacks and whites remains large: about 10–12 points.[118] Moreover, the gap between whites and blacks of high socioeconomic status is larger than that between whites and blacks of lower socioeconomic status.[119] In other words, it is a mistake to imagine that as black socioeconomic levels improve, the IQ gap will automatically disappear. In addition, it is a statistical fallacy to correct for socioeconomic differences and then compare racial groups for the simple reason that intelligence affects socioeconomic status. In other words, if intelligent families are on average more affluent, then the correlation between family income and high scores may simply be the result of a third factor, namely IQ, propelling both figures upward.[120] Socioeconomic corrections frequently have the misleading effect of comparing a small fraction of top-scoring African Americans with a very large group of whites of average performance.

My conclusion is that it is an illusion to believe that racial differences between blacks and whites are largely a phenomenon of socioeconomic class and that such differences will disappear with the current menu of preschool and public-school government interventions. Thus we should be skeptical of future reports of the latest remedial panacea, although it is certainly possible that new initiatives, heretofore unknown, will overcome our justified skepticism.

THE QUESTION OF CULTURAL BIAS

In recent years IQ tests have come under strong indictment for racial and cultural bias. Such charges have been launched by groups such as the Association of Black Psychologists, the NAACP, the National Education Association, and the Mexican American Legal Defense Fund. These organizations have expressed their opposition to all forms of IQ and standardized testing, apparently on the grounds that the results of such testing show substantial racial differences in test scores.[121] Alleging cultural bias, James Comer and Alvin Poussaint advise black families, "Beware of IQ tests for black children."[122] J. L. Dillard writes, "It is no more a disgrace to make a low score on the other man's test than it is to lose money playing poker with the other fellow's deck of cards."[123]

The accusation of cultural bias is a direct product of the assumptions of cultural relativism. Since all cultures are equal, tests that show group differences are presumed to be culturally biased. In other words, the allegation of cultural bias emanates from the existence of racial differences itself. In this view, tests could only avoid accusations of bias by producing identical group average scores. Cultural relativists argue that group cultures can only be evaluated or criticized from within. Otherwise an external scale of values is being arbitrarily imposed on a particular culture, which is regarded as inferior when it is merely different. In this view, if young people from different ethnicities are socialized differently, then they are not likely to approach the test from the same cultural background. Consequently they cannot be expected to score equally well.

In its radical form, the charge of cultural bias is unanswerable, because it dogmatically refuses to consider the possibility that groups could score differently on a legitimate test. In most areas other than race, such an argument is not likely to command rational assent. If we proclaimed at the outset that men and women are (or should be) equally tall and dismissed all tape measures that consistently show one group to be, on average, taller than the other, most scholars would regard us, rather than the tape measure, as in need of professional attention. In more moderate forms, however, the accusation of bias does not insist outright upon equal outcomes, but expresses doubt that measurements which produce unequal outcomes are valid.

IQ critics such as Richard Lewontin, Steven Rose, and Leon Kamin have publicized horror stories in which students are asked to answer questions that are heavily loaded with cultural content. During World War I, we hear, the U.S. army asked immigrants to identify products manufactured by Smith and Wesson, and to give the names of professional baseball teams. One test showed foreign newcomers a picture of a tennis court without the net and asked them to identify what was missing. Even today, Richard Lewontin writes, things have hardly improved. "What do IQ tests measure? They ask such things as: Who was Wilkins McCawber? What is the meaning of *sudiferous?* What should a girl do if a boy hits her (Hitting him back is *not* the correct answer.)" Lewontin concludes, "How do we know that someone who does well on such a test is intelligent?"[124] Such examples almost always rely on a small number of cases usually drawn from tests administered decades ago when psychological testing was in its very early stages. Since then tests have been carefully prepared and extensively reviewed to minimize if not eliminate problems of bias, so that the predictive power of the tests is greatly increased.

Contrary to Lewontin's claim, virtually no tests administered today require a familiarity with baseball teams or an acquaintance with Wilkins McCawber. Rather, they include such things as block designs, in which plastic blocks each with two red sides, two white sides and two red-and-white sides must be assembled into a given pattern. Tests also include mazes, in which young people are asked to track their way to the other end without running into a dead end. Tests typically include basic mathematical problems: if a bicycle can travel at 15 miles an hour, how far can it go in 40 minutes? Some tests seek to measure visuospatial ability: in a multiple choice question, if a cone is rotated in the manner depicted in a diagram, which of the four given cones represents the next position in its journey? Then there are digit span tests, which require the subject to repeat a series of three, four, or five digits—a test of simple memory—and then to repeat them backwards—a test of conceptual ability because the mind has to picture the digits in reverse order. IQ tests such as Raven's Progressive Matrices and the Cattell Culture Fair test have very little specific cultural content. The Raven's test includes a series of designs printed on flat surfaces, and the problem is to detect uniform features running through and expanding regularly in the sequences of designs. Only blindness, it seems, could prevent someone from taking this test. Similarly the Cattell test offers rows of drawings that form a logical series; the problem is to select from given multiple choices the item that completes the series. No writing is required on either of these tests.

Hundreds of studies of black and white performance have been conducted, and scholars have reached what appears to be a strong consensus: the tests are not biased against African Americans, who do no better on verbal questions than on mathematics questions, whose scores do not improve when tests move from high cultural content to little or no cultural content. Indeed black Americans do worse on IQ tests than Eskimos and immigrants from Far Eastern countries whose way of life is far more distant from white middle-class norms. African American performance is generally poorest on tests that require conceptual, visuospatial, and reasoning ability. By and large, blacks have no trouble identifying the missing net from the tennis court.[125] In addition, as Stephen Jay Gould admits, IQ tests predict academic success equally well for blacks as for whites.[126]

Given these embarrassing findings, scholars and activists have tried for many years to come up with a test on which blacks do not do worse than other groups. After all, if blacks, Hispanics, and American Indians are not less intelligent than whites, there must be some test that actually shows this. Perhaps the best example in this category is the Goodenough Draw-A-Man test, devised by Florence Goodenough in the 1920s and administered to children from some fifty countries around the world.[127] In the Draw-A-Man test, children between the ages of six and seven are asked simply to draw a person including as many features as they can remember. American Indian students outperform whites on this test, which is sometimes taken as proof that genuinely culture-free tests allow the manifestation of true intelligence. Yet even the Draw-A-Man test proved to have cultural limitations when researchers found that Bedouin children from Arab countries scored lowest in the world, apparently in large part because Islamic doctrine prohibits representative art as a form of idolatry.[128] The most serious problem with tests like Draw-A-Man, however, is that they do not seem to predict performance in anything except the specific task involved. The results of most IQ tests parallel each other closely because they all measure general reasoning ability, whereas the results of the Draw-a-Man test stand virtually alone.[129] Another classic in the same genre is a test called the Black Intelligence Test of Cultural Homogeneity, developed by Robert Williams. It includes questions such as the following:

> Who wrote the Negro National Anthem? (a) Langston Hughes, (b) James Weldon Johnson, (c) Paul Laurence Dunbar, (d) Frederick Douglass
> A yawk is: (a) gun, (b) fishing hook, (c) high boat, (d) heavy coat
> I know you shame means: (a) you don't hear very well, (b) you are a racist, (c) you don't mean what you're saying, (d) you are guilty.[130]

Both the Draw-a-Man test and the Black Intelligence Test illustrate a sense in which IQ tests *are* culturally biased. IQ tests are not administered in a cultural vacuum. They measure skills and abilities that are highly valued in a modern technological society. And those skills and abilities are culture bound. Consequently, it is futile to measure them with a culture-free or even a culture-fair test. Indeed the English psychologist Philip Vernon has categorically asserted that "there is no such thing as a culture-fair test, and never can be."[131] Psychologists across the spectrum are in general agreement on this point.[132] "All definitions of intelligence are shaped by the time, place and culture in which they evolve," Howard Gardner writes. "Placing logic and language on a pedestal reflects the values of our Western culture."[133]

Throughout history, various human communities have emphasized certain skills of survival and achievement and these vary enormously. American IQ tests do not measure, nor do they seek to measure, the ability to herd sheep in the Sudan, or the capacity to elude a hungry lion, or the skills to survive in the mountains of Tibet. The requirements of life in the Arctic or the rain forests are likely to differ considerably from those in the West. Indeed skills such as mathematical equations and reading comprehension may be largely irrelevant for successful adaptation in those environments.[134] It is possible to envision a wide range of techniques and skills that are ignored by IQ tests. We can imagine life in radically different social contexts in which the ensemble of modern requirements disappears or recedes into insignificance. If we lived on Mars, perhaps, we would not need the same kinds of communication, comprehension, and reasoning skills that our society demands. In communities that rely for subsistence on hunting, perceptual ability would most likely be far more important than numerical ability as a measure of relevant intelligence. But the fact is that we do not live in those worlds. IQ tests are biased in favor of the kind of intelligence sought in the modern world, because we have no choice but to inhabit it. As Andrew Hacker writes:

> Tests reflect not a racial or national corpus of knowledge, but a wider modern consciousness. Modern now stands for the mental and structural modes that characterize the developed world. It calls for a commitment to science and technology, as well as the skills needed for managing administrative systems. The modern world rests on a framework of communication and finance, increasingly linked by common discourse and rules of rationality.[135]

The issue is the functional utility of the tests, not their importance as a Platonic index of pure intelligence. Unlike, say, the Amish, who consciously reject modernity and many aspects of Western civilization—and are admired for it—African Americans and immigrants seek full membership in the institutions of the modern West: they want to be on the board at General Motors, they want tenured positions in the universities, they want political power. Those who embrace the goals of the contemporary West must be committed to the acquisition of the resources which are necessary to reach those ends.

Thus the charge that IQ tests are culturally biased is true but irrelevant. Tests are culturally biased in favor of those intellectual demands imposed by a changing and increasingly competitive global market. If blacks as a group lack those skills because they have not been exposed to the culture of reading comprehension and mathematical problem solving, then it is not the tests but black cultural mores that appear to require reform. Contrary to the assumptions of cultural relativism, the problem, it seems, is not test bias but the functional inadequacy of African American culture.

IS IQ TESTING RACIST?

Let us now take up the question of whether racial measurements of IQ are racist because they have historically served to promote nativism and bigotry, and because they justify segregation and discrimination against African Americans. Stephen Jay Gould's *The Mismeasure of Man* is largely devoted to an attack on the nineteenth century scientific racists. Gould writes, "What craniometry was for the nineteenth century, intelligence testing has become for the twentieth."[136] Charles Lane publicizes what he terms the "tainted sources" of *The Bell Curve* and Alvin Poussaint deplores the book's "racist effect."[137] Stefan Kuhl in *The Nazi Connection* insists that contemporary IQ testing bears "striking similarities to earlier studies that provided the scientific basis for Nazi measures."[138] The National Research Council worries that IQ data "could become a tool of racial and ethnic prejudice, generating feelings of superiority in some groups and inferiority in others."[139]

Gould's attack on the nineteenth-century phrenologists has gone largely unchallenged, mainly because the practice has been obsolete for the better part of a century. Without bothering to defend the craniologists, Arthur Jensen responded to Gould by arguing that current work in physical anthropology, psychometrics, and behavioral genetics cannot be tarred by associating it with late nineteenth-century and early twentieth-century tests which were admittedly devised when these modern sciences were in their primitive stage. Gould deserves little congratulation, in Jensen's view, for trying to "condemn the modern automobile by pointing out the faults of the Model T."[140]

Much more keenly felt, however, are the assaults by Gould, Kamin, and others on the motives of the leading early IQ testers such as H. H. Goddard, who brought IQ testing to America, or Lewis Terman, who developed the widely used Stanford-Binet test, or Robert Yerkes, who convinced the U.S. Army to test more than a million men during the World War I period. The racism of some of these early IQ theoreticians is hard to deny. In 1916 Terman wrote that low intelligence "is very common among Spanish-Indian and Mexican families and also among Negroes. Their dullness appears to be racial, or at least inherent in the family stocks from which they come. . . . From a eugenic point of view they constitute a grave problem because of their unusually prolific breeding."[141]

In the 1920s, psychologist Carl Brigham published *A Study of American Intelligence* which used the low IQ scores of immigrants from southern and eastern Europe to advocate that they be kept out and immigration restricted to people of Nordic heritage.[142] In his introduction to Brigham's book, Robert Yerkes wrote, "The author presents not theories or opinions but facts. No one of us as a citizen can afford to ignore the menace of race deterioration."[143] These psychological findings were trumpeted by popular authors such as Madison Grant and Lothrop Stoddard who campaigned aggressively against immigration and in favor of eugenic breeding.[144] Not only are such arguments morally repulsive, Leon Kamin argues, but he also maintains that advocates of eugenics like psychologist Henry Goddard administered tests which produced the ridiculous result that more than 80 percent of Jews, Russians, Hungarians, and Italians were "feebleminded." For Kamin and many others who rely on his claim, the self-evident absurdity of Goddard's conclusion is taken as irrefutable proof of the worthlessness of the tests and the racist motives of the testers.[145]

There is no denying that some of the early IQ testers were true believers in white supremacy and advocates of restricted immigration. How much influence they had on the Immigration Act of 1924 remains a matter of dispute. Historian Carl Degler, who has investigated the matter, reports that "the role of intelligence testing in the law's enactment was insignificant."[146] More seriously, when Mark Snyderman and Richard Herrnstein reviewed Goddard's early research, they found that for testing purposes he had preselected immigrants who showed signs of being of borderline intelligence or below. In other words, Goddard never claimed to be testing a representative sample of immigrants. On the contrary, he specifically stated that his study "makes no attempt to determine the percentage of feeble-minded among immigrants in general or even of the special groups named—the Jews, Hungarians, Italians and Russians."[147] No credence can be given to Kamin's account of the apparent unreliability of Goddard's tests in light of this evidence of scholarly ignorance or distortion.

Although Stefan Kuhl alleges that American and German hereditarians admired each other's work, there is no evidence that American IQ research inspired or supported Hitler's genocidal campaign to exterminate the Jews. IQ critics do charge, however, as Richard Lerner puts it in *Final Solutions,* that the consequences of attributing intellectual deficiencies to nature can lead to great atrocities, while the consequences of attributing them to environment are "less often socially pernicious."[148] The Nazis did advocate their own theories of racial supremacy and used them to justify mass killings—undoubtedly their hereditarian dogma about race helped to inspire genocide. What Lerner fails to mention, however, is that any computation of the casualties of hereditarianism would also have to admit that the opposite doctrine, which claims that human nature is infinitely plastic and can be remade in order to generate radical equality, has also been invoked to justify the mass murder of millions. Mao in China and Stalin in Russia have rivaled and even exceeded Hitler in the grisly business of human extermination, including massive systems of slave labor, and their excuse was not hierarchy but egalitarianism.

Because of their commitment to relativism, many American intellectuals seem peculiarly vulnerable to ignoring and apologizing for Marxist atrocities.[149] Indeed academic groups such as the American Anthropologist Association have consistently refused to condemn Communist mass murder in Afghanistan, Cambodia, and Ethiopia.[150] African Nobel laureate Wole Soyinka deplores the way in which Western liberals, who claim to be partisans of freedom, engaged in "passionate reconstructions of reality" and "tortuous rationalizations" for Stalinist and Marxist totalitarianism.[151] Eugene Genovese notes that while the collapse of Nazism produced a major moral accounting on the part of those who silently acquiesced in Hitler's crimes, the collapse of Soviet communism has generated no comparable soul-searching on the part of American leftist intellectuals.[152]

The deepest fear of IQ critics who employ the *reductio ad Hitlerum*—an argument is necessarily false if Hitler happened to share the same view—is the apocalyptic possibility of a revival of public pressures for eugenics and racial discrimination. Discussing Richard Herrnstein and Charles Murray, Adolph Reed raises the familiar specter of "extermination, mass sterilization and selective breeding."[153] Richard Lewontin warns that America might undo all its civil rights laws and revive the worst horrors of the *ancien régime:* "Should all black men be unskilled laborers and all black women clean other women's houses?"[154] Such concerns are not entirely unjustified, but they seem wildly exaggerated. They rely entirely for corroboration on the infrequent proposals of eccentrics, such as that of some California members of the high-IQ society Mensa who recently proposed euthanasia for the mentally defective.[155]

Yet if we have no reason to fear the Frankenstein-like experiments that Lewontin and others warn about, I am equally unconvinced by the argument, advanced by Richard Herrnstein and Charles Murray, that even though inherited IQ differences probably exist between the races, no policy implications follow and we can all celebrate multicultural difference and embrace Martin Luther King, Jr.'s precept to judge people as individuals, based on the content of their character. Herrnstein and Murray's reasons for arriving at this brisk conclusion are clear: they wish to forestall unpleasant questions about whether they favor a return to policies of officially sanctioned segregation and discrimination. Yet it is not clear that they have confronted the implications of their views. If IQ differences between racial groups are inherited and are substantial, then it is impossible to close the Pandora's Box and we have to ask the alarming questions: was the Southern racist position basically correct, and are some forms of segregation and discrimination justified?

An example may clarify why such an inquiry logically follows from Herrnstein and Murray's premises. Men are faster and stronger than women, which gives them a natural advantage in such sports as running and playing tennis. This does not mean that every man is quicker or more powerful than every woman; yet group differences do exist on average, and they are substantial. We may postulate that very few women could play competitively among the thousand highest-ranked male tennis players, or that the average female runner would fall between the 10th and the 15th percentile of male runners as a group. The consequence of such large differences, of course, is that (despite the protestations of some radical feminists) men and women do not compete against each other in running and in tennis. The reason is that such competition would be grossly unfair: women would lose virtually all the time. In order to avoid this, we have what may accurately be termed *segregation:* men and women compete in the same sport, but only against other members of their own group.

There are two implications to this argument, neither of which fit harmoniously into Herrnstein and Murray's vision of a race-blind society. The first is that sizable inherited IQ differences between groups do provide a rational basis under certain circumstances for segregation and for discrimination. After all, in terms of some conventional measures of academic achievement, blacks fall about two years behind whites of the same age. Does this mean that blacks who are old enough to be in the seventh grade should take fifth-grade courses? Michael Levin has called for both segregation and discrimination against blacks based on their alleged biological inferiority.[156] And the newsletter *American Renaissance,* which routinely reports IQ findings, welcomed *The Bell Curve* as "a remarkable achievement—a milestone on the road back to national sanity" and rejoiced that it may soon be possible for someone to stand up and say: "No I don't want blacks moving into the neighborhood because they are not like us."[157] Although these are extreme voices, liberal critics are correct that uninterrupted movement down this path would surely lead to unpleasant and unjust consequences.

The second implication of Herrnstein and Murray's work is that large inherited differences in IQ, far from undermining the case for affirmative action, as the authors intend, may actually strengthen it.[158] After all, if blacks cannot compete on a level playing field with whites and Asians, a humane argument can be made for preferences to artificially elevate their status. Since as John Rawls points out, people do not deserve their ration in the genetic lottery,[159] hereditary deficiencies can provide a strong ground for egalitarian correction. If nature produces radical inequality, then racial preferences on a permanent basis could be defended to raise blacks to the same plane as everyone else.

A new argument for affirmative action now emerges based not on the aspiration to equality of opportunity but on the evidence for cognitive equality. This is where contemporary liberalism appears to be headed. Consider the controversy early in 1995 at Rutgers University, where President Francis Lawrence, in a speech denouncing standardized tests and promoting affirmative action, blurted out that blacks don't have the "genetic hereditary background to have a higher average."[160] Although Lawrence insisted that he had misspoken, many believe that he had mistakenly spoken publicly a private conviction that since blacks cannot compete they should not be judged by the same standards as everyone else.

Consider also this: The National Merit Scholarship Board is so embarrassed about the tiny number of blacks who win its annual scholarships that it has established a "separate but equal" scholarship program for blacks.[161] This is liberal paternalism, which bears a close and uncanny resemblance to the old Southern paternalism. Like their Southern predecessors, many contemporary liberals seem to support racial preferences on the grounds that since blacks cannot compete, they should be treated philanthropically. Liberal segregation doesn't require geographical separation, but it does require a multiple-track racial system in which members of each group run within their own ethnic lanes. In this view, blacks continue to attend schools with whites, but they are admitted and judged by different standards. Blacks vote with whites, but they get specially designed minority districts. Blacks work alongside whites, but they are hired and promoted according to different criteria. Although implemented with a view to fighting racist claims of black inferiority, contemporary liberal social policy appears increasingly premised on precisely that assumption.

No one should be surprised if many liberal activists heatedly deny this; by their actions we should judge them.

To sum up, IQ tests are not automatically discredited by their disreputable origins—on this point the critics exaggerate their case—but tests which show substantial differences between racial groups do open the door to discrimination—on this point the critics are correct. What these critics fail to add, however, is that IQ gaps can be invoked to justify discrimination in favor of blacks as well as discrimination against blacks. Racists and liberal paternalists could both advocate preferences: the former to encourage survival of the fittest, the latter to ensure proportional success for the unfittest; the former to enable intellectually superior groups to forge ahead; the latter to forestall racial hierarchy, alienation, and conflict.

THE ICEMAN COMETH

Before conceding the natural basis of IQ differences and accepting the legitimacy of racial discrimination, however, let us examine the basis for critics' skepticism about how such gaps could have developed. Theories of natural inferiority, to be plausible, must account for the possible source of substantial inherited gaps in reasoning ability. The liberal assumption—articulated by Clifford Geertz—is that despite evolutionary changes "different groups of *homo sapiens* must be regarded as equally competent" because they "vary anatomically within a very narrow range."[162] Stephen Jay Gould has emphasized evolutionary theories that suggest that all human beings are descended from a common ancestor "Eve" who lived in Africa perhaps 100,000 years ago. Gould argues that such recent shared origins would not be likely to provide enough time for a "race gene" to develop. Indeed Gould triumphantly points out that "we have found no race genes . . . fixed in certain races and absent from all others."[163] Others like Christopher Hitchens and Susan Sperling seem to rely on Gould in repeating this claim.[164]

But Gould's argument is fallacious. First, it is no longer clear that all human beings have a recent shared origin. In a fascinating revival of polygenism, the "Eve" hypothesis has been strongly contested by what scientists call the "candelabra" hypothesis which holds that the races may have evolved separately under different climatic conditions in Asia, Africa, and Europe. Anthropologist Dennis Etler argues, "The evidence suggests that no one region of the world is the exclusive area from which modern humans evolved."[165] Since advocates of multiregional evolution like anthropologist Milford Wolpoff argue for a divergence of human populations perhaps a million years ago, this would be plenty of time for substantial racial variations to develop in both physical and mental characteristics.

In addition, the "race gene" argument dethrones a straw man. There is no gene for race, just as there is no gene for brown eyes or blue eyes. None of the experts in IQ testing have ever claimed that there is a specific gene or even an identifiable group of genes that produces the whole range of IQ differences. Rather, they assert that racial differences are polygenic: they are the result of different frequencies produced by large numbers of genes interacting in complex ways. Even under the "Eve" scenario, there is no scientific reason for why racial groups could not have evolved different frequency distributions of overlapping genes, resulting in marked variation among groups. Psychologist Lloyd Humphreys terms Gould's race-gene rhetoric and similar arguments to be "science fiction" and "political propaganda" calculated to deceive the ignorant.[166]

Yet the fact that racial differences in IQ could have developed does not mean that they did. For decades, advocates of IQ testing have struggled to give plausible cultural or evolutionary explanations for why Jews seem to score highest, why Asians score higher than whites, and why blacks score lowest of all groups. In one provocative theory—in an area that abounds with them—Hans Eysenck suggests that perhaps African Americans have relatively low intellectual ability because they were selected by slave traders on the basis of physical strength rather than intellectual prowess; Eysenck hints that perhaps the smartest ones got away.[167] Nathaniel Weyl accounts for high Jewish IQ scores and Jewish overrepresentation among entrepreneurs, lawyers, and scientists by hypothesizing that for most of Western history the most intelligent Christians joined the priesthood and took vows of celibacy, while the intelligent Jews became rabbis and traders and multiplied. Weyl also suggests that the Jewish population was "winnowed out" by centuries of persecution, leaving a residue of men and women of steely determination and superior intelligence.[168]

The most comprehensive theories that seek to explain racial gaps in IQ rely on the evolutionary concept of natural selection. Psychologist Richard Lynn argues that a tabulation of IQ test results from around the world shows a consistent pattern: Asians have the highest IQs, whites fall in the middle, and blacks are far behind. Lynn contends that black Africans have IQs virtually at the retarded level: 80 in Uganda and Ghana, 75 in Nigeria, 65 in Zaire, with an African average of about 70. Lynn theorizes that

Caucasians and especially Mongoloids who migrated to the cold climates of northern Europe and Asia were forced to contend with the cognitive demands of enduring mountainous terrain and frigid winters. By contrast, blacks remained in the relatively warm and benign latitudes, where they could survive without extensive use of their heads. In Lynn's view, whites and Asians were forced to develop, through natural selection, strong visuospatial abilities in order to make distinctions in a snow-driven environment. He writes of "the ability to isolate slight variations in visual stimulation from a relatively featureless landscape, such as the movement of a white Arctic hare against a background of snow and ice." Also, Lynn argues, whites and Asians evolved, out of necessity, such group characteristics as individual resourcefulness and collective future-oriented planning in order to capture and store food. Lynn adds that blacks, however, found the challenges of eating and clothing themselves relatively undemanding, and storage could even be counterproductive since food goes bad quickly in hot weather.[169]

An even more flamboyant theory comes from the Canadian psychologist J. Philippe Rushton. Rushton argues that races differ not simply in mean intelligence but in virtually every human characteristic: they have different brain sizes, brain weights, maturation rates, personality and temperament, sexual hormone levels, reproductive behavior, and social organization. Races even differ, Rushton maintains, in their rates of identical and fraternal twinning. He adds, "There is a black-white difference in testosterone levels." Rushton regards all these differences, including cultural differences, as having a genetic and specifically evolutionary origin. Rushton insists that, adjusted for body size, Asian brains are bigger than Caucasian brains, and Caucasian brains are bigger than Negroid brains. Drawing on some relatively old data, he also claims that (I was surprised to discover) Asian penises are smaller than Caucasian penises, and agrees with the earliest European racists: blacks have the largest penises. Rushton weaves these items into a theory that seeks to account for why Asians are the most intelligent and the most sexually restrained, while blacks are the least intelligent and the most promiscuous, with whites falling into the unremarkable middle. In a theory that calls to mind the Afrocentric distinction between "ice people" and "sun people," Rushton proposes that evolutionary pressures in early times imposed on Asians a "K" type reproductive strategy, in which Asians produce few eggs and work to maximize parental care of their offspring, while a different set of circumstances caused blacks to adopt an "r" strategy, in which they produce maximum offspring with minimum parental involvement. These different strategies, which optimize survival chances in intensely cold and warm climates respectively, Rushton argues, are central to an understanding of contemporary race differences in IQ and sexuality.[170]

What is one to make of these disturbing claims? Many biologists and physical anthropologists are dubious about these theories on scientific grounds, entirely apart from their inflammatory political content. First there is the questionable validity of drawing conclusions based on international comparisons of IQ tests. Since brain weight, brain protein, and DNA and RNA all increase during the early months of life, it is reasonable to assume that malnutrition could account for much or all of the measured deficiencies in African cognitive capacity. Arthur Jensen concedes that "prolonged severe malnutrition, as occurs in some Third World countries, can stunt mental growth by as much as 20 IQ points or more."[171] This would suggest a response that did not merely observe evolutionary differences, but worked to improve African infants' diets with milk and vitamin supplements in order to maximize the human potential of those children. Even more important, since IQ tests are normed on Western populations, and measure the kind of intelligence currently valued by modern technocratic society, it seems risky to administer them to rural Africans and then proclaim them intellectually deficient. How well would American students fare on an IQ test devised by the headmen of those tribes?

Finally there is the question of what scientists really know about the evolution of racial differences. Very few scholars doubt that blacks are now more susceptible to sickle-cell anemia because their ancestors in Africa developed immunities to malaria. The sickle-cell mutation, which is not unique to Africa, offers the malarial parasite less favorable breeding ground than normal cells do. Thus Africans could endure the mosquitos that quickly disabled and killed Europeans in earlier centuries.[172] Variations in skin color almost certainly evolved as a consequence of differential exposure to the ultraviolet radiation of the sun. Melanin, the colorizing agent in the skin, protects against sunburn and skin cancer. Light skin is valuable in temperate climates because it assures maximum penetration of sunlight and adequate supplies of vitamin D. Light skin may also be less vulnerable to frostbite, although it makes Caucasians more prone to skin cancer.[173] Other minor differences in stature, nose shape, and hair form could also have developed in this way. Some African peoples have longer limbs and bodies that diffuse heat more easily. Mongolians and Eskimos who live in the coldest climates have flatter noses which are less exposed to cold, and rounder frames that are better equipped for storing food and fat. The Mongolian epicanthic fold, or skin lining covering the eye, may have evolved in order to protect the eye from the glare and force of blizzards and snow drifts.[174] Yet these are only surmises by scholars who acknowledge that the precise evolutionary pressures operating upon different groups and the adaptive significance of particular racial features are not well understood. Why, for instance, do white males seem to go bald more frequently than males of other races? Why do the Bantus and the Pygmies, two of the world's tallest and shortest groups, inhabit the same tropical environment? Why does the skin of blacks and Asians seem to resist wrinkling, compared with that of whites? In many cases, there are no answers, only hypotheses.[175]

Although there is much in this area that remains to be discovered, most scholars now agree that the genes that account for racially distinguishing characteristics are a very small fraction of the human genetic makeup. Even if it is possible to identify some intellectual and temperamental differences between groups, scientists know of no evidence that the genes that produce physical differences between people are the same genes that produce mental or psychological differences. The melanocytes, for example, which are the cells that produce pigment in the skin, eyes, and hair, are not in any way connected with intellectual activity. It is not blackness that makes anyone dull or lazy, nor whiteness that makes anyone smart or hardworking; if this were so, albinos would be Nobel laureates. Even ardent hereditarians make this point: as one scholar writes, "Race and intelligence are not logically or scientifically related."[176]

Beyond this, however, the evolutionary argument raises further questions. It seems farfetched to believe that whites and Asians do well on American measures of academic achievement because their ancestors had to develop skills in storing food and hunting polar bears. James Flynn argues that theories of evolutionary adaptation can be tailored to fit virtually any set of facts. If blacks scored higher on IQ tests than whites, he writes, "it would be easy to argue that selective pressures were really more severe in the tropical jungle than in the Arctic cold." Flynn concludes, cautiously but sensibly, that Lynn and Rushton's evolutionary arguments are "too suspect to count."[177]

The plausibility of the evolutionary view must be set against its alternative, which is that groups score differently on IQ tests for cultural reasons. This alternative does not deny evolution, but builds upon it to argue that for *homo sapiens,* the most important agent of evolution has been cultural rather than biological. The reason is that, virtually unrivaled in nature, man has the ability to transcend biological instinct and creatively manipulate his circumstances. By contrast with insects, whose behavior is genetically fixed, human beings are capable of education and improvisation. Indeed it is this capacity, rather than brute strength, which is of the greatest survival value for humans. So while it is quite possible that the races developed different physical attributes in order to cope with evolutionary pressures, even under conditions of separate evolution, they could all have similar patterns of intellectual development as a consequence of encountering diverse but comparably demanding mental challenges. This is especially true of modern society. As Theodosius Dobzhansky puts it, "Differential adaptations of the races of man are most probably concerned with environments of a remote past, largely superseded by the environments created by civilization."[178]

Sociobiologist E. O. Wilson puts it somewhat differently: while biological evolution is Darwinian, cultural evolution is Lamarckian. Lamarck, who argued that acquired traits could be inherited, turned out to be wrong: as Darwin showed, evolution operates by natural selection, so that nothing we learn is genetically transmitted to our children. But in the domain of culture, acquired traits can be transmitted to our offspring. We can speak of a kind of cultural DNA, which transfers knowledge and values from one generation to the next. Socialization and education, not sex, are the means for this. Evolutionary theories that seek to account for high Asian and poor black IQ test performance by invoking equatorial sunbathing and Mongolian treks through the snow seem simplistic, even ludicrous, unless they also take into account the large intervening history of cultural evolution.

THE CULTURAL ALTERNATIVE

Let us imagine that those who believe in the existence of a genetically superior race are correct: it would seem to follow that through all the vagaries of history, this group would have maintained a permanent and decisive civilizational advantage over all other groups. But in fact this is nowhere the case. No race has a monopoly on achievement. Civilizational levels have dramatically shifted throughout recorded history. Perhaps the first human civilizations developed not in the coldest climates but in the moderate environs of North Africa and the Mediterranean. Sumerian, Babylonian, Egyptian, and Greek civilization can hardly be attributed to the pressures of enduring snowdrifts. These were mixed-race civilizations located at the juncture where Asians, Africans, and Europeans met and exchanged goods and ideas.

By contrast, as Ernest Gellner points out, "The regions of the world which produced most of the innovations which lie at the base of modern industrial civilization were themselves cultural backwaters a small number of generations earlier . . . yet it is unlikely that their gene pool changed radically."[179] Even in the industrial age, civilizational development has not been closely correlated with race. At the risk of offending some people, we may discreetly recall that the blond white-skinned Scandinavians have contributed little to Western civilization, then or subsequently. Hardly any major advances in scientific theory or major inventions have come from Sweden, Norway, or Iceland, whatever the visuospatial skills of their inhabitants. In the same vein, we should recall that China and the Islamic world were once great civilizations, their gene pool has remained relatively constant, but their cultural fortunes have changed dramatically. After a long ascendancy, both empires collapsed. China now seems to be making an economic comeback, but much of the Islamic world, once a center of scientific learning, seems resistant to the electric currents of modernity, preferring the pleasures of religious devotion instead. Japan, once a samurai culture of swordsmen, is now a pacific society which invests its resources in the technological paraphernalia of modern capitalism. These examples suggest that people from the same gene pool respond differently when incentives and circumstances change. And in the contemporary global marketplace, as Joel Kotkin and Lawrence Harrison document, successful groups such as the Mormons, Gujaratis, Parsees, and Ibo rely not on genetic uniqueness but on developed cultural traits such as hard work and entrepreneurship to distinguish themselves.[180]

Even within the United States, Thomas Sowell offers evidence for a cultural basis for IQ differences between groups. Sowell points out that the measured intelligence of numerous white ethnic groups has risen since the early part of this century. Indeed the gap between whites then and now is about 15 points—the same as the black-white gap today. Since the gene pool has not changed dramatically, these rises must have an environmental explanation.[181] As if to confirm the slow but steady upward trend for ethnic groups, the performance of black students on standardized tests such as the NAEP and the SAT has risen slowly but steadily, narrowing the black-white gap by about 20 percent: undoubtedly better nutrition, greater opportunities, and improved socioeconomic circumstances have contributed to this.[182]

Scholars who study Asian Americans have advanced plausible cultural explanations for the group's relatively strong academic performance. Asian Americans have IQs that are slightly higher than those of whites, yet American Indians—who originally migrated from Asia—score lower than whites. Even among Asians, some groups such as the H'mong, who came to the United States from Laos and are now settled in the Midwest, demonstrate weak academic performance and high dropout rates.[183] In a comparative study of whites and Asians, psychologist James Flynn found that the two groups do not perform much differently on IQ tests administered at an early age. Asians do, however, perform far better in school and university for what Flynn concludes are largely cultural reasons: Asians come from close families, they attach a high value to education and entrepreneurship, and they study and work harder.[184]

Finally an increasing body of research shows that child-rearing and socialization practices during the first few years have a decisive impact on brain functioning. Recent advances in neuroscience and cognitive development reveal that brain cell formation occurs mostly during pregnancy, but brain maturation continues during childhood and adolescence, and is particularly vigorous in the early years. In a process called synaptogenesis, the brain produces a surplus of synapses, which are pruned and modified in response to external stimuli. What this research confirms is that the mind is not a fixed but an adaptive structure, and that there is a symbiotic relationship between genes and environment: nature and nurture literally shape each other.[185]

Awkward though this may be, we have to look at black family structure and socialization practices which could partly explain the IQ gap. We know that IQ is affected by such prenatal and postnatal factors as the health of the mother during gestation, whether or not the mother smokes, drinks, or takes drugs during pregnancy, whether the child is premature, the birth weight of the baby, infant nutrition, early sensory deprivation, infant socialization, relationship with parents and other siblings, and so on.[186] There is a good deal of evidence that black and white children are not equal on these measures: for example, black children are more likely to be born prematurely, to have low birth weight, and to be deprived of conditions for optimum development in the home.[187] Psychologists have known for some time that the first child in a family tends on average to have the highest IQ and, as Arthur Jensen puts it, "each successive child has on average a slightly lower IQ."[188] The reasons for this continue to be debated, but one implication is that blacks, who have substantially larger families than whites, are likely on that account alone to have lower average IQ scores.

Two researchers, Elsie Moore and Zena Blau, have conducted studies which purport to show that early socialization differences between white and black parents explain a large component of the IQ gap between white and black children. Moore, an African American scholar, reviews research that distinguishes between white and black "behavioral styles." Black mothers, for example, are less likely to teach children how to cope with intellectual problems ("Why don't you work on it one section at a time?") and more likely to express general disapproval and hostility ("You could do better than this if you really tried").[189] Blau traces IQ differences to varied levels of available human, material, and intellectual resources in the children's home environment. She finds, for instance, that "black children in father-present homes average significantly higher achievement scores than those in father-absent homes." Blau argues that IQ scores can be raised through such practices as reading to children, imbuing in them the belief that hard work generates rewards, and encouraging from an early age their curiosity and talents in music, art, numbers and science. Blau's conclusion is that IQ differences "are social, not genetic, in origin."[190]

Moore and Blau's small-scale studies must be read in the context of the far more authoritative twin studies and transracial studies cited earlier which do not provide grounds for heady optimism about raising IQ scores in the near term. The conclusion of most scholars is that despite many caveats, there is no scientific basis for rejecting the possibility that race differences in IQ are partly hereditary. Howard Gardner says he has "deliberately avoided" investigating the question, partly because "appropriate studies . . . might suggest differences across groups."[191] This, by the way, is also Stephen Jay Gould's newfound position: retreating from earlier claims, Gould now declares the issue of race-based differences in IQ "a complex case that can yield only agnosticism."[192]

Most people, myself included, do not want to live in a racial caste society. Yet *The Bell Curve* makes a strong case that cannot be ignored. Whatever the book's shortcomings, it remains an undisputed fact that the fifteen-point IQ difference between blacks and whites has remained roughly constant for more than three quarters of a century, even though the environmental conditions for African Americans have vastly improved during that period. It is possible to reject the fatalism of genetic theories of IQ differences, as I do. My view is that of psychologist Rogers Elliott: while physical differences between the races are hereditary, it is a "reasonable hypothesis" that IQ differences can be explained by culture and environment.[193] In order to substantiate this hypothesis, however, it is not enough to hurl epithets or blame societal racism for blacks' poor scores on tests of numerical and logical reasoning. Rather, we need to examine the controversial subject of internal environment, or cultural dysfunctionalities in the black community. Both external and internal environments interacting together may account for why blacks are not competitive with other groups on measures of IQ and academic performance. No such investigation is possible, however, if we continue to insist upon the liberal dogma that all cultures are equal. Only by reconsidering relativism can liberals provide an adequate answer to Richard Herrnstein and Charles Murray and thereby refute charges of inherited black inferiority.

12

UNCLE TOM'S DILEMMA

Pathologies of Black Culture

Sometimes I believe the hype, man,
We mess it up ourselves, and blame the white man.
—Ice Cube[1]

The last few decades have witnessed nothing less than a breakdown of civilization within the African American community. This breakdown is characterized by extremely high rates of criminal activity, by the normalization of illegitimacy, by the predominance of single-parent families, by high levels of addiction to alcohol and drugs, by a parasitic reliance on government provision, by a hostility to academic achievement, and by a scarcity of independent enterprises. Civilizing institutions such as the small business, the church, and the family are now greatly weakened and in some areas they are on the verge of breaking down altogether. The next generation of young blacks is especially vulnerable. The crisis in black America is privately acknowledged by black scholars and activists, who discuss it incessantly among themselves.[2]

"We talked 30 years ago about genocide," Jesse Jackson told an audience of black government workers in 1993. "It's now fratricide. At this point, the Klan is not nearly the threat that your next-door neighbors are."[3] Jewelle Taylor Gibbs in *Young, Black and Male in America: An En-*

dangered Species describes a world in which African American youths "sell drugs openly on major thoroughfares without fear of apprehension, teenage girls have multiple out-of-wedlock pregnancies without fear of ostracism, youthful gangs terrorize neighborhoods without fear of retaliation, and young teenagers loiter aimlessly at night on street corners without fear of reprobation."[4] Anthony Walton argues that even racism loses its appeal when blacks cease to be worth exploiting. "We are in danger of becoming superfluous people in this society. We are not essential or even integral to the economy. White folks don't need us anymore."[5] Marian Wright Edelman of the Children's Defense Fund says, "We have a black child crisis worse than any since slavery."[6]

The civilizational crisis of the black community is not the result of genes and it is not the result of racism. This can be shown indisputably by the fact that this crisis did not exist a generation ago. In 1960, 78 percent of all black families were headed by married couples; today that figure is less than 40 percent.[7] Similarly in the 1950s, black crime rates were higher than those for whites, but they were vastly lower than they are today. During that period the black gene pool has not changed substantially, and racism was far worse, especially in its ability to deny blacks access to basic rights and opportunities. The conspicuous pathologies of blacks are the product of catastrophic cultural change that poses a threat both to the African American community and to society as a whole. These pathologies are far more serious than the fact that, for whatever reason, there are too few black math professors and nuclear physicists.

Although African American intellectuals and civil rights activists are well aware of the problem, oddly there seems to be a powerful public taboo preventing a national debate about it. This taboo is perhaps understandable when it comes to whites discussing the cultural deficiencies of blacks: ever since the 1960s, when Daniel Patrick Moynihan issued his hapless report on the black family, mainstream black scholars and civil rights activists have been quick to attribute public notice of African American pathology to white racism.[8] Yet even when blacks publicly engage in moral criticism of these pathologies, they find themselves castigated and reviled. This fury has been especially directed against black conservatives.

• Michael Williams, an African American who promoted race-neutral scholarships as a senior official in the Bush administration, was denounced by Spike Lee as an Uncle Tom who deserves to be "dragged into the alley and beaten with a Louisville Slugger."[9]

• Commenting on the writings of Thomas Sowell, columnist Carl

Rowan of the *Washington Post* observed that "Sowell is giving aid and comfort to those who . . . are taking food out of the mouths of black children. Vidkun Quisling in his collaboration with the Nazis surely did not do as much damage . . . as Sowell is doing."[10]

• Rowan seems equally outraged about Clarence Thomas, insisting that "if you give Thomas a little flour on his face, you'd think you had David Duke."[11]

• Speaking of Gary Franks, who was until recently the only black Republican in the House of Representatives, Congresswoman Cynthia McKinney admits that he is treated with abuse and contempt by most of his African American colleagues: "I'm one of the few members of the Black Caucus who treats him as a person."[12]

• In 1993 the Congressional Black Caucus sponsored an attempt, later reversed, to oust Franks from membership in the group. Congressman William Clay argued that Franks showed "callous disregard for the basic rights and freedoms" of African Americans, and that his views were "inimical to the permanent interests of black folk."[13]

• Writing in *Black Enterprise,* Frank McCoy accuses Franks of harboring "racially traitorous views."[14]

• "It is a clear distortion of the term dissenter to apply it to black conservatives," warns Martin Kilson, who accuses Clarence Thomas, Shelby Steele, and others of being "akin to client or satellite states . . . who do the ideological bidding of the WASP establishment."[15]

• Former NAACP head Benjamin Hooks denounces African American conservatives as "a new breed of Uncle Tom . . . some of the biggest liars the world ever saw."[16]

• Discussing the views of Supreme Court Justice Clarence Thomas, political scientist Manning Marable charges that "ethnically, Thomas has ceased to be an African American."[17]

• Invoking an old slaveowner image, Spike Lee calls Thomas "a handkerchief-head, chicken-and-biscuit eating Uncle Tom."[18]

• In a similar vein, author June Jordan condemns Thomas as a "virulent Oreo phenomenon," a "punk ass," and an "Uncle Tom calamity."[19]

• Columnist Julianne Malveaux fumes that "these people such as Thomas who claim to have pulled themselves up by the bootstraps are very likely to use the bootstraps to strangle people."[20]

• Nikki Giovanni writes, "The Thomas Sowells, Shelby Steeles and the Clarence Thomases . . . are trying to justify the gross neglect of the needs of black America. We know that such conservatives have no character. They are in opportunistic service."[21]

• Civil rights activist Roger Wilkins accuses Sowell of being hostile to "the weakest and the poorest of his brethren . . . an enemy of the interests of his people."[22]

• Drawing on colonial analogies, literary critic Houston Baker terms Thomas Sowell and Glenn Loury "prospectors on the new frontiers of an urban dark continent. Gentrification and black genocide go hand in hand. Sowell and others are capitalism's and the state's new Livingstones in blackface."[23]

• Alvin Poussaint and Price Cobbs diagnose such men as suffering from what they call Token Black Syndrome, a mental disorder in which African American conservatives internalize white stereotypes about blacks and then try to escape them and win white approval.[24]

• For retired New York judge Bruce Wright, an African American, blacks on the bench who impose sentences no different from white judges are "Afro-Saxons" who are acting "white in their . . . reaction to black defendants."[25]

• Political scientist Alphonso Pinkney alleges that blacks who dissent from the policies of the civil rights establishment "are not unlike government officials in South Vietnam who supported American aggression against their own people."[26]

• Writing in *Emerge* magazine, Playthell Benjamin ridicules "neocon Negroes" who, for him, are simply "colored quislings" suffering from an obsequious "Sambo personality."[27]

• Afrocentric historian John Henrik Clarke goes even further, warning that "black conservatives are really frustrated slaves crawling back to the plantation."[28]

This rhetoric, in its vehemence and ferocity, is unrivaled in any other area of contemporary debate. Roger Wilkins argues in favor of the enforcement of black orthodoxy:

> For black Americans who live in a society where racism exists, it is legitimate to set parameters. In arguing about how best to struggle, there is some political and intellectual behavior in which you engage that keeps you from being a black person. Every oppressed community has drawn lines and says certain behavior puts you outside the community.[29]

Curiously community standards, as Wilkins defines them, are imposed not to regulate pathological forms of behavior by blacks, but to restrict attempts to point out such behavior. For many scholars and activists, whites who criticize black pathologies are racist, and blacks who do so are mouthpieces for white bigots, craven apostates, virtual black impersonators who deserve ostracism, if not physical punishment. "The leadership has successfully imposed a gag rule on the black community," remarks Robert Woodson.[30] Orlando Patterson says, "In America, if you break away from the party line, you are seen as a reactionary. It's very crippling."[31]

What accounts for the truculent resistance to criticism on the part of the civil rights establishment? The reason is the politics of victimization which has been endorsed by white liberals and perfected by activist groups like the NAACP. Claims of victimization are established by blaming societal racism for the problems of blacks. Such blame serves two purposes: to rationalize the pathologies of the black underclass, and to legitimize racial preferences and set-asides for the black middle class. Civil rights organizations are singlemindedly devoted to white bigotry as the primary explanation for black suffering. They raise money from their donors and appeal for government funding for programs in order to combat the effects of this racism. If racism was not the primary obstacle currently facing blacks, many in the civil rights industry would have to find something else to do.

Activists denounce criticism of black pathologies as a callous form of "blaming the victim." This term was made famous in the late 1960s and early 1970s by sociologist William Ryan.[32] Today it is repeatedly invoked to deflect criticism of even the most outrageous and destructive forms of behavior. Kimberle Crenshaw argues that culture, rather than race, represents the fashionable contemporary technique for inferiorizing blacks.[33] Henry Louis Gates, Jr. asserts that whites create the barriers that force blacks to fail, and then accuse blacks of being pathological and inferior.[34] David Wellman argues that culture, like biology, is now used as a "rationalization and justification for the superior position of whites." Wellman rejects all theories that "place the reason for inequality with the oppressed people themselves—their biology, their psyche, their culture."[35]

Yet if the problems endured by African Americans today are substantially the result of cultural pathologies on the part of blacks, these individuals would not be victims but perpetrators. The notion that blacks cannot be perpetrators is a legacy of cultural relativism. Since all cultures are equal, all inequalities between groups are considered to be the unnatural product of historical and continuing oppression. Thus offensive or atrocious behavior is a symbol not of civilizational defects but of externally inflicted deformation. In this view blacks are portrayed as living largely involuntary lives, wholly manipulated by the structures of visible and invisible racism. Therefore, this logic holds, it is unfair to criticize the culture of the group that is failing, because to do so is to avert one's gaze from the conduct of the oppressor. Moreover, such criticism is said to reinforce the oppressor's self-serving racist perception of the victim group as somehow inferior. Black self-criticism, in this paradigm, becomes a form of self-hate.

Of course no one is to blame for being a victim. But if as a reaction to being victimized, a group develops dysfunctional or destructive patterns of behavior which perpetuate a vicious cycle of poverty, dependency, and violence, then continuing to inveigh against the oppressor cannot offer the victim much relief. As African American scholar Milton Morris puts it, "When black people slaughter other black people on the street, they all come back to: look what the white people made us do."[36] In dealing with pathologies like black-on-black violence, it may be the victim who is in the best position to address the problem, even though the victim was not entirely responsible for causing it. Unless victim groups are considered utterly prostrate and helpless, there are measures that they can take to remedy their plight. This does not absolve society of its obligation to help, but it also means that victims should recognize the benefits of taking responsibility even for cultural traits that they did not freely choose, and that were to some extent imposed on them.

This chapter is a frank examination of black pathologies which are so flagrant that no one can ignore them. It identifies these in explicit detail, because it is impossible to address a problem that is not first named and confronted. It also shows how mainstream African American intellectuals and activists are ideologically prevented from seriously discussing ways to deal with black pathologies. Finally it identifies a small but intrepid group of reformers who are trying to reestablish civilizational norms.

AN OPPOSITIONAL CULTURE

For all their regional and economic diversity, blacks in America do share a culture. This culture is not racial but ethnic. It is the product not of a physiological likeness but of a shared history. Black culture emerged out of the crucible of racism and historical oppression directed specifically at blacks. Earlier we saw that as a result of slavery, blacks who came from diverse tribes speaking different languages and practicing varied ways of life forged a distinct African American identity in the new country. This identity was further solidified under segregation, when blacks were involuntarily united by the one-drop rule. Although black culture contains elements of Southern rural culture, modern urban culture, and low-class culture, it has fused these elements into a distinct amalgam. The term "African American" is an accurate one in that—like Italian American or Jewish American—it signifies a coherent ethnic identity. Lawrence Levine in *Black Culture and Black Consciousness* describes the traditions and institutions that evolved in the black community during slavery and segregation. Among these traditions are "the mask" for concealing true feelings, the theme of "struggle" as an instrument of spiritual and political liberation, and the celebration of the "trickster" and the "bad nigger" as wily and heroic resisters of white oppression. Even today blacks as a group exhibit characteristic patterns of speech and behavior that can be traced back to the group's historical experience in the old South.[37]

Some scholars view black culture as largely, if not wholly, imposed from the outside. These scholars are structural determinists: like Marxists, they tend to view culture as the epiphenomenal product of external forces such as poverty and oppression. William Julius Wilson argues that "cultural values grow out of specific circumstances and life changes and reflect one's position in the class structure." Wilson is right to see ghetto pathologies partly as a response to lack of opportunity. Yet he goes too far in asserting that "cultural values do not determine behavior or success."[38] Contrary to Wilson, culture is not simply an expression of external circumstances; it is also a powerful instrument in shaping those circumstances. Even under the extreme deprivations of slavery, segregation and racism, black culture was never entirely controlled from without, but also generated from within. As Manning Marable writes, "Blackness or African American identity . . . is not something our oppressors forced upon us. It is a cultural and ethnic awareness that we have collectively constructed for ourselves."[39]

The notion of culture as to some degree inwardly generated should not lead to the opposite extreme of cultural determinism.[40] Cultural determinists tend to view culture as the unique set of attitudes and orientations of a particular group which persist across the vicissitudes of time and space. What this view misses is the fact that cultures frequently change in response to the restrictions and opportunities generated by particular circumstances. The most balanced view of culture, therefore, is dynamically interactionist. It views culture as both the product of external conditions and of internal choices for adapting to those conditions.

The concept of culture as an adaptation is of course central to Boasian relativism. In this view, all cultures are inherently legitimate social adjustments to local conditions. Yet what happens when circumstances change and yet old cultural patterns of behavior persist and become impediments in the new climate? The concept of maladaptive or dysfunctional cultures represents a departure from relativism, and imposes a higher standard than the Boasian one. It suggests that cultures can be judged to be functionally deficient based on a civilizational standard that is not entirely relative. In the American multicultural context, this possibility suggests that cultures of failure can learn from cultures of success.

Blacks in America seem to have developed what some scholars term an "oppositional culture" which is based on a comprehensive rejection of the white man's worldview.[41] Alvin Poussaint articulates a position popular among African American leaders: "For blacks to mindlessly strive to be like the white middle class in a white racist, capitalist, exploitative society is without question detrimental to the cause of black people."[42] It is not hard to see how this oppositional culture would develop in a black community which has historically suffered so much at the hands of whites. Until recently, Eugene Genovese says, "There was hardly any room at the top or in the middle for blacks who tried to play by the rules of bourgeois society." Under slavery it made sense to do as little work as possible, because slaves received no share in the master's profits. In some cases even extreme forms of violence constituted a reasonable adaptation, because it was the only way to preserve dignity. Yet as Genovese says, "What constituted strategies for survival under one set of circumstances have now emerged, in an entirely different context, as celebrations of self-indulgence and irresponsibility." Today black culture has become an obstacle, because it prevents blacks from taking advantage of rights and opportunities that have multiplied in a new social environment.

African Americans are not the only group to develop something resembling an oppositional culture. Poor Italian immigrants growing up in New York in the earlier part of this century were raised in a culture that held that going to college and taking up a profession was something alien and unattainable; therefore the very effort was sometimes condemned as a ridiculous form of WASP imitation. Yet at the same time Italian grandmothers taught their grandchildren to look up to, and seek to emulate, successful members of the community. "Look at Uncle Mario and what he has done." By an anomaly of history, however, the oppositional culture of African Americans causes even many middle-class and upper-middle-class blacks to permit blackness to be defined by the underclass. Middle-class behavior by African Americans is seen as inauthentic, while low-class behavior is seen as genuinely black—a reversal of what Du Bois had in mind with his Talented Tenth. Thus while most immigrant groups tend to look to their most successful citizens for emulation and self-definition, on many issues the moral tone in the black community is set from below. The underclass exercises such a powerful influence in shaping black cultural norms because this group is perceived as the most oppositional of all: it is remote from, and organized in resistance to, white middle-class standards.

Almost a century ago, Booker T. Washington warned of the existence of pathologies that both strengthened white racism and inhibited black development. Those pathologies have existed in the black community since slavery, but they have been restricted and contained both by white-imposed discipline and by black-imposed norms enforced by churches and local community institutions. But those institutions have been greatly weakened since the 1960s, and in a new environment of social permissiveness and government subsidy, black pathologies have proliferated. Today they pose a serious threat to the survival of blacks as a group as well as to the safety and integrity of the larger society.

Black pathologies, of course, are not uniformly distributed throughout the African American community. There are millions of blacks who work hard, maintain cohesive families, raise their children with productive and humane morals, eschew crime, and find a way to live decently even though they endure destabilizing economic and social pressures.[43] In many desolate neighborhoods, the black church remains a bulwark of stability, calling members to personal responsibility in holding jobs and discharging family obligations.[44] Many individuals and groups work against considerable political and financial odds to maintain enclaves of decency. Yet their work is made more difficult because of the prevalence of pathological norms, especially strong in the black underclass, which mock and resist all efforts at neighborhood restoration. It should also be obvious that these pathologies are not exclusively African American problems: to some degree, they are national problems. Yet they are disproportionately concentrated in the black community, and they often affect people who are least equipped to cope. Rich whites, for example, may adopt cocaine habits but they can take advantage of expensive treatment programs that are unavailable to the crack addict. Similarly when middle-class white teenagers get pregnant they frequently draw on the support of parents and grandparents; these resources do exist among poor blacks, but they are scarce. Historically there is a tendency for both those at the top and those at the bottom of society to rebel against middle-class norms, but the people at the top can afford it.[45]

No culture is entirely positive or negative, and black culture is no exception. Despite external hardships, blacks have built what is in many ways a kaleidoscopic and creative cultural tradition—a tradition of jazz and blues, epitomized by the performances of Duke Ellington, Charlie Parker, Count Basie, and Miles Davis; a tradition of popular music, as evident in the success of Nat King Cole, Ray Charles, Dionne Warwick, Diana Ross, Michael Jackson, and Whitney Houston; a tradition of poetry and literature, characterized by the work of Richard Wright, Langston Hughes, Zora Neale Hurston, Ralph Ellison, James Baldwin, and Toni Morrison; a tradition of performing in films and on television, as seen in the films of Sidney Poitier, Sammy Davis Jr., Bill Cosby, and Morgan Freeman; and a tradition of athletic distinction, as is obvious from the careers of Reggie Jackson, Muhammad Ali, Carl Lewis, Jackie Joyner-Kersee, and Michael Jordan. American popular culture is highly influenced and frequently enriched by the contributions of blacks.[46] Wynton Marsalis, the musician and jazz artist, recently observed, in a passage of lyrical beauty:

> Jazz is the most modern expression of the way black people look at the world. It's not like what black people did in sports, where they reinterpreted the way the game could be played, bringing new dimensions to competitive expression in boxing, basketball and so forth. Jazz is something Negroes *invented,* and it said the most profound things not only about us and the way we look at things, but about what modern democratic life is really about. It is the nobility of the race put into sound; it is the sensuousness of romance in our dialect; it is the picture of the people in all their glory, which is what swinging is.[47]

Yet black culture also has a vicious, self-defeating, and repellent underside that it is no longer possible to ignore or euphemise. As more and more blacks seem to realize, no good is achieved by dressing these pathologies in sociological cant, complete with the familiar vocabulary of disadvantage and holding society to account. Society must do its part, and blacks must do theirs. But first, the magnitude of the civilizational crisis facing the black community must be recognized. This crisis points to deficiencies not of biology but of culture; yet they are deficiencies, and they should be corrected.

RACISM AS AN EXCUSE

The first dysfunctional aspect of black culture is racial paranoia—a reflexive tendency to blame racism for every failure, even those that are intensely personal. Historically African Americans had every justification for suspecting the controlling influence of racism and discrimination on their everyday lives. Yet now, when racism is no longer so prevalent, many blacks experience it vicariously. Like someone looking to buy a Volkswagen, that's all they see on the road. Goaded by the propaganda of the civil rights establishment, which has a stake in recycling racist horror stories, many blacks seem to live in the haunted house of the past, apparently patrolled by the ghosts of white racism. In 1992 the *Wall Street Journal* investigated reports of a large and growing market for racist memorabilia, such as hand-made slave shackles and Little Black Sambos from the segregationist South. Yet what looked like evidence of white racists on a spending spree turned out to be middle-class blacks seeking to preserve recollections of past suffering.[48] Others attend racism workshops, where through film and oratory they can experience the outrages of the antebellum period, an experience that seems both horrifying and, in a perverse way, profoundly satisfying.

Sometimes racism is all too real, but it is bad enough to endure real racism without having to suffer imaginary racism as well. Racism appears to have become the opiate of many middle-class blacks. For society, promiscuous charges of racism are dangerous because they undermine the credibility of the charge and make it more difficult to identify real racists. For blacks, the risk of exaggerated and false charges of racism is that they divert attention from the possibilities of the present and the future. Excessive charges of racism set up a battle with an adversary who sometimes does not exist. Consequently, blacks are in a struggle that they always lose. Racism itself becomes a scapegoat: it is blamed for problems that have little to do with racism, such as blacks failing math tests. This sets up blacks in a classic situation where some of them pursue the white whale of racism with Ahab-like determination. The displacement of personal or group problems onto the bugaboo of racism inspires a frenetic assault on society at large. But since racism is not the problem, the assault proves futile. The problem endures, and the frustration mounts. Once again, racism becomes the culprit, now accused of having taken an even subtler and more insidious shape. A wider campaign for extirpating racism becomes necessary. Ultimately some blacks like Colin Ferguson become convinced that the universe has been designed to oppress them personally. Bitterness, cynicism, and thoroughgoing alienation are the result.

• In May 1994 Louis Farrakhan asserted that white racism was responsible for black people killing other blacks. The reason that whites do not stop black-on-black violence, he added, was that whites need the organ donations. "When you're killing each other, they can't wait for you to die," Farrakhan told a large audience in Toledo, Ohio. "You've become good for parts."[49] Farrakhan's intimations of a homicidal white plot are not unique. In 1990, in a poll of black Americans, 60 percent said it was true or possibly true that the government was deliberately encouraging drug use among African Americans, and 29 percent suspected that scientists deliberately created the AIDS infection in order to decimate the black population.[50] "Many of us are convinced there is a conspiracy to anesthetize and ultimately do away with as many blacks in American society as possible," the Reverend Cecil Williams of San Francisco's Glide Methodist Church told *Newsweek.* "This is genocide, 1990s style."[51] "It's a deep-seated suspicion," remarks Andrew Cooper, publisher of the *City Sun,* a black weekly in New York. "I believe it. It's almost an accepted fact."[52] Recent articles in the black press carry titles such as "Black Male Genocide: A Final Solution to the Race Problem in America."[53] Even Spike Lee alleges that "it is no mistake that the majority of drugs in this country is being deposited in black and Hispanic neighborhoods," and actor Bill Cosby says he has a "feeling" that AIDS had been concocted "to get after certain people."[54]

• The health care system is not the only site for apparent black paranoia. In his book *Black Men: Obsolete, Single, Dangerous?* Haki Madhubuti warns of an organized plan by the "white supremacy system" seeking to "drive black men out of the economic sector," to "disrupt black families," to "use the prison system as a breeding ground for black men who . . . will return and prey on their own communities," to "drive African American men crazy," and to "make them into so-called *women,* where homosexual and bisexual activity become the norm."[55] According to a recent book, *I Heard It Through the Grapevine,* blacks are remarkably susceptible to rumors that there is a racist plot to destroy the race. Among the false reports that have received widespread circulation and serious treatment in the African American community: Church's Fried Chicken is owned by the Ku Klux Klan, which uses ingredients that make black men sterile; the FBI was responsible for the killing of twenty-eight black children in Atlanta as part of an experiment in the genocidal elimination of all blacks in

America; some popular brands of athletic clothing and footwear are sold by racist groups like Skinheads and the Ku Klux Klan; Reebok sneakers are made in South Africa and the profits of sales helped to sustain the apartheid regime; popular fruit juices such as Tropical Fantasy are secretly manufactured by white supremacist organizations, once again to reduce black sexual potency.[56]

• Nowhere are strong claims of racism more evident than in the criminal justice system. The Rodney King beating, according to one African American activist, means that "Negroes are lynched in America."[57] A columnist for the *Los Angeles Sentinel,* the largest African American newspaper on the West Coast, offered the King verdict as further proof that "the United States is on the verge of becoming a police state, if it is not there already." The author noted "many similarities between present-day USA and early stages of the Nazi Third Reich in prewar Germany."[58] In early 1992 former boxing heavyweight Mike Tyson was accused of raping a contestant in a beauty pageant. Even though Tyson's accuser was black, and he was convicted by a jury of his peers, Ishmael Reed compared his incarceration to a lynching. "As soon as a black man wins the heavyweight championship, a movement begins among some whites to dethrone him."[59] In a similar vein, Spike Lee said the system was trying to "demoralize" Tyson because "he was making too much money" for an African American.[60] When Washington, D.C., mayor Marion Barry was arrested on charges of purchasing and smoking crack cocaine, leading figures in the black community promptly launched charges of a racist conspiracy. According to NAACP head Benjamin Hooks, Barry's arrest was part of a "pattern of harassment of black elected officials." Jesse Jackson charged that Barry was not being prosecuted but rather "persecuted." Mary Frances Berry of the U.S. Commission on Civil Rights declared, "All black officials ought to assume that someone is after them because of racism." Eventually Barry was convicted, served his sentence, and has publicly acknowledged and apologized for his wrongdoing. Subsequently, he was reelected to office.[61]

• Although African Americans routinely receive racial preferences in universities and the work force, this does not seem to have inhibited imaginative accusations of racism where none seems evident. When black poet Amiri Baraka was denied tenure at Rutgers University in 1990, he accused fellow professors and administrators of being Nazis and Ku Klux Klansmen in disguise. "We must unmask these powerful Klansmen. These enemies of people's democracy and Pan American culture must not be allowed to prevail. Their intellectual presence makes a stink across the campus like the corpses of rotting Nazis."[62] In 1992, after St. Mary's College in Maryland threatened to terminate the teaching contract of Reginald Savage for not showing up for work for months and teaching during that time at another college, Savage argued that he was unable to function at St. Mary's as a result of being traumatized by the level of racism on campus. He produced a report from a psychiatrist diagnosing him as suffering from "situational anxiety." Asked to cite examples of racism, Savage noted that several years earlier the college president had confessed that he had trouble hiring black professors because of the national shortage of black Ph.D.s. Others in his department said that Savage was in the habit of charging everyone who disagreed with him of racism.[63] In *Racism: American Style,* Dempsey Travis accuses heads of major companies of being "Klansmen in pin-striped suits." He compares various job rejection letters that one of his friends received, and is struck by the ominous similarity of their tone and language. Without irony, Travis writes:

> The letters of rejection are so similar in tone and content that they raise the specter of corporate officers from across the country gathered in back rooms deciding on a kinder and gentler language for rejecting black applicants. Such gatherings could be called a conspiracy and it is undeniable that such schemes are in place.[64]

• No public report of racism in recent years turned out to be as spectacularly false as the case of Tawana Brawley. Although she claimed to have been attacked and defiled by three white men, who allegedly smeared her with excrement and wrote "KKK" and "Nigger" on her body, police soon discovered that Brawley had not been attacked and that she had perversely faked the incident in order to make herself appear a victim of racism. Even though a New York grand jury concluded that Brawley fabricated the offense that she sought to blame on white racists, some leading African American activists and scholars declared that if Brawley's accusation was literally false, it remained figuratively or metaphorically true. Remarked Otis Brown, president of the Atlanta chapter of the NAACP, "It doesn't matter to me whether Brawley did it or not, because of all the pressure these black students are under at these predominantly white schools. If this will highlight it . . . I have no problem with that."[65] Legal scholar Patricia Williams wrote:

> Tawana Brawley has been the victim of some unspeakable crime. No matter who did it to her—and even if she did it to herself. Her condition was clearly the expression of . . . some tremendous violence, some great violation.[66]

THE RAGE OF THE PRIVILEGED CLASS

A second dysfunctional aspect of black culture, a feature mainly of middle-class African American life, is a rage that threatens to erupt in an orgy of destruction or self-destruction. Ironically when middle-class blacks found their opportunities severely restricted under segregation, black rage was either submerged or less apparent. But now that middle-class blacks find themselves on the receiving end of racial preferences and government set-asides, many are beside themselves with anger. "I do not believe that we can restore and expand the freedoms that our lives require," June Jordan writes, "until we embrace the justice of our rage."[67]

Actually, this rage is not so difficult to comprehend. It represents post–affirmative action angst, the frustration of pursuing unearned privileges and then bristling when they do not bring something that has to be earned, the respect of one's peers. Moreover, black rage arises out of the recognition that even as middle-class activists deplore the pathologies of the underclass, by moving out of inner-city neighborhoods they have sometimes contributed to those pathologies and are dependent on their continuation for the race-based privileges they enjoy. The effect of this molten frustration is what William Grier and Price Cobbs, in their book *Black Rage,* term "a posture close to paranoid thinking and mental disorder."[68] In *Living with Racism,* Joe Feagin and Melvin Sikes sympathetically portray middle-class blacks describing their state of mind. Written by two activist scholars, one white and the other black, the book is intended to spotlight white racism; instead, it provides illuminating insight into some blacks' questionable grip on reality.

> I come in here and scream! I talk to my friends. I come in here and talk to my assistant. She's even seen me cry because I'm so angry that I am to the point of violence. But I know that I have to really, really be cognizant of what I'm doing, because why go to jail for nothing?

> On a scale of one or ten, my level of anger is a ten. Mine has had time to grow over the years more and more until I now feel that my grasp on handling myself is tenuous. I think that now I would strike out to the point of killing, and not think about it. I really wouldn't care.

> One step from suicide! The psychological warfare games that we have to play every day just to survive. It's a mental health problem. It's a wonder we haven't all gone out and killed somebody or killed ourselves.[69]

These are the observations of relatively well-placed men and women: an executive, a government worker, and a college professor. Since no reasons are given that would justify such reactions, one might conclude that we are dealing with cases of people who live in a world of make-believe, in mental prisons of their own construction. For them, apparently, antiracist militancy is carried to the point of virtual mental instability. It is hard to imagine whites feeling secure working with such persons: surely such inflamed ethnic sensitivities are not what companies have in mind when they extol the diversity of work environments. Yet if these individuals are cranks, they are in respectable company. Leading African American writers and scholars seem to share their persecution complex and the attendant rage. Here is a fairly typical incident described by law professor Patricia Williams:

> A man with whom I used to work once told me that I made too much of my race. "After all," he said. "I don't even think of you as black." Yet sometime later, when another black woman became engaged in an ultimately unsuccessful tenure battle, he confided to me that he wished the school could find more blacks like me.

It is not hard to envision the scene: a white colleague, probably eager to please, tells Williams that he tries to judge her by her ability rather than her skin color. Apparently confronted on another occasion with an affirmative action candidate seeking a tenured appointment, the colleague expresses to Williams the hope that the university will find more qualified African American scholars like herself. Here is how Williams reacts:

> I felt myself slip in and out of a shadow, as I become non-black for the purposes of inclusion and black for the purposes of exclusion. I felt the boundaries of my very body manipulated, casually inscribed by definitional demarcations that did not refer to me.

Williams is not finished. Reflecting on similar cases in a kind of stream-of-consciousness rhetoric, she eventually explodes:

> I am afraid of being alien and suspect. . . . My rage feels dangerous, full of physical violence, like something that will get me arrested. All this impermissible danger floats around in me, boiling, exhausting. I can't kill and I can't teach everyone. So I protect myself. I don't deal with other people if I can help it. I don't risk exposing myself to the rage that will get me arrested.[70]

We have to remind ourselves that this is a highly paid professor at a distinguished university, and one of the leading black female scholars in the nation. Yet her sentiments are shared by others. "I'm a volunteer slave," announces Jill Nelson, an African American, upon being hired as a reporter for the *Washington Post*. "My price? A house, a Volvo, and the illusion of disposable income." This seems to be the kind of servitude that most Americans of any background would settle for. Nelson, however, calls herself a "race woman": she seems both uncomfortable and angry about being a successful African American working in a mainstream profession.

> Middle-class black folk, especially those with straight or pseudo-straight hair who are nearer light-skinned than dark, tend to grow up feeling we have something to prove—not just to white folks, but to just about everyone, including each other. We greet one another with skepticism, treating each other as potential Eurocentric sellouts until proven otherwise.

Nelson's suspicions of Eurocentrism become more intense when an editor at her newspaper informs her that another black writer, Juan Williams, has concerns about the way one of her stories was written. "Williams is the perfect Negro, at least in the eyes of white folks," Nelson reacts. Williams, who is of Panamanian descent, is "a black Republican type . . . an opportunist *à la* Clarence Thomas." Such blacks, Nelson writes, "mouth the prejudices of white immigrants in blackface." Indeed Nelson does not even describe Williams as black; rather, "he appears to be black." He is, she bluntly asserts, "a vicious, competitive Uncle Neocon son of a bitch." She confronts him about his objections to her story and the following exchange occurs, an exchange rendered more believable in that it is reported not by Williams but by Nelson herself.

> WILLIAMS: I was trying to help.
> NELSON: Listen, Juan, don't fuck with me. You know, you're worse than a Negro who carries white folks' water for them, because your own water is dirtier than theirs could ever be. Don't get into my business again, because if you fuck with me, I'll destroy you.[71]

Nelson eventually resigned from the *Post* after being suspended for signing an editor's initials on one of her travel vouchers. Nevertheless, it seems from her account that Nelson is out of place in a mainstream integrated environment, experiencing the pea of racial victimization under many mattresses and engaging in conduct that is, by most commonly accepted standards insecure, paranoid, and uncivil.

In Brent Staples's autobiography *Parallel Time*, the African American writer describes how, as a graduate student, he spent his time stalking white people in order to scare them. He invested many weeks in tracking the novelist Saul Bellow but apparently without much success. Here is a man who is conversant with philosophy and literature, and who should seemingly have better things to do with his time, relishing a game that he, to his own great amusement, calls Scatter the Pigeons.

> I became expert in the language of fear. Couples locked arms or reached for each other's hand when they saw me. Some crossed to the other side of the street. People who were carrying on conversations went mute and stared straight ahead, as though avoiding my eyes would save them. A few steps beyond them I stopped and howled with laughter . . . I felt a surge of power: these people were mine: I could do with them as I wished. If I'd been younger, with less to lose, I'd have robbed them, and it would have been easy.[72]

Recalling these incidents many years later, Staples might be expected to have some regrets about his bizarre youthful behavior, perhaps to offer critical analysis of what was wrong with the situation and his response to it. Yet Staples's perspective on his stalking days seems exactly the same today as it was then. Despite his training as a student of psychology, Staples offers a recollection devoid of analytical self-consciousness. Obviously Staples is simply blind to the immaturity and strangeness of his conduct. The conclusion is hard to avoid: one of America's leading black intellectuals gets kicks out of playing hoodlum, and then proceeds to accuse whites of racism for engaging in what, under the circumstances, can only be termed rational avoidance of blacks like him.

Another infuriated African American is Derrick Bell, whose national recognition and hefty income do not inhibit him from describing his social status as below that of the most ignorant and unemployed white man. Bell's writings are filled with images of holocaust: he imagines a group of Citizens for Black Survival whose mission is "to build a nationwide network of secret shelters to house and feed black people in the event of a black holocaust." Bell is not speaking here of Ethiopia or Rwanda but the United States:

> What precisely would you do if they came for you? How would you protect your family? Where would you go? How would you get there? You have money. Could you get access to it if the government placed a hold on the assets in your checking and savings accounts?

Bell is not finished. He now conjures up an elaborate case study of white Americans selling blacks into slavery to aliens from outer space. Predictably, Bell's account features a black conservative, Gleason Golightly, who supports the white proposal and is tragically, though deservedly, betrayed by whites who use him as a puppet. Bell imagines white TV evangelists holding massive rallies in the Houston Astrodome, where they inform the nation that it is blasphemous not to sell African Americans to the Martians. Finally Bell achieves his psychic release:

> On the dunes above the beaches, guns at the ready, stood U.S. guards. There was no escape, no alternative. Heads bowed, arms now linked by slender chains, black people left the New World as their forebears had arrived.

All this could be dismissed as macabre science fiction, but Bell is deadly serious. Drawing on these literary fantasies about white racism, Bell proposes a practical *Weltanschauung* for young blacks, using a phrase he learned from an angry woman: "I lives to harass white folks."[73]

GOVERNMENT AS THE BIG HOUSE

Another destructive stance that seems deeply ingrained in African Americans, especially those in the middle class, is a heavy dependence on government, accompanied by the belief that public programs are the way to solve virtually all social problems. Not only are blacks heavily reliant on the state, but as a group they are remarkably weak in developing independent businesses that have proved, for many ethnic groups, to be a durable source of employment and income. "Capitalism and its institutions are basically individualistic," James Hund writes in *Black Entrepreneurship.* "But the ethos of the black community is collectivistic."[74] Thomas Kochman writes that while whites view their social advantages as earned—"I worked for what I have"—blacks tend to view theirs as the fruit of political activism—"We fought for it" or "We struggled for it."[75]

Today a large fraction of middle-class blacks works for the government. Although blacks make up 10 percent of the civilian work force, about 24 percent of blacks (compared with 14 percent of whites) are employed by the federal, state, and local governments.[76] State and local agencies which service a poor and predominantly black clientele, such as housing and welfare, employ substantial proportions of African Americans: 38 and 23 percent respectively.[77] According to sociologist Bart Landry, about half of black professional males and two-thirds of black professional females work for some arm of the state.[78] In addition, 50 percent of blacks (more than 15 million persons) live in households that receive some form of welfare, compared with 19 percent of whites. Blacks are between two and five times more likely than whites to receive means-tested cash assistance and food stamps, and to live in subsidized or public housing.[79] In short, much of the black community is parasitic on government for its basic livelihood.

According to a recent survey, 67 percent of blacks believe that the government, rather than private business or individuals, has the greatest responsibility for creating jobs. Poor and middle-class blacks both shared this belief. By contrast, whites were far less likely to look to government for jobs; even among the poorest whites, less than 50 percent cited the government's responsibility. Sixty-eight percent of blacks compared with 36 percent of whites insisted that increases in government spending were the way to invigorate the economy and provide employment. A typical comment was from Della Simmons, an African American who told the *Wall Street Journal*: "Employment is the big issue the government needs to be dealing with."[80]

Meanwhile, blacks have done very poorly in the one area that is a rapid source of jobs and social mobility for other groups: small business. According to U.S. government data, in 1987 blacks, who make up 12 percent of the population, owned about 420,000 businesses in America with receipts of $19 billion. By contrast, Asians, who make up 3 percent of the population, owned 350,000 businesses with receipts of $33 billion.[81] African Americans currently start and run less than 3 percent of the nation's businesses, and take in less than 1 percent of the nation's gross receipts. Black enterprise is so fragile that 60 percent of its receipts come from the government; many black businesses would collapse instantly if they were taken off government contracting preferences and set-asides. A substantial majority of black enterprises are tiny, with receipts of less than $5,000 a year. About 80 percent are family-run enterprises, employing no outside workers. Only about 4 percent of African American spending each year goes to black-owned enterprises.[82]

The reliance on government is a relatively recent development in black culture, and it stands in sharp contrast with the way that whites have traditionally viewed government. Like the American founders, many whites view the government with suspicion, as an obstacle to rights. The Bill of Rights with its repetitious "Congress shall not" clauses was intended as a restraint on government. Yet for blacks, government has been the protector and guarantor of rights. It was federal intervention in the 1860s that freed the slaves. The basic right of blacks to equal protection of the laws was recognized in the Fourteenth Amendment to the Constitution, which was somewhat incongruous with the rest of the document in that it was passed to expand federal power. In the twentieth century, black leaders found themselves compelled to turn to the federal government to combat state-sanctioned segregation and private discrimination. Government was recruited as an ally out of necessity, not preference. Today many black scholars affirm their faith in political struggle and state provision.

• In *The Origins of the Civil Rights Movement,* Aldon Morris offers a romantic picture of how "the tradition of protest is transmitted across generations by older relatives, black institutions, churches and protest organizations. Blacks interested in social change inevitably gravitate to this protest community, where they hope to find solutions."[83]

• James Farmer of the Congress of Racial Equality wrote, "We might think of the demonstration as a rite of initiation in which the black man is mustered into the sacred order of freedom."[84]

• Civil rights activist Julian Bond says that blacks are much more likely than whites to view government as "a positive helpful force" for the simple reason that they "have seen government make an enormous difference in their lives. Government eliminated discrimination in the ballot box, government ended segregation."[85]

• Linda Faye Williams, an African American scholar who conducts research for the Congressional Black Caucus Foundation, agrees. "The reason blacks put far more emphasis than other groups on government," she says, "is because of what we've seen. It took the government for us to get these voting rights. It took the government to do the Great Society programs."[86]

All of this is true, but the contemporary problems of blacks are less susceptible to a federal solution. It is much more difficult to envision how the government could keep black families intact, or force mothers to monitor their children's study habits, or counteract the strong peer appeal of juvenile gangs. None of these problems can be easily addressed by marching to or from Selma, or by signing more civil rights legislation. Black reliance on government, once justified, may now have become a liability.

"When I graduated from college," Nikki Giovanni writes in *Racism 101,* "The only true credential I had for a job was that I was pretty good at picketing."[87] Giovanni has fortunately made a career for herself writing books and verse about racism, but most blacks who pursue the vocation of revolutionary poet find themselves at a career dead end. The only detour is into the racism industry, where protest becomes a way of life and indignation becomes a job qualification. Meanwhile, other ethnic groups are selling cars and computer software, and moving to the suburbs. Black confusion about the entrepreneurial success on the part of Koreans and other groups is indicated by the widespread suspicion in the inner city that the U.S. government is secretly providing capital to Koreans.[88]

Economist John Kasarda argues many Asians establish small businesses in order to overcome the obstacles that newcomers to this country face: problems of language and access to credit. Kasarda points out that economic solidarity helps Koreans to keep capital circulating within their community. "This is what used to happen in the black community during segregation," Kasarda says. "A single dollar would turn over five or six times, because it would be spent on goods and services provided by other blacks."[89] Other scholars such as Ivan Light and Timothy Bates have written about how Asian groups establish rotating credit associations for the purpose of pooling capital and investing it in new enterprises.[90] Ironically this research points to the fact that, used correctly, ethnocentrism can be a business asset. People from a homogeneous group who trust each other can avoid the legal and bureaucratic structures that are necessary to administer the transactions of strangers. Groups that succeed through the private sector don't need many civil rights leaders, only entrepreneurs. Yet although blacks as a group have a gross and per capita income that exceeds that of many industrialized nations, very little of this money is spent on products sold by black-owned business. Despite a few modestly successful "buy black" campaigns,[91] African Americans who are famous for their political solidarity as a group to date show no comparable sense of economic solidarity. Indeed at a recent black family gathering on the mall in Washington, D.C., many of those present were outraged to see Koreans and not their own people manning the stores selling Malcolm X T-shirts, African paraphernalia, and food.

Despite the opportunities provided by entrepreneurship,[92] and the limitations of government in solving social problems, many black leaders continue to counsel resistance as a means to secure greater transfers of wealth from the public treasury to the African American community. Manning Marable defines "the contemporary challenge" as calling for "a renaissance of black militancy" in order to generate "new organizations for collective resistance." Bell Hooks issues a call for "systematic resistance to the existing social order" on the grounds that "as long as black people believe that our liberation lies in aping ruling-class white culture, we help to perpetuate white supremacist capitalist patriarchy."[93] Congressman John Lewis offers advice that is more moderate but just as futile: "We have an obligation to organize and mobilize the African American community like never before. We must continue to push, continue to agitate, continue to get the government to say yes when it may have a desire to say no."[94]

Government, of course, has a legitimate role in providing needed services and a safety net. But the degree of black reliance on government is dysfunctional because it prevents many African Americans from being "spurred by necessity," as John Kasarda puts it, into the risks and rewards of entrepreneurship. Like the Big House in times of slavery, government can provide security. But frequently that protection from cradle to grave comes at the cost of self-reliance and private initiatives which offer better long-term rewards and, perhaps more important, an abiding sense of personal freedom.

IT'S A WHITE THING—YOU WOULDN'T UNDERSTAND

A further dysfunctional feature of black culture is its repudiation of standard English and academic achievement as forms of "acting white." (By the same token, white students who adopt a black walk, listen to rap music, speak in broken English, and do poorly in school are sometimes called "wiggers.") Resistance to "acting white" is widespread among the African American underclass, but it also seems to exist for many middle-class blacks. The problem must be viewed in the context of the educational crisis facing black America: a large proportion of the African American population is illiterate, many adults cannot read beyond the fourth-grade level, the performance of blacks in school lags behind that of whites on every measure of performance, only about one third of blacks who go to college graduate within six years.[95] African Americans seem woefully lacking in the skills needed to compete effectively in a multiracial society.

In the face of this crisis, one might expect a vigorous campaign to improve vocabulary skills, clarity of expression, numerical facility, and general academic standards among African Americans. Instead many students seem to have adopted, with the approval of their elders and civil rights leaders, a hostile stance toward the values of the white world, including the values of scholarship and study. Among some blacks, "getting ignorant" is considered a virtue and a source of self-esteem. Indeed several studies have shown, contrary to popular wisdom, that the self-esteem of young black males is higher than that of any other group.[96] Apparently those who do not value educational success do not feel bad when they fail at something they don't care about.

Skepticism toward the values of whites may be a cultural stance that served blacks well in the past: it was a technique for refusing to be defined by the categories of the oppressor. Under slavery, we saw, if whites held stealing to be bad, the slaves under some circumstances would consider it to be good. That historical inversion of values is reflected even today in black lingo: the term "bad" often means "good." White values have been historically identified with an assertion of Western cultural superiority, which provided a justification for racism. Also blacks in the past who did try to assimilate in white society often found themselves rebuffed and scorned. So now an attitude of rejection seems to have set in, and values identified as white are spurned by many blacks.

• Proviso West is a racially mixed school outside of Chicago where the grades and test scores of black students fall consistently behind those of white students. A reporter for the *New York Times* found an atmosphere of ignorance: Herbert Hoover was identified as "the vacuum guy" and Lloyd George was confused with "Boy George." More telling, the caliber of writing submitted by African American students is conveyed by the following excerpts: "The pepel from wen Martin Luther King Jr. Lived and did not wrly get along." "It was three boys with some mast up hair coming into my house. I cute their hair, because they need it." "Once I saw a boy get shot at a fair where I lived at it was about three people got shot that night." Black students, the *Times* reported, avoid the company of whites and accuse blacks who are in honors tracks of being "nerds" and "sell-outs." They are frequently taunted, "Why are you in a class with all the white kids?" and "Why are you using a white man's book?" Laura Banks, a senior, complains, "We're not accepted by the white people because they think we're not smart enough. We're not accepted by black people because they think we're too smart."[97]

• When Nwamaegwu Jeremi Duru, president of the student body at Montgomery Blair High School in the Washington, D.C., area, stepped up to the podium to receive a Gannett Foundation scholarship in 1991, he told parents and educators present that he felt constant pressure from other blacks not to study hard, and that as a result of his success he had been nicknamed "whitey." Duru argued that young blacks had been taught to believe that "it is somehow bad for black men to achieve academically" and that violent and disorderly behavior constituted more romantic expressions of black identity.[98]

• Za'kettha Blaylock, a high-performing student at a middle school in Oakland, California, told *Time* magazine in 1992 that she is regularly harassed by other students, who telephone her with threats of violence. These threats come from low-achieving blacks, according to Blaylock, who "think that because you're smart, they can go around beating you up." The hoodlums set the social tone in school, Blaylock reports, in part because they identify themselves with genuine blackness, and accuse students like her of behaving like a white person.[99]

• In 1994 the *Wall Street Journal* profiled Cedric Jennings, a hardworking student at Frank Ballou High School in Washington, D.C. Jennings acknowledged that he had almost no friends at school, that he had been called names and threatened, and that most students in his school performed poorly and regarded him as a racial apostate. "The charge of wanting to be white, where I'm from, is like treason," Jennings says. "Doing well here means you better not show your face." Another student derided academically successful blacks: "Everyone knows that they're trying to be white, get ahead in the white man's world." Phillip Atkins, an acquaintance of Jennings, says that despite his own intellectual potential and good grades in junior high, he ensures that his high school grades do not exceed a C average. "The best way to avoid trouble," he says, "is to never get all the answers right on a test." Teachers at the school describe what they call the crab-bucket syndrome: when some crabs try to crawl out of the bucket, the rest pull them back down. And academic awards at the school are often given in secret, because otherwise no students would show up.[100]

• Nomathombi Martin, a nineteen-year-old student at the University of California at Berkeley, recently recalled the intense pressures he encountered in high school to avoid speech and behavior identified as white. "I got a lot of criticism about speaking proper speech," he says. "I don't speak street talk and I never did. When I try I sound really weird. I don't pronounce words wrong like *wif, birfday, bafroom,* and things like that. They would say: why do you talk so proper? Why do you talk like you're white?"[101]

Many teachers acknowledge the pressures that African American students fall under—peer pressure not to succeed, but to fail. Marc Elrich, who teaches fourth grade in suburban Maryland, writes that black students treat fellow students of color who try and succeed as white "wannabes." Such wannabes invite amusement and contempt, according to Elrich, "because they pretend to be what they can't be."[102] And the resistance to "acting white" is not restricted to African Americans; it can also be found among lower-class Chicanos.[103] Yet it seems most pervasive in the black community. In an influential article in the *Urban Review,* two black scholars, Signithia Fordham and John Ogbu, describe the "acting white" phenomenon among African American students and give specific examples of such objectionable behavior: speaking standard English, listening to classical music, going to the opera or ballet, spending time at the library studying, working hard to get good grades in school, winning academic honors of any kind, going to the Smithsonian Institution, doing volunteer work, going camping or hiking, engaging in civil conversation at a cocktail party, being on time, and reading and writing poetry.[104]

Fordham and Ogbu seem to recognize the educational disadvantages of the "acting white" approach. In another paper Fordham concedes that successful black students tend to have strong beliefs in equality of opportunity and merit. Yet in typical relativist fashion, Fordham and Ogbu interpret the cultural resistance to "acting white" as an adaptive response to the fear of failure. Consequently, they offer few proposals for how blacks can or should behave differently. Remarkably Fordham condemns blacks who seek to transcend their racial identity and conform to the requirements of academic success. She criticizes these students as "raceless," complains that they have "subordinated their identity as black Americans to their identity as Americans," and accuses them of being "clear examples of internalizing oppression."[105] On a more popular note, rapper Chuck D of Public Enemy took credit for the role that rap music has played in reinforcing black students' rejection of the academic ethos. "You know," he told the *Village Voice,* "You walk into a fourth or fifth grade black school today, I'm telling you, you're finding chaos right now, 'cause rappers came in the game and threw that confusing element in it, and kids is like, Yo, fuck this."[106]

Perhaps one of the clearest ways for black students to distance themselves from whites is to communicate with each other in the distinctive lingo of Black English. Scholars estimate that around 80 percent of African Americans use some form of black dialect.[107] There is little doubt, as linguists point out, that ghetto idiom does possess, like most forms of communication, its own coherent form and structure.[108] Yet it seems equally clear that if African American students wish to succeed in American society, they cannot do it with Black English. "I'm not so sure about that," Alvin Poussaint says. "If you want to be a rapper, then black English is what you need." True, but such language would not work so well in a legal brief, and more blacks are likely to succeed as lawyers than as rappers.

In an intriguing study, *Twice as Less,* Eleanor Wilson Orr argues that because of its use of unorthodox terms and tense, Black English hampers African American students in their logical and mathematical reasoning, because relationships of time, place, and number become garbled.[109] Yet African American linguist Geneva Smitherman argues in favor of Black English instruction. June Jordan exults, "If it's wrong in standard English, it's probably right in Black English." And a recent article in a black studies journal declared, "Whites should not become reference points for how black children are to speak and behave. Black children's encounter with the white world should be filtered through a black frame of reference, which includes the use of Black English."[110]

CULT OF THE "BAD NIGGER"

Violence has now become a tragic defining feature of life in the black underclass. African Americans in this group seem divided into two factions: perpetrators, and potential victims. Indeed violence unleashed by blacks seems to have reached a point where it threatens the future of the African American community and the stability of society as a whole.

- In 1992 the violent crime rate for blacks was the highest ever recorded.[111]
- That same year, almost half of all murder victims were African American. Ninety-four percent of murdered blacks were killed by other blacks.[112]
- Black males are about twice as likely as white males to be victims of robbery, theft, and aggravated assault, and seven times more likely to be victims of murder.[113]
- The life expectancy of black men in central Harlem is shorter than that of men in Bangladesh.[114]
- In the District of Columbia, black residents are more likely to be killed than are people in war-torn regions such as Northern Ireland and the Middle East.[115]
- Partly as a consequence of black crime, American crime rates are the highest in the industrialized world.[116]

One of the main sources for this violence is the African American cultural orientation of the "bad nigger." As we have seen, this outlaw figure has been a revered archetype since slavery. In the view of many blacks, his very badness becomes a symbol of heroic resistance to white oppression. As Eugene Genovese writes, "Oppressed peoples cannot avoid admiring their own nihilists, who are the ones dramatically saying No! and reminding others that there are worse things than death."[117] Harnessed constructively, the "bad nigger" stance can be converted into revolutionary or reformist zeal, as the examples of Frederick Douglass, W. E. B. Du Bois, and Malcolm X suggest. But the "bad nigger" always had a gross and homicidal underside. Orlando Patterson remarks:

> There was a distinct underclass of slaves. They were the incorrigible blacks of whom the slaveowner class was forever complaining. They ran away. They were idle. They were compulsive liars. They seemed immune to punishment. We can trace the underclass, as a persisting social phenomenon, back to this group.[118]

The "bad nigger" orientation persisted into the twentieth century. Writing in 1937, John Dollard observed in *Caste and Class in a Southern Town* that blacks "seem to have a touch of Homeric attractiveness . . . as a result of prison experience or a shooting affair. They are envied their freedom of aggressive expression as well as their superior ability to take care of themselves.[119] Similarly, Claude Brown wrote in *Manchild in the Promised Land* that in Harlem, people respected those who had killed somebody, and children looked up to adults who could protect themselves from violence by fast talk if possible, and by reciprocal and deadly force if necessary. Brown described the inner-city black as "more cunning, more devious and often more vicious than his middle-class counterpart."[120] Today, if the statistics are any indication, the culture of the "bad nigger" flourishes in a permissive social climate.

Most African American scholars simply refuse to acknowledge the pathology of violence in the black underclass, apparently convinced that black criminals as well as their targets are both victims: the real culprit is societal racism. Activists recommend federal jobs programs and recruitment into the private sector. Yet it seems unrealistic, bordering on the surreal, to imagine underclass blacks with their gold chains, limping walk, obscene language, and arsenal of weapons doing nine-to-five jobs at Procter and Gamble or the State Department. Many of these young men seem lacking in the most basic skills required for steady employment: punctuality, dependability, willingness to perform routine tasks, acceptance of authority. Moreover, studies show that even when jobs are available, many young blacks refuse them, apparently on the grounds that the jobs don't pay enough or that crime is more profitable.[121]

Black scholars who do write about underclass violence typically do so in a tone of moral neutrality. In their book *Cool Pose,* Richard Majors and Janet Mancini Billson outline many of the characteristics that have gained acceptance in the inner city as a contemporary form of coolness: a way to establish a "rep" or reputation, a way to be "in."[122] According to Majors and Billson, being cool is a kind of public pose, a self-defense strategy as well as an evasion of responsibility. Style substitutes for substance, so that being unemployed with a criminal record, acting "loco" or deranged, and speaking in slurred obscenities are no obstacle but rather essential techniques for being cool. Majors and Billson are virtually anthropological in their account of the oppositional "bad nigger" archetype at work.

> African American gangs have their own rules and culture. They are consumed with symbols that identify and promote masculine cultural display: distinctive handshakes, hairstyles, stance, walks, battle scars, turf wars, hand signals, language and nicknames. Clothing can signify solidarity: baseball caps, jackets, sweatsuits, bandannas, and leather sneakers. Use of certain colors or the wearing of gold chains can signify loyalty. Gang violence can be used to achieve symbolic gains: drive-by shootings, the placing of a black wreath on a person's door (serving notice that the gang wants to execute that person), or a Colombia Necktie displayed at the site of someone's death—a murder victim's throat is cut, and the tongue is pulled through the cut.

Yet despite their nonjudgmental tone, the authors seem to recognize the pathological consequences of what they call the cool pose. "The second leading cause of death among young black males is accidents," Majors and Billson write. "Many single-car fatalities are the result of aggressive, high-risk driving such as leaning-in-the-car, one-arm driving, and drag racing." Being cool can also entail heavy drug and alcohol use; statistics show that black males have far higher rates of addiction and alcohol dependence than white males.[123] For all their social prestige, "bad niggers" often end up in jail, in the hospital, or in the morgue.

Yet statistics and scholarly description do not convey what the culture of the "bad nigger" means on the street level. For this one has to turn to the real experts: members and former members of the black underclass. Some recent writings and statements by members of this group give a revealing look at what such a social posture entails. In his book *The Ice*

Opinion, subtitled "Who Gives a Fuck?", rapper Ice T describes the ghetto as a kind of jungle:

> In the jungle, masculinity is at a premium. Anybody weaker than the next man will be victimized. In the 'hood, violence and even murder become something honorable. You've got this walk, this attitude, that says: Don't fuck with me. Everybody walks around looking at each other crazy.[124]

Ice T contends that conventional learning is simply irrelevant to the life of the black underclass; consequently, communication often takes place in newly developed forms of sign language.

> You're given books to read and learn from about shit that just seems so far-fetched from what you are and what you know and how you live. . . . All these gangs have their own hand signals. A Hoover Crip would throw two fingers down and put another finger across, to look like an H. The Crips hold up a C. A Blood will make his fingers look like a B. Even the hand signals are intricate. They can tell each other to fuck off from one set to another by throwing up their hand signals.

Although his financial success has enabled him to move away from the ghetto, Ice T continues to celebrate the ethos of the black underclass, informing blacks who move to the suburbs: "You can still be a homeboy. You can keep the same attitude once you start breaking out of the ghetto. I'm very proud I associate with convicts." He issues a resounding condemnation of the system. "The ghetto is set up like a concentration camp. . . . The biggest criminals in this country aren't the street hustlers or the men behind bars. They are probably the small, nameless group of people who actually run this country." Looters and rioters, Ice T concludes, "look at the big stores as being the system, and the system owes them. They're saying: pay muthafucka."

In his recent book *Monster,* Sanyika Shakur, a former Los Angeles gang member, offers candid reflections on the life of the black underclass, "armed and dangerous," as he describes it, "prowling the concrete jungle." He articulates an unconventional approach to the work ethic: "Work does not always constitute shooting someone, though this is the ultimate. Anything from spitting on someone to fighting—it's all work. And I was a hard worker." Monster's narrative is not always easy to follow because it uses the distinct vocabulary of the inner city, with passages such as, "We gon' kill yo' muthafuckin' ass in the mo'nin', crab. Fuck you slob-ass muthafucka, this is ET muthafuckin' G, fool." Yet it is impossible to misunderstand Monster's stark accounts of his comrades-in-arms boasting about their shootings:

> "So what's up with them niggas across the way? Y'all been droppin' bodies or what?"
>
> "Aw, nigga, I thought you knew!" said Li'l Crazy De. "Tell him Joker."
>
> "Monsta, we caught this fool the other night in the hood, writin' on the wall. Cuz, in the 'hood. Can you believe that shit? Anyway, we roll up on boy and ask him: Yo, what the fuck you doin'? Boy breaks and runs and . . ."
>
> "I cut his ass down wit' a thirty-oh-six wit' a infrared scope!" interrupted Li'l De. "Aw, Monsta, I fucked cuz up! He was all squirmin' and shit, suffer-in' and stuff, so . . ."
>
> "I put this," Joker said, pulling out a Colt 45 from his waistband. "And Ka-boom! To the brain, you know. Couldn't stand to see the bitch-made mutha-fucka sufferin' and shit."
>
> "Who was he?" I said.
>
> "Shit, we ain't heard yet."[125]

In his new incarnation as a black Muslim, Sanyika Shakur has joined a group called the Republic of New Afrika. He has not eschewed violence; rather, he wants to mobilize blacks to direct their revolutionary violence against whites. Shakur's current agenda is to organize, as part of a repara-tions campaign, a forced African American seizure and occupation of five states: South Carolina, Mississippi, Alabama, Georgia, and Louisiana. Shakur is so alienated from society that he calls whites "Americans." He is confident that he has unmasked the basic problem facing his comrades in the ghetto. "Although I was, like very other person of color on this planet, oppressed, I didn't know it."

The life of hoodlums like Monster is vividly described by journalist Leon Bing in her book *Do or Die*. Bing offers further insight into the pathological behavior and rationalizations that have become common-place in the African American underclass. Bing records and transcribes a typical conversation among young men.

> "What y'all call me, nigger?"
>
> "I'll kick you in yo' place, you call me that again!. Don't you *never* call *me* no bitch!"
>
> "How about I call you a dick-eatin' ho?"
>
> "I'll kick the shit outta you, you think you so down, you dick-eatin' little homo!"[126]

At times this rap-style repartee disintegrates into virtual incoherence:

But *fuck* slobs. That's what he's sayin'. Right, Cuz? Yeeeeeeh. Regardless—fuck slobs, that's what we all sayin'. Fuck all snoops, nigger. Bang! Bang Mighty West Side Crip gang. Unnhhh! They busters and they all gonna die—*fuck* them niggers!

Bing provides vignettes of underclass black culture by simply quoting its members' descriptions of their lifestyle.

When I was younger I was a straight killer. They'd have me killin'—everythin'. And when you eleven years old and you get you a gun, you got to be a little shook up. Then you get used to it, no problem. You got to prove a lot when you first start, see. You gotta prove that you down. Then, like I said, you get used to it—it ain't no thing.

My homeboys be doin' rapes. They'll just rape a girl, any girl, if she look good and she don't wanna kick in. Hey, if they want it bad enough, they gonna take it. All of them together. And beat on her too if she try to hold back.

See, when you shoot someone, like with a 45 automatic, one that goes, pow-pow-pow, like that—br-r-r-r-r. Make a big hole. It look real nasty. Take they brain right out. Afterward, you might feel like you want to throw up. Like: Hey, I did this? Just sittin' there, watchin' somebody's brains come out. I saw it. Looked like oatmeal.

We put him in the car and went over to a field and put a rope over that thing you hook a trailer on with. We tied him on it and drag him in the field. He got skinned up all bad, tore his scalp half off. Got all dirt and gravel and stuff stuck in the blood. Then we put him back in the car and drove him over to where one of the homies had two pit bulls in the back yard, and we threw him in there with them. Man, they chewed him up—big ole chunks of meat comin' off his arms and legs, blood pourin' out, and him just screaming and cryin' for us to take him on outta there. After we let him out the yard we made him kneel down and say stuff like: I'll suck your dicks.

Virtually without exception these morally anaesthetized muggers, drug pushers, and rapists refuse to consider themselves responsible for their behavior, placing the blame instead on whites and the government. Gang member G-Roc says:

The big enemy is the system, this government. They say they want to help you, they say they are helping you, but then, really, they ain't doin' nothing but killin' you off with words. The government don't want any of us to get no kinda good jobs. And that's based on the color of our skins. So you feel as though, well, I need money and I need it now. So you will go out and try to hurt whoever you can. The government plays a big part in why we kill our own kind.

In a similar vein, gang leader Li'l Monster appears on ABC's *Nightline* and informs Ted Koppel that he is not surprised that Asians succeed while African Americans like him are targeted by the police. "Because when you get a foreigner, they can come to this country and step to a bank and get $20,000 with no problem, they can open a business anywhere they want to, you see what I'm saying? But now here I am, I can't even get a bank account, born and raised in America."[127] Recently an Omaha drug dealer explained his illegal activity as the understandable response to societal oppression. "Society is set up so that black people can't get ahead. I'm not supposed to have the American dream and all that. I'm supposed to be in jail."[128] Fight the Power. Tawana Told the Truth. No Justice, No Peace. Understand the Rage. This familiar rhetoric seems to have been picked up by black criminals and derelicts from the civil rights establishment and from mainstream African American intellectuals.[129]

Bruce Wright, a retired New York judge, seems untroubled by gang lawlessness by his fellow African Americans, because they are simply violating "a social contract that was not of their making in the first place." Wright focuses his outrage on societal neglect of education and prison conditions. "Prisoners complain that they are punished for breaking rules they never knew existed," Wright argues. He calls for prisons that provide "middle-class vacation comforts" such as tennis and computers. Of African American murderers and rapists he urges: "Let them have swimming pools, saunas and prisons without walls."[130]

In *Why Blacks Kill Blacks,* Alvin Poussaint argues that "economic and psychological survival has often meant that blacks have had to participate in 'anti-social' acts." Rather than engage in "facile labelling," Poussaint argues, we should learn "to distinguish deviant behavior from what is, in fact, *different* behavior." Poussaint blames white racism for making black life unlivable and black violence understandable.

Reacting to the futility of his life, the individual derives an ultimate sense of power when he holds the fate of another human being in his hands. . . . Similarly, frustrated men may beat their wives and children in order to feel manly. Expectedly, these impulses are exaggerated in men who are hungry and without work. Violent acts and crime often become an outlet for a desperate man struggling against feelings of inferiority. Needless to say, black men often do not have access to legitimate means of making it in our society.[131]

Derrick Bell insists that black crime is a natural response to the fact that society simply doesn't care enough. "Victimized themselves by an uncaring society, some blacks vent their rage on victims like themselves, thereby perpetuating the terror that whites once had to invoke directly."[132] For Bell, solutions are unlikely not because African American criminals cannot change their behavior, but because whites don't want them to do so. Bell offers a scenario to explain why any cure for the problem of black crime would be against white interests.

> The Black Crime Cure drastically undermined the crime industry. Thousands of people lost jobs as police forces were reduced, court schedules cut back, and prisons closed. Manufacturers who provided weapons, uniforms and equipment of all forms to law enforcement agencies were brought to the brink of bankruptcy. Estimates of the dollar losses ran into the hundreds of millions of dollars.[133]

As with mainstream black scholars, leading African American politicians and civil rights activists have endorsed the activities of criminals and gang members. The alliance between hoodlums and mainstream civil rights activists came into public view after the Los Angeles riots, when Representative Maxine Waters brought gang leaders before the Congressional Black Caucus to denounce white racism and demand public funding. Waters introduced three young men as "friends, brothers, who are leaders in my community." One of the three said he had been in prison for three years, another for ten years. The third, who did not reveal his prison record, told news photographers that together the three had probably killed about thirty people. "We ask for jobs," these gang members complained, "yet when they bring us jobs, it's only 10 jobs, but there are 500 gang members."[134] Former NAACP head Benjamin Chavis offered similar credibility to gang leaders, who were invited by him to a "summit" where they declared "truces" and signed "peace treaties" like diplomats. Although the treaties turned out to be short-lived, Chavis announced at the time, "This summit has demystified who gang members are. It has shattered the stereotype that gang members are social deviants. They are some of the best members of society, who just need a chance and some encouragement."[135]

RAP SHEETS

All cultures have their characteristic forms of communication and artistic expression, which provide a revealing look at the group. Rap music conveys the distinctive tone of the culture of young African Americans. Many whites, especially young people, find rap music appealing because of its rebellious and anti-establishment themes. The renegade appeal of rap is suggested by the names of several groups: Above the Law, Arrested Development, The Alkaholiks, Black Sheep, Criminal Nation, Convicts, Brokin English, Fat Joe Da Gangsta, Geto Boys, Jungle Brothers, Naughty by Nature, Niggers With Attitude, Poison Clan, Public Enemy. Titles of rap songs are similarly antisocial: "How I Could Just Kill a Man," "Illegal Business," "I'm Your Pusher," "Treat Her Like a Prostitute" and "Fuck tha Police." Yet what for whites is nothing more than an in-your-face esthetic has far more serious consequences for blacks. Alice Walker recalls the way in which black men frequently address black women: "Hey, Brown Coat! Come here, Black Jacket! Hey, girl! Cutie! Won't speak, huh? What you need is a good fucking, bitch!" Walker adds, "These were all things addressed to me while attempting to get my shopping done in the past two days."[136] Linguist Geneva Smitherman in *Black Talk* has assembled a lexicon of distinctively African American terms, many of them not found in traditional dictionaries, which provide a window into life in urban black America.

Bad: Good, excellent, great, fine.
Bad Nigga: One who "doan take no shit from nobody."
Bitch: A generic term for any female.
Blue-eyed devil: A European-American.
Drive-by: Shooting from a vehicle and then driving on.
Gangsta: One who refuses to buckle under white norms.
Glass dick: The pipe used to smoke crack.
Go out: Die or be killed.
Head hunter: A woman who performs sex for drugs.
Ho: A generic reference to any female.
Put a baby: To claim as father of your child one who is not.
Rat pack: A group that gangs up to beat somebody up.
Shit: Can refer to almost anything.[137]

The debate about rap has focused on the conflict between inflammatory lyrics and cries of censorship. Critics of rap, such as film star Charlton

Heston, have pointed to songs such as Ice T's "Cop Killer" which describe rape, arson, and the murder of policemen.[138] Defenders of rap point out that rap music deserves to be protected as freedom of expression. They also argue that some rap music is socially constructive, advocating parental responsibility and study; such lyrics do exist, but they are rare. Finally rap enthusiasts maintain that even at its earthy core, rap does not promote antisocial behavior; rather, it is a vivid and accurate reflection of actual life in the inner-city. As Ice Cube puts it, "We call ourselves underground street reporters."[139] Taking this claim at face value, let us examine rap as a kind of mirror, providing a revealing portrait of the African American underclass. Lawrence Stanley's book *Rap: The Lyrics* reveals the consistent rap themes of violence and sexual exploitation. One famous tune celebrates the joys of being a "menace to society," a vocation that includes remorseless beatings and slayings "'cause sympathy is for the pathetic and the victim." A policeman, in the view of another song, is simply "a sucker in a uniform waitin' to get shot by me or another nigger." Even sadistic rape and necrophilia are presented in a positive light:

Her body's beautiful so I'm thinkin' rape
Shouldn't have had her curtains open so that's her fate.

The rapper proceeds to give a gruesome account of how he "grabbed the bitch," then "slammed her down on the couch," drew his knife, and "commenced to fucking." The young girl's pleas went unheeded, as the rapist "slit her throat and watched her shake till her eyes close[d]." At this point he "had sex with the corpse before [he] left her." Another consistent theme that surfaces in *Rap: The Lyrics* is the excuses given for violent and irresponsible behavior:

The system is designed to lead us astray
So we turn to guns and drugs for pay.[140]

Although rappers sometimes present themselves as observers rather than participants in underclass black culture, several so-called "raptivists" have become public advocates for the values of their communities. Ice Cube has endorsed the Nation of Islam's *Secret Relationship Between Blacks and Jews,* and Professor Griff of Public Enemy accuses Jews of collaborating with the South African white supremacists to perform AIDS experiments on blacks.[141] Moreover, the highly publicized problems of leading rap stars suggest that for some rappers there is a fine line between rhetoric and action. Rapper Eazy-E, founder of the group Niggers With

Attitude, boasted that he had fathered seven children by six different women; sadly, one of his sexual expeditions apparently resulted in his contracting AIDS, which took his life in April 1995. William Drayton, who goes by the name of Flavor Flav in the rap group Public Enemy, was arrested on weapons and attempted murder charges after allegedly shooting at a man he suspected was having sex with his girlfriend. Earlier Flav served time in jail for assaulting the same woman. Snoop Doggy Dog, another rapper, was recently charged with being an accessory to murder because he was driving a car from which an associate fired shots that killed a Los Angeles man. And Tupac Shakur, whose publicity packet boasts of his "revolutionary credentials" and whose music celebrates violence against policemen, has been arrested several times on various charges: sexual abuse, assault with a baseball bat against a fellow rapper, and shooting two off-duty police officers. "We are who we are," Shakur candidly says. "It's beyond good and evil."[142]

It should surprise no one that young fans of rappers look to them as role models. Lol Hayes, a thirteen-year-old Harlem youth, told *Newsweek* that he viewed Tupac Shakur not as a felon but as a freedom fighter. "There ain't been nobody like him since Malcolm. He shot those white cops in Atlanta and didn't miss a step."[143] Many mainstream black intellectuals and activists, although quick to condemn Rush Limbaugh and other talk-show hosts for incendiary rhetoric that allegedly provoked the Oklahoma bombing of a federal building, refuse to recognize that the ideas and example set by "gangsta rappers" also have consequences. Instead of seeking to counter the cultural influence of rap, leading African American figures unabashedly condone and celebrate rap music as the embodiment of black authenticity.

• Houston Baker in his book *Black Studies, Rap and the Academy* argues that rap musicians are the "black poets of the contemporary urban scene." Baker credits them with being "the last voices in America talking bravely back and black."[144] Informed that 2 Live Crew promotes "vile, juvenile, puerile and misogynistic" lyrics that celebrate illegal drug use and violence, Baker remarks, "Well, that's fine. I got nothing against that."[145]

• For Cornel West, rappers are offering nothing less than "a subversive critique of society . . . of the power structure as a whole." Indeed in West's view they are supposedly "part of a prophetic tradition."[146]

• Michael Eric Dyson commends rappers as "urban griots" who should be credited with "refining the art of oral communication" even as they "take delight in undermining 'correct' English usage."[147] And rappers return the compliment: Dyson's latest book contains a blurb from rapper Chuck D who praises Dyson as a "bad brother."[148]

• Ishmael Reed praises barely literate youths badmouthing each other's mothers as a form of high art: "Along come the rappers with a style that is sassy, militant, energetic, original and avant-garde. Some uptight folks find this difficult to deal with, just like their ideological ancestors, the Salem Puritans."[149]

• In *Raising Black Children,* James Comer and Alvin Poussaint draw on the insights of rap music to give parents the inside story on black cultural lingo: "Today the use of *motherfucker* has so changed that some young blacks use it as a term of endearment and respect. The terms *shit, bitch* and *nigger* also serve as both epithets and expressions of endearment within sections of the black community."[150]

• Henry Louis Gates, Jr. defends the lyrics of the rap group 2 Live Crew not on legitimate First Amendment grounds, but on the more dubious esthetic grounds that its music is "brilliant . . . astonishing and refreshing . . . exuberant hyperbole." For Gates, the group's "so-called obscenity" is comparable to Shakespeare's lyrics. "Many of the greatest classics of Western literature contain quote-unquote lewd words," Gates declares. 2 Live Crew's "nursery rhymes" were "part of a venerable Western tradition." At the same time, Gates pronounces the rap group part of a sophisticated African literary tradition of "signifying" and says the group has earned its place "in the history of black culture."[151] Unbelievably, Gates seems not to have listened to 2 Live Crew's homegrown version of Romeo and Juliet. The group hails the pleasurers of forced intercourse ("I'll break you down, and dick you long," "So we try real hard just to break the walls," "I'll bust your pussy, then break your backbone") and proceeds with a coarse and degrading sexual account that even Harvard libertines should find objectionable:

> Suck my dick, bitch, and make it puke
> Lick my ass up and down
> Lick it till your tongue turn doo-doo brown.[152]

UNMARRIED, WITH CHILDREN

Perhaps the most serious of African American pathologies—no less serious than violence—is the routinization of illegitimacy as a way of life. The bastardization of black America is confirmed by the fact that nearly 70 percent of young black children born in the United States today are illegitimate, compared with 22 percent of white children.[153] More than 50 percent of black households are headed by women.[154] Almost 95 percent of black teen mothers are unmarried, compared with 55 percent of their white peers.[155] Illegitimacy and single-parent households are not exclusive characteristics of the black underclass: college-educated African American women have children outside of marriage at a rate about seven to eight times higher than that of college-educated white women.[156] The result is what sociologist Andrew Cherlin terms an "almost complete separation of marriage and childbearing among African Americans."[157]

Whites too have a problem with illegitimacy, but to date the white norm remains the two-parent household. What is significant in the African American community is that illegitimacy is normalized, both statistically and morally. Studies have shown that "the black community is more tolerant about births for unwed mothers than society at large."[158] Yet as anthropologist David Murray remarks, "No community can survive over the long term without the family as a viable institution." Murray argues that "marriage is a productive institution because it makes relatives out of strangers. It provides a matrix of support for children that no other structure can provide."

It is dangerous to euphemize the problem of broken families because it is connected with a range of other social pathologies. According to the Centers for Disease Control, the AIDS rate among African Americans is about three times higher than among the U.S. population overall, and more than 50 percent of children with AIDS are black.[159] Part of the reason for this is the common practice of poor black women exchanging sex for drugs. Robert Hampton writes that "sexual abuse, physical child abuse, and family violence are arguably among the most serious social problems in the black community."[160] Richard Majors reports that wife abuse is four times more common among blacks than among whites, and that black men kill their wives at a higher rate than any other ethnic group.[161] These interrelated pathologies are evident in the Robert Taylor Homes and Cabrini Green, the largest and second largest housing projects in Chicago. William Julius Wilson reports that in Robert Taylor Homes, with a virtually all-black population of twenty thousand, 90 percent of households are headed by women, and 81 percent are on welfare. Although less than 1 percent of Chicago's population lives in the project, residents commit about 10 percent of all assaults, rapes, and murders in the city. In Cabrini Green, with a population of fourteen thousand, once again the single-parent families numbered about 90 percent, and 70 percent were supported by welfare. Within a few weeks, Wilson counted ten murders and thirty-five woundings by gunshot in that project.[162]

In an authoritative review, *Single Mothers and Their Children,* Irwin Garfinkel and Sara McLanahan show that single parenthood is closely correlated with, and contributes to, poverty and lack of opportunity. Garfinkel and McLanahan point out that mother-only families are five times more likely than two-parent families to be poor. Indeed, of all black families with children below the poverty line in 1991, 83 percent were single-parent households headed by a woman; only 13 percent were married-couple families.[163] Moreover, daughters of single parent families are more likely to have illegitimate children themselves. Garfinkel and McLanahan conclude, "The scientific evidence suggests that children who grow up in families headed by single mothers do worse as adults than children who grow up in families with two parents."[164]

As we have seen, high black illegitimacy rates cannot be blamed on slavery or segregation.[165] For much of the twentieth century, Sidney Kronus reports, "The personal standards of conduct and behavior of the black middle class were modeled after the prevailing norms of the middle-class white community which stressed responsibility and the leading of the respectable life."[166] After remaining relatively stable for the first half of this century, the black illegitmacy rate seems to have reached a critical mass during the 1960s and simply exploded since then. Scholars continue to debate whether welfare causes illegitimacy. Garfinkel and McLanahan draw a cautious but sensible conclusion: "Increases in welfare benefits contributed to, but were not the major cause of, the growth of mother-only families."[167] Perhaps the best way of putting it is that welfare makes it possible for many young women who (for whatever reason) get pregnant to have their children and set up residence on their own.

To understand illegitimacy in the black underclass, one must turn to the work of urban anthropologist Elijah Anderson, who—in his book *Street-wise* and other articles—describes the inner city in the same immersed and detailed way that some Western scholars portray tribes in distant lands. Walk through urban African American neighborhoods, Anderson writes, and you will see young black men at intersections, boasting about their sexual exploits, laughing, and strutting. Another common sight is that of many pregnant young women with distended bellies, their youthful faces belying the fact that they are often close to delivering their second or third child. Thirty-two-year-old black grandmothers abound, and the status of great-grandmother is sometimes attained before the age of fifty. These women, Anderson argues, are the complicit agents of a highly reproductive culture of sexually rapacious black males. With some discomfort, we see that there is some truth to the historical stereotype of the black male stud, or, at least in the case of the black underclass, what used to be a stereotype now contains an ingredient of truth.

These young men are "streetwise," in Anderson's term. "To be streetwise is to risk one's claim to decency, for decency is generally associated with being lame or square." Rejecting such conventional strategies of upward mobility such as getting a job, young men resort to a flourishing underground economy of drugs, alcohol, prostitution, mugging, carjacking, gambling, and other forms of criminal revenue. Within this culture, Anderson says, African American males take pride in seducing women with extravagant but dishonest promises of commitment and marriage, getting them pregnant, then abandoning them contemptuously and repeating the process with another woman. "The girls have a dream," Anderson writes, "the boys a desire." The seduction begins with the "rap," Anderson says. Rap constitutes "the verbal element of the game," whose winnings are described as "hit and run" or "booty." Anderson writes that "the boys know what the girls want and play that role to get sex. To many boys, sexual conquests become so many notches on one's belt." Young men who fail at booty—getting sex—are taunted by their peers as "bitches" and "sissies." Raising one's own children can also be viewed as being "pussy-whipped." Ruthless abandonment, sometimes accompanied by insult—"That baby ain't mine, bitch"—is regarded as the authentic black maneuver when a boy makes a girl pregnant. Such abuse—distinctive for its flagrancy and celebration of cruelty—is part of a culture of what Anderson terms "immediate self-gratification."

In most societies young men cannot readily impregnate and leave young women because these females are protected by their fathers and male relatives. In the black underclass, however, fathers are scarce and male relatives are either in prison or themselves responsible for producing illegitimate offspring with one or more women. Anderson points out that unmarried fathers typically do not provide for their children but frequently use government support for the child to provide for themselves. The welfare economy, he argues, supplements the underground economy as a source of income for young black males. Indeed some youths speak of "mother's day," a reminder to visit their girlfriends because the welfare check has arrived. Anderson argues that the women, too, are using the men although in a less blatant and irresponsible manner. The typical young woman does not seek children outside of marriage—on the contrary, "she wants desperately to believe that if she becomes pregnant he will marry her or at least be more obligated to her." Many young black women frequently offer sex "as a gift in bargaining for the attentions of a young man." Yet once they become pregnant, they find that having illegitimate children "becomes a rite of passage to adulthood." Suddenly these sad young women have something that they can call their own, and "the teenage mother derives status from her baby." They become part of what Anderson calls the "baby club": many other similarly placed women welcome the newcomer into their fold. "Becoming a mother," Anderson writes, "can seem to be a means to authority, maturity and respect."

Welfare is not the reason for getting pregnant, Anderson insists. But it affords "a limited but steady income" which becomes the means for teenagers to escape the often painful circumstances of their own homes, and to establish their own single-family household "and at times attract other men who need money." Welfare even encourages young women to endorse the denial of their male sexual partner who does not want to claim paternity. "This incentive is the prospect of a check from the welfare office, which is much more dependable than the irregular support payments of a sporadically employed youth." Because of the relative security and emancipation that illegitimate children can bring, Anderson argues that bastardy has—despite the condemnation of some churches—lost most of its earlier stigma and now become "socially acceptable."[168]

It is easy to appreciate the difficulties of young single girls raising their children with no sources of financial support except the government. Broken homes reduce the chances for children to be socialized in an environment that provides adequate attention, firm yet consistent discipline, and intellectual and social stimulation. All too often, such families degenerate into institutions of neglect, where shrieking and slapping is common and the child's mental development is virtually ignored. From a very early age, children learn about sex and drugs, and that violence is an acceptable way to resolve problems.[169] Despite the scandalous pain generated by illegitimacy in the underclass, leading African American intellectuals abstain from criticizing and go so far as to revel in what they describe as another alternative lifestyle.

• Julianne Malveaux is appalled that anyone would question the lifestyle of welfare mothers who live off taxpayers or seek to impose work requirements on them; she insists that "being on welfare is hard work."[170]

• Bell Hooks contends that female-headed households are part of a tradition of "meaningful and productive lifestyles that do not conform to white societal norms."[171]

• Alice Walker argues that single motherhood is an honorable vocation for African Americans and the European tradition of marriage is obsolete and should be abolished.[172]

• June Jordan says that it is a "heartless joke" to "blame the black family for not being white. . . . We have never been standard or predictable or stabilized in any normative sense." Jordan calls for a revival of African kinship and extended family systems as a possible solution for the breakdown of conventional marriage in the black community.[173]

• Similarly Johnnetta Cole finds nothing wrong with single-parent families. "The 'problem' with these households is that they are deprived of decent food, shelter, medical care, and education." Moreover, in Cole's view, if families abuse their children or if children take to crime and drugs, society is to blame. "Deprivation breeds frustration that can become so intense as to drive a mother to neglect or abuse her children, and propel a youngster into destructive and self-destructive behavior." Cole's solutions include exploring "a range of alternatives . . . from a fairly permanent state of singleness to lesbianism to significant-othering."[174]

• For Toni Morrison the problem is not that unmarried black women are getting pregnant, but that societal sexism refuses to acknowledge women as heads of households. Taking a cue from Margaret Mead, Morrison proposes an abandonment of societal restraints and a return to the elemental urge of nature. The ghetto is the new Samoa.

> The little nuclear family is a paradigm that just doesn't work. Why we are hanging onto it, I don't know. I don't think a female running a house is a problem. It's perceived as one because of the notion that a head is a man. . . . The child's not going to hurt the women. Who cares about the schedule? What is this business that you have to finish school at 18? The body is ready to have babies. Nature wants it done then. I want to take them all in my arms and say: Your baby is beautiful and so are you. . . . And when you want to be a brain surgeon, call me—I will take care of your baby.[175]

TAKING RESPONSIBILITY

As should be clear by now, the mainstream of black intellectuals simply refuses to criticize African American pathologies or to seek internal reform. All that the scholars and activists of the civil rights establishment have to offer is what may be termed excuse theory: an extensive literature offering literally hundreds of reasons for why external constraints make it impossible for blacks to succeed. For William Julius Wilson, black pathologies are the product (and not a contributory cause) of a lack of jobs: in Wilson's view, blacks just happened to arrive in the cities around the time that unskilled jobs were leaving.[176] Douglas Massey and Nancy Denton argue that residential separation accounts for the formation and persistence of the underclass.[177] Bernard Boxill even argues that black pathologies should be classed as a cultural injury which entitles African Americans to further subsidies from the government.[178]

One problem with this approach is that by emphasizing how poverty and deprivation cause crime and other pathologies, excuse theorists cannot explain why the majority of poor people remain law abiding. Another problem is that by focusing almost entirely on the cause of pathologies, excuse theorists offer no coherent vision about what to do about them. Since external factors are always to blame, these activists cannot do better than propose societal remedies like redoubled federal funding, more social engineering, or a renewed campaign to root out white racism. In some cases government programs may help, yet none of them show much prospect of reducing the pathologies themselves. The reason for the moral paralysis of mainstream black intellectuals is that their relativist framework makes it impossible for them to identify black pathology without placing the onus for causing and remedying it on society at large.

The "prophetic" philosophy of Cornel West illustrates the deficiencies of excuse theory. West eloquently describes black nihilism, spiritual despair, and self-destructive wantonness—"the eclipse of hope, the unprecedented collapse of meaning, the incredible disregard for human life and property, and empty quest for pleasure, property and power."[179] Yet his biblical-style pronouncements are promptly directed against two external groups: society in general and white racists in particular. "We indeed must criticize and condemn immoral acts of black people," West writes, "but we must do so cognizant of the circumstances into which people are born and under which they live."[180] This passage illustrates the basic incoherence of West's position: blacks are not responsible for their circumstances, yet they should be criticized and condemned for engaging in behavior that is really someone else's fault. This is the Du Boisian problem all over again. West, who consciously places himself in the tradition of Du Bois, begins by seeking to reform black culture and ends up fulminating about the inadequacies of American culture. West's solutions are a quixotic combination of watered-down Marxism, radical feminism, and homosexual rights advocacy, none of which offers any realistic hope for ameliorating black pathologies.[181]

The only people who are seriously confronting black cultural deficiencies and offering constructive proposals for dealing with them are members of a group we can call the reformers.[182] Many of them are conservatives such as Clarence Thomas, Colin Powell, Thomas Sowell, Glenn Loury, Shelby Steele, Alan Keyes, Walter Williams, Robert Woodson, John Sibley Butler, Stanley Crouch, Tony Brown, Anne Wortham, Elizabeth Wright, Ken Hamblin, and Armstrong Williams. Conservative thought can be found in two new magazines: *Destiny,* edited by Emanuel McLittle, and *National Minority Politics,* edited by Willie Richardson. Since the 1960s, black conservatives have been a *vox clamantis in deserto,* a voice in the wilderness calling for the community to improve through self-help and entrepreneurship. For their efforts, these thinkers have received nothing but relentless abuse and virtual excommunication. Yet in the last few years the conservatives have been getting some credit for being farsighted in predicting the cultural crisis of the black community. Indeed some of their themes have been taken up by a group whose members would insistently describe themselves as liberals: Randall Kennedy, Orlando Patterson, Carol Swain, Anthony Appiah, Gerald Early, Nancy Fitch, Stephen Carter, William Raspberry, Clarence Page, Juan Williams, Hugh Price, Michael Meyers, Hugh Pearson, Mark Mathabane, and Itabari Njeri. Of late these liberals have been under assault for adopting unorthodox positions and supporting black conservatives like Clarence Thomas.[183] At a surface level, what unites both conservative and liberal reformers is the invective to which they are subjected. But at a deeper level, these groups are on the same side of the battle to oppose destructive and pathological trends. And their best hope is to strengthen the morale and expand the resources of thousands of inner-city pastors and school teachers, who are politically liberal but culturally conservative. Heretofore unknown and unrecognized, these figures are striving heroically to make the underclass not respectable but (a crucial difference) worthy of respect.

The reformers stress three basic themes. The first is that while racism exists, it no longer controls the destiny of African Americans as a group, and it should not be used as a pretext for blacks to avoid dealing with their own problems. "I continue to experience racial indignities and slights," Shelby Steele writes. "Yet I have also come to realize that I have been more in charge of my fate than I always wanted to believe."[184] Mark Mathabane, a black South African who now lives in South Carolina, writes that during his speeches before African American groups "many people seem disappointed when I cannot relate harrowing stories of persecution at the hands of hooded Klansmen."[185] Orlando Patterson writes:

> America, while still flawed in its race relations, is now the least racist white-majority society in the world; has a better record of legal protection of minorities than any other society, white or black; offers more opportunities to a greater number of black persons than any other society, including all of Africa; and has gone through a dramatic change in its attitudes toward miscegenation over the past 25 years.[186]

Hugh Price, the new president of the Urban League, argues that "we must not let ourselves and especially our children fall into the paranoid trap of thinking that racism accounts for all that plagues us."[187] In a similar vein, Colin Powell tells African American students, "Don't use racism as an excuse for your own shortcomings."[188] Clarence Thomas warns young blacks that "unlike me, you must not only overcome the repressiveness of racism, you must also overcome the lure of excuses."[189] Stephen Carter writes that blacks should not feel too bitter about sometimes having to work harder than everyone else. "It would not be a bad thing at all for us as a race to develop as our defining characteristic: Oh, you know these black people, they always work twice as hard as everybody else."[190] Thomas Sowell stresses the destructive effects of blaming omnipresent racism: "How are you going to tell a young black to work hard or study hard in order to get ahead, when many so-called black leaders are constantly telling him that everything is rigged against him?"[191] William Raspberry writes:

> Racism has become our all-purpose explanation for every disadvantage. We spend precious resources, time, energy, imagination and political capital searching, always successfully, for evidence of racism, while our problems get worse. . . . The difference between us and Asian Americans is that our myth is that racism accounts for our shortcomings. Theirs is that their own efforts can make a difference, no matter what white people think.[192]

The second theme of the reformers is that black pathologies need to be boldly identified and squarely confronted. "A group can never get cleaner over time," Thomas Sowell writes, "if the suggestion that it was ever dirty was only a figment of bigots' imaginations."[193] Colin Powell tells black audiences that "the worst kind of poverty is not economic poverty" but rather "the poverty of values."[194] Randall Kennedy urges that blacks show less solicitude for the rights of criminals and more concern for the rights of African Americans victimized by them.[195] Deploring the "exhibitionism of nonachievement" in which some black activists engage, Glenn Loury writes, "Further progress toward the attainment of equality depends most crucially at this juncture on the acknowledgment and rectification of the dysfunctional behaviors which plague black communities, and which so offend and threaten others."[196] The irresponsible underclass male, Anne Wortham writes, wants freedom but "the only way he can obtain it is by force and destruction . . . the freedom he seeks is freedom from the judgement of others."[197] Orlando Patterson writes:

> Black American ethnicity has encouraged the intellectual reinforcement of aspects of black life that are just plain rotten. The street culture of petty crime, drug addiction, paternal irresponsibility, whoring, pimping, and superfly inanity, all of which damage and destroy fellow blacks, instead of being condemned by black ethnic leaders has, until recently, been hailed as the embodiment of black soul.[198]

Third, the reformers are skeptical of the capacity of external sources such as the government to address black pathologies; rather, they argue, the primary initiative should come from the pursuit of excellence and entrepreneurship within the black community. "Enforcement of civil rights can assure us only a place at the starting gate," William Raspberry writes. "What is required for victory is that we run like hell."[199] Although a supporter of moderate forms of affirmative action as a remedy for existing forms of white nepotism, Randall Kennedy argues that blacks should seek the strict enforcement of meritocratic standards for all groups.[200] Shelby Steele puts it more bluntly, "Representation can be manufactured. Development is always hard-earned."[201]

Voicing a bold criticism of the civil rights establishment as ideologically resistant to cultural reform, Stanley Crouch inveighs against the unproductive "tantrum politics" of the race merchants.[202] Michael Meyers says that mainstream civil rights institutions "have become moribund, dysfunctional and self-destructive" and warns that many black leaders have embraced the principles of the racists—in his words, they "really do believe that skin color determines personality, culture and even intelligence."[203] Juan Williams alleges that some African American leaders exploit the issue of racism for monetary gain, fueling "the idea that blacks can be bought and that the civil rights movement is for sale."[204] Clarence Page urges that groups such as the NAACP "move on to new strategies to revive inner-city economies, educate our young, fight street crime and empower embattled parents in low-income households."[205]

"No people can be genuinely free," Glenn Loury writes, "so long as they look to others for their deliverance." Loury argues that self-help is not a substitute but a prerequisite for assistance from society, because people are more disposed to help groups that are doing for themselves.[206] Tony Brown argues that African Americans need to come together as a group to develop institutions that promote entrepreneurship and self-help. "We have conducted the most successful economic boycott in history—against ourselves."[207] Alan Keyes emphasizes moral renewal and the need to strengthen the black church and the black family.[208] Orlando Patterson writes, "As long as African Americans remained outsiders, we were forced to concentrate on the central issue of getting in and, in the process, to downplay the many problems that beset us. I think the time has now come to confront those problems squarely."[209] Stanley Crouch says it in the simplest way possible, "The values of civilized behavior must be reestablished."[210]

Uncle Tom's dilemma becomes apparent. During the days of slavery and segregation Uncle Tom recognized the cultural superiority of his oppressor, even as he accommodated himself to the system of oppression. Thus Uncle Tom became a figure who could be understood but not admired. Instead, the oppositional culture of the "bad nigger" became normative for the black community. But now the historical meaning of these terms is obsolete. In today's America, where the slavemasters and segregationists are gone and blacks enjoy the same legal status as whites, the "bad nigger" and his oppositional culture have become a menace to African Americans and the larger society. By contrast, the African American reformers who are derided as contemporary Uncle Toms are the true civilizational forces in the black community. In the success of their efforts lies our hope.

13

THE END OF RACISM

A New Vision for a Multiracial Society

Race consciousness is a deadly explosive on the tongues of men.
—Zora Neale Hurston[1]

This book has traced the origins of racism as a modern doctrine of the superiority of Western civilization. It has also documented the twentieth-century rise of liberal antiracism, which uses the ideology of cultural relativism—the presumed equality of all cultures—to debunk the old racist hierarchy. As we have seen, cultural relativism is the source of the legal doctrine of proportional representation, as well as of the educational ideology of multiculturalism. The unquestioned assumption of contemporary liberalism is that racism is responsible for black failure, and that given the persistence of racism in society, there is no alternative to institutionalizing race as the basis of job hiring, voting, law, and education. This study has sought to demonstrate the intellectual and moral bankruptcy of this form of liberalism.

Racism undoubtedly exists, but it no longer has the power to thwart blacks or any other group in achieving their economic, political, and social aspirations. It cannot be denied that African Americans suffer slights in terms of taxidrivers who pass them by, pedestrians who treat them as a security risk, banks that are reluctant to invest in black neighborhoods, and other forms of continued discrimination. Some of this discrimination is irrational, motivated by bigotry or faulty generalization. Much of it, as we have seen, is behavior that is rational from the point of view of the discriminator and at the same time harmful for black individuals who do not conform to the behavioral pattern of their peers. Such incidents undoubtedly cause pain, and invite legitimate public sympathy and concern. But they do not explain why blacks as a group do worse than other groups in getting into selective colleges, performing well on tests, gaining access to rewarding jobs and professions, starting and successfully operating independent businesses, and maintaining productive and cohesive communities.

Racism cannot explain most of the contemporary hardships faced by African Americans, even if some of them had their historical roots in oppression. Activists like Derrick Bell may deny it, but America today is not the same place that it was a generation ago. African Americans now live in a country where a black man, Colin Powell, who three decades ago could not be served a hamburger in many Southern restaurants, became chairman of the Joint Chiefs of Staff; where an African American, Douglas Wilder, was elected governor of Virginia, the heart of the Confederacy; where a former Dixiecrat like Senator Strom Thurmond supported the nomination of Clarence Thomas, a black man married to a white woman, for the Supreme Court; and where an interracial jury convicted Byron De La Beckwith for killing civil rights activist Medgar Evers a generation after two all-white juries acquitted him.

Many scholars and civil rights activists continue to blame racism for African American problems; yet if white racism controls the destiny of blacks today, how has one segment of the black community prospered so much over the past generation, while the condition of the black underclass has deteriorated? Since black women and black men are equally exposed to white bigotry, why are black women competitive with white women in the workplace, while black men lag behind all other groups? In major cities in which blacks dominate the institutions of government, is it realistic to assume that white racism is the main cause of crime, delinquency, and dilapidation? It also is not at all clear how racism could prevent the children of middle-class blacks from performing as well as whites and Asians on tests of mathematical and logical reasoning. Black pathologies such as illegitimacy, dependency, and crime are far more serious today than in the past, when racism was indisputably more potent and pervasive. "No one who supports the contemporary racism thesis," William Julius Wilson acknowledges, "has provided adequate or convincing answers to these questions."[2]

Even if racism were to disappear overnight, the worst problems facing black America would persist. Single parenthood and welfare dependency among the black underclass would not cease. Crack and AIDS would continue to ravage black communities. The black crime rate, with its disproportionate impact on African American communities, would still extract a terrible toll.[3] Indeed drugs and black-on-black crime kill more blacks in a year than all the lynchings in U.S. history. Racism is hardly the most serious problem facing African Americans in the United States today. Their main challenge is a civilizational breakdown that stretches across class lines but is especially concentrated in the black underclass. At every socioeconomic level, blacks are uncompetitive on those measures of achievement that are essential to modern industrial society. Many middle-class African Americans are, by their own account, distorted in their social relations by the consuming passion of black rage. And nothing strengthens racism in this country more than the behavior of the African American underclass, which flagrantly violates and scandalizes basic codes of responsibility, decency, and civility. As far as many blacks are concerned, as E. Franklin Frazier once wrote, "The travail of civilization is not yet ended."[4]

Racism began in the West as a biological explanation for a large gap of civilizational development separating blacks from whites. Today racism is reinforced and made plausible by the reemergence of that gap within the United States. For many whites the criminal and irresponsible black underclass represents a revival of barbarism in the midst of Western civilization. If this is true, the best way to eradicate beliefs in black inferiority is to remove their empirical basis. As African American scholars Jeff Howard and Ray Hammond argue, if blacks as a group can show that they are capable of performing competitively in schools and the work force, and exercising both the rights and the responsibilities of American citizenship, then racism will be deprived of its foundation in experience.[5] If blacks can close the civilization gap, the race problem in this country is likely to become insignificant. African Americans in particular and society in general have the daunting mission to address the serious internal problems within black culture. That is the best antiracism now.

In private, some activists like Jesse Jackson will tentatively acknowledge black pathologies. Yet it is difficult for liberal whites and mainstream black leaders to confront these problems publicly because of the deep-rooted ideology of cultural relativism. If all cultures are equal, on what grounds can the standards of mainstream society be applied to evaluate the performance and conduct of African Americans? If such standards are

entirely relative and culture-bound, on what basis can blacks who are productive and law-abiding establish valid norms for blacks who are not? As
Elijah Anderson argues, the inner city is characterized by two rival cultures: a hegemonic culture of pathology and a besieged culture of decency. By refusing to acknowledge that one culture is better than another—by
erasing the distinction between barbarism and civilization—cultural relativism cruelly inhibits the nation from identifying and working to ameliorate pathologies that are destroying the life chances of millions of African
Americans. Thus we arrive at a singular irony: cultural relativism, once the
instrument of racial emancipation for blacks, has now become an obstacle
to confronting real problems that cannot be avoided. One may say that
today the most formidable ideological barrier facing blacks is not racism
but antiracism.

Rethinking Relativism

As we have seen, liberals in the twentieth century embraced relativism because it offered a basis for affirming and working to secure racial equality.
Undoubtedly the relativist proclamation of the equality of all cultures provided liberals with a powerful rationale to reject the classic racist assertion
of white civilizational superiority. But as often happens, the solution to an
old problem becomes the source of a new one. Relativism has now imprisoned liberals in an iron cage that prevents them from acknowledging
black pathology, makes it impossible for them to support policies that uphold any standard of responsibility, and compels them to blame every
problem faced by blacks on white racism or its institutional legacy. This
explains the interminable liberal rhetoric about the "root causes" of
poverty, the "bitter hoax" of the American dream, the mysterious disappearance of "meaningful" jobs, the prospect of a "resurgence" of "hate,"
the danger of "imposing one's morality," the need to avoid "code words,"
and how we should all "understand the rage." Pondering what he concedes are the shocking behavior patterns of the black underclass, columnist Michael Massing can only ask, "what has driven these people to
engage in such excesses?"[6] By denying that blacks can fail on their own,
cultural relativism denies them the possibility of achieving success. Seeking to cover up black failure, relativism suppresses cultural autonomy, refusing to grant blacks control over their destiny.

Modern liberals are well aware of the differences in academic achievement, economic performance, family structure, and crime rates between

blacks and other groups. Given that these differences persist at all socio-economic levels, there are three possible explanations: genes, culture, and racial discrimination (or some combination of these factors). Since many liberals are committed to the precept that all cultures are or should be equal, it follows that observable group differences are the product of either discrimination or genes. If discrimination cannot fully explain why blacks do not perform as well as whites on various measures of performance, then the conclusion cannot be escaped: according to the liberal paradigm, blacks must be genetically inferior. Arthur Jensen and Charles Murray wait in the wings.

Since relativism makes it impossible for liberals to confront the issue of black cultural pathology—to do so is seen as "blaming the victim"—the desire to avoid a genetic explanation forces liberals to blame group differences on racism. At first glance it seems difficult, if not impossible, to argue that African Americans as a group perform substantially worse in intellectual and economic ventures than whites and Asians of similar background because they are passed up by racist cabdrivers or because shopkeepers follow them around in stores. Yet despite their absurdity, such suggestions are required by a liberal ideology that requires white racism to explain black failure. If racism cannot be located in individuals, it must be diagnosed in institutional structures. The charge of racism becomes a kind of incantation intended to ward off the demons of black inferiority. It offers a bewitched understanding that makes nonsense of everyday perception and empirical reality by alleging the subtle workings of unfriendly ghosts. In this Ptolemaic universe, the idea of racism serves the function of corrective epicycles that need to be invoked constantly to preserve the liberal edifice of cultural relativism and liberal confidence in black capacity. Raising the question of "why so many young men are engaging in what amounts to self-inflicted genocide," Andrew Hacker provides the prescribed answer. "It is white America that has made being black so disconsolate an estate."[7]

Thus begins the liberal project to offer an elaborate and shifting rationale for black incapacity. If African Americans do not do well on tests, that is because the tests are biased, and because white society has deprived them of the necessary skills. If they drop out of school, they have been driven out by racism which injures black self-esteem. If they have illegitimate children, this is because society refuses to provide black males with steady jobs. If they are convicted of a disproportionate number of violent crimes, this is because the police, judges, and juries are racist. Those who have committed crimes have been pressured to do so by undeserved economic hardship. Riots are automatically attributed to legitimate outbursts of black rage. In short, the liberal position on black failure can be reduced to a single implausible slogan: Just say racism. Yet liberals recognize that old forms of segregation and overt discrimination have greatly eroded, so where is this racism that is supposedly holding African Americans back at every juncture? Bull Connor does not serve in the Princeton admissions office, where he keeps blacks out with hoses and dogs; Bull Connor is dead. The main obstacle to more blacks getting into Princeton is the university's selective admissions standards. Consequently many liberals find that they must now treat merit itself as a mere cover for racism. In case after case, liberals are destroying legitimate institutions and practices in order to conceal the embarrassing reality of black failure.

In the view of its founders, such as Locke, liberalism is a philosophy that seeks to establish fair rules so that people with different interests have the freedom to pursue their goals within a framework of state neutrality. In modern liberal society, democratic elections, free markets, and civil liberties are all instruments that aim at maximizing freedom without dictating results. Liberalism does not tell you who to vote for, what to buy, or how to exercise your freedom of religion and speech. Liberal procedures such as the jury system and the presumption of innocence are intended to secure basic rights. Yet in order to compel the relativist outcome of substantive racial equality, liberals are forced to subvert these very principles. The easiest way to ensure that more blacks enter selective colleges and receive well-paying jobs is to lower admissions and hiring standards. If companies prove recalcitrant, the civil rights laws invert the premise of Western justice and treat defendants who fail to hire a proportional number of blacks as "guilty until proven innocent." In order to ensure that blacks are elected to represent blacks, voting districts are drawn in such a way as to virtually foreordain the result. In some cases, free speech is subordinated to the goals of sensitivity and diversity, as in so-called hate speech and hate crimes laws. At every stage, fundamental liberal principles are being sacrificed at the altar of cultural relativism. In its fanatical commitment to the relativist ideology of group equality, liberalism is inexorably destroying itself.

In the 1960s, many liberals supported civil rights because of a deep confidence in color-blind rules that would give blacks a fair chance to compete on their merits. The results of the last few decades have eroded this faith, so that now many of these same white liberals mainly produce alibis for black failure. These apologies take on a ritualistic and sometimes comic aspect, and there is some question about whether they are even believed by their advocates. Shelby Steele points out that many of the same activists who offer extensive arguments for why grades and standardized aptitude and achievement tests are meaningless nevertheless demonstrate intense private concern about how their own sons and daughters do on such measures of performance. If this double standard exists, it shows that many activists don't want to get rid of standards altogether, they want to get rid of standards *for blacks.* Eventually such self-deception becomes corrosive; many liberals may cease to believe in their own ingenious excuses and become like lawyers who suspect, finally, that their client may be guilty. Indeed before the moral tribunal of liberalism, blacks seem to stand publicly exculpated but privately convicted. White liberals do not want blacks to fail but many seem to behave as though, in every competition that is not rigged, they expect them to do so. Moreover, the routine abridgment of standards for blacks makes it more likely that blacks will fail at tasks for which they are inadequately prepared. Liberalism, which began as an ideology of equal rights, has degenerated into the paternalism of rigged results.

While contemporary liberalism destroys its principles, it clears the pathway for various species of illiberalism. Ironically liberalism which has for much of this century been the ideology of antiracism is now establishing the foundation for a new racism, black and white. Today's invocations of white power are based upon an appeal to cultural integrity and racial pride; on what grounds can liberal relativists criticize groups like Jared Taylor's "American Renaissance" which assert the right to defend their own cultural norms? Similarly white liberals find it difficult to condemn Afrocentric extremism and black racism because those ideologies are also constructed on the foundation of Boasian relativism. Instead, all the threats and actions of black racists must be blamed on societal racism or on liberalism itself: "Look what we made them do."[8] Not only does liberal relativism legitimate white and black racism, but it also concedes the high ground to the forces of bigotry: white racists become the unchallenged custodians of Western civilization, and black racists become the most clear-eyed diagnosticians of our social problems.

By denying civilizational standards, liberal relativism performs the philosophical spadework that permits irresponsible behavior to flourish without public accountability. This is not merely an African American problem; it is a national problem. The American crime rate has risen dramatically over the past few decades, and juvenile homicide has reached catastrophic proportions. Alarming numbers of high school students use drugs, get pregnant, or carry weapons to class. And as many observers have pointed out, the white illegitimacy rate today is approximately the same as the African American rate when Daniel Patrick Moynihan wrote his report on the black family in the mid-1960s. Cultural relativism now prevents liberals from publicly asserting and enforcing civilizational standards for everyone, not just for African Americans.

This is the phenomenon that Moynihan terms "defining deviancy down": in contemporary rhetoric, deviant and pathological behavior such as high crime rates and illegitimacy become socially acceptable. Conversely, as Charles Krauthammer points out, traditional institutions such as heterosexual courtship and the family are treated as deviant settings for sexual abuse and domestic violence.[9] In a moral inversion, the normal becomes abnormal and vice versa. We have gone from civil rights to uncivil liberties—the liberty to abuse freedom and then claim entitlement. As Gertrude Himmelfarb argues, liberal demoralization is a direct result of the denial of moral and civilizational norms.[10] Consider this: if all welfare recipients were white, most liberals would probably support legal measures that make benefits contingent upon responsible behavior. But since a disproportionate number of welfare mothers are black, many liberals are ideologically compelled to resist any serious proposals that link benefits to work or accountability. The liberal line is summarized by columnist Judy Mann, who terms illegitimacy "a moralistic word" and condemns welfare restrictions and work requirements as part of "a war against poor women whose misfortune has been to have children they can't support."[11] It is not irresponsible behavior, but the attempt to point it out and discourage it, that invites liberal condemnation. The logic of this argument suggests that since African Americans cannot be held responsible, no one can be.

It is time for well-meaning liberals to reconsider their allegiance to relativism. The doctrine that all cultures are equal, the intellectual foundation of liberal antiracism, was functional and useful in its day. But now relativism has become a kind of virus, attacking the immune systems of institutional legitimacy and public decency, and preventing Americans from confronting a civilizational crisis that affects all groups although it is most concentrated among poor blacks. John Dewey once wrote that the test of political doctrines is whether they are "socially beneficial or harmful." Relativism should at least be abandoned on pragmatic grounds—it no longer works for us. Like elements of black culture, relativism has become dysfunctional in a new environment and a new era.

Yet it is not enough for liberals to reject relativism and return to a philosophy of individual rights. When the American founders articulated their vision of rights they took for granted a moral fabric that is now badly lacerated. American society in general, and black culture in particular, cannot be reconstructed on a liberal foundation of rights without also recovering an older language and ethic of responsibility. What liberals should consider now is a return to the classical conception of natural rights, and the distinction made by the ancient Greeks between civilization and barbarism. This is a proposal, we may say, to "turn back the clock" not to the 1950s but to the fifth century B.C.

Since the Boasian revolution, talk of "civilization" is scandalous to many liberals because they associate the term with the *mission civilisatrice* of colonialism and with the most arrogant claims of white racism. The concepts of "nature" and "civilization," like most good ideas, have been abused in the past; as we have seen, they provided a justification for bigotry and oppression. Western technological superiority supplied the means not only for the conquest of nature but also for the conquest of other human beings. Since modernity is largely Western, the advance of modern science provided a rationale for the racist view that only whites were suited to civilization; other peoples were members of a lower natural order, if their humanity was granted at all. Yet the Greek understanding of nature and civilization is not exclusively Western, and it does not rely on scientific or technological superiority. The Greeks offer an idea of civilization that is free of racist overtones, one that is vitally needed in America today.

The Greeks did not use the term "civilization," which is modern. Rather, they spoke of the *polis.* The Greeks were fiercely attached to their *polis,* because they viewed civilization as a fragile phenomenon which could not be taken for granted. Civilized people are held together by a common understanding of virtue and depravity, of greatness and degradation. As we have seen, the Greeks were ethnocentric: they showed a preference for their own. Such tribalism they would have regarded as natural, and indeed we now know that it is universal. In some situations an instinctive ethnocentrism is inevitable, as when one's society is under external armed attack and one must rally to its defense. Yet the Greeks also understood that ethnocentrism can be narrow and blinding, as when we automatically assume that our own customs and beliefs are necessarily the best or the true ones. The investigations of Socrates were devoted to an interrogation of conventional mores and assumptions, in order to discover a transcendent way of life that realizes what is best in human nature.

As we have seen, the Greeks acknowledged physical differences and even joked about them. They did not, however, attach any significance to race. The Greeks had no quarrel with the concept of superior and inferior cultures, but they did not link such differences to biology. In the Aristotelian tradition, the line between civilization and barbarism is not racial; it runs through every human being. Barbarism represents the natural and untutored state. Civilization is not inborn but acquired through dedication and effort, aimed at taming our savage impulses through various higher attachments, and at the formation of a discriminating mind and the cultivation of taste. The Greek view of civilization was aristocratic, in that it implied a hierarchy of excellence and achievement, but it was also egalitarian, in that the possibility of the civilized life is in principle open to all. In modern parlance, the Greeks acknowledged the multiplicity of races but affirmed civilization as a universal human possibility.

The modern assumption is that the antithesis of a relativist is an absolutist. The Greeks found a way to escape this false dichotomy. Aristotle was neither a relativist nor an absolutist. In Aristotle's view absolutism is against nature because it is an effort to establish tyrannical rule over it—to remake human beings. Absolutism shares with relativism a false belief in the complete plasticity of human nature. Aristotle held that human nature imposes limits on freedom. Aristotle might have agreed that science has taught modern man to conquer nature, an achievement for which he would have displayed only qualified enthusiasm. At the same time, he would have denied that human nature can be similarly conquered—at least not without the destruction of humanity. Whatever the achievements of technology, it is unlikely to abolish selfishness or envy. Material progress does not entail moral progress. The limits that the ancients envisioned in human nature are fully consistent with the findings of modern biology.

Aristotle parted with modern science, however, in his conviction that human beings have a shared nature which was not merely physical but also moral. For Aristotle, man was the "beast with the red cheeks," capable of placing himself under ethical judgment and thus capable of shame. Aristotle's conception of virtue was rational and practical: good actions were simply those which were "in accordance with nature," actions that promoted *eudaimonia* or happiness. For the Greeks, the purpose of society was to cultivate good citizens. They did not speak of "values" but of "virtues," yet their term *arete* means something closer to "excellence." Aristotle understood *arete* not as theological virtue—he was no early incarnation of Pat Robertson—but as those human qualities like courage, magnanimity, and prudence which make possible an honorable and happy life. Aristotle understood that virtues are transmitted through law and through education, mainly through the device of repetition or habit. Eventually, learned practice becomes "second nature." Central to Aristotle's thought is the distinction between *sophia* (wisdom) and *phronesis* (practical wisdom), because it suggests that while the nature or end of man is fixed, right actions are not simply general laws but determined in the context of given situations. For Aristotle, pragmatism was not an end but a means to an end. The classical virtues of prudence and moderation help to chart a middle course between the twin excesses of relativism and absolutism.

Modern liberal society was founded in resistance to the classical vision, as a preferable alternative to it. Unlike the Greeks, we speak the language of rights rather than duty. In its original conception liberalism is radically individualistic; it detaches man from society in order to discover rights that human beings enjoy in the "state of nature." As Locke and Hobbes have it, man enters into a social contract in which he exchanges his natural rights for civil rights. The American principle of limited government is largely based on this modern understanding. It emphasizes freedom, rather than virtue, as the highest political good. The great achievement of liberal democracy is to recognize that civilization and virtue cannot be coerced; wisdom must be vindicated by consent. The great weakness of this system is its tendency to reduce virtue to consent, or to deny its existence. Thus, as Plato understood, liberal democracy is peculiarly vulnerable to relativism.

We cannot literally return to the past, but we can learn from the past. America is currently experiencing what is called a culture war, but what is more accurately termed a civilizational crisis. This crisis arises out of the breakdown of the compromise between the Judeo-Christian ethic and liberal democracy, between the old world and the new. Tocqueville, who appreciated the blessings of free and democratic societies, also understood that they required a continual replenishment of moral capital from the deeper springs of the *ancien régime*. The old world, of course, is the world of Athens and Jerusalem, of natural reason and revealed religion. Despite the long-standing dispute between the philosophers and the poets (or priests) about theology, there is a general agreement between Athens and Jerusalem about morality. Morality refers to what is loosely called the

Judeo-Christian ethic, but what is more accurately described as the ethical norms without which contemporary civilized life in the West becomes difficult, if not impossible.

Absent a major religious revival—a prospect not entirely out of the question—it seems pointless to argue for the social desirability of a return to God. (No one embraces theology for the sake of public utility.) But it is time for liberals to recover a public ethic of responsibility which Christians derive from religion, yet which can also be derived—as the Greeks derived it—from nature. A healthy modern society seeks to combine the liberal doctrine of rights with a conservative ethic of accountability. Here is the meeting ground between sensible liberals and conservatives: conservatives agree to conserve the liberal doctrine of rights, while liberals agree to respect the conservative insistence on social responsibility and civic virtue. By recovering the Greek and Christian notion of a "common good" that transcends our particular interests, we can restore a public ethic that integrates rights and duties, so that freedom does not degenerate into license, and civilization into barbarism.

The purpose of this discussion is to suggest a new philosophic ground for public policy. What it means, in practical terms, is that Americans should work toward a system of laws which recognizes natural rights and expands opportunity, but in return expects responsible and productive behavior from its citizens. In private, people should have maximum liberty to pursue their competing visions of happiness, but in the public sphere, people should be held to the high standards of democratic citizenship. If all persons and groups are equally capable of exercising rights, they should be equally accountable for how those rights are exercised. Democratic citizenship means that people govern themselves in both senses of the term: they are expected both to exercise the responsibility of collective self-rule, and to regulate their own aggressive and vicious impulses so that they do not trespass on the rights of others. Democracy, more than other forms of government, permits self-expression; also more than other forms of government, democracy requires self-restraint.[12]

Today there is a great deal of talk about the "new citizenship," but the concept is vague. We can give it content by insisting that the instruments of policy (such as outlawing certain forms of behavior, providing incentives and disincentives through regulation and the tax code, and public exhortation) be used to promote decent and productive habits of behavior that are necessary for modern American civilization to endure. In *Rethinking Social Policy,* Christopher Jencks specifies three principles that constitute the basic minimum of an American civilizational code: working men are generally expected to keep steady jobs; women should not bear illegitimate children they cannot support; and everyone should refrain from violence.[13] Meeting these three criteria hardly establishes that one is civilized, yet no society can thrive when these norms are systematically violated. Insisting upon them is a prerequisite to civilizational renewal.

We hear many new proposals for how to address such glaring social problems as crime and dependency. One proposal is for criminals to pay mandatory restitution to those they have wronged; if they lack the resources, they should be required to do physical labor. A second proposal is to hold parents partly responsible for the crimes of their minor-age children. A third is to limit welfare benefits for mothers who continue to have children while on welfare. A fourth is to insist that teenage welfare mothers take up education, training, or work. A fifth is to strengthen paternity and child support laws. A sixth is to modify the tax code to strengthen rather than penalize two-parent families. Which of these proposals should be enacted? All of them. This is not to say that public policy should not promote structural changes, such as providing job training or incentives for investment in the inner city. But we have to recognize that poverty and pathology today do not merely arise from the absence of opportunity but also from the inability or refusal to take advantage of opportunity. There is a dynamic interplay between external incentives and cultural responses to them. What we have now is a downward spiral produced by dysfunctional cultural orientations and destructive social policies. We need to reverse the trend, to generate an upward spiral in which social structures and cultural habits work together to generate greater productivity and social responsibility. This should be the test of every public policy measure: the degree to which it expands opportunity while at the same time fostering productive and responsible behavior on the part of citizens.

RETHINKING RACISM

So what about racism? The conclusion of our inquiry into the history and nature of racism suggests that it is not reducible to ignorance or fear. Not only is the liberal remedy for racism incorrect; the basic diagnosis of the malady is wrong. Racism is what it always was: an opinion that recognizes real civilizational differences and attributes them to biology. Liberal relativism has been based on the denial of the differences. Liberals should henceforth admit the differences but deny their biological foundation. Thus liberals can continue to reject racism by preserving the Boasian distinction between race and culture. This is not a denial of the fact that individuals do differ or even the possibility that there are some natural differences between groups. Yet liberals can convincingly argue that whatever these may be, they are not significant enough to warrant differential treatment by law or policy. In other words, intrinsic differences are irrelevant when it comes to the ability of citizens to exercise their rights and responsibilities. Liberals can explain group differences in academic and economic performance by pointing to cultural differences, and acknowledging that some cultures are functionally superior to others. The racist fallacy, as Anthony Appiah contends, is the act of "biologizing what is culture."[14]

Yet this new liberal understanding should not make the present mistake—duplicated in thousands of sensitivity classes—of treating racism the way a Baptist preacher considers sin. Rather, it should recognize racism as an opinion, which may be right or wrong, but which in any case is a point of view that should be argued with and not suppressed. Antiracist education is largely a waste of time because it typically results in intellectual and moral coercion. Heavy-handed bullying may produce public acquiescence but it cannot compel private assent. Increasingly it appears that it is liberal antiracism that is based on ignorance and fear: ignorance of the true nature of racism, and fear that the racist point of view better explains the world than its liberal counterpart.

For a generation, liberals have treated racism as a form of psychological dementia in need of increasingly coercive forms of enlightenment. But liberal societies should not seek to regulate people's inner thoughts, nor should they outlaw ideas however reprehensible we find them. Hate speech and hate crime laws that impose punishment or enhanced penalties for proscribed motives and viewpoints are inherently illiberal and destructive of intellectual independence and conscience. Americans should recognize that racism is not what it used to be; it does exist, but we can live with it. This is not to say that racism does not do damage, only that the sorts of measures that would be needed to eradicate all vestiges of racist thought can only be totalitarian. Efforts to root out residual racism often create more injustice than they eliminate.

The crucial policy issue is what to do about discrimination. Irrational discrimination of the sort that inspired the civil rights laws of the 1960s is now, as we have seen, a relatively infrequent occurrence. Although such discrimination continues to cause harm, it is irrelevant to the prospects of blacks as a group because it is selective rather than comprehensive in

scope. For a minority like African Americans, discrimination is only catastrophic when virtually everyone colludes to enforce it. Consider what
would happen if every baseball team in America refused to hire blacks.
Blacks would suffer most, because they would be denied the opportunity
to play professional baseball. And fans would suffer, because the quality
of games would be diminished. But what if only a few teams—say the
New York Yankees and the Los Angeles Dodgers—refused to hire blacks?
African Americans as a group would suffer hardly at all, because the best
black players would offer their services to other teams. The Yankees and
the Dodgers would suffer a great deal, because they would be deprived of
the chance to hire talented black players. Eventually competitive pressure
would force the Yankees and Dodgers either to hire blacks, or to suffer
losses in games and revenue.[15] As Gary Becker has pointed out, in a free
market, selective discrimination imposes the heaviest cost on the discriminator, which is where it should be. Some people will undoubtedly continue to eschew blacks because of their "taste for discrimination," but most
will continue to deal with them because of their taste for profit.[16] Rational
discrimination, on the other hand, is likely to persist even in a fully competitive market.

There are four possible policy remedies for dealing with persistent discrimination: the first two embrace the one-drop rule, the last two reject it.
The first approach is to maintain the status quo, perhaps even to expand
the logic of proportional representation for all racial groups. The approach, as we have seen, is a radical application of cultural relativism,
which becomes the basis for an enforced egalitarianism between racial
groups. This approach, which necessarily entails racial preferences, was
perhaps necessary and inevitable in the late 1960s—it sought to eliminate
comprehensive discrimination against blacks in many areas, to kick in a
closed door. Now such comprehensive discrimination, which stretches
across entire sectors of the work force, is nonexistent, yet we have become used to doing business through the legerdemain of preferences and
relaxed standards. Proportional representation also entails administrative
benefits: it establishes an enforceable arithmetical standard for implementing civil rights laws. These paltry benefits, however, are overridden
by the destructive impact of proportional representation.

First, the concept is incoherent. As we have seen, there is no reason
whatsoever to believe that in the absence of discrimination, all groups
would perform equally in every area. Equality of rights for individuals
does not necessarily translate into equality of result for groups. Just as

racism is a distortion of the principle of merit, so proportional representation is a distortion of the principle of equality. If different groups of runners hit the finishing tape at different times, it does not follow that the race has been rigged. Our current civil rights laws, therefore, are built on an intellectual foundation of quicksand.

In addition, proportional representation fails the test of social justice. Columnist Michael Kinsley argues that race is a "rough and ready shorthand for disadvantage,"[17] but that facile equation does not hold true any more. When W. E. B. Du Bois wrote in the early part of this century, the vast majority of blacks were indeed poor. But now the African American community has bifurcated into a middle class and an underclass. There is no justification for giving a university admissions preference to the government official's son who attends a private school in Washington, D.C., just because he belongs to an underrepresented group, over the daughter of an Appalachian coal miner or a Vietnamese refugee. Another problem with proportional representation is that it frequently subsidizes the children of new immigrants, who have played no part in American history, at the expense of the sons and daughters of native-born citizens. Those who are not disadvantaged should not get preferences, and debts that are not owed should not be paid.

Proportional representation also erodes the principle of merit which constitutes the only unifying principle for a multiracial society. People can live with inequality of result if they are assured equality of rights, just as we can endure losing a race as long as all competitors started on the same line. James Fallows writes that "America's radius of trust is expanded not by racial unity but by the belief that everyone is playing by the same rules."[18] Majorities, no less than minorities, need the assurance that they are being treated fairly, otherwise they are sure to mobilize through democratic channels to affirm their interests. By not only tolerating racial nepotism for minorities but enshrining it in law, proportional representation is rapidly balkanizing the country along racial lines, destroying the confidence of citizens that the law will treat them equally and provoking a strong and largely justified backlash.

Finally, proportional representation assures an unceasing racialization of American society. By seeking to fight discrimination by practicing it, proportional representation multiplies the wounds inflicted by race-based decisions. Far from compensating old victims, it creates new ones. Proportional representation seeks to institutionalize race and make it a permanent feature of American public life. It has normalized and legitimized a neurotic obsession with race that maims our souls. If Americans acquiesce in this prescription, it will set them on a perpetual treadmill of racial recrimination and conflict. At least the old discrimination existed anomalously with the American creed; the new discrimination, embedded in law and policy, corrupts the nation's institutions and makes them purveyors of injustice.

What, then, sustains proportional representation? I believe it is the liberal conviction that the social outcomes produced by merit alone would prove painful and humiliating for blacks. If the Massachusetts Institute of Technology selected students solely based on merit, the number of blacks at MIT might well fall to around 2 percent.[19] Similarly blacks would be scarce in some professions, and virtually absent from others. Proportional representation will end only when we have the courage to say that we are willing to live with these outcomes, until blacks are able to raise their own standards to compete at the highest levels.

A second option, favored by some scholars, is to abolish racial preferences for all groups except one: African Americans. Andrew Kull writes, "The moral awkwardness of asking black Americans to be content with nondiscrimination should not stop us from giving that answer to everyone else."[20] Orlando Patterson, Nathan Glazer, and Eugene Genovese argue that blacks have faced a unique history in this country which does not place them in the same position as other immigrants.[21] Genovese argues that African Americans should be permitted to identify themselves as culturally (as opposed to racially) black and benefit from a carefully selected range of preferences restricted to that group. This approach has the advantage of acknowledging the absurdity of preferring newcomers from Paraguay over locals from Peoria. It sensibly seeks to narrow the range of beneficiaries to the group that has suffered the unmitigated evils of slavery, segregation, and widespread discrimination. It would preserve preferences as exceptional, rather than typical. And it would continue to view them as temporary.

The problem with this attractive strategy is that while it has a chance of working in a black and white milieu, it is increasingly unsustainable in a multiracial society. When there are many groups with different ancestral histories, there are bound to be competing claims. These can be rejected out of hand, but if we are going to insist that middle-class blacks deserve preference for admissions and jobs over the poorest members of all other groups, this will not only produce acute resentment, it will probably stigmatize African Americans as inherently inferior. Whites, Hispanics, Asians, and native Americans would all be competing together, with a kind of Special Olympics held for blacks. The moral and psychological damage wrought by such an approach would almost certainly outweigh any tangible short-term benefits, so that the only workable scheme is one proposed by Lawrence Fuchs: limit affirmative action now to African Americans and set a date, perhaps 2010, when "all counting by race should be phased out."[22]

The two remaining options for dealing with discrimination reject the one-drop rule and thus avoid the risk, as Hugh Davis Graham puts it, of "our racist past being institutionalized in the present and hence poisoning the future."[23] Both options are premised on an embrace of equality of rights rather than equality of result. Both proceed from the belief that for government to judge people on the basis of race or other arbitrary features is immoral and illegal. Thus they would require the agencies of government to stop classifying citizens by race and forbid race-based decisions by the state. As African American writer Itabari Njeri puts it, "If our interest is in the elimination of oppression, then the elimination of classifications based on race is the only solution that makes sense. We should be challenging the nomenclature of oppression and attacking the philosophical underpinnings of racism."[24]

The first option is a blanket nondiscrimination rule, which establishes a right not to be discriminated against; consequently, it requires the enforcement of color-blind principles in both the private and the public sector. This is the approach that Martin Luther King favored, and the one that was written into law in the Civil Rights Act of 1964. Many liberals such as Jim Sleeper, Randall Kennedy, William Julius Wilson, and Clarence Page, as well as conservatives such as Newt Gingrich and Jack Kemp, are trying to revive this approach now, typically combined with a demand for class-based affirmative action.[25] This approach concedes that race can provide the basis for private identity, but not for public forms of conduct. Thus it is perfectly fine for persons to insist that they will date only members of their own race—obviously in the process discriminating against members of all other groups—but it would be illegal to discriminate in hiring for a job or selling a home.

Socioeconomic affirmative action can work if it is pursued in a prudent and targeted manner. Some form of preference is defensible in college admissions, on the grounds that in many cases students from disadvantaged backgrounds have not had the opportunity to demonstrate their true potential. It makes no sense, however, to extend class-based preferences to faculty hiring: colleges cannot hire history and math professors who do not meet the usual standards on the grounds that they are poor. Similarly, the federal government can provide set-asides for small businesses and training programs for the economically disadvantaged, but it defies common sense to require private and public employers to hire substandard workers simply because they come from impoverished families.

Whether accompanied by socioeconomic affirmative action or not, the benefit of any nonracial or color-blind approach is that it would use a single standard to implement civil rights laws. Whites and blacks would enjoy the same degree of protection, and so would other groups. An even-handed nondiscrimination rule would acknowledge some forms of discrimination as rational, yet would still outlaw them as immoral and socially harmful. Resources currently invested in promoting proportional representation could be more sensibly invested in strictly enforcing antidiscrimination laws. As Richard Posner has suggested, violators could be punished, and potential violators deterred, by awards of double or triple damages.[26]

One difficulty with a broad-based color-blind rule is that it is not easy to enforce. Private discrimination is hard to prove when the discriminator seeks to conceal his motives. Yet the obstacle is not insurmountable. Courts could use an intent standard and yet examine all available circumstantial evidence to determine whether an act of illegal discrimination has occurred. Thus if companies treat black applicants differently from similarly situated whites, that discrepancy provides strong prima facie proof of intentional discrimination. Although such an approach requires case-by-case prosecution that some enforcement agencies consider cumbersome, it is justified by the fact that it is discriminators rather than the entire workforce that the law seeks to penalize.

A more serious problem with the Martin Luther King approach is that if applied consistently and even-handedly, it would require the government to make it illegal for minority companies to give preferences to members of their own group. Peek into the back of a Korean grocery store and you often see Korean workers in addition to the owners. Similarly, many black-owned businesses insist upon hiring African American employees. Should the government prohibit these obvious displays of minority ethnocentrism? I am reluctant to approve of such interference. Yet I am also unwilling to live with a double standard that forces whites to be race neutral while minorities are allowed to discriminate in favor of their own group. Thus I am forced to conclude that while a broadly enforced color-blind rule would be a great improvement over current policy, it would not be the best approach for a civil rights policy that seeks to be principled as well as pragmatic.

What we need is a long-term strategy that holds the government to a rigorous standard of race neutrality, while allowing private actors to be free to discriminate as they wish. In practice, this means uncompromising color blindness in government hiring and promotion, criminal justice, and the drawing of voting districts. Yet individuals and companies would be allowed to discriminate in private transactions such as renting an apartment or hiring for a job. Am I calling for a repeal of the Civil Rights Act of 1964? Actually, yes. The law should be changed so that its nondiscrimination provisions apply only to the government.

In a recent book, legal scholar Richard Epstein argues for precisely such an approach, which has so far remained outside the mainstream of the race debate. Arguing that "discrimination laws represent the antithesis of freedom of contract," Epstein asserts that people should be free to hire and fire others for good reason, bad reason, or no reason at all. Epstein challenges the strongly held belief of many Americans that they have a right not to be discriminated against: in a free society, he counters, people have a right to enter into voluntary transactions that other parties should be at liberty to accept or refuse. Epstein admits that while competitive markets would make irrational discrimination costly and relatively rare, companies would continue to practice rational discrimination. He argues that it is not unjust for an employer to refuse to hire even the most qualified black because the job is the employer's to give and the rejected applicant is no worse off than before applying for the job.[27]

Without putting it this way, Epstein is defending ethnocentrism as not only natural but also justifiable. As we have seen, it is a universal practice to prefer members of one's own group over strangers. Epstein implies, and I agree, that this is a defensible and in some cases even admirable trait. What is the argument for preventing people from giving jobs and benefits, which are theirs to give, to those whom they favor? Admittedly in some cases the job goes to the nephew of the boss. This, in the boss's mind, is his nephew's "merit"—to be related to him. Such nepotism, although reprehensible in the public sector where the government has an obligation to treat citizens equally, need not be restricted in the competitive private sector where the economic cost of selecting the less competent falls on the individual or company making the selection.

At this point I can already hear the gasps of civil rights activists. Absent legal penalties, they will warn, many companies would simply refuse to hire blacks even when they have demonstrated that they are the best-qualified candidates for jobs. Since such behavior makes no economic sense, we can expect that it would be relatively infrequent in a competitive market. Some employers undoubtedly would discriminate against blacks. Precisely how many is unknown, although after a generation of hiring preferences in favor of minorities, sometimes without external coercion, there is no reason to believe that comprehensive discrimination will make a comeback. Indeed I would go further: based on existing evidence, today's corporate culture exhibits more discrimination in favor of blacks than against blacks. Consequently, faced with the alternative of an enforced race-blind approach that would outlaw discrimination in either direction, many African Americans who recognize the pervasiveness of contemporary minority preferences might well prefer to see those private benefits continue, and would be willing to pay the price of tolerating a few relatively isolated employers who would refuse to hire backs. Thus we arrive at the greatest paradox of all: the best way for African Americans to save private-sector affirmative action is to repeal the Civil Rights Act of 1964.

The issue of private discrimination is important, but whichever way it is settled, the central choice facing American society is whether its agencies of government are going to embrace the one-drop rule and practice racial discrimination, or reject it and treat citizens equally under the law. The one-drop rule reveals the way in which our current antidiscrimination policy is premised upon the ideological foundation established by the old racists. It endorses and perpetuates racial discrimination, even while purporting to fight it. Although current policy professes to promote "benign" discrimination, all discrimination is benign for its beneficiary and invidious for its victim. America will never liberate itself from the shackles of the past until the government gets out of the race business.

Some activists agree that in an ideal world the government would not classify and prefer citizens on the basis of race; yet in today's society, these self-styled realists contend, race-based policies are indispensable because, as Cornel West puts it, "race matters." But precisely because race matters, one can argue that the government should not play favorites. Consider the analogy of separation of church and state. The reason for its enactment in the West was not that religion didn't matter. On the contrary, precisely because people were killing each other over their faith, some form of separation became an appealing and indispensable solution. What we need now is what Jennifer Roback calls "separation of race and state."[28] The justification of separation is not that race is not a fact; rather, insofar as the government is concerned, in Leon Wieseltier's words, "Race is not a value."[29] Separation is based on the recognition of the harm that government-imposed racial classifications have done. The best safety of citizens, consequently, lies in refusing to trust the state with a power that they are unable to trust themselves to use wisely. As John Courtney Murray writes, when it came to religion, the American founders established not "articles of faith" but "articles of peace."[30] This model, as it turns out, is also extremely helpful in thinking about how the nation can deal with the challenge of multiculturalism.

RETHINKING MULTICULTURALISM

As we have seen, advocates of multiculturalism such as Stanley Fish tend to view opposition to immigration as inherently racist. Others, such as Ronald Takaki, go beyond this to argue that it is no less bigoted to expect nonwhite immigrants to assimilate to the norms of the American mainstream. Advocates of multiculturalism typically indict the West for inflicting racist oppression on other cultures, arguing that America should modify dominant European institutions both in the classroom and in society, so as to give equal recognition and representation to non-Western cultures. In this view, what Americans have in common is their ethnic and cultural diversity and we should learn to celebrate that.

Yet to say that all that unites Americans is their diversity is another way of saying that there is nothing that unites Americans. This is not only untrue, it is unworkable. Consider the dispute over a common language. Even more than homogeneous societies, multiracial societies need a *lingua franca*. If most Americans spoke English and new immigrants all spoke Spanish, a bilingual compromise could be reached in which natives learned Spanish as a second language and immigrants learned English. But in a society with many groups and many ancestral languages—Spanish, Hindustani, Urdu, and Tagalog—we risk an American Babel, a breakdown of communication, if everyone does not speak a shared language. For reasons of practicality, this language must be English, which is rapidly becoming the global medium of intercultural communication.[31]

The relativist proposition that all cultures should be equally respected and accommodated within American borders is equally unrealistic. Indeed such demands do not take the concept of culture seriously. Culture originates in the *cult*—the deepest wellsprings of human belief and endeavor.[32] Cultures generally arise out of religion: thus one can speak of Islamic culture or Hindu culture. In their pursuit of the good life, cultures have competing visions which are often radically at odds with each other. Consequently Horace Kallen's vision of a federation or mosaic of harmoniously coexisting cultures ignores the fact that a society cannot simultaneously embrace multiple and contradictory worldviews.

Consider some customs and practices that are found in non-Western countries. Many cultures reject romantic love as the basis for marriage, so parents find mates for their children. Customarily, children are responsible for taking care of their parents when they are old. Many cultures regard age as synonymous with wisdom: thus young people are expected to show deference bordering on obeisance to the elderly. Several cultures, notably Islamic ones, permit polygamy. Some African and Arab nations practice clitoral removal in adolescent girls. Female infanticide is common in China and other places. Similarly the political institutions of non-Western cultures frequently clash with those of America. To take the Islamic world as a single example, many of these countries reject democracy in favor of some form of theocracy. Citizens are expected to live by religious codes prescribed by mullahs. In several Muslim regions it is illegal to lend money for interest. Schools are sometimes forbidden from showing the human body or teaching about sex and reproduction. The Darwinian theory of evolution is flatly prohibited. Freedom of speech is subordinated to higher considerations of order and religious truth, as the Salman Rushdie case illustrated. The Islamic attitude toward convicted criminals is suggested by Abdul Hadi Awang, a senior official of the Islamic regime in Malaysia, who opposed medical attention for thieves whose hands were cut off on the grounds that "if doctors and surgeons start re-attaching the hands, the whole purpose is defeated."[33]

No society can absorb unlimited diversity. When immigrants import to the United States attitudes and mores that clash with those of natives, there is bound to be reciprocal tension and suspicion. Opposition to immigration that is arbitrarily based on skin color is undoubtedly racist. Yet hostility to high levels of immigration in Texas, California, and Florida seems to be primarily based on issues of competition over scarce resources and regional cultural indigestion. Such concerns are legitimate and not evidence of bigotry. Americans are entitled to preserve their way of life and determine for themselves what level of immigration benefits the country, and how many newcomers can be reasonably absorbed in a given year.

"Paradoxical as it may seem," George Fredrickson writes, "it is democratic values of Anglo-American origin that make multiculturalism conceivable in the United States."[34] For example, a relatively large number of Hindus, Muslims, Sikhs, and Buddhists can be admitted each year and given wide latitude to practice their diverse religious faiths as long as the institution of separation of church and state is preserved. Some conflict is inevitable. In America today, Muslims who take their religion seriously cannot believe in separation of church and state: tolerance and religious pluralism are concepts alien to the Koran. Consequently Muslims in the United States should be allowed to practice their religion but not to the point where it threatens the religious freedom of others, as through the practice of *jihad* against non-Muslims. Charles Taylor rightly observes that "liberalism is not a possible meeting ground for all cultures, but is the political expression of one range of cultures."[35]

The reason that a liberal framework makes possible a broad social tolerance for diversity is the unique Western distinction between the private and the public sphere. Thus the idea of separation of church and state can be extended to ethnicity. Religious separation is based on the conviction that privatizing dogmatic beliefs and keeping them out of the public square permits individuals and voluntary groups to practice their faith unmolested. In this framework, the state remains respectfully distant from religion, with the only exception being a token "civil religion" based on anthems and invocations whose religious content is generic and functions mainly as part of a secular patriotic creed.[36] Separation of ethnicity and state would domesticate group passions and—with the exception of symbolic public events such as St. Patrick's Day and Columbus Day—permit diversity to flourish within the private sphere. In this model, citizens would be free to cherish their group identities and organize along ethnic lines if they so choose. They could even teach their children ethnic dogma. Yet this ethnocentric lore would be kept out of the public schools and receive no state approval. State neutrality makes practical sense because in a multiethnic society, it is simply impossible for the public school and the public square to entertain every group's claims, especially when those claims are metaphysical and conflict with one another. Just as Jewish immigrants who in the early part of this century could give their children a yeshiva education, but at home or through privately subsidized institutions, so ethnic groups today should be encouraged to celebrate their own diverse identities without foisting them on others.

America, complains literary critic Sacvan Bercovitch, seems "intrinsically tied to a certain kind of liberal pluralism. America can absorb blacks, women, native Americans provided that they conform to a particular pattern of life, and that they define freedom in terms of a liberal society."[37] This is exactly right. Another way of saying it is that America can become a multiracial society but not a multicultural society. In fact, a multiracial society is only possible because race is not the same as culture; thus people of different skin tones can live under the same set of laws within a shared liberal understanding of the rights and obligations of citizenship. For better or worse, America's future is likely to be racially diverse, but culturally Western.

Contrary to the claims of nativists and multiculturalists, who insist that nonwhite immigrants cannot and will not assimilate, newcomers from Seoul, Karachi, and San Salvador seem to be doing just that. Studies show that Asian immigrants are aggressively assimilationist, and even Hispanics who want to preserve the Spanish language strongly embrace American culture and want their children to learn English.[38] None of this is very surprising; in fact, immigration is one of the most stunning refutations of cultural relativism, because immigrants are voting with their feet against their own culture and in favor of American culture. As novelist Bharati Mukherjee points out, since immigrants come to the United States in search of a new kind of freedom and a new way of life, they can hardly be assumed to want a restoration of their old cultures in America. Indeed now as in the past, many immigrants wholeheartedly embrace their adopted country and sound more patriotic than native-born Americans.[39]

The strident claims of some ethnic activists aside, most immigrants seem to want little more from America than token recognition of their sartorial styles and folk festivals. Surely this is not too much to ask of a liberal society. Yet multicultural identity, Richard Rodriguez writes, cannot be reduced to "tacos and serapes and weekend trips to Mexican resort towns."[40] Rather, it is best discovered by answers to such questions as how immigrants view their elders, how they find their wives and husbands, and how they practice their religion. Here, the process of assimilation to the mores of the new world is rapid, irreversible, and easily confirmed simply by looking at the difference in an airport between an Urdu-speaking woman in a veil and her thoroughly Westernized children. Of course new immigrants from Asia, Africa, and Latin America frequently face problems of language, gaining access to credit, and the feeling of alienation in an unfamiliar society. But these problems are temporary, and they are precisely the obstacles that were faced by older generations of immigrants.

It should hardly come as a surprise that many immigrants experience a sense of uprootedness, of moral confusion and social conflict. Their geographic displacement is not accompanied by a full cultural displacement. Feeling like exiles at first, they are magnetically drawn into the safe haven of ethnic colonies, social clubs, restaurants, burial and insurance societies, churches, and groceries, all serving their special needs. Over time, even in the presence of turmoil and self-consciousness, most immigrants opt to leave their cultural enclaves and acquire a new language, new tastes in food, new esthetic styles, new mannerisms, new terms of affection and insult, new modes of courtship, and new ways of forming relationships with acquaintances, friends, and family. These changes are often accompanied by nostalgia—a desire to preserve the family heirlooms, if only as antiques of affectionate recollection. Yet assimilation also brings rewards. As the strongest defenders of bilingualism recognize, "very few people can thrive in this country without a good working knowledge of English."[41] And research by Alejandro Portes and others shows that there is "a positive relationship between immigrant economic success and changes of values, lifestyle and language in a direction congruent with the host culture."[42] As Portes recognizes, however, in some cases full-scale assimilation can prove deleterious, as when second- and third-generation Asian students internalize the lackadaisical work ethic of the public schools and witness their test scores drop.[43]

Certainly there appears to be a steady and inexorable pattern of Americanization, punctuated by forward and backward steps by different immigrant groups. In an interesting theory that the experience of many families corroborates, Marcus Hansen suggested what has come to be known as Hansen's law: the first immigrant generation remains largely foreign in its language and customs, the second assimilates with a vengeance, and the third seeks to rediscover some of the ancestral roots that have since been forgotten. But Hansen's law—"what the son wishes to forget, the grandson wishes to remember"—does not imply a rejection of assimilation, only psychological landmarks en route to assimilation.[44]

So immigrants change America a little, and are themselves changed a lot. They do not entirely give up their foreign identity; rather, like earlier generations of Americans, they choose what significance their origins will have in shaping their destiny in the new world. Mario Cuomo is an Italian, but he is not an Italian in the same sense as his grandfather. While the elder Cuomo had no choice in the matter, his offspring live in a cosmopolitan world in which being Italian is only one aspect of their American identity. Similarly studies by Orlando Patterson show that West Indian immigrants who live half the year in the Caribbean and half in the United States frequently present themselves as white at home, where it is considered upper-class to be light-skinned, but black in this country, where there are benefits of political solidarity and racial preferences to be had.[45] Skin color is immutable, but as sociologist Alan Wolfe says, "Ethnicity has become a commodity. We can shop for it."[46]

Despite today's hot-tempered debate about immigration, America has shown that it can absorb fairly large numbers of newcomers provided that its policies encourage assimilation and reward work rather than dependency. At approximately one million a year, immigration levels to the United States are high, but still amount to less than half of one percent of the U.S. population. Scholars continue to debate whether immigrants help or hurt the American economy. The most balanced research suggests that the net effect is a slight plus, although the United States could enhance these benefits by modifying immigration laws to attract more foreigners who would contribute to America rather than becoming a taxpayer liability.[47] Yet without policy disincentives that discourage work and assimilation, there is every reason to believe that immigrants will prove both compatible and competitive with natives. So there seems to be hardly any similarity between their circumstances and those of indigenous minorities, and the ideology of multiculturalism can now be seen to provide rainbow diversion from the specific problems faced by one group, African Americans.

THE END OF RACISM

Once we have set aside the false remedies premised on relativism—proportional representation and multiculturalism—it is possible to directly address America's real problem, which is partly a race problem and partly a black problem. The solution to the race problem is a public policy that is strictly indifferent to race. The black problem can be solved only through a program of cultural reconstruction in which society plays a supporting role but which is carried out primarily by African Americans themselves. Both projects need to be pursued simultaneously; neither can work by itself. If society is race neutral but blacks remain uncompetitive, then equality of rights for individuals will lead to dramatic inequality of result for groups, liberal embarrassment will set in, and we are back on the path to racial preferences. On the other hand, if blacks are going to reform their community, they have a right to expect that they will be treated equally under the law. Although America has a long way to go, many mistakes have been made, and current antagonisms are high, still there are hopeful signs that the nation can move toward a society in which race ceases to matter, a destination that we can term "the end of racism."

While politicians and pundits continue to debate who should benefit from race-based programs, the country is entering a new era in which old racial categories are rapidly becoming obsolete. The main reason for this is intermarriage. Exogamy rates have been extremely high for white ethnic groups for almost a generation. Intermarriage rates for Asians and Hispanics are also substantial and rising. Some 25 percent of Hispanics now marry outside their group. About one-third of Asians living in the United States are married to non-Asians. Although many states as late as 1967 outlawed such unions, today about 5 percent of blacks marry whites. Ten percent of African American men between the ages of fifteen and thirty-four are married to white women. Each year approximately fifty thousand births are recorded to black and white couples.[48]

The rapid increase in mixed-race children means that, in the not-too-distant future, it will be virtually impossible to sort Americans into precise categories for the purposes of maintaining government statistics and enforcing racial preferences. Already the Census Bureau has been compelled by demographic necessity to consider abandoning its archaic system of classification which forces all citizens into a Procrustean bed of six basic groups: white, black, Hispanic, Asian/Pacific Islander, American Indian, and other. For some civil rights activists, such change is an alarming prospect. Consequently, many vehemently oppose a proposal being entertained by the government to introduce a new "multiracial" category, because it might diminish the size of the black population and reduce its affirmative action claims in voting and the work force. "To relinquish the notion of race," black studies professor Jon Michael Spencer says, "is to relinquish our fortress against the powers and principalities that still try to undermine us."[49]

Yet by ending racial classification, and limiting government use of ethnic data for scholarly research, Americans across the ideological spectrum can take an important step toward transcending the historic barriers of race. Far from treating mixed-race children as an embarrassment to the existing regime of racial head-counting, liberals should welcome the emerging *café au lait* society. It is also time to reject the advice of an older generation of scholars who continue to fight the old battles of the civil rights movement, and to place confidence in the new generation of young people, who are a hopeful sign for the twenty-first century.

All the evidence shows that young people today are strongly committed to the principle of equality of rights. They are not disfigured by the racism that afflicted earlier generations of Americans. For most young whites born after the civil rights movement, it is absurd and unthinkable to place people of a different race in the back of the bus, or to require them to drink out of a separate water fountain. Yet these young people who go to the same schools as blacks, dress in similar ways, and listen to the same music, find it just as ridiculous to arbitrarily single out African Americans or other groups for special preferences based on color. A recent survey by Peter Hart's polling firm showed vast majorities of whites and blacks united in their agreement that success should be the result of education, hard work, and equal treatment under the law.[50]

Older whites mistake young people's sense of fair play, which produces a resistance to racial nepotism, for a resurgence of racism. Here is an amazing spectacle: a new generation, which has no record of legal discrimination and which is by all evidence not racist, is accused of racism by an earlier generation which has demonstrated its racist ideology and participated in the enforcement of legal discrimination against blacks. Against their better instincts, young people are being corrupted into thinking of themselves in racial terms and into developing identities and hostilities that will only prove a barrier to further reducing the vestiges of racism in America. An incredible fund of goodwill is being squandered.

Liberals should stop listening to the fashionable prophets of despair who once led the nation nobly and admirably, but who have now become reactionary fogies. So committed are they to the paradigm of racial struggle that they are unable to see and seize new opportunities. Civil rights mythographers are fond of painting Martin Luther King as the Moses of the movement, who, in his own prophetic words, would never reach the Promised Land. What has not been noted is the obvious corollary to this elegant myth: like the Hebrews whom Moses shepherded through the desert for 40 years, today's civil rights leaders are too steeped in the mentality of Egypt to be admitted into Canaan; they may have to die out altogether before a new generation can arise to claim the fruits of their long and largely successful struggle against racial discrimination in this country. These bitter and bewildered old idolators should invest their earnings from racial soothsaying and take a well-earned retirement from the civil rights debate. A new liberal vision, which can strengthen and inspire the burgeoning idealism of the younger generation, would reject biology as the basis for group claims of superiority, acknowledge dysfunctionalities in black culture, insist upon strict government race neutrality, and support policies that encourage productive habits of behavior among African Americans and indeed all citizens.

Blacks as a group stand at a historic junction. Very few people in the civil rights leadership recognize this: convinced that racism of a hundred varieties stands between African Americans and success, most of the activists are ready to do battle once again with this seemingly elusive and invincible foe. Yet the agenda of securing legal rights for blacks has now been accomplished, and there is no point for blacks to increase the temperature of accusations of racism. Historically whites have used racism to serve powerful entrenched interests, but what interests does racism serve now? Most whites have no economic stake in the ghetto. They have absolutely nothing to gain from oppressing poor blacks. Indeed the only concern that whites seem to have about the underclass is its potential for crime and its reliance on the public purse.

By contrast, it is the civil rights industry which now has a vested interest in the persistence of the ghetto, because the miseries of poor blacks are the best advertisement for continuing programs of racial preferences and set-asides. No one is more committed to the one-drop rule, and more likely to resist its demise, than these professional blacks whose livelihoods depend on maintaining a large and resentful African American coalition. Publicly inconsolable about the fact that racism continues, these activists seem privately terrified that it has abated. Formerly a beacon of moral argument and social responsibility, the civil rights leadership has lost much of its moral credibility, and has a fair representation of charlatans who exploit the sufferings of the underclass to collect research grants, minority scholarships, racial preferences, and other subsidies for themselves. Progressive blacks who wish to keep the spirit of the civil rights movement alive might consider a sit-in at the offices of the NAACP at which they demand that the organization commit itself to measures to address the plight of the poorest blacks.

The real issue in America today is not whether Cornel West can get a taxi. If he dresses well he is less likely to be mistaken for a criminal, and if one cab passes him by, another will come along to take him to the dining room at the Harvard faculty club. The supreme challenge faced by African Americans is the one that Booker T. Washington outlined almost a century ago: the mission of building the civilizational resources of a people whose culture is frequently unsuited to the requirements of the modern world. Writes African American pastor Eugene Rivers:

> Unlike many of our ancestors, who came out of slavery and entered this century with strong backs, discipline, a thirst for literacy, deep religious faith, and

hope in the face of adversity, we have produced . . . a new jack generation ill-equipped to secure gainful employment even as productive slaves.[51]

Sadly, the habits that were needed to resist racist oppression or secure legal rights arc not the ones needed to exercise personal freedom or achieve success today. As urged by black reformers, both conservative and liberal, the task ahead is one of rebuilding broken families, developing educational and job skills, fostering black entrepreneurship, and curbing the epidemic of violence in the inner cities. Since the government is not in a good position to improve socialization practices among African Americans, the primary responsibility for cultural restoration undoubtedly lies with the black community itself. "When we finally achieve the right of full participation in American life," Ralph Ellison wrote, "what we make of it will depend upon our sense of cultural values, and our creative use of freedom, not upon our racial identification."[52]

Reformers like Glenn Loury, William Raspberry, and John Sibley Butler have offered specific recommendations for black self-improvement. Raspberry has proposed that middle-class African Americans voluntarily establish Big Brother programs in which they "adopt" poor black children and expose them to more productive habits of behavior. The National Urban League has a pilot program to convince successful blacks who have benefited from affirmative action to invest in the economic revitalization of inner cities. Another proposal is for black groups to conduct summer camps in which students are taught entrepreneurial skills. John Sibley Butler argues that blacks should emulate Koreans and set up rotating credit associations which establish pools of capital for members to set up new businesses. Reformers such as Robert Woodson, Charles Ballard, Kimi Gray, Jesse Peterson, Johnny Ray Youngblood, and Reginald Dickson are going beyond advocacy, setting up teen-pregnancy programs, family support initiatives, community job training, instruction in language and social demeanor, resident supervision of housing projects, and privately run neighborhood schools. Even some of the old civil rights veterans are starting to realize that old panaceas won't work. As Harlem's Reverend Calvin Butts puts it, "Our community has now become the dumping ground for every social service in the world. Harlem's salvation is not more AIDS hostels, drug rehab centers, homeless shelters, or low-income housing, but more businesses and middle-class people who buy condos or coops."[53]

We can sympathize with the magnitude of the project facing African Americans. In order to succeed, they must rid themselves of aspects of their past that are, even now, aspects of themselves.[54] The most telling refutation of racism, as Frederick Douglass once said about slavery, "is the presence of an industrious, enterprising, thrifty and intelligent free black population."[55] For many black scholars and activists, such proposals are anathema because they seem to involve ideological sellout to the white man and thus are viewed as not authentically black. Frantz Fanon, a leading black anticolonialist writer, did not agree. What is needed after the revolution, Fanon wrote, is "the liberation of the man of color from himself. However painful it may be for me to accept this conclusion, I am obliged to state it: for the black man, there is only one destiny, and it is white."[56] In this Fanon is right: for generations, blacks have attempted to straighten their hair, lighten their skin, and pass for white.[57] But what blacks need to do is to "act white," which is to say, to abandon idiotic Back-to-Africa schemes and embrace mainstream cultural norms, so that they can effectively compete with other groups.

There is no self-esteem to be found in Africa or even in dubious ideologies of blackness. "Let the sun be proud of its achievement," Frederick Douglass said.[58] Instead, African Americans should take genuine pride in their collective moral achievement in this country's history. Blacks as a group have made a vital contribution to the expansion of the franchise of liberty and opportunity in America. Through their struggle over two centuries, blacks have helped to make the principles of the American founding a legal reality not just for themselves but also for other groups. As W. E. B. Du Bois put it, "There are no truer exponents of the pure human spirit of the Declaration of Independence than the American Negroes."[59]

Yet rejection in this country produced what Du Bois termed a "double consciousness," so that blacks experience a kind of schizophrenia between their racial and American identities. Only now, for the first time in history, is it possible for African Americans to transcend this inner polarization and become the first truly modern people, unhyphenated Americans. Black success and social acceptance now are both tied to rebuilding the African American community. If blacks can achieve such a cultural renaissance, they will teach other Americans a valuable lesson in civilizational restoration. Thus they could vindicate both Booker T. Washington's project of cultural empowerment and Du Bois's hope for a unique African American "message" to the world. Even more, it will be blacks themselves who will finally discredit racism, solve the American dilemma, and become the truest and noblest exemplars of Western civilization.

NOTES

Chapter 1. The White Man's Burden

1. James Baldwin, *Notes of a Native Son,* Beacon Press, Boston, 1955, p. 175.

2. Evans was retried and convicted of first degree murder. See Paul Duggan and Cindy Loose, "Mistrial Declared in Hill Killing," *Washington Post,* April 27, 1994, p. A-1; Paul Duggan, "D.C. Man Convicted, in Second Trial, of Slaying Senate Aide," *Washington Post,* September 7, 1994, p. D-1.

3. Randall Kennedy, "The Angry Juror," *Wall Street Journal,* September 30, 1994.

4. Sharon Theimer, "Black Militia Vows War on Property," *Los Angeles Times,* September 11, 1994, p. A-7; Isabel Wilkerson, "Call for Black Militia Stuns Milwaukee," *New York Times,* April 6, 1990, p. A-12.

5. Robert I. Friedman, "The Color of Rage," *Vanity Fair,* January 1995, pp. 32, 49; Rorie Sherman, "Crime's Toll on the U.S.: Fear, Despair and Guns," *National Law Journal,* April 18, 1994, p. A-1.

6. Cornel West, *Race Matters,* Beacon Press, Boston, 1993, p. 1.

7. Ice T, *The Ice Opinion,* St. Martin's Press, New York, 1994, p. 151.

8. Audrey Edwards and Craig K. Polite, *Children of the Dream: The Psychology of Black Success,* Doubleday, New York, 1992, p. 190.

9. Jewelle Taylor Gibbs, *Young, Black and Male in America: An Endangered Species,* Auburn House, Dover, MA, 1988, p. 19.

10. Robert Boynton, "Professor Bell, Sage of Black Rage," *New York Observer,* October 10, 1994, p. 1.

11. Ellis Cose, *The Rage of a Privileged Class,* HarperCollins, New York, 1993, p. 38.

12. U.S. Bureau of the Census, *Statistical Abstract of the United States 1994,* Washington, DC, pp. 48, 62, 80, 88, 92, 94, 139, 177, 215–16, 418, 472–73.

13. Alvin F. Poussaint, *Why Blacks Kill Blacks,* Emerson Hall Publishers, New York, 1972, p. 114.

14. John Edgar Wideman, *Fatheralong: A Meditation on Fathers and Sons, Race and Society,* Pantheon Books, New York, 1994, p. xvii.

15. Cited in Peter Collier and David Horowitz, eds., *Second Thoughts About Race in America,* Madison Books, Lanham, MD, 1991, p. 137.

16. Sister Souljah, *No Disrespect,* Times Books, New York, 1994, p. 350.

17. Cited by Barbara Grizzuti Harrison, "Spike Lee Hates Your Cracker Ass," *Esquire,* October 1992, p. 137.

18. Gerald Early, "Race, Rage and the Bonds of History," *Washington Post,* December 12, 1994, p. B-1.

19. *Klanwatch Intelligence Report,* Southern Poverty Law Center, February 1994. In the Florida case, the two assailants were charged and convicted of kidnapping, robbery, and attempted murder. See James Martinez, "Two Whites Convicted in Burning of Black," *Washington Times,* September 8, 1993, p. A-1.

20. Michael Barkun, *Religion and the Racist Right,* University of North Carolina Press, Chapel Hill, 1994, pp. viii–ix, 158; see also Andrew Hazlett, "Identity Crisis: White Supremacists Armed with a New Theology," *Diversity and Division,* Fall 1993, pp. 16–18.

21. Cited by John Harris and Dan Balz, "Affirmative Action Divides Democrats," *Washington Post,* March 10, 1995.

22. Howard Kohn, "Service with a Sneer," *New York Times Magazine,* November 6, 1994, pp. 43–47, 58, 78–79; see also Carlos Sanchez and Maria Odum, "2 Denny's Said to Refuse Service to Black Choir," *Washington Post,* June 5, 1993; Philip Hager, "Suit Accuses Denny's of Racial Bias, Discrimination," *Los Angeles Times,* March 25, 1993.

23. Alphonso Pinkney, *The Myth of Black Progress,* Cambridge University Press, Cambridge, 1984, p. 53.

24. Ralph Wiley, *Why Black People Tend to Shout,* Birch Lane Press, New York, 1991, p. 81.

25. William G. Mayer, *The Changing American Mind,* University of Michigan Press, Ann Arbor, 1992, pp. 22–28; see also Judith Lichtenberg, "Racism in the Head, Racism in the World," *Report from the Institute for Philosophy and Public Policy* 12 (Spring-Summer 1992), pp. 3–5.

26. According to an April 1995 *Newsweek* poll, 79 percent of whites oppose racial preferences in employment and college admissions while only 14 percent support them. "Race and Rage," *Newsweek,* April 3, 1995, p. 25. See also the results of a recent USA Today/CNN poll, reported in Andrea Stone and Jim Norman, "Affirmative Action: Fairness Key to Support," *USA Today,* March 24, 1995, pp. 1-A, 3-A; David Moore, "Americans Dubious About Affirmative Action Today," Gallup Poll News Service, March 9, 1995; "Where the Public Stands," *Los Angeles Times,* February 27, 1995, p. A-5.

27. Cited by R. Drummond Ayres, "Conservatives Forge New Strategy to Challenge Affirmative Action," *New York Times,* February 16, 1995, p. A-22.

28. Cited by Paul Barrett and G. Pascal Zachary, "Race, Sex Preferences Could Become a Target in Voter Shift to Right," *Wall Street Journal,* January 11, 1995, p. A-11.

29. Cited in Peter Behr, "Crucial Break or Unjustified Crutch?" *Washington Post,* March 10, 1995, p. A-14.

30. "Campus Protest Against Slurs," *New York Times,* February 16, 1995, p. A-22.

31. Mona Charen, "The Ruckus at Rutgers and What It Portends," *Washington Times,* February 15, 1995, p. A-16.

32. Tony Snow, "Affirmative Action at Risk? Deadly Political Symptoms," *Washington Times,* February 21, 1995, p. A-16.

33. Patrick Buchanan, "Affirmative Action Quicksand?" *Washington Times,* January 23, 1995, p. A-16.

34. U.S. Bureau of the Census, *Statistical Abstract of the United States 1994,* pp. 10–13.

35. Several polls over the past few years have indicated that most Americans now favor tighter immigration laws. In 1993, *Time* reported the results of a Yankelovich poll showing that 73 percent of Americans want to "strictly limit immigration"; "Not Quite So Welcome," *Time,* special issue, Fall 1993, p. 10. In 1994, a *Los Angeles Times* poll showed 82 percent in favor of immigration cutbacks. Cited in "Shutting the Golden Door," *U.S. News & World Report,* October 3, 1994, p. 36. For a summary of the results of opinion polls on immigration from 1992 to 1994, see "Reduce the Flow," *The American Enterprise,* March–April 1995, p. 104.

36. Wayne Lutton and John Tanton, *The Immigration Invasion,* Social Contract Press, Petoskey, MI, 1994, pp. 7, 39.

37. Quotations are from a U.S. English newspaper ad. See also *Democracy or Babel,* U.S. English, Washington DC, 1991.

38. Cited by Ellis Cose, *A Nation of Strangers: Prejudice, Politics and the Populating of America,* William Morrow, New York, 1992, p. 194.

39. Jon Nordheimer, "Where the Sounds of Spanish Grate," *New York Times,* August 22, 1994, p. A-10.

40. Cited by Laurence R. Stains, "The Latinization of Allentown, Pa.," *New York Times Magazine,* May 15, 1994, p. 61.

41. Cited in Anti-Defamation League of B'nai B'rith, *Hate Groups in America,* New York, 1988, p. 18.

42. "Race and IQ," *The New Republic,* October 31, 1994.

43. Samuel Francis, "Prospects for Racial and Cultural Survival," *American Renaissance,* March 1995.

44. Robert Blauner, "Talking Past Each Other: Black and White Languages of Race," *The American Prospect,* Summer 1992, p. 63.

45. Arnold Rose, "Postscript 20 Years Later," in Gunnar Myrdal, *An American Dilemma: The Negro Problem and Modern Democracy,* Pantheon Books, New York, 1962 edition, pp. xliii–xliv.

46. See, e.g., Elena Neuman, "Blacks of the '90s Often Segregate Themselves," *Washington Times,* June 8, 1994; Mary Jordan, "College Dorms Reflect Trend of Self-Segregation," *Washington Post,* March 6, 1994, p. A-1; David Dent, "The New Black Suburbs," *New York Times Magazine,* June 14, 1992; Isabel Wilkerson, "Separate Senior Proms Reveal an Unspanned Racial Divide," *New York Times,* May 5, 1991, p. A-1; Institute for the Study of Social Change, *The Diversity Project: Final Report,* University of California, Berkeley, 1991.

47. Cited by Rochelle Stanfield, "The Split Society," *National Journal,* April 2, 1994, p. 764.

48. Cited by Jim Sleeper, "The Decline and Rise of Bigotry," *Cosmopolitan,* June 1994, p. 208.

49. West, *Race Matters,* p. 64; Carl Rowan, "Activist Racism," *Baltimore Sun,* January 11, 1995; Kevin Johnson, "In California, Debate Rages on Affirmative Action,"

USA Today, February 16, 1995; R. Drummond Ayres, "Conservatives Forge New Strategy to Challenge Affirmative Action"; Rod Dreher, "Kemp Urges Affirmative Action Based on Economics," *Washington Times,* February 20, 1995, pp. A-1, A-9; Rod Dreher, "Jesse Jackson Hit for Slurs on Religious Right," *Washington Times,* December 8, 1994, pp. A-1, A-13; Paul Farhi and Kevin Merida, "House Rejects Tax Break," *Washington Post,* February 22, 1995, p. A-4; "Marching to a New War," *U.S. News & World Report,* March 6, 1995, p. 32.

50. David Goldberg, *The Anatomy of Racism,* University of Minnesota Press, Minneapolis, 1990; Naomi Zack, *Race and Mixed Race,* Temple University Press, Philadelphia, 1994, p. 24; J. Angelo Corlett, "Racism and Affirmative Action," *Journal of Social Philosophy* 24, No. 1 (Spring 1993), p. 163.

51. Joe R. Feagin and Melvin P. Sikes, *Living with Racism: The Black Middle Class Experience,* Beacon Press, Boston, 1994, p. 20.

52. Martin Kilson, "Realism About the Black Experience," *Dissent,* Fall 1990, p. 520; Martin Kilson and Clement Cottingham, "Thinking About Race Relations," *Dissent,* Fall 1991, pp. 520–29.

53. Joel Kovel, *White Racism: A Psychohistory,* Columbia University Press, New York, 1984, pp. xi, 32.

54. Molefi Kete Asante, *Afrocentricity,* Africa World Press, Trenton, 1988, p. 35.

55. Cited by Richard Majors and Jacob Gordon, eds., *The American Black Male: His Present Status and His Future,* Nelson Hall, Chicago, 1994, p. 171.

56. Ali A. Mazrui, "Dr. Schweitzer's Racism," *Transition,* Issue 53, 1991, p. 97.

57. Kovel, *White Racism,* pp. 48–49.

58. James M. Jones, "Racism in Black and White," in Phyllis Katz and Dalmas Taylor, *Eliminating Racism: Profiles in Controversy,* Plenum Press, New York, 1988, p. 131; Christine Bennett, *Comprehensive Multicultural Education,* Allyn & Bacon, Boston, 1990, p. 46.

59. Sut Jhally and Justin Lewis, *Enlightened Racism: The Cosby Show, Audiences and the Myth of the American Dream,* Westview Press, Boulder, 1992.

60. Thomas Powell, "Feel Good Racism," *New York Times,* May 24, 1992; Samuel L. Gaertner and John F. Dovidio, "Racism Among the Well-Intentioned," in E. Clausen and J. Bermingham, eds., *Pluralism, Racism and Public Policy,* G. K. Hall, Boston, 1981.

61. Cited by William Welch, "A New Frontier: Survival," *USA Today,* January 6, 1994, p. 6-A.

62. Leon Bing, *Do or Die,* HarperPerennial, New York, 1991, pp. 121–22.

63. Julius Lester, "The Lives People Live," in Paul Berman, ed., *Blacks and Jews: Alliances and Arguments,* Delacorte Press, New York, 1994, p. 170.

64. Cited by Luis Rodriguez, "Deciphering L.A. Smoke Signals," *National Catholic Reporter,* May 22, 1992, p. 20.

65. Toni Morrison, *Playing in the Dark: Whiteness and the Literary Imagination,* Harvard University Press, Cambridge, 1982, p. 63.

66. Richard Delgado, "Does Voice Really Matter?" *Virginia Law Review* 76 (1990), pp. 105–6.

67. Kenneth B. Clark, "Racial Progress and Retreat: A Personal Memoir," in Her-

bert Hill and James L. Jones, Jr., *Race in America: The Struggle for Equality,* University of Wisconsin Press, Madison, 1993, p. 18.

68. Kovel, *White Racism,* pp. ix, xxxi, 177.

69. Derrick Bell, *Faces at the Bottom of the Well: The Permanence of Racism,* Basic Books, New York, 1992, pp. 1, 3, 10, 152.

70. Andrew Hacker, *Two Nations: Black and White, Separate, Hostile, Unequal,* Ballantine Books, New York, 1992, p. 24; Lynne Duke, "The White Stuff: A Theory of Race," *Washington Post,* April 14, 1992, p. B-1, B-3.

71. Charles Lawrence, "The Id, the Ego, and Equal Protection: Reckoning with Unconscious Racism," *Stanford Law Review* 39 (1987), pp. 322–23, 330.

72. Renato Rosaldo, *Culture and Truth: The Remaking of Social Analysis,* Beacon Press, Boston, 1993, p. 196.

73. Cited by Frank Swoboda, "Glass Ceiling Firmly in Place, Panel Finds," *Washington Post,* March 16, 1995, p. A-18.

74. Cited by Pierre Thomas, "Deval Patrick and the Great Moral Imperative," *Washington Post,* October 26, 1994.

75. Michael Omi and Howard Winant, *Racial Formation in the United States,* Routledge & Kegan Paul, New York, 1986, p. 6.

76. Cited by Scott Jaschik, "Affirmative Action Under Fire," *Chronicle of Higher Education,* March 10, 1995, p. A-22.

77. Eduardo Galeano, *We Say No: Chronicles 1963–1991,* W. W. Norton, New York, 1992, p. 234.

78. Cited by Lynne Duke, "Cultural Shifts Bring Anxiety for White Men," *Washington Post,* January 1, 1991, p. A-14.

Chapter 2. Ignoble Savages

1. Kwaku Person-Lynn, "Language Keeps Racism Alive," *Los Angeles Times,* November 29, 1994, p. B-2.

2. Frantz Fanon, *Black Skin, White Masks,* Grove Weidenfeld, New York, 1967, p. 189.

3. Paula Rothenberg, *Racism and Sexism: An Integrated Study,* St. Martin's Press, New York, 1988, p. 270.

4. Christine Bolt, *Victorian Attitudes to Race,* Routledge & Kegan Paul, London, 1971, p. 131.

5. Richard Rorty, "Human Rights, Rationality and Sentimentality," in Stephen Shute and Susan Hurley, eds. *On Human Rights: The Oxford Amnesty Lectures,* Basic Books, New York, 1993, pp. 111–34.

6. Cited in Bob Trebilcock, "Reading, 'Riting, 'Rithmetic . . . Racism," *Redbook,* October 1993, p. 101.

7. Andrew Hacker, *Two Nations: Black and White, Separate, Hostile, Unequal,* Ballantine Books, New York, 1992, p. 19.

8. *Webster's New World Dictionary,* Prentice Hall, New York, 1994, p. 1106.

9. "Racism is any set of beliefs that organic, genetically transmitted differences (whether real or imagined) between human groups are intrinsically associated with

the presence or the absence of certain socially relevant abilities, hence that such differences are a legitimate basis of invidious distinctions between groups socially defined as races." Pierre Van den Berghe, *Race and Racism,* John Wiley & Sons, New York, 1978, p. 11.

"Racism in its simplest and most obvious form is defined as the belief that groups of human beings differ in their values and social accomplishments solely as a result of the impact of biological heredity." William B. Cohen, *The French Encounter With Africans: White Response to Blacks, 1530–1880,* Indiana University Press, Bloomington, 1980, p. 95.

"Racism rests upon two basic assumptions: (1) the moral qualities of a human group are positively correlated with their physical characteristics, and (2) all humankind is divisible into superior and inferior stocks upon the basis of the first assumption." Robert Berkhofer, Jr., *The White Man's Indian: Images of the American Indian from Columbus to the Present,* Alfred A. Knopf, New York, 1978, p. 55.

"Racism assumes inherent racial superiority or the purity and superiority of certain races; also, it denotes any doctrine or program of racial domination based on such an assumption." Louis L. Snyder, *The Idea of Racialism,* D. Van Nostrand, Princeton, NJ, 1962, p. 10.

Racism refers to "patterns of belief and related actions that overtly embrace the notion of genetic or biological differences between human groups." Gerald David Jaynes and Robin M. Williams, eds., *A Common Destiny: Blacks and American Society,* National Academy Press, Washington, DC, 1989, p. 566.

10. Martin Luther King, Jr., *Where Do We Go From Here: Chaos or Community?* Beacon Press, Boston, 1968, p. 48.

11. George Fredrickson, *White Supremacy: A Comparative Study in American and South African History,* Oxford University Press, New York, 1981, p. xii.

12. David Hume, "Of National Characters," in David Hume, *Essays: Moral, Political and Literary,* edited by T. H. Green and T. Grose, Longmans, Green and Co., London, 1875, Vol. 1, p. 252.

13. Immanuel Kant, *Observations on the Feeling of the Beautiful and Sublime,* translated by John Goldthwait, University of California Press, Berkeley, 1960, pp. 111–13.

14. Georg Wilhelm Friedrich Hegel, *The Philosophy of History,* Dover Publications, New York, 1956, pp. 95–99.

15. Oscar Handlin, *Race and Nationality in American Life,* Doubleday, New York, 1957, p. 71.

16. Joel Kovel, *White Racism: A Psychohistory,* Columbia University Press, New York, 1984, p. xlvii.

17. Tzvetan Todorov, *On Human Diversity: Nationalism, Racism and Exoticism in French Thought,* Harvard University Press, Cambridge, 1993, p. 91.

18. Stephen Jay Gould, *The Mismeasure of Man,* W. W. Norton, New York, 1981, p. 31.

19. Thomas F. Gossett, *Race: The History of an Idea in America,* Southern Methodist University Press, Dallas, 1963, p. 23.

20. Ibid., p. 4; see also Orlando Patterson, *Slavery and Social Death,* Harvard University Press, Boston, 1982, p. 176.

21. See David Brion Davis, *The Problem of Slavery in Western Culture,* Oxford University Press, New York, 1988, p. 51.

22. Nirad Chaudhuri, *The Continent of Circe,* Oxford University Press, New York, 1966, p. 45.

23. Selby Bangani Ngcobo, "The Bantu Peoples," in G. H. Calpin, ed., *The South African Way of Life,* Columbia University Press, New York, 1954, p. 55.

24. Cited by Bernard Lewis, *Race and Slavery in the Middle East,* Oxford University Press, New York, 1990, p. 48.

25. See Rabindranath Tagore, *A Tagore Reader,* Beacon Press, Boston, 1966, p. 186; Stanley Wolpert, *A New History of India,* Oxford University Press, New York, 1989, pp. 29–30; Romila Thapar, *A History of India,* Penguin Books, New York, 1990, pp. 34–38; M. N. Srinivas, "The Caste System in India," in Andre Beteille, ed., *Social Inequality: Selected Readings,* Penguin Books, Baltimore, 1969; Louis Dumont, *Homo Hierarchicus: The Caste System and Its Implications,* Weidenfeld and Nicholson, London, 1970.

26. G. F. Hudson, *Europe and China: A Survey of Their Relations from the Earliest Times to 1800,* Edward Arnold, London, 1931, pp. 237–47; Rhoads Murphey, *The Outsiders: The Western Experience in India and China,* University of Michigan Press, Ann Arbor, 1977, pp. 131–55.

27. Audrey Butt, *The Nilotes of the Sudan and Uganda,* International African Institute, London, 1964, p. 41; Orlando Patterson, *Ethnic Chauvinism,* Stein and Day, New York, 1977, p. 43; E. O. Wilson, *On Human Nature,* Harvard University Press, Cambridge, 1978, p. 92.

28. Bernard Lewis, *Race and Slavery in the Middle East,* p. 47.

29. Ibn al-Faqih, "Mukhtasar Kitab al-Buldan," cited by Bernard Lewis, *Islam,* Vol. II, Oxford University Press, New York, 1987, p. 209.

30. See Frank Snowden, *Before Color Prejudice,* Harvard University Press, Cambridge, 1985, p. 76, for discussion of a Central African creation myth in which the Negro "regards himself as perfectly cooked but the white man as underdone because of a defect in the creator's oven." See also Patricia Limerick, *The Legacy of Conquest: The Unbroken Past of the American West,* W. W. Norton, New York, 1987, p. 221, for "The Well Baked Man," a Pueblo Indian creation story.

31. In the classic definition of William Graham Sumner, ethnocentrism "is the technical name for the view of things in which one's own group is the center of everything and all others are scaled and rated with reference to it." See William Graham Sumner, *Folkways,* Ginn and Co., Boston, 1906, p. 13.

32. In ancient America, the Inca considered themselves the original model for all humanity and destined for leadership; they used a name for themselves which means "royal" or "archetypal." Similarly the Aztecs interpreted their own name as "people who explain themselves and speak clearly," thus differentiating them from others, variously named "the people who go hunting" and "the people who are wild and barbarous." See Ronald Wright, *Stolen Continents: The Americas Through Indian Eyes Since 1492,* Houghton Mifflin, New York, 1992, p. 72; Tzvetan Todorov, *The Conquest of America,* HarperPerennial, New York, 1984, p. 72.

Traveling in India, the Islamic scholar Alberuni was impressed by the level of learning, but not as impressed as the native Indians themselves. He commented, "The Indians believe that there is no country but theirs, no nation like theirs, no king like theirs, no religion like theirs, no science like theirs." As if to confirm his own tribal sentiments, Alberuni added that compared with the Muslim world, "I can only compare their mathematical and astronomical knowledge to a mixture of pearls and sour dates, or of pearls and dung. . . . The Indians are in a state of utter confusion." Cited by Thapar, *A History of India,* p. 239.

Writing in the eighteenth century, Adam Smith asked his readers to "suppose that the great empire of China, with all its myriads of inhabitants, was suddenly swallowed up by an earthquake." What would be the expected reaction in Europe? After the mandatory expressions of great sorrow, and perhaps a word or two about the vicissitudes of fate, Smith predicted that the most enlightened humanists would continue their lives "with the same ease and tranquillity as if no such accident had happened." When our own reactions to tragedies that strike close to home are compared with our response to distant afflictions, we will probably admit that despite attempts to moderate tribalism with altruism, the human impulse seems to endure. See Adam Smith, *A Theory of Moral Sentiments,* J. Richardson, London, 1822, Vol. 3, p. 186.

33. Ruth Benedict, *Race: Science and Politics,* Modern Age Books, New York, 1940, p. 155; Ruth Benedict, *Race and Racism,* Routledge & Kegan Paul, London, 1942, p. 99.

34. Orlando Patterson, *Ethnic Chauvinism: The Reactionary Impulse,* Stein and Day, New York, 1977, p. 43.

35. In the words of Edmund Burke, "To be attached to the subdivision, to love the little platoon we belong to in society, is the first principle of public affections." Edmund Burke, *Reflections on the Revolution in France,* Penguin Books, New York, 1982, p. 135.

36. Many scholars argue that self-love or narcissism is the most basic human feeling, essential to self-protection and survival. Tribalism is merely an extension of narcissism to the group, whether extended family or clan or religion or country. "The compelling imperative for self-preservation is self-love. Self-love is a governing tyrannical principle of human experience, to which aggression responds as a bonded servant." Gregory Rochlin, *Man's Aggression: The Defense of the Self,* Gambit Press, Boston, 1973, p. 1. See also Gerhard Lenski, *Power and Privilege: A Theory of Social Stratification,* McGraw-Hill, New York, 1966, p. 30.

37. See, e.g., Vernon Reynolds, Vincent Falger, and Ian Vine, *The Sociobiology of Ethnocentrism,* University of Georgia Press, Athens, 1987.

38. Richard Dawkins, *The Selfish Gene,* Oxford University Press, New York, 1989.

39. Pierre Van Den Berghe, *The Ethnic Phenomenon,* Elsevier Press, New York, 1981, pp. xi, 15–36, 239.

40. Bradford Cornell, "An Hypothesis Regarding the Origins of Ethnic Discrimination," Finance Working Paper, February 1994, UCLA Graduate School of Management.

41. See, e.g., Claude Lévi-Strauss, "Race and History," in Leo Kuper, ed., *Race, Science and Society,* The UNESCO Press, Paris, 1975.

42. For evidence of Roman tolerance toward the Jews compared to Christians,see E. Mary Smallwood, *The Jews Under Roman Rule,* E.J. Brill, Leiden, Netherlands, 1976, pp. 539–43.

43. Solomon Grayzel notes that on account of substantial Jewish conversion during the Middle Ages, "there is a great deal of Jewish blood in the veins of the population of modern Europe." Solomon Grayzel, *A History of the Jews,* New American Library, New York, 1984, p. 320.

44. See, e.g., Jane S. Gerber, *The Jews of Spain: A History of the Sephardic Experience,* Free Press, New York, 1992. Yet Norman Roth argues that most Jews who converted to Christianity were sincere. Norman Roth, *Conversos, Inquisition and the Expulsion of the Jews from Spain,* University of Wisconsin Press, Madison, 1994.

45. Grayzel, *A History of the Jews,* pp. 359–60.

46. David Brion Davis, *Slavery and Human Progress,* Oxford University Press, New York, 1984, p. 96.

47. Robert S. Wistrich, *Antisemitism: The Longest Hatred,* Pantheon Books, New York, 1991, p. 36; for a detailed account, see Bernard Lewis, *Semites and Antisemites: An Inquiry Into Conflict and Prejudice,* W. W. Norton, New York, 1986, pp. 81–84.

48. Solomon Grayzel, *A History of the Jews,* pp. 554–57, 661–62.

49. Pierre Van Den Berghe, *Race and Racism,* p. 12.

50. For some exponents of this view, see Marvin Harris, *Patterns of Race in the Americas,* Greenwood Press, Westport, CT, 1964, p. 70; Stephen Steinberg, *The Ethnic Myth: Race, Ethnicity and Class in America,* Beacon Press, Boston, 1989, p. 30, and Donald Noel, ed., *The Origins of American Slavery and Racism,* Charles E. Merrill, Columbus, OH, 1972.

51. Eric Williams, *Capitalism and Slavery,* Capricorn Books, New York, 1966, p. 7.

52. Basil Davidson, *The African Slave Trade,* Little, Brown, Boston, 1980, p. 25.

53. "Racism first flowered as a means for legitimizing the lucrative slave trade, and was patently economic in origin." Salman Rushdie, *Imaginary Homelands,* Penguin Books, New York, 1991, p. 145. See also Lerone Bennett, *Before the Mayflower: A History of Black America,* Penguin Books, New York, 1993, p. 45.

54. Winthrop Jordan, *White Over Black: American Attitudes Toward the Negro, 1550–1812,* University of North Carolina Press, Chapel Hill, 1968, p. 134. For a summary of this thesis, see Winthrop Jordan, *The White Man's Burden,* Oxford University Press, New York, 1974.

55. Alexis de Tocqueville, *Democracy in America,* edited by J. P. Mayer, Harper & Row, New York, 1988, p. 343.

56. Cited by William S. McFeely, *Frederick Douglass,* W. W. Norton, New York, 1991, p. 94.

57. Orlando Patterson, *Slavery and Social Death: A Comparative Study,* Harvard University Press, Cambridge, 1982, p. vii.

58. Isaac Mendelsohn, *Slavery in the Ancient Near East,* Greenwood Press, New York, 1949; C. Martin Wilbur, *Slavery in China During the Former Han Dynasty,* Field Museum of Natural History, Chicago, 1943; Orlando Patterson, *Freedom in the Making of Western Culture,* Vol. I, Basic Books, New York, 1991, p. 21; A. M. Bakir, *Slavery in Pharaonic Egypt,* Cairo, 1952; Dev Raj Chanana, *Slavery in Ancient India,* People's Publishing House, New Delhi, 1960; Moses Finley, *Slavery in Classical Antiquity,* W. Heffer & Sons, Cambridge, 1960; William Westermann, *The Slave Systems of Greek and Roman Antiquity,* American Philosophical Society, Philadelphia, 1955.

59. See, e.g., Patterson, *Slavery and Social Death;* Davis, *Slavery and Human Progress;* Lewis, *Race and Slavery in the Middle East;* Bernard Lewis, *The Muslim Discovery of Europe,* W. W. Norton, New York, 1982, pp. 188–92; John Blassingame, *The Slave Community,* Oxford University Press, New York, 1979, pp. 49–62.

60. According to Orlando Patterson's analysis of fifty-five slaveholding societies, 75 percent had populations in which slaves and masters were from the same general group, 21 percent had populations in which masters and slaves were from different racial groups, and 4 percent had populations in which some slaves were of the same racial group as masters while others were not. Patterson, *Slavery and Social Death,* p. 176.

61. Snowden, *Before Color Prejudice,* p. 70.

62. Audrey Smedley, *Race in North America,* Westview Press, Boulder, 1993, p. 148; Davis, *Slavery and Human Progress,* pp. 32–33.

63. Grace Hadley Beardsley, *The Negro in Greek and Roman Civilization,* Arno Press, New York, 1979, pp. 36, 66, 111.

64. Patterson, *Slavery and Social Death,* p. 176. See also Lewis, *Race and Slavery in the Middle East.*

65. William D. Phillips, *Slavery From Roman Times to the Early Transatlantic Trade,* University of Minnesota Press, Minneapolis, 1965, p. 162; Davis, *Slavery and Human Progress,* p. 35.

66. Davis, *The Problem of Slavery in Western Culture,* p. 44.

67. In Greece, slave women were not permitted to marry free men, and in Rome slaves were segregated from the rest of society. See Davis, *The Problem of Slavery in Western Culture,* p. 49. For a study of the common techniques of oppression and degradation employed by slaveholding societies, see Patterson, *Slavery and Social Death.*

68. "In Greece and Rome . . . manumissions were remarkably common. The ex-slave in fifth century Athens bore no stigma from his servile past, and some rose to positions of political and economic power." Moreover, "If Romans usually showed more sensitivity to social distinctions between slaves and freemen, they seldom appeared conscious of racial differences." Davis, *The Problem of Slavery in Western Culture,* p. 55. Additionally, Moses Finley argues that the typical slave in the Greco-Roman world had a Greek or Roman name, spoke Latin, shared the tan complexion of his owners, and could easily shed the cultural markings of slave identity; but even if not, he carried a stigma not of race but of culture, and that could be erased over time through intermarriage, education, and cultivation. Moses Finley, *Slavery in Classical Antiquity,* p. 110; Moses Finley, *Ancient Slavery and Modern Ideology,* Penguin, New York, 1980, p. 97. On manumission as a social instrument for assimilation, see Thomas Wiedemann, *Greek and Roman Slavery,* Johns Hopkins University Press, Baltimore, 1981, p. 13.

69. Patterson, *Slavery and Social Death,* p. 278.

70. Van Den Berghe, *The Ethnic Phenomenon,* p. 135.

71. Na'im Akbar, *Visions for Black Men,* Winston-Derek Publishers, Nashville, 1991, p. 27.

72. Marimba Ani, *Yurugu: An African-centered Critique of European Cultural Thought and Behavior,* Africa World Press, Trenton, 1994, pp. 127, 258.

73. Michael Bradley, *The Iceman Inheritance,* Kayode Publications, New York, 1978, p. 3.

74. Snowden, *Before Color Prejudice,* p. 63, 77. Frank Snowden, *Blacks in Antiquity,* Harvard University Press, Cambridge, 1970, pp. 144, 146–47, 175, 178, 179–80, 192, 194–96, 217. Frank Snowden, "Asclepiades' Didyme," *Greek, Roman and Byzantine Studies* 32, No. 3 (1991), p. 239. The subsequent account of Snowden's work is based on these sources.

75. See Michael Grant, *The Founders of the Western World: A History of Greece and Rome,* Scribner's, New York, 1991, for a general discussion of Greek attitudes toward aliens and foreigners.

76. Martin Bernal, *Black Athena: The Afroasiatic Roots of Classical Civilization,* Rutgers University Press, New Brunswick, 1987, p. 28. The general argument of this book is considered dubious by most scholars, but Bernal is certainly right on this point. I cite him because his work is respected among Afrocentric scholars, and Afrocentrists are the ones most likely to argue that racism has always existed among white peoples.

77. Gossett, *Race: The History of an Idea in America,* pp. 5–6.

78. Aristotle, *The Politics,* Penguin Books, New York, 1981, p. 69.

79. Ibid., p. 73.

80. Aristotle, "Politica," cited by Gossett, *Race,* p. 6.

81. Aristotle, *The Politics,* p. 61.

82. Cited in Finley, *Ancient Slavery and Modern Ideology,* p. 120.

83. Forrest Wood, *The Arrogance of Faith: Christianity and Race in America from the Colonial Era to the Twentieth Century,* Alfred A. Knopf, New York, 1990, pp. xviii, 50, 83.

84. "Natives were outside the pale of humanity, but this was regarded as a consequence of the fact that they were not Christians, not of the fact that they belonged to the darker races." Benedict, *Race and Racism,* p. 107. See also Lewis, *Race and Slavery in the Middle East,* p. 17.

85. Saint Augustine, *The City of God,* Book XXII, Modern Library, New York, 1950, pp. 864–65.

86. Galatians 3:28. In another related passage, Paul writes, "There cannot be Greek and Jew, circumcised and uncircumcised, barbarian, Scythian, slave, free man, but Christ is all, and in all." Colossians 3:11.

87. Bernal, *Black Athena,* Vol. I, p. 242.

88. Snowden, *Blacks in Antiquity,* pp. 198, 204.

89. Jerry H. Bentley, *Old World Encounters: Cross-Cultural Contacts and Exchanges in Pre-Modern Times,* Oxford University Press, New York, 1993, pp. 33, 80\N81; William H. McNeill, *The Rise of the West,* Mentor Books, New York, 1963, pp. 332, 563–66.

90. Bentley, *Old World Encounters.* See esp. p. 182. "In earlier centuries, technology had not strengthened the hand of a single people in quite the same way that it favored Europeans during early modern times. . . . No single people was able to gain a permanent or even a long-term monopoly on advanced techniques."

91. Alvin Poussaint, *Why Blacks Kill Blacks,* Emerson Hall Publishers, New York, 1972, p. 37.

92. Elie Kedourie, *Politics in the Middle East,* Oxford University Press, New York, 1992, p. 2.

93. Bernard Lewis, *Race and Slavery in the Middle East,* pp. 17, 21.

94. Ibid., p. 52.

95. Ibn Butlan, Shira al-Raqiq, cited by Lewis, *Islam,* Vol. II, p. 249.

96. Lewis, *The Muslim Discovery of Europe,* p. 139.

97. "There is nobody among them, of whatever class, who does not eat onions every day and no house in which it is not eaten morning and evening. This is what has corrupted their imagination, harmed their brains, confused their senses, altered their intelligence, spoiled their complexions, and so disturbed their constitutions that they see things, or at any rate most things, as the opposite of what they really are." Ibn Hawqal, Surat-al-Ard, cited by Bernard Lewis, *Islam,* Vol. II, p. 93.

98. Ibn Battuta, *Travels in Asia and Africa, 1325–1354,* Augustus Kelley, New York, 1969, pp. 330–31.

99. Ibn Khaldun, *The Muqaddimah,* translated by Franz Rosenthal, Princeton University Press, New Jersey, 1967, pp. 59, 63.

100. Distinguishing between white and black slaves, Khaldun writes, "Negro nations are, as a rule, submissive to slavery, because Negroes have little that is essentially human and have attributes that are quite similar to dumb animals." Ibid., p. 117.

101. Bernard Lewis, "The Crows of the Arabs," in Henry Louis Gates, ed., *"Race," Writing and Difference,* University of Chicago Press, Chicago, 1986, pp. 111–15. See also Lewis, *Race and Slavery in the Middle East,* pp. 15, 51–53, 89, 93. See also Ronald Sanders, *Lost Tribes and Promised Lands,* HarperPerennial, New York, 1992, p. 55.

102. Philip Snow, *The Star Raft: China's Encounter with Africa,* Cornell University Press, Ithaca, 1988, pp. 3–4, 14, 189. See also J. J. L. Duyvendak, *China's Discovery of Africa,* Arthur Probsthain, London, 1949, p. 30. For a description of Chinese maritime technology and mention of African landings, see Jacques Gernet, *A History of Chinese Civilization,* Cambridge University Press, Cambridge, 1989, pp. 326–27.

103. Eugenia Shanklin, *Anthropology and Race,* Wadsworth Publishing, Belmont, CA, 1994, pp. iv, 73.

104. Michael Banton and Jonathan Harwood argue that between the sixteenth and the eighteenth centuries, the term race "was used with growing frequency in a literary sense, as denoting simply a class of persons. . . . In the 19th and increasingly in the 20th century, this loose usage began to give way and the word came to signify groups that were distinguished biologically." Michael Banton and Jonathan Harwood, *The Race Concept,* Praeger, New York, 1975, p. 13. "Race was, from its inception, a folk classification, a product of popular beliefs about human differences that evolved from the 16th through the 19th centuries." Audrey Smedley, *Race in North America: Origin and Evolution of a Worldview,* Westview Press, Boulder, 1993, p. 25.

105. Bolt, *Victorian Attitudes To Race,* p. ix.

106. H. W. Janson, *Apes and Ape Lore in the Middle Ages and the Renaissance,* University of London Press, London, 1952, pp. 74–75. Richard Bernheimer, *Wild Men*

in the Middle Ages, Harvard University Press, Cambridge, 1952. See Lewis Hanke, *Aristotle and the American Indians,* Henry Regnery, Chicago, 1959, p. 4.

107. Malcolm Letts, ed., *Mandeville's Travels: Texts and Translations,* Hakluyt Society, London 1953, Vol. I. For a discussion of Mandeville, see Stephen Greenblatt, *Marvelous Possessions: The Wonder of the New World,* University of Chicago Press, Chicago, 1991, p. 31.

108. Greenblatt, *Marvelous Possessions,* p. 74.

109. The British voyager and courtier Walter Raleigh uncritically embraced reports of natives in the new world with "eyes in their shoulders and their mouths in the middle of their breasts." In 1540, Francisco de Orellana gave the biggest river in South America the name "Amazon" based on Gaspar de Carvajal's eyewitness reports of a tribe of female warrior giants who supposedly ruled in the area, and several decades later a unicorn was reported in the state of Florida. As late as 1635, John Swan in his *Speculum Mundi* declared his belief in mermaids and unicorns, but he rejected the possibility of a phoenix on the grounds that Noah would not have accepted in the ark an animal that didn't have a partner for a mate. See Richard Hakluyt, *Voyages and Discoveries,* edited by Jack Beeching, Penguin Books, New York, 1972, p. 278; Lewis Hanke, *Aristotle and the American Indians,* pp. 5–6; Emir Rodriguez Monegal, ed., *The Borzoi Anthology of Latin American Literature,* Alfred A. Knopf, New York, 1983, p. 57; Norman Hampson, *The Enlightenment,* Penguin Books, New York, 1968, p. 33.

110. Marco Polo, *The Travels,* edited by Ronald Latham, Penguin Books, New York, 1958.

111. Gomes Eannes de Azurara, Prince Henry's chronicler, mentions "news of Prester John" as one of the motivations for the Portuguese voyages along the African coast. See Ronald Sanders, *Lost Tribes and Promised Lands,* 1992, p. 38. See also Barnet Litvinoff, *1492: The Decline of Medievalism and the Rise of the Modern Age,* Avon Books, New York, 1991, p. 27.

112. Sanders, *Lost Tribes and Promised Lands,* p. 6.

113. Leo Africanus, *Description of Africa,* translated by John Pory in 1600, reprinted by the Hakluyt Society, London, 1896.

114. See, e.g., Janet Abu-Lughod, *Before European Hegemony: The World System A.D. 1250–1350,* Oxford University Press, New York, 1989; Immanuel Wallerstein, *The Modern World System,* Academic Press, New York, 1974; Philip Curtin, *Cross-Cultural Trade in World History,* Cambridge University Press, Cambridge, 1984.

115. McNeill, *The Rise of the West;* J. M. Roberts, *The Triumph of the West,* Little Brown, Boston, 1985; Carlo Cipolla, *Guns, Sails and Empires: Technological Innovation and the Early Phases of European Expansion, 1400–1700,* Pantheon Books, New York, 1966; E. L. Jones, *The European Miracle,* Cambridge University Press, Cambridge, 1981. For a more skeptical account of the European rise to power, see Michael Adas, *Machines as the Measure of Men: Science, Technology and Ideologies of Western Dominance,* Cornell University Press, Ithaca, 1989.

116. For a discussion of the "enchanted world," and its abandonment as a key ingredient of modernity, see Ernest Gellner, *Plough, Sword and Book,* University of Chicago Press, Chicago, 1989.

117. Jacob Bronowski, *The Ascent of Man,* Little, Brown, Boston, 1973; J. B. Bury, *The Idea of Progress: An Inquiry Into Its Origin and Growth,* Dover Publications, New York, 1960.

118. David C. Lindberg, *The Beginnings of Western Science,* University Of Chicago Press, Chicago, 1992; Joel Mokyr, *The Lever of Riches: Technological Creativity and Human Progress,* Oxford University Press, New York, 1990; David Landes, *The Unbound Prometheus,* Cambridge University Press, Cambridge, 1969; Adas, *Machines as the Measure of Men;* see also McNeill, *The Rise of the West,* pp. 641–52.

119. William H. McNeill, *A World History,* Oxford University Press, New York, 1979, p. 513. See also Herbert Butterfield, *The Origins of Modern Science,* Free Press, New York, 1965.

120. Margaret Aston, *The Fifteenth Century: The Prospect of Europe,* W. W. Norton, New York, 1968.

121. This list is given by Stanley Alpern, "The New Myths of African History," *Bostonia,* Summer 1992, p. 29. See also Aston, *The Fifteenth Century,* pp. 9, 67; Litvinoff, *1492,* p. xx.

122. Isaac Asimov, *Asimov's Chronology of Science and Discovery,* Harper & Row, New York, 1989.

123. McNeill, *The Rise of the West,* pp. 652–58, 705–8.

124. John Garraty and Peter Gay, "Sub-Saharan Africa," *The Columbia History of the World,* Harper & Row, New York, 1986, pp. 300–303.

125. Wright, *Stolen Continents,* pp. 50, 68. The achievements of Aztec, Inca, and Maya civilizations are given full treatment in Alvin Josephy, Jr., *The Indian Heritage of America,* Alfred A. Knopf, New York, 1971.

126. George W. Stocking, Jr., *Victorian Anthropology,* Free Press, New York, 1987, pp. 275, 280–83; David Tomas, "Tools of the Trade: The Production of Ethnographic Observations of the Andaman Islands," in George W. Stocking, Jr., ed., *Colonial Situations,* Univeristy of Wisconsin Press, Madison, 1991, p. 77; Lévi-Strauss, "Race and History," pp. 99, 122–23, 157. For a list of the "reservoirs of savage and barbarian life" which operated outside the "immediate radius of civilized societies," see McNeill, *The Rise of the West,* p. 254.

127. Robert Hughes, *The Fatal Shore,* Collins Harvill, London, 1987, pp. 12–15, 273.

128. Robert Edgerton, *Sick Societies: Challenging the Myth of Primitive Harmony,* Free Press, New York, 1992, pp. 47–50.

129. Thomas Sowell argues that "the continent of Europe had virtually every geographical advantage, whether in navigable waterways, more fertile soil, more ample and reliable rainfall, and a climate that does not support devastating tropical diseases." Thomas Sowell, *Race and Culture,* Basic Books, New York, 1994, p. 13.

130. Richard W. Bulliet, *The Camel and the Wheel,* Harvard University Press, Cambridge, 1975.

131. Josephy, *The Indian Heritage of America,* p. 29.

132. McNeill, *The Rise of the West,* p. 53.

133. Josephy, *The Indian Heritage of America,* p. 29; Harold Driver, *Indians of North America,* University of Chicago Press, Chicago, 1975, p. 212; Jacob Bronowski,

The Ascent of Man, p. 194; E. L. Jones, *The European Miracle,* p. 156; J. M. Roberts, *The Penguin History of the World,* Penguin Books, New York, 1990, p. 447.

134. Asimov, *Asimov's Chronology of Science and Discovery,* p. 20.

135. Roberts, *The Penguin History of the World,* p. 447. See also L. H. Gann and Peter Duignan, *Africa South of the Sahara,* Hoover Institution Press, Stanford, 1981, p. 2. "Almost no African community south of the Sahara managed to harness draft animals to pull plows and wagons until European newcomers introduced these new methods of traction in the nineteenth and twentieth centuries." See also Harold Driver, *Indians of North America,* p. 77: "The plow was totally unknown in the New World until it was introduced by the Europeans, and draft animals were not used in farming."

136. Kwasi Wiredu, "African Philosophical Tradition: A Case Study of the Akan," *The Philosophical Forum* 24, Nos. 1–3, 1992–1993, p. 36.

137. Asimov, *Asimov's Chronology of Science and Discovery,* p. 20.

138. Josephy, *The Indian Heritage of America,* p. 13; John McKay et. al., *A History of World Societies,* Houghton Mifflin, Boston, 1988, Vol. I, p. 474; W. Gordon East, *The Geography Behind History,* W. W. Norton, New York, 1965, p. 161.

139. Basil Davidson, *A History of West Africa,* Anchor Books, New York, 1966, pp. 164–66. Discussing formal education, Davidson writes, "With some exceptions, important though few, it was a matter of word-of-mouth teaching of skills, customs, laws, traditions, and the like. It was done for the most part without the aid of writing and reading: the culture was non-literate."

140. Thus Basil Davidson, the Marxist writer, admits that south of the Sahara a subsistence community prevailed, lacking scientific invention and not feeling the need for it, with the result that "increasingly, these peoples fell into a relative inferiority to Europe in military, commercial and mechanical power." In *How Europe Underdeveloped Africa* the Marxist historian Walter Rodney writes, "In the centuries before colonial rule, Europe increased its economic capacity by leaps and bounds, while Africa appeared to have been almost static."

Even Chiekh Anta Diop, the godfather of Afrocentrism, in his book *Precolonial Black Africa* portrays a simple tribal society clothed in loincloths and animal skins, fed and protected with javelins and bows and arrows, which traded in barter and cowry shells, whose musical instruments were made of reeds and gourds and wooden drumsticks; accumulations of wealth, Diop argues, were simply unnecessary in such a subsistence economy.

Ngugi wa Thiong'o, the African novelist and political activist, writes that "the precolonial African world . . . was on the whole characterized by the low level of development of productive forces. Hence it was dominated by an incomprehensible and unpredictable nature, or rather by a nature to an extent only knowable through ritual, magic and divination."

See Davidson, *A History of West Africa,* pp. 108, 152–53; Walter Rodney, *How Europe Underdeveloped Africa,* Howard University Press, Washington, DC, 1982; Chiekh Anta Diop, *Precolonial Black Africa,* Lawrence Hill Books, Chicago, 1987, esp. p. 158; Ngugi wa Thiong'o, *Decolonizing the Mind: The Politics of Language in African Literature,* Heinemann, Portsmouth, NH, 1986, p. 65.

141. Olaudah Equiano describes his native country of Benin before he was cap-

tured and brought to the new world. "Agriculture is our chief employment, and everyone, even the children and women, are engaged in it." There were no plows and no beasts of husbandry," so the land was tilled with hoes and pointed iron. "Our manners are simple, our luxuries are few." Olaudah Equiano, *The Life of Olaudah Equiano or Gustavus Vassa, the African,* Humanities Press, New York, 1969, p. 17.

142. Cited by Ali A. Mazrui, *Cultural Forces in World Politics,* James Currey, London, 1990, p. 134; see also Ali A. Mazrui, "Wole Soyinka as a Television Critic: A Parable of Deception," *Transition,* Issue 54, 1991, p. 171.

143. Christine Bennett, *Comprehensive Multicultural Education: Theory and Practice,* Allyn & Bacon, Boston, 1990, p. 72.

144. Johnnetta B. Cole, *Conversations: Straight Talk With America's Sister President,* Anchor Books, New York, 1993, p. 61.

145. Gary Nash, *Red, White and Black: The Peoples of Early America,* Prentice Hall, Englewood Cliffs, NJ, 1974, p. 158; Gary Nash and Richard Weiss, *The Great Fear: Race in the Mind of America,* Holt, Rinehart and Winston, New York, 1970, p. 13.

146. Harris, *Patterns of Race in the Americas,* p. 3.

147. "Generally speaking, the level of mastery over the environment attained in Mexico and Peru by 1500 seems very similar to what the ancient Mesopotamians and Egyptians had achieved by 2500 B.C. A four thousand year lag." McNeill, *A World History,* p. 278. Discussing Africa, a more more charitable comparison is given by Philip D. Curtin in *The Image of Africa,* University of Wisconsin Press, Madison, 1964 p. 31: "If Africa was behind, it was hardly more than a thousand years behind. The technology of most African societies of about 1750 A.D. had reached and in some respects passed the level of technology prevalent in northwest Europe in 750 A.D." For the comment about the Stone Age, see Roberts, *Penguin History of the World,* p. 447. A similar reference appears in Garraty and Gay, *Columbia History of the World,* p. 297.

148. "But when the side that has the physical force has intellectual superiority too, it is rare for the conquered to become civilized; they either withdraw or are destroyed. For this reason one can say that, generally speaking, savages go forth in arms to seek enlightenment but do not accept it as a gift." Tocqueville, *Democracy in America,* pp. 330–31.

149. George Louis Leclerc Buffon, *Natural History,* translated by William Smellie, London, 3rd edition, 1791, III, pp. 201–4.

150. Curtin, *The Image of Africa,* p. 236; Jordan, *The White Man's Burden,* p. 9.

151. Jordan, *White Over Black,* p. 12.

152. Philip D. Curtin, *Imperialism,* Harper & Row, New York, 1971, p. xv; see also Curtin, *The Image of Africa,* p. 30.

153. Davis, *The Problem of Slavery in Western Culture,* p. 168.

154. Brewton Berry, *Race and Ethnic Relations,* Houghton Mifflin, New York, 1965, p. 86.

155. Limerick, *The Legacy of Conquest,* pp. 181–87.

156. Fredrickson, *White Supremacy,* p. 39.

157. Davis, *The Problem of Slavery in Western Culture,* p. 172.

158. Christopher Columbus, *The Four Voyages,* J. M. Cohen, trans., Penguin Books, New York, 1969, p. 221.

159. Jordan, *White Over Black,* p. 7. See also Kovel, *White Racism,* p. 62.

160. Jordan, *White Over Black,* p. 7. See also Nash and Weiss, *The Great Fear,* p. 11; Barry Schwartz, ed., *White Racism,* Laurel Leaf Books, New York, 1978, p. 6.

161. "It is surely more than a coincidence that in Africa and Asia as well as Europe, black is associated with unpleasantness, disaster or evil." Carl N. Degler, *Neither Black Nor White: Slavery and Race Relations in Brazil and the United States,* Macmillan, New York, 1971, p. 211. "Recent research has shown a pancultural preference for light over dark, presumably derived from the worldwide fear of the night together with the association of daylight with fear reduction and need satisfaction." Thomas Pettigrew, George Fredrickson, Dale Knobel, Nathan Glazer, and Reed Ueda, *Prejudice,* Harvard University Press, Cambridge, 1982, p. 15. See also Harry Levin, *The Power of Blackness,* Ohio University Press, Athens, 1980; Davis, *Slavery and Human Progress,* p. 38; Kathy Russell, Midge Wilson, and Ronald Hall, *The Color Complex,* Harcourt Brace Jovanovich, New York, 1992, p. 37.

162. See Winthrop Jordan, *White Over Black,* esp. p. 29.

163. Edward Tyson, *Orang-Outang, Sive Homo Sylvestris: Or the Anatomy of a Pygmie Compared with That of a Monkey, an Ape, and a Man,* Thomas Bennet and Daniel Brown, London, 1699.

164. Smedley, *Race in North America,* p. 162.

165. Eugene Genovese, *Roll, Jordan, Roll: The World the Slaves Made,* Vintage Books, New York, 1972, pp. 458–59.

166. Davis, *The Problem of Slavery in Western Culture,* p. 469.

167. Cited by Davis, *The Problem of Slavery in Western Culture,* pp. 452–53; Jordan, *White Over Black,* p. 34.

168. Edward Long, *The History of Jamaica,* London, 1774. Cited by Davis, *The Problem of Slavery in Western Culture,* pp. 455, 462–63. See also Jordan, *The White Man's Burden,* pp. 197–98.

169. *Compact Edition of the Oxford English Dictionary,* Oxford University Press, New York, 1971, p. 2002.

170. Jordan, *The White Man's Burden,* pp. 106, 197.

171. "Not to mention our colonies, there are Negro slaves dispersed all over Europe, of which none ever discovered any symptoms of ingenuity; though low people, without education, will start up amongst us, and distinguish themselves in every profession." Hume, "Of National Characters," p. 252.

172. Immanuel Kant, *Observations on the Feeling of the Beautiful and Sublime,* pp. 111–13.

173. "If only your doctrine . . . could serve mankind better! What purpose does it serve to persuade lesser peoples living in abject conditions of barbarism or slavery that, such being their racial status, they can do nothing to better themselves, to change their habits, or to ameliorate their status?" Tocqueville also termed Gobineau's theories "probably quite false" and "certainly very pernicious." Alexis de Tocqueville, *The European Revolution and Correspondence with Gobineau,* edited by John Lukacs, Greenwood Press, Westport, CT, 1959, pp. 286–88.

174. Michael Biddiss, introduction to Joseph Arthur Gobineau, *Selected Political Writings,* Harper & Row, New York, 1970.

175. "No full-blooded Negro has ever been distinguished as a man of science, a

poet or an artist, and the fundamental equality claimed for him is belied by the whole history of the race." *Encyclopaedia Britannica,* 9th edition, London, 1884, Vol. 17, p. 318.

176. See, e.g., Leon Poliakov, *The Aryan Myth: A History of Racist and Nationalist Ideas in Europe,* Basic Books, New York, 1971.

177. Arthur de Gobineau, *The Inequality of Human Races,* translated by Adrian Collins, Howard Fertig, New York, 1967, pp. 27, 37–38, 54, 74–75, 154, 168, 180.

Chapter 3. An American Dilemma

1. Mark Twain, *The Adventures of Huckleberry Finn,* Bantam Books, New York, 1981, p. 213.

2. Michael Eric Dyson, *Reflecting Black: African American Cultural Criticism,* University of Minnesota Press, Minneapolis, 1993, p. 183.

3. See, e.g., Johnnetta B. Cole, *Conversations: Straight Talk with America's Sister President,* Anchor Books, New York, 1993, p. 58; Alphonso Pinkney, *Black Americans,* Prentice Hall, Englewood Cliffs, NJ, 1969, p. 1.

4. Andrew Hacker, *Two Nations: Black and White, Separate, Hostile, Unequal,* Ballantine Books, New York, 1992, p. 14.

5. Ibid.

6. Stephen Steinberg, *The Ethnic Myth: Race, Ethnicity and Class in America,* Beacon Press, Boston, 1989, p. 293.

7. Alvin Poussaint, *Why Blacks Kill Blacks,* Emerson Hall Publishers, New York, 1972, p. 99.

8. Patricia Williams, *The Alchemy of Race and Rights,* Harvard University Press, Cambridge, 1991, p. 24; Molefi Kete Asante, "Afrocentricity and the Question of Youth Violence," in *Malcolm X as Cultural Hero and Other Afrocentric Essays,* Africa World Press, Trenton, NJ, 1993, pp. 117–19.

9. "I try to imagine what it would have been like to have a discontented white man buy me . . . I wonder what it would have been like to have a 35-year-old man own the secrets of my puberty, which he bought to prove himself sexually as well as to increase his lifestock of slaves . . . I imagine trying to please, with the yearning of adolescence, a man who truly did not know I was human . . . I try to envision being casually threatened with sale from time to time, teeth and buttocks bared to interested visitors." Williams, *The Alchemy of Race and Rights,* p. 18.

10. Cornel West, "Philosophy and the Urban Underclass," in Bill Lawson, ed., *The Underclass Question,* Temple University Press, Philadelphia, 1992, p. 195.

11. Derrick Bell, *Faces at the Bottom of the Well: The Permanence of Racism,* Basic Books, New York, 1992, p. 12.

12. Jenifer Warren, "Demanding Repayment for Slavery," *Los Angeles Times,* July 6, 1994, pp. A-1, A-5; Lena Williams, "Group of Blacks Presses the Case for Reparations for Slavery," *New York Times,* July 21, 1994, p. B-10.

13. David Swinton, "The Key to Black Wealth: Ownership," *Black Enterprise,* July 1994, p. 24; Lori S. Robinson, "Economist: Inequities of the Past Block Progress," *Emerge,* October 1993, pp. 18–19.

14. "If I am kidnapped and forced to work for subsistence and my meager earnings are then confiscated, I am not only owed compensation for the confiscation of those earnings; far more important, I am also owed compensation for what I would have produced had I not been kidnapped. And if I am not around to claim my compensation, my descendants, to whom I would have bequeathed it, can claim it as their right. This is the case in relation to the slaves and their descendants." Bernard Boxill, *Blacks and Social Justice,* Rowman & Littlefield, Lanham, MD, 1992, p. 36.

15. Sam Haselby, "Muscular Humanism: An Interview with Henry Louis Gates, Jr.," *Hungry Mind Review,* Fall 1994, p. 23.

16. See, e.g., James Forman, "The Black Manifesto," in Robert S. Lecky and H. Elliot Wright, eds., *Black Manifesto: Religion, Racism, and Reception,* Sheed & Ward, New York, 1969, pp. 115–26; Arnold Schuchter, *Reparations: The Black Manifesto and Its Challenge to White America,* J. B. Lippincott, Philadelphia, 1970; Boris Bittker, *The Case for Black Reparations,* Random House, New York, 1973.

17. "Tax Report," *Wall Street Journal,* October 19, 1994, p. A-1; Marsha Ginsburg, "Slavery Payback Is Only a Dream," *Washington Times,* October 23, 1994, p. A-5.

18. Richard F. America, ed., *The Wealth of Races: The Present Value of Benefits from Past Injustices,* Greenwood Press, New York, 1990, p. 41, 100, and 118; Haki R. Madhubuti, *Black Men: Obsolete, Single, Dangerous?,* Third World Press, Chicago, 1990, p. 28.

19. As a metaphor for the high emotions raised by the subject see, e.g., Tamara Jones, "Living History or Undying Racism: Colonial Williamsburg Slave Auction Draws Protest, Support," *Washington Post,* October 11, 1994, pp. A-1, A-18.

20. Although in its 1976 hardcover edition Doubleday marketed *Roots* as nonfiction, subsequent research by historians shows that—in the words of *The Village Voice,* a sympathetic source—"Haley invented 200 years of family history." Haley claimed that much of his information was provided by a griot, or oral historian, who turned out not to be a griot after all. Haley apparently relied on more conventional sources: he copied several passages from Harold Courlander's 1967 slave novel *The African.* He also lifted passages from other books such as *Travels of Mungo Park* and *The Story of Phillis Wheatley.* Haley's pristine village of Juffure turns out to have been a major slave-trading post. Juffure's residents, far from being slaves, captured and sold other Africans into slavery. Indeed Haley himself admitted that "I was just trying to give my people a myth to live by." See Philip Nobile, "Alex Haley's Hoax," *The Village Voice,* February 23, 1993; David C. Moore, "Routes," *Transition,* Issue 64, 1995, pp. 4–21.

21. Stanley Elkins, *Slavery: A Problem in American Institutional and Intellectual Life,* University of Chicago Press, Chicago, 1976. To follow the debate over this book, see Ann Lane, ed., *The Debate Over Slavery: Stanley Elkins and His Critics,* University of Illinois Press, Urbana, 1971.

22. Bell Hooks, *Yearning: Race, Gender and Cultural Politics,* South End Press, Boston, 1990, p. 57.

23. Dennis Farney, "As America Triumphs, Americans Are Awash in Doubt," *Wall Street Journal,* July 27, 1992, p. A-1; John Hope Franklin, "The Moral Legacy of the Founding Fathers," *University of Chicago Magazine,* Summer 1975, pp. 10–13.

24. Nathan Irvin Huggins, *Black Odyssey: The African American Ordeal in Slavery,* Vintage Books, New York, 1990, pp. xi–xii, 113.

25. Thurgood Marshall, address to the San Francisco Patent and Trademark Law Association, May 6, 1987.

26. "What, to the American slave, is your fourth of July? I answer: a day that reveals to him, more than all other days in the year, the gross injustice and cruelty to which he is the constant victim. To him, your celebration is a sham; your boasted liberty, an unholy license; your national greatness, swelling vanity; your sounds of rejoicing are empty, all heartless; your denunciation of tyrants, brass-fronted impudence; your shouts of liberty and equality, hollow mockery; your prayers and hymns, your sermons and thanksgivings, with all your religious parade and solemnity are, to him, mere bombast, fraud, deception, impiety, and hypocrisy—a thin veil to cover up crimes which would disgrace a nation of savages."

See Frederick Douglass, speech at Rochester, New York, July 5, 1852, in Carter G. Woodson, ed., *Negro Orators and Their Orations,* Russell & Russell, New York, 1925, pp. 197, 209. For William Lloyd Garrison's view of the constitution, see Carl Becker, *The Declaration of Independence,* Alfred A. Knopf, New York, 1956, p. 242. For agreement between Douglass and William Lloyd Garrison, see Frederick Douglass, *Life and Times of Frederick Douglass,* Collier Books, New York, 1962, pp. 260–61.

27. Eric Williams, *Capitalism and Slavery,* Capricorn Books, New York, 1966.

28. Statement by Senator Bill Bradley before the town hall of Los Angeles on March 23, 1992; reprinted in "The Real Lesson of L.A," *Harper's,* July 1992, p. 10.

29. Cited by Forrest McDonald, *Novus Ordo Seclorum,* University Press of Kansas, Lawrence, 1985, p. 51.

30. Orlando Patterson, *Slavery and Social Death: A Comparative Study,* Harvard University Press, Cambridge, 1982, pp. 27–28.

31. David Brion Davis, *Slavery and Human Progress,* Oxford University Press, New York, 1984, pp. 15–16.

32. Huggins, *Black Odyssey,* p. 86.

33. Oscar Handlin, *Race and Nationality in American Life,* Doubleday, New York, 1957, pp. 4–5.

34. Richard A. Easterlin, David Ward, William S. Bernard, and Reed Ueda, *Immigration,* Harvard University Press, Cambridge, 1982, p. 77.

35. Gordon Wood, *The Radicalism of the American Revolution,* Vintage Books, New York, 1993, pp. 53–54; see also George Fredrickson, *White Supremacy: A Comparative Study in American and South African History,* Oxford University Press, New York, 1981, p. 60.

36. Bernard Lewis, *Race and Slavery in the Middle East,* Oxford University Press, New York, 1990. See esp. pp. 11–12, 48, 75–76. Paul Rycaut, *The Present State of the Ottoman Empire,* Arno Press, London, 1971, pp. 33–35. Patterson, *Slavery and Social Death,* p. 421.

37. Thomas Sowell, *Race and Culture,* Basic Books, New York, 1994, p. 188; for a full account, see Murray Gordon, *Slavery in the Arab World,* New Amsterdam Books, New York, 1989.

38. Orlando Patterson, *Freedom in the Making of Western Culture,* Basic Books, New York, 1991, p. 12.

39. Theda Perdue, *Slavery and the Evolution of Cherokee Society,* University of Tennessee Press, Knoxville, 1979, p. 4.

40. Patterson, *Slavery and Social Death,* p. 84.

41. Ibid., p. 81. See also Patterson, *Freedom in the Making of Western Culture,* pp. 14–16.

42. Gary B. Nash, *Red, White and Black: The Peoples of Early America,* Prentice Hall, Englewood Cliffs, NJ, 1974, p. 159.

43. For a comprehensive discussion, see Suzanne Miers and Igor Kopytoff, *Slavery in Africa: Historical and Anthropological Perspectives,* University of Wisconsin Press, Madison, 1977. This book has separate essays on slavery among the Igbo, the Mende, the Wolof, and other tribes. For the item on Mansa Musa, see David Brion Davis, *Slavery and Human Progress,* pp. 46–47. Commenting on Mali and Songhay, Chiekh Anta Diop writes, "Domestic slavery at this time was rife in African society." Chiekh Anta Diop, *Precolonial Black Africa,* Lawrence Hill Books, Chicago, 1987, p. 91. On white slaves in West Africa, see John Blassingame, *The Slave Community,* Oxford University Press, New York, 1979, p. 51. The funeral rites of the king of Dahomey are mentioned in Pierre Van Den Berghe, *The Ethnic Phenomenon,* Elsevier Press, New York, 1981, p. 117. See also Orlando Patterson, *Slavery and Social Death,* p. viii, 40.

44. Paul Lovejoy, *Transformations in Slavery: A History of Slavery in Africa,* Cambridge University Press, Cambridge, 1983, p. 278.

45. John Thornton, *Africa and Africans in the Making of the Atlantic World, 1400–1680,* Cambridge University Press, Cambridge, 1992, pp. 74–76, 95.

46. Ibid., p. 97. "The capture, purchase, transport and sale of slaves was a regular feature of African society. This preexisting social arrangement was thus as much responsible as any external force for the development of the Atlantic slave trade."

47. Basil Davidson, *The African Slave Trade,* Little, Brown, Boston, 1980, pp. 42, 105–6, 208. Davidson argues that the view that Europeans imposed the slave trade on Africa "mirrors a familiar notion of African incapacity, and has no place in the historical record. . . . If everyone in Liverpool was investing in the trades that derived from slave labor in the Americas, so was everyone in the Congo. There grew up along the coast a tightly organized and self-defending system of monopoly." See also p. 164.

48. Peter Kolchin, *American Slavery, 1619–1877,* Hill & Wang, New York, 1993, p. 20.

49. David Brion Davis, *The Problem of Slavery in Western Culture,* Oxford University Press, New York, 1988, p. 183. "In general, Europeans had little contact with the actual process of enslavement," Davis adds. See also Patterson, *Slavery and Social Death,* p. 119, and Davidson, *The African Slave Trade,* pp. 101–5.

50. E. Franklin Frazier, *Race and Culture Contacts in the Modern World,* Beacon Press, Boston, 1957, p. 149.

51. Ibid., p. 67.

52. Zora Neale Hurston, *Dust Tracks on a Road,* HarperPerennial, New York, 1991, p. 145.

53. Audrey Smedley, *Race in North America,* Westview Press, Boulder, 1993, p.

95; Winthrop Jordan, *The White Man's Burden,* Oxford University Press, New York, 1974, p. 40.

54. Black slaves arrived in the New World around 1502, although the Portuguese had been shipping natives from the Guinea coast for sale in Lisbon as early as 1444. See Davis, *The Problem of Slavery in Western Culture,* p. 8; Barnet Litvinoff, *1492: The Decline of Medievalism and the Rise of the Modern Age,* Avon Books, New York, 1991, p. 28.

55. In 1642 a Virginia judge sentenced two white servants to an additional year of service for trying to run away, and a black servant to labor for the rest of his life for the same offense. John Hope Franklin, *Race and History,* Louisiana State University Press, Baton Rouge, 1989, p. 334. In 1661 the Virginia assembly passed a law making white servants who ran away with blacks responsible for serving the life tenure of a Negro. Many such rules, decisions, and practices became embedded in the fabric of colonial society. Smedley, *Race in North America,* pp. 95–96. For a study of the rise of slavery in Virginia, see Handlin, *Race and Nationality in American Life.* For a full account of the evolution of slavery in the United States, see John Hope Franklin, *From Slavery to Freedom,* Alfred A. Knopf, New York, 1980.

56. There is an ongoing debate among specialists about precisely how many slaves left Africa, how many perished en route, and how many arrived in the Americas. Scholars seem to be converging on the estimate of 12 million departures and 10 million arrivals. Philip D. Curtin, *The Atlantic Slave Trade: A Census,* University of Wisconsin Press, Madison, 1969; Herbert S. Klein, *The Middle Passage: Comparative Studies in the Transatlantic Slave Trade,* Princeton University Press, Princeton, 1978; James Rawley, *The Transatlantic Slave Trade: A History,* W. W. Norton, New York, 1981; Paul Lovejoy, "The Volume of the Atlantic Slave Trade: A Synthesis," *Journal of African History* 23 (1982), pp. 473–502.

57. McDonald, *Novus Ordo Seclorum,* p. 50.

58. See U.S. Bureau of the Census, *Negro Population of the United States: 1790–1915,* Washington, DC, p. 56. See also Peter Parish, *Slavery: History and Historians,* Harper & Row, New York, 1989, p. 27; Kenneth Stampp, *The Peculiar Institution: Slavery in the Antebellum South,* Vintage, New York, 1956, pp. 30–31.

59. Stampp, *The Peculiar Institution,* p. 30.

60. Lerone Bennett, *The Shaping of Black America,* Penguin, New York, 1993, p. 101

61. Blassingame, *The Slave Community,* p. 211.

62. Perdue, *Slavery and the Evolution of Cherokee Society,* pp. 38–39, 58. See also Ronald Wright, *Stolen Continents: The Americas Through Indian Eyes Since 1492,* Houghton Mifflin, Boston, 1992, p. 208.

63. Arthur L. Tolson, *The Black Oklahomans, A History: 1541–1972,* Edwards Printing, New Orleans, 1966, pp. 36–37.

64. Stampp, *The Peculiar Institution,* p. 194.

65. The U.S. Census of 1860 listed nearly four million slaves and 488,000 free black men and women. See Ira Berlin, *Slaves Without Masters: The Free Negro in the Antebellum South,* Pantheon, New York, 1974, Table 6, p. 136; Joel Williamson, *The Crucible of Race: Black-White Relations in the American South Since Emancipation,* Oxford University Press, New York, 1984, p. 36.

66. See Juliet Walker, "Racism, Slavery and Free Enterprise: Black Entrepreneurship in the U.S. Before the Civil War," *Business History Review* 60 (Fall 1986), pp. 343–82.

67. Jordan, *The White Man's Burden*, p. 41.

68. John H. Russell, "Colored Freemen and Slave Owners in Virginia," *Journal of Negro History*, July 1916, pp. 234–35, 241–42.

69. Davis, *The Problem of Slavery in Western Culture*, p. 263.

70. Eugene Genovese, *Roll, Jordan, Roll: The World the Slaves Made*, Vintage Books, New York, 1972, pp. 406–7.

71. Carter G. Woodson, "Free Negro Owners of Slaves in the United states in 1830," *Journal of Negro History* 9, January 1924, p. 41.

72. Berlin, *Slaves Without Masters*, p. 275.

73. Gary B. Mills, *The Forgotten People: Cane River's Creoles of Color*, Louisiana State University Press, Baton Rouge, 1977, p. 117.

74. H. E. Sterkx, *The Free Negro in Antebellum Louisiana*, Fairleigh Dickinson University Press, Rutherford, NJ, 1972, pp. 54, 202.

75. Abram Harris, *The Negro as Capitalist*, Arno Press, New York, 1936, pp. 4–5; Genovese, *Roll, Jordan, Roll*, p. 748; W. E. B. Du Bois, *Black Reconstruction*, S. A. Russell, New York, 1935 p. 6; John Sibley Butler, *Entrepreneurship and Self-Help Among Black Americans*, State University of New York Press, Albany, 1991, pp. 43–45.

76. Mills, *The Forgotten People*, p. 220; Thomas Holt, *Black Over White: Negro Political Leadership in South Carolina During Reconstruction*, University of Illinois Press, Urbana, 1977, p. 46; Larry Koger, *Black Slaveowners: Free Black Slave Masters in South Carolina, 1790–1860*, University of South Carolina Press, Charleston, 1985, pp. 21, 23.

77. Mills, *The Forgotten People*, p. 108; Harris, *The Negro as Capitalist*, pp. 4–5. See also Butler, *Entrepreneurship and Self-Help Among Black Americans*, p. 44; Bennett, *The Shaping of Black America*, p. 300; Berlin, *Slaves Without Masters*, pp. 274–75; Sterkx, *The Free Negro in Antebellum Louisiana*, p. 237; for a general survey, see Woodson, "Free Negro Owners of Slaves," pp. 41–85.

78. Michael P. Johnson and James L. Roark, *Black Masters: A Free Family of Color in the Old South*, W. W. Norton, New York, 1984, see esp. pp. 23, 132, 135–36, 141, 308; see also Michael P. Johnson and James L. Roark, *No Chariot Let Down: Charleston's Free People of Color on the Eve of the Civil War*, W. W. Norton, New York, 1984.

79. Johnson and Roark, *Black Masters*, pp. 128, 203–4.

80. Mills, *The Forgotten People*, p. xxix; Holt, *Black Over White*, p. 63, 230; see also Sterkx, *The Free Negro in Antebellum Louisiana*, p. 212.

81. Stampp, *The Peculiar Institution*, p. 194; Butler, *Entrepreneurship and Self-Help Among Black Americans*, p. 43; Harris, *The Negro As Capitalist*, p. 4.

82. Koger, *Black Slaveowners*, pp. xiii, 1, 81.

83. "If racial characteristics meant nothing to the English settlers, it is difficult to see how slavery based on race ever emerged, how the concept of complexion as the mark of slavery ever entered the colonists' minds." Winthrop Jordan, *White Over*

Black: American Attitudes Toward the Negro, 1550–1812, University of North Carolina Press, Chapel Hill, 1968, p. 97.

84. Largely owing to the influence of religion, the lifetime enslavement of white Christians had virtually ended in Europe, so that it was impossible to purchase large numbers of whites for servitude, except as paid servants. African blacks were relatively easy and inexpensive to acquire, compared to slaves from other continents, and they were a good investment compared to European indenured laborers because they worked for life without pay.

85. Eugene Genovese, *The World the Slaveholders Made,* Wesleyan University Press, Middletown, CT, 1988, p. 4.

86. See, e.g., Oliver C. Cox, *Caste, Class and Race,* Doubleday, New York, 1948, p. 393: Cox defines racism as "a social attitude propagated among the public by an exploiting class for the purpose of stigmatizing some group as inferior so that the exploitation of either the group itself or its resources may both be justified."

87. C. R. Boxer, *Race Relations in the Colonial Portuguese Empire,* Oxford University Press, New York, 1963, p. 56.

88. Davis, *The Problem of Slavery in Western Culture,* p. 49.

89. In the seventeenth and early eighteenth centuries, many masters did, in fact, brand slaves as they branded cattle. This was not to establish their status as slaves, but to identify them as belonging to a particular plantation. Edmund S. Morgan, *American Slavery, American Freedom: The Ordeal of Colonial Virginia,* W. W. Norton, New York, 1975, p. 386.

90. Cited by Du Bois, *Black Reconstruction,* p. 39.

91. Carl Degler, *Neither Black Nor White: Slavery and Race Relations in Brazil and the United States,* Macmillan, New York, 1971, p. 67. In a study of the sugar islands of Latin America, Richard Dunn concludes that slavery there became "one of the harshest systems of servitude in Western history." Richard Dunn, *Sugar and Slaves,* University of North Carolina Press, Chapel Hill, 1972, p. 224. Although Herbert Klein points out that legal protections for slaves, including the regulation of "such things as health standards, diets, working hours, clothing, and even minimum housing standards" were enacted by the Spanish and the Portuguese governments, Marvin Harris shows that such rules meant little across the ocean, on the plantations of the Americas. Herbert Klein, *Slavery in the Americas: A Comparative Study of Virginia and Cuba,* Ivan R. Dee, Chicago, 1967, p. 85; Marvin Harris, *Patterns of Race in the Americas,* Greenwood Press, Westport, CT, 1964, pp. 74–76.

92. Davis, *The Problem of Slavery in Western Culture,* p. 233.

93. This argument, most strongly advanced by Frank Tannenbaum and Stanley Elkins, has not been contested by their critics, who have simply disputed whether or not Latin American laws were widely applicable, whether they were enforced, and whether or not they fundamentally changed the nature of Latin American slavery compared to that in the United States. See Frank Tannenbaum, *Slave and Citizen: The Negro in the Americas,* Vintage Books, New York, 1963; Elkins, *Slavery: A Problem in American Institutional and Intellectual Life.* The Tannenbaum-Elkins thesis is generally supported by Klein, *Slavery in the Americas.*

94. Gilberto Freyre, *New World in the Tropics: The Culture of Modern Brazil,* Al-

fred A. Knopf, New York, 1959, pp. 195–201; Gilberto Freyre, *The Masters and the Slaves*, Alfred A. Knopf, New York, 1964; Florestan Fernandes, *The Negro in Brazilian Society*, Columbia University Press, New York, 1969. See also Tannenbaum, *Slave and Citizen*, pp. 62–64, 98; Degler, *Neither Black Nor White*, pp. 35–37. Scholars continue to dispute the practical importance of these protections. Most of the slaves in Latin America were male; as a result of this disproportion, families often did not form. Cohabitation rather than marriage seemed to be the norm on several plantations.

95. Edward Long of Jamaica went so far as to assert, "He who should presume to shew any displeasure against such a thing as simple fornication, would for his pains be accounted a simple blockhead, since not one in 20 can be persuaded that there is either sin or shame in cohabiting with his slave." Cited by Jordan, *The White Man's Burden*, p. 71. See also Brewton Berry, *Race and Ethnic Relations*, Houghton Mifflin, New York, 1965, pp. 137, 171.

96. Elkins, *Slavery: A Problem in American Institutional and Intellectual Life*, p. 241.

97. Davis, *The Problem of Slavery in Western Culture*, p. 266.

98. Mestizos were children of whites and Indians. Mulattoes (whose name derives from mules) were the children of blacks and whites. Zambos were children of Indians and blacks. Quadroons were the children of mulattoes and whites. More obscure categories included castizos, moriscoes, lobos, zambaigos, barconos, chamiscoes, pardoes, mustees, mustifinos, and quintroons. See Carlos Fuentes, *The Buried Mirror: Reflections on Spain and the New World*, Houghton Mifflin, New York, 1992, p. 234; Forrest Wood, *The Arrogance of Faith: Christianity and Race in America from the Colonial Era to the Twentieth Century*, Alfred A. Knopf, New York, 1990, p. 51; Pierre Van Den Berghe, *Race and Racism*, John Wiley and Sons, New York, 1978 edition, p. 52.

99. There were several U.S. cases of slaveowners acknowledging and freeing their mulatto children, but this practice was much rarer than in Latin America. See Davis, *The Problem of Slavery in Western Culture*, p. 280.

100. "The United States is unique so far as I know in drawing an arbitrary line that classifies everyone as either black or white and calls all people with any apparent African intermixture Negroes or blacks." C. Vann Woodward, *The Future of the Past*, Oxford University Press, New York, 1989, p. 44. See also Degler, *Neither Black Nor White*, p. 102. This mode of classification persists to the present, with far-reaching consequences outlined in future chapters.

101. Degler, *Neither Black Nor White*, p. 219.

102. In practice, owing to the liberties taken by some masters with their female slaves, a substantial number of white and slave children on the plantation were, literally, half-brothers and half-sisters. But the slave system relied on obscuring this observed reality, and denying it at the level of law.

103. Harris, *Patterns of Race in the Americas*, p. 37.

104. "All the evidence now being accumulated to prove the existence and severity of white racism in Brazil cannot explain away the chasm that separates Brazil from the United States in rate of intermarriage, access of blacks to positions of respect

and power, and the integration of people of color into a single nationality." Genovese, *Roll, Jordan, Roll,* p. 179. See also Degler, *Neither Black Nor White,* p. 95; Fredrickson, *White Supremacy,* p. 134.

105. This section was deleted by the Continental Congress. Cited by Carl Becker, *The Declaration of Independence,* Random House, New York, 1942, p. 147.

106. Duncan MacLeod, *Slavery, Race and the American Revolution,* Cambridge University Press, Cambridge, 1974, pp. 16–17.

107. James Boswell, *The Life of Samuel Johnson,* edited by C. G. Osgood, Charles Scribner, New York, 1945, p. 353.

108. *Dred Scott v. Sandford,* 60 U.S. 393 (1857).

109. Huggins, *Black Odyssey,* p. 116.

110. Jordan, *White Over Black,* p. 95.

111. Louis Dumont, *Homo Hierarchicus: The Caste System and Its Implications,* Weidenfeld and Nicholson, London, 1970, p. 214.

112. "Racism . . . was the formula to purge the guilt of men who believed in liberty but were the masters of slaves." Handlin, *Race and Nationality in American Life,* p. 33. See also Albert Memmi, *Dominated Man: Notes Toward a Portrait,* Orion Press, New York, 1968, p. 192.

113. Vine Deloria, Jr., *Custer Died for Your Sins,* Macmillan, New York, 1969, p. 171.

114. Jordan, *White Over Black,* p. 241.

115. "The demise of Indian bondage can probably be attributed to the fact that the African wrenched from his homeland with no opportunity to escape and return represented a better investment. . . . Slaveowners had special problems with Indians because of the geographical proximity of their kinsmen. . . . Revolts seemed a troublesome possibility. . . . The presence of Indian slaves also made it difficult to establish rapport with other tribes." Perdue, *Slavery and the Evolution of Cherokee Society,* p. 37. See also Jordan, *White Over Black,* pp. 89–90; Fredrickson, *White Supremacy,* p. 58. For the problems of Indians in coping with settled agriculture, see A. L. Kroeber, *Cultural and National Areas of North America,* University of California Press, Berkeley, 1939, pp. 146–49; Ruth M. Underhill, *Red Man's America,* University of Chicago Press, Chicago, 1952, pp. 67, 87.

116. Jordan, *White Over Black,* p. 90.

117. Some states included Indians, Mongolians, Malays, and other "persons of color" in their statutes forbidding miscegenation, but most states limited the restrictions to "any person who has in his or her veins any Negro blood whatever," as an Arkansas statute specified. For a list of the terminology in several state laws on miscegenation, see Ashley Montagu, *Race: Man's Most Dangerous Myth,* World Publishing, New York, 1964, Appendix G, pp. 421–24.

118. Thomas Jefferson, letter to Benjamin Hawkins, February 18, 1803; Thomas Jefferson, letter to Baron von Humboldt, December 6, 1813. Cited in Ralph Lerner, "Reds and Whites: Rights and Wrongs," *The Thinking Revolutionary: Principle and Practice in the New Republic,* Cornell University Press, Ithaca, 1987, p. 163. See also Gary B. Nash and Richard Weiss, *The Great Fear: Race in the Mind of America,* Holt, Rinehart and Winston, New York, 1970, p. 20.

119. Nancy Stepan, *The Idea of Race in Science,* Archon Books, Hamden, CT, 1982, p. xii.

120. Leon F. Litwack, *North of Slavery: The Negro in the Free States, 1790–1860,* University of Chicago Press, Chicago, 1965, p. 65, 75, 93, 97, 153, 168; Ira Berlin, *Slaves Without Masters,* pp. 8–9, 96–97; Joel Williamson, *New People: Miscegenation and Mulattoes in the United States,* Free Press, New York, 1980, pp. 8, 10–11; Duncan MacLeod, *Slavery, Race and the American Revolution,* pp. 164–65.

121. Eric Williams, *Capitalism and Slavery,* p. 19.

122. Du Bois, *Black Reconstruction,* p. 13.

123. Walter Rodney, *How Europe Underdeveloped Africa,* Howard University Press, Washington, DC, 1982, p. 83.

124. Davis, *The Problem of Slavery in Western Culture,* p. 10.

125. Rodney, *How Europe Underdeveloped Africa,* p. 87.

126. Robert Fogel and Stanley Engerman, *Time on the Cross: The Economics of American Negro Slavery,* Little, Brown, Boston, 1974.

127. Ibid., pp. 8–9.

130. Allan J. Lichtman, "A Benign Institution?" *The New Republic,* July 6 and 13, 1974, pp. 22–24; Christopher Dell, "In Money Terms, It Worked Fine," *The Nation,* October 5, 1974, pp. 310–11.

129. For a scholarly expression of this perspective, see Ulrich Bonnell Phillips, *American Negro Slavery,* New York, 1918.

130. Mary Boykin Chesnut, *Diary from Dixie,* edited by B. A. Williams, Houghton Mifflin, Boston, 1949, pp. 172, 184, 244.

131. For a sampling of criticism, see Herbert Gutman, *Slavery and the Numbers Game: A Critique of "Time on the Cross,"* University of Illinois Press, Urbana, 1975; Paul David, Herbert Gutman, Richard Sutch, Peter Temin and Gavin Wright, *Reckoning With Slavery: Critical Essays in the Quantitative History of American Negro Slavery,* Oxford University Press, New York, 1976.

132. This point is extensively documented in Eugene Genovese, *Roll, Jordan, Roll,* p. 59, with accompanying footnotes.

133. For a full account of urban slavery in the South, see Richard Wade, *Slavery in the Cities: The South 1820–1860,* Oxford University Press, New York, 1964.

134. Huggins, *Black Odyssey,* p. 129.

135. Thomas Sowell, "The Economics of Slavery," *Markets and Minorities,* Basic Books, New York, 1981, p. 92.

136. Frederick Law Olmstead, *The Cotton Kingdom,* Modern Library Books, New York, 1969, p. 215.

137. Robert Fogel, *Without Consent or Contract: The Rise and Fall of American Slavery,* W. W. Norton, New York, 1989, p. 18.

138. Genovese, *Roll, Jordan, Roll,* p. 5. See also Genovese, *The World the Slaveholders Made,* pp. 98–99.

139. This evidence is reviewed in Peter Parish, *Slavery: History and Historians,* p. 65.

140. Kolchin, *American Slavery,,* p. 113; Fogel, *Without Consent Or Contract,* p. 137.

141. Cited by Andrew Greeley, *That Most Distressed Nation,* Quadrangle Books, New York, 1972, pp. 34–35.

142. William McFeely, *Frederick Douglass,* W. W. Norton, New York, 1991, p. 126.

143. Cecil Woodham-Smith, *The Great Hunger: Ireland 1845–1849,* Penguin, New York, 1991; Greeley, *That Most Distressed Nation.*

144. Here is the typical diary entry of a slaveowner, describing the daily routine of his slaves:

> Finished picking, ginning, and pressing cotton and hauling it in wagons to the point of shipment; killed hogs and cut and salted the meat; cut and hauled wood; cut and mauled fence rails; repaired buildings and tools; spread manure; cleared and repaired ditches; cleared new ground by rolling and burning logs and grubbing stumps; knocked down corn and cotton stalks and burned trash; plowed and bedded up corn and cotton fields; planted vegetables.

Cited by Kenneth Stampp, *The Peculiar Institution,* p. 45.

145. Two vivid accounts of slave life are given by Stampp in *The Peculiar Institution,* and Genovese in *Roll, Jordan, Roll.*

146. Each of these items is extensively reviewed in the literature on slavery. See, e.g., John Blassingame, *The Slave Community,* p. 47: "The Southern plantation system was not a rationally organized institution designed to crush every manifestation of individual will or for systematic extermination. . . . The Africans learned that their labors, and therefore their lives, were of considerable value to their masters. As a result, they were assured of the bare minimum of food, shelter and clothing. Although provisions were often inadequate and led to many complaints, they survived." In *Roll, Jordan, Roll,* p. xvi, Genovese writes, "For a complex of reasons of self-interest, common humanity and Christian sensibility, masters could not help contributing to their slaves' creative survival."

147. *Farmer's Register,* IV (1836), cited by Kenneth Stampp, *The Peculiar Institution,* p. 279.

148. Alexis de Tocqueville, *Democracy in America,* edited by J. P. Mayer, Harper & Row, New York, 1988, p. 361.

149. This quotation comes from a speech delivered by Douglass in Belfast in December 1845. Cited by McFeely in *Frederick Douglass,* p. 128.

150. Douglass continued as follows:

> Mr Covey succeeded in *breaking* me—in body, soul and spirit. My natural elasticity was crushed; my intellect languished; the disposition to read departed; the cheerful spark that lingered about my eye died out; the dark night of slavery closed in upon me; and behold a man was transformed into a brute.

Frederick Douglass, *The Life and Times of Frederick Douglass,* Collier Books, New York, 1962, p. 124.

151. Du Bois, *Black Reconstruction,* p. 9.

152. Patterson, *Slavery and Social Death,* p. 78.

153. Bennett, *The Shaping of Black America,* p. 147.

154. Parish, *Slavery: History and Historians,* p. 73, 86.

155. Genovese, *Roll, Jordan, Roll,* pp. 33, 471.

156. The most comprehensive documentation is in Kenneth Stampp, *The Pecu-*

liar Institution, see esp. pp. 197–98, 219, 221. In 1669 the Virginia assembly passed a law saying it was not murder for a master to kill his slave "since it cannot be presumed that malice (which alone makes murder felony) should induce any man to destroy his own estate." Cited by Morgan, *American Slavery, American Freedom,* p. 312. This was admittedly an extreme case. Through most of the eighteenth and nineteenth centuries, most states did have laws classifying the killing of slaves as murder, and penalizing masters for cruelty and sadistic punishment. The extreme logic of slavery is spelled out with ruthless clarity by Judge Thomas Ruffin in 1829: "With slavery . . . the end is the profit of the master, his security and public safety. The power of the master must be absolute to render the submission of the slave perfect. I must freely confess my sense of the harshness of this proposition. As a principle of moral right, every person . . . must repudiate it. But in the actual condition of things, it must be so." *State v. Mann,* 13 N.C. 263 (1829).

157. For examples of state penalties for teaching slaves to read and write, see Note 2 in Booker T. Washington and W. E. B. Du Bois, *The Negro in the South,* Carol Publishing, New York, 1970, pp. 198–99. Alabama, for instance, stipulated that teaching a slave to "spell, read or write" was subject to a fine of between $250 and $500; Georgia prescribed "fine and whipping" for blacks who taught slaves to read, and imprisonment or fines for whites guilty of the same offense. See also Genovese, *Roll, Jordan, Roll,* p. 41.

158. Traveling in Maryland, Frederick Douglass wrote, "I never met a slave in that part of the country who could tell me with any certainty how old he was. Masters allowed no questions concerning their ages to be put to them by slaves. Such questions were regarded by the masters as evidence of an impudent curiosity." Frederick Douglass, *The Life and Times of Frederick Douglass,* p. 27.

159. Rayford Logan, *The Negro in American Life and Thought,* Dial Press, New York, 1954, pp. 240, 266.

160. James Baldwin, *The Fire Next Time,* Dial Press, New York, 1963, p. 95.

161. See, e.g., Sidney W. Mintz and Richard Price, *The Birth of African American Culture,* Beacon Press, Boston, 1992.

162. See, e.g., Lorenzo Turner, *Africanisms in the Gullah Dialect,* University of Michigan Press, Ann Arbor, 1973; Melville Herskovits, *The Myth of the Negro Past,* Harper & Bros., New York, 1941; Sterling Stuckey, *Slave Culture: Nationalist Theory and the Foundations of Black America,* Oxford University Press, New York, 1987. For less ambitious claims about the endurance of African ways in America, see the chapter "Enslavement, Acculturation and African Survivals," in Blassingame, *The Slave Community.* For a list of West African proverbs allegedly imported into slave discourse, see Mary Frances Berry and John Blassingame, *Long Memory,* Oxford University Press, New York, 1982. For an account of the African priest and "medicine man" tradition in the United States, see W. E. B. Du Bois, "The Religion of the American Negro," *New World,* December 1900, p. 618.

163. J. L. Dillard, *Black English: Its History and Usage in the United States,* Vintage Books, New York, 1972, p. ix.

164. Mintz and Price, *The Birth of African-American Culture,* pp. 3, 20.

165. Ibid., p. 3.

166. Kenneth Stampp estimates that about 50 percent of slaveholders owned fewer than five slaves, 72 percent owned fewer than ten, and 88 percent owned fewer than twenty. Kenneth Stampp, *The Peculiar Institution,* p. 30. See also Peter Kolchin, "Reevaluating the Antebellum Slave Community: A Comparative Perspective," *Journal of American History* 70 (1983), pp. 582–88; and E. Franklin Frazier, *The Negro Family in the United States,* University of Chicago Press, Chicago, 1966, p. 6.

167. E. Franklin Frazier, *The Negro Family in the United States,* pp. 6–7; E. Franklin Frazier, *Black Bourgeoisie,* Collier Books, New York, 1957, p. 17. The point about African conversions is made, with strong anti-Christian bias, by Forrest G. Wood, *The Arrogance of Faith: Christianity and Race in America from the Colonial Era to the Twentieth Century,* Alfred A. Knopf, New York, 1990.

168. See Albert Murray, *The Omni-Americans: New Perspectives on Black Experience and American Culture,* Outerbridge & Dienstfrey, New York, 1970, pp. 17–18.

169. Genovese, *Roll, Jordan, Roll;* Lawrence Levine, *Black Culture and Black Consciousness,* Oxford University Press, New York, 1978; Mintz and Price, *The Birth of African American Culture.*

170. Mintz and Price, *The Birth of African American Culture,* p. 51. See also Blassingame, *The Slave Community.*

171. For a classic account of the role of the church, see E. Franklin Frazier, *The Negro Church in America,* Schocken Books, New York, 1974.

172. The sacred world of the slaves, argues Lawrence Levine, "created the necessary space between the slaves and their owners and the means of preventing legal slavery from becoming spiritual slavery. . . . The slaves created a world apart which they shared with each other and which remained their own domain, free of control of those who ruled the earth." Levine, *Black Culture and Black Consciousness,* p. 80. See also Blassingame, *The Slave Community,* p. 145.

173. For a full discussion, Genovese, *Roll, Jordan, Roll,* pp. 161–255.

174. Frazier, *The Negro Church in America,* p. 33.

175. See W. E. B. Du Bois, *The Negro American Family,* MIT Press, Cambridge, 1970 edition, first published 1908; E. Franklin Frazier, *The Negro Family in the United States;* Robert E. Park, *Race and Culture,* Free Press, Glencoe, IL, 1950, p. 75; Daniel P. Moynihan, "The Negro Family: The Case for National Action," in Lee Rainwater and William Yancy, eds., *The Moynihan Report and the Politics of Controversy,* MIT Press, Cambridge, 1967.

176. Du Bois, *The Negro American Family,* pp. 151–52.

177. Herbert Gutman, *The Black Family in Slavery and Freedom,* Pantheon Books, New York, 1976.

178. An exaggerated account of slave revolts is given in Herbert Aptheker, *American Negro Slave Revolts,* International Publishers, New York, 1943. Many of Aptheker's examples are hardly "revolts" of any significance or magnitude; they represent highly local, sometimes individual, acts of rebellion.

179. For an account of how American slaves stopped working as soon as the overseer's eyes moved away from them, see Frederick Law Olmsted, *A Journey in the Seaboard Slave States,* Dix & Edwards, New York, 1856, pp. 434–36. Tocqueville wrote, "Slavery dishonors labor; it introduces idleness to society, and with idleness, ignorance

and pride, luxury and distress. It enervates the powers of the mind and benumbs the activity of man." See Alexis de Tocqueville, *Democracy in America,* p. 35. Commenting on the legacy of slavey in South America, the Venezuelan writer Carlos Rangel writes that among the factors that inhibit the development of societies formerly based on slavery are "the passive resistance to work that is the earmark of the slave" and "a rhythm of life so little concerned with punctuality." Carlos Rangel, *The Latin Americans,* Harcourt Brace, New York, 1977, p. 193. The black economist W. Arthur Lewis writes, "Slaves are notoriously inefficient and unwilling. . . . Their sense of justice revolts against a system which uses their labor to enrich others." W. Arthur Lewis, *A Theory of Economic Growth,* Richard Irwin Publishers, Homewood, IL, 1955, p. 107.

180. Du Bois, *Black Reconstruction,* p. 40.

181. W. E. B. Du Bois, *The Gift of Black Folk,* Kraus-Thomson, Millwood, NY, 1975, p. 77. Du Bois adds, "The white laborer therefore brought to America the habit of regular, continuous toil which he regarded as a great moral duty. The black laborer brought the idea of toil as a necessary evil ministering to the pleasure of life." See p. 79.

182. Raymond Bauer and Alice Bauer, "Day to Day Resistance to Slavery," *Journal of Negro History* 27 (October 1942), pp. 388–419; see also Willie Lee Rose, *Slavery and Freedom,* edited by William H. Freehling, Oxford University Press, New York, 1982, p. 94; Morgan, *American Slavery, American Freedom,* p. 318; Benjamin Quarles, *The Negro in the Making of America,* Collier Books, New York, 1987, p. 75.

183. Cited by Genovese, *Roll, Jordan, Roll,* p. 626. Genovese discusses this issue on pp. 626–29.

184. W. J. Cash, *The Mind of the South,* Vintage Books, New York, 1991 edition, p. 67.

185. Stampp, *The Peculiar Institution,* p. 125.

186. Genovese, *Roll, Jordan, Roll,* p. 602. Genovese discusses the issue of theft at pp. 599–612.

187. Frederick Douglass, *The Life and Times of Frederick Douglass,* p. 105.

188. Ibid., p. 437.

189. Richard Wright, "How Bigger Was Born," in *Native Son,* HarperPerennial, New York, 1993 (first published 1940), p. 508.

190. See the story "Stagolee" in Julius Lester, *Black Folktales,* Grove Weidenfeld, New York, 1969, p. 113.

191. See, e.g., Geneva Smitherman, *Black Talk: Words and Phrases From the Hood to the Amen Corner,* Houghton Mifflin, Boston, 1994, p. 52. Smitherman offers the following definition: "Bad: good, excellent, great, fine; powerful, tough, aggressive, fearless."

192. Orlando Patterson, "Toward a Study of Black America," *Dissent,* Fall 1989, p. 480.

193. This point is made by African American writer Stanley Crouch. "It is important to face the fact that there was no great African debate over the moral meaning of slavery itself. There is no record whatsoever of any African from a tribe that wasn't being enslaved arguing against the very practice of capturing and selling other Africans." Stanley Crouch, "Who Are We? Where Did We Come From?" in Gerald

Early, ed., *Lure and Loathing: Essays On Race, Identity and the Ambivalence of Assimilation,* Penguin Books, New York, 1993, p. 92.

194. This question is taken up in Orlando Patterson's *Freedom in the Making of Western Culture.* Tracing the roots of freedom in secular Athens and Christian Europe, Patterson maintains that "freedom has been the core value of Western culture throughout its history." But its realization, he concludes, depended crucially on the experience of slavery. "Freedom was generated from the experience of slavery." See esp. pp. x, xiii, xiv, xvi.

195. J. M. Roberts, *The Penguin History of the World,* Penguin Books, New York, 1990, p. 727.

196. Lewis, *Race and Slavery in the Middle East,* p. 78.

197. Genovese, *The World the Slaveholders Made,* p. 131.

198. See Larry Tise, *Proslavery: A History of the Defense of Slavery in America,* University of Georgia Press, Athens, 1987.

199. Chancellor William Harper, *A Memoir on Slavery,* Walter and Burke Printers, Charleston, 1845. A virtually identical remark comes from the senator from South Carolina, James Hammond, who told the U.S. Senate, "In all social systems, there must be a class to do the menial duties, to perform the drudgery of life. This is a class requiring but a low order of intellect and but little skill. . . . Fortunately for the South, she found a race adapted to that purpose. We call them slaves." Cited by Franklin, *Race and History,* p. 335.

200. Davis, *Slavery and Human Progress,* p. 114.

201. See, e.g., Richard Cralle, ed., *The Works of John C. Calhoun,* Appleton, New York, 1854.

202. Cited by Kolchin, *American Slavery,* p. 188; see also George Fitzhugh, *Cannibals All, or Slaves Without Masters,* Harvard University Press, Cambridge, 1960, first published 1857, p. 69.

203. Eugene Genovese, *The Slaveholders' Dilemma,* University of South Carolina Press, Columbia, 1992, p. 61.

204. Cited by George Fredrickson, *The Black Image in the White Mind: The Debate on Afro-American Character and Destiny, 1817–1914,* Harper & Row, New York, 1971, pp. 63–64.

205. Van Den Berghe, *Race and Racism,* p. 18.

206. Morgan, *American Slavery, American Freedom.*

207. Cited by Harry V. Jaffa, *Crisis of the House Divided,* University of Chicago Press, Chicago, 1959, p. 32.

208. Martin A. Klein, *Breaking the Chains: Bondage and Emancipation in Modern Africa and Asia,* University of Wisconsin Press, Madison, 1993, p. 14.

209. For a comprehensive study of abolition, see Robert W. Fogel, *Without Consent or Contract.* In a provocative analysis of the antislavery movement, George Fredrickson argues that the abolitionist William Lloyd Garrison was motivated by "perfectionist Christianity" whereas the former slave Frederick Douglass was inspired by American political ideals of equality. George M. Fredrickson, *The Arrogance of Race: Historical Perspectives on Slavery, Racism and Social Inequality,* Wesleyan University Press, Middletown, CT, 1988, pp. 13, 76, 81.

210. Thomas Hobbes, *Leviathan,* edited by Richard Tuck, Cambridge University Press, Cambridge, 1991.

211. John Locke, *Two Treatises on Government,* edited by Peter Laslett, Cambridge University Press, London, 1988, pp. 284, 287–88.

212. Davis, *Slavery and Human Progress,* p. 143.

213. Alexis de Tocqueville, "On the Emancipation of Slaves," cited in ibid., p. 110; see also Tzvetan Todorov, *On Human Diversity: Nationalism, Racism and Exoticism in French Thought,* Harvard University Press, Cambridge, 1993, pp. 191–92.

214. Davis, *Slavery and Human Progress,* p. 131.

215. Roger Anstey, *The Atlantic Slave Trade and British Abolition, 1760–1810,* Humanities Press, New York, 1975; David Eltis and James Walvin, eds., *The Abolition of the Atlantic Slave Trade,* University of Wisconsin Press, Madison, 1981; for a debate on English abolitionism, see David Turley, *The Culture of English Antislavery, 1780–1860,* Routledge, London, 1991.

216. The activists of the French Revolution had outlawed slavery in 1791, but in 1802 Napoleon restored it in France and in the colonies, so that slavery had to be abolished once again. See William B. Cohen, *The French Encounter with Africans,* Indiana University Press, Bloomington, 1980, p. 118.

217. Davidson, *The African Slave Trade,* p. 255; see also L. H. Gann and Peter Duignan, *Africa South of the Sahara,* Hoover Institution Press, Stanford, 1981, p. 4.

218. Martin Klein, "Servitude Among the Wolof and Sereer of Senegambia," in Suzanne Miers and Igor Kopytoff, ed., *Slavery in Africa,* University of Wisconsin Press, Madison, 1977, p. 352; Mohamed Mbodj, "The Abolition of Slavery in Senegal," in Martin Klein, eds., *Breaking the Chains,* p. 199.

219. Cited by John R. Baker, *Race,* Oxford University Press, New York, 1974, p. 364.

220. "Placing on men the ignominious title, slave," John Woolman wrotes, "dressing them in uncomely garments, keeping them to servile labor, in which they are often dirty, tends gradually to fix a notion in the mind, that they are a sort of people below us in nature." Cited by Winthrop Jordan, *The White Man's Burden,* p. 115.

221. For an examination of the racial views of the abolitionists, see James McPherson, *The Struggle for Equality: Abolitionists and the Negro in the Civil War and Reconstruction,* Princeton University Press, Princeton, 1964.

222. Cited by Henry Louis Gates, *Loose Canons: Notes on the Culture Wars,* Oxford University Press, New York, 1992, pp. 51–53.

223. Cited by McDonald, *Novus Ordo Seclorum,* p. 160.

224. Dumas Malone, *Jefferson and His Time: Jefferson the Virginian,* Little, Brown, Boston, 1948–1981, Vol. I, pp. 163, 391; MacLeod, *Slavery, Race and the American Revolution,* p. 134.

225. Thomas Jefferson, *Notes on the State of Virginia,* W. W. Norton, New York, 1982, p. 163.

226. Jefferson advanced his "suspicion" that blacks were intellectually inferior to whites. "In general, their existence appears to participate more of sensation than reflection. . . . Comparing them by their faculties of memory, reason and imagination, it appears to be that in memory they are equal to the whites, in reason much inferior,

as I think one could scarcely be found capable of tracing and comprehending the investigations of Euclid, and that in imagination they are dull, tasteless and anomalous." Ibid., pp. 139, 143.

Yet Jefferson wrote Benjamin Banneker on August 30, 1791, "Nobody wishes more than I do to see such proofs as you exhibit, that nature has given to our black brethren talents equal to those of other colors of man, and that the appearance of a want of them is owing merely to the degraded condition of their existence both in Africa and in America." Merrill D. Peterson, ed., *The Portable Thomas Jefferson,* Penguin Books, New York, 1975, p. 454.

227. Benjamin Franklin regarded blacks as "not deficient in natural understanding" and Alexander Hamilton asserted that "their natural faculties are probably as good as ours." Cited by Winthrop Jordan, *The White Man's Burden,* p. 117.

228. Thomas Jefferson, letter to Henri Gregoire, February 25, 1809, in Peterson, *The Portable Thomas Jefferson,* p. 517. Jefferson offered an analogy: just because Newton might be more intelligent than other Europeans, it did not follow that he was entitled to be "lord of the person and property of others." Blacks, Jefferson concluded, "are gaining daily in the opinion of nations, and hopeful advances are being made toward their reestablishment on an equal footing with other colors of the human family."

229. Thomas Jefferson, letter to John Holmes, April 22, 1820, in ibid., p. 568.

230. Madison's proposal is contained in a letter to Robert J. Evans, June 15, 1819. Cited in Drew McCoy, *The Last of the Fathers: James Madison and the Republican Legacy,* Cambridge University Press, Cambridge, 1989, p. 280.

231. Black leaders such as Paul Cuffe and Martin Delany supported the idea of a black state in Africa. The American Colonization Society was founded in 1816. Invoking the example of the British settlement of former slaves in Sierra Leone, members of the Society over the years explored several possible sites for American blacks: Madagascar, Sandwich Island, St. Helena. Some ex-slaves did settle in Liberia, where they proceeded to subjugate the local natives. But most American blacks proved uninterested in a return to Africa. See Benjamin Quarles, *Lincoln and the Negro,* Oxford University Press, New York, 1962; Charles Johnson, *Bitter Canaan,* Transaction Books, New Brunswick, NJ, 1987, p. 17.

232. Eugene Genovese, *The Southern Tradition: The Achievement and Limitations of an American Conservatism,* Harvard University Press, Cambridge, 1994, p. 28.

233. See Herbert Storing, "Slavery and the Moral Foundations of the American Republic," in Robert H. Horwitz, ed., *The Moral Foundations of the American Republic,* University of Virginia Press, Charlottesville, 1986.

234. Andrew Kull, *The Color-Blind Constitution,* Harvard University Press, Cambridge, 1992, p. 20.

235. Garry Wills, *Lincoln at Gettysburg: The Words That Remade America,* Simon & Schuster, New York, 1992, p. 147.

236. Jaffa, *Crisis of the House Divided,* p. 375.

237. "Now I protest against this counterfeit logic which concludes that because I do not want a black woman for a *slave* I must necessarily want her for a *wife.*" Notice that Lincoln does not oppose racial intermarriage; he simply asserts that racial inter-

marriage does not automatically result from a recognition of the black woman's right not to be a slave. Lincoln continues do discuss the status and rights of the black woman in the same vein: "In some respects, she is certainly not my equal, but in her natural right to eat the bread she earns with her own hands without asking leave of anyone else, she is my equal, and the equal of all others." Abraham Lincoln, "Speech on the Dred Scott Decision," June 26, 1857, in Mario Cuomo and Harold Holzer, eds., *Lincoln on Democracy,* HarperCollins, New York, 1990, p. 90.

"Certainly the Negro is not our equal in color—perhaps not in many other respects; still, in the right to put into his mouth the bread that his own hands have earned, he is the equal of every other man, white or black. In pointing out that more has been given you, you cannot be justified in taking away the little which has been given him. All I ask for the Negro is that if you do not like him, let him alone. If God gave him little, that little let him enjoy." Abraham Lincoln, speech at Springfield, Illinois, July 17, 1858, ibid., p. 120.

238. Abraham Lincoln, "Speech on the Dred Scott Decision," Springfield, Illinois, June 26, 1857, in ibid., pp. 90–91.

239. Frederick Douglass, "Address for the Promotion of Colored Enlistments," July 6, 1863, in Philip S. Foner, ed., *The Life and Writings of Frederick Douglass,* International Publishers, New York, 1950, Vol. 3, p. 365.

240. Woodward, *The Future of the Past,* p. 149.

241. See, e.g., Michelle Faul, "Slavery Alive and Well as Mauritania Looks On," *Washington Times,* April 6, 1992; James Brooke, "Slavery on Rise in Brazil, as Debt Chains Workers," *New York Times,* May 23, 1993, p. A-3; Charles Jacobs and Mohamed Athie, "Bought and Sold," *New York Times,* July 13, 1994, p. A-19; "Slavery," *Newsweek,* May 4, 1992, pp. 30–39. For a scholarly discussion, see Murray Gordon, *Slavery in the Arab World,* New Amsterdam Books, New York, 1989.

242. Fredrickson, *White Supremacy,* p. 93.

243. Zora Neale Hurston, *Dust Tracks on a Road,* pp. 206–8; Zora Neale Hurston, "How It Feels To Be Colored Me," excerpted in Henry Louis Gates, ed., *Bearing Witness,* Pantheon Books, New York, 1991, pp. 34–35.

244. Booker T. Washington, *Selected Speeches,* edited by E. Davidson Washington, Doubleday, New York, 1932, p. 37; Booker T. Washington, *Up From Slavery,* Penguin Books, New York, 1986, p. 16.

245. Phillis Wheatley's view is expressed in one of her poems.

> 'Twas mercy brought me from my pagan land,
> Taught my benighted soul to understand
> That there's a God, that there's a Savior too,
> Once I redemption neither sought nor knew.

Cited by Bennett, *Before the Mayflower,* p. 71.

246. For a detailed discussion, see Herbert Storing, "The School of Slavery: A Reconsideration of Booker T. Washington," in Robert Goldwin, ed., *100 Years of Emancipation,* Rand McNally Chicago, 1963, pp. 47–79.

247. Asked what society should do for blacks after emancipation, Douglass answered, "Do nothing with them. Mind your business, and let them mind theirs. . . .

The best way to help them is just to let them help themselves." Philip S. Foner, *The Life and Writings of Frederick Douglass,* International Publishing House, New York, 1950, pp. 188–90.

248. Frederick Douglass, "What Are the Colored People Doing for Themselves?" *The North Star,* July 14, 1848.

249. Leon Wieseltier, "Scar Tissue," *The New Republic,* June 5, 1989.

Chapter 4. The Invention of Prejudice

1. Charles Darwin, *The Descent of Man, and Selection in Relation to Sex,* Rand Mc-Nally, Chicago, 1874, p. 152.

2. Anna Quindlen, "Black and White and Gray," *New York Times,* February 25, 1990, p. E-19; Anna Quindlen, "The Great White Myth," *New York Times,* January 15, 1992, p. A-21; Anna Quindlen, "Across the Divide," *New York Times,* May 3, 1992, p. E-17.

3. Associated Press Report, "United Church of Christ Urges Fight Against Rising Racism," *New York Times,* January 15, 1991.

4. Duster's remarks cited by Dana Takagi, *The Retreat from Race: Asian American Admissions and Racial Politics,* Rutgers University Press, New Brunswick, 1992, p. 146.

5. William McDougall, *Is America Safe for Democracy?,* Charles Scribner, New York, 1921, p. 66.

6. Elazar Barkin, *The Retreat of Scientific Racism,* Cambridge University Press, Cambridge, 1992, p. 3; Phillis Katz and Dalmas Taylor, eds., *Eliminating Racism: Profiles in Controversy,* Plenum Press, New York, 1988, p. 7; Melville Herskovits, introduction to Franz Boas, *The Mind of Primitive Man,* Free Press, New York, 1938, p. 5. Many dictionaries only include the term "racism" after World War II.

7. Albert Memmi, *Dominated Man: Notes Toward a Portrait,* Orion Press, New York, 1968, p. ix.

8. See, e.g., Eugenia Shanklin, *Anthropology and Race,* Wadsworth Publishing, Belmont, CA, 1994, pp. 2–3; Robert Berkhofer, *The White Man's Indian: Images of the American Indian from Columbus to the Present,* Alfred A. Knopf, New York, 1978, p. 61.

9. Thomas H. Huxley, "Emancipation—Black and White," *Science and Education,* Collier Books, New York, 1901, pp. 64–67.

10. Editorial by E. L. Godkin, *The Nation* 56, January 19, 1893, p. 43.

11. Joan London, *Jack London and His Times,* Doubleday, New York, 1939, pp. 212–13; see also Cynthia Russett, *Darwin in America: The Intellectual Response, 1865–1912,* W. H. Freeman, San Francisco, 1976, pp. 175, 179.

12. Margaret Sanger, letter to Clarence Gamble, October 19, 1939, Sanger manuscripts, Smith College; see also Margaret Sanger, *The Pivot of Civilization,* Brentano's Publishers, New York, 1922. Sanger's views are also described in David M. Kennedy, *Birth Control in America: The Career of Margaret Sanger,* Yale University Press, New Haven, 1970; George Grant, *Grand Illusions: The Legacy of Planned Parenthood,* Wolgemuth & Hyatt, Brentwood, TN, 1988; Andrew Zappia, "Unnatural Selection: Planned Parenthood's Campaign Against Minorities," *Diversity,* March-April 1992.

13. For uncritical use of the term "pseudoscientific," see, e.g., Louis Snyder, *The*

Idea of Racialism: Its Meaning and History, Van Nostrand, Princeton, 1962, pp. 26–27; Ralph Ellison, *Shadow and Act,* Random House, New York, 1964, p. 304; Philip D. Curtin, *The Image of Africa,* University of Wisconsin Press, Madison, 1964, p. 363; Stephen Molnar, *Human Variation: Races, Types, and Ethnic Groups,* Prentice Hall, Englewood Cliffs, NJ, 1983, p. 12; Michael Adas, *Machines as the Measure of Men: Science, Technology and the Ideologies of Western Dominance,* Cornell University Press, Ithaca, 1989, p. 122; J. M. Blaut, *The Colonizer's Model of the World: Geographical Diffusionism and Eurocentric History,* Guilford Press, New York, 1993, p. 63; Stephen Steinberg, *The Ethnic Myth: Race, Class and Ethnicity in America,* Beacon Press, Boston, 1989, p. 1; Peter Kolchin, *American Slavery, 1619–1877,* Hill & Wang, New York, 1993, p. 193.

14. "Those who gave scientific racism its credibility and respectability were often first-rate scientists struggling to understand what appeared to them to be deeply puzzling problems of biology and human society." Nancy Stepan, *The Idea of Race in Science: Great Britain, 1800–1960,* Archon Books, Hamden, CT, 1982, p. xvi.

15. Henry Louis Gates, Jr., ed., *"Race," Writing and Difference,* University of Chicago Press, Chicago, 1986, p. 4.

16. Tzvetan Todorov, "Race, Writing and Culture," in ibid., p. 370.

17. Naomi Zack, *Race and Mixed Race,* Temple University Press, Philadelphia, 1994, pp. 3–4.

18. Joel Williamson, *New People: Miscegenation and Mulattoes in the United States,* Free Press, New York, 1980, p. xii.

19. Shanklin, *Anthropology and Race,* pp. 1, 18.

20. Marvin Harris, *Cultural Anthropology,* Harper & Row, New York, 1987, p. 34.

21. Claude Levi-Strauss, "Race and History," in Leo Kuper, ed., *Race, Science and Society,* UNESCO Press, Paris, 1975, p. 96.

22. Clifford Geertz, *The Interpretation of Cultures: Selected Essays,* Basic Books, New York, 1973, pp. 26, 49.

23. Melville Herskovits, *Cultural Relativism: Perspectives in Cultural Pluralism,* Vintage Books, New York, 1973, pp. 14, 19, 38, 43.

24. George Stocking writes that since the 1930s "the term savage ceased being acceptable in the mainstream of Anglo-American anthropology." Octave Mannoni writes that in contemporary discourse "the word primitive can be used only in inverted commas, as if to show that we no longer believe in it." See George Stocking, Jr., *Victorian Anthropology,* Free Press, New York, 1987, p. xv; George Stocking, Jr., *Colonial Situations: Essays on the Contextualization of Ethnographic Knowledge,* University of Wisconsin Press, Madison, 1991, p. 43; Octave Mannoni, *Prospero and Caliban: The Psychology of Colonization,* Frederick Praeger, New York, 1968, p. 21.

25. Andrew Hacker, *Two Nations: Black and White, Separate, Hostile, Unequal,* Ballantine Books, New York, 1992, p. 26.

26. Johnnetta B. Cole, *Anthropology for the Nineties,* Free Press, New York, 1988, p. 5.

27. Cited by Ernest Gellner, *Plough, Sword and Book,* University of Chicago Press, Chicago, 1989, p. 11.

28. Alexis de Tocqueville, *Democracy in America,* edited by J. P. Mayer, Harper & Row, New York, 1988, pp. 343–44.

29. Joel Williamson, *The Crucible of Race: Black-White Relations in the American South Since Emancipation,* Oxford University Press, New York, 1984, p. 109.

30. Stepan, *The Idea of Race in Science,* p. 1.

31. Tocqueville, *Democracy in America,* p. 357.

32. George Stocking, Jr., *Race, Culture and Evolution,* University of Chicago Press, Chicago, 1982, p. 37.

33. For a detailed account, see Barkin, *The Retreat of Scientific Racism.*

34. Adas, *Machines as the Measure of Men,* p. 134.

35. Cited by Thomas F. Gossett, *Race: The History of an Idea in America,* Southern Methodist University Press, Dallas, 1963, pp. 32–33.

36. Ibid., p. 35; Audrey Smedley, *Race in North America,* Westview Press, Boulder, 1993, pp. 163–64.

37. "Upon the whole," Buffon wrote, "every circumstance concurs in proving that mankind are not composed of species essentially different from each other; on the contrary, there was originally but one species, who after multiplying and spreading over the whole surface of the earth, have undergone various changes by the influence of climate, food, mode of living, epidemic disease, and the mixture of dissimilar individuals." See Gossett, *Race: The History of an Idea in America,* pp. 35–36; Smedley, *Race in North America,* pp. 165–66.

38. That Blumenbach took an ironic view of racial superiority is suggested by his remark, "If a toad could speak and were asked which was the loveliest creature upon God's earth, it would say simpering that modesty forbade it to give a real opinion on that point." See Gossett, *Race: The History of an Idea in America,* pp. 37–39; Audrey Smedley, *Race in North America,* pp. 166–67.

39. George Cuvier, *The Animal Kingdom,* Carvill, New York, 1831.

40. Stepan, *The Idea of Race in Science,* pp. 2, 4, 29.

41. William Stanton, *The Leopard's Spots: Scientific Attitudes Toward Race in America,* University of Chicago Press, Chicago, 1960, pp. 15–16; Stocking, *Race, Culture and Evolution,* pp. 44–45.

42. Charles White, *An Account of the Regular Gradation in Man,* C. Dilly, London, 1709. See also Winthrop Jordan, *The White Man's Burden,* Oxford University Press, New York, 1974, pp. 199–200; Stanton, *The Leopard's Spots,* pp. 16–18. White argued that Negroes may have a better capacity for memory than whites, but this did not invalidate his progression because "those domestic animals with which we are best acquainted, as the horse and the dog, excel the human species in this faculty." As for those who insisted that Negroes have abilities that apes don't, White responded that apes had been underestimated. "They have been taught to play upon musical instruments, as the pipe and the harp." See Gossett, *Race: The History of an Idea in America,* pp. 47–49.

43. David Brion Davis, *The Problem of Slavery in Western Culture,* Oxford University Press, New York, 1988, p. 454; William B. Cohen, *The French Encounter With Africans,* Indiana University Press, Bloomington, 1980, p. 12.

44. George Stocking, *Race, Culture and Evolution,* p. 38.

45. Cited by Thomas Gossett, *Race: The History of an Idea in America,* pp. 44–45.

See also William B. Cohen, *The French Encounter With Africans,* p. 67; Audrey Smedley, *Race in North America,* p. 169; Philip Curtin, *The Image of Africa,* p. 42.

46. Samuel Stanhope Smith, *Essay on the Causes of the Variety of Complexion and Figure,* J. Simpson, New Brunswick, NH, 1810; see also Stanton, *The Leopard's Spots,* pp. 3, 4, 7, 8, 12; Gossett, *Race: The History of an Idea in America,* pp. 39–40; Jordan, *The White Man's Burden,* pp. 200–201. Monogenists like Smith and the American abolitionist Benjamin Rush found some strange support for their environmental theories in the case of a former slave named Henry Moss. Born in Virginia, and a veteran of the American revolution, Moss began to develop white spots on his body and over a period of several years he apparently turned entirely white. Through Smith and Rush's arrangements, Moss was placed on exhibit in Philadelphia in 1796 as corroborating evidence of the veracity of the monogenist position. Moss got so much publicity and attention that, according to one writer, his name was as familiar to the reading public in America as that of James Madison and John Adams. See Gossett, *Race,* pp. 40–41; Stanton, *The Leopard's Spots,* pp. 5–6.

47. Stephen Jay Gould, *The Mismeasure of Man,* W. W. Norton, New York, 1981.

48. John Michael, "A New Look at Morton's Craniological Research," *Current Anthropology* 29, No. 2 (April 1988), pp. 349–54.

49. Although Morton disavowed the label, his work was hailed as a major contribution to phrenology in Europe, where the Edinburgh-based *Phrenological Journal* and other publications routinely trumpeted the findings of British, French, and German scientists. These men were busy comparing countless racial specimens for two things: facial angle and cranial or cephalic index. The facial angle was the degree of protrusion of the face and jaw. Sharp facial angles were termed prognathous, and small angles were termed orthognathous. The cranial index was the ratio of maximum width to maximum length of the skull. Short skulls were called brachycephalic, and long skulls dolichocephalic. Sharp facial angles and short skulls were regarded as clear signs of intellectual deficiency.

The most eminent of the European polygenists was Paul Broca, a professor of clinical surgery and founder of the Anthropological Society of Paris. Using instruments such as the caliper, the andrometer, dynomometer, and spirometer, Broca and others produced thousands of measurements to confirm the claim for diversity of the human species, and the congenital inferiority of the blacks. In London, James Hunt, the founder of the Anthropological Society, concluded, based on the emerging evidence, that human equality was a scientifically untenable doctrine, and that it would be as improbable for the primitives of the world to embrace civilization as "for a monkey to understand a problem of Euclid." This scholarly group informally described itself as the Cannibal Club and used, as its gavel, a mace in the form of a Negro head. At the Anthropological Society of Paris, Gratiolet in 1856 argued that the Negro's cranium "closes itself upon the brain like a prison. It is no longer a temple divine, but a sort of helmet for resisting heavy blows."

These claims were resisted by liberal cosmopolitans such as the traveler and author Alexander von Humboldt, who found them narrow-minded and repellant, but their objections were dismissed as dilettantish and unscientific. "I have noticed for a long time," one follower of Morton and Broca wryly observed, "that in general those who deny the intellectual importance of the brain's volume have small heads."

See Stanton, *The Leopard's Spots,* p. 51; Reginald Horsman, *Race and Manifest Destiny: The Origins of American Racial Anglo-Saxonism,* Harvard University Press, Cambridge, 1981, pp. 57–59, 125; Paul Broca, *On the Phenomena of Hybridity in the Genus Homo,* translated by C. C. Blake, Longman, Green, Longman & Roberts, London, 1864; Stocking, *Race, Culture and Evolution,* p. 48; Stocking, *Victorian Anthropology,* p. 252; Smedley, *Race in North America,* p. 261; D. J. Cunningham, "Anthropology in the Eighteenth Century," *Journal of the Royal Anthropological Institute* (London) 38 (1908), p. 12; T. Wingate Todd, "An Anthropologist's Study of Negro Life," *Journal of Negro History* 16 (1931), p. 36; Gould, *The Mismeasure of Man,* p. 112.

50. Samuel Morton, *Crania Americana,* J. Dobson, Philadelphia, 1839; Samuel Morton, *Crania Aegyptiaca,* , J. Pennington, Philadelphia, 1844.

51. William Stanton, *The Leopard's Spots;* for an alternative interpretation, see George Fredrickson, *The Black Image in the White Mind: The Debate on Afro-American Character and Destiny,* Harper & Row, New York, 1971.

52. "Whilst we maintain the unity of the human species, we at the same time repel the depressing assumption of superior and inferior races of men." Alexander von Humboldt, *Cosmos,* London, 1849; see also John Bachman, *The Doctrine of the Unity of the Human Race,* C. Canning, Charleston, 1850, pp. 208–210.

53. Josiah Nott, "Statistics of Southern Slave Population," *DeBow's Review* 4 (1847), pp. 275–89. See also Stanton, *The Leopard's Spots,* p. 80.

54. William Stanton, *The Leopard's Spots,* pp. 61–62.

55. Josiah Nott and George Gliddon, *Types of Mankind,* Lippincott & Grambo, Philadelphia, 1855. See also Horsman, *Race and Manifest Destiny,* pp. 129, 152–55; Stanton, *The Leopard's Spots,* pp. 50, 65–68, 155–63. The term "muleology" is from Williamson, *New People,* p. 96.

56. See, e.g., Russett, *Darwin in America,* p. 91; Steinberg, *The Ethnic Myth,* pp. 77–81.

57. "Although the existing races of man differ in many respects as in color, hair, shape of skull, proportions of the body, etc., yet if their whole structure be taken into consideration, they are found to resemble each other closely in a multitude of points. Many of these differences are so unimportant or of so singular a nature that it is extremely improbable that they should have been independently acquired by aboriginally distinct species or races." Darwin, *The Descent of Man,* p. 174.

58. Cited by Stocking, *Race, Culture and Evolution,* p. 46.

59. Josiah Nott, letter to Ephraim Squier, August 22, 1860; cited in Reginald Horsman, *Josiah Nott of Mobile: Southerner, Physician and Racial Theorist,* Louisiana State University Press, Baton Rouge, 1987, p. 249.

60. Cited by Russett, *Darwin in America,* p. 92.

61. Stocking, *Victorian Anthropology,* p. 326.

62. Charles Darwin *On the Origin of Species,* Harvard University Press, Cambridge, 1964, p. 63.

63. "When we reflect on this struggle, we may console ourselves with the full belief that the war of nature is not incessant, that no fear is felt, that death is generally

prompt, and that the vigorous, the healthy, and the happy survive and multiply." Ibid., p. 79.

64. "There is no doubt that the various races, when carefully compared and measured, differ from each other. . . . It would be an endless task to specify the numerous points of structural difference. The races differ also in constitution, in acclimatization, and in liability to certain diseases. Their mental characteristics are likewise very distinct, chiefly it would appear in their emotional, but partly in their intellectual, faculties." Darwin, *The Descent of Man,* pp. 163–64.

65. Ibid., p. 178.

66. Ibid., pp. 130, 612.

67. According to Carl Degler, Darwin endorsed the view that "the differences in levels of culture or civilization which occurred among the diverse peoples of the world derived from differences in their biological capacities. Some cultures were higher than others because the peoples in those societies were biologically superior." Carl Degler, *In Search of Human Nature,* Oxford University Press, New York, 1991, p. 61. See also Stocking, *Race, Culture and Evolution,* pp. 113–14.

68. Charles Darwin, *The Voyage of the Beagle,* Anchor Books, Garden City, NY, 1962 edition, pp. 205–6, 213, 251.

69. Darwin, *The Descent of Man,* p. 613.

70. Huxley argued that "the difference in the volume of the cranial cavity of different races of mankind is far greater, absolutely, than that between the lowest man and the highest ape." Cited by Stocking, *Victorian Anthropology,* p. 148.

71. Huxley, "Emancipation—Black and White," pp. 64–67.

72. For a discussion, see J. B. Bury, *The Idea of Progress,* Dover Publications, New York, 1960; Robert Nisbet, *History of the Idea of Progress,* Basic Books, New York, 1980.

73. Degler, *In Search of Human Nature,* p. 13.

74. A. R. Wallace, *Natural Selection and Tropical Nature,* Macmillan, London, 1895; see also Malcolm Kottler, "Charles Darwin and Alfred Russel Wallace: Two Decades of Debate over Natural Selection," in David Kohn, ed., *The Darwinian Heritage,* Princeton University Press, Princeton, 1985; Stepan, *The Idea of Race in Science,* pp. 66–67; Degler, *In Search of Human Nature,* pp. 59–60.

75. This notion of racism as an immanentizing of the eschaton—bringing heaven down to earth—is conveyed by Eric Voegelin. See Thomas Heilke, *Voegelin on the Idea of Race,* Louisiana State University Press, Baton Rouge, 1990, pp. 141–42.

76. See Richard Hofstadter, *Social Darwinism in American Thought,* George Braziller, New York, 1959. This subject is also discussed in the chapter, "Race and Social Darwinism," in Gossett, *Race: The History of an Idea in America.*

77. Francis Galton, *Hereditary Genius: An Inquiry into the Laws of Consequences,* World Publishing, New York, 1962, pp. 40–41.

78. Degler, *In Search of Human Nature,* p. 41.

79. Herbert Spencer, *First Principles,* P. F. Collier, New York, 1902, p. 537.

80. Herbert Spencer, *Social Statics,* Robert Schalkenbach Foundation, New York, 1954, pp. 315–17.

81. Spencer's leading student in the United States was William Graham Sumner

of Yale, one of the founders of American sociology, who believed that black inferiority was ingrained and whose magnum opus, *Folkways,* argued the hopelessness of trying to use laws to change embedded social traits.

Sociology textbooks routinely reflected this viewpoint. Fairly typical was *Principles of Sociology,* published in 1896 by Frank Giddings of Columbia University, who placed the Negro on the lowest rung of the ladder of civilization. Applying Darwinian language, Giddings said that the Indian was "intellectually superior" to the Negro, but had "shown less ability to adapt himself to new conditions." Asians were in the same league as native Americans. "These people have been in existence much longer than the European race, and have accomplished immeasurably less. We are therefore warranted in saying that they have not the same inherent abilities."

The leading figure in the emerging field of American psychology in the first decade of the twentieth century was William McDougall of Harvard University, whose textbooks dominated the profession. An advocate of Nordic superiority and keeping the dark-skinned immigrants out, McDougall was dogmatic in his insistence that racial differences in intelligence were hereditary and could not be reduced by altering the environment.

See William Graham Sumner, *Folkways,* Ginn and Co., Boston, 1906; Frank Henry Giddings, *Principles of Sociology,* Macmillan, New York, 1896, pp. 328–29; McDougall, *Is America Safe for Democracy?;* Edward Youmans, *Herbert Spencer on the Americans and the Americans on Herbert Spencer,* D. Appleton, New York, 1883.

82. James Q. Wilson and Richard J. Herrnstein, *Crime and Human Nature,* Simon & Schuster, New York, 1985, p. 72; Degler, *In Search of Human Nature,* p. 36.

83. Stocking, *Victorian Anthropology,* pp. 219, 229.

84. Lewis Henry Morgan, *Ancient Society,* Holt, Rinehart and Winston, New York, 1877.

85. Josiah Strong, *Our Country: Its Possible Future and Present Crisis,* Cambridge University Press, Cambridge, 1963, first published 1885.

86. George Fredrickson, *White Supremacy: A Comparative Study in American and South African History,* Oxford University Press, New York, 1981, pp. 199–225. For an examination of racism in the labor movement, see Herbert Hill, "Black Labor and Affirmative Action: An Historical Perspective," in Steven Schulman and William Darity, Jr., *The Question of Discrimination,* Wesleyan University Press, Middletown, 1989.

87. A curious 1854 Supreme Court decision illustrates how scientific racism routinely became the chosen instrument for racial exclusion and white privilege. The California case of *People v. Hall* involved the right of Chinese persons to testify as eyewitnesses in a murder case against a white man. State law prohibited testimony from blacks, mulattoes, and Indians, but these restrictions did not seem to apply to Asians.

Not so, the court ruled, because the most recent scientific research from ethnology and anthropology showed that Indians were really mongoloid peoples who migrated to the Americas across the Bering Strait tens of thousands of years ago. Thus, Chief Justice J. Murray concluded, the Chinese were prohibited by law from giving evidence against whites in California because they were ethnically identical to American Indians, "a race of people whom nature has marked as inferior, who are incapable of progress or intellectual development beyond a certain point . . . between whom and ourselves nature has placed an impassable difference."

People v. Hall, October 1, 1854; reprinted in Robert Heizer and Alan Almquist, *The Other Californians: Prejudice and Discrimination Under Spain, Mexico and the United States to 1920,* University of California Press, Berkeley, 1971, pp. 229–34.

88. Ronald Takaki, *Strangers from a Different Shore: A History of Asian Americans,* Penguin Books, New York, 1989.

89. "During their entire settlement in California the Chinese have never adapted themselves to our habits, mode of dress, or our educational system, have never learned the sanctity of an oath, never desired to become citizens, or to perform the duties of citizenship, never discovered the difference between right and wrong, never ceased the worship of their idol gods, or advanced a step beyond the traditions of their native hive." Cited by Barbara Benton, *Ellis Island,* Facts on File, New York, 1987, p. 34.

90. Cited by Ronald Takaki, *A Different Mirror: A History of Multicultural America,* Little, Brown, Boston, 1993, p. 206.

91. Ronald Takaki, "A Tale of Two Decades: Race and Class in the 1880s and the 1980s," in Herbert Hill and James Jones, eds., *Race in America: The Struggle for Equality,* University of Wisconsin Press, Madison, 1993, p. 402.

92. Roger Daniels, *Coming to America: A History of Immigration and Ethnicity in American Life,* HarperCollins, New York, 1990, pp. 271–72.

93. Ibid., p. 255.

94. Cited by Takaki, *Strangers from a Different Shore,* pp. 296–97.

95. Arthur Schlesinger, Jr., *The Disuniting of America,* W. W. Norton, New York, 1992.

96. Bonnie Angelo, "The Pain of Being Black," *Time,* May 22, 1989; Toni Morrison, "On the Backs of Blacks," *Time,* special issue, Fall 1993, p. 57.

97. Stanley Fish, *There's No Such Thing as Free Speech, and It's a Good Thing Too,* Oxford University Press, New York, 1994, p. 87.

98. Reed Ueda, *Postwar Immigrant America: A Social History,* St. Martin's Press, Boston, 1994, p. 11.

99. U.S. Bureau of the Census, "Immigration: 1820 to 1991," *Statistical Abstract of the United States, 1993,* Washington, DC, p. 10; see also George Borjas, *Friends or Strangers: The Impact of Immigrants on the U.S. Economy,* Basic Books, New York, 1990, p. 6. Between 1820 and 1870, only 26,000 Italians came to the United States; by 1900 that number had increased by more than a million. Russian emigration went from 4,000 to three quarters of a million. From Poland, over the same period, immigration rose from 4,000 to 160,000. See Ellis Cose, *A Nation of Strangers: Prejudice, Politics and the Populating of America,* William Morrow, New York, 1992, p. 60.

100. Richard Easterlin, David Ward, William Bernard, and Reed Ueda, *Immigration,* Harvard University Press, Cambridge, 1982, pp. 8–9; Alejandro Portes and Robert L. Bach, *Latin Journey: Cuban and Mexican Immigrants in the United States,* University of California Press, Berkeley, 1985, p. 31.

101. Cited by Edward A. Ross, *The Old World in the New,* Century Co., New York, 1914, pp. 285–86.

102. The term Know-Nothings was used by Horace Greeley to describe a nativist anti-Catholic movement during the 19th century that developed national strength, but was especially influential in New York, Massachusetts, Pennsylvania, Maryland and Kentucky. See Cose, *A Nation of Strangers,* p. 33.

103. Francis Walker, "The Tide of Economic Thought," *Publications of the American Economic Association* 6 (January-March 1891), p. 37.

104. Cited by Barry Schwartz, ed., *White Racism,* Laurel Leaf Books, New York, 1978, p. 58.

105. Leon Litwack, *North of Slavery: The Negro in the Free States, 1790–1860,* University of Chicago Press, Chicago, 1965, p. 163.

106. John Higham, *Strangers in the Land: Patterns of American Nativism, 1860–1925,* Atheneum Books, New York, 1963.

107. Will Herberg, *Protestant, Catholic, Jew: An Essay in American Religious Sociology,* Anchor Books, New York, 1960, p. 6, 27.

108. See, e.g., Horace Kallen, *Culture and Democracy in the United States,* Arno Press, New York, 1924.

109. Cited by Robert Bellah, *The Broken Covenant,* Seabury Press, New York, 1975, p. 90.

110. Ueda, *Postwar Immigrant America,* p. 84.

111. Milton Gordon, *Assimilation in American Life,* Oxford University Press, New York, 1964, p. 106.

112. See Oscar Handlin, *The Uprooted: The Epic Story of the Great Migrations That Made the American People,* Grosset & Dunlap, New York, 1951; Higham, *Strangers in the Land.*

113. Gordon, *Assimilation in American Life,* pp. 126–27.

114. Cited by Ueda, *Postwar Immigrant America,* p. 124.

115. Cited by Michael Novak, *The Rise of the Unmeltable Ethnics,* Macmillan, New York, 1971, p. 140.

116. Nathan Glazer, *Ethnic Dilemmas, 1964–1982,* Harvard University Press, Cambridge, 1983, p. 99.

117. Gordon, *Assimilation in American Life,* pp. 115–33.

118. "Great has been the Greek, the Latin, the Celt, the Teuton and the Saxon," William Jennings Bryan proclaimed, "but greater than any of these is the American, who combines the virtues of them all." Cited by Robert E. Park and Ernest W. Burgess, *Introduction to the Science of Sociology,* University of Chicago Press, Chicago, 1969, p. 734.

119. Higham, *Strangers in the Land,* pp. 136–44.

120. Daniel Kevles, *In the Name of Eugenics: Genetics and the Uses of Human Heredity,* Alfred A. Knopf, New York, 1985, p. 47.

121. Madison Grant, *The Passing of the Great Race,* 4th edition, Charles Scribner, New York, 1926, pp. xxviii–xxix, xxxi, 77, 167.

122. Cited by Easterlin et al., *Immigration,* p. 97.

123. Cited by Higham, *Strangers in the Land,* p. 300.

124. Gould, *The Mismeasure of Man,* p. 232.

125. The way in which the new law controlled the racial composition of immi-

grants was to annually restrict nationality totals to 2 percent of the size of each group as counted in the U.S. Census of 1890. This assured that English, Irish, German, and Scandinavian immigrants would be favored over later arrivals from Italy, Austria, Russia, and Poland. See Gossett, *Race: The History of an Idea in America,* p. 406; Stanley Lieberson, *A Piece of the Pie: Black and White Immigrants Since 1880,* University of California Press, Berkeley, 1980, p. 29; Ueda, *Postwar Immigrant America,* p. 20.

126. H. S. Jennings, *The Biological Basis of Human Nature,* W. W. Norton, New York, 1930, pp. 280–82.

127. Statement by a committee of the American Breeders' Association, cited by Degler, *In Search of Human Nature,* p. 43.

128. 274 U.S. 200 (1927).

129. Eduardo Galeano, *We Say No: Chronicles 1963–1991,* W. W. Norton, New York, 1992, p. 80.

130. Elazar Barkin argues that the "social diversification" of the scientific community was "an important factor in the redefinition of the race concept." Barkin, *The Retreat of Scientific Racism,* p. 343; see also Degler, *In Search of Human Nature,* p. 201.

131. Cited in Jane Howard, "Angry Storm Over South Seas of Margaret Mead," *Smithsonian* 14 (April 1983), p. 67.

132. Margaret Mead, *Coming of Age in Samoa,* William Morrow, New York, 1961, first published 1928, pp. 83, 104–8.

133. Cited by Derek Freeman, *Margaret Mead and Samoa: The Making and Unmaking of an Anthropological Myth,* Harvard University Press, Cambridge, 1983, p. 97.

134. George Stocking, *Race, Culture and Evolution,* p. 306.

135. Ruth Benedict, *Patterns of Culture,* Penguin Books, New York, 1934.

136. Mary Catherine Bateson, *With a Daughter's Eye: A Memoir of Margaret Mead,* William Morrow, New York, 1984, p. 125; E. Michael Jones, *Degenerate Moderns,* Ignatius Press, San Francisco, 1993, p. 35.

137. Degler, *In Search of Human Nature,* p. 61.

138. Gossett, *Race: The History of an Idea in America,* p. 418.

139. Boas voted socialist as early as 1918, and became an admirer of Soviet communism. Even when he grew critical in later years of the suppression of intellectual freedom in the Soviet Union, he refused to criticize the Communist government. He even refused to make his criticisms public during the period of the Nazi-Soviet pact. Boas fully earned George W. Stocking's label of "scientific activist." George Stocking, Jr., *The Ethnographer's Magic: And Other Essays in the History of Anthropology,* University of Wisconsin Press, Madison, 1992, pp. 106–110.

140. Ibid., p. 106. "It is clear from Boas' correspondence that he saw the work of Herskovits on the physical anthropology of the Negro, of Mead on Samoan adolescence, and of Klineberg on racial mental differences as part of a coordinated attack on the problem of the cultural factor in racial differences. . . . The Boasian viewpoint, which in 1919 was still distinctly a minority current, by 1934 was on the verge of becoming social science orthodoxy."

141. Cited by Stocking, *Race, Culture and Evolution,* p. 148, see also pp. 135, 150–51.

142. Franz Boas, *Changes in the Bodily Form of Descendants of Immigrants,* Senate Document 208, 61st Congress, Washington, DC, 1911, pp. 1–7.

143. Boas, *The Mind of Primitive Man;* see also Franz Boas, *Anthropology and Modern Life,* Dover Publications, New York, 1928.

144. There are no entries for "slave" or "slavery" in Boas's study of the Kwakiutl. See Franz Boas, *Kwakiutl Ethnology,* edited by Helen Codere, University of Chicago Press, Chicago, 1966. Boas's omission is criticized by Leland Donald, "Liberty, Equality, Fraternity: Was the Indian Really Egalitarian?" in James A. Clifton, ed., *The Invented Indian,* Transaction Books, New Brunswick, 1990, pp. 154–55.

145. Boas, *The Mind of Primitive Man,* pp. 270–71.

146. Matthew Arnold, *Culture and Anarchy,* Yale University Press, New Haven, 1994, first published in 1869, pp. 8, 34–35.

147. Cited by Stocking *Race, Culture and Evolution,* p. 73.

148. Ibid., pp. 200, 203. See also Degler, *In Search of Human Nature,* p. 71. "By the end of the 1890s, Boas was using culture in the plural, as we do today—every society exhibits a culture. . . . Boas almost single-handedly developed in America the concept of culture which, like a powerful solvent, would in time expunge race from the literature of social science."

149. Here is what T. S. Eliot includes under the term culture: "Derby Day, Henley Regatta, Cowes, the twelfth of August, a cup final, the dog races, the pin table, the dart board, Wensleydale cheese, boiled cabbage cut into sections, beetroot in vinegar, nineteenth-century Gothic churches and the music of Elgar." T. S. Eliot, *Christianity and Culture,* Harcourt Brace Jovanovich, New York, 1939, p. 104.

150. Stocking, *The Ethnographer's Magic,* p. 110.

151. "The differences between the races are so small that they lie within the narrow range in the limits of which all forms may function equally well." Boas, *Anthropology and Modern Life,* p. 41.

152. Ruth Bunzel, introduction to Boas, *Anthropology and Modern Life,* pp. 9–10.

153. "Boas wrote as a skeptic of received belief rather than as a staunch advocate of racial equipotentiality." Stocking, *Race, Culture and Evolution,* p. 189.

154. "The Boasians saw themselves as scientific innovators. Their innovation has a definitely Kuhnian character. Substantively, the conception of culture and of cultural determinism implicit in Boas' critique of evolutionism provided the basis for a radically different disciplinary worldview, although its implications were slow to be developed." See Stocking, *The Ethnographer's Magic,* p. 123.

155. Alfred L. Kroeber, "The Morals of Uncivilized People," *American Anthropologist* 12 (July-September 1910), pp. 443–46; Alfred L. Kroeber, *The Nature of Culture,* University of Chicago Press, Chicago, 1952; Robert Lowie, *Culture and Ethnology,* Boni and Liveright, New York, 1917.

158. Ruth Benedict, "Obituary of Franz Boas," *Science* 97 (1963), p. 60.

157. Margaret Mead, *Sex and Temperament in Three Primitive Societies,* William Morrow, New York, 1963 (first published in 1935), p. 280.

158. Otto Klineberg, "Race and Psychology," in Leo Kuper, ed., *Race, Science and Society,* p. 204.

159. Melville Herskovits, *Cultural Anthropology,* Alfred A. Knopf, New York, 1965 edition, p. 364.

160. Phyllis Grosskurth, *Margaret Mead,* Penguin Books, New York, 1988, pp. 21, 25, 26.

161. Michel de Montaigne, "On Cannibals," in *Essays,* Penguin Books, Balti more, 1958, p. 117.

162. Franz Boas, introduction to Mead, *Coming of Age in Samoa.*

163. Grosskurth, *Margaret Mead,* p. 88.

164. Derek Freeman, *Margaret Mead and Samoa,* pp. 91, 94, 241, 242, 250, 291–92; see also Edwin McDowell, "New Samoa Book Challenges Margaret Mead's Conclusions," *New York Times,* January 31, 1983, p. A-1.

165. Eleanor Leacock, "In Search of a Culture," in Lenora Foerstel and Angela Gilliam, ed., *Confronting the Margaret Mead Legacy,* Temple University Press, Philadelphia, 1992, p. 4.

166. Cited in Cheryl Fields, "Controversial Book Spurs Scholars' Defense of the Legacy of Margaret Mead," *Chronicle of Higher Education,* May 11, 1983, p. 27.

167. Annette B. Weiner, "Ethnographic Determinism: Samoa and the Margaret Mead Controversy," *American Anthropologist* 85 (1983), p. 918.

168. Colin Turnbull, "Trouble in Paradise," *The New Republic,* March 28, 1983, pp. 32–34.

169. Bradd Shore, "Paradox Regained: Freeman's *Margaret Mead and Samoa,*" *American Anthropologist* 85 (1983), p. 936.

170. Peter Worsley, "Foreword," in Foerstel and Gilliam, *Confronting the Margaret Mead Legacy,* p. xvi.

171. Benedict, *Patterns of Culture,* pp. 73–75, 263.

172. Melville Herskovits, *The Myth of the Negro Past,* Harper & Bros., New York, 1941, pp. 70–71. Herskovits's comparative style is clear in his solemn treatment of supernatural "divining techniques" among African tribes. "Divination is principally based on a complex system of combinations and permutations arrived at by throwing a set number of seeds," he noted. "The very period of study required to become a diviner, between five and ten years, suggests an analogy with the doctorate of philosophy or medicine among ourselves."

173. Ibid., p. 30. "To the extent that the past of a people is regarded as praiseworthy, their own self-esteem will be high and the opinion of others will be favorable." Ibid., p. 299.

174. Claude Lévi-Strauss, "Race and History," in Kuper, *Race, Science and Society,* p. 97.

175. Ruth Benedict, *Race: Science and Politics,* Modern Age Books, New York, 1940, pp. 133–34, 199; Benedict, *Race and Racism,* Routledge and Kegan Paul, London, 1942, p. 90; Benedict, *Patterns of Culture,* p. 2.

176. Herskovits, *Cultural Anthropology,* pp. 123, 360.

177. Benedict, *Patterns of Culture,* p. 33; Benedict, *Race and Racism,* pp. viii, 10.

178. Melville Herskovits, "On the Values in Culture," *Scientific Monthly* 54 (1942), pp. 557–60.

179. See Robert Edgerton, *Sick Societies: Challenging the Myth of Primitive Harmony,* Free Press, New York, 1992.

180. Renato Rosaldo, *Culture and Truth: The Remaking of Social Analysis,* Beacon Press, Boston, 1993, pp. 1, 10.

181. "Values constitute an essential ingredient of culture." A. L. Kroeber, *The Nature of Culture,* University of Chicago Press, Chicago, 1952, p. 5. "Every society through its culture seeks and in some measure finds values." A. L. Kroeber and Clyde Kluckholn, cited by George Stocking, *Race, Culture and Evolution,* p. 199.

182. Ernest Gellner, *Legitimation of Belief,* Cambridge University Press, Cambridge, 1974, p. 48.

183. Theodosius Dobzhansky, *Mankind Evolving: The Evolution of the Human Species,* Yale University Press, New Haven, 1962, p. 9.

184. In a 1910 book *Social and Mental Traits of the Negro* Odum emphasized the intrinsic limitations of black capability. A Negro "may be assisted to be a good Negro," Odum concluded, "but that is the highest privilege that can be given him." But a few years later Odum was quoting from Boas on the importance of culture over race, and his later work emphasized that blacks should not be judged inferior to whites. "It would clearly be impossible for the Negro children to show the same manifestations of mental traits as white children, after having been under the influence of entirely different environments for many generations." Odum added, "Injustice would be done to Negro children if harsh judgment be passed upon them because they do not maintain the standard of the white children." See Howard Odum, *Social and Mental Traits of the Negro,* Columbia University Press, New York, 1910, p. 294; Howard Odum, "Negro Children in the Public Schools of Philadelphia," *Annals of the American Academy of Political and Social Science* 49 (September 1913), pp. 200, 205–6.

185. Sociologist Charles Ellwood of the University of Missouri and educational psychologist William Bagley are two examples of leading scholars whose views changed under the Boasian sway. In 1901 Ellwood was convinced that the Negro's intellectual performance was due to innate incapacity. "The Negro child, even when reared in a white family under the most favorable conditions, fails to take on the mental and moral characteristics of the Caucasian." After reviewing the Boas studies on immigrants, however, Ellwood greatly modified his estimation of the importance of race, giving more prominence to the effects of "differences in social equipment." See Charles Ellwood, "The Theory of Imitation in Social Psychology," *American Journal of Sociology* 6 (May 1901), p. 573; Charles Ellwood, review of William Benjamin Smith's *The Color Line, American Journal of Sociology* 11 (January 1906), p. 572.

A firm believer in innate differences, Bagley continued to assert in the 1920s that "There is a fair degree of probability that the Negro race will never produce so large a proportion of highly gifted persons as will the white races." But he no longer believed that public policy should make "invidious distinctions" between groups and he asserted that the "hereditarian solution is openly inhumane and anti-democratic." See William Bagley, *Determinism in Education,* Warwick and York, Baltimore, 1925, pp. 45, 129–31.

186. Degler, *In Search of Human Nature,* p. 187.

187. Adolf Hitler, *Mein Kampf,* Houghton Mifflin, Boston, 1962 edition, p. 339.

188. Stepan, *The Idea of Race in Science,* p. 140.

189. As late as 1933 the *Eugenical News* commented, "One may condemn the Nazi policy generally, but specifically it remained for Germany to lead the great nations of the world in recognition of the biological foundations of national character." Three years later the president of the Eugenics Research Association wrote in the same journal: "It is unfortunate that the anti-Nazi propaganda with which all countries have been flooded has gone so far as to obscure the correct understanding and the great importance of the German racial policy. No earnest eugenicist can fail to give approbation to such a policy." See H. H. Laughlin and C. B. Davenport, "Race Integrity," *Eugenical News* 18 (July-August 1933), p. 76; C. M. Goethe, "The German Racial Policy," *Eugenical News* 21 (March-April 1936), p. 25.

190. Gossett, *Race: The History of an Idea in America,* pp. 427–28.

191. Pat Shipman, *The Evolution of Racism,* Simon & Schuster, New York, 1994, pp. 191, 219.

192. Cited by Degler, *In Search of Human Nature,* p. 203.

193. For example:

> The American Anthropological Association repudiates statements now appearing that Negroes are biologically and in innate mental ability inferior to whites, and reaffirms the fact that there is no scientifically established evidence to justify the exclusion of any race from the rights guaranteed by the Constitution of the U.S. The basic principles of equality of opportunity and equality before the law are compatible with all that is known about human biology. All races possess the abilities needed to participate fully in the democratic way of life and in modern technological civilization.

Statement of the Council of Fellows, American Anthropological Association, November 17, 1961.

194. Cited in Kuper, ed., *Race, Science and Society,* pp. 176, 345; see also Degler, *In Search of Human Nature,* p. 204.

195. This point is made by Carl Degler. "A convenient measure of the triumph of the concept of culture among social scientists may be found in a single book . . . Gunnar Myrdal's *An American Dilemma.*" Carl Degler, *In Search of Human Nature,* p. 215.

196. Gunnar Myrdal, *An American Dilemma: The Negro Problem and Modern Democracy,* Harper & Bros., New York, 1962 (first published in 1944). Myrdal's influence is well described in David Southern, *Gunnar Myrdal and Black-White Relations,* Louisiana State University Press, Baton Rouge, 1987; see also Walter A. Jackson, *Gunnar Myrdal and America's Conscience,* University of North Carolina Press, Chapel Hill, 1990.

197. Myrdal, *An American Dilemma,* pp. lxxxv, 49, 75–76, 92, 106–8, 115–16, 146–47, 669.

198. Pierre Van Den Berghe, *The Ethnic Phenomenon,* Elsevier Press, New York, 1981, p. 2.

199. Bruno Bettelheim and Morris Janowitz, *Dynamics of Prejudice,* Harper & Bros., New York, 1950.

200. T. W. Adorno, Else Frenkel-Brunswik, Daniel Levinson, and R. Nevitt Sanford, *The Authoritarian Personality,* Harper & Bros., New York, 1950.

201. Gordon W. Allport, *The Nature of Prejudice,* Addison-Wesley, Reading, MA, 1979 edition, pp. 6, 27.

202. "Prejudice can be thought of as irrationally based, negative attitudes against certain ethnic groups and their members. . . . Ethnic prejudice simultaneously violates two basic norms—the norm of rationality and the norm of human heartedness." Thomas Pettigrew, George Fredrickson, Dale Knobel, Nathan Glazer, and Reed Ueda, *Prejudice,* Harvard University Press, Cambridge, 1982, pp. 2–3.

"Prejudice is a negative or hostile attitude toward a person or group formed without just or sufficient knowledge." Anti-Defamation League of B'nai B'rith, *A World of Difference,* curricular materials package.

203. Pettigrew et al., *Prejudice,* p. 7.

204. Anti-Defamation League of B'nai B'rith, *A World of Difference.*

205. Ibid.

206. Pettigrew et al., *Prejudice,* p. 16.

Chapter 5. A Dream Deferred

1. Martin Luther King, Jr., "I Have A Dream," in James Melvin Washington, ed., *A Testament of Hope: The Essential Writings of Martin Luther King, Jr.,* HarperSan Francisco, 1986, p. 219.

2. On November 2, 1983, President Reagan signed into law a bill designating the third Monday in January a federal holiday in honor of Martin Luther King, Jr..

3. Derrick Bell, *And We Are Not Saved: The Elusive Quest for Racial Justice,* Basic Books, New York, 1987, p. 22.

4. David Troutt, "The Dream of Integration Is Dead for Some," *Los Angeles Times,* January 17, 1995.

5. "Generation X: A Conversation with Spike Lee and Henry Louis Gates, Jr.," *Transition,* Issue 56, 1992, p. 56.

6. William Bennett reported these responses from Jackson and Norton when he cited King's "content of our character" theme. See William J. Bennett, *The De-Valuing of America,* Summit Books, New York, 1992, p. 191.

7. Roy Brooks, *Rethinking the American Race Problem,* University of California Press, Berkeley, 1990, pp. 89, 165–66.

8. Bernard Boxill, *Blacks and Social Justice,* Rowman and Littlefield, Lanham, MD, 1992, p. 11.

9. John Hope Franklin, *The Color Line: Legacy for the Twenty First Century,* University of Missouri Press, Columbia, 1993, p. 44.

10. William Allen, Drew Days, Benjamin Hooks, and William Bradford Reynolds, "Affirmative Action and the Constitution," seminar at American Enterprise Institute, May 21, 1985, Washington, DC, p. 3.

11. "Affirmative Action on the Edge," *U.S. News & World Report,* February 13, 1995, p. 35.

12. Randall Kennedy, "Still a Pigmentocracy," *New York Times,* July 21, 1993.

13. Lani Guinier, *The Tyranny of the Majority: Fundamental Fairness in Representative Democracy,* Free Press, New York, 1994, p. 176.

14. Charles Lawrence, "The Id, the Ego and Equal Protection: Reckoning with Unconscious Racism," *Stanford Law Review* 49 (1987), pp. 317, 326.

15. Patricia Williams, *The Alchemy of Race and Rights,* Harvard University Press, Cambridge, 1980, pp. 49, 101, 120.

16. Robert Carter, "Thirty Five Years Later: New Perspectives on *Brown,*" in Herbert Hill and James Jones, eds., *Race in America: The Struggle for Equality,* University of Wisconsin Press, Madison, 1993, p. 89.

17. Kimberle Williams Crenshaw, "Race, Reform and Retrenchment: Transformation and Legitimation in Antidiscrimination Law," *Harvard Law Review* 101 (1988), pp. 1341–44.

18. Adolph Reed and Julian Bond, "Equality: Why We Can't Wait," *The Nation,* December 9, 1991, p. 736.

19. Statement of Commissioners Blandina Ramirez and Mary Frances Berry, *Toward an Understanding of Stotts,* U.S. Commission on Civil Rights, January 1985; see also Robert Pear, "Civil Rights Agency Splits in Debate on Narrowing Definition of Equality," *New York Times,* October 14, 1985, p. A-17.

20. "During the late 1960s, the civil rights community began to splinter and, certainly by the mid-1970s, much of its leadership had become preoccupied with equality of results. . . . And it has made support for the redistribution of these rights a precondition for being part of the movement." Morris Abram, "Affirmative Action: Fair Shakers and Social Engineers," *Harvard Law Review* 99 (1986), pp. 1313, 1325.

21. Frederick Douglass, "The Destiny of Colored Americans," *The North Star,* November 16, 1849.

22. Andrew Kull, *The Color-Blind Constitution,* Harvard University Press, Cambridge, 1992, pp. 55–69.

23. Eric Foner, *Reconstruction: America's Unfinished Revolution, 1863–1877,* Harper & Row, New York, 1988, p. 26.

24. Kull, *The Color-Blind Constitution,* p. viii.

25. James Baldwin, *The Fire Next Time,* Laurel Books, New York, 1963, p. 127.

26. Kull, *The Color-Blind Constitution,* p. 183. See also Nathan Glazer's analysis: "In 1964, we declared that no account should be taken of race. . . . Yet no sooner had we made this national assertion than we entered into a period of color and group-consciousness with a vengeance." Nathan Glazer, *Affirmative Discrimination: Ethnic Inequality and Public Policy,* Basic Books, New York, 1975, p. 18.

27. Chancellor Williams, *The Destruction of Black Civilization,* Third World Press, Chicago, 1987, pp. 302–3.

28. Tony Brown, "Why Integration Fails America's Blacks," *Issues and Views,* Fall 1991, p. 3.

29. Derrick Bell, "*Brown v. Board of Education* and the Interest-Convergence Dilemma," *Harvard Law Review* 93 (1980), p. 518; Derrick Bell, *And We Are Not Saved,* pp. 5, 22, 63; Derrick Bell, *Faces at the Bottom of the Well: The Permanence of Racism,* Basic Books, New York, 1992, pp. 13–14.

30. Taylor Branch, *Parting the Waters: America in the King Years, 1954–1963,*

Simon & Schuster, New York, 1988; David Garrow, *Bearing the Cross: Martin Luther King and the Southern Christian Leadership Conference,* Vintage Books, New York, 1988; Ralph Abernathy, *And the Walls Came Tumbling Down,* Harper & Row, New York, 1989; Stephen B. Oates, *Let the Trumpet Sound: The Life of Martin Luther King, Jr.,* Mentor Books, New York, 1982; Vincent Harding, *There Is a River: The Black Struggle for Freedom in America,* Harcourt Brace Jovanovich, New York, 1991; Henry Hampton and Steve Fayer, *Voices of Freedom: An Oral History of the Civil Rights Movement from the 1950s Through the 1960s,* Bantam Books, New York, 1991; Peter J. Albert and Ronald Hoffman, eds., *We Shall Overcome: Martin Luther King, Jr., and the Black Freedom Struggle,* Da Capo Press, New York, 1993; Jack Greenberg, *Crusaders in the Courts,* Basic Books, New York, 1994.

31. Bell Hooks, *Black Looks: Race and Representation,* South End Press, Boston, 1992, p. 168; Lerone Bennett, *Before the Mayflower: A History of Black America,* Penguin Books, New York, 1993, p. 257.

32. Cited by W. E. B. Du Bois, *Black Reconstruction,* S. A. Russell, New York, 1935, p. 405.

33. See, e.g., Pete Daniel, *The Shadow of Slavery: Peonage in the South, 1901–1969,* University of Illinois Press, Urbana, 1972; Nicholas Lemann, *The Promised Land: The Great Black Migration and How It Changed America,* Vintage Books, New York, 1991.

34. Eric Foner, *A Short History of Reconstruction, 1863–1877,* Harper & Row, New York, 1990, pp. 151–52; Du Bois, *Black Reconstruction,* pp. 77–78; Bennett, *Before the Mayflower,* pp. 214–15; Benjamin Quarles, *The Negro in the Making of America,* Collier Books, New York, 1987, pp. 134–35.

35. Thomas Holt, *Black Over White: Negro Political Leadership in South Carolina During Reconstruction,* University of Illinois Press, Urbana, 1977, p. 1.

36. Eric Foner, "African Americans in Public Office During the Era of Reconstruction: A Profile," *Reconstruction* 2, No. 2 (1993), pp. 20–32.

37. Herbert Hill, "Black Labor and Affirmative Action: An Historical Perspective," in Steven Shulman and William Darity, Jr., eds., *The Question of Discrimination: Racial Inequality in the U.S. Labor Market,* Wesleyan University Press, Middletown, CT, 1989, p. 190.

38. Stephan Thernstrom, *The Other Bostonians: Poverty and Progress in the American Metropolis, 1880–1970,* Harvard University Press, Cambridge, 1973, pp. 194–97.

39. Cited by Foner, *A Short History of Reconstruction,* p. 193.

40. See, e.g., Leon Litwack, *North of Slavery: The Negro in the Free States, 1790–1860,* University of Chicago Press, Chicago, 1961, pp. 60–61, 93–94, 153–70.

41. A sample of the Black Codes in action:

Mississippi declared that "Any freedman, free Negro or mulatto committing riots, routs, affrays, trespasses, malicious mischief and cruel treatment to animals, seditious speeches, insulting gestures, exercising the functions of a minister of the gospel without a license," etc. would be subjected to fines and imprisonment.

Florida made it illegal for blacks to "own, use or keep in possession any bowie-knife, dirk, sword, firearms or ammunition of any kind" on penalty of "whipping not exceeding thirty nine stripes."

For the offenses of "assault upon a white woman, impersonating her husband, raising an insurrection, stealing a horse, a mule or baled cotton," South Carolina decreed capital punishment for blacks.

For a full account, see Du Bois, *Black Reconstruction,* especially pp. 171–72, 176.

42. David M. Chalmers, *Hooded Americanism: The History of the Ku Klux Klan,* Duke University Press, Durham, 1987, pp. 9–10; James Ridgeway, *Blood in the Face: The Ku Klux Klan, Aryan Nation, Nazi Skinheads and the Rise of a New White Culture,* Thunder's Mouth Press, New York, 1990, p. 33.

43. Chalmers, *Hooded Americanism,* p. 9; Thomas Gossett, *Race: The History of an Idea in America,* Southern Methodist University Press, Dallas, 1963, p. 260.

44. Frank Shay, *Judge Lynch: His First Hundred Years,* Patterson Smith, Montclair, NJ, 1969, pp. 20–25.

45. Eugene Genovese estimates, for example, that between 1840 and 1860 approximately three hundred lynchings took place in the country, of which probably less than 10 percent were black. Eugene Genovese, *Roll, Jordan, Roll: The World the Slaves Made,* Vintage Books, New York, 1972, p. 32. According to a table of recorded lynchings compiled by Joe Feagin, approximately 750 white and 730 blacks were lynched between 1882 and 1891. Between 1891 and 1921, however, 510 whites were lynched compared with 2,384 blacks. Joe Feagin, *Racial and Ethnic Relations,* Prentice Hall, Englewood Cliffs, NJ, 2nd edition, 1984, p. 224. For a general account, see John Higham, *Strangers in the Land,* Atheneum Books, New York, 1963.

43. Kenneth Jackson, *The Ku Klux Klan in the City,* Ivan R. Dee Publishers, Chicago, 1992, p. vii.

46. Thomas Dixon, *The Leopard's Spots: A Romance of the White Man's Burden,* Grosset & Dunlap, New York, 1902; Thomas Dixon, *The Clansman: An Historical Romance of the Ku Klux Klan,* Doubleday and Page, New York, 1905.

48. See John Hope Franklin, *Race and History,* Louisiana State University Press, Baton Rouge, 1989, pp. 11–12. Dixon's career is described in Raymond Allen Cook, *Fire From the Flint: The Amazing Careers of Thomas Dixon,* John Blair, Winston-Salem, 1968.

49. Chalmers, *Hooded Americanism,* pp. 25–27; Franklin, *Race and History,* pp. 16–17.

50. Cited by Jackson, *The Ku Klux Klan in the City,* p. 19.

51. Chalmers, *Hooded Americanism,* p. 33.

52. "It must have provided a real thrill to go scooting through the shadowy roads, to meet in pine woods and flog other men. . . . It was perpetual Halloween." See Leonard Cline, "In Darkest Louisiana," *The Nation* 116 (1923), pp. 292–93. See also Chalmers, *Hooded Americanism,* p. 118: "With its highly accented sense of mystery, patriotism, communal guardianship and nocturnal ramblings, the Ku Klux Klan gave to the Klansman the chance to live a second, more fulfilling life within the Invisible Empire. Where else could anyone get so much for ten dollars?"

53. Richard Wright, *White Man, Listen!,* Greenwood Press, Westport, CT, 1957, p. 81.

54. Jackson, *The Ku Klux Klan in the City,* pp. vii–viii, 251; Chalmers, *Hooded Americanism,* p. 57; Bill Stanton, *Klanwatch: Bringing the Ku Klux Klan to Justice,* Mentor Books, New York, 1991, p. 87.

55. Rayford Logan, "The Negro as Portrayed in Representative Northern Magazines and Newspapers," in Barry Schwartz, ed., *White Racism,* Laurel Leaf Books, New York, 1978, pp. 393–95.

56. James Weldon Johnson, *Black Manhattan,* Plenum Publishing, New York, 1991 (first published 1930), p. 93.

57. A. Leon Higginbotham, "Racism in American and South African Courts: Similarities and Differences," *New York University Law Review* 65 (1990), pp. 542–43.

58. Charles Carroll, *The Negro a Beast,* American Book and Bible House, St. Louis, 1900; Charles McCord, *The American Negro as a Dependent, Defective and Delinquent,* Benson Printing, Nashville, 1914; Robert Shufeldt, *The Negro, A Menace to American Civilization,* F. A. Davis, Philadelphia, 1907; Robert Shufeldt, *America's Greatest Problem: The Negro,* F. A. Davis, Philadelphia, 1915.

59. John H. Franklin, *From Slavery to Freedom,* Alfred A. Knopf, New York, 1967, p. 341.

60. Cited by A. Leon Higginbotham in Introduction to Genna Rae McNeil, *Groundwork: Charles Hamilton Houston and the Struggle for Civil Rights,* University of Pennsylvania Press, Philadelphia, 1983, p. xvi.

61. Cited by Lemann, *The Promised Land,* p. 47.

62. For example, when a false rumor appeared in the newspapers that he had invited a Negro to a White House function, President Cleveland responded, "It so happens that I have never in my official position, either when sleeping or waking, alive or dead, on my head or on my heels, dined, lunched, supped or invited to a wedding reception any colored man, woman or child." For a more detailed account, see G. Sinkler, *The Racial Attitudes of American Presidents,* Doubleday, New York, 1971, esp. pp. 225–27. For an account of segregation in federal buildings, see Rayford Logan, *The Betrayal of the Negro,* Macmillan, New York, 1965, esp. p. 361.

63. Donald Nieman, *Promises to Keep: African Americans and the Constitutional Order,* Oxford University Press, New York, 1991, p. 119.

64. Neil McMillen, *Dark Journey: Black Mississippians in the Age of Jim Crow,* University of Illinois Press, Urbana, 1989, p. 234.

65. In the 1880s and 1890s "lynching reached the most staggering proportions ever reached in the history of that crime," C. Vann Woodward writes. Scholars differ somewhat in their estimates of the number of black lynchings, although virtually all estimates fall between two thousand and three thousand. See C. Vann Woodward, *The Strange Career of Jim Crow,* Oxford University Press, New York, 1955, p. 43; Franklin, *From Slavery to Freedom,* p. 439; Gunnar Myrdal, *An American Dilemma,* Harper and Bros., New York, 1962 edition, p. 560.

66. Nieman, *Promises to Keep,* p. 121.

67. W. J. Cash, *The Mind of the South,* Vintage Books, New York, 1991 (first published 1941), p. 113.

68. Joel Williamson, *The Crucible of Race: Black-White Relations in the American South Since Emancipation,* Oxford University Press, New York, 1984, esp. p. 181.

69. Raymond Nixon, *Henry W. Grady: Spokesman of the New South,* Alfred A. Knopf, New York, 1943, pp. 213–15.

70. Cited by Woodward, *The Strange Career of Jim Crow,* p. 68.

71. *Plessy v. Ferguson,* 163 U.S. 537 (1896).

72. "One of the strangest things about the career of Jim Crow was that the system was born in the North and reached an advanced age before moving South in force." Woodward points out that under slavery, segregation of the races made no sense at all. But just when most Northern states abolished their segregation laws, Southern states adopted them to keep free Negroes "in their place." Woodward, *The Strange Career of Jim Crow,* esp. pp. 12–13, 17–19; see also Litwack, *North of Slavery,* p. 97.

73. Hinton Helper, *Nojoque,* G. W. Carleton, New York, 1867, p. 251.

74. George Fitzhugh, *Sociology for the South,* A. Morris, Richmond, 1854, p. 96; George Fitzhugh, *Cannibals All!,* Harvard University Press, Cambridge, 1960 (first published 1857), p. 69.

75. Williamson, *The Crucible of Race,* p. 254.

76. The philosophy of the Southern conservatives is discussed in George Fredrickson, *The Black Image in the White Mind: The Debate on Afro-American Character and Destiny, 1817–1914,* Harper & Row, New York, 1971.

77. The pervasiveness of segregation is documented in Woodward, *The Strange Career of Jim Crow.* For a case study of Jim Crow in Mississippi, see McMillen, *Dark Journey.* See also Nieman, *Promises to Keep,* pp. 108–9; John Ogbu, *Minority Education and Caste,* Harcourt Brace Jovanovich, New York, 1978, p. 121.

78. Jennifer Roback, "The Political Economy of Segregation: The case of Segregated Streetcars," *Journal of Economic History* 46 (1986), pp. 893–917; see also Edward L. Ayers, *The Promise of the New South: Life After Reconstruction,* Oxford University Press, New York, 1992, p. 143.

79. For a discussion of the one-drop rule, which he terms the principle of "hypodescent," see Marvin Harris, *Patterns of Race in the Americas,* Greenwood Press, Westport, CT, 1964, p. 56.

80. Cited by Williamson, *The Crucible of Race,* p. 147.

81. Winthrop Jordan, *White Over Black: American Attitudes Toward the Negro, 1550–1812,* University of North Carolina Press, Chapel Hill, 1968, pp. 171–73.

82. Charles Chesnutt, *The House Behind the Cedars,* Penguin Books, New York, 1993 (first published 1900), p. xiv.

83. Joel Williamson, *New People: Miscegenation and Mulattoes in the United States,* Free Press, New York, 1980, p. 62.

84. Ibid., p. 114.

85. Thomas Sowell, *Markets and Minorities,* Basic Books, New York, 1981, p. 61.

86. John Sibley Butler, *Entrepreneurship and Self-Help Among Black Americans: A Reconsideration of Race and Economics,* State University of New York Press, Albany, 1991; see also Abram Harris, *The Negro as Capitalist,* Arno Press, New York, 1936.

87. See Oscar Handlin, *The Newcomers,* Harvard University Press, Cambridge, 1959.

88. Reynolds Farley and Walter Allen, *The Color Line and the Quality of Life in America,* Oxford University Press, New York, 1989, p. 190.

89. See, e.g., Cary D. Wintz, *Black Culture and the Harlem Renaissance,* Rice University Press, Houston, 1988.

90. Cited by Nathan Huggins, *Harlem Renaissance,* Oxford University Press, New York, 1971, p. 24.

91. Among those of mulatto or mixed-race ancestry were Countee Cullen, Lena Horne, Langston Hughes, Jean Toomer, and James Weldon Johnson.

92. See Williamson, *New People,* p. 117.

93. For an insightful commentary on this subject, see Albert Murray, *The Omni-Americans: Black Experience and American Culture,* Outerbridge & Dienstfrey, New York, 1970.

94. Cited by Johnson, *Black Manhattan,* p. 270.

95. Alphonso Pinkney, *White Hate Crimes,* Third World Press, Chicago, 1994, p. 29; Martin Kilson, "Anatomy of Black Conservatism," *Transition,* Issue 59 (1994), p. 15.

96. Louis Harlan, *Booker T. Washington: The Wizard of Tuskegee, 1901–1915,* Oxford University Press, New York, 1983.

97. David Levering Lewis, *W.E.B. Du Bois: Biography of a Race,* Henry Holt, New York, 1993.

98. "I have been a slave once in my life—a slave in body," Washington wrote. "But I long since resolved that no inducement and no influence would ever make me a slave in soul." See Booker T. Washington and W. E. B. Du Bois, *The Negro in the South,* George W. Jacobs, New York, 1907, p. 10.

99. Booker T. Washington, *Up From Slavery,* Penguin Books, New York, 1986, p. 201.

100. Ibid., p. 223.

101. Ibid., p. 208; Booker T. Washington, "The Awakening of the Negro," *The Atlantic Monthly,* September 1896.

102. Lewis, *W.E.B. Du Bois,* p. 26.

103. Ibid., esp. p. 80.

104. For a portrait of Du Bois as a person as well as a sympathetic analysis of his agenda, see Arnold Rampersad, *The Art and Imagination of W. E. B. Du Bois,* Schocken Books, New York, 1990.

105. W. E. B. Du Bois, *The Souls of Black Folk,* Penguin Books, New York, 1969.

106. W. E. B. Du Bois, "The Talented Tenth," in Booker T. Washington et al., *The Negro Problem,* Arno Press, New York, 1969, p. 33.

107. Philip S. Foner, ed., *W.E.B. Du Bois Speaks: Speeches and Addresses 1890–1919,* Pathfinder Books, New York, p. 4.

108. Booker T. Washington, "For Old and New Students," speech to student body at Tuskegee delivered during the school term of 1913–1914, cited in Emmett J. Scott and Lyman Beecher Stowe, *Booker T. Washington: Builder of a Civilization,* Doubleday, Garden City, NY, 1917, p. 231.

109. Washington and Du Bois, *The Negro in the South,* pp. 181–82.

110. Booker T. Washington, "The Southern Sociological Congress as a Factor for Social Welfare," delivered May 8, 1914 in Memphis, Tennessee, reprinted in E. Davidson Washington, ed., *Selected Speeches of Booker T. Washington,* Doubleday, Garden City, NY, 1932, p. 237.

111. W. E. B. Du Bois, "The Conservation of Races," in Foner, *W.E.B. Du Bois Speaks,* pp. 82–84. Du Bois also wrote, "Unless we conquer our present vices they will conquer us. We are diseased, we are developing criminal tendencies, and an alarmingly large percentage of our men and women are sexually impure." See also W. E. B. Du Bois, *The Negro American Family,* MIT Press, Cambridge, 1970, p. 37;

W. E. B. Du Bois, *The Philadelphia Negro,* University of Pennsylvania Press, Philadelphia, 1899, pp. 389–90.

112. Foner, *W. E. B. Du Bois Speaks,* p. 176.

113. Washington, *Up From Slavery,* pp. 41, 229.

114. W. E. B. Du Bois, "The Conservation of Races," American Negro Academy Paper, 1897. For an analysis of the endorsement of race thinking implicit and sometimes explicit in this paper, see Anthony Appiah, "The Uncompleted Argument: Du Bois and the Illusion of Race," in Henry Louis Gates, Jr., ed., *"Race," Writing and Difference,* University of Chicago Press, Chicago, 1986, pp. 21–37.

115. Rampersad, *The Art and Imagination of W. E. B. Du Bois,* p. 74; Williamson, *The Crucible of Race,* p. 403.

116. Du Bois invited Boas to a conference on the Negro at Atlanta University in 1905; Boas returned later that year to give the graduation address. See Carl Degler, *In Search of Human Nature,* Oxford University Press, New York, 1991, p. 76.

117. Du Bois, *The Souls of Black Folk,* p. 45.

118. Foner, *W. E. B. Du Bois Speaks,* p. 78.

119. Harlan, *Booker T. Washington,* pp. 244–51.

120. *The Crisis,* May 1911, p. 24.

121. "The Niagara Movement," statement of the delegates to the First General Meeting, July 11-13, 1905; reprinted in Leslie H. Fishel, Jr. and Benjamin Quarles, eds., *The Black American: A Documentary History,* Scott, Foresman, Glenview, IL, 1967, pp. 372–74. See also Foner, *W.E.B. Du Bois Speaks,* pp. 43, 47, 52, 56, 171–72, 219–20; Myrdal, *An American Dilemma,* p. 820; Johnson, *Black Manhattan,* p. 141. Johnson writes, "The platform adopted (by the NAACP) was practically the same as that of the Niagara Movement."

122. Franz Boas, "The Outlook of the American Negro," in George W. Stocking, Jr., ed., *The Shaping of American Anthropology, 1883–1911: A Franz Boas Reader,* Basic Books, New York, 1974, pp. 310–16; see also Richard Kluger, *Simple Justice: The History of Brown v. Board of Education and Black America's Struggle for Equality,* Vintage Books, New York, 1977, p. 98.

123. See David M. Chalmers, *Hooded Americanism.* Whereas the Klan had between two and five million members in the mid 1920s, Chalmers estimates that by 1930 membership was down to a few hundred thousand.

124. "In 1936 and 1937, the number of Negroes lynched was eight. The following year it was reduced to six. In 1939 it dropped to three." Cash, *The Mind of the South,* p. 371; see also Walter A. Jackson, *Gunnar Myrdal and America's Conscience: Social Engineering and Racial Liberalism, 1938–1987,* University of North Carolina Press, Chapel Hill, 1990, p. 7.

125. "The war led to increased black migration to urban and Northern areas, provided greater economic opportunities for blacks, brought many blacks and whites into close social contact for the first time, broadened the social and political horizons of many blacks, and led increasingly to the views that racist ideology and practice were evils inconsistent with basic democratic principles." Gerald Jaynes and Robin M. Williams, eds., *A Common Destiny: Blacks and American Society,* National Academy Press, Washington, DC, 1989, p. 60.

126. As former NAACP head Roy Wilkins put it, "It was grim to have a young black man in uniform get an orientation in the morning on wiping out Nazi bigotry and that same evening be told he could buy a soft drink only in the colored post exchange." Roy Wilkins, *The Autobiography of Roy Wilkins,* Viking, New York, 1982, pp. 184–85.

127. Cited by Ronald Takaki, *A Different Mirror: A History of Multicultural America,* Little, Brown, Boston, 1993, p. 374.

128. Lerone Bennett, Jr., *The Shaping of Black America,* Penguin Books, New York, 1993, p. 273; Hugh Davis Graham, *The Civil Rights Era: Origins and Development of National Policy,* Oxford University Press, New York, 1990, pp. 10–11.

129. Franklin, *Race and History,* p. 146.

130. Manning Marable, *Race, Reform and Rebellion: The Second Reconstruction of Black America, 1945–1982,* University Press of Mississippi, Jackson, 1989, p. 15; Harvard Sitkoff, *The Struggle for Black Equality 1954–1992,* Hill & Wang, New York, 1993, p. 11.

131. *Shelley v. Kraemer,* 334 U.S. 1 (1948).

132. Robert W. Mullen, *Blacks in America's Wars,* Monad Press, New York, 1973, pp. 60–61.

133. Michael Sovern, *Legal Restraints on Racial Discrimination in Employment,* Columbia University Press, New York, 1966, pp. 10–17; Graham, *The Civil Rights Era,* pp. 9–14.

134. During the period from 1930 to 1950, black life expectancy rose from forty-nine years to sixty-one years—eight years below the white rate. The proportion of blacks in school went up from 60 percent to 75 percent—10 percent below the white rate. Black college enrollment went from 27,000 to more than 110,000. And black family income rose from $489 in 1930 to more than $2,000 in 1950, which was for the first time over 50 percent of the average family income for whites. See *Historical Statistics of the United States, Colonial Times to 1970,* U.S. Department of Commerce, Washington, DC, 1975, Vol. I, pp. 55–56, 303, 370.

135. *Plessy v. Ferguson,* 163 U.S. 537 (1896); Editorial, "Justice Harlan Concurring," *New York Times,* May 23, 1954.

136. *Plessy v. Ferguson,* ibid. at 559.

137. Kull, *The Color-Blind Constitution,* pp. 113–26.

138. See, e.g., McNeil, *Groundwork.*

139. In 1930, for example, Southern school spending on black students per capita was only 37 percent of what it was for white students. The average salary for black teachers was substantially below, sometimes as low as one half, that for white teachers. Black teachers had less training and education, by and large, than their white counterparts. Black schools had a shorter academic year as well. Moreover, black students had grown accustomed to taking long rides to schools which were often in poor physical condition, where they used secondhand textbooks, many of them out of date. See John Ogbu, *Minority Education and Caste,* pp. 113–14, 118; Jaynes and Williams, *A Common Destiny,* p. 29; Stanley Lieberson, *A Piece of the Pie: Blacks and White Immigrants Since 1880,* University of California Press, Berkeley, 1980, p. 141, 144.

140. Ogbu, *Minority Education and Caste,* p. 118.

141. One of Thurgood Marshall's first victories as NAACP counsel was to compel the University of Maryland, which had rejected his own application on racial grounds many years earlier, to admit its first black students. When Donald Murray enrolled at the Baltimore campus in the fall of 1935, the acerbic columnist H. L. Mencken observed, "There will be an Ethiop among the Aryans when the larval Blackstones assemble next Wednesday." Cited by Kluger, *Simple Justice,* p. 192.

Another NAACP victory came in 1938. After graduating from Lincoln University in Missouri, Lloyd Gaines applied for admission to the University of Missouri Law School. Since blacks were not allowed there, the state asked Gaines to go to school out of state, or else they would establish a law school on demand at Lincoln University. With NAACP assistance and under Charles Hamilton Houston's direction, Gaines sued, and the Supreme Court decided in his favor in *Missouri ex rel. Gaines v. Canada,* on the grounds that no makeshift law school at Lincoln could compensate for the facilities and opportunities of a full-fledged institution like the state university. *Missouri ex rel. Gaines v. Canada,* 305 U.S. 337 (1938).

A little over a decade later, in *Sweatt v. Painter,* the Supreme Court agreed with the argument presented by the NAACP's Marshall on behalf of his black client, a mail carrier named Herman Sweatt. The court ruled that Sweatt could attend the University of Texas Law School unless the state provided for him a black law school with facilities and privileges comparable in every significant respect, including such intangibles as the university's "standing in the community, traditions and prestige." *Sweatt v. Painter,* 339 U.S. 629 (1950).

142. Kluger, *Simple Justice,* p. 314.

143. Max Deutscher and Isidor Chein, "The Psychological Effects of Enforced Segregation: A Survey of Social Science Opinion," *Journal of Psychology* 26 (1948), p. 259.

144. Kluger, *Simple Justice,* pp. 556–57.

145. Ibid., p. 353; see also Kenneth Clark, *Prejudice and Your Child,* Wesleyan University Press, Middletown, CT, 1963; Kenneth Clark, "Racial Progress and Retreat: A Personal Memoir," in Herbert Hill and James Jones, eds., *Race in America: The Struggle for Equality,* University of Wisconsin Press, Madison, 1993.

146. Daniel Goleman, "Black Child's Self-View Is Still Low, Study Finds," *New York Times,* August 31, 1987, p. A-13.

147. *Brown v. Board of Education of Topeka,* 347 U.S. 483 (1954).

148. Among the works cited in the famous Footnote 11 are Kenneth Clark, *Effect of Prejudice and Discrimination on Personality Development,* Midcentury White House Conference on Children and Youth, 1950; Deutscher and Chein, "The Psychological Effects of Enforced Segregation; and Myrdal, *An American Dilemma.*

149. *Brown v. Board of Education,* 347 U.S. 483 (1954) at 494.

150. Kull, *The Color-Blind Constitution,* pp. 154–55.

151. Cited by Sitkoff, *The Struggle for Black Equality,* p. 22.

152. Martin Luther King, Jr., *I Have A Dream: Writings and Speeches That Changed the World,* edited by James Melvin Washington, HarperSanFrancisco, 1992, p. 24.

153. Cited in Washington, ed., *A Testament of Hope,* p. 211. "Many great anthropologists, Margaret Mead and Ruth Benedict and Melville Herskovits and others, have pointed out that there are no superior races and no inferior races."

154. Ibid., pp. 98, 105, 151.

155. King's moral universalism is clearly articulated in his Nobel Prize acceptance speech. See ibid., pp. 224–26.

156. These phrases are from King's "I Have A Dream" speech, reprinted in ibid., pp. 289–302.

157. Cited in Garrow, *Bearing the Cross,* p. 156.

158. Cited in Washington, ed., *A Testament of Hope,* pp. 212, 246, 489–90.

Chapter 6. The Race Merchants

1. Cited by William O. Douglas, *The Court Years, 1939–1975,* Random House, New York, 1980, p. 149.

2. J. Paul Brownridge, "Economic Rights: A Matter of Access for All," *Los Angeles Times,* August 23, 1993.

3. Patrice Gaines and DeNeen Brown, "Before March, a Search for Unity, Direction," *Washington Post,* August 28, 1993, p. A-8.

4. Henry Louis Gates, Jr., "Two Nations . . . Both Black," *Forbes,* September 14, 1992, p. 138.

5. Carl Upchurch, "I Still Have A Dream," *New York Times,* August 27, 1993, p. A-29.

6. Joel Williamson, *New People: Miscegenation and Mulattoes in the United States,* Free Press, New York, 1980, p. 2.

7. Mary C. Waters, *Ethnic Options: Choosing Identities in America,* University of California Press, Berkeley, 1990, p. 18.

8. F. James Davis, *Who Is Black? One Nation's Definition,* Pennsylvania State University Press, University Park, 1991, pp. 137, 139, 168, 180.

9. Nathan Glazer, *Ethnic Dilemmas, 1964–1982,* Harvard University Press, Cambridge, 1983, p. 159–60.

10. Cited in Ellis Cose, "One Drop of Bloody History," *Newsweek,* February 13, 1995, p. 72.

11. Editorial, "A Dinosaur Ruling," *New York Times,* June 30, 1993, p. A-14.

12. The movement, after all, was a spontaneous and temporary coalition of blacks (and whites) from all walks of life who sought a specific goal: the removal of race from the fabric of American law. This objective was achieved, yet new objectives have taken its place.

13. Cited by Tom Kenworthy, "Whites See Jobs on Line in Debate," *Washington Post,* June 4, 1991, p. A-4.

14. Michael Eric Dyson, *Making Malcolm: The Myth and Meaning of Malcolm X,* Oxford University Press, New York, 1995, p. xiii.

15. Ellis Cose, "Interview: Orlando Bagwell," *Newsweek,* January 7, 1994, p. 65.

16. Malcolm X, *The Autobiography of Malcolm X,* as told to Alex Haley, Ballantine Books, New York, 1964.

17. Malcolm X, *By Any Means Necessary,* Pathfinder Books, New York, 1970, p. vii.

18. Malcolm X, *Malcolm X Speaks: Selected Speeches and Statements,* Pathfinder Books, New York, 1965, p. 26.

19. Malcolm X, *The End of White World Supremacy: Four Speeches by Malcolm X,* edited by Imam Benjamin Karim (Benjamin 2X), Arcade Publishing, New York, 1971, pp. 51–63. For a discussion of how Malcolm's views may have been modified toward the end of his life see George Breitman, *The Last Year of Malcolm X,* Pathfinder Books, New York, 1967.

20. Malcolm X, *Malcolm X Speaks,* p. 9.

21. Bruce Perry, *Malcolm: The Life of a Man Who Changed Black America,* Station Hill, Barrytown, NY, 1992, p. 211.

22. Cited by Harvard Sitkoff, *The Struggle for Black Equality, 1954–1992,* Hill & Wang, New York, 1993, p. 119.

23. Malcolm X, *By Any Means Necessary,* p. 120; Malcolm X, *The Autobiography of Malcolm X,* p. 245.

24. "The only way the black people caught up in this society can be saved is not to integrate into this corrupt society, but to separate from it, to a land of our own." Malcolm X, *The Autobiography of Malcolm X,* p. 246.

25. Cornel West, *Keeping Faith: Philosophy and Race in America,* Routledge, New York, 1993, pp. 280–81.

26. James Farmer, *Freedom—When?,* Random House, New York, 1965, p. 87.

27. C. Vann Woodward, *The Strange Career of Jim Crow,* Oxford University Press, New York, 1974, (first published in 1955), pp. 197–98.

28. Philip S. Foner, ed., *The Black Panthers Speak,* J. B. Lippincott, Philadelphia, 1970, pp. 1, 3; see also Sitkoff, *The Struggle for Black Equality,* p. 204.

29. Stokely Carmichael and Charles V. Hamilton, *Black Power: The Politics of Liberation in America,* Vintage Books, New York, 1967, pp. xi, 5, 41, 44, 54.

30. James Cone, *Black Theology and Black Power,* Seabury Press, New York, 1969, p. 18.

31. Julius Lester, *Look Out, Whitey! Black Power's Gon' Get Your Mama,* Dial Press, New York, 1968, p. 137.

32. Henry Hampton and Steve Fayer, *Voices of Freedom: An Oral History of the Civil Rights Movement from the 1950s Through the 1980s,* Bantam Books, New York, 1991, pp. 571–72, 576.

33. Woodward, *The Strange Career of Jim Crow,* pp. 193–94.

34. Sitkoff, *The Struggle for Black Equality,* pp. 185–89; Manning Marable, *Race, Reform and Rebellion: The Second Reconstruction in Black America,* University Press of Mississippi, Jackson, 1989, pp. 102–3.

35. Gary Orfield, *The Reconstruction of Southern Education,* Wiley Books, New York, 1968, p. 1.

36. Julian Bond, introduction to Juan Williams, *Eyes on the Prize: America's Civil Rights Years, 1954–1965,* Viking, New York, 1974, p. xii.

37. Woodward, *The Strange Career of Jim Crow,* p. 187.

38. Nicholas Lemann, *The Promised Land: The Great Black Migration and How It Changed America,* Vintage Books, New York, 1991.

39. Woodward, *The Strange Career of Jim Crow,* p. 192.

40. Cited by David Garrow, *Bearing the Cross: Martin Luther King and the Southern Christian Leadership Conference,* Vintage Books, New York, 1988, p. 540.

41. *Report of the National Advisory Commission on Civil Disorders,* New York Times Company, New York, 1968, pp. 2, 10–12.

42. Ibid., p. 2.

43. Martin Luther King, Jr., *Where Do We Go from Here: Chaos or Community,* Beacon Press, Boston, 1968, p. 34.

44. Bayard Rustin, "From Protest to Politics: The Future of the Civil Rights Movement," *Commentary,* February 1965, pp. 25–27.

45. Daniel Patrick Moynihan, *The Negro Family: The Case for National Action,* U.S. Department of Labor, Office of Policy Planning and Research, March 1965, summary introduction.

46. *Regents of the University of California v. Bakke,* 438 U.S. 265 (1978).

47. Michael Rosenfeld, *Affirmative Action and Justice: A Philosophical and Constitutional Inquiry,* Yale University Press, New Haven, 1991, p. 45.

48. Richard Cohen, "Diversity Kick," *Washington Post,* January 13, 1994.

49. Clifford Alexander, "What Affirmative Action Really Means," *New York Times,* December 16, 1991.

50. Benjamin Hooks, "Self-Help Just Won't Do It All," *Los Angeles Times,* July 10, 1990, p. B-7.

51. Cited by Jimmie Briggs, "Hope of Our Past," *Emerge,* March 1994, p. 23.

52. Lyndon Johnson, "Howard University Address," June 4, 1965, reprinted in Lee Rainwater and William L. Yancey, *The Moynihan Report and the Politics of Controversy,* MIT Press, Cambridge, 1967, p. 126.

53. See, e.g., Burke Marshall, "A Comment on the Nondiscrimination Principle in a Nation of Minorities," *Yale Law Journal* 93 (1984), pp. 1006–1007. "The problem is that ours is not an ideal society. Discrimination is not . . . against individuals. It is discrimination against a people. And the remedy, therefore, has to correct and cure and compensate for the discrimination against the people and not just the discrimination against identifiable persons. . . . Disadvantages to white males need not be tested by the same grudging judicial standards as racial discrimination against blacks."

54. Whitney Young of the National Urban League prepared a position paper in 1963 in which he insisted that "employers who throughout the years have never considered a Negro for top jobs in their institutions must now recruit qualified Negro employees and give preference to their employment." But this proposal was not adopted by the trustees of the Urban League. By contrast, Gordon Carey, national program director for the Congress of Racial Equality, said publicly that "CORE has begun recently to change its line on the national level. We used to talk simply of merit employment. But now CORE is talking in terms of compensatory hiring." Cited by Hugh Davis Graham, *The Civil Rights Era: Origins and Development of National Policy,* Oxford University Press, New York, 1990, pp. 105, 111-12.

55. Senator Harrison Williams: "How can the language of equality favor one race over another? Equality can have only one meaning. Those who say that equality means favoritism do violence to common sense." *Congressional Record* 110 (1964), p. 8921.

Senators Case and Clark: "There is no requirement in Title VII that an employer maintain a racial balance in his work force. On the contrary, any deliberate attempt to maintain a racial balance, whatever such a balance may be, would involve a violation of Title VII because maintaining a balance would require an employer to hire or to refuse to hire on the basis of race." *Congressional Record* 110 (1964), p. 7213.

Senator Hubert Humphrey: "We seek to give people an opportunity to be hired on the basis of merit. Title VII does not limit the employer's freedom to hire, fire, promote or demote for any reason, or no reason, so long as his action is not based on race, color, religion, national origin or sex." *Congressional Record* 110 (1964), pp. 5423, 6548–49.

For a debate over the meaning of Title VII of the Civil Rights Act of 1964, see *United Steelworkers v. Weber,* 443 U.S. 193, especially the dissent by Justice William Rehnquist, which reviews the history in some detail.

56. *Congressional Record* 110 (1964), p. 7420.

57. Civil Rights Act of 1964, 42 U.S.C. Section 2000e-2(j).

58. McGeorge Bundy, "The Issue Before the Court: Who Gets Ahead in America," *The Atlantic,* November 1977, pp. 44–45.

59. Cited by Lesley Oelsner, "More Blacks Turning to the Study of Law," *New York Times,* October 9, 1969.

60. Nancy Hicks, "Califano Says Quotas Are Necessary to Reduce Bias in Jobs and Schools," *New York Times,* March 18, 1977, pp. A-1, A-13.

61. Stephen Steinberg, "Et Tu Brute: The Liberal Betrayal of the Black Liberation Struggle," *Reconstruction* 2, No. 1 (1992), p. 32.

62. Graham, *The Civil Rights Era,* p. 117.

63. William O. Douglas, dissenting opinion, *DeFunis v. Odegaard,* 416 U.S. 312, 341 (1974).

64. "Having found support in the Constitution for equality, they now claim support for inequality under the same Constitution." Alexander Bickel, *The Morality of Consent,* Yale University Press, New Haven, 1975, p. 133.

65. See, e.g., Rosenfeld, *Affirmative Action and Justice;* Gertrude Ezorsky, *Racism and Justice: The Case for Affirmative Action,* Cornell University Press, Ithaca, 1991; Alfred Blumrosen, *Modern Law: The Law Transmission System and Equal Employment Opportunity,* University of Wisconsin Press, Madison, 1993; Roy Brooks, *Rethinking the American Race Problem,* University of California Press, Berkeley, 1992; J. Skelly Wright, "Color-Blind Theories and Color-Conscious Remedies," *University of Chicago Law Review* 47 (1980), pp. 213–45; James L. Jones, "The Bugaboo of Employment Quotas," *Wisconsin Law Review* 278 (1970), pp. 340–403; Alfred W. Blumrosen, "Strangers in Paradise: *Griggs v. Duke Power Co.* and the Concept of Employment Discrimination," *Michigan Law Review* 71 (1972), p. 59; Ronald Dworkin, "How to Read the Civil Rights Act," in Ronald Dworkin, ed., *A Matter of Principle,* Harvard University Press, Cambridge, 1985; Randall Kennedy, "Persuasion and Distrust: A Comment on the Affirmative Action Debate," *Harvard Law Review* 99 (1986), p. 1335.

66. See, e.g., Bickel, *The Morality of Consent;* "An Interview with Bayard Rustin," *New Perspectives,* Winter 1985; Morris Abram, "Affirmative Action: Fair Shakers and Social Engineers," *Harvard Law Review* 99 (1986), p. 1312; William Van Alstyne, "Rites of Passage: Race, the Supreme Court and the Constitution," *University of*

Chicago Law Review 46 (1979), p. 775; Nathan Glazer, *Affirmative Discrimination: Ethnic Inequality and Public Policy,* Basic Books, New York, 1978; Daniel Patrick Moynihan, "State v. Academe," *Harper's,* December 1980; Hubert Humphrey, *Beyond Civil Rights: A New Day for Equality,* Random House, New York, 1968.

67. *International Brotherhood of Teamsters v. United States,* 431 U.S. 324 (1977).

68. Writing as late as 1972, Alfred Blumrosen asserted that "the argument for population parity among journeymen electricians must be construed as an argument for a rapid increase in the number of minority electricians." In other words, Blumrosen resisted strict enforcement of a proportional representation standard, but argued that some standard was necessary in order to dramatically boost black representation. Blumrosen, "Strangers in Paradise," p. 63.

69. Cited by Barry L. Goldstein, "The Historical Case for Goals and Timetables," *New Perspectives,* U.S. Commission on Civil Rights, Summer 1984, p. 20.

70. "The contractor will take affirmative action to ensure that applicants are employed and that employees are treated during employment without regard to their race, color, religion, sex or national origin." This is a kind of kamikaze sentence, in that it begins by calling for special treatment or affirmative action, but that special treatment, it turns out, is a means to assure nondiscrimination. In other words, special treatment is a means to the end of no special treatment.

71. Cited by Thomas B. Edsall and Mary D. Edsall, *Chain Reaction: The Impact of Race, Rights and Taxes on American Politics,* W. W. Norton, New York, 1992, p. 86.

72. Laurence Silberman, "The Road to Racial Quotas," *Wall Street Journal,* August 11, 1977, p. 14.

73. *Griggs v. Duke Power Co,* 401 U.S. 424 (1971).

74. At an EEOC meeting on December 22, 1977, Eleanor Holmes Norton outlined her strategy. "We do not see evidence that validated tests have in fact gotten black and brown bodies into places. . . . Therefore, I see some very positive advantages in encouraging an employer to look at what the ultimate goal is. That is to say, did your workforce have some minorities and females before the test was validated or does it have an appreciable number now that the test has been validated? And if you really don't want to go through that, but you are interested in getting excluded people in your workforce, we would encourage you to do that." EEOC transcript; see also Robert Detlefsen, *Civil Rights Under Reagan,* Institute for Contemporary Studies, San Francisco, 1991, p. 37.

75. "In order to achieve such interim goals or targets, an employer may consider race, sex and/or national origin in making selections from among qualified or qualifiable applicants." Equal Employment Opportunity Commission, *Affirmative Action Guidelines,* January 19, 1979, p. 4425.

76. Herman Belz, *Equality Transformed: A Quarter Century of Affirmative Action,* Transaction Publishers, New Brunswick, 1991, p. 21.

77. In the *Bakke* decision, the Supreme Court in 1978 allowed Bakke to be admitted to the medical school at University of California at Davis, but upheld the constitutionality of racial preferences as one factor in decision making. Voluntary race-based quotas specifying 50 percent black representation in training programs

were approved by the Supreme Court in the *Weber* decision in 1979, which held that Title VII does not prohibit discrimination against whites. In 1980, the court in *Fullilove v. Klutznick* upheld as constitutional a federal quota statute requiring at least 10 percent of federal funds granted for local public works to go to minority-owned contractors and subcontractors. In *United States v. Paradise* the Court in 1987 permitted the Alabama State Police force to enforce a color-coded hiring system to overcome the present effects of past discrimination. The *Croson* decision of 1989 struck down a Richmond, Virginia law mandating quotas but allowed that minority preferences were legal as long as they were narrowly crafted to remedy the present consequences of past discrimination within the institution. The next year the Supreme Court announced that the rights of whites are not violated if the Federal Communications Commission grants a range of racial preferences in selling radio and TV stations to minorities for the purpose of promoting "broadcast diversity." See *Regents of the University of California v. Bakke,* 438 U.S. 265 (1978); *United Steelworkers of America v. Weber,* 443 U.S. 193 (1979); *Fullilove v. Klutznick,* 448 U.S. 448 (1980), *United States v. Paradise,* 480 U.S. 149 (1987); *City of Richmond v. J.A. Croson,* 488 U.S. 469 (1989); *Metro Broadcasting v. F.C.C.,* 497 U.S. 547 (1990). In *Adarand Constructors v. Pena* the Supreme Court in June 1995 ruled that federal affirmative action programs must survive "strict scrutiny," that is, they must be narrowly drawn to remedy past and present discrimination within the particular field in which they operate.

78. Civil Rights Act of 1991, Public Law 102-166.

79. Burt Soloman, "Clinton's Gang, " *National Journal,* January 16, 1993; Associated Press, "Starting to Look a Bit More Like America," *Los Angeles Times,* December 12, 1992, p. B-7.

80. Pierre Van Den Berghe, "Encountering American Race Relations," in John Stanfield, ed., *A History of Race Relations Research,* Sage Publications, Newbury Park, CA, 1993, p. 244.

81. Thurgood Marshall asserted, "The only thing that the court is dealing with is whether or not race can be used. What we want from the court is the striking down of race." Later, in a discussion with Justice Felix Frankfurter, Marshall said, "Whatever district lines they draw, if the lines are drawn on a natural basis, without regard to race or color, then I think that nobody would have any complaint." 347 U.S. 483, Brief for Appellants on Reargument. Cited by Graham, *The Civil Rights Era,* p. 370. See also Diane Ravitch, "The Ambiguous Legacy of *Brown v. Board of Education,*" *New Perspectives,* Summer 1994, p. 10; Mark Tushnet, *Making Civil Rights Law: Thurgood Marshall and the Supreme Court, 1936–1961,* Oxford University Press, New York, 1994, p. 177.

82. "Classifications and distinctions based on race or color have no moral or legal validity in our society." NAACP brief, *Sipuel v. Board of Regents of the University of Oklahoma,* 332 U.S. 631 (1948).

83. Leon Friedman, ed., *Argument: The Oral Argument Before the Supreme Court in Brown v. Board of Education of Topeka,* Chelsea House, New York, 1969, p. 47, 375, 402; Andrew Kull, *The Color Blind Constitution,* Harvard University Press, Cambridge, 1992, pp. 146–49.

84. White Citizens Councils issued threats. The Ku Klux Klan converted these into bloody execution. Leading southern politicians issued a manifesto pledging to resist enforcement of the court's ruling. Many districts in the South passed so-called pupil placement rules and other devices which were race-neutral in appearance but could be administered to maintain segregation. (Pupil placement laws call for school assignment to be based on "the suitability of established curricula," "the adequacy of a pupil's academic preparation," "the possiblity of breaches of the peace or ill will," and other criteria seemingly designed to permit the exclusion of blacks.) Some counties shut down their public schools altogether rather than comply with the mandate of the *Brown* decision. The Southern resistance is described in detail in Raymond Wolters, *The Burden of Brown: Thirty Years of School Desegregation,* University of Tennessee Press, Knoxville, 1984; see also Richard Kluger, *Simple Justice: The History of Brown v. Board of Education and Black America's Struggle for Equality,* Vintage Books, New York, 1977.

85. In Alabama, Georgia, Louisiana, Mississippi, and the Carolinas, "The rule of segregation remained unbroken." Woodward, *The Strange Career of Jim Crow,* pp. 160–61; see also Jennifer Hochschild, *The New American Dilemma: Liberal Democracy and School Desegregation,* Yale University Press, New Haven, 1984, p. 27.

86. King advocated an end to state-sponsored segregation; integration for him was a moral goal which he hoped that Americans over time would freely choose for themselves. See James Melvin Washington, ed., *A Testament of Hope: The Essential Writings of Martin Luther King, Jr,* HarperSanFrancisco, 1986, pp. 118, 123.

87. This example is given by Walter Williams, "Civil Rightspeak," *New Perspectives,* Winter-Spring 1986, p. 15.

88. "Desegregation means the assignment of students to public schools and within such schools without regard to their race, color, religion or national origin, but desegregation shall not mean the assignment of students to public schools in order to overcome racial imbalance." Section 407, Civil Rights Act of 1964.

89. "The distinction between the right and its exercise is the basis for the distinction between the public and private or between state and society that characterizes constitutional democracy. By means of this distinction, government is limited because it acts for society, that is, for citizens in their private capacities; it facilitates the exercise of those capacities but does not prescribe how they are to be exercised. Government remains limited insofar as it maintains and respects the distinction between securing rights, which is the business of government, and exercising them, which is not." Harvey Mansfield, *America's Constitutional Soul,* Johns Hopkins University Press, Baltimore, 1991, p. 93.

90. In *United States v. Jefferson County,* a 1966 case decided in the Fifth Circuit Court, Justice John Minor Wisdom displayed all the usual symptoms. Scorning "the supposed difference between desegregation and integration," he impatiently asserted, "The only school desegregation plan that meets constitutional standards is one that works." He then outlined his underlying legal philosophy. "The Constitution is both color blind and color conscious . . . But the Constitution is color conscious to prevent discrimination being perpetuated and to undo the effects of past discrimination. The

criterion is the relevancy of color to a legitimate governmental purpose." See *United States v. Jefferson County Board of Education,* 272 F. 2nd 836 (Fifth Circuit, 1966).

91. *Green v. School Board of New Kent County,* 391 U.S. 430 (1968). Coincidentally, this was the same year affirmative action was introduced by the Nixon administration in the Philadelphia Plan. At the behest of the NAACP, the Court found that a Virginia county freedom-of-choice plan allowing parents to send their children to any school they wanted would violate constitutional desegregation standards if it did not result in integrated student populations. Just as hiring goals and timetables were justified by invoking the noble goal of integrating the work force, so also forced racial reassignment was defended by the court by demanding that "the schools must take affirmative action to integrate their student bodies." Thus *Green* performed the legal spadework for subsequent decisions that would mandate school busing.

92. "All things being equal, with no history of discrimination, it might well be desirable to assign pupils to schools nearest their homes. But all other things are not equal in a system that has been deliberately constructed and maintained to enforce racial segregation." Chief Justice Burger, *Swann v. Charlotte-Mecklenburg Board of Education,* 402 U.S. 1 (1971).

93. *Keyes v. Denver School District No. 1,* 413 U.S. 189 (1973).

94. In *Plessy* the court approved segregation as a reasonable application of the constitutional guarantee of equal rights under the law and rejected the claim that it imposed psychological inferiority on blacks. *Brown* reached a different result, but without enunciating a color-blind principle. In *Brown,* the court held that because segregation injures black self-esteem, it cannot be permitted; the clear inference is that if facilities were truly equal and blacks did not emerge psychologically scarred, segregation would survive constitutional scrutiny. In *Swann,* the court similarly sought to use race to achieve its desired goal of an ethnically balanced student body.

95. *Marsh v. Board of Education of City of Flint,* 476 U.S. 1137 (1986), Justice Marshall dissenting.

96. Lani Guinier, "The Triumph of Tokenism: The Voting Rights Act and the Theory of Black Electoral Success," *Michigan Law Review* 89 (1991), p. 1077; Lani Guinier, "Don't Scapegoat the Gerrymander," *New York Times Magazine,* January 8, 1995, p. 37.

97. Kull, *The Color-Blind Constitution,* p. 215.

98. M. J. Rossant, introduction to Abigail Thernstrom, *Whose Votes Count? Affirmative Action and Minority Voting Rights,* Harvard University Press, Cambridge, 1987. Rossant is summarizing the thesis of Thernstrom's study.

99. Peter Skerry, *Mexican Americans: The Ambivalent Minority,* Free Press, New York, 1993, pp. 252, 331.

100. Guinier, "Don't Scapegoat the Gerrymander," p. 36.

101. Dale Russakoff, "Lani Guinier's Second Act," *Washington Post Magazine,* December 12, 1993, p. 19; see also Lani Guinier, *The Tyranny of the Majority: Fundamental Fairness in Representative Democracy,* Free Press, New York, 1994.

102. John C. Calhoun, *A Disquisition on Government,* Bobbs-Merrill, Indianapolis, 1953.

103. Guinier, *The Tyranny of the Majority,* p. 46.

104. Ibid., p. 56.

105. Carol M. Swain, *Black Faces, Black Interests: The Representation of African Americans in Congress,* Harvard University Press, Cambridge, 1993. The quotation appears on p. ix. See also Daniel Polsby and Robert Popper, "Racial Lines," *National Review,* February 20, 1995, and Steven Holmes, "Civil Rights Group Disputes Election Analysis on Black Districts," *New York Times,* December 1, 1994, for reports on the controversy over the effect of racial gerrymandering on the 1994 election outcome.

106. Daniel Wattenberg, "The GOP Divides to Conquer," *Insight,* June 3, 1991, pp. 13–19.

107. See, e.g., David Savage, "High Court Rules Against Racial Gerrymandering," *Los Angeles Times,* June 29, 1993, p. A-1; Joan Biskupic, "Race-Consious District Reinstated in Louisiana," *Washington Post,* August 12, 1994, p. A-3.

108. Shawn Deyo, "King: Focus on Changing America," *The Diamondback,* University of Maryland, February 16, 1994, p. 1.

109. Gerald David Jaynes and Robin M. Williams, *A Common Destiny: Blacks and American Society,* National Academy Press, Washington, DC, 1989, p. 13.

110. Ibid., p. 188; "Calendar of Events 1994," *Black Enterprise*/Kraft General Foods.

111. Cited by E. L. Thornbrough, ed., *Booker T. Washington,* Prentice Hall, Englewood Cliffs, NJ, 1969, p. 57.

112. Daniel Patrick Moynihan, *The Negro Family: The Case for National Action,* U.S. Department of Labor, Office of Policy Planning and Research, Washington, DC, 1965.

113. See Lee Rainwater and William Yancey, *The Moynihan Report and the Politics of Controversy,* MIT Press, Cambridge, 1967.

114. Cited by William Bennett, "Reflections on the Moynihan Report," *The American Enterprise,* January-February 1995, p. 30.

115. Carlos Sanchez and Maria Odum, "Two Denny's Said to Refuse Service to Black Choir," *Washington Post,* June 5, 1993; Rudolph Pyatt, Jr., "Denny's Racial Bias Case Raises Questions of Responsibilities," *Washington Post,* July 8, 1993; Philip Hager, "Suit Accuses Denny's of Racial Bias, Discrimination," *Los Angeles Times,* March 25, 1993; Sam Fulwood, "Denny's Signs Pact Assuring Minority Hires," *Los Angeles Times,* July 2, 1993; Pierre Thomas, "Denny's to Settle Bias Cases," *Washington Post,* May 24, 1994; Ann LoLordo, "Denny's Owner Improves Slowly on Race Relations," *Baltimore Sun,* September 20, 1994; Howard Kohn, "Service with a Sneer," *New York Times Magazine,* November 6, 1994; Jay Mathews, "Denny's Says Black Firm Will Own 47 Outlets," *Washington Post,* November 9, 1994; "Sharing in Denny's Award," *New York Times,* May 25, 1994.

116. Benjamin Holden, "A Law Firm Shows Civil Rights Can Be a Lucrative Business," *Wall Street Journal,* June 10, 1993, p. A-1.

117. "Denny's Pact Combats Racism," *Chicago Sun-Times,* May 30, 1994, p. 17.

118. Lynne Duke, "That Was Then, This Is Now," *Washington Post Magazine,* December 18, 1994; Jack E. White, "Let's Scrap the NAACP," *Time,* February 13, 1995, p. 70.

119. For a comprehensive listing, see Mark Eddy, "Minority and Women-Owned Business Programs of the Federal Government," Congressional Research Service, Library of Congress, Washington, DC, March 18, 1993; see also George LaNoue, "Split Visions: Minority Business Set-Asides," *Annals of the American Academy of Political and Social Science* 523, (September 1992), pp. 104–116.

120. Jeanne Saddler, "Going It Alone," *Wall Street Journal*, April 3, 1992, p. R-14.

121. Michael Barone, "Race Decisions That Backfire," *U.S. News and World Report*, July 12, 1993, p. 34; Evan Gahr, "FCC Preferences: Affirmative Action for the Wealthy," *Insight*, February 7, 1993, pp. 6–9, 22; Jonathan Rauch, "Color TV," *The New Republic*, December 19, 1994.

122. George LaNoue, "Social Science and Minority Set-Asides," *The Public Interest*, Winter 1993, pp. 49–62; George LaNoue, "But For Discrimination: How Many Minority Businesses Would There Be?" *Columbia Human Rights Law Review* 24, No. 1 (Winter 1992–1993); Roger Clegg, ed., *Racial Preferences in Government Contracting*, National Legal Center for the Public Interest, Washington, DC, 1993; Dorothy Gaither, "Court Ruling Makes Discrimination Studies a Hot New Industry," *Wall Street Journal*, August 13, 1993.

123. Cited in *Black Enterprise*, February 1992, p. 78.

124. Jim Preston, "The Business of Diversity," *Diversity*, November 1992, pp. 2–3; "Program Ensures Minorities, Women Get Equal Chance," *Diversity*, November 1992, p. 14.

125. Udayan Gupta, "Affirmative Buying," *Wall Street Journal*, April 3, 1992, p. R-12.

126. Ford Foundation, *1993 Annual Report*, New York, March 1994.

127. Mexican American Legal Defense and Education Fund, *Annual Report 1993–1994*, Los Angeles, 1994.

128. Daniel P. Moynihan, "Report to the President," March 19, 1969, cited by Graham, *The Civil Rights Era*, p. 311.

129. Jill Nelson, *Volunteer Slavery: My Authentic Negro Experience*, Noble Press, Chicago, 1993, p. 10.

130. Vivian Gordon, "How Do We Rage Safely?" in Haki Madhubuti, ed., *Why L.A. Happened: Implications of the '92 Los Angeles Rebellion*, Third World Press, Chicago, 1993, p. 61.

131. Davis, *Who Is Black?*, pp. 137–39, 180.

132. For studies of the effects of civil rights laws in promoting and accelerating black economic progress see, e.g., Richard Freeman, "Black Economic Progress Since 1964," *The Public Interest*, Summer 1978; Jonathan Leonard, "The Impact of Affirmative Action on Employment," *Journal of Labor Economics* 2 (October 1984), pp. 269–301; *Affirmative Action to Open the Doors of Job Opportunity*, Citizens' Commission on Civil Rights, Washington, DC, 1984; Finis Welch, *Affirmative Action in Employment: An Overview and Assessment of Effects*, U.S. Commission on Civil Rights paper, Washington, DC, March 1985; James Smith and Finis Welch, *Closing the Gap: Forty Years of Economic Progress for Blacks*, Rand Corporation, Santa Monica, CA, 1986; James Heckman and Hoult Verkerke, "Racial Disparity and Employment Discrimination Law: An Economic Perspective," *Yale Law and Policy Review* 8 (1990), p. 276; James Heckman and Brook Payner, "Determining the Impact of Federal An-

tidiscrimination Policy on the Economic Status of Blacks: A Study of South Carolina," *American Economic Review* 79 (1989), p. 138.

133. Bart Landry, *The New Black Middle Class,* University of California Press, Berkeley, 1987, p. 3.

134. U.S. Bureau of the Census, *Statistical Abstract of the United States 1994,* Washington, DC, pp. 457, 471.

135. Stephen Carter, *Reflections of an Affirmative Action Baby,* Basic Books, New York, 1991, p. 71.

136. William Julius Wilson, *The Declining Significance of Race,* University of Chicago Press, Chicago, 1980, p. 2.

137. Bayard Rustin, "The Blacks and the Unions," *Harper's,* May 1971, pp. 73–76.

138. William Raspberry, "PUSHed and Pulled," *Washington Post,* national weekly edition, September 3–9, 1990.

139. Nathan Hare, *The Black Anglo-Saxons,* Collier Books, New York, 1965, pp. 42–43, 46–47.

140. Glenn Loury, *One by One from the Inside Out: Essays and Reviews on Race and Responsibility,* Free Press, New York, 1995, p. 47.

141. Jaynes and Williams, *A Common Destiny,* p. 169.

142. Cited by Harold Cruse, *The Crisis of the Negro Intellectual,* William Morrow, New York, 1967, p. 283.

143. This argument is developed both in Wilson's *The Declining Significance of Race* and in his *The Truly Disadvantaged: The Inner City, the Underclass and Public Policy,* University of Chicago Press, Chicago, 1987.

144. In 1993, whites contributed an average of 2.1 percent of their annual income to charity. Blacks contributed 1.8 percent. These percentages were fairly steady across socioeconomic levels. See *Giving and Volunteering in the United States: Findings From a National Survey,* Independent Sector, Washington, DC, 1994, p. 39.

Chapter 7. Is America a Racist Society?

1. Marian Wright Edelman, *The Measure of Our Success: A Letter to My Children and Yours,* Beacon Press, Boston, 1992, p. 23.

2. See, e.g., Robert Blauner, "Talking Past Each Other: Black and White Languages of Race," *American Prospect,* Summer 1992.

3. Cited by Salman Rushdie, *Imaginary Homelands,* Penguin Books, New York, 1991, p. 13.

4. Michael Sovern, *Legal Restraints on Discrimination in Employment,* Twentieth Century Fund, New York, 1966, pp. 7–8.

5. Lena Williams, "Growing Black Debate: Racism or an Excuse?" *New York Times,* April 5, 1992, p. A-1.

6. Johnnetta B. Cole, *Conversations: Straight Talk with America's Sister President,* Anchor Books, New York, 1993, pp. 54, 57.

7. Cited by Audrey Edwards and Craig K. Polite, *Children of the Dream,* Doubleday, New York, 1992, p. 222.

8. Richard Delgado, "Words That Wound: A Tort Action," in Mari J. Matsuda, Charles R. Lawrence, Richard Delgado, and Kimberle Williams Crenshaw, *Words That Wound: Critical Race Theory, Assaultive Speech and the First Amendment,* Westview Press, Boulder, 1993, p. 90.

9. Henry Louis Gates, Jr., *Loose Canons: Notes on the Culture Wars,* Oxford University Press, New York, 1992, p. 50.

10. Kimberle Crenshaw, "Race, Reform and Retrenchment: Transformation and Legitimation in Antidiscrimination Law," *Harvard Law Review* 101 (1988), p. 1131.

11. Cornel West, *Keeping Faith: Philosophy and Race in America,* Routledge, New York, 1993, p. 236.

12. Joe R. Feagin and Melvin P. Sikes, *Living With Racism: The Black Middle Class Experience,* Beacon Press, Boston, 1994, pp. ix, 17.

13. Cosell later apologized for the remarks. See Leonard Shapiro, "Cosell's Remark Raises Ire," *Washington Post,* September 6, 1983.

14. James Barron, "Rooney, Back on the Air, Has Some New Questions," *New York Times,* March 5, 1990, p. C-14.

15. Jane Gross, "Coach Suspended over Ethnic Slurs," *New York Times,* July 30, 1991.

16. "Deep Thoughts," *The New Republic,* November 1, 1993, p. 8.

17. Claire Smith, "Baseball Bans Cincinnati Owner for a Year over Racial Remarks," *New York Times,* February 4, 1993, p. A-1.

18. Helen Dewar, "NAACP Chief Calls Hollings an Embarrassment for Remark," *Washington Post,* December 16, 1993, p. A-15.

19. Dorothy Gaiter, "White Teacher's Use of a Racial Pejorative Roils a Black Campus," *Wall Street Journal,* September 26, 1994, p. A-1.

20. Matsuda et al., *Words That Wound.* As Matsuda argues, "Tolerance of hate speech is not tolerance borne by the community at large. Rather, it is a psychic tax imposed on those least able to pay." See p. 18.

21. Commenting on black students at the University of Pennsylvania who destroyed thousands of copies of a conservative newspaper which published an article criticizing affirmative action, Catharine MacKinnon said, "There is expressive value in what the students did, and there is also expressive value in letting the paper publish." Symposium, "The First Amendment Under Fire from the Left," *New York Times Magazine,* March 3, 1994, p. 42.

22. Stanley Fish, *There's No Such Thing as Free Speech—and It's a Good Thing Too,* Oxford University Press, New York, 1994, p. 114.

23. "True Colors," ABC *Prime Time Live,* September 26, 1991.

24. Andrew Hacker, *Two Nations: Black and White, Separate, Hostile, Unequal,* Ballantine Books, New York, 1992, p. 32.

25. Derrick Bell, *Faces at the Bottom of the Well: The Permanence of Racism,* Basic Books, New York, 1992, pp. 158–94.

26. Henry Louis Gates, Jr., "Two Nations . . . Both Black," *Forbes,* September 14, 1992.

27. Cornel West, *Race Matters,* Beacon Press, Boston, 1993, p. x.

28. Cited by Studs Terkel, *Race,* New Press, New York, 1992, p. 360.

29. Hacker, *Two Nations,* p. 20.

30. Gregory Wright, "Fare Game," *Washington Post,* June 20, 1993, p. C-8.

31. Hamil R. Harris, "For Blacks, Cabs Can Be Hard To Get," *Washington Post,* July 21, 1994, p. A-1, A-2.

32. "Fact Sheet," Fair Taxicab Service Project, issued by the Department of Human Rights, Government of the District of Columbia, July 16, 1990. See also Wright, "Fare Game."

33. J. R. Green, "Cabbies Practice Passenger Selectivity to Protect Themselves," *New York Times,* March 22, 1990.

34. Harris, "For Blacks, Cabs Can Be Hard to Get," p. A-2.

35. Gabriel Escobar, "Rash of Violence Prompts Cabdrivers to Bypass Law," *Washington Post,* June 27, 1989, pp. A-1, D-9.

36. Brian Reilly, "Cabbie Killing Revives Debate," *Washington Times,* August 10, 1994, p. C-6.

37. Guy Toscano and William Weber, "Violence in the Workplace," Bureau of Labor Statistics, Washington, DC, April 1995.

38. See, e.g., Herbert Hyman and Paul Sheatsley, "Attitudes Toward Desegregation," *Scientific American,* December 1956, pp. 35–39; Herbert Hyman and Paul Sheatsley, "Attitudes Toward Desegregation," *Scientific American,* July 1964, pp. 16–23; Andrew Greeley and Paul Sheatsley, "Attitudes Toward Racial Integration," in Lee Rainwater, ed., *Inequality and Justice,* Aldine Books, Chicago, 1974; Paul Sheatsley, Andrew Greeley, and Garth Taylor, "Attitudes Toward Racial Integration," *Scientific American,* June 1978, pp. 42–50; Richard Apostle and Charles Glock, *The Anatomy of Racial Attitudes,* University of California Press, Berkeley, 1983; J. R. Kluegel and E. R. Smith, *Beliefs About Equality: American's Views of What Is and What Ought to Be,* Aldine Books, New York, 1986.

39. Howard Schuman, Charlotte Steeh, and Lawrence Bobo, *Racial Attitudes in America,* Harvard University Press, Cambridge, 1985, pp. 9, 16–17, 74–75.

40. Charlotte Steeh and Howard Schuman, "Young White Adults: Did Racial Attitudes Change in the 1980s?" *American Journal of Sociology* 98, No. 2 (September 1992), pp. 340–67. The quotation is from page 340.

41. Cole, *Conversations,* p. 56.

42. Patricia Williams, *The Alchemy of Race and Rights,* Harvard University Press, Cambridge, 1991, p. 103.

43. Anthony Lewis, "It Can Happen Here," *New York Times,* November 11, 1991, p. A-15.

44. Jennifer Hochschild, *The New American Dilemma: Liberal Democracy and School Desegregation,* Yale University Press, New Haven, 1984, p. 203.

45. For a summary of the symbolic racism argument, see David O. Sears, "Symbolic Racism," in Phyllis Katz and Dalmas Taylor, eds., *Eliminating Racism: Profiles in Controversy,* Plenum Press, New York, 1988, pp. 53–84. See also Donald Kinder, "The Continuing American Dilemma: White Resistance to Racial Change 40 Years After Myrdal," *Journal of Social Issues* 42 (1986); John B. McConahay and J. C. Hough, "Symbolic Racism," *Journal of Social Issues* 32 (1976), pp. 23–45; David O.

Sears, Carl P. Hensler and Leslie K. Speer, "Whites' Opposition to Busing: Self-Interest or Symbolic Politics?" *American Political Science Review* 73 (1979), pp. 369–84; Donald Kinder and David Sears, "Prejudice and Politics: Symbolic Racism Versus Racial Threats to the Good Life," *Journal of Personality and Social Psychology* 40, No. 3 (1981), pp. 414–31; J. B. McConahay, "Modern Racism and Modern Discrimination: The Effects of Race, Racial Attitudes, and Context on Simulated Hiring Decisions," *Personality and Social Psychology Bulletin* 9, No. 4 (1983), pp. 551–58; J. B. McConahay, B. B. Hardee, and V. Batts, "Has Racism Declined in America?" *Journal of Conflict Resolution* 25 (1981), pp. 563–79.

46. Sears, "Symbolic Racism," pp. 78, 80.

47. McConahay and Hough, "Symbolic Racism," pp. 23–45.

48. Kinder, "The Continuing American Dilemma," pp. 151–52.

49. Anti-Defamation League of B'nai B'rith, *Highlights from Survey on Racial Attitudes in America,* June 1993, New York, pp. 64–67.

50. Gerald David Jaynes and Robin M. Williams, *A Common Destiny: Blacks and American Society,* National Academy Press, Washington, DC, 1989, pp. 141–42.

51. Seymour Martin Lipset, "Equality and the American Creed," Progressive Policy Institute paper, June 1991, p. 23.

52. See, e.g., Tom W. Smith and Paul B. Sheatsley, "American Attitudes Toward Race Relations," *Public Opinion,* October 1984, p. 53; Vern E. Smith, "Busing: How to Get Everyone Mad; In a Model of Integration, Parents of Both Races Now Question the Benefits," *Newsweek,* March 7, 1988, pp. 39–40.

53. See, e.g., Lawrence Bobo, "Whites' Opposition to Busing: Symbolic Racism or Realistic Group Conflict?" *Journal of Personality and Social Psychology* 45, No. 6 (1983), pp. 1196–1210; Irwin Katz, Joyce Wackenhut, and R. Glen Hass, "Racial Ambivalence, Value Duality and Behavior," in John Dovidio and Samuel Gaertner, eds., *Prejudice, Discrimination and Racism,* Harcourt Brace Jovanovich, New York, 1986, pp. 35–40.

54. Stephen Johnson, "Reverse Discrimination and Aggressive Behavior," *Journal of Psychology* 104 (1980), pp. 11–19.

55. See Paul Sniderman and Thomas Piazza, *The Scar of Race,* Harvard University Press, Cambridge, 1993; Paul Sniderman and Philip E. Tetlock, "Symbolic Racism: Problems of Motive Attribution in Political Analysis," *Journal of Social Issues* 42 (1986), pp. 129–50; Paul Sniderman, Thomas Piazza, Philip E. Tetlock, and Ann Kendrick, "The New Racism," *American Journal of Political Science* 35 (1991), pp. 423–47.

56. Sniderman et al., "The New Racism," p. 425.

57. Ibid., pp. 427–30.

58. Ibid., pp. 434–37.

59. Sniderman and Piazza, *The Scar of Race,* p. 28.

60. Anti-Defamation League of B'nai B'rith, *Highlights from Survey on Racial Attitudes,* p. 10.

61. See, e.g., Lynne Duke, "Whites' Racial Stereotypes Persist: Most Retain Negative Beliefs About Minorities," *Washington Post,* January 9, 1991, p. A-1. "A majority

of whites . . . said they believe blacks and Hispanics are likely to prefer welfare to hard work and tend to be lazier than whites, more prone to violence, less intelligent and less patriotic."

62. Michelle Singletary, "Life and Death Decisions," *Washington Post,* October 4, 1993, Washington Business Section, p. 14.

63. Cited by Ellis Cose, *The Rage of a Privileged Class,* HarperCollins, New York, 1993, p. 34.

64. Ibid., p. 1.

65. Alejandro Brown, "Do People Misjudge You?" *Parade,* "Fresh Voices" Section, January 26, 1990.

66. Larry Aubry, "Are Black Males the Nation's Throw-Aways?" *Los Angeles Sentinel,* January 16, 1992.

67. Cited by Howard Kurtz, "Some Journalists Link Crime Coverage, Racism," *Washington Post,* July 29, 1994.

68. Martin Kilson and Clement Cottingham, "Thinking About Race Relations," *Dissent,* Fall 1991, p. 522.

69. Federal Bureau of Investigation, *Crime in the United States 1992,* summarized in U.S. Bureau of the Census, *Statistical Abstract of the United States 1994,* Table 315, Washington, DC, p. 205.

70. About 95 percent of prison inmates are male, only 5 percent are female. U.S. Bureau of Justice Statistics, *Survey of State Prison Inmates 1991,* summarized in U.S. Bureau of the Census, *Statistical Abstract of the United States 1994,* Table 340, p. 215.

71. About 90 percent of male prison inmates are between the ages of eighteen and forty-four, whereas less than 10 percent are older. Ibid.

72. "Losing Ground," *Newsweek,* April 6, 1992, p. 20.

73. Marc Mauer, "Young Black Men and the Criminal Justice System: A Growing National Problem," The Sentencing Project, Washington, DC, February 1990, p. 3. See also Jason DeParle, "Young Black Men in Capital: Study Finds 42 Percent in Courts," *New York Times,* April 18, 1992, p. A-1. For comparable figures see David Savage, "1 of 4 Young Black Men Are in Jail or on Parole," *San Francisco Chronicle,* February 27, 1990, p. A-1; Elaine Rivera, "High Jail Rate for Minorities," *Newsday,* October 4, 1990, p. 8.

74. Susan Fry and Vincent Schiraldi, "Young African American Men and the Criminal Justice System in California," National Center on Institutions and Alternatives, October 1990, p. 2; see also Sonia Nazario, "Odds Grim for Black Men in California," *Washington Post,* December 12, 1993, p. A-23.

75. Jerome G. Miller, "Hobbling a Generation: Young African American Males in Washington D.C.'s Criminal Justice System," National Center on Institutions and Alternatives, April 1992, pp. 1, 6.

76. National Center on Institutions and Alternatives, "Hobbling a Generation: Young African American Males in the Criminal Justice System of America's Cities: Baltimore, Maryland," 1992, pp. 1–7; see also "Race and Crime: Don't Mention It," *The Economist,* September 12, 1992, p. 33.

77. Sanyika Shakur, *Monster: The Autobiography of an L.A. Gang Member,* Penguin Books, New York, 1993, p. 72.

78. Elijah Anderson, *Streetwise: Race, Class and Change in an Urban Community,* University of Chicago Press, Chicago, 1990, pp. 164–67, 176; see also Elijah Anderson, "Race and Neighborhood Transition," in Paul E. Peterson, ed., *The New Urban Reality,* The Brookings Institution, Washington, DC, 1985.

79. Ishmael Reed, *Airing Dirty Laundry,* Addison-Wesley, Reading, MA, 1993, pp. 7, 70; Ishmael Reed, "Stats, Lies & Videotape," *Emerge,* April 1994.

80. Richard Majors and Jacob Gordon, ed., *The American Black Male: His Present Status and His Future,* Nelson Hall Publishers, Chicago, 1994, p. xi.

81. John Hurst, "Jackson Forms Panel to Fight Bias in Media," *Los Angeles Times,* June 27, 1994, p. B-4.

82. See, e.g., Howard Kurtz, "Our Politically Correct Press," *Washington Post,* January 20, 1991; Christopher Hitchens, "Sensitive to a Fault," *Vanity Fair,* April 1994.

83. See, e.g., "Man Rapes and Robs Two Women in Chelsea," *New York Times,* May 27, 1993. While the *Times* described the suspect as "muscular" and "wearing a red long-sleeved sweatshirt," the *New York Post* added a relevant detail: "a muscular black man." See "Two Women in Rape Nightmare," *New York Post,* May 27, 1993.

84. Statement by executive editor Gregory Favre, *Sacramento Bee,* November 2, 1991.

85. Dovidio and Gaertner, *Prejudice, Discrimination and Racism,* pp. 6–8.

86. Robert Lichter, Linda Lichter, and Stanley Rothman, *Watching America,* Prentice Hall, New York, 1991, p. 198; see also Robert Lichter, Linda Lichter, Stanley Rothman, and Daniel Amundson, "Prime Time Prejudice: TV Images of Blacks and Hispanics," *Public Opinion,* July-August 1987, pp. 13–16; Robert Lichter and Linda Lichter, *Prime Time Crime,* The Media Institute, Washington, DC, 1983.

87. "Imagine That," *Washington Times,* April 1, 1992, p. A-6.

88. Sut Jhally and Justin Lewis, *Enlightened Racism: The Cosby Show, Audiences and the Myth of the American Dream,* Westview Press, Boulder, 1992, pp. 74, 91, 97, 110.

89. Henry Louis Gates, Jr., "TV's Black World Turns—But Stays Unreal," *New York Times,* November 12, 1989, pp. B-1, B-40.

90. See, e.g., Garry Trudeau, "Street Calculus," *New York Times,* April 29, 1994, p. A-27; Ed Koch, "Blacks, Jews, Liberals and Crime," *National Review,* May 16, 1994; Judith Lichtenberg, "Racism in the Head, Racism in the World," *Report From the Institute for Philosophy and Public Policy* 12 (Spring-Summer 1992), pp. 3–5.

91. Michael Levin, "Responses to Race Differences in Crime," *Journal of Social Philosophy* 23 (Spring 1992), pp. 5–29; Michael Levin, "Reply to Adler, Cox and Corlett," *Journal of Social Philosophy* 25 (Spring 1994), pp. 5–19. The quotations from Levin that follow are from these articles.

92. J. Angelo Corlett, "Racism and Affirmative Action," *Journal of Social Philosophy* 24 (Spring 1993), pp. 164–65.

93. Ibid., p. 166.

94. Jonathan E. Adler, "Crime Rates by Race and Causal Relevance," *Journal of Social Philosophy* 24 (Spring 1993), p. 182.

95. Lichtenberg, "Racism in the Head, Racism in the World."

96. Reed, *Airing Dirty Laundry,* p. 48.

97. Cited by Lynne Duke, "Confronting Violence," *Washington Post,* January 8, 1994, p. A-10; see also "A New Civil Rights Frontier," *U.S. News and World Report,* January 17, 1994.

98. Cole, *Conversations,* p. 46.

99. William Oliver, *The Violent Social World of Black Men,* Lexington Books, New York, 1994, p. 2.

100. See, e.g., Jeanne Sadler, "Greatest Threat to Washington D.C.'s Health May Be Growing Exodus of Black Middle Class," *Wall Street Journal,* September 7, 1994, p. A-16.

101. Cited by Thomas Byrne Edsall and Mary D. Edsall, *Chain Reaction: The Impact of Race, Rights and Taxes on American Politics,* W. W. Norton, New York, 1992, p. 236.

102. Edmund Burke, *Reflections on the Revolution in France,* Penguin Books, New York, 1982, p. 183.

103. Henry Louis Gates, Jr., "Talkin' That Talk," in Henry Louis Gates, Jr., ed., *"Race," Writing and Difference,* University of Chicago Press, Chicago, 1986, pp. 403–4.

104. *Encyclopedia Britannica,* Encyclopedia Britannica Inc., Chicago, 1977, p. 360.

105. Thomas Pettigrew, George Fredrickson, Dale Knobel, Nathan Glazer, and Reed Ueda, *Prejudice,* Harvard University Press, Cambridge, 1982, pp. 2–3.

106, Christine Bennett, *Comprehensive Multicultural Education: Theory and Practice,* Allyn & Bacon, Boston, 1990, p. 26.

107. Joe Feagin, *Racial and Ethnic Relations,* Prentice Hall, Englewood Cliffs, NJ, 1984, p. 11.

108. *Webster's New World Dictionary,* Prentice Hall, New York, 1994, p. 1314.

109. Gordon Allport, *The Nature of Prejudice,* Addison-Wesley Co, Reading, MA, 1979, p. 23.

110. George Jean Nathan and H. L. Mencken, *The American Credo,* Alfred A. Knopf, New York, 1920.

111. National Conference on Christians and Jews, *Taking America's Pulse: The National Conference Survey on Intergroup Relations,* pp. 6–11. See also Steven Holmes, "Survey Finds Minorities Resent One Another Almost as Much as They Do Whites," *New York Times,* March 3, 1994, p. B-8.

112. "The vast majority of Americans do have regular contact with people of different races and ethnic backgrounds." National Conference on Christians and Jews, *Taking America's Pulse,* p. 26. See also Anti-Defamation League of B'nai B'rith, *Highlights from Survey on Racial Attitudes,* pp. 71–76.

113. Hacker, *Two Nations,* p. 62.

114. Thomas Kochman, *Black and White: Styles in Conflict,* University of Chicago Press, Chicago, 1981, pp. 107, 131.

115. Grace Hadley Beardsley, *The Negro in Greek and Roman Civilization,* Arno Press, New York, 1979, p. 21.

116. Cited by Bernard Lewis, *Race and Slavery in the Middle East,* Oxford University Press, New York, 1990, pp. 93–94.

117. Cited by Bernard Lewis, *Islam,* Volume II: *Religion and Society,* Oxford University Press, New York, 1987, pp. 210–11.

118. Ibn Khaldun, *The Muqaddimah,* translated by Franz Rosenthal, Princeton University Press, Princeton, 1967, p. 63.

119. Taylor Cox, *Cultural Diversity in Organizations,* Berrett-Koehler Publishers, San Francisco, 1993, p. 92.

120. Richard Gambino, *Blood of My Blood: The Dilemma of Italian-Americans,* Doubleday, New York, 1974.

121. Thomas Sowell, *Ethnic America: A History,* Basic Books, New York, 1981; Nathan Glazer and Daniel P. Moynihan, *Beyond the Melting Pot,* MIT Press, Cambridge, 1970.

122. Paul Robeson, "Thoughts on the Color Bar," *The Spectator,* August 8, 1931, p. 178; reprinted in Philip S. Foner, ed., *Paul Robeson Speaks: Writings, Speeches, Interviews,* Brunner-Mazel, New York, 1978, p. 84–85.

123. Ralph Ellison, *Shadow and Act,* Random House, New York, 1964, p. 88.

124. Ralph Wiley, *Why Black People Tend to Shout,* Birch Lane Press, Carol Publishing, New York, 1991, p. 39.

125. James Anyike, *African American Holidays: A Historical Research and Resource Guide to Cultural Celebrations,* Popular Truth, Chicago, 1991, p. 1.

126. Thomas Gossett, *Race: The History of an Idea in America,* Southern Methodist University Press, Dallas, 1963, p. 11.

127. William Helmreich, *The Things They Say Behind Your Back,* Doubleday, New York, 1982, pp. 16, 21, 50, 92–97, 143–45, 220, 244.

128. Allport, *The Nature of Prejudice,* pp. 6, 87–88.

129. Harry Triandis, "The Future of Pluralism Revisited," in Phyllis Katz and Dalmas Taylor, eds., *Eliminating Racism, p. 41.*

130. M. W. Giles and A. Evans, "The Power Approach to Intergroup Hostility," *Journal of Conflict Resolution* 30, No. 3 (1986), pp. 469–86.

131. As philosopher Steven Goldberg writes, "It is self-defeating to ask people to pretend that they have not seen what they have seen." Steven Goldberg, "Are Stereotypes True?" *When Wish Replaces Thought,* Prometheus Books, Buffalo, NY, 1991, p. 154.

132. Bell, *Faces at the Bottom of the Well,* p. 5.

133. Jaynes and Williams, eds., *A Common Destiny,* p. 155.

134. Margery Austin Turner, Michael Fix and Raymond Struyk, *Opportunities Denied, Opportunities Diminished: Racial Discrimination in Hiring,* Urban Institute Press, Washington, DC, 1991.

135. Lynne Duke, "Entry Level Hiring Bias Found Here," *Washington Post,* May 15, 1991, p. A-3.

136. Gary Becker, *The Economics of Discrimination,* University of Chicago Press, Chicago, 1957; see also Kenneth Arrow, "The Theory of Discrimination," in Orley Ashenfelter and Albert Rees, eds., *Discrimination in Labor Markets,* Princeton University Press, Princeton, 1973.

137. For a discussion of search costs, see, e.g., Kenneth Arrow, "The Theory of Discrimination," pp. 3–33; Richard A. Posner, *The Economics of Justice,* Harvard University Press, Cambridge, 1981, p. 362.

138. Joleen Kirschenman and Kathryn Neckerman, "The Meaning of Race for

Employers," in Christopher Jencks and Paul Peterson, eds., *The Urban Underclass*, Brookings Institution, Washington DC, 1991, pp. 204–31.

139. Paulette Thomas, "Federal Data Detail Pervasive Racial Gap in Mortgage Lending," *Wall Street Journal*, March 31, 1992, p. A-1.

140. Andrew Brimmer, "The Cost of Bank Bias," *Black Enterprise*, July 1992, p. 43.

141. "There's No Whites Only Sign But. . . ," *Business Week*, October 26, 1992, p. 78.

142. See, e.g., Bill Dedman, "Blacks Denied S&L Loans Twice As Often as Whites," *Atlanta Journal and Constitution*, January 22, 1989, p. A-1; Eugene Carlson, "Battling Bias," *Wall Street Journal*, April 3, 1992, p. R-1, R-16; Michael Quint, "Anti-Black Bias Still Found in Mortgage Applications," *New York Times*, October 2, 1992, pp. D-1, D-11; Joel Glenn Brenner and Liz Spayd, "A Pattern of Bias in Mortgage Loans," *Washington Post*, June 6, 1993, pp. A-1, A-24; Carolyn Brown, "How to Fight Mortgage Discrimination—And Win," *Black Enterprise*, July 1993, pp. 48–57; William D. Bradford, "Money Matters: Lending Discrimination in African American Communities," in *The State of Black America*, National Urban League, New York, 1993, pp. 109–120.

143. See, e.g., "U.S. Probes Bank Records for Race Bias," *Wall Street Journal*, May 19, 1992, p. A-2, A-6; John H. Cushman, Jr., "Clinton Proposes Tough New Rules on Bias by Banks," *New York Times*, December 9, 1993, p. A-1; "Shawmut Settles: Will Pay $960,000," *USA Today*, December 14, 1993, p. 2-B; Kenneth Bacon, "Under Strong Pressure, Banks Extend Loans for Inner-City Homes," *Wall Street Journal*, February 23, 1994, p. A-1; Steve Cocheo, "Justice Opens Fire on Fair-Lending Issues," *ABA Banking Journal*, March 1994, pp. 32–38; Ann Mariano, "U.S. Drafts Rules to End Housing Bias," *Washington Post*, April 9, 1994, p. E-1; Michelle Singletary, "Chevy Chase Settles Case Over Bias," *Washington Post*, August 23, 1994; Jonathan Macey, "Banking by Quota," *Wall Street Journal*, September 7, 1994, p. A-14; Keith Bradsher, "Regulators Join Banks in Protesting U.S. Discrimination Suits," *New York Times*, October 30, 1994, p. A-34.

144. Statement by Lawrence Lindsey, member of the board of governors of the Federal Reserve, before the Committee on Banking, Finance and Urban Affairs, U.S. House of Representatives, May 14, 1992, reprinted in *Federal Reserve Bulletin*, July 1992, pp. 500–4.

145. Sam Roberts, *Who We Are: A Portrait of America Based on the Latest U.S. Census*, Times Books, New York, 1993, p. 169.

146. Peter Brimelow and Leslie Spencer, "The Hidden Clue," *Forbes*, January 4, 1993, p. 48.

147. David Horne, "Evaluating the Role of Race in Mortgage Lending," *FDIC Banking Review*, Spring-Summer 1994; Stan Liebowitz, "A Study That Deserves No Credit," *Wall Street Journal*, September 1, 1993; Ed Rubenstein, "Banking on Racism," *National Review*, November 21, 1994, p. 16.

148. Brimelow and Spencer, "The Hidden Clue"; see also Gary Becker, "The Evidence Against Banks Doesn't Prove Bias," *Business Week*, April 19, 1993, p. 18.

149. Glenn Canner, Wayne Passmore, and Dolores Smith, "Residential Lending

to Low-Income and Minority Families: Evidence from the 1992 HMDA Data," *Federal Reserve Bulletin,* February 1994, pp. 79–108.

150. Scott Minerbrook, "Home Ownership Anchors the Middle Class," *Emerge,* October 1993, p. 45.

151. U.S. Bureau of Justice Statistics, *Survey of Prison Inmates 1991,* summarized in U.S. Bureau of the Census, *Statistical Abstract of the United States 1994,* Washington, DC, Table 340, p. 215.

152. See, e.g., Ruth Marcus, "Racial Bias Widely Seen in Criminal Justice System," *Washington Post,* May 12, 1992, p. A-4.

153. Bruce Wright, *Black Robes, White Justice,* Carol Publishing, New York, 1987, p. 153.

154. Lawrence Vogelman, "The Big Black Man Syndrome," *Fordham Urban Law Journal* 20 (1993), p. 571.

155. Cited by Tony Mauro, "Experts, the Public, Ask Why," *USA Today,* May 1, 1992, p. 4-A.

156. According to a 1983 study by the Rand Corporation, "Social science researchers have been addressing the question of discrimination in the system for more than 30 years but have failed to reach consensus on almost every point. Studies have offered evidence both for and against racial bias in arrests, prosecution, conviction, sentencing, correction and parole." Joan Petersilia, *Racial Disparities in the Criminal Justice System,* Rand Corporation, Santa Monica, 1983, p. vi.

For a California study which found no discrimination in the criminal justice system, once relevant factors such as prior record were taken into account, see Stephen Klein, Joan Petersilia, and Susan Turner, "Race and Imprisonment Decisions in California," *Science,* February 16, 1990, pp. 812–16. Reviewing several studies, James Q. Wilson and Richard Herrnstein find no good evidence for racial bias in the justice system. See James Q. Wilson and Richard Herrnstein, *Crime and Human Nature,* Simon & Schuster, New York, 1985; see also William Wilbanks, *The Myth of a Racist Criminal Justice System,* Brooks-Cole Publishing, Monterey, CA, 1987.

For a study that found considerable discrimination against African Americans, see T. Jones, "Blacks in the American Criminal Justice System: A Study of Sanctioned Deviance," *Journal of Sociology and Social Welfare* 5 (1978), pp. 356–73. Based on his review of numerous studies, Ronald B. Flowers concludes that "there can be little doubt that minority members face some form of discriminatory treatment in every phase of the criminal justice system." Ronald Barri Flowers, *Minorities and Criminality,* Greenwood Press, Westport, CT, 1988; see also Coramae Richey Mann, *Unequal Justice: A Question of Color,* Indiana University Press, Bloomington, 1993.

Perhaps the conclusion to which most scholars would give assent is that "although at one time discrimination was quite likely, at the present time the general conclusion is that race remains an important factor only in selected contexts." See Joseph Sheley, "Structural Influences on the Problem of Race, Crime, and Criminal Justice Discrimination," *Tulane Law Review* 67 (1993), pp. 2273, 2278.

157. See, e.g., Hacker, *Two Nations,* p. 183; Patrick Langan, "Racism on Trial: New Evidence to Explain the Racial Composition of Prisons in the United States,"

Journal of Criminal Law and Criminology 76 (1985), p. 666; Michael Hindelang, "Variations in Sex-Race-Age-Specific Incidence Rates of Offending," *American Sociological Review* 46 (1981), p. 461; Michael Hindelang, "Race and Involvement in Common Law Personal Crimes," *American Sociological Review* 43 (1978), p. 93.

158. Alfred Blumstein, "On the Racial Disproportionality of United States Prison Populations," *Journal of Criminal Law and Criminology* 73 (1982), pp. 1259–81.

159. In 1930, the prison population was 77 percent white and 22 percent black. In 1950 it was 70 percent white and 30 percent black. In 1970 it was 60 percent white and 36 percent black. In other words, despite changes for the better in racial attitudes and the introduction of numerous safeguards the proportion of blacks in jail has continuously increased. See Hacker, *Two Nations,* p. 197.

160. Wilbanks, *The Myth of a Racist Criminal Justice System,* p. 146.

161. Blumstein estimates that "80 percent of the actual racial disproportionality in incarceration rates is accounted for by the differential involvement in arrest." Blumstein, "On the Racial Disproportionality of United States Prison Populations," p. 1268.

162. David Baldus, George Woodworth, and Charles A. Pulanski, Jr., *Equal Justice and the Death Penalty: A Legal and Empirical Analysis,* Northeastern University Press, Boston, 1990, p. 401.

163. *McCleskey v. Kemp,* 481 U.S. 279 (1987).

164. "Capital Punishment in America, 1978–1993," *Facts on File,* 1993, p. 349.

165. *McCleskey v. Kemp* at 276.

166. See, e.g., Marvin Wolfgang and Marc Riedel, "Race, Judicial Discretion and the Death Penalty," *Annals of the American Academy of Political and Social Science* 407 (1973), pp. 119–33. This study examined capital rape convictions between 1945 and 1965 and found that if the defendant is black and the victim white, the chance of a capital conviction is about eighteen times higher than when the defendant and victim are in any other racial combination.

167. Klein and Rolph concluded that "nonwhite offenders who killed white victims were no more likely to be sentenced to death than were white offenders who killed white victims." See, e.g., Stephen Klein and John Rolph, "Relationship of Offender and Victim Race to Death Penalty Sentences in California," *Jurimetrics Journal* 32 (Fall 1991), pp. 33–44.

168. William Wilbanks, *The Myth of a Racist Criminal Justice System,* pp. 17–18.

169. Blumstein, "On the Racial Disproportionality of United States Prison Populations," p. 1276.

170. Helen Dewar, "Senate Bows to Braun on Symbol of Confederacy," *Washington Post,* July 23, 1993, p. A-1; for the full debate, see *Congressional Record,* July 22, 1993, S-9251 to S-9271.

171. See, e.g., Douglas Lederman, "Old Times Not Forgotten: A Battle Over Symbols Obscures University of Mississippi's Racial Changes," *Chronicle of Higher Education,* October 20, 1993, p. A-51.

172. These distinctions can be seen clearly in the terminology employed by R. K. Merton, who used a fourfold classification: the unprejudiced nondiscriminator, the unprejudiced discriminator, the prejudiced nondiscriminator, and the prejudiced

discriminator. See R. M. MacIver, ed., *Discrimination and the National Welfare,* Harper & Bros., New York, 1947.

173. Christopher Jencks, *Rethinking Social Policy: Race, Poverty and the Underclass,* Harvard University Press, Cambridge, 1992, p. 46.

174. Jimmie Briggs, "Hope of Our Past: Interview with John Hope Franklin," *Emerge,* March 1994, pp. 21–22.

Chapter 8. Institutional Racism and Double Standards

1. James Dao, "Minority Contract Rules Raise Issues of How to Measure Discrimination," *New York Times,* August 30, 1992.

2. Thomas Pettigrew, George Fredrickson, Dale Knobel, Nathan Glazer, and Reed Ueda, *Prejudice,* Harvard University Press, Cambridge, 1982, pp. 4–5.

3. James Jones, *Prejudice and Racism,* Addison-Wesley, Reading, MA, 1972, p. 131.

4. David T. Wellman, *Portraits of White Racism,* Cambridge University Press, Cambridge, 1977, pp. xviii, 235.

5. Nathan Glazer writes, "Judges, lawyers and government officials operate on the assumption that if there were no discrimination, an even distribution of blacks or any other ethnic groups in the occupations and educational institutions of society would occur." Nathan Glazer, *Affirmative Discrimination: Ethnic Inequality and Public Policy,* Basic Books, New York, 1978, p. 153.

6. "Suppose that 100 whites and 100 blacks applied for 50 jobs. If there were no adverse impact in the examining procedure used to select for these jobs, one would expect to see 25 blacks and 25 whites hired." Letter from Richard Seymour, Lawyers' Committee for Civil Rights Under Law, cited by Morris Abram, "Affirmative Action: Fair Shakers and Social Engineers," *Harvard Law Review* 99 (1986), pp. 1312, 1317.

"If employment, housing and educational opportunities were truly open and nondiscriminatory, we should reasonably expect that over a period of time there would be no significant disparity in the distribution of social problems between Americans of different races." Roy Brooks, *Rethinking the American Race Problem,* University of California Press, Berkeley, 1990, p. 5.

"Once discriminatory forces cease . . . the racial composition of the labor market should approach that of the population." Martin J. Katz, "The Economics of Discrimination: The Three Fallacies of *Croson,*" *Yale Law Journal* 100 (1991), p. 1039.

7. David A. Strauss, "The Law and Economics of Racial Discrimination in Employment: The Case for Numerical Standards," *Georgetown Law Journal* 79 (1991), pp. 1619–1620.

8. Alan Farnham, "Holding Firm on Affirmative Action," *Fortune,* March 13, 1989, pp. 87–88.

9. "Race in the Workplace: Is Affirmative Action Working?" *Business Week,* July 8, 1991, p. 56.

10. Stephen S. Hsu, "Minority Business Leaders Uneasy over Disney Hiring," *Washington Post,* July 25, 1994, pp. B-1, B-5.

11. Joan Rigdon, "KFC Scouts for Blacks and Women for Its Top Echelons," *Wall Street Journal,* November 13, 1991, p. 1.

12. Cited by Peter Brimelow and Leslie Spencer, "When Quotas Replace Merit, Everybody Suffers," *Forbes,* February 15, 1993, p. 81.

13. In a typical case, Liberty National Bank & Trust of Louisville, Kentucky, found itself under government pressure to hire more black tellers and clerical workers, even though it already had 16 percent African American representation in 1989. Yet because 32 percent of those who applied for the bank's vacancies were black, Liberty was judged presumptively guilty of discrimination for not giving approximately one-third of new jobs to blacks. In 1991 Liberty agreed under duress to offer jobs to eighteen African Americans it had previously rejected, and to pay them whatever income they had lost as a consequence of not being employed with the bank two years earlier. See John Filiatreau, "How the Right Thing Went Awry," *Business Week,* July 8, 1991, p. 56.

14. "Airline Creates Affirmative Action Program to Settle Job Bias Suit," *New York Times,* May 12, 1991.

15. Alicia Shepard, "High Anxiety: The Call for Diversity in the Newsroom Has White Men Running Scared," *American Journalism Review,* November 1993, pp. 19–21.

16. Andrew Hazlett, "FBI's Most Wanted: Diversity," *The American Experiment,* Summer 1993, p. 3; Christopher Kerr, "Nominee Gone, but Remedies Linger On," *Washington Times,* June 14, 1993, p. E-4; Sharon LaFraniere, "Agents Say FBI Has Adopted Hiring, Promotion Quotas," *Washington Post,* June 17, 1991, p. A-1.

17. Ford Cooper, "Selecting Envoys: Is Diversity or Merit Key?" *Foreign Service Journal,* February 1994, pp. 16–20; Marc Sievers, "Clear Policy Wanted," *Foreign Service Journal,* March 1994, p. 8; see also Ruth Larson, "Foreign Service Officers Cite Bias Against White Males," *Washington Times,* June 7, 1994, p. A-6; James Workman, "Gender Norming," *The New Republic,* July 1, 1991, p. 16.

18. "Affirmative, Yes—But Is it Fair?" *Business Week,* July 4, 1994, pp. 74–76; Eleena DeLisser, "Independent Bankers Get Big-Name Help," *Wall Street Journal,* May 12, 1994, p. B-1; James White, "Minorities and Women Gain a Bigger Role in Money Management," *Wall Street Journal,* March 13, 1991.

19. "The Thin White Line," *U.S. News and World Report,* August 15, 1994, pp. 53–54.

20. Sonia Nazario, "Many Minorities Feel Torn by Experience of Affirmative Action," *Wall Street Journal,* June 27, 1989, pp. A-1, A-10.

21. Ken McLaughlin, "Ethnic Diversity in S.J. Hiring Ignites Reverse Bias Outcry," *San Jose Mercury News,* May 6, 1993.

22. Jimmie Gates, "Hiring of White Urged for Hinds County Personnel Post," *Clarion-Ledger,* Jackson, MS, April 26, 1994.

23. Cited in Lee Rainwater and William L. Yancey, *The Moynihan Report and the Politics of Controversy,* MIT Press, Cambridge, 1967, p. 3.

24. Derrick Bell, "Remembrances of Racism Past: Getting Beyond the Civil Rights Decline," in Herbert Hill and James Jones, eds., *Race in America,* University of Wisconsin Press, Madison, 1993, p. 78.

25. Wellman, *Portraits of White Racism,* pp. 8, 41.

26. Paul Gewirtz, "Discrimination Endgame," *The New Republic,* August 12, 1991, p. 19.

27. Joel Kovel, *White Racism: A Psychohistory,* Columbia University Press, New York, 1984, p. xiv.

28. Alfred Blumrosen, *Modern Law: The Law Transmission System and Equal Employment Opportunity,* University of Wisconsin Press, Madison, 1993, p. 230.

29. Richard Delgado, "Does Voice Really Matter?" *Virginia Law Review* 76 (1990), pp. 105, 107; Richard Delgado, "Critiques of Stephen Carter's *Reflections of an Affirmative Action Baby,"* *Reconstruction* 1, No. 4 (1992), p. 121.

30. Gertrude Ezorsky, *Racism and Justice: The Case for Affirmative Action,* Cornell University Press, Ithaca, NY, 1984, pp. 9–10.

31. Strauss, "The Law and Economics of Racial Discrimination in Employment," p. 1629.

32. Michael J. Perry, "The Disproportionate Impact Theory of Racial Discrimination," *University of Pennsylvania Law Review* 125 (1977), pp. 540, 557.

33. Michael Rosenfeld, *Affirmative Action and Justice: A Philosophical and Constitutional Inquiry,* Yale University Press, New Haven, 1991, p. 288.

34. This argument, attributed to Hardy Jones, is summarized in Robert Detlefson, *Civil Rights Under Reagan,* Institute for Contemporary Studies Press, San Francisco, 1991, p. 54.

35. Thomas Sowell, *Civil Rights: Rhetoric or Reality,* William Morrow, New York, 1984, pp. 54–55.

36. "A selection rate for any race, sex or ethnic group which is less than four-fifths or 80 percent of the rate for the group with the highest rate will generally be regarded by the federal government enforcement agencies as evidence of adverse impact." See Equal Employment Opportunity Commission, *Uniform Guidelines on Employee Selection Procedures,* Washington, DC, 1978. These guidelines have been subsequently reissued and are now routinely referred to as the 1989 Uniform Guidelines.

37. Robert Follett and Finis Welch, "Testing for Discrimination in Employment Practices," *Law and Contemporary Problems* 46 (1983), p. 172.

38. Richard Epstein, *Forbidden Grounds: The Case Against Employment Discrimination Laws,* Harvard University Press, Cambridge, 1992, p. 223.

39. Thomas Sowell, *Preferential Policies: An International Perspective,* William Morrow, New York, 1990, p. 129.

40. Ibid., pp. 132–33; see also Donald Horowitz, *Ethnic Groups in Conflict,* University of California Press, Berkeley, 1985, p. 677; Myron Weiner, "The Pursuit of Ethnic Inequalities Through Preferential Policies: A Comparative Public Policy Perspective," in Robert B. Goldmann and A. Jeyaratnam Wilson, *From Independence to Statehood,* Frances Pinter, London, 1984, p. 64.

41. Stanley Lieberson, *A Piece of the Pie: Blacks and White Immigrants Since 1880,* University of California Press, Berkeley, 1980, p. 379.

42. Leon F. Bouvier and David Simcox, *Foreign Born Professionals in the United States,* Center for Immigration Studies, Washington, DC, April 1994, p. 2.

43. Christopher Jencks, *Rethinking Social Policy: Race, Poverty and the Underclass,* Harvard University Press, Cambridge, 1992, p. 28.

44. Andrew Hacker, *Two Nations: Black and White, Separate, Hostile, Unequal,* Ballantine Books, New York, 1992, p. 94.

45. Jencks, *Rethinking Social Policy,* p. 37.

46. *The Economic Status of Black Women: An Exploratory Investigation,* Staff Report, U.S. Commission on Civil Rights, Washington, DC, 1990, p. 12; Jencks, *Rethinking Social Policy,* p. 40; Hacker, *Two Nations,* p. 95.

47. See, e.g., Johnnetta B. Cole, *Conversations: Straight Talk With America's Sister President,* Anchor Books, New York, 1993, p. 85. "When sexism is superimposed on racism, we find the worst nightmare of all. . . . African American women, confronted with racism on the one hand and sexism on the other, find themselves between a rock and a hard place."

48. U.S. Bureau of the Census, *We the American Hispanics,* Washington, DC, 1993, p. 4; *We the First Americans,* Washington, DC, 1993, p. 3; *We the American Blacks,* Washington, DC, 1993, p. 2; Claudia Bennett, *The Black Population in the United States,* U.S. Department of Commerce, March 1992, p. 1; Sidney Goldstein, "Profile of American Jewry," *American Jewish Year Book,* American Jewish Committee and Jewish Publication Society, New York, 1992, pp. 105–6.

49. U.S. Bureau of the Census, *We the Asian Americans,* Washington, DC, 1993, p. 2; *We the American Hispanics,* p. 3; *We the First Americans,* p. 3; *We the American Blacks,* pp. 3–4; Bennett, *The Black Population in the United States,* p. 27.

50. Claudia Bennett, "The Black Population," in U.S. Department of Commerce, *Population Profile of the United States 1993,* Washington, DC, May 1993, p. 34; Susan Lapham, "The Hispanic Population," ibid., pp. 36–37; Claudia Bennett, "The Asian and Pacific Islander Population," ibid., pp. 38–39.

51. June O'Neill, "The Role of Human Capital in Earnings Differences Between Black and White Men," *Journal of Economic Perspectives* 4, No. 4 (Fall 1990), pp. 25–45; see also June O'Neill, "The Changing Economic Status of Black Americans," *The American Enterprise,* September-October 1992, pp. 71–79.

52. Data supplied by the College Board, Princeton, New Jersey.

53. John A. Dossey, Ina V.S. Mullins, and Chancey O. Jones, *Can Students Do Mathematics Problem Solving?,* National Center for Education Statistics, Washington, DC, August 1993, pp. 14, 173–74, 193.

54. Ina Mullins and Lynn Jenkins, *The Reading Report Card, 1971–1988,* Educational Testing Service, Princeton, NJ, 1988, pp. 63–64; John Dossey, Ina Mullins, Mary Lindquist, and Donald Chambers, *The Mathematics Report Card,* Educational Testing Service, Princeton, NJ, 1988, pp. 141–42.

55. A. Applebee, J. Langer, and I. Mullins, "Crossroads in American Education," in *The Nation's Report Card,* Educational Testing Service, Princeton, NJ, 1989, p. 17.

56. *Summary Report 1992: Doctorate Recipients from United States Universities,* National Academy Press, Washington, DC, 1993, see Appendix A, pp. 44–47.

57. Irwin S. Kirsch, Ann Jungeblut, Lynn Jenkins, and Andrew Kolstad, *Adult Literacy in America,* National Center for Education Statistics, Department of Education, Washington, DC, 1993, pp. 32–37.

58. U.S. Department of Defense, *Population Representation in the Military Services: Fiscal Year 1992*, Washington, DC, October 1993. See table A-6.

59. Rogers Elliott, "Tests, Abilities, Race and Conflict," *Intelligence* 12 (1988), p. 343.

60. Gregory R. Anrig, Margaret E. Goertz, and Regina C. McNeill, "Teacher Competency Testing: Realities of Supply and Demand in This Period of Educational Reform," *Journal of Negro Education* 55 (1986), pp. 316–55; American Association of Colleges of Teacher Education, "Pass Rates on Teacher Competency Tests in 10 States," cited in Gerald David Jaynes and Robin M. Williams, *A Common Destiny: Blacks and American Society*, National Academy Press, Washington, DC, 1989, p. 364; see also Andrew Hacker, *Two Nations*, p. 173.

61. Mark Kelman, "Concepts of Discrimination in General Ability Testing," *Harvard Law Review* 104 (1991), p. 1192.

62. Race norming is described in detail and defended in John Hartigan and Alexandra Wigdor, *Fairness in Employment Testing: Validity Generalization, Minority Issues and the General Aptitude Test Battery*, National Academy Press, Washington, DC, 1989; see also Linda Gottfredson, "When Job Testing Fairness Is Nothing but a Quota," *Wall Street Journal*, December 6, 1990.

63. See, e.g., Timothy Noah, "Job Tests Scored on Racial Curve Stir Controversy," *Wall Street Journal*, April 26, 1991, p. B-1; Stuart Taylor, "Rigging Test Scores by Race," *Legal Times*, May 13, 1991, p. 17; Laurence Barrett, "Cheating on Test," *Time*, June 3, 1991, p. 57; Robert Holland, "Race Norming by Any Other Name," *National Review*, July 29, 1991, p. 36. For Linda Gottfredson's own recent account, see Linda Gottfredson, "The Science and Politics of Race Norming," *American Psychologist*, November 1994, pp. 955–63.

64. The Civil Rights Act of 1991 embraced the disparate impact theory that courts have used to legitimize racial preferences. At the same time, Congress outlawed race norming. See Civil Rights Act of 1991, Public Law 102–166, Section 703 (l).

65. Nathan Glazer writes, "The demand for competence meets as a first barrier the fact that different percentages of key ethnic and racial groups achieve different levels of competency. The critics of testing . . . attack the tests as discriminatory because more blacks fail them. Direct employment by racial quota . . . seems the unstated but clear objective of the attack on testing." See Nathan Glazer, "The Problem With Competence," in John Bunzel, ed., *Challenge to American Schools*, Oxford University Press, New York, 1985, pp. 216, 228; see also Kenneth Carson, "New Civil Rights Law Shoots Itself in the Foot," *Wall Street Journal*, November 22, 1991.

66. Kenneth J. Cooper, "Exams Opposed over Potential Harm to Minorities," *Washington Post*, June 12, 1991, p. A-21.

67. "Race Norming," *Wall Street Journal*, April 4, 1991, p. A-18.

68. Richard Seymour, "Why Plaintiffs' Counsel Challenge Tests, and How They Can Successfully Challenge the Theory of Validity Generalization," *Journal of Vocational Behavior* 33 (1988), pp. 331–64.

69. Faustine Jones-Wilson, "The State of African-American Education," in Kofi Lomotey, ed., *Going to School: The African-American Experience*, State University of New York Press, Albany, 1990, p. 47.

70. Cited by Heather MacDonald, "The Diversity Industry," *The New Republic*, July 5, 1993, p. 24.

71. Sonia Nieto, *Affirming Diversity: The Sociopolitical Context of Multicultural Education*, Longman, New York, 1992, pp. 290–91, 295.

72. Geneva Gay, "Ethnic Minorities and Educational Equality," in James A. Banks and Cherry McGee Banks, eds., *Multicultural Education: Issues and Perspectives*, Allyn & Bacon, Boston, 1989, pp. 168, 179.

73. Derrick Bell, *Faces at the Bottom of the Well: The Permanence of Racism*, Basic Books, New York, 1992, p. 56.

74. Michael Eric Dyson, *Reflecting Black: African American Cultural Criticism*, University of Minnesota Press, Minneapolis, 1993, p. 138.

75. See, e.g., Stanley Fish, *There's No Such Thing as Free Speech, and It's a Good Thing Too*, Oxford University Press, New York, 1994, p. 4; Gary Peller, "Espousing a Positive Vision of Affirmative Action Policies," *Chronicle of Higher Education*, December 18, 1991, p. B-1; Blumrosen, *Modern Law*, p. 269.

76. Cited by John Leo, "A University's Sad Decline," *U.S. News and World Report*, August 15, 1994, p. 20.

77. Andrew Hacker, "An Affirmative Vote for Affirmative Action," *Academic Questions*, Fall 1992, p. 25.

78. See, e.g., Ezorsky, *Racism and Justice*, p. 41.

79. For a discussion of banding, see Frank L. Schmidt, "Why All Banding Procedures in Personnel Selection Are Logically Flawed," *Human Performance* 4 (1991), pp. 265–77; Wayne Cascio et al., "Statistical Implications of Six Methods of Test Score Use in Personnel Selection," *Human Performance* 4 (1991), pp. 233–64.

80. Geneva Gay, "Ethnic Minorities and Educational Equality," in Banks and Banks, *Multicultural Education*, p. 182. Gay argues that "narrative reports, developmental profiles . . . and anecdotal records should replace letter and symbol grades." She also contends that minorities should not be enrolled in difficult subjects. "If minority students are already failing science, taking more of it means they will have even greater opportunities to fail."

81. Kelman, "Concepts of Discrimination in General Ability Job Testing," p. 1158.

82. Fish, *There's No Such Thing as Free Speech*, p. 63.

83. Several studies are reviewed in Stanley Sue and Jennifer Abe, *Predictors of Academic Achievement Among Asian Students and White Students*, College Entrance Examination Board, Princeton, NJ, 1988; Robert Klitgaard, *Choosing Elites*, Basic Books, New York, 1985; Warren Willingham, Charles Lewis, Rick Morgan, and Leonard Ramist, *Predicting College Grades: An Analysis of Institutional Trends Over Two Decades*, Educational Testing Service, Princeton, NJ, 1990.

84. See, e.g., F. L. Schmidt, "The Problem of Group Differences in Ability Test Scores in Employment Selection," *Journal of Vocational Behavior* 33 (1988), pp. 272–92; Frank L. Schmidt, John E. Hunter, and Nambury S. Raju, "Validity Generalization and Situational Specificity," *Journal of Applied Psychology* 73 (1988), pp. 665–72; John E. Hunter, "Cognitive Ability, Cognitive Aptitudes, Job Knowledge and Job Performance," *Journal of Vocational Behavior* 29 (1986), pp. 340–62; Frank L. Schmidt, John E. Hunter, Alice N. Outerbridge, and M. H. Trattner, "The Impact

of Job Selection Methods on Size, Productivity and Payroll Cost of the Federal Workforce," *Personnel Psychology* 39 (1985), pp. 1–29; John Hunter and Frank Schmidt, "Forty Questions About Validity Generalization and Meta-Analysis," *Personnel Psychology* 38 (1985), p. 697; Frank Schmidt and John Hunter, "Individual Differences in Productivity," *Journal of Applied Psychology* 68 (1983), pp. 407–14; Frank L. Schmidt, John E. Hunter, and Kenneth Pearlman, "Progress in Validity Generalization," *Journal of Applied Psychology* 67 (1982), pp. 835–45; Frank Schmidt and John Hunter, "Employment Testing: Old Theories and New Research Findings," *American Psychologist* 36 (1981), pp. 1128–37; Frank Schmidt and John Hunter, "Development of a General Solution to the Problem of Validity Generalization," *Journal of Applied Psychology* 62 (1977), pp. 529–40.

85. Hartigan and Wigdor, *Fairness in Employment Testing*, p. 5. Hartigan and Wigdor estimate the predictive validity of the GATB in the range of 0.25 to 0.35.

86. See, e.g., Jan H. Blits and Linda Gottfredson, "Employment Testing and Job Performance," *The Public Interest*, Winter 1990.

87. David Owen, *None of the Above: Behind the Myth of Scholastic Aptitude*, Houghton Mifflin, New York, 1985, p. 222.

88. Carol Innerst, "Tilt to Minorities Upsets Some Takers," *Washington Times*, February 23, 1992, p. A-6.

89. Carol Innerst, "Revised Tests Still Show Bias, Critics Complain," *Washington Times*, February 23, 1992, p. A-6.

90. Since 1977, the racial gap between blacks and whites on the math section of the SAT has been approximately 15–18 points greater than the gap on the verbal section of the test. National Center for Education Statistics, *The Condition of Education*, U.S. Department of Education, Washington, DC, 1993, pp. 54, 244.

91. James Crouse and Dale Trusheim, *The Case Against the SAT*, University of Chicago Press, Chicago, 1988, pp. 96–98. Crouse and Trusheim write, "Colleges' prediction equations from a combined sample of blacks and whites typically overestimate the freshman grades of blacks. . . . These findings may come as a surprise to some people, since a popular belief among blacks and critics of the SAT is that high school records and SAT scores underestimate blacks' college performance."

92. A. K. Wigdor and W. R. Garner, *Ability Testing: Uses, Consequences and Controversies*, National Academy Press, Washington DC, 1982, Vol. I, p. 77.

93. Jacqueline Fleming, "Standardized Test Scores and the Black College Environment," in Kofi Lomotey, ed., *Going to School*, pp. 143–52.

94. Oddly, Hartigan and Wigdor proceed to endorse race norming. Their reasoning is that since no test is perfectly predictive, any modestly predictive test like the GATB will produce some candidates who fail the test yet would perform as good workers (false negatives) and others who pass the test yet would not do as well on the job (false positives). Although these risks are inherent in any test that does not show 100 percent predictive validity, Hartigan and Wigdor conclude that "the disproportionate impact of selection error" on blacks provides adequate justification for artificially raising African American scores. See Hartigan and Wigdor, eds., *Fairness in Employment Testing*, pp. 6–7. For a critique of Hartigan and Wigdor's policy proposals, see Blits and Gottfredson, "Employment Testing and Job Performance."

95. Lawrence Feinberg, "Study Rejects Bias Charges in Job Tests," *Washington Post,* February 3, 1982.

96. Ellis Cose, "The Myth of Meritocracy," *Newsweek,* April 3, 1995, p. 34.

97. "Notions like merit and fairness are always presented as if their meanings were perspicuous to anyone no matter what his or her political affiliation, educational experience, ethnic tradition, gender, class, institutional history, etc. In fact merit and fairness will have different meanings in relation to different assumptions and background conditions." See Fish, *There's No Such Thing as Free Speech,* esp. pp. 4–12.

98. "The Other Minorities Get Their Due," *Business Week,* July 8, 1991, p. 62.

99. Randall Kennedy, "Competing Conceptions of Racial Discrimination," *Harvard Journal of Law and Public Policy,* Winter 1991, p. 99.

100. Martin Kilson, "Anatomy of Black Conservatism," *Transition,* Issue 59 (1994), p. 11.

101. The Jefferson quotation is cited by Gordon Wood, *The Radicalism of the American Revolution,* Vintage Books, New York, 1993, p. 182. The Adams quotation is cited by Gordon Wood, *The Creation of the American Republic,* W. W. Norton, New York, 1972, p. 71.

102. John Gardner, *Excellence: Can We Be Equal and Excellent Too?,* W. W. Norton, New York, 1984, p. 63.

103. Cited by Daniel Bell, "On Meritocracy and Equality," *The Public Interest,* Fall 1972, p. 43.

104. Glazer, *Affirmative Discrimination,* p. 67.

105. Herman Belz, *Equality Transformed: A Quarter Century of Affirmative Action,* Transaction Books, New Brunswick, NJ, 1991, p. 83; Blumrosen, *Modern Law,* p. 175. In 1973, in a widely publicized case, AT&T signed a consent decree agreeing to more than $30 million in back pay. More significant, AT&T agreed to a preferential hiring policy that increased minority representation from 6.7 percent of black employees and 2.4 percent of black managers in 1969 to 22.3 percent minority workers and 14.4 percent managers in 1979. Melvin Urofsky, *A Conflict of Rights: The Supreme Court and Affirmative Action,* Charles Scribner, New York, 1991, pp. 21–22.

106. Cited by Belz, *Equality Transformed,* p. 84.

107. Blumrosen, *Modern Law,* pp. 33, 165.

108. Andrew Kull, *The Color-Blind Constitution,* Harvard University Press, Cambridge, 1982, p. 200.

109. Glazer, *Affirmative Discrimination,* p. 58.

110. Stuart Taylor, "Clinton and the Quota Game," *Legal Times,* December 28, 1992, p. 23.

111. Tama Starr, "Who's Gonna Sue Me Next?" *Across the Board,* July-August 1993, pp. 59–60.

112. James Bovard, *Lost Rights: The Destruction of American Liberty,* St. Martin's Press, New York, 1994, pp. 169–70.

113. Information Office, OFCCP, U.S. Department of Labor.

114. Information Office, EEOC.

115. See, e.g., *Regents of University of California v. Bakke,* 438 U.S. 265 (1978);

United Steelworkers v. Weber, 443 U.S. 193 (1979); *Fullilove v. Klutznick,* 448 U.S. 448 (1980); *United States v. Paradise,* 480 U.S. 149 (1987).

116. In the 1975 case of *Albemarle Paper v. Moody,* the court decided that it was not enough for a company to prove that its merit criteria were job related; the plaintiff could still win the case by showing that the employer could have used other criteria that produced a smaller disproportionate impact in hiring rates between groups. In *Connecticut v. Teal,* decided in 1982, the Supreme Court held that companies should be scrutinized for adverse impact not only at the final selection stage but at every step of the selection process. In 1988, the Supreme Court in *Watson v. Fort Worth Bank & Trust Co* declared that employers who fail to achieve proportional representation based on race would have to prove that not only were standardized tests and other generally objective criteria required by "business necessity," but also all subjective standards such as interview questions, candidate demeanor, and so on. *Albemarle Paper Co v. Moody,* 422 U.S. 405 (1975), *Connecticut v. Teal,* 457 U.S. 440 (1982); *Watson v. Fort Worth Bank & Trust Co,* 487 U.S. 977 (1988).

117. "Race in the Workplace: Is Affirmative Action Working?" *Business Week,* July 8, 1991, p. 56.

118. Steven A. Holmes, "Affirmative Action Plans Are Part of Business Life," *New York Times,* November 22, 1991, p. A-20.

119. Anne B. Fisher, "Businessmen Like to Hire by the Numbers," *Fortune,* September 16, 1985, pp. 26, 28. "Most large American corporations want to retain their affirmative action programs, numerical goals and all." Some senior corporate executives are quoted saying that even if the government stopped requiring minority hiring, they would continue to maintain race-based targets anyway.

120. "Twenty years after the enactment of the Civil Rights Act of 1964, there has been no systematic inquiry into the effects of affirmative action on American society, neither its costs to the nation's economy nor its impact on our country's morale. In an age of program evaluation, when most other social experiments are studied almost to death, our profession has shown a resolute ignorance about an extraordinarily controversial policy that has been in place for over two decades. It is as if affirmative action has assumed the status of a religious article of faith, and professionals choose to avoid studying its effects for fear of what they might find out." William Beer, "Resolute Ignorance: Social Science and Affirmative Action," *Society,* May-June 1987, p. 63.

121. Jencks, *Rethinking Social Policy,* p. 57.

122. Ibid., p. 54; Hacker, *Two Nations,* p. 133.

123. Richard Posner writes that the threat of civil rights litigation "makes it more costly for a firm to operate in an area where the labor pool contains a high percentage of blacks, by enlarging the firm's legal exposure. There, when deciding where to locate a new plant or whether to expand an existing one, a firm will be attracted, other things being equal, to areas that have only small percentages of blacks in their labor force." Richard Posner, "The Efficiency and Efficacy of Title VII," *University of Pennsylvania Law Review* 136 (1987), p. 519..

124. About 76 percent of whites oppose racial preferences for college admissions. About 90 percent of whites oppose racial preferences in hiring and job promotion.

See Paul Sniderman and Thomas Piazza, *The Scar of Race,* Harvard University Press, Cambridge, 1993, p. 131.

125. Anti-Defamation League of B'nai B'rith, *Survey on Racial Attitudes,* November 1992, pp. 70–71.

126. Martin Kilson, "Anatomy of Black Conservatism," *Transition,* Issue 59, 1994, p. 14.

127. Sniderman and Piazza, *The Scar of Race,* pp. 8, 101–4.

128. Anti-Defamation League of B'nai B'rith, *Survey on Racial Attitudes,* pp. 32–33.

129. William Raspberry, "Why Civil Rights Isn't Selling," *Washington Post,* March 13, 1991, p. A-17.

130. One case is that of Philip and Paul Malone, who took a Civil Service Test in order to qualify for the Boston fire department. They scored below the city average, making it unlikely that the two white men would be hired. But then the brothers discovered that Boston, like other cities, routinely recruits black and other minority applicants with lower scores in order to increase their representation on the force. The Malones found an old photograph of a great grandmother whom they claim was black, and listed themselves as minorities. After several years, when their names appeared on a list of black firefighters due for a promotion, supervisors challenged their authenticity. They were accused of being whites posing as blacks, and fired from the department. According to Boston city officials, as many as sixty firefighters have been accused of faking their identity as minorities, and the problem occurs in other areas of public hiring. See Peggy and John Ellement, "Effort to Advance Spotlighted Claim of Firefighters," *Boston Globe,* September 29, 1988; Susan Diesenhouse, "Boston Case Raises Questions on Misuse of Affirmative Action," *New York Times,* October 9, 1988.

131. Frederick Lynch, *Invisible Victims: White Males and the Crisis of Affirmative Action,* Praeger, New York, 1991.

132. Tom Kenworthy and Thomas B. Edsall, "Whites See Jobs on the Line," *Washington Post,* June 4, 1991, pp. A-1, A-4.

133. Testimony of John Velde, offered before the Subcommittee on Transportation, U.S. Senate Committee on Public Works, November 19, 1985, p. 2.

134. Cited in "Battleground Chicago," *Newsweek,* April 3, 1995, p. 30.

135. Edward W. Jones, Jr., "Black Managers: The Dream Deferred," *Harvard Business Review,* May-June 1986, pp. 84–93.

136. Cornel West, *Race Matters,* Beacon Press, Boston, 1993, p. 52.

137. Stephen Carter, *Reflections of an Affirmative Action Baby,* Basic Books, New York, 1991.

138. See, e.g., Nazario, "Many Minorities Feel Torn by Experience of Affirmative Action," pp. A-1, A-10. "If I had to do it over again," Roland Lee, a San Francisco fireman, says, "I would get my promotion" without preferences. "That would give me back my credibility." Migdia Chinea-Varela, a Hispanic screenwriter, says, "I'm reluctantly appreciative of the affirmative action jobs I've had. But at the same time, they made me really depressed."

139. "American business is not considering the same affirmative action and diversity

issues it espouses in hiring and promotion when it moves to slash jobs." See Caroline V. Clarke, "Downsizing Trounces Diversity," *Black Enterprise,* February 1994, p. 69.

140. Bill McAllister, "Postal Official: Too Many Blacks Hired," *Washington Post,* August 3, 1994, pp. A-1, A-5; Robert Rosenblatt, "Blacks Dominate Postal Service, Latino Charges," *Los Angeles Times,* August 3, 1994, p. A-3.

141. See, e.g., Taylor Cox, *Cultural Diversity in Organizations: Theory, Research and Practice,* Berrett-Koehler Publishers, San Francisco, 1993, pp. 178–79. For some of the extensive literature on managing diversity, see Susan Jackson, ed., *Diversity in the Workplace: Human Resource Initiatives,* Guilford Press, New York, 1992; D. Jamieson and J. O'Mara, *Managing Workforce 2000: Gaining the Diversity Advantage,* Jossey-Bass, San Francisco, 1991; M. Loden and J. B. Rosener, *Workforce America! Managing Employee Diversity as a Vital Resource,* Business Irwin, Homewood, IL, 1991; S. B. Thiederman, *Bridging Cultural Barriers for Corporate Success,* Lexington Books, Lexington, MA, 1991.

142. Alex Jones, "Editors Take on Conflicts of News Staff Diversity," *New York Times,* April 9, 1992; Frederick Lynch, "Multiculturalism Comes to the Workplace," *Wall Street Journal,* October 26, 1992.

143. "CEO Roundtable: Hispanics and Corporate America," *Hispanic,* January-February 1994, p. 95.

144. Elsa McDowell, "Avon Thrives on Diversity," *The Post and Courier* (Charleston, SC), November 15, 1991, p. 7-B.

145. Cited by Heather MacDonald, "The Diversity Industry," *The New Republic,* July 5, 1993, p. 23.

146. "The Challenge of Managing Diversity in the Workplace," *Black Enterprise,* July 1993, p. 90; Drew Clark, "Getting Along: Workplace Diversity Consultants Take Corporate World by Storm," *Washington Business Journal,* March 25–31, 1994, pp. 29, 32.

147. "1994 Hispanic 100," *Hispanic,* January-February 1994; see also Coca-Cola ad, *Wall Street Journal,* April 3, 1992, p. R-3.

148. Mark Land, "Where Diversity Survives Hard Times," *USA Today,* January 8, 1992, p. 8-B.

149. MacDonald, "The Diversity Industry," p. 25.

150. Anheuser-Busch advertisement, "Our Partnership with the Community Is More than a Promise. It's a Commitment," *Emerge,* April 1994.

151. Sybil Evans, "Pfizer: Spirit of Citizenship, Commitment to Diversity," *Cultural Diversity at Work,* July 1993.

152. Sybil Evans, "The Prudential," *Cultural Diversity at Work,* March 1992.

153. MacDonald, "The Diversity Industry," p. 25.

154. R. Roosevelt Thomas, *Beyond Race and Gender: Unleashing the Power of Your Total Work Force by Managing Diversity,* American Management Association, New York, 1991; R. Roosevelt Thomas, *Differences Do Make a Difference,* American Institute for Managing Diversity, Atlanta, 1991.

155. Cox, *Cultural Diversity in Organizations,* p. 60.

156. Fernandez, *Managing a Diverse Work Force,* Lexington Books, Lexington, MA, 1991, p. 191.

157. Cited by Frederick Lynch, "Workforce Diversity: PC's Final Frontier," *National Review,* February 21, 1994, p. 36.

158. Cited in "White, Male and Worried," *Business Week,* January 31, 1994, p. 51.

159. Cited by Bill Gifford, "The Unbearable Whiteness of Being," *Washington City Paper,* November 12, 1993, p. 30.

160. Cited by Penny Lunt, "Should You Do Diversity Training?" *ABA Banking Journal,* August 1994, pp. 53–54.

161. Fernandez, *Managing A Diverse Workforce,* p. 47.

162. Cox, *Cultural Diversity in Organizations,* p. 207.

163. Jackson, *Diversity in the Workplace,* p. 7.

164. Cox, *Cultural Diversity in Organizations,* pp. 33–34.

165. Fernandez, *Managing a Diverse Workforce,* pp. 209, 282; Cox, *Cultural Diversity in Organizations,* p. 209; Jackson, *Diversity in the Workplace,* pp. 52, 54, 63.

166. "Public Seminar Schedule," American Institute for Managing Diversity, Atlanta, Georgia, 1994.

167. See, e.g., Jack Gordon, "Rethinking Diversity," *Training,* January 1992, pp. 23–30; Joyce Price, "Classes in How to Get Along Are Becoming Big Business," *Washington Times,* January 13, 1994; Max Boot, "Oppression Studies Go Corporate," *Wall Street Journal,* August 24, 1994, p. A-8.

168. MacDonald, "The Diversity Industry."

169. Thomas Sowell, "Effrontery and Gall, Inc," *Forbes,* September 27, 1993, p. 52.

170. Amy Stevens, "Antidiscrimination Training Haunts Employer in Bias Suit," *Wall Street Journal,* July 31, 1991, p. B-1, Shari Caudron, "Employees Use Diversity Training Exercise Against Lucky Stores in Intentional Discrimination Suit," *Personnel Journal,* April 1993, p. 52.

171. Thomas McCarroll, "It's a Mass Market No More," *Time,* special issue on multiculturalism, Fall 1993, p. 80.

172. Ibid., p. 81.

173. Marketing research has shown, for example, that black car buyers show a preference for large cars. Black men are more likely than white men to buy certain brands of cologne such as Pierre Cardin and Brut and less likely to buy Mennen deodorant. Blacks tend to chew Wrigleys gum, while whites prefer Trident. Blacks use Listerine mouthwash, whites Scope or Signal. Blacks on average drink a lot more Bacardi rum than whites, who seem to incline toward Smirnoff vodka. One analyst writes, "Prestige, status, pride and reassurance of product quality appeal to the black consumer because blacks have historically been denied these things." See W. Keith Tunnell, "Not Colorblind," *Madison Avenue,* March 1984, pp. 20–23; see also Alphonzia Wellington, "Traditional Brand Loyalty," *Advertising Age,* May 18, 1981, p. S-2.

174. Michael E. Porter, *Competitive Advantage,* Free Press, New York, 1985, p. 390.

175. Bradford Cornell, "An Hypothesis Regarding the Origins of Ethnic Discrimination," Finance Working Paper, UCLA Management School, February 1994.

176. Cox, *Cultural Diversity in Organizations,* pp. 34, 37.

177. Louis Gerstner, Jr., "Our Schools Are Failing: Do We Care?" *New York Times,* May 27, 1994.

178. Brimelow and Spencer, "When Quotas Replace Merit, Everybody Suffers," p. 82.

179. Michael Porter, *The Competitive Advantage of Nations,* Free Press, New York, 1990, p. 8.

Chapter 9. Is Eurocentrism a Racist Concept?

1. Chinua Achebe, *Hopes and Impediments: Selected Essays,* Doubleday, New York, 1988, p. 16.

2. J. M. Blaut offers the standard definition of Eurocentrism as "a label for all the beliefs that postulate past or present superiority of Europeans over non-Europeans and over minority people of non-European descent." J. M. Blaut, *The Colonizer's Model of the World: Geographical Diffusionism and Eurocentric History,* Guilford Press, New York, 1993, p. 8.

3. See, e.g., U.S. Department of Education, *The Condition of Education 1993,* Washington, DC; International Assessment of Educational Progress, *A World of Difference,* National Center for Education Statistics, U.S. Department of Education, Washington, DC, 1989; National Endowment for the Humanities, *American Memory: A Report on the Humanities in the Nation's Public Schools,* Washington, DC, 1987; John Dossey, Ina Mullins, and Chancey Jones, *Can Students Do Mathematical Problem Solving?,* Educational Testing Service, Washington, DC, August 1993.

4. Edward Said, "Identity, Authority and Freedom," *Transition,* Issue 54, 1991, p. 5.

5. James Baldwin, "Stranger in the Village," *Notes of a Native Son,* Beacon Press, Boston, 1955, pp. 159–75.

6. See, e.g., Claude M. Steele, "Race and the Schooling of Black Americans," *The Atlantic Monthly,* April 1992, pp. 26–58.

7. Ishmael Reed, *Airing Dirty Laundry,* Addison-Wesley, Reading, MA, 1993, p. 87.

8. Alice Walker, *In Search of Our Mothers' Gardens,* Harcourt Brace Jovanovich, New York, 1983, p. 8.

9. June Jordan, *Technical Difficulties: African American Notes on the State of the Union,* Vintage Books, New York, 1994, p. 202.

10. Andrew Hacker, "Conceptions of Academic Qualifications," *The Journal of Blacks in Higher Education,* Autumn 1993, p. 32.

11. Toni Morrison, "Unspeakable Things Unspoken: The Afro-American Presence in American Literature," *Michigan Quarterly Review,* Winter 1989, p. 8.

12. Christine Bennett, *Comprehensive Multicultural Education: Theory and Practice,* Allyn & Bacon, Boston, 1990, p. 71.

13. Bell Hooks, *Black Looks: Race and Representation,* South End Press, Boston, 1992, p. 18.

14. Molefi Kete Asante, "Multiculturalism: An Exchange," *The American Scholar,* Spring 1991, p. 268.

15. Gerald J. Pine and Asa Hilliard III, "Rx for Racism: Imperatives for America's Schools," *Phi Delta Kappan,* April 1990, pp. 593–600; Asa Hilliard, "Why We Must Pluralize the Curriculum," *Educational Leadership,* December 1991–January 1992, pp. 12–13.

16. Martin Bernal, *Black Athena: The Afroasiatic Roots of Classical Civilization,* Rutgers University Press, New Brunswick, 1987, p. 73.

17. Cited by James Traub, "Separate and Equal," *The Atlantic,* September 1991, p. 30. Some scholars maintain that busing contributes to slightly improved academic perfomance, although even they usually defend the practice mainly because it improves social interactions between the races. See Gerald David Jaynes and Robin M. Williams, eds., *A Common Destiny: Blacks and American Society,* National Academy Press, Washington, DC, 1989, p. 19.

18. John A. Murphy, "Busing: No Substitute for High Quality Education," *Washington Post,* April 29, 1994.

19. See, e.g., a review of several studies by Walter Stephan, "School Desegregation: An Evaluation of Predictions Made in *Brown v. Board of Education," Psychological Bulletin* 85, No. 2 (March 1978), pp. 217–28.

20. Jacqueline Fleming, *Blacks in College,* Jossey-Bass, San Francisco, 1984, p. 143.

21. Neal Krause, "Interracial Contact in Schools and Black Children's Self-Esteem," in Harriette Pipes McAdoo and John Lewis McAdoo, eds., *Black Children: Social, Educational and Parental Environments,* Sage Publications, Beverly Hills, 1985, p. 259.

22. Robert Joiner, "Black Mayors Driving Away from Busing," *Emerge,* March 1994, pp. 52–55.

Prince George's County, Maryland has for more than two decades spent a great deal of money and time busing students without much return on its investment in terms of improved schools. The *Washington Post* reports that programs often involve transporting students from schools that are three-fourths black to schools that are one-half black. In 1993 Democratic state delegate Michael Arrington, an African American, said of busing, "We've had this thing over our heads for 20 years, and it's an albatross." Finally, with support of blacks and whites, Prince George's County announced plans to end busing and adopt a new system of enhanced neighborhood schools. See Lisa Leff, "Demographics Foil PG Schools' Efforts to Achieve Racial Balance," *Washington Post,* September 12, 1993, pp. A-1, A-24; Lisa Leff, "For Schools, Court Order Provided No Shortcut to Excellence," *Washington Post,* September 13, 1993, p. A-1; Retha Hill, "PG Schools Want to End Racial Busing," *Washington Post,* July 21, 1994, p. A-1.

See also Mirsha Mah and Charles P. Wilson, "The Desegregation Mess," *Delaware Today,* June 1994, pp. 24–32.

23. Asa G. Hilliard, "Conceptual Confusion and the Persistence of Group Oppression Through Education," *Equity and Excellence* 24, No. 1 (1988), p. 38.

24. An excellent example of this is Outcomes Based Education. Advocates of OBE argue that traditional standards such as grades, tracking, and discipline can be injurious to the self-esteem of young people. As the National Center for OBE puts it, "Failure should be removed from our vocabulary and thoughts. . . . Competition in the classroom is destructive." An OBE proposal in Pennsylvania calls for students to be required "to understand and appreciate their worth as unique and capable individuals . . . to preserve and promote their cultural heritage . . . and to exhibit self-esteem." A Virginia proposal specifies similar outcomes: "personal self-concept,"

"cultural endeavors," "civic participation," and "environmental stewardship." Some Ohio educators want their students to "maintain physical, emotional and social well-being." See Bruno Manno, "Outcomes Based Education: Miracle Cure or Plague?" *Hudson Briefing Paper* No. 165, June 1994; Carol Innerst, "Parents Rebel as Outcomes Replace Three Rs," *Washington Times,* September 7, 1994, pp. A-1, A-8.

25. Steven Muller, "How to Restore Excellence in Society," *Cosmos* 4 (1994), p. 6.

26. Charles Taylor, *Multiculturalism and "The Politics of Recognition,"* Princeton University Press, Princeton, 1992.

27. Andrew Mecca, Neil Smelser, and John Vasconcellos, *The Social Importance of Self-Esteem,* California Task Force to Promote Self-Esteem, University of California Press, Berkeley, 1989, pp. 15, 84, 139, 177–78.

28. International Assessment of Educational Progress, *A World of Difference,* National Center for Education Statistics, U.S. Department of Education, Washington, DC, 1989.

29. Cited by Richard Cohen, "Snake Oil for DC Schools," *Washington Post,* September 10, 1993.

30. Mary Ann Scheirer and Robert Kraut, "Increasing Educational Achievement Via Self-Concept Change," *Review of Educational Research* 49, No. 1 (1979), pp. 131–49.

31. Cited by Jo Thomas, "U.S. Panel's Model Looks Beyond Europe," *New York Times,* November 11, 1994, p. A-1.

32. Allan Bloom, *The Closing of the American Mind,* Simon & Schuster, New York, 1988.

33. E. D. Hirsch, *Cultural Literacy,* Houghton Mifflin, Boston, 1987.

34. Arthur Schlesinger, *The Disuniting of America,* W. W. Norton, New York, 1991, p. 137.

35. Gerald Graff, "Teach the Conflicts," *South Atlantic Quarterly* 89, No. 1 (Winter 1990), p. 53.

36. Barbara Herrnstein-Smith, "Cult-Lit: Hirsch, Literacy and the National Culture," ibid., p. 71.

37. Stanley Fish, *There's No Such Thing as Free Speech—And It's a Good Thing Too,* Oxford University Press, New York, 1984, pp. 7–8.

38. Barbara Johnson, ed., *Freedom and Interpretation: The Oxford Amnesty Lectures 1992,* Basic Books, New York, 1993, p. 7.

39. Richard Rorty, *Consequences of Pragmatism: Essays 1972–1980,* University of Minnesota Press, Minneapolis, 1982, p. 204; see also Richard Rorty, *Objectivity, Relativism and Truth: Philosophical Papers,* Cambridge University Press, Cambridge, 1991, Vol. I, p. 23; Richard Rorty, *Philosophy and the Mirror of Nature,* Princeton University Press, Princeton, 1979, p. 360; Renato Rosaldo, *Culture and Truth: The Remaking of Social Analysis,* Beacon Press, Boston, 1993.

40. Cited in Bill Moyers, *A World of Ideas,* Doubleday, New York, 1989, p. 209.

41. Matthew Arnold, *Culture and Anarchy,* Yale University Press, New Haven, 1994, p. 5.

42. Mary Louise Pratt, "Humanities for the Future: Reflections on the Western Culture Debate at Stanford," *South Atlantic Quarterly* 89, No. 1 (Winter 1990), p. 9.

43. Charles Taylor, *The Ethics of Authenticity,* Harvard University Press, Cambridge, 1991, p. 50.

44. Taylor, *Multiculturalism and "The Politics of Recognition,"* pp. 42, 66.

45. Cited in *The Diversity Report,* Institute for the Study of Social Change, University of California at Berkeley, November 1991, p. 16.

46. Gayatri Chakravorty Spivak, "Three Women's Texts and a Critique of Imperialism," in Henry Louis Gates, Jr., ed., *"Race," Writing and Difference,* University of Chicago Press, Chicago, 1986, p. 262.

47. Edward Said, *Culture and Imperialism,* Alfred A. Knopf, New York, 1993, p. 22.

48. Michael Omi and Howard Winant, *Racial Formation in the United States,* Routledge & Kegan Paul, New York, 1986, p. 72.

49. "There is an historical connection between the Third World abroad and the Third World within. Racial groups in America are and have been colonized peoples. . . . Our own development proceeded on the basis of Indian conquests and land seizures, on the enslavement of African peoples, and in terms of a westward expansion that involved war with Mexico and the incorporation of half of that nation's territory." Robert Blauner, *Racial Oppression in America,* Harper & Row, New York, 1972, pp. 12, 52.

50. Henry Louis Gates, Jr., *Loose Canons: Notes on the Culture Wars,* Oxford University Press, New York, 1992, p. 35.

51. James A. Banks, *Multiethnic Education: Theory and Practice,* Allyn & Bacon, Boston, 1981, pp. 25, 242.

52. Deborah A. Batiste and Pamela Harris, "A Holistic Approach to Multicultural Education," National Multicultural Institute, Washington, DC, 1994.

53. Ellen K. Coughlin, "New History of America Attempts to Make Good on the Claims of Multiculturalism," *Chronicle of Higher Education,* May 26, 1993, p. A–9; Ronald Takaki, *A Different Mirror: A History of Multicultural America,* Little, Brown, Boston, 1993, p. 426.

54. James Banks, "Multicultural Education: Characteristics and Goals," in James Banks and Cherry McGee Banks, eds., *Multicultural Education: Issues and Perspectives,* Allyn & Bacon, Boston, 1989, p. 198.

55. Renato Rosaldo, *Culture and Truth,* p. xvii.

56. For popular accounts of the controversy over Columbus, see, e.g., Joyce Price, "Goodbye Columbus," *Washington Times,* March 26, 1991; Barbara Vobejda, "Columbus: Which Legacy?" *Washington Post,* October 11, 1992.

57. Public statement by Russell Means on November 24, 1989; cited by Robert Royal, *1492 and All That,* Ethics and Public Policy Center, Washington, DC, 1992, p. 19.

58. Winona LaDuke, "We Are Still Here," *Sojourners,* October 1991, p. 16.

59. "A Faithful Response to the 500th Anniversary of the Arrival of Christopher Columbus," National Council of Churches, governing board resolution, May 17, 1990.

60. "Even Columbus," *Wall Street Journal,* October 12, 1992, p. A-10.

61. Stephen Greenblatt, *Marvelous Possessions: The Wonder of the New World,* University of Chicago Press, 1991, p. 136.

62. Reed, *Airing Dirty Laundry*, p. 228.

63. Christine Slater, "White Racism," *Multicultural Education*, Spring 1994, pp. 5, 7.

64. Bell Hooks, *Outlaw Culture: Resisting Representations*, Routledge, New York, 1994, p. 198.

65. Francis Jennings, *The Invasion of America*, W. W. Norton, New York, 1976, p. 15.

66. Lynne Duke, "As Some Celebrate Columbus, Others See Pattern of Conquest," *Washington Post*, October 11, 1992, p. A-10.

67. Kirkpatrick Sale, *The Conquest of Paradise: Christopher Columbus and the Columbian Legacy*, Alfred A. Knopf, New York, 1990, p. 69.

68. Cited by Louis Uchitelle, "In the Aztec's Land, Muted Hurrah for Columbus," *New York Times*, September 6, 1990, p. A-4.

69. See, e.g., Garry Wills, "Goodbye Columbus," *New York Review of Books*, November 22, 1990, p. 6; Gary B. Nash, *Red, White and Black: The Peoples of Early America*, Prentice Hall, Englewood Cliffs, NJ, 1974, p. 3; Takaki, *A Different Mirror*, p. 23.

70. Daniel Boorstin, *The Discoverers*, Vintage Books, New York, 1983, pp. 211–12, 215.

71. See, e.g., Wilcomb Washburn, "The Meaning of 'Discovery' in the Fifteenth and Sixteenth Centuries," *American Historical Review* 68, No. 1 (1962).

72. Leszek Kolakowski, *Modernity on Endless Trial*, University of Chicago, Chicago, 1990, p. 4.

73. Nash, *Red, White and Black*, p. 28.

74. Sale, *The Conquest of Paradise*, p. 76, 87, 96, 113, 316.

75. Christopher Columbus, *The Journal of Christopher Columbus*, translated by Cecil Jane, Bonanza Books, New York, 1989, pp. 33, 58, 116, 196; see also Tzvetan Todorov, *The Conquest of America: The Question of the Other*, HarperPerennial, New York, 1984, pp. 36–39.

76. Pedro Alvares Cabral, who was the first European to land in Brazil in 1500, reported a similarly enthusiastic portrait of the natives. Amerigo Vespucci, the Italian sailor who gave his name to the continent of the Americas, described peaceful and idyllic relations with the Guarani Indians. Equally enthusiastic impressions were registered by Magellan, Verrazano, and Martin Frobisher. The English explorer Walter Raleigh reported that "We found the people most gentle, loving and faithful, void of all guile and treason, and such as live after the manner of the golden age." See Wilcomb Washburn, "The First European Contacts with the American Indians," Instituto de Investigacao Cientifica Tropical, Lisbon, 1988, pp. 439–43; Norman Hampson, *The Enlightenment*, Penguin Books, New York, 1968, p. 27.

77. Bernal Diaz, *The Conquest of New Spain*, translated by J. M. Cohen, Penguin Books, New York, 1963, p. 229. Diaz's account is corroborated by a contemporary source, Alvin M. Josephy, Jr., in *The Indian Heritage of America*, Alfred A. Knopf, New York, 1971, p. 216. Josephy writes:

> Many of the rituals required the sacrificing of thousands of human victims to the gods, whose strength needed perpetual renewal with the most spiritually powerful of all foods: human hearts and blood. Victims were led up the steep steps of pyra-

mids to temples on top, where their hearts were cut out and their heads impaled on skull racks. Other victims were flayed, and their skins worn by priests, who themselves often practiced rituals of self-sacrifice, drawing blood from their tongues, ears and other parts of their body.

78. Diaz, *The Conquest of New Spain,* p. 183.

79. Marvin Harris, *Cannibals and Kings: The Origins of Cultures,* Vintage, New York, 1991, p. 164.

80. Ibid., p. 163; Barnet Litvinoff, *1492: The Decline of Medievalism and the Rise of the Modern Age,* Avon Books, New York, 1991, p. 141; Ronald Wright, *Stolen Continents: The Americas Through Indian Eyes Since 1492,* Houghton Mifflin, New York, 1992, pp. 34–35.

81. Igor Shafarevich, *The Socialist Phenomenon,* Harper & Row, New York, 1980, p. 138.

82. Josephy, *The Indian Heritage of America,* pp. 248–49.

83. George Stocking Jr., *Victorian Anthropology,* Free Press, New York, 1987, p. 105.

84. Sale, *The Conquest of Paradise,* pp. 131–32, 319.

85. "That his own religion centered on expiatory sacrifice and upon the symbolic eating and drinking of his god's body and blood does not inhibit Bernal Diaz's horrified response to what his culture construed as the weirdly literal Aztec equivalents." Greenblatt, *Marvelous Possessions,* pp. 134–35.

86. Isabel Schon, "Recommended and Not Recommended Books About Hispanics for Children and Adolescents," *Multicultural Review* 3, No. 1 (March 1994), pp. 18–19. It may be thought that young people should not be exposed to harsh practices such as human sacrifice, but multicultural advocates are enthusiastic about exposing them to other harsh institutions such as American slavery.

87. Pascal Bruckner, *The Tears of the White Man,* Free Press, New York, 1986, p. 93.

88. Sale, *The Conquest of Paradise,* p. 161.

89. Claude Lévi-Strauss, *Tristes Tropiques,* Atheneum, New York, 1974, p. 109.

90. Todorov, *The Conquest of America,* p. 5.

91. Josephy, *The Indian Heritage of America,* pp. 52–53.

92. John P. McKay, Bennett D. Hill, and John Buckler, *A History of World Societies,* Houghton Mifflin, Boston, 1988, Vol. I, p. 559.

93. Ibid.; see also Boyce Rensberger, "A Mummy's Revelation: TB Came to New World Before Columbus," *Washington Post,* March 15, 1994, p. A-15.

94. William H. McNeill, *Plagues and Peoples,* Doubleday, New York, 1976.

95. Litvinoff, *1492,* p. 243; Josephy, *The Indian Heritage of America,* p. 217.

96. Mario Vargas Llosa, "Questions of Conquest," *Harper's,* December 1990, pp. 45–53; Mario Vargas Llosa, "The Disputed Legacy of Christopher Columbus," *Bostonia,* Summer 1992, pp. 45–48; Mario Vargas Llosa, *A Writer's Reality,* Syracuse University Press, New York, 1991, pp. 28–33.

97. Carlos Fuentes, *The Buried Mirror: Reflections on Spain and the New World,* Houghton Mifflin, Boston, 1992, p. 83.

98. Lewis Hanke, *Aristotle and the American Indians,* Henry Regnery, Chicago, 1959, p. 37.

99. Bartolome de las Casas, *A Short Account of the Destruction of the Indies,* Penguin Books, New York, 1992.

100. Cited by Boorstin, *The Discoverers,* p. 635.

101. The Sepulveda–Las Casas debate is authoritatively discussed in Lewis Hanke, *Aristotle and the American Indians.*

102. Cited in ibid., p. 19.

103. For a discussion of Vitoria, see Robert A. Williams, Jr., *The American Indian in Western Legal Thought,* Oxford University Press, New York, 1990, pp. 97–100; see also Royal, *1492 and All That,* pp. 78–81. For a discussion of Suarez, see Wilcomb Washburn, *Red Man's Land, White Man's Law,* Charles Scribner, New York, 1971, pp. 5, 18–20.

104. Ronald Sanders, *Lost Tribes and Promised Lands: The Origins of American Racism,* HarperPerennial, New York, 1992, pp. 128–31, 219–20, 229–31.

105. Alvin Josephy, *The Indian Heritage of America,* pp. 32–33; Jack Weatherford, *Indian Givers: How the Indians of the Americas Transformed the World,* Ballantine Books, New York, 1988, pp. 59–77.

106. Takaki, *A Different Mirror,* p. 12.

107. Thomas Riley, "History and Foodstuffs," *National Review,* November 19, 1990, p. 4.

108. Josephy, *The Indian Heritage of America,* pp. 34–35.

109. Weatherford, *Indian Givers,* p. 135.

110. Benjamin Franklin to James Parker, March 20, 1754, in Leonard Labaree, ed., *The Papers of Benjamin Franklin,* Yale University Press, New Haven, 1961, pp. 118–19.

111. Elisabeth Tooker, "The United States Constitution and the Iroquois League," *Ethnohistory* 35, No. 4 (Fall 1988), reprinted in James A. Clifton, ed., *The Invented Indian,* Transaction Publishers, New Brunswick, 1990.

112. See, e.g., Washington Irving, *The Life and Voyages of Christopher Columbus,* G. P. Putnam and Sons, New York, 1897; Samuel Eliot Morison, *Admiral of the Ocean Sea,* Little, Brown, New York, 1942.

113. Marianna Torgovnick, *Gone Primitive: Savage Intellects, Modern Lives,* University of Chicago Press, Chicago, 1990, p. 83.

114. Conor Cruise O'Brien, "American Identities," *Partisan Review* 61, No. 3 (1994), p. 486.

115. Robert Edgerton, *Sick Societies: Challenging the Myth of Primitive Harmony,* Free Press, New York, 1992, pp. 81, 134, 136–37; Nawal El Saadawi, "Circumcision of Girls," in Stuart Hirschberg, *One World, Many Cultures,* Macmillan, New York, 1992; "Female Genital Mutilation in Africa," *Freedom Review,* March-April 1994, p. 27.

116. Manning Marable, "The Black Male: Searching Beyond Stereotypes," in Richard Majors and Jacob Gordon, eds., *The American Black Male,* Nelson Hall Publishers, Chicago, 1994, p. 70.

117. C. Vann Woodward, *The Future of the Past,* Oxford University Press, New York, 1989, p. 47.

118. Takaki, *A Different Mirror,* p. 428.

119. Molefi Kete Asante, *Afrocentricity,* Africa World Press, Trenton, 1988, pp. 5, 29.

120. The seven principles of the *Nguzo Saba* are: *umoja* or unity, *kujichagulia* or self-determination, *ujima* or collective responsibility, *ujamaa* or cooperative economics, *nia* or group purpose, *kuumba* or creativity, and *imani* or ancestral faith. See Maulana Karenga, *The African American Holiday of Kwanzaa,* University of Sankore Press, Los Angeles, 1988; Cedric McClester, *Kwanzaa,* Gumbs & Thomas, New York, 1993, pp. 3–4.

121. See, e.g., Lerone Bennett, *Before the Mayflower: A History of Black America,* Penguin Books, New York, 1993, p. 24 (where Bennett finds "parallels between African philosophy and modern subatomic physics"); Ralph Wiley, *Why Black People Tend to Shout,* Carol Publishing, New York, 1991, pp. 168–69 (where Wiley credits blacks with inventing the phonograph and the cotton gin and with pioneering open heart surgery).

122. See, e.g., Thomas Midgette and Eddie Glenn, "African-American Male Academies: A Positive View," *Journal of Multicultural Counseling and Development,* 21 (April 1993), pp. 69–78; William Oliver, "Black Males and Social Problems: Prevention Through Afrocentric Socialization," *Journal of Black Studies* 20 (September 1989), pp. 15–39; Na'im Akbar, *Visions for Black Men,* Winston-Derek, Nashville, 1991, p. 36; Derrick Bell, "The Case for a Separate Black School System," in Willy Smith and Eva Chunn, eds., *Black Education: A Quest for Equity and Excellence,* Transaction Books, New Brunswick, 1991, pp. 136–45.

123. Schlesinger, *The Disuniting of America;* Robert Hughes, *The Culture of Complaint: The Fraying of America,* Oxford University Press, New York, 1993; see also Lynne Duke, "African-Centered Curricula: Reclaiming History or Rewriting It?" *Washington Post,* November 27, 1992, pp. A-1, A-34.

124. Joint Center for Political and Economic Studies, survey of attitudes of African Americans, released July 8, 1992.

125. Kenneth J. Cooper, "Broadening Horizons: Afrocentrism Takes Root in Atlanta Schools," *Washington Post,* November 27, 1992, pp. A-1, A-33.

126. For a longer list of Swahili words included as part of the school's curriculum, see the Swahili answer sheet, *African-American Infusion: Social Studies Resource Guide,* Martin Luther King Elementary School, Milwaukee, Wisconsin.

127. Kenneth J. Cooper, "Broadening Horizons: Afrocentrism Takes Root in Atlanta Schools," 1992, pp. A-1, A-33; Swahili Answer Sheet, *African-American Infusion: Social Studies Resource Guide,* Martin Luther King Elementary School, Milwaukee, Wisconsin.

128. Sari Horwitz, "Unlicensed College Provided D.C. Afrocentric Training," *Washington Post,* August 14, 1993, pp. A-1, A-10; "Abena Walker's Curriculum," *Washington Times,* August 14, 1993; Sari Horwitz and Cindy Loose, "Afrocentric Program Gets Go-Ahead," *Washington Post,* September 4, 1993, p. A-1; Russell Adams, "Neophytes in Afrocentrism," *Washington Post,* September 9, 1993, p. A-21; Sari Horwitz, "Participants Laud Afrocentric Program, Blast Media," *Washington Post,* September 23, 1993, p. B-1; Sari Horwitz, "District to Expand Afrocentric Classes," *Washington Post,* July 25, 1994, p. B-1; Maria Koklanaris, "Afrocentrism Gets Good Report Card," *Washington Times,* September 22, 1994, p. C-4.

129. Nsenga Warfield-Coppock, "Saving the African American Child Through

Academic and Cultural Excellence," National Alliance of Black School Educators, Largo, Maryland, May 30, 1992; see also Laura Litvan and Carol Innerst, "Confidence Builder or Raw Racism: Self-Esteem Program Debated in PG," *Washington Times,* July 3, 1992, pp. A-1, A-8.

130. Sanyika Shakur, *Monster: The Autobiography of an L.A. Gang Member,* Penguin Books, New York, 1993, pp. 256–57.

131. Molefi Kete Asante, *Afrocentricity,* pp. 5, 42–43, 45, 48, 56; Molefi Kete Asante, *Kemet, Afrocentricity, and Knowledge,* Africa World Press, Trenton, NJ, 1990, pp. vi, 5, 15, 115; Molefi Kete Asante, *Malcolm X as Cultural Hero and Other Afrocentric Essays,* Africa World Press, Trenton, NJ, 1993, pp. x, 3, 5, 42, 49, 120; Molefi Kete Asante, *The Afrocentric Idea,* Temple University Press, Philadelphia, 1987, p. 159.

132. Janice Hale-Benson, *Black Children: Their Roots, Culture and Learning Styles,* Johns Hopkins University Press, Baltimore, 1986, p. 42; Asa Hilliard, *Alternatives to IQ Testing: An Approach to the Identification of Gifted "Minority" Children,* Final Report to the California State Department of Education, 1976, pp. 38–39.

133. Molefi Kete Asante, "African-American Studies: The Future of the Discipline," *The Black Scholar* 22, No. 3 (Summer 1992), p. 25.

134. Jawanza Kunjufu, *Countering the Conspiracy to Destroy Black Boys,* African American Images, Chicago, 1985, Vol. 2, p. 33.

135. Akbar, *Visions for Black Men,* p. ix.

136. Cited by Marshall Frady, "The Children of Malcolm," *New Yorker,* October 12, 1992, p. 68.

137. Chancellor Williams, *The Destruction of Black Civilization: Great Issues of a Race from 4500 B.C. to 2000 A.D.,* Third World Press, Chicago, 1987, pp. 26, 157, 284.

138. Molefi Kete Asante, *Kemet, Afrocentricity and Knowledge,* pp. 21–22.

139. Letter from David Baurac, public information director, Argonne National Laboratory, to Erich Martel, May 22, 1991; cited in Erich Martel, "Afrocentric Historical Claims: An Examination of the Portland, Oregon African-American Baseline Essays," *World History Bulletin* 3, No. 2 (Fall-Winter 1991–1992).

140. According to Asa Hilliard, Egypt "was from its beginning and during its greatest periods of cultural development an indigenous black African civilization. Its birthplace was inner equatorial Africa. It remained at its core culturally unified with the rest of ancient Africa." See Asa Hilliard, "The Meaning of KMT (Ancient Egyptian) History for Contemporary African American Experience," *Phylon* 49, Nos. 1, 2 (1992), p. 10. See also Yosef Ben-Jochanan, *Africa, Mother of Western Civilization,* Black Classic Press, Baltimore, 1988; Bernal, *Black Athena.*

141. Michael Harris, "African-American Art Traditions and Developments," *African American Baseline Essays,* Portland Public Schools, Portland, OR, 1987, p. A-6.

142. Chiekh Anta Diop, *The African Origin of Civilization: Myth Or Reality?,* Lawrence Hill Books, Chicago, 1974, pp. xiv, 238.

143. Williams, *The Destruction of Black Civilization,* p. 18.

144. Frank Yurco, "Unconscious of Race: Were the Ancient Egyptians Black or White?" *Biblical Archaeology Review* 15, No. 5 (September-October 1989).

145. Frank M. Snowden, Jr., "Bernal's Blacks, Herodotus and Other Classical Evidence," *Arethusa,* Fall 1989, pp. 83–95; see also Frank M. Snowden, Jr., "Did

Herodotus Say the Egyptians Were Black?" *Biblical Archaeological Review,* March-April 1990.

146. Kathryn Bard, "Ancient Egyptians and the Issue of Race," *Bostonia,* Summer 1992, pp. 33–34.

147. Williams, *The Destruction of Black Civilization,* p. 127.

148. Ivan Van Sertima, "Future Directions for African and African-American Content in the School Curriculum," in Asa Hilliard, ed., *Infusion of African and African American Content in the School Curriculum,* Aaron Press, Morristown, NJ, 1989, p. 95.

149. Kwasi Wiredu, *Philosophy and an African Culture,* Cambridge University Press, Cambridge, 1980, pp. 4, 15, 28, 48.

150. Williams, *The Destruction of Black Civilization,* pp. 131, 149.

151. See, e.g., Ibn Battuta, *Travels in Asia and Africa, 1325–1354,* Augustus Kelley, New York, 1969; Ibn Khaldun, *The Muqaddimah,* translated by Franz Rosenthal, Princeton University Press, Princeton, 1967; Bernard Lewis, ed., *Islam,* Oxford University Press, New York, 1987.

152. Van Sertima, "Future Directions for African and African-American Content in the School Curriculum," pp. 87–88, 95; Ivan Van Sertima, "African Science Before the Birth of the New World," *The Black Collegian,* January-February 1992, p. 69.

153. Na'im Akbar, *Visions for Black Men,* p. 48.

154. John G. Jackson, *Introduction to African Civilizations,* Carol Publishing, New York, 1970, p. 23.

155. Hunter Havelin Adams III, "African and African-American Contributions to Science and Technology," *African-American Baseline Essays,* p. S-53.

156. Van Sertima, "Future Directions for African and African American Content in the School Curriculum," pp. 91, 99.

157. Orlando Patterson, *Ethnic Chauvinism: The Reactionary Impulse,* Stein and Day, New York, 1977, pp. 23, 70.

158. Wade Nobles, *African Psychology: Toward Its Reclamation, Reascension & Revitalization,* Black Family Institute, Oakland, CA, 1986, p. 24.

159. Asante, *Malcolm X As Cultural Hero and Other Afrocentric Essays,* p. 93.

160. George G. M. James, *Stolen Legacy: Greek Philosophy Is Stolen Egyptian Philosophy,* Africa World Press, Trenton, NJ, 1992, pp. 156–57, 160.

161. See, e.g., Mary Lefkowitz, "Not Out of Africa," *The New Republic,* February 10, 1992; Mary Lefkowitz, "Afrocentrism Poses a Threat to the Rationalist Tradition," *Chronicle of Higher Education,* May 6,1992; Mary Lefkowitz, "Ethnocentric History from Aristobolus to Bernal," *Academic Questions,* Spring 1993; Frank Snowden, "Whither Afrocentrism?" *Georgetown Magazine,* Winter 1992, pp. 7–8.

162. Snowden, "Whither Afrocentrism?" pp. 7–8.

163. Akbar, *Visions for Black Men,* p. 28.

164. James, *Stolen Legacy,* p. 153.

165. Nobles, *African Psychology,* p. 26.

166. Akbar, *Visions for Black Men,* p. 29.

167. Jackson, *Introduction to African Civilizations,* p. 299.

168. Snowden, "Whither Afrocentrism?" p. 8; Snowden, "Bernal's Blacks, Herodotus and Other Classical Evidence," p. 90.

169. Williams, *The Destruction of Black Civilization,* p. 135.

170. Diop, *The African Origin of Civilization,* p. xiv.

171. Laurie Goodstein, "Religion's Changing Face: More Churches Depicting Christ as Black," *Washington Post,* March 26, 1991, pp. A-1, A-6; Robin Wilson, "A Professor Who Sees Jews as a Soul Brother," *Chronicle of Higher Education,* June 16, 1993, p. A-7.

172. Williams, *The Destruction of Black Civilization,* pp. 162–63, 169.

173. Ibid., pp. 174–75.

174. Van Sertima, "African Science Before the Birth of the New World," pp. 69–70.

175. Akbar, *Visions for Black Men,* p. 57.

176. Williams, *The Destruction of Black Civilization,* p. 231.

177. Ivan Van Sertima, *They Came Before Columbus,* Random House, New York, 1976, pp. xiv, 25–26, 28–33, 155–74, 242–70; see also Michael Bradley, *The Black Discovery of America,* Personal Library, Toronto, 1981.

178. Jackson, *Introduction to African Civilizations,* pp. 75, 260.

179. Letter from David C. Grove to Erich Martel, November 7, 1991.

180. Philip D. Curtin, letter to Erich Martel, September 26, 1991.

181. Glyn Daniel, "America B.C," *New York Times Book Review,* March 13, 1977, pp. 8, 12.

182. Williams, *The Destruction of Black Civilization,* pp. 205, 207.

183. Ibid., pp. 164–65.

184. Hunter Havelin Adams, III, "African and African American Contributions to Science and Technology," pp. S-15, S-19, S-27–30, S-36–38, S-41, S-52–54.

185. Bernard Ortiz De Montellano, "Multicultural Pseudoscience: Spreading Scientific Illiteracy Among Minorities," *Skeptical Inquirer* 16 (Fall 1991), pp. 47–50; Bernard Ortiz De Montellano, "Avoiding Egyptocentric Pseudo-Science," *Chronicle of Higher Education,* March 25, 1992, pp. B-1, B-2.

186. Na'im Akbar, *Visions for Black Men,* p. 47.

187. Nathan Hare and Julia Hare, *Bringing the Black Boy to Manhood,* Black Think Tank, San Francisco, 1985, p. 43.

188. Cited in "African Dreams," *Newsweek,* September 23, 1991, p. 45; see also Henry Louis Gates, Jr., "Black Demagogues and Pseudo-Scholars," *New York Times,* July 20, 1992.

189. Kwame Anthony Appiah, "Europe Upside Down: Fallacies of the New Afrocentrism," *Times Literary Supplement,* February 12, 1993, pp. 24–25.

190. Nicholas Lemann, "Black Nationalism on Campus," *Atlantic Monthly,* January 1993, p. 47.

191. Akbar, *Visions for Black Men,* p. 38.

192. Marimba Ani (Dona Richards), *Yurugu: An African-Centered Critique of European Cultural Thought and Behavior,* Africa World Press, Trenton, 1994, pp. 8, 22, 63, 98.

193. In her lexicon, *Black Talk,* Geneva Smitherman defines "tricknology" as

"European American technological innovations, viewed as things to be distrusted." Geneva Smitherman, *Black Talk: Words and Phrases from the Hood to the Amen Corner,* Houghton Mifflin, Boston, 1994, p. 227.

194. Bernal, *Black Athena,* Vol. 1. pp. 9, 436. Bernal dismisses the criticism of scholars such as Frank Snowden on the grounds that "blacks will not be able to accept the conformity to white scholarship of men like Professor Snowden."

195. Molefi Kete Asante, *Afrocentricity,* pp. 20, 80–82; Molefi Kete Asante, *The Afrocentric Idea,* p. 98.

196. Nobles, *African Psychology,* p. 39.

197. Anthony Appiah, "Fallacies of Eurocentrism and Afrocentrism," Bradley Lecture, American Enterprise Institute, Washington, DC, May 10, 1993.

198. Cited in John J. Miller, ed., *Alternatives to Afrocentrism,* Manhattan Institute, Washington, DC, 1994, pp. 18–20.

199. John G. Jackson, *Introduction to African Civilization,* p. 313.

200. Michael Bradley, *The Iceman Inheritance,* Kayode Publications, New York, 1978, pp. xxiii, 26, 103; see also the introduction by John Henrik Clarke.

201. Martin Bernal, "*Black Athena* and the APA," *Arethusa,* Fall 1989, p. 30; Bernal, *Black Athena,* p. 242. Bernal's comment about segregated restaurants was made in a debate with me at Cornell University on September 21, 1994.

202. Molefi Kete Asante, "Racism, Consciousness and Afrocentricity," in Gerald Early, ed., *Lure and Loathing: Essays on Race, Identity, and the Ambivalence of Assimilation,* Penguin Books, New York, 1993, p. 142.

203. Chiekh Anta Diop, *The African Origin of Civilization,* p. 117.

204. Frank Yurco, "How to Teach Ancient History: A Multicultural Model," *American Educator,* Spring 1994, p. 36; Michael Specter, "Was Nefertiti Black?" *Washington Post,* February 26, 1990, p. A-3.

205. "Black Columnist Sets Off a Furor With Call to Arms," *New York Times,* February 16, 1992.

206. Ramon Saldivar, *Chicano Narrative: The Dialects of Difference,* University of Wisconsin Press, Madison, 1990, p. 8.

207. See, e.g., Richard Rorty, *Philosophy and the Mirror of Nature*; Richard Rorty, *Consequences of Pragmatism*; Richard Rorty, *Contingency, Irony and Solidarity,* Cambridge University Press, Cambridge, 1989; Stanley Fish, *There's No Such Thing As Free Speech.*

208. Rorty calls himself an anti-anti-ethnocentrist. See Rorty, "On Ethnocentrism," in *Objectivity, Relativism and Truth,* vol. 1, pp. 203–10. Rorty has risked his multicultural reputation by championing ethnocentrism as a justification for patriotism. See Richard Rorty, "The Unpatriotic Academy," *New York Times,* February 13, 1994, p. E-15.

209. Richard Delgado, "When a Story Is Just a Story: Does Voice Really Matter?" *Virginia Law Review* 76 (1990), p. 95; Renato Rosaldo, *Culture and Truth,* pp. 172–73; Ian Haney-Lopez, "Community Ties, Race and Faculty Hiring: The Case for Professors Who Don't Think White," *Reconstruction* 1, No. 3 (1991).

210. See, e.g., Bob Seter, "Black Prof. Fails Political Test," *Chicago Sun-Times,* December 11, 1994. In this case, activist professors and students successfully op-

posed tenure for Northwestern University law professor Maria Hylton partly on the grounds that Hylton, though of both African and Latin American descent, did not ally herself with multicultural causes or support the progressive agenda.

211. Bennett, *Comprehensive Multicultural Education,* p. 311.

212. Taylor, *Multiculturalism and "The Politics of Recognition",* pp. 68–69.

213. "A European who says that all cultures are equal does not normally mean that he would like to have his hand cut off if he is caught falsifying his tax return, or be subjected to a public flogging. To say in such a case—this is the law of the Koran and we must respect traditions other than our own—essentially amounts to saying: that would be dreadful if it happened here, but for those savages it's just the right thing." Leszek Kolakowski, *Modernity on Endless Trial,* p. 21.

214. Claude Lévi-Strauss, "Race and History," in Leo Kuper, ed., *Race, Science and Society,* UNESCO Press, Paris, 1975, p. 116.

215. This point is made by I. C. Jarvie, *Rationality and Relativism,* Routledge & Kegan Paul, London, 1984, pp. 35–38.

216. Christine Bennett argues that the American Indian belief that the native peoples lived eternally in the Americas should be taught on an equal plane with the scientific view that they migrated across the Bering Straits. Bennett argues that the Bering Straits theory has no claim to priority since "there is absolutely no evidence except logic to support it." Bennett advocates that "data derived from archaeology should be supplemented by Indian traditional literature." Bennett, *Comprehensive Multicultural Education,* p. 287.

217. Johnnetta Cole, *Conversations: Straight Talk with America's Sister President,* Anchor Books, New York, 1993, p. 173.

218. Thomas Kuhn, *The Structure of Scientific Revolutions,* University of Chicago Press, Chicago, 2nd ed., 1970, pp. 198–99, 206.

219. This position is defended in A. J. Ayer, ed., *Logical Positivism,* Free Press, New York, 1955, and A. J. Ayer, *Language, Truth and Logic,* Dover Books, New York, 1952.

220. Fish, *There's No Such Thing As Free Speech,* p. 135. Fish argues that "the opposition between reason and belief is a false one" and that "every situation of contest should be recharacterized as a quarrel between two sets of belief with no possibility of recourse to a mode of deliberation that is not itself an extension of belief."

221. Abraham Lincoln, letter to Boston Republicans, in Mario Cuomo and Harold Holzer, eds., *Lincoln on Democracy,* HarperCollins, New York, 1990, p. 155.

222. John Henry Cardinal Newman, *The Idea of a University,* Image Books, New York, 1959, p. 149.

Chapter 10. Bigotry in Black and White

1. Bill Adler, "Hiphoprisy: A Conversation with Ishmael Reed and Michael Franti," *Transition,* Issue 56 (1992), p. 159.

2. William Robertson Boggs, "Racial Differences: Why They Matter," *American Renaissance,* January 1993, p. 5.

3. Thomas Jackson, "Which Way, Western Man?" *American Renaissance,* May 1993, p. 7.

4. "De Gustibus," *American Renaissance,* May 1993, p. 8.

5. "Another Black Thing," *American Renaissance,* August 1993, p. 9.

6. Samuel Taylor and Marian Evans, "Who Still Believes in Integration?" *American Renaissance,* September-October 1993, p. 9.

7. Gedahlia Braun, "Forgotten Black Voices," *American Renaissance,* September-October 1993, p. 10.

8. Paul Kittering, "Letters," *American Renaissance,* November 1993, p. 2.

9. Samuel Taylor, "A Reply," *American Renaissance,* December 1993, p. 4.

10. John Kelly, "Another Reply to Doubters," *American Renaissance,* February 1994, p. 4.

11. "The Beginning of the End," *American Renaissance,* June 1994, p. 7.

12. Francis's speech was later published. See Samuel Francis, "Why Race Matters," *American Renaissance,* September 1994, pp. 1–6.

13. See, e.g., Jack Moore, *Skinheads Shaved for Battle: A Cultural History of American Skinheads,* Bowling Green State University Press, Ohio, 1993; Michael Barkun, *Religion and the Racist Right: The Origins of the Christian Identity Movement,* University of North Carolina Press, Durham, 1994; Kevin Flynn, *The Silent Brotherhood: Inside America's Racist Underground,* Free Press, New York, 1989; Tyler Bridges, *The Rise of David Duke,* University of Mississippi Press, Jackson, 1994.

14. See, e.g., "Klanwatch Reports Hate Groups Up 25 Percent," *Washington Post,* February 20, 1992; Ronald Smothers, "Report Sees Increase in White Supremacy Groups," *New York Times,* February 19, 1992.

15. Alphonso Pinkney, *The Myth of Black Progress,* Cambridge University Press, Cambridge, 1984, p. 69.

16. Joe R. Feagin and Hernan Vera, *White Racism: The Basics,* Routledge, New York, 1995, p. 78.

17. These figures were obtained in 1995 directly from the Anti-Defamation League of B'nai B'rith, and matched against comparable figures from the Southern Poverty Law Center. See also ADL, *Hate Groups in America: A Record of Bigotry and Violence,* New York, 1988; ADL, *Neo-Nazi Skinheads: A 1990 Status Report,* New York, 1990.

18. Cited by Jules Loh, "This Time, It Looks As If the Klan Is Gone for Good," *Washington Times,* December 21, 1994, p. A-8.

19. Bill Stanton, *Klanwatch,* Mentor Books, New York, 1991, pp. 91, 260–64; Morris Dees, *A Season for Justice,* Simon & Schuster, New York, 1991, pp. 330–31.

20. Morris Dees, *A Season for Justice,* p. 337.

21. Stephen Kinzer, "Klan Seizes on Germany's Wave of Racist Violence," *New York Times,* November 3, 1991.

22. See, e.g., John Roll, "Klan Foes Muffle Maryland Rally," *Washington Times,* October 30, 1994, p. A-8.

23. Robert Branch, "Boardwalk Bigotry: The Day the Klan Came Marching Through My Ocean City Weekend," *Washington Post,* September 6, 1992, p. C-5.

24. "Eight Held in Plots to Kill Blacks in Los Angeles," *New York Times,* July 16, 1993, p. A-10.

25. *Klanwatch Intelligence Report,* February 1994, p. 5.

26. David Chalmers, *Hooded Americanism: The History of the Ku Klux Klan,* Duke University Press, Durham, 1987, pp. xi–xii.

27. Cited in ibid., p. 432.

28. David Van Biema, "When White Makes Right," *Time,* August 9, 1993, p. 42.

29. Michael Riley, "White and Wrong: New Klan, Old Hatred," *Newsweek,* July 6, 1992, p. 26.

30. Book List No. 0792, Liberty Bell Publications, Reedy, WV.

31. Paul Sniderman and Thomas Piazza, *The Scar of Race,* Harvard University Press, Cambridge, 1993, pp. 46–51.

32. *Resurgence,* Skylight Pictures, released September 1981.

33. Stanton, *Klanwatch,* p. 268.

34. Kenneth T. Jackson, *The Ku Klux Klan in the City,* Ivan Dee Publishers, Chicago, 1992, p. 255.

35. Elaine Jones, "In Peril: Black Lawmakers," *New York Times,* September 11, 1994.

36. Feagin and Vera, *White Racism,* p. 81.

37. Branch, "Boardwalk Bigotry."

38. Cited by Feagin and Vera, *White Racism,* p. 21.

39. "Hate Groups in Bitter Struggle Over Public Image," *Klanwatch Intelligence Report,* No. 59 (February 1992), p. 3.

40. William Gayley Simpson, *Which Way, Western Man?,* National Alliance, Washington, DC, 1978, pp. 82, 89, 92–93, 181, 478.

41. Wilmot Robertson, *The Dispossessed Majority,* Howard Allen Publishers, Cape Canaveral, 1981, pp. 301, 328.

42. Wilmot Robertson, *The Ethnostate,* Howard Allen Publishers, Cape Canaveral, 1992, pp. ix, 7, 52, 98, 202–3.

43. Resource Packet, "The Politics and Background of David Duke," Louisiana Coalition Against Racism and Nazism, December 1991.

44. Associated Press report, "Confederate Flag Raises Passions Again in Deep South," *Washington Times,* July 26, 1994, p. A-8.

45. W. E. B. Du Bois, "Back to Africa," *Century,* February 1923, cited by John Henrik Clarke, ed., *Marcus Garvey and the Vision of Africa,* Vintage Books, New York, 1974, pp. 101, 117, 134; see also John Hope Franklin and August Meier, *Black Leaders of the Twentieth Century,* University of Illinois Press, Urbana and Chicago, 1982, pp. 132–34.

46. Bruce Perry, *Malcolm: The Life of a Man Who Changed Black America,* Station Hill Press, Barrytown, NY, 1991, p. 358. Perry provides extensive evidence for the Malcolm X–Ku Klux Klan meeting; these citations are on page 503. See also Clayborne Carson, *Malcolm X: The FBI File,* Carroll and Graf, New York, 1991, pp. 29, 203–4. For Malcolm's comment about Jews, see Marshall Frady, "The Children of Malcolm," *New Yorker,* October 12, 1992, p. 70.

47. Michael Bradley, *Chosen People from the Caucasus,* Third World Press, Chicago, 1992, pp. 22–23, 25, 27, 76, 199, 213, 220, 222.

48. Michael Bradley, "The Lesson of Rodney King," in Haki Madhubuti, ed.,

Why L.A. Happened: Implications of the '92 Los Angeles Rebellion, Third World Press, Chicago, 1993.

49. See, e.g., Sandra Van Dyk, "The Evaluation of Race Theory," *Journal of Black Studies,* September 1993, pp. 83–84.

50. Todd Gillman, "Panthers, Supremacists Call for U.S. Overthrow; Dallas Rally Urges Revolution to Achieve Goals," *Dallas Morning News,* May 30, 1992, p. 37-A.

51. Anti-Defamation League of B'nai B'rith, *Hate Groups in America,* p. 5.

52. See, e.g., Juan Williams, "Black Power's New Dilemma," *Washington Post,* May 12, 1991, p. C-1; Charles Lane, "Over the Rainbow: Washington's Black-Hispanic Split," *The New Republic,* June 10, 1991; Steven Holmes, "Minority Leaders See a Clash of Hues in a Rainbow Coalition," *New York Times,* June 16, 1991, p. E-4.

53. Mark Mathabane, *Kaffir Boy in America,* Collier Books, New York, 1989, p. 257; Mark Mathabane, *Love in Black and White,* HarperCollins, New York, 1992, pp. 9, 198.

54. Walter Williams, "Gleaned from the Fine Print," *Washington Times,* July 3, 1992.

55. Khalid Abdul Muhammad, transcript of Kean College address, November 29, 1993. Muhammad's remarks, delivered in a conversational tone and punctuated by obscenity, have been slightly edited for clarity.

56. Thomas B. Edsall, "Clinton Stuns Rainbow Coalition," *Washington Post,* June 14, 1992, pp. A-1, A-8.

57. Sister Souljah, *360 Degrees of Power,* Epic Records, 1992.

58. Alex Safian, "Pacifica: Broadcasting Hate," *Comint,* Center for the Study of Popular Culture, Spring-Summer 1993, pp. 32–37.

59. Joseph Boyce, "Struggle Over Hospital in Los Angeles Pits Minority vs. Minority," *Wall Street Journal,* April 1, 1991, p. A-1.

60. Anderson Thompson, "The Los Angeles Rebellion: Seizing the Historical Moment," in Madhubuti, *Why L.A. Happened,* pp. 49–59.

61. Ice Cube, *Death Certificate,* Priority Records, 1991; Ice Cube, cited in *Black Beat Special,* Lexington Library, New York, 1992, p. 15.

62. Jesse Birnbaum, "When Hate Makes a Fist," *Time,* April 26, 1993, p. 30; "Freedom to Hate," *The Economist,* May 8, 1993, p. 33.

63. Amy Wallace, "Whites Face a New Fear: Being Judged by Color," *Los Angeles Times,* June 15, 1992, p. A-1; "Denny Trial Is Told of Scene at Flash Point in 1992 Riots," *Washington Post,* August 24, 1993, p. A-8; transcript, "Nightline in South Central," ABC-TV *Nightline,* May 4, 1992, p. 2; Seth Mydans, "A Target of Rioters, Koreatown Is Bitter, Armed and Determined," *New York Times,* May 3, 1992, p. A-1.

64. Nathan McCall, *Makes Me Wanna Holler: A Young Black Man in America,* Random House, New York, 1994, pp. 3–4.

65. James Barron, "Portrait of Suspect Emerges in Shooting on L.I. Train," *New York Times,* December 9, 1993, pp. A-1, B-8; Susanne Lee and Samuel Cacas, "Suburbs Under Siege: The Garden City Killings," *Asian Week,* December 17, 1993, p. 1; "Black Rage: In Defense of a Mass Murderer," *Time,* June 6, 1994, p. 31; Robert I. Friedman, "The Color of Rage," *Vanity Fair,* January 1995.

66. David Evanier, "Invisible Man: The Lynching of Yankel Rosenbaum," *The New Republic,* October 14, 1991, pp. 21–26; Eric Breindel, "Shameful Verdict," *Washington Times,* November 8, 1992; Eric Breindel, "Race and Riots in New York," *Wall Street Journal,* November 18, 1992; Alison Mitchell, "Adult Count to Be Sought in Crown Heights Trial," *New York Times,* August 13, 1994.

67. "*Klanwatch* Reports Surge in Hate Violence by Blacks," Southern Poverty Law Center, December 13, 1993; "Hate Violence Not Restricted to One Group or Race," *Klanwatch Intelligence Report,* February 1993, pp. 6–7; Peter Applebome, "Rise Is Found in Hate Crimes Committed by Blacks," *New York Times,* December 13, 1993, p. A-12; "Law Center: Hate Crime Reversal," *USA Today,* December 14, 1993, p. 3-A.

68. "The statements made in recent months by self-appointed representatives of the black community . . . are as vile and as racist as any made by a group of white supremacists. There are no excuses or mitigating circumstances. Some white racist groups also provide services and assistance to their members, but that doesn't excuse their racism, cross-burnings and lynchings." Vernon Jordan, "Racists, Anti-Semites and the Rights of Humanity," *Washington Post,* May 8, 1994, p. C-7.

"Oddly the Ku Klux Klan preached these very hatreds. It's as if these [black] demagogues are saying that all the ugly stereotypes our oppressors have long used against us are valid—except they apply not to us but to others." Jack Greenberg, "Identity Crisis," *New York Times,* May 23, 1994, p. A-15.

See also Barbara Jordan, "The Democratic Party Will Change," excerpt from keynote address delivered at the Democratic National Convention, *Washington Post,* July 14, 1992; Cornel West, *Race Matters,* Beacon Press, Boston, 1993, pp. 76–77; Henry Louis Gates, Jr., "Black Demagogues and Pseudo-Scholars," *New York Times,* July 20, 1992.

69. Anna Quindlen, "All of These You Are," *New York Times,* June 30, 1992.

70. Stanley Fish, "Reverse Racism," *The Atlantic Monthly,* November 1993, p. 130; Stanley Fish, *There's No Such Thing as Free Speech—And It's a Good Thing Too,* Oxford University Press, New York, 1994, p. 76.

71. Spike Lee, "The Playboy Interview," *Playboy,* July 1991, p. 52; "The Spike Lee Interview," *Rolling Stone,* July 11–25, 1991; see also "Final Cut: Spike Lee and Henry Louis Gates, Jr. Rap on Race, Politics and Black Cinema," *Transition,* Issue 52 (1991), p. 198.

72. Joel Kovel, *White Racism: A Psychohistory,* Columbia University Press, New York, 1984, p. xxxvii.

73. Coramae Richey Mann, "The Reality of a Racist Criminal Justice System," *Criminal Justice Research Bulletin* 3, No. 5 (1987), p. 2.

74. Paula Rothenberg, ed., *Racism and Sexism: An Integrated Study,* St Martin's Press, New York, 1988, p. 6.

75. Sean Piccoli, "Malcolm X, the Legacy: Does Black Racism Exist?" *Washington Times,* November 18, 1992, pp. E-1, E-2.

76. Ibid.

77. Danyel Smith, "Harry Allen: Hip Hop's Intellectual Assassin," *San Francisco Weekly,* February 13, 1991, p. 1.

78. Stokely Carmichael and Charles V. Hamilton, *Black Power: The Politics of Liberation in America,* Vintage Books, New York, 1967, p. 47.

79. Kenneth B. Clark, *Dark Ghetto: Dilemmas of Social Power,* Harper & Row, New York, 1965, p. 238.

80. Whitney Young, *Beyond Racism,* McGraw-Hill, New York, 1969, p. 85.

81. Malcolm X, *The End of White World Supremacy: Four Speeches,* edited by Imam Benjamin Karim (Benjamin 2X), Little, Brown, Boston, 1971, p. 82.

82. Eldridge Cleaver, *Soul on Ice,* McGraw Hill, New York, 1968, pp. 4, 14.

83. "The Hate That Hate Produced" aired in the late 1950s. For a transcript, see Louis Lomax, "Black Racism: The Hate That Hate Produced," in Barry N. Schwartz, ed., *White Racism,* Laurel Leaf Books, New York, 1978.

84. Derrick Bell, *Faces at the Bottom of the Well: The Permanence of Racism,* Basic Books, New York, 1992, p. 9.

85. William Schneider, "An Insider's View of the Election," *The Atlantic Monthly,* July 1988, p. 36.

86. Andrew Hacker, *Two Nations: Black and White, Separate, Hostile, Unequal,* Ballantine Books, New York, 1992, p. 208.

87. Thomas B. Edsall, "Conflicting Trends Seen in Whites' Willingness to Vote for Blacks," *Washington Post,* December 19, 1993, p. A-27.

88. Anthony Lewis, "A Lost Country," *New York Times,* May 3, 1992, p. E-17.

89. William Wilbanks, "Frequency and Nature of Inter-racial Crime," *The Justice Professional* 6, No. 1 (Winter 1992), pp. 1–17. Wilbanks uses 1988 data, but similar figures exist for subsequent years.

90. U.S. Department of Justice, *Uniform Crime Reports 1993,* Washington, DC, pp. 16–17; see also U.S. Department of Justice, *Criminal Victimization in the United States 1992,* Washington, DC, March 1994, p. 61; William Wilbanks, *The Myth of a Racist Criminal Justice System,* Brooks Cole Publishing, Monterey, CA, 1987, p. 19.

91. Frantz Fanon, *The Wretched of the Earth,* Grove Weidenfeld, New York, 1963, p. 93.

92. Albert Memmi, *Dominated Man,* Beacon Press, Boston, 1969, p. 9.

93. The Nation of Islam refuses to disclose its membership. The estimate given here is from *Emerge* magazine, March 1994.

94. William A. Henry III, "Pride and Prejudice," *Time,* February 28, 1994, p. 22.

95. Mari Matsuda, "Public Response to Racist Speech," in Mari J. Matsuda, Charles R. Lawrence III, Richard Delgado, and Kimberle Williams Crenshaw, *Words That Wound: Critical Race Theory, Assaultive Speech and the First Amendment,* Westview Press, Boulder, 1993, pp. 38–39.

96. William A. Henry III, "Pride and Prejudice"; see also Arch Puddington, "Black Anti-Semitism and How It Grows," *Commentary,* April 1994, p. 21.

97. Juan Williams, "The Farrakhan Paralysis: How the Demagogues of the Disenfranchised Are Silencing Black Leaders," *Washington Post,* February 13, 1994, p. C-2.

98. "Final Cut: Spike Lee and Henry Louis Gates, Jr. Rap on Race, Politics and Black Cinema," p. 186.

99. Lynne Duke, "Congressional Black Caucus and Nation of Islam Agree on Al-

liance," *Washington Post,* September 17, 1993, p. A-3; Steven A. Holmes, "Farrakhan Is Warned over Aide's Invective," *New York Times,* January 25, 1994, p. A-12.

100. John Henrik Clarke, "Black Pseudo-Scholars Are in with White America, but They Deserve to Be Outed," *City Sun,* New York, August 26–September 1, 1992, pp. 8, 37; "A Dialogue With John Henrik Clarke," *Emerge,* February 1992, pp. 11–12.

101. Avi Weiss, "What About Anti-Semitism at Howard?" *Washington Post,* May 8, 1994, p. C-8; Richard Cohen, "A Nasty Night at Howard," *Washington Post,* March 1, 1994, p. A-19.

102. Jon Nordheimer, "Angry Echoes of Campus Speech," *New York Times,* January 26, 1994, pp. B-1, B-4.

103. Nation of Islam, *The Secret Relationship Between Blacks and Jews,* Chicago, 1991, pp. vii, 122, 157, 211.

104. Tony Martin, *The Jewish Onslaught,* The Majority Press, Dover, MA, 1993; see also Denise Magner, "A Charge of Anti-Semitism," *Chronicle of Higher Education,* January 12, 1994, p. A-14.

105. Andrew Hacker, "Jewish Racism, Black Racism," in Paul Berman, ed., *Blacks and Jews: Alliances and Arguments,* Delacorte Press, New York, 1994, p. 154.

106. Anti-Defamation League of B'nai B'rith, "ADL Survey on Anti-Semitism and Prejudice in America," November 16, 1992, pp. 30–32; Jennifer Golub, "What Do We Know About Black Anti-Semitism?" American Jewish Committee Working Paper, New York, 1990, pp. 21, 28–29; Harold Quinley and Charles Glock, *Anti-Semitism in America,* Transaction Books, New Brunswick, NJ, 1983, pp. xx, 55, 70; Richard Morin, "Study Cites Drop in Anti-Semitism," *Washington Post,* June 21, 1994, p. A-8; Robert S. Wistrich, *Anti-Semitism: The Longest Hatred,* Pantheon Books, New York, 1991, p. 123.

107. Ice Cube, *Death Certificate,* Priority Records, 1991; see also Eric Breindel, "Rap Star to Koreans: We'll Burn Your Stores," *New York Post,* December 5, 1991, p. 29.

108. Felicia Lee, "Brooklyn Blacks and Koreans Forge Pact," *New York Times,* December 21, 1988, p. B-1.

109. Peg Tyre and Beth Holland, "Battered and Shocked," *Newsday,* May 14, 1990, p. 5; "The Race Baiters Exposed," *New York Post,* June 4, 1990; William McGowan, "Race and Reporting," *City Journal,* Summer 1993, pp. 48–56; Jiyun Lee, "Racism Comes in All Colors: The Anti-Korean Boycott in Flatbush," *Reconstruction* 1, No. 3 (1991), pp. 72–75.

110. Jack Miles, "Blacks vs. Browns," *The Atlantic Monthly,* October 1992, p. 41; Steven Chin, "Innocence Lost: LA's Koreans Fight to Be Heard," *San Francisco Examiner,* May 9, 1992, p. 1; Associated Press, "Korean Leaders Are Alarmed at Violence in Los Angeles," *Oakland Tribune,* May 3, 1992, p. B-1; Jeff Pelline, "Lasting Blow to LA Neighborhoods," *San Francisco Chronicle,* May 2, 1992, p. 1; Marie Lee, "We Koreans Need an Al Sharpton," *New York Times,* December 12, 1991.

111. Seth Mydans, "A Target of Rioters, Koreatown Is Bitter, Armed and Determined," *New York Times,* May 3, 1992, p. A-1.

112. Kenneth Clark, "Candor on Negro-Jewish Relations," *Commentary,* February 1946; James Baldwin, *Notes of a Native Son,* Beacon Press, Boston, 1962, quotation on

p. 28; James Baldwin, "Negroes Are Anti-Semitic Because They Are Anti-White," *New York Times Magazine,* April 9, 1967; James Baldwin, "The Harlem Ghetto," *Commentary,* February 1948.

113. Cited by Itabari Njeri, "Sushi and Grits," in Gerald Early, ed., *Lure and Loathing: Essays on Race, Identity, and the Ambivalence of Assimilation,* Penguin Books, New York, 1993, p. 31; see also Edna Bonacich, "Making It in America," *Sociological Perspectives* 30 (October 1987), pp. 461–64; Edna Bonacich and Ivan Light, *Immigrant Entrepreneurs: Koreans in Los Angeles,* University of California Press, Berkeley, 1988, pp. 318, 324–36.

114. Thomas Sowell, "Middleman Minorities," *The American Enterprise,* May-June 1993, pp. 30–41; Thomas Sowell, *Race and Culture,* Basic Books, New York, 1994, p. 17.

115. See, e.g., Joel Garreau, "Koreans Strive to Make a Living in a World Where Cultures Collide," *Washington Post,* July 7, 1992, pp. A-1, A-10.

116. See, e.g., Jonathan Kaufman, *Broken Alliance: The Turbulent Times Between Blacks and Jews in America,* Charles Scribner, New York, 1988.

117. Anti-Defamation League of B'nai B'rith, *Survey on Racial Attitudes,* New York, November 1992, pp. 79–86. The survey shows that Jews are least likely to accept negative characterizations of blacks as a group, and most likely to attribute black difficulties to discrimination and unfair societal treatment.

118. Harold Cruse, *The Crisis of the Negro Intellectual,* William Morrow, New York, 1967, p. 484.

119. See, e.g., Edward Shapiro, *A Time for Healing: American Jewry Since World War II,* Johns Hopkins University Press, Baltimore, 1993. Shapiro points out that Jews, who make up 3 percent of the population, are vastly overrepresented among the nation's lawyers, doctors, editors, advertising executives, professors, TV producers, investment bankers, and scientists.

120. James Traub, "The Hearts and Minds of City College," *New Yorker,* June 7, 1993, p. 45.

121. Glenn C. Loury, *One by One from the Inside Out: Essays and Reviews on Race and Responsibility in America,* Free Press, New York, 1995, p. 85.

122. Traub, "The Hearts and Minds of City College," p. 48.

123. Ralph A. Austen, "The Uncomfortable Relationship: African Enslavement in the Common History of Blacks and Jews," *Tikkun* 9 (March-April 1994), pp. 60–65; David Brion Davis, "The Slave Trade and the Jews," *New York Review of Books,* December 22, 1994, pp. 14–16; Selwyn Cudjoe, "Time for Serious Scholars to Repudiate Nation of Islam's Diatribe Against Jews," *Chronicle of Higher Education,* May 11, 1994, pp. B-3, B-5; Harold Brackman, "Jews Had Negligible Role in Slave Trade," *New York Times,* February 14, 1994, p. A-16; Harold Brackman, *Farrakhan's Reign of Historical Error,* Simon Wiesenthal Center Reports, Los Angeles, 1992; Cornel West, "How We Fight Xenophobia," *Time,* February 28, 1994, p. 31.

124. Mark Mooney, "Ex-Dinkins Organizer Boasts He's Anti-White," *New York Post,* October 21, 1989; Jonathan Reider, "Trouble in Store: Behind the Brooklyn Boycott," *The New Republic,* July 2, 1990, p. 21; Tamar Jacoby, "Sonny Carson and the Politics of Protest," *City Journal,* Summer 1991, p. 29.

125. Michael Young, *The Rise of the Meritocracy, 1870–2033,* Random House, New York, 1959.

126. Shiva Naipaul, *North of South: An African Journey,* Penguin Books, New York, 1980, p. 76.

127. Cited by Jeffrey Goldberg, "My Anti-Semite," *New York,* October 24, 1994, p. 44.

128. Leon Jaroff, "Teaching Reverse Racism: A Strange Doctrine of Black Superiority is Finding Its Way into Schools and Colleges," *Time,* April 4, 1994, pp. 74–75.

129. Molefi Kete Asante, *The Afrocentric Idea,* Temple University Press, Philadelphia, 1987, pp. 62–63.

130. Cited by Thomas Byrne Edsall and Mary D. Edsall, *Chain Reaction: The Impact of Race, Rights and Taxes on American Politics,* W. W. Norton, New York, 1992, p. 239.

131. Frances Cress Welsing, *The Isis Papers: The Keys to the Colors,* Third World Press, Chicago, 1989, pp. ii, iv, 5, 8, 13, 23, 86, 171, 192. For an application of melanin theory to an understanding of the Los Angeles riots, see Frances Cress Welsing, "The Symbolism, Logic and Meaning of Justifiable Homicide in the 1980s," in Madhubuti, *Why L.A. Happened,* pp. 83–94.

132. Wade Nobles, *African Psychology: Toward Its Reclamation, Reascension & Revitalization,* Black Family Institute, Oakland, CA, 1986, pp. 65, 73, 85–87, 104.

133. Richard King, *African Origin of Biological Psychiatry,* Seymour-Smith Press, Germantown, TN, 1990.

134. Michael Eric Dyson, "Melanin Madness," *Emerge,* February 1992, p. 33.

135. Massimo Calabresi, "Skin Deep 101," *Time,* February 14, 1994, p. 16.

136. Leon Jaroff, "Teaching Reverse Racism," *Time,* April 4, 1994, pp. 74–75.

137. Marimba Ani (Dona Richards), *Yurugu: An African-centered Critique of European Cultural Thought and Behavior,* Africa World Press, Trenton, 1994, pp. 466–67, 469–70.

138. For a summary of what is known scientifically about melanin, see Christopher Wills, "The Skin We're In," *Discover,* November 1994, pp. 77–81.

139. Bernard Ortiz De Montellano, "Magic Melanin: Spreading Scientific Illiteracy among Minorities," *Skeptical Inquirer* 16 (Winter 1992).

140. Ani, *Yurugu,* pp. 402, 416, 485.

141. Jackson, *The Ku Klux Klan in the City,* p. 247.

142. See, e.g., David Jackson, "Profit and Promises," *Chicago Tribune,* March 12–14, 1995 (three-part series).

143. Na'im Akbar, *Visions for Black Men,* Winston-Derek Publishers, Nashville, 1991, p. 33.

144. "Propagandists or Saviors?" *U.S. News and World Report,* September 12, 1994, p. 40.

145. Haki Madhubuti, *Black Men: Obsolete, Single, Dangerous?,* Third World Press, Chicago, 1990, pp. vi, 8, 53, 57, 101, 109; Madhubuti, *Why L.A. Happened,* p. 103.

146. For the subsequent account see C. Eric Lincoln, *The Black Church Since Frazier,* Schocken Books, New York, 1974.

147. Elijah Muhammad, *Message to the Blackman in America,* United Brothers Communications System, Newport News, VA, 1992, pp. 53, 134.

148. See, e.g., Jerry Seper, "Leader Urges Black Exodus," *Washington Times,* February 28, 1990, pp. A-1, A-8; Don Terry, "Minister Farrakhan: Conservative Militant," *New York Times,* March 3, 1994, pp. A-1, B-9.

149. David Jackson, "Ascent and Grandeur," *Chicago Tribune,* March 15, 1995.

Chapter 11. The Content of Our Chromosomes

1. Richard Herrnstein and Charles Murray, *The Bell Curve: Intelligence and Class Structure in American Life,* Free Press, New York, 1994.

2. Jesse Jackson, *"Bell Curve* Exemplifies the Retreat on Race," *Los Angeles Times,* October 23, 1994.

3. Bob Herbert, "Throwing a Curve," *New York Times,* October 26, 1994, p. A-27.

4. Adolph Reed, Jr., "Looking Backward," *The Nation,* November 28, 1994, pp. 654, 659, 660.

5. Jacob Weisberg, "Who? Me? Prejudiced?" *New York,* October 17, 1994, p. 30.

6. Editorial, "Race and IQ Tests," *Atlanta Constitution,* October 14, 1994, p. A-12.

7. Stephen Jay Gould, "Curveball," *The New Yorker,* November 28, 1994, pp. 139, 147–148.

8. Leon Kamin, "Behind the Curve," *Scientific American,* February 1995, pp. 99–102.

9. This candor is suggested by comments every few years by Japanese politicians which raise a furor in the United States. In 1986, for example, Prime Minister Nakasone suggested that the low intelligence of blacks was largely responsible for America's educational and economic failures. Nakasone's remarks met with widespread condemnation, and black activists issued demands that he be subjected to sensitivity education, and that Japan be pressured to invest more money in black businesses in America. See, e.g., "A Slip of the Lip Heard Across the Pacific," *U.S. News and World Report,* October 6, 1986, p. 10; James Treece, "Nakasone's Ugly Remark Says a Lot About Today's Japan," *Business Week,* October 13, 1986, p. 66; James Fallows, *More Like Us,* Houghton Mifflin, Boston, 1989, p. 6.

10. For some examples of scholars expressing concern that valid research will be deterred because of political pressures, see Christopher Winship, "Lessons Beyond *The Bell Curve,*" *New York Times,* November 15, 1994, p. A-29; John C. Loehlin, "Should We Do Research on Race Differences in Intelligence?" *Intelligence* 16 (1992), pp. 1–4; Sandra Scarr, "Race and Gender as Psychological Variables," *American Psychologist,* January 1988, p. 56. The academic freedom concerns of several psychologists and biogenetics researchers are quoted in Charles Mann, "Behavioral Genetics in Transition," *Science,* June 17, 1994, p. 1686; Charlotte Allen, "Gray Matter, Black and White Controversy," *Insight,* January 5, 1992, pp. 4–9, 22–28.

11. Arthur Jensen, "How Much Can We Boost IQ and Scholastic Achievement?" *Harvard Educational Review* 39 (1969), p. 1.

12. "Interview: William Shockley," *Playboy,* August 1980, pp. 69–102; see also Roger Pearson, ed., *Shockley on Eugenics and Race,* Scott-Townsend Publishers, Washington, DC, 1992.

13. Richard Herrnstein, "IQ," *The Atlantic Monthly,* September 1971, pp. 43–64; Letters, "More About IQ," *The Atlantic Monthly,* December 1971, p. 101. The letter cited is from William Brazziel, an education professor at the University of Connecticut.

14. Cited by Daniel J. Kevles, *In the Name of Eugenics: Genetics and the Uses of Human Heredity,* Alfred A. Knopf, New York, 1985, p. 280.

15. This incident was mentioned by Boston University economist Glenn Loury in a symposium on political correctness. See "The Politics of Political Correctness," *Partisan Review* 60, No. 4 (1993), p. 618. James Q. Wilson confirms this incident.

16. Lynne Duke, "Controversy Flares Over Crime, Heredity," *Washington Post,* August 19, 1992, p. A-4; David Wheeler, "U. of Maryland Conference That Critics Charge Might Foster Racism Loses NIH Support," *Chronicle of Higher Education,* September 2, 1992, p. A-6; "Race and Crime: Don't Mention It," *The Economist,* September 12, 1992, p. 33.

17. Joann Gutin, "End of the Rainbow," *Discover,* November 1994, pp. 71–75.

18. Robert Sternberg is cited in "Why IQ Isn't Destiny," *U.S. News and World Report,* October 24, 1994, p. 75. Stephen Ceci is cited in Ellen K. Coughlin, "Class, IQ and Heredity," *Chronicle of Higher Education,* October 26, 1994, p. A-12.

19. Editorial, "A High Ignorance Quotient," *Boston Globe,* August 10, 1994.

20. Stephen Jay Gould, "Human Equality Is a Contingent Fact of History," *Natural History,* November 1984, p. 32.

21. Jacob Weisberg is citing Harvey Mansfield. Weisberg, "Who? Me? Prejudiced?" p. 26.

22. For a detailed discussion of the case of *Larry P. v. Riles* (1979), see Rogers Elliott, *Litigating Intelligence: IQ Tests, Special Education, and Social Science in the Classroom,* Auburn House, Dover, MA, 1987.

23. Editorial, "A High Ignorance Quotient," *Boston Globe,* August 10, 1994.

24. Cited by Richard Lacayo, "For Whom the Bell Tolls," *Time,* October 24, 1994, p. 67.

25. Byron M. Roth, *Prescription for Failure: Race Relations in the Age of Social Science,* Transaction Books, New Brunswick, NJ, 1994, p. 36.

26. Nathan Glazer, "The Lying Game," *The New Republic,* October 31, 1994, p. 16.

27. Cited by Ashley Montagu, *Race, Science and Humanity,* Van Nostrand, Princeton, 1963, pp. 1–2; see also Boyce Rensberger, "The Emergence of *Homo Sapiens,*" in Phillip Whitten and David Hunter, eds., *Anthropology: Contemporary Perspectives,* HarperCollins, New York, 1990, p. 31.

28. For a popular account summarizing recent research, see Michael Gazzaniga, *Nature's Mind: The Biological Roots of Thinking, Emotions, Sexuality, Language and Intelligence,* Basic Books, New York, 1992.

29. See, e.g., Robert Plomin, *Nature and Nurture,* Wadsworth, Belmont, CA, 1990.

30. See, e.g., "A Gene That Says: No More," *Newsweek,* December 12, 1994; John Sedgwick, "The Mentality Bunker," *GQ,* November 1994, p. 231.

31. See, e.g., Theresa Overfield, *Biologic Variation in Health and Illness,* Addison-Wesley, Reading, MA, 1985; Anthony P. Polednak, *Racial and Ethnic Differences in Disease,* Oxford University Press, New York, 1989.

32. James P. Comer and Alvin F. Poussaint, *Raising Black Children,* Penguin, New York, 1992, pp. 26, 137.

33. *World Almanac and Book of Facts,* Funk and Wagnall, Mahwah, NJ, 1994, pp. 841–43, 923.

34. Amby Burfoot, "White Men Can't Run," *Runner's World,* August 1992, pp. 89–95. The subsequent account draws on research cited in this article.

35. Steven Goldberg, "Black Athletic Superiority: Why Are Blacks Better Athletes," in *When Wish Replaces Thought,* Prometheus Books, Buffalo, 1991, p. 122.

36. John George, "The Virtual Disappearance of the White Male Sprinter in the United States: A Speculative Essay," *Sociology of Sport Journal,* No. 11 (1994), pp. 70–78.

37. Stanley Eitzen, "Black Athletes in American Society Since 1940," paper prepared for the Committee on the Status of Black Americans, cited in Gerald David Jaynes and Robin M. Williams, *A Common Destiny: Blacks and American Society,* National Academy Press, Washington, DC, 1989, p. 96

38. David K. Wiggins, "Great Speed But Little Stamina: The Historical Debate Over Black Athletic Superiority," *Journal of Sport History* 16, No. 2 (Summer 1989), pp. 158–85.

39. Alfonso de Garay, Louis Levine, and J. E. Lindsay Carter, eds., *Genetic and Anthropological Studies of Olympic Athletes,* Academic Press, New York, 1974.

40. See, e.g., Robert Malina, "Racial and Ethnic Variation in the Motor Development and Performance of American Children," *Canadian Journal of Sports Science* 13 (1988), pp. 136–43; Claude Bouchard, "Racial Differences in Performance" and "Genetic Basis of Racial Differences," ibid., pp. 103–9. Bouchard argues that "a firm conclusion cannot be enunciated" about whether race differences in athletic capacity are hereditary; Malina told me that he inclines toward a "partly genetic and partly environmental" explanation.

41. "Black Dominance," *Time,* May 9, 1977, pp. 57–60; "Calvin Hill Interview," *Journal of Sports History,* Winter 1988, pp. 334–35.

42. Murray Chass, "Campanis Is Out; Racial Remarks Cited by Dodgers," *New York Times,* April 9, 1987, p. B-13; Michael Goodwin, "CBS Dismisses Snyder," *New York Times,* January 17, 1988, p. E-1. For a discussion, see Lloyd R. Cohen, "The Puzzling Case of Jimmy the Greek," *Society,* July-August 1994, pp. 43–50.

43. "Remark Ends a Job Candidacy," *New York Times,* July 29, 1993, p. A-21.

44. Martin Kane, "An Assessment of Black Is Best," *Sports Illustrated,* January 18, 1971, pp. 72–83.

45. See, e.g., Harry Edwards, "The Sources of the Black Athlete's Superiority," *The Black Scholar,* November 1971, pp. 32–41; Harry Edwards, "20th Century Gladiators for White America," *Psychology Today,* November 1973, pp. 43–52; Harry Edwards, "On the Issue of Race in Contemporary American Sports," *Western Journal of Black Studies* 6, No. 3 (1982), pp. 139–44.

46. Richard Cohen, "The Greek's Offense," *Washington Post,* January 19, 1988, p. A-15.

47. Anti-Defamation League of B'nai B'rith, *Survey of Racial Attitudes,* New York, November 1992, pp. 11–12.

48. Rogers Elliott, "Tests, Abilities, Race and Conflict," *Intelligence* 12 (1988), pp. 333–50.

49. David Wechsler, who developed one of the most widely used IQ tests, maintains that "intelligence is the aggregate capacity of the individual to . . . think rationally and to deal effectively with his environment." David Wechsler, *The Measurement and Appraisal of Adult Intelligence,* Williams & Wilkins, Baltimore, 1958, p. 7.

50. Binet administered tests aimed at identifying children who needed special education by comparing them to other children of the same age. He developed the concept of "mental age" to reflect the relative cognitive capacity of young people. A few years later, a German psychologist named W. Stern divided the mental age by the chronological age to come up with an intelligence quotient or IQ.

51. Charles Spearman, "General Intelligence Objectively Defined and Measured," *American Journal of Psychology* 15 (1904), pp. 201–93; Charles Spearman, *The Abilities of Man,* Macmillan, New York, 1927.

52. Arthur Jensen, "How Much Can We Boost IQ and Scholastic Achievement?" p. 9.

53. For a review of many studies, see, e.g., Audrey Shuey, *The Testing of Negro Intelligence,* Social Science Press, New York, 1966; John C. Loehlin, Gardner Lindzey, and James N. Spuhler, *Race Differences in Intelligence,* W. H. Freeman, San Francisco, 1975; Herrnstein and Murray, *The Bell Curve.*

54. Stephen Jay Gould, *An Urchin in the Storm,* W. W. Norton, New York, 1987, p. 127.

Leon Kamin of Northwestern University admits, "The clear fact that, on average, American blacks have lower IQ scores than American whites . . . has been well known since the first world war. The difference is about 15 points. The fact is not in dispute: the argument has revolved around how to interpret that evidence."

Surveying IQ and cognitive ability tests administered in different places and at different ages, the National Academy of Science concluded a few years ago that the 15 point IQ gap persists "between blacks and whites on all given tests and at all grade levels. . . . Differences of approximately this magnitude were found at the sixth, ninth and twelfth grades."

See Leon Kamin, "Some Odds and Ends," in H. J. Eysenck and Leon Kamin, *The Intelligence Controversy,* John Wiley, New York, 1981, p. 140; W. Garner and A. Wigdor, *Ability Testing: Uses, Consequences and Controversies,* National Academy Press, Washington, DC, 1982, Vol. I, pp. 71–72; Vol. 2, p. 365; see also Robert Sternberg, "Negro Intelligence," in R. J. Sternberg, ed., *Encyclopedia of Human Intelligence,* Macmillan, New York, 1994, pp. 899–907; Richard Lewontin, "Race and Intelligence," in N. J. Block and Gerald Dworkin, *The IQ Controversy: Critical Readings,* Pantheon Books, New York, 1976, p. 88.

55. Mark Snyderman and Stanley Rothman, *The IQ Controversy: The Media and Public Policy,* Transaction Books, New Brunswick, NJ, 1988, pp. 71, 92–96, 284.

56. Linda Gottfredson, "Reconsidering Fairness: A Matter of Social and Ethical Priorities," *Journal of Vocational Behavior* 33 (December 1988), pp. 293–319.

57. Linda Gottfredson, "Societal Consequences of the g Factor in Employment," *Journal of Vocational Behavior* 29 (1986), pp. 379–410.

58. U.S. Bureau of the Census, *Statistical Abstract of the United States 1994,* Washington, DC, p. 407; Sam Roberts, *Who We Are: A Portrait of America Based on the Latest U.S. Census,* Times Books, New York, 1993, p. 107.

59. Brett Pulley and Jeff Bailey, "Pool of Qualified Blacks Expands, but Very Few Sit on Corporate Boards," *Wall Street Journal,* June 28, 1994, p. B-1.

60. Gottfredson, "Societal Consequences of the g Factor in Employment."

61. Herrnstein and Murray, *The Bell Curve,* pp. 71–89.

62. For data on the two-to-four-year gap in reading, prose, comprehension, and quantitative test scores between blacks and whites, see R. L. Venezky, C. F. Kaestle, and A. M. Sum, *The Subtle Danger: Reflections on the Literacy Abilities of America's Young Adults,* Educational Testing Service, Princeton, NJ, 1987.

Although blacks made up about 16 percent of the enrollment in public schools between 1976 and 1984, blacks made up about 38 percent of the population of students classified as "educable mentally retarded." See Willy D. Smith and Eva W. Chunn, *Black Education: A Quest for Equity and Excellence,* Transaction Publishers, New Brunswick, NJ, 1991, p. 102.

"African American students continue to complete college at one of the lowest rates: approximately one-third of all African American four-year entrants graduates within six years." See Deborah Carter and Reginald Wilson, *Minorities in Higher Education,* American Council on Education, Washington, DC, 1993, p. 4.

For data on the scarcity of black mathematicians at America's leading universities, see Theodore Cross and Robert Slater, "Only Five Black Mathematicians at America's 25 Top-Ranked Universities," *Journal of Blacks in Higher Education,* No. 4 (Summer 1994), pp. 72–75.

The National Science Foundation reports that blacks made up 1.9 percent of employed Ph.D. scientists in 1991. See Karen Fox, "A Question of Identity," *Science* 262 (November 12, 1993), p. 1090.

63. See, e.g., Nathaniel Weyl, *The Geography of American Achievement,* Scott-Townsend, Washington, DC, 1989. Weyl examines books such as *Who's Who, American Men and Women of Science,* as well as Nobel Prize recipients. He concludes that Asian Americans are overrepresented in these lists by 200–1000 percent, while blacks appear with about 10 percent of the expected frequency.

64. John Baker, *Race,* Oxford University Press, New York, 1974, p. 503.

65. See, e.g., Walter Lippmann's famous series of articles in *The New Republic* attacking IQ tests: "The Mental Age of Americans," October 25, 1922; "The Mystery of the A-Men," November 1, 1922; "The Reliability of Intelligence Tests," November 8, 1922; "The Abuse of the Tests," November 15, 1922; "Tests of Hereditary Intelligence," November 22, 1922; "The Future of the Tests," November 29, 1922.

66. Ashley Montagu, *Race and IQ,* Oxford University Press, New York, 1975, p. 3.

67. Robert L. Williams, "On Black Intelligence," *Journal of Black Studies,* September 1973, p. 30.

68. Jensen, "How Much Can We Boost IQ and Scholastic Achievement," p. 5.

69. Louis Thurstone, *Primary Mental Abilities,* University of Chicago Press, Chicago, 1938.

70. Raymond B. Cattell, "Theory of Fluid and Crystalized Intelligence: A Critical Experiment," *Journal of Educational Psychology* 54 (1963), pp. 1–22.

71. Daniel Seligman, *A Question of Intelligence,* Carol Publishing, New York, 1994, p. 34.

72. John Gardner, *Excellence: Can We Be Equal and Excellent Too?,* W. W. Norton, New York, 1984, p. 116.

73. Howard Gardner, *Multiple Intelligences: The Theory in Practice,* Basic Books, New York, 1993, pp. 8–9, 38; see also Howard Gardner, *Frames of Mind: The Theory of Multiple Intelligences,* Basic Books, New York, 1983; Howard Gardner, *Creating Minds,* Basic Books, New York, 1993.

74. Robert Sternberg, *Beyond IQ: A Triarchic Theory of Human Intelligence,* Cambridge University Press, New York, 1985; Robert Sternberg and Richard Wagner, *Practical Intelligence: Nature and Origins of Competence in the Everyday World,* Cambridge University Press, New York, 1986. Sternberg argues for the existence of three basic types of intelligence: conceptual, which involves information processing; creative, which entails applying mental concepts in new and interesting ways; and contextual, which refers to the application of ideas to the everyday problems of the real world.

75. Henry Louis Gates, Jr., *Loose Canons: Notes on the Culture Wars,* Oxford University Press, New York, 1992, pp. 48, 50.

76. Christopher Hitchens, "Minority Report," *The Nation,* November 28, 1994, p. 640; Steven A. Holmes, "You're Smart If You Know What Race You Are," *New York Times,* October 23, 1994.

77. "Three Is Not Enough," *Newsweek,* February 13, 1995.

78. Less than 25 percent of African Americans are considered to be of purely African ancestry. Blacks on average are estimated to derive almost one-third of their ancestry from whites. See William Boyd, "Four Achievements of the Genetical Method in Physical Anthropology," *American Anthropologist* 65 (1963), pp. 243–52; Pat Shipman, "Facing Racial Differences—Together," *Chronicle of Higher Education,* August 3, 1994, p. B-1 (citing research by Luigi Cavalli-Sforza); Melville Herskovits, *The American Negro,* Alfred A. Knopf, New York, 1928, p. 9; Joel Williamson, *New People: Miscegenation and Mulattoes in the United States,* Free Press, New York, 1980, p. 111.

79. "Race," *The Columbia Encyclopedia,* Houghton Mifflin, Boston, 1993, p. 2265.

80. Holmes, "You're Smart If You Know What Race You Are."

81. Hitchens, "Minority Report."

82. John Baker writes, "Large scale hybridization between races and subraces has in fact occurred." Baker, *Race,* p. 5.

83. Louis L. Snyder, *The Idea of Racialism: Its Meaning and History,* D. Van Nostrand, Princeton, 1962, p. 19.

84. L. C. Dunn, "Race and Biology," in Leo Kuper, ed., *Race, Science and Society,* UNESCO Press, Paris, 1975, p. 41.

85. See Theodosius Dobzhansky, *Mankind Evolving: The Evolution of the Human Species,* Yale University Press, New Haven, 1962, p. 266; Snyder, *The Idea of Racialism,* p. 12.

86. Jared Diamond, "Race Without Color," *Discover,* November 1994, p. 89; see also Boyce Rensberger, "Forget the Old Labels: Here's a New Way to Look at Race," *Washington Post,* November 16, 1994, pp. H-1, H-6.

87. Cited by David L. Wheeler, "A Growing Number of Scientists Reject the Concept of Race," *Chronicle of Higher Education,* February 17, 1995, p. A-15.

88. "Race," *Columbia Encyclopedia,* p. 2265.

89. Farai Chideya, *Don't Believe the Hype: Fighting Cultural Misinformation About African-Americans,* Penguin, New York, 1995, p. 155.

90. Pat Shipman, *The Evolution of Racism,* Simon & Schuster, New York, 1994, p. 269.

91. See, e.g., Baker, *Race,* p. 459; Herrnstein and Murray, *The Bell Curve,* pp. 105–6.

92. Leon Kamin, *The Science and Politics of IQ,* John Wiley, New York, 1974, p. 67; Leon Kamin, "In Conclusion," in Eysenck and Kamin, *The Intelligence Controversy,* p. 154.

93. Richard Lewontin, *Biology as Ideology,* HarperPerennial, New York, 1993, p. 96.

94. Thomas J. Bouchard, Auke Tellegen, David T. Lykken, Kimerly J. Wilcox, Nancy L. Segal, and Stephen Rich, "Personality and Similarity in Twins Reared Together and Apart," *Journal of Personality and Social Psychology* 54, No. 6 (1988), pp. 1031–39; Thomas J. Bouchard and Matthew McGue, "Genetic and Rearing Environmental Influences on Adult Personality: An Analysis of Adopted Twins Reared Apart," *Journal of Personality* 58 (1990), pp. 263–93; Thomas J. Bouchard, David Lykken, Matthew McGue, Nancy Segal, and Auke Tellegen, "Sources of Human Psychological Differences: The Minnesota Study of Twins Reared Apart," *Science* 250 (1990), pp. 223–28.

95. Robert Plomin, "The Nature and Nurture of Cognitive Abilities," in R. J. Sternberg, ed., *Advances in the Psychology of Human Intelligence,* Erlbaum, Hillsdale, NJ, Vol. 4, 1988; Robert Plomin, "The Role of Inheritance in Behavior," *Science* 248 (1990), pp. 183–88; Robert Plomin, Michael J. Owen, and Peter McGuffin, "The Genetic Basis of Complex Human Behaviors," *Science* 264 (1994), pp. 1733–39.

96. Stephen Jay Gould, *The Mismeasure of Man,* W. W. Norton, New York, 1981, p. 155; Stephen Jay Gould, "Racist Arguments and IQ," in Ashley Montagu, ed., *Race and IQ,* Oxford University Press, New York, 1975, p. 149.

97. R. C. Lewontin, Steven Rose, and Leon Kamin, *Not in Our Genes: Biology, Ideology and Human Nature,* Pantheon, New York, 1984, pp. 267–68.

98. Arthur Jensen, *Straight Talk About Mental Tests,* Free Press, New York, 1981, p. xiv.

99. Richard Lewontin, "Race and Intelligence," *Science and Public Affairs,* March 1970, pp. 2–8.

100. Gould, "Curveball," p. 140.

101. Arthur Jensen, for example, writes: "Formally, the heritability of a trait with-

in populations cannot tell us the heritability of the difference between population means. High heritability within populations, however, adds to the plausibility of the hypothesis that genetic factors are involved in the difference between populations." See Arthur Jensen, *Educability and Group Differences,* Harper and Row, New York, 1973, p. 356.

102. In a famous study in the 1930s, Otto Klineberg, a student of Franz Boas, showed that blacks in the urban North scored higher on IQ tests than both blacks and whites in the rural South. Critics of Klineberg attributed this to selective migration—perhaps the most intelligent blacks went north—but Klineberg showed that the longer black families had stayed in the North, the better their children did on tests. In other words, the external environment seemed largely responsible for black performance. See Otto Klineberg, *Negro Intelligence and Selective Migration,* Columbia University Press, New York, 1935; see also Carl Degler, *In Search of Human Nature,* Oxford University Press, New York, 1991, pp. 179–81.

103. Arthur Jensen, "Cumulative Deficit in IQ of Blacks in the Rural South," *Developmental Psychology* 13, No. 3 (1977).

104. Herrnstein and Murray, *The Bell Curve,* p. 301.

105. These experiments are not entirely free of complications. For example, there is the possibility that since young people are placed for adoption not by intelligence testers but by adoption agencies, those agencies will choose adoptive families that resemble the child's biological family. If so, heredity estimates would be hard to calculate, since placement practices of this sort would increase the likelihood of IQ similaries between adoptive children and their natural parents.

106. Gould, "Curveball," p. 142.

107. Cited by J. R. Flynn, *Race, IQ and Jensen,* Routledge & Kegan Paul, London, 1980, pp. 84–102; see also Loehlin, Lindzey, and Spuhler, *Race Differences in Intelligence,* pp. 126–27. The German study is mentioned by Herrnstein and Murray, *The Bell Curve,* p. 310.

108. Sandra Scarr and Richard Weinberg, "IQ Test Performance of Black Children Adopted by White Families," *American Psychologist* 31 (1976), pp. 726–39; Sandra Scarr and Richard Weinberg, "Intellectual Similarities Within Families of Both Adopted and Biological Children," *Intelligence* 1 (1977), pp. 170–91; Sandra Scarr and Richard Weinberg, "The Influence of Family Background on Intellectual Attainment," *American Sociological Review* 43 (1978), pp. 674–92; Richard Weinberg, Sandra Scarr, and Irwin Waldman, "The Minnesota Transracial Adoption Study: A Follow-Up of IQ Test Performance at Adolescence," *Intelligence* 16 (1992), pp. 117–35; Sandra Scarr, Richard Weinberg, and Irwin Waldman, "IQ Correlations in Transracial Adoptive Families," *Intelligence* 17 (1993), pp. 541–55.

109. Oscar Lewis, "The Culture of Poverty," *Scientific American* 215 (October 1966), pp. 19–25; Oscar Lewis, "The Culture of Poverty," in Daniel P. Moynihan, ed., *On Understanding Poverty: Perspectives from the Social Sciences,* Basic Books, New York, 1968, pp. 187–220; Oscar Lewis, *La Vida: A Puerto Rican Family in the Culture of Poverty,* Random House, New York, 1965.

110. Howard Garber, *The Milwaukee Project: Preventing Mental Retardation in Children at Risk,* American Association on Mental Retardation, Washington, DC,

1988; Arthur Jensen, "Raising IQ Without Increasing g: A Review of the Milwaukee Project," *Developmental Review* 9 (1989), pp. 234–58. For a review of several unsuccessful efforts to substantially raise IQ and educational performance, including the Milwaukee Project and the Perry Preschool Program, see Herman Spitz, *The Raising of Intelligence,* Lawrence Erlbaum, Hillsdale, NJ, 1986.

111. John Ogbu, *Minority Education and Caste,* Academic Press, New York, 1978, p. 94.

112. Peter Skerry, "The Charmed Life of Head Start," *The Public Interest* 73 (Fall 1983), pp. 18–39; Charles Haskins, "Beyond Metaphor: The Efficacy of Early Childhood Education," *American Psychologist* 44 (1989), pp. 274–82; Constance Holden, "Head Start Enters Adulthood," *Science,* May 23, 1990, pp. 1400–1402.

113. For a summary of studies of Chapter I, see Jaynes and Williams, *A Common Destiny,* pp. 346–48.

114. *Journal of Blacks in Higher Education,* No. 1 (Autumn 1993), p. 21.

115. The College Board, "National College Bound Seniors: 1994 Profile of SAT and Achievement Test Takers," Princeton, NJ.

116. The College Board, "SAT Scores for Each Ethnic Group by Highest Level of Parental Education, 1994," August 1994, p. 16.

117. Dana Takagi, *The Retreat from Race: Asian American Admissions and Racial Politics,* Rutgers University Press, New Brunswick, 1992, p. 198.

118. Irwin S. Kirsch and Ann Jungeblut, *Literacy: Profiles of America's Young Adults,* National Assessment of Educational Progress, Princeton, 1986; see also Loehlin, Lindzey, and Spuhler, *Race Differences in Intelligence,* p. 235; Herrnstein and Murray, *The Bell Curve,* p. 289.

119. Herrnstein and Murray, *The Bell Curve,* p. 288.

120. Herrnstein, "IQ," pp. 43–64.

121. Allen, "Gray Matter, Black and White Controversy," p. 5.

122. Comer and Poussaint, *Raising Black Children,* p. 234.

123. J. L. Dillard, *Black English: Its History and Usage in the United States,* Vintage Books, New York, 1972, p. 30.

124. Lewontin, *Biology as Ideology,* p. 34; see also Lewontin, Rose, and Kamin, *Not in Our Genes,* p. 88; Gould, *The Mismeasure of Man,* p. 200.

125. Herrnstein and Murray, *The Bell Curve,* p. 282; Arthur Jensen, *Bias in Mental Testing,* Free Press, New York, 1980, p. 552.

126. "All these authors swear up and down and I agree with them completely that the tests are not biased in the statistician's definition. Lack of S-bias means that the same score, when it is achieved by members of different groups, predicts the same thing, that is a black and a white person with identical scores will have the same probabilities for doing anything that IQ is supposed to predict." Gould, "Curveball," p. 145.

127. Florence Goodenough, *The Measurement of Intelligence by Drawings,* Harcourt Brace Jovanovich, New York, 1926.

128. Otto Klineberg, "Race and Psychology," in Kuper, ed., *Race, Science and Society,* pp. 184–85.

129. Randy W. Kamphaus, *Clinical Assessment of Children's Intelligence,* Allyn & Bacon, Boston, 1993, pp. 334–38.

130. R. L. Williams, "The BITCH-100: A Culture Specific Test," paper presented at the annual convention of the American Psychological Association, Honolulu, 1972.

131. Philip E. Vernon, *Intelligence and Cultural Environment,* Methuen, London, 1969, pp. 25, 98.

132. Arthur Jensen acknowledges that IQ tests are "implicitly shaped by the educational traditions of Europe and North America," that in this sense they are "a rather narrow and select sample of all the various forms of human learning," and that "the particular constellation of abilities we call intelligence . . . has been singled out from the total galaxy of mental abilities mainly because of the nature of our system of formal education and the occupational structure with which it is coordinated."

Anthropologist John Ogbu, who studies cross-cultural definitions of intelligence, argues that even though the underlying brain functions are the same, "members of various cultures possess distinctly different intelligences." He writes that "the primary purpose of IQ tests is to predict how well children in Western cultures learn the cognitive skills taught in Western schools, families and other settings . . . that are required for successful participation as adults in the occupational environment of Western societies."

See Arthur Jensen, "How Much Can We Boost IQ and Scholastic Achievement?" pp. 7, 19; John Ogbu, "Human Intelligence Testing: A Cultural-Ecological Perspective," *National Forum: The Phi Kappa Phi Journal,* Spring 1988, p. 24.

133. Gardner, *Multiple Intelligences,* p. 231.

134. John Ogbu, *Minority Education and Caste,* Harcourt Brace Jovanovich, New York, 1978, p. 33.

135. Andrew Hacker, *Two Nations: Black and White, Separate, Hostile, Unequal,* Ballantine Books, New York, 1992, p. 145.

136. Gould, *The Mismeasure of Man,* pp. 21, 25.

137. Charles Lane, "The Tainted Sources of *The Bell Curve,*" *New York Review of Books,* December 1, 1994, pp. 14–19; Alvin Poussaint is cited by Tom Morganthau, "IQ: Is It Destiny?" *Newsweek,* October 24, 1994, p. 53.

138. Stefan Kuhl, *The Nazi Connection: Eugenics, American Racism and German National Socialism,* Oxford University Press, New York, 1994, p. 106.

139. John Hartigan and Alexandra Wigdor, *Fairness in Employment Testing: Validity Generalization, Minority Issues and the General Aptitude Test Battery,* National Academy Press, Washington, DC, 1989, p. 26.

140. Arthur Jensen, "The Debunking of Scientific Fossils and Straw Persons," *Contemporary Education Review* 1, No. 2 (Summer 1982), pp. 121–35.

141. Lewis M. Terman, *The Measurement of Intelligence,* Houghton-Mifflin, Boston, 1916, pp. 91–92; cited by Lewontin, Rose, and Kamin, *Not in Our Genes,* p. 86.

142. Carl C. Brigham, *A Study of American Intelligence,* Princeton University Press, Princeton, 1923, pp. 197–210.

143. Ibid., p. vii.

144. See, e.g., Madison Grant, *The Passing of the Great Race,* Charles Scribner, New York, 1922; T. L. Stoddard, *The Revolt Against Civilization,* Macmillan, New York, 1922.

145. Leon Kamin, "Some Historical Facts About IQ Testing," in Eysenck and Kamin, *The Intelligence Controversy,* p. 91; Lewontin, Rose, and Kamin, *Not in Our Genes,* pp. 83–88. For a repetition of Kamin's claim that the early tests found more than three-fourths of Hungarians and Jews to be feebleminded, see Gould, *The Mismeasure of Man,* p. 166; James Fallows, *More Like Us,* Houghton-Mifflin, Boston, 1989, p. 145; Joe R. Feagin, *Racial and Ethnic Relations,* Prentice Hall, Englewood Cliffs, NJ, 1984, p. 113.

146. Degler, *In Search of Human Nature,* p. 52.

147. H. H. Goddard, "Mental Tests and the Immigrant," *The Journal of Delinquency* No. 2 (1917), pp. 243–77, Mark Snyderman and R. J. Herrnstein, "Intelligence Tests and the Immigration Act of 1924," *American Psychologist,* September 1983, pp. 986–95.

148. Richard M. Lerner, *Final Solutions: Biology, Prejudice, and Genocide,* Pennsylvania State University Press, University Park, 1992, p. xx.

149. See Paul Hollander, *Political Pilgrims: Travels of Western Intellectuals to the Soviet Union, China and Cuba,* Oxford University Press, New York, 1981.

150. See Wilcomb Washburn, "Cultural Relativism, Human Rights and the AAA," *American Anthropologist* 89 (December 1987).

151. Wole Soyinka, *Art, Dialogue and Outrage,* Pantheon Books, New York, 1993, pp. 199–215; see esp. pp. 201–2.

152. See Eugene Genovese, "The Question," *Dissent,* Summer 1994.

153. Reed, "Looking Backward," p. 654.

154. Richard Lewontin, "Further Remarks on Race and the Genetics of Intelligence," in Block and Dworkin, *The IQ Controversy,* p. 111.

155. "Mensa Faulted for Articles Advocating Extermination," *The Baltimore Sun,* January 11, 1995.

156. Many such proposals are contained in Michael Levin's forthcoming book *Why Race Matters,* which he was kind enough to send me. Levin argues, for instance, that since blacks tend to be more present-oriented than whites, "black time budgets may make it unwise to offer blacks the same safety net that it is prudent for whites to offer each other."

157. "Breakthrough on Race?" *American Renaissance,* December 1994, p. 8; Samuel Taylor, "For Whom the Bell Curves," *American Renaissance,* February 1995, p. 9.

158. This point is made in Bernard Boxill, *Blacks and Social Justice,* Rowman & Littlefield, Lanham, MD, 1992, p. 155.

159. "No one deserves his greater natural capacity nor merits a more favorable starting place in society." John Rawls, *A Theory of Justice,* Harvard University Press, Cambridge, 1971, p. 102.

160. See Tom Knott, "Lawrence Apology Simply Won't Do," *Washington Times,* February 10, 1995, p. B-7; Roger Hernandez, "Skirting the Real Issue—Racism,"

Washington Post, February 10, 1995, p. A-23; Richard Cohen, "Activist Or Racist?" *Washington Post,* February 14, 1995, p. A-15.

161. George Garriguez, "National Merit Scholarships: A Major Dash of Jim Crow," *Journal of Blacks in Higher Education,* No. 3 (Spring 1994), pp. 60–64.

162. Clifford Geertz, *The Interpretation of Cultures: Selected Essays,* Basic Books, New York, 1973, p. 69.

163. Gould, *The Mismeasure of Man,* p. 323.

164. Hitchens writes, "There is no gene for IQ." Susan Sperling claims that "modern genetic data indicate the extreme genetic closeness of all living humans." Christopher Hitchens, "Minority Report: Intelligence and Race," *The Nation,* November 28, 1994, p. 640; Susan Sperling, "Beating a Dead Monkey," ibid., p. 664.

165. Alan G. Thorne and Milford H. Wolpoff, "The Multiregional Evolution of Humans," *Scientific American* 266 (1992), pp. 76–83. For popular reports on the controversy over evolutionary origins, see Herbert M. Watzman, "Question of Human Origins Debated Anew As Scientists Put to Rest the Idea of a Common African Ancestor," *Chronicle of Higher Education,* September 16, 1992; Boyce Rensberger, "Skulls from China Support New Hypothesis on Humans," *Washington Post,* June 4, 1992, p. A-3; "The Search for Adam and Eve," *Newsweek,* January 11, 1988, pp. 46–52; James Shreeve, "Argument over a Woman: Science Searches for the Real Eve," *Discover,* August 1990, pp. 15–21; "How Man Began," *Time,* March 14, 1994, pp. 81–87.

166. Lloyd Humphreys, review of Stephen Jay Gould's *The Mismeasure of Man, American Journal of Psychology* 96 (Fall 1983), pp. 407–15; see also Lloyd Humphreys, "Trends in Levels of Academic Achievement of Blacks and Other Minorities," *Intelligence* 12 (1988), pp. 231–60; Jensen, *Straight Talk About Mental Tests,* pp. 83, 227. Jensen writes, "A gross misconception is that there are white genes and black genes for intelligence. This is nonsense. A polygenic theory assumes that the very same genes that produce variation in intelligence among persons of the same race can produce variation between races. The gene pools of such groups are hypothesized to possess different frequencies of the same genes that enhance the trait in question."

167. Hans Eysenck, *The IQ Argument,* Library Press, New York, 1971, p. 42.

168. Weyl, *The Geography of American Achievement,* pp. 130–58.

169. Richard Lynn, "The Intelligence of the Mongoloids: A Psychometric, Evolutionary and Neurological Theory," *Personality and Individual Differences* 8, No. 6 (1987), pp. 813–44; Richard Lynn, "Race Differences in Intelligence," *The Mankind Quarterly* 31 (1991), pp. 254–96; Richard Lynn, "The Evolution of Racial Differences in Intelligence," *The Mankind Quarterly* 32 (1991), pp. 99–121. For data on African test scores, as measured by the Raven's Standard Progressive Matrices, see K. Owen, "The Suitability of Raven's Standard Progressive Matrices for Various Groups in South Africa," *Personality and Individual Differences* 13 (1992), pp. 149–59.

170. J. Philippe Rushton, "Race Differences in Behavior: A Review and Evolutionary Analysis," *Personality and Individual Differences* 9, No. 6 (1988), pp.

1009–24; J. Philippe Rushton, "The Reality of Racial Differences: A Rejoinder and New Evidence," *Personality and Individual Differences* 9, No. 6 (1988), pp. 1035–40. Rushton's comment about testosterone levels is cited by Allen, "Gray Matter, Black and White Controversy," p. 8. Rushton's theory is summed up in J. Philippe Rushton, *Race, Evolution and Behavior: A Life History Perspective*, Transaction Books, New Brunswick, NJ, 1995.

171. Jensen, *Straight Talk About Mental Tests*, p. 170.

172. Dobzhansky, *Mankind Evolving*, pp. 150–54.

173. L. C. Dunn, "Race and Biology," in Kuper, *Race, Science and Society*, p. 61.

174. For good summaries of the scientific evidence, see Dobzhansky, *Mankind Evolving*, and C. Loring Brace, "Nonracial Approaches Toward Human Diversity," in Ashley Montagu, ed., *The Concept of Race*, Free Press, Glencoe, IL, 1964.

175. Boyce Rensberger, "Racial Odyssey," *Science Digest*, January-February 1981.

176. Seymour W. Itzkoff, *The Road to Equality: Evolution and Social Reality*, Praeger, Westport, CT, 1992, p. 86; see also Baker, *Race*, p. 159.

177. James Flynn, response to Richard Lynn, in J. Lynch et al., *Cultural Diversity and the Schools*, Falmer Press, London, 1992, p. 381; James Flynn, "Rushton, Evolution and Race: An Essay on Intelligence and Virtue," *The Psychologist: Bulletin of the British Psychological Society*, September 1989, pp. 363–66.

178. Dobzhansky, *Mankind Evolving*, p. 271. Anthropologist Sherwood Washburn writes, "No race has evolved to fit the selective pressures of the modern world. Technical civilization is new and the races are old." S. L. Washburn, "The Study of Race," in Montagu, *The Concept of Race*, p. 253.

179. Ernest Gellner, *Relativism and the Social Sciences*, Cambridge University Press, Cambridge, 1985, p. 98.

180. Joel Kotkin, *Tribes: How Race, Religion and Identity Determine Success in the New Global Economy*, Random House, New York, 1993; Lawrence Harrison, *Who Prospers? How Cultural Values Shape Economic and Political Success*, Basic Books, New York, 1992.

181. Thomas Sowell, "Ethnicity and IQ," *The American Spectator*, February 1995.

182. U.S. Bureau of the Census, "Proficiency Test Scores for Selected Subjects, by Characteristic: 1977 to 1990," in *Statistical Abstract of the United States 1994*, Washington, DC, p. 175; see also David J. Armor, "Why Is Black Educational Achievement Rising?" *The Public Interest*, Summer 1992, pp. 65–80.

183. See, e.g., "The H'mong in Wisconsin," *Wisconsin Policy Research Institute Report* 4, No. 2 (April 1991); Roy Beck, "The Ordeal of Immigration in Wausau," *The Atlantic Monthly*, April 1994, pp. 84–97.

184. James R. Flynn, *Asian Americans: Achievement Beyond IQ*, Lawrence Erlbaum Associates, Hillsdale, NJ, 1991.

185. This research is summed up in Rosemary Rosser, *Cognitive Development: Psychological and Biological Perspectives*, Allyn and Bacon, Boston, 1994; Mark H. Johnson, ed., *Brain Development and Cognition*, Blackwell, Cambridge, 1993; Geraldine Dawson and Kurt Fischer, *Human Behavior and the Developing Brain*, Guilford Press, New York, 1994; Lawrence Barsalou, *Cognitive Psychology: An Overview for Cognitive Scientists*, Lawrence Erlbaum, Hillsdale, NJ, 1992. For two popular accounts see

Carnegie Corporation, "Starting Points," New York, April 1994; Rochelle Sharpe, "To Boost IQs, Aid Is Needed in First Three Years," *Wall Street Journal,* April 12, 1994.

186. Sarah Broman, Paul Nichols, and Wallace Kennedy, *Preschool IQ: Prenatal and Early Developmental Correlates,* John Wiley, New York, 1975.

187. Children's Defense Fund, *Progress and Peril: Black Children in America,* Washington, DC, 1993, pp. 27–28, 37–38, 51–52.

188. Jensen, *Bias in Mental Testing,* p. 43; Jensen, *Straight Talk About Mental Tests,* p. 171; Jensen, "How Much Can We Boost IQ and Scholastic Achievement?" p. 74.

189. Elsie Moore, "Family Socialization and the IQ Test Performance of Traditionally and Transracially Adopted Black Children," *Developmental Psychology* 22, No. 3 (1986), pp. 317–26.

190. Zena Smith Blau, *Black Children, White Children: Competence, Socialization and Social Structure,* Free Press, New York, 1981. The quotations are on pp. xv and 58.

191. Gardner, *Multiple Intelligences,* p. 47.

192. Gould, "Curveball," p. 141.

193. Elliott, "Tests, Abilities, Race and Conflict," p. 333.

Chapter 12. Uncle Tom's Dilemma

1. Ice Cube, *Death Certificate,* Priority Records, 1991.

2. Haki Madhubuti in *Black Men: Obsolete, Single, Dangerous?* describes the destructive patterns of behavior of the African American who "buys few books . . . gravitates toward incompetence and mediocrity . . . has a welfare-conscious, get-it-for-nothing attitude . . . loves sexual conquests . . . does not want children or responsibility of home life . . . actively fights against discipline . . . is involved in black-on-black crime . . . rejects criticism . . . and is drug-dependent."

Education for many young black men is "streetwork" rather than "homework," James Vigil writes. These lessons often "take the form of learning how to plan and prepare a drive-by shooting or retaliation."

Mark Naison identifies "urban outlaws" of the black underclass who "use children as shields in gun battles, spray street corners with automatic weapons, kill fellow black teenagers for jackets and sneakers, and rob congregations during church services."

William Oliver writes in *The Violent Social World of Black Men* that "many lower class black males tend to define masculinity in terms of dominance and the sexual exploitation of women."

See Haki Madhubuti, *Black Men: Obsolete, Single, Dangerous?,* Third World Press, Chicago, 1990, p. 9; James Vigil, "Gangs, Social Control and Ethnicity," in Shirley B. Heath and Milbrey W. McLaughlin, eds., *Identity and Inner-City Youth,* Teachers College Press, New York, 1993, p. 108; Mark Naison, "Outlaw Culture and Black Neighborhoods," *Reconstruction* 1, No. 4 (1992), p. 128; William Oliver, *The Violent Social World of Black Men,* Lexington Books, New York, 1994, p. 27.

3. "Jackson Urges Blacks to Excel in Government Jobs," *Washington Post,* August 24, 1993.

4. Jewelle Taylor Gibbs, ed., *Young, Black and Male in America: An Endangered Species,* Auburn House, Dover, MA, p. 19.

5. Anthony Walton, "Patriots," in Gerald Early, ed., *Lure and Loathing: Essays on Race, Identity and the Ambivalence of Assimilation,* Penguin Books, New York, 1993, p. 261.

6. Barbara Vobedja, "Black Adults Are Pessimistic About Prospects of Children," *Washington Post,* May 27, 1994, p. A-2.

7. Andrew Billingsley, *Climbing Jacob's Ladder: The Enduring Legacy of African-American Families,* Simon & Schuster, New York, 1992, p. 36.

8. Lee Rainwater and William L. Yancey, ed., *The Moynihan Report and the Politics of Controversy,* MIT Press, Cambridge, 1967.

9. "Final Cut: Spike Lee and Henry Louis Gates, Jr. Rap on Race, Politics and Black Cinema," *Transition,* Issue 52, (1991), p. 185.

10. "Backlash Against Sowell," *Business Week,* November 30, 1981, p. 119.

11. Cited by L. Gordon Crovitz in his introduction to Clarence Thomas, *Confronting the Future,* Regnery Gateway, Washington, DC, 1992, p. 14.

12. Kenneth J. Cooper, "Rep. Franks Revisits Voting Rights Dispute," *Washington Post,* July 25, 1994, p. A-5.

13. John McManus, "CBC: Dissension in the Ranks," *The New American,* September 6, 1993, p. 17; see also Kenneth J. Cooper, "The Black Caucus's Odd Man In," *Washington Post,* September 1, 1993, p. C-1.

14. Frank McCoy, "Can the Black Caucus Be Bipartisan?" *Black Enterprise,* January 1994, p. 22.

15. Martin Kilson, "The Anatomy of Black Conservatism," *Transition,* Issue 59 (1993), pp. 14–16.

16. "Civil Rights and Wrongs," *Wall Street Journal,* July 19, 1990, p. A-10.

17. Manning Marable, "Clarence Thomas and the Crisis of Black Political Culture," in Toni Morrison, ed., *Race-ing Justice, En-gendering Power,* Pantheon Books, New York, 1992, p. 82.

18. Cited in "On the Record," *National Review,* August 12, 1991.

19. June Jordan, *Technical Difficulties: African American Notes on the State of the Union,* Vintage Books, New York, 1994, pp. 206, 217.

20. Julianne Malveaux, "Black Conservatives in the Spotlight," *San Francisco Examiner,* July 6, 1991.

21. Nikki Giovanni, *Racism 101,* William Morrow, New York, 1994, p. 52.

22. Roger Wilkins, "Sowell Brother," *The Nation,* October 10, 1981, p. 333.

23. Houston Baker, "Caliban's Triple Play," in Henry Louis Gates, Jr., ed., *"Race," Writing and Difference,* University of Chicago Press, Chicago, 1986, p. 387.

24. Cited in Arch Puddington, "Clarence Thomas and the Blacks," *Commentary,* February 1992, p. 150.

25. Bruce Wright, *Black Robes, White Justice,* Carol Publishing, New York, 1987, p. 65.

26. Alphonso Pinkney, *The Myth of Black Progress,* Cambridge University Press, Cambridge, 1984, p. 17.

27. Playthell Benjamin, "Black Neocon Artists: Living Large, Thinking Small," *Emerge,* November 1991, p. 48.

28. John Henrik Clarke, "Black Pseudo-Scholars Are in with White America, but They Deserve to Be Outed," *City Sun,* New York, August 26–September 1, 1992.

29. Lena Williams, "In a '90s Quest for Black Identity, Intense Doubts and Disagreement," *New York Times,* November 30, 1991, pp. A-1, A-26.

30. Cited by Judith Colb, "He's Black, Conservative, Hates Elitism," *Washington Times,* August 14, 1991, p. E-1.

31. Chris Raymond, "Controversial Harvard Sociologist Relishes His Role as a Maverick," *Chronicle of Higher Education,* March 4, 1992, p. A-8.

32. See William Ryan, *Blaming the Victim,* Vintage Books, New York, 1971.

33. Kimberle Crenshaw, "Race, Reform and Retrenchment: Transformation and Legitimation in Antidiscrimination Law," *Harvard Law Review* 101 (1988), p. 1379.

34. Henry Louis Gates, Jr., "Why Now?" *The New Republic,* October 31, 1994, p. 10.

35. David T. Wellman, *Portraits of White Racism,* Cambridge University Press, Cambridge, 1977, pp. 39, 42.

36. Cited in "Endangered Family," *Newsweek,* August 30, 1993, p. 29.

37. Lawrence Levine, *Black Culture and Black Consciousness: Afro-American Thought from Slavery to Freedom,* Oxford University Press, New York, 1978; see also John Roberts, *From Trickster to Badman: The Black Folk Hero in Slavery and Freedom,* University of Pennsylvania Press, Philadelphia, 1989; Charles P. Henry, *Culture and African American Politics,* Indian University Press, Bloomington, 1990; Thomas Kochman, *Rappin' and Stylin' Out: Communication in Urban Black America,* University of Illinois Press, Urbana, 1972.

38. William Julius Wilson, *The Truly Disadvantaged: The Inner City, the Underclass and Public Policy,* University of Chicago Press, Chicago, 1987, p. 14.

39. Manning Marable, "Race, Identity and Political Culture," in Michele Wallace, *Black Popular Culture,* Bay Press, Seattle, 1992, p. 295.

40. Thomas Sowell comes close to determinism when he traces the success of ethnic groups around the world to cultural patterns that go back hundreds, if not thousands of years. "Group cultural patterns may indeed be the products of environments, but often of environments that existed on the other side of an ocean, in the lives of ancestors long forgotten, yet transmitted over the generations as distilled values, preferences, skills and habits." See Thomas Sowell, *Race and Culture,* Basic Books, New York, 1994, p. x.

41. See, e.g., John Ogbu, "A Cultural Ecology of Competence Among Inner-City Blacks," in Margaret B. Spencer, Geraldine K. Brookins and Walter R. Allen, eds., *Beginnings: The Social and Affective Development of Black Children,* Lawrence Erlbaum Associates, Hillsdale, NJ, 1985, p. 66; John Ogbu, *Minority Education and Caste,* Harcourt Brace Jovanovich, New York, 1978; Elijah Anderson, "The Code of the Streets," *The Atlantic Monthly,* May 1994, p. 82.

42. Alvin F. Poussaint, *Why Blacks Kill Blacks,* Emerson Hall Publishers, New York, 1972, p. 19.

43. For two studies of the values of working class blacks, see Elliot Liebow, *Tally's Corner: A Study of Negro Streetcorner Men,* Little, Brown, Boston, 1967; Mitchell Duneier, *Slim's Table: Race, Respectability and Masculinity,* University of Chicago Press, Chicago, 1992.

44. See, e.g., Tucker Carlson, "That Old Time Religion," *Policy Review,* Summer 1992.

45. This point is made by Myron Magnet, *The Dream and the Nightmare: The Sixties' Legacy to the Underclass,* William Morrow, New York, 1993.

46. For an appreciation of black culture, see, e.g., Ralph Ellison, *Shadow and Act,* Random House, New York, 1964; for a more recent tribute, see "The Beauty of Black Art," *Time,* October 10, 1994, pp. 66–75.

47. Wynton Marsalis, "Why We Must Preserve Our Jazz," *Ebony,* February 1986, p. 131.

48. Carol Hernandez, "Black Memorabilia Find Big Demand," *Wall Street Journal,* August 10, 1992.

49. Associated Press report, "Farrakhan Links Race to Transplants," *New York Times,* May 2, 1994, p. A-18.

50. Jason DeParle, "Talk Grows of Government Being Out to Get Blacks," *New York Times,* October 29, 1990, pp. B-6, B-7.

51. "Losing Ground," *Newsweek,* April 6, 1992, p. 21.

52. Howard Kurtz, "Drug Scourge Is Conspiracy by Whites, Some Blacks Say," *Washington Post,* December 29, 1989, p. A-1.

53. Robert Staples, "Black Male Genocide: A Final Solution to the Race Problem in America," *The Black Scholar,* May-June 1987, p. 2.

54. Spike Lee's comments are cited in Arch Puddington, "The Question of Black Leadership," *Commentary,* January 1991; Bill Cosby's remarks are cited in "Bill Cosby's AIDS Conspiracy," *New York Post,* December 4, 1991.

55. Madhubuti, *Black Men,* pp. 73–74.

56. Patricia A. Turner, *I Heard It Through the Grapevine: Rumor in African-American Culture,* University of California Press, Berkeley, 1993.

57. William Mandel, "What Los Angeles Means: Negroes Are Lynched in America," in Haki R. Madhubuti, ed., *Why L.A. Happened: Implications of the '92 Los Angeles Rebellion,* Third World Press, Chicago, 1993, p. 157.

58. James Cashing, Jr., "You Bet Your Life! (And Mine Too!)" *Los Angeles Sentinel,* May 28, 1992, p. A-7.

59. Andy Logan, "Around City Hall," *New Yorker,* March 2, 1992, p. 81; "Talking About Crime," *Wall Street Journal,* February 27, 1992, p. A-12; Bill Brubaker, "Tyson's Descent from Glory Continues in Depths of Prison," *Washington Post,* February 14, 1993, p. D-1; Ishmael Reed, *Airing Dirty Laundry,* Addison-Wesley, Reading, MA, 1993, pp. xiv, 68.

60. Lena Williams, "Growing Black Debate: Racism or an Excuse?" *New York Times,* April 5, 1992.

61. "D.C. Mayor Arrested on Drug Charge," *Facts on File,* January 19, 1990, p. 29; "Hooks Sees Selective Prosecution," *Facts on File,* January 26, 1990, p. 47; Lena Williams, "Growing Black Debate: Racism or an Excuse?" p. 28; Jonathan Agronsky,

Marion Barry: The Politics of Race, British American Publishing, Latham, NY, 1991, pp. 64, 74.

62. Robert Hanley, "Black Poet Says Faculty Nazis Blocked Tenure," *New York Times,* March 15, 1990.

63. Denise Magner, "Charges of Racism Mark Dispute over a Professor's Leave," *Chronicle of Higher Education,* November 25, 1992, p. A-12.

64. Dempsey Travis, *Racism: American Style,* Urban Research Press, Chicago, 1991, p. 100.

65. Robert McFadden, et al., *Outrage: The Story Behind the Tawana Brawley Hoax,* Bantam Books, New York, 1990; see also Alan Dershowitz, "Racial Hoax with a Sour Echo," *Washington Times,* June 26, 1990; Jim Sleeper, "New York Stories," *The New Republic,* September 10, 1990, p. 21.

66. Patricia J. Williams, *The Alchemy of Race and Rights,* Harvard University Press, Cambridge, 1991, pp. 169–70.

67. Jordan, *Technical Difficulties,* p. 178.

68. William Grier and Price M. Cobbs, *Black Rage,* Basic Books, New York, 1986, p. 206.

69. Joe R. Feagin and Melvin P. Sikes, *Living with Racism: The Black Middle-Class Experience,* Beacon Press, Boston, 1994, pp. 221, 294; see also Joe R. Feagin, "Blacks Still Face the Malevolent Reality of White Racism," *Chronicle of Higher Education,* November 27, 1991, p. A-44.

70. Williams, *The Alchemy of Race and Rights,* pp. 9–10, 129.

71. Jill Nelson, *Volunteer Slavery: My Authentic Negro Experience,* The Noble Press, Chicago, 1993, pp. 54, 56, 67, 90–91, 98.

72. Brent Staples, *Parallel Time: Growing Up in Black and White,* Pantheon Books, New York, 1994, pp. 202–4.

73. Derrick Bell, *Faces at the Bottom of the Well: The Permanence of Racism,* Basic Books, New York, 1992, pp. xii, 93–94, 184–85, 194.

74. James M. Hund, *Black Entrepreneurship,* Wadsworth Publishing, Belmont, CA, 1970, p. 119.

75. Thomas Kochman, *Black and White: Styles in Conflict,* University of Chicago Press, Chicago, 1981, p. 41.

76. Robert L. Boyd, "The Allocation of Black Workers into the Public Sector," *Sociological Focus* 27, No. 1 (1994), p. 36; see also Equal Employment Opportunity Commission, EEO Profile of Private and Public Employers, summary of findings, March 1991; Richard Zweigenhaft and G. William Domhoff, *Blacks in the White Establishment,* Yale University Press, New Haven, 1991, p. 175.

77. Gerald David Jaynes and Robin Williams, *A Common Destiny: Blacks and American Society,* National Academy Press, Washington, DC, 1989, p. 244.

78. Cited in "Have Capital, Will Flourish," *The Economist,* February 27, 1993, pp. 33–34; see also Alphonso Pinkney, *The Myth of Black Progress,* p. 171.

79. U.S. Bureau of the Census, *Poverty in the United States,* Current Population Reports, Washington, DC, 1992, Table 7, pp. 33–37.

80. These results are from a September 1994 NBC News/*Wall Street Journal* survey. Cited by Gerald F. Seib and Joe Davidson, "Whites, Blacks Agree on Problems;

the Issue Is How to Solve Them," *Wall Street Journal,* September 29, 1994. See also Michael Dawson, "Black Discontent: The Preliminary Report on the 1993–1994 National Black Politics Study," University of Chicago, April 1994.

81. U.S. Department of Commerce, *Survey of Minority Owned Business Enterprises,* Washington, DC, August 1991, p. 2.

82. Ibid., p. 81; National Urban League, *The State of Black America 1993,* Washington, DC, 1993, pp. 94, 101.

83. Aldon D. Morris, *The Origins of the Civil Rights Movement: Black Communities Organizing for Change,* Free Press, New York, 1984, p. x.

84. James Farmer, *Freedom—When?,* Random House, New York, 1965, p. 36.

85. Cited in Michael McQueen, "Voter Response to Poll Discloses Huge Chasm Between Social Attitudes of Blacks and Whites," *Wall Street Journal,* May 17, 1991.

86. Alayna A. Gaines, "Expanding Political Clout," *Emerge,* April 1994, p. 29.

87. Giovanni, *Racism 101,* p. 138.

88. See, e.g., Jonathan Rieder, "Trouble in Store," *The New Republic,* July 2, 1990, p. 20. Rieder quotes a black organizer of a Brooklyn boycott against Koreans saying, "They are given money to establish themselves. How can poor people like that just come to this country and do that unless they have been given a fund? There's no one doing that for black people."

89. Kasarda's comment is based on a personal interview. But for a summary of his general argument, see John Kasarda, "City Jobs and Residents on a Collision Course: The Urban Underclass Dilemma," *Economic Development Quarterly* 4 (November 1990).

90. Ivan H. Light, *Ethnic Enterprise in America,* University of California Press, Berkeley, 1972; Ivan Light and Edna Bonacich, *Immigrant Entrepreneurs: Koreans in Los Angeles, 1965–1982,* University of California Press, Berkeley, 1988; Timothy Bates and Constance Dunham, "Asian-American Success in Self-Employment," *Economic Development Quarterly* 7, No. 2 (1993), pp. 199–214.

91. See, e.g., Calvin Sims, "Buying Black Approach Paying Off in Los Angeles," *New York Times,* May 23, 1993, p. E-5.

92. See Shelly Green and Paul Pryde, *Black Entrepreneurship in America,* Transaction Publishers, New Brunswick, NJ, 1989.

93. Manning Marable, "Race, Identity and Political Culture," in Michele Wallace, ed., *Black Popular Culture,* p. 302; Bell Hooks, "Dialectically Down with the Critical Program," ibid, p. 49.

94. Joe Davidson, "Dialogue with John Lewis," *Emerge,* July-August 1993, pp. 15–16.

95. National Center for Education Statistics, *Digest of Education Statistics,* Department of Education, U.S. Government Printing Office, Washington, DC, 1993, Tables 105, 108, 109, 112, 113, 116, 120–124, 302, 385.

96. Mary Ann Scheirer and Robert Kraut, "Increasing Educational Achievement Via Self-Concept Change," *Review of Educational Research* 49, No. 1 (1979), pp. 131–49.

97. H. G. Bissinger, "We're All Racist Now," *New York Times Magazine,* May 29, 1994, pp. 27–33, 43, 50, 53–56.

98. Nwamaegwu Jeremi Duru, "You're Just Trying to Act White," *Washington Post,* May 19, 1991.

99. "The Hidden Hurdle," *Time,* March 16, 1992, p. 44.

100. Ron Susskind, "In Rough City School, Top Students Struggle to Learn—and Escape," *Wall Street Journal,* May 26, 1994, pp. A-1, A-8; Ron Susskind, "Poor, Black and Smart, An Inner-City Teen Tries to Survive MIT," *Wall Street Journal,* September 22, 1994, pp. A-1, A-6.

101. Cited by Lise Funderburg, *Black, White, Other: Biracial Americans Talk About Race and Identity,* William Morrow, New York, 1994, pp. 115–16.

102. See, e.g., Retha Hill, "Scarce Men on Campus," *Washington Post,* March 21, 1994, p. A-8; Marc Elrich, "The Stereotype Within," *Educational Leadership,* April 1994, p. 13. See also Seth Mydans, "Academic Success Seen as Selling Out," *New York Times,* April 25, 1990; Linda Stewart, "Some Black Students Bear a Burden By Being Smart," *Detroit Free Press,* September 24, 1991.

103. See, e.g., Maria Eugenia Matute-Bianchi, "Ethnic Identities and Patterns of School Success and Failure Among Mexican-Descent and Japanese-American Students in a California High School: An Ethnographic Analysis," *American Journal of Education,* November 1986, pp. 232–55.

104. Signithia Fordham and John Ogbu, "Black Student School Success: Coping With the Burden of Acting White," *Urban Review* 18, No. 3 (1986), pp. 176–206.

105. Signithia Fordham, "Racelessness as a Factor in Black Students' School Success: Pragmatic Strategy or Pyrrhic Victory?" *Harvard Educational Review* 58, No. 1 (February 1988), pp. 54–84.

106. Robert Christgau and Greg Tate, "Chuck D All Over the Map," *Village Voice,* October 22, 1991, Rock and Roll Quarterly Insert, p. 16.

107. Johnnetta B. Cole, *Anthropology for the Nineties,* Free Press, New York, 1988, p. 109; J. L. Dillard, *Black English: Its History and Usage in the United States,* Random House, New York, 1972. Dillard gives an estimate of 80 percent and Cole 85 percent.

108. See, e.g., John Baugh, *Black Street Speech: Its History, Structure and Survival,* University of Texas Press, Austin, 1983; William Labov, ed., *Language in the Inner City: Studies in the Black English Vernacular,* University of Pennsylvania Press, Philadelphia, 1972.

109. Eleanor Wilson Orr, *Twice as Less: Black English and the Performance of Black Students in Mathematics and Science,* W. W. Norton, New York, 1987. Orr argues that students who think in Black English "arrive at different mental constructs of some given information" than speakers of standard English, and in some cases they suffer from "an inability to arrive at a workable mental construct at all." Orr argues that prepositions, conjunctions, and relative pronouns are crucial to identify and solve quantitative problems. Black English, she charges, obscures "distinctions that standard English modes of expression identify." The double negative, widely used in Black English, is a disaster when applied to logical reasoning.

110. Felicia Lee, "Grappling with How to Teach Young Speakers of Black Dialect," *New York Times,* January 5, 1994; Betty G. Davis and Hollis Armstrong, "The Impact of Teaching Black English on Self-Image and Achievement," *The Western Journal of Black Studies* 5, No. 3 (1981), pp. 208–15.

111. John DiIulio, Jr., "The Question of Black Crime," *The Public Interest,* Fall 1994, p. 4.

112. U.S. Department of Justice, *United States Crime Reports 1993,* Washington, DC, p. 17.

113. Jaynes and Williams, *A Common Destiny,* pp. 23, 464; see also Christopher Jencks, *Rethinking Social Policy: Race, Poverty and the Underclass,* Harvard University Press, Cambridge, 1992, p. 182.

114. "Who Will Help the Black Man?" *New York Times Magazine,* December 4, 1994, p. 74.

115. "Uncivil Wars," *The Economist,* October 7, 1989, p. 38.

116. According to *National Review,* the white crime rate for murder and robbery in America is comparable to the crime rates of Britain, France, Germany, and Italy. Yet this data, cited by James Kouri of the National Association of Chiefs of Police, is challenged by political scientist James Q. Wilson, who provides Interpol statistics to show that, even subtracting the African American crime rate, U.S. crime rates are still substantially higher than those of Europe. See *National Review,* May 16, 1994, p. 45; "Crime in America," *Commentary,* February 1995, p. 20.

117. Eugene Genovese, *Roll, Jordan, Roll: The World the Slaves Made,* Vintage Books, New York, 1972, p. 629.

118. Orlando Patterson, "Toward a Study of Black America," *Dissent,* Fall 1989, p. 480.

119. John Dollard, *Caste and Class in a Southern Town,* University of Wisconsin Press, Madison, 1937, p. 275.

120. Claude Brown, *Manchild in the Promised Land,* Macmillan, New York, 1965, pp. 301–9; Claude Brown, "Manchild in Harlem," *New York Times Magazine,* September 16, 1984, p. 40.

121. Christopher Jencks cites a survey by the National Bureau of Economic Research in which unemployed young blacks were asked how hard they thought it would be to find a minimum wage job. More than 70 percent said it would be "very easy" or "somewhat easy," leading Jencks to conclude that "a lot of idleness is voluntary." While some blacks said they wanted to work, Jencks remarks that "many do not want to work so badly that they will take or keep a minimum wage job." Jencks, *Rethinking Social Policy,* p. 127; see also Lawrence Mead, *The New Politics of Poverty,* Basic Books, New York, 1992, p. 107.

122. Richard Majors and Janet Mancini Billson, *Cool Pose: The Dilemmas of Black Manhood in America,* Simon & Schuster, New York, 1992. The subsequent quotations are from this book. See pp. 3–4, 21, 39, 46, 51, 87–88.

123. National Center for Health Statistics, *Vital Statistics of the United States, 1989,* Public Health Service, Washington, DC, 1993, p. 131; see also Samuel Dixon, "Contributions of Cultural, Social and Psychological Factors to the Etiology of Alcoholism in African Americans," *Western Journal of Black Studies* 15, No. 3 (1991), pp. 133–37.

124. Ice T, *The Ice Opinion: Who Gives a Fuck?,* St. Martin's Press, New York, 1994. The subsequent quotations are from this book. See pp. 7, 10, 14, 16, 25, 60, 62, 147.

125. Sanyika Shakur, *Monster: The Autobiography of an L.A. Gang Member*, Penguin Books, New York, 1993. The subsequent quotations are from this book. See pp. 52, 111, 133, 142, 215, 240.

126. Leon Bing, *Do or Die*, HarperPerennial, New York, 1991. The subsequent quotations are from this book. See pp. x–xi, 18, 59–61, 177, 194, 198, 200.

127. Transcript, "Nightline in South Central," ABC News, May 4, 1992, p. 9.

128. Jane Mayer, "In the War on Drugs, the Toughest Foe May be the Alienated Youth," *Wall Street Journal*, September 8, 1989, p. A-7.

129. Taking note of high rates of black involvement in crime, delinquency and drugs, Alphonso Pinkney offers the standard line, "The racist nature of American society frequently forces them to resort to nonconforming behavior as a means of surviving the daily hazards to which they are subjected." Alphonso Pinkney, *Black Americans*, Prentice-Hall, Englewood Cliffs, NJ, 1969, p. 136; see also Pinkney, *The Myth of Black Progress*, p. 117.

Similarly Johnnetta Cole argues, "The dependence on drugs and the rampant violence which stalk our communities are clearly in some ways related to the frustration and despair that result when people are without those social services necessary to sustain a decent life." Johnnetta Cole, *Conversations: Straight Talk with America's Sister President*, Anchor Books, New York, 1993, p. 142.

"For many black males," Clyde Franklin writes, "aggressiveness, violence, cool poses, and dominance . . . are logical strategies to function reasonably well in their day-to-day activities." Clyde Franklin, "Men's Studies, the Men's Movement and the Study of Black Masculinities," in Richard Majors and Jacob Gordon, eds., *The American Black Male: His Present Status and His Future*, Nelson Hall Publishers, Chicago, 1994, p. 15.

William Harvey justifies black crimes against the most vulnerable members of society on the grounds that members of the underclass live in a "subculture of exasperation" in which they are "unable to strike back at those in power, whom they feel are responsible for their societal positions and for their inability to obtain the possessions that are considered most desirable." William B. Harvey, "Homicide Among Young Black Adults: Life in the Subculture of Exasperation," in Darnell F. Hawkins, ed., *Homicide Among Black Americans*, University Press of America, Lanham, MD, 1986, pp. 153, 160.

Bernard Boxill argues that black violence is understandable because it is perpetrated by people "in order to survive and retain their sanity and equilibrium in impossibly unjust situations." Bernard Boxill, *Blacks and Social Justice*, Rowman & Littlefield, Lanham, MD, 1992, p. 157.

130. Bruce Wright, *Black Robes, White Justice*, Carol Publishing, New York, 1987, pp. 207, 213.

131. Poussaint, *Why Blacks Kill Blacks*, pp. 52, 72.

132. Bell, *Faces at the Bottom of the Well*, p. 196.

133. Derrick Bell, *And We Are Not Saved: The Elusive Quest for Racial Justice*, Basic Books, New York, 1987, pp. 246–47.

134. Ralph Hallow, "Blacks Blame Republicans for Riots but Are Less Liberal Than the Press Says," *Washington Times*, September 25, 1992.

135. Sylvester Monroe, "Trading Colors," *Emerge,* July-August 1993, p. 49; see also Alex Kotlowitz, "A Bridge Too far?" *New York Times Magazine,* June 12, 1994.

136. Alice Walker, *In Search of Our Mothers' Gardens,* Harcourt Brace Jovanovich, San Diego, 1983, p. 323.

137. Geneva Smitherman, *Black Talk: Words and Phrases From the Hood to the Amen Corner,* Houghton Mifflin, Boston, 1994, pp. 52–53, 59, 63, 101, 119, 126–127, 132, 135, 187, 191, 202.

138. Charlton Heston, "Just A Song?" *National Review,* August 17, 1992, pp. 37, 53; see also Chuck Phillips, "Music to Kill Cops By?" *Washington Post,* September 20, 1992, pp. G-1, G-10.

139. Cited by Robin Kelley, *Race Rebels: Culture, Politics and the Black Working Class,* Free Press, New York, 1994, p. 190.

140. Lawrence A. Stanley, ed., *Rap: The Lyrics,* Penguin Books, New York, 1992. The subsequent quotations are from this book. See pp. 53, 140, 237, 368.

141. "Rap and Race," *Newsweek,* June 29, 1992, p. 48; Terry Teachout, "Rap and Racism," *Commentary,* March 1990, p. 61.

142. "Thousands Pack Church for Rapper's Funeral," *Washington Times,* April 9, 1995, p. A-2; Ronald Smothers, "Rapper Charged in Shootings of Off-Duty Officers," *New York Times,* November 2, 1993, p. A-8; Richard Harrington, "Guns 'N Rappers: 3 Arrested In Shootings," *Washington Post,* November 3, 1993, p. C-7; Malcolm Gladwell, "Shakur Guilty of Sex Abuse," *Washington Post,* December 2, 1994, p. F-1; Charisse Jones, "For a Rapper, Life and Art Converge in Violence," *New York Times,* December 1, 1994, p. A-1.

143. Cited in "Double Trouble for 2Pac," *Newsweek,* December 12, 1994, p. 63.

144. Houston Baker, *Black Studies, Rap and the Academy,* University of Chicago Press, Chicago, 1993, p. xi.

145. Houston Baker, "You Cain't Trus' It," in Wallace, ed., *Black Popular Culture,* p. 136.

146. Cited by Bill Moyers, *A World of Ideas,* Anchor Books, New York, 1990, Vol. 2, p. 106.

147. Michael Eric Dyson, *Reflecting Black: African American Cultural Criticism,* University of Minnesota Press, Minneapolis, 1993, p. 3, 12.

148. Michael Eric Dyson, *Making Malcolm: The Myth and Meaning of Malcolm X,* Oxford University Press, New York, 1995.

149. Ishmael Reed, *Airing Dirty Laundry,* Addison-Wesley, Reading, MA, 1993, p. 234.

150. James P. Comer and Alvin F. Poussaint, *Raising Black Children,* Penguin, New York, 1992, p. 327.

151. Henry Louis Gates, Jr., "2 Live Crew Decoded," *New York Times,* June 19, 1990, p. A-23; Laura Parker, "Rap Lyrics Likened to Literature," *Washington Post,* October 20, 1990; Dexter Filkins, "Witness in 2 Live Crew Trial Hails Group's Brilliant Art," *Boston Globe,* October 20, 1990; Mike Clary, "Professor Calls 2 Live Crew Refreshing," *Los Angeles Times,* October 20, 1990; see also Luther Campbell and John Miller, *As Nasty As They Wanna Be: The Uncensored Story of Luther Campbell of the 2 Live Crew,* Barricade Books, Fort Lee, NJ, 1992.

152. Cited by Dyson, *Reflecting Black,* p. 168.

153. In 1991, 68 percent of black childbirths were to unmarried women. U.S. Bureau of the Census, *Statistical Abstract of the United States: 1994,* Washington, DC, 1994, p. 80.

154. U.S. Bureau of the Census, *Marital Status and Living Arrangements,* Current Population Reports, U.S. Government Printing Office, Washington, DC, 1994, Table 9, p. 75.

155. U.S. Bureau of the Census, *Fertility of American Women,* Current Population Reports, Washington, DC, 1993, Table B, p. x.

156. In 1989, the illegitimacy rate among white women with college degrees was 3.5 percent; among black women with college degrees, it was 23.2 percent. National Center for Health Statistics, *Vital Statistics of the United States: 1989,* pp. 200–201; see also Christopher Jencks, "Is the American Underclass Growing?" in Christopher Jencks and Paul E. Peterson, eds., *The Urban Underclass,* Brookings Institution, Washington, DC, 1991, p. 88.

157. Cited in "Endangered Family," *Newsweek,* August 30, 1993, p. 18.

158. Irwin Garfinkel and Sara S. McLanahan, *Single Mothers and Their Children: A New American Dilemma,* Urban Institute Press, Washington, DC, 1989, p. 84.

159. Centers for Disease Control and Prevention, "Facts About HIV/AIDS and U.S. Blacks," October 1993; see also "Blacks Far More Likely Than Whites to Have AIDS, Agency Says," *New York Times,* September 9, 1994, p. A-16.

160. Robert L. Hampton, *Violence in the Black Family: Correlates and Consequences,* Lexington Books, Lexington, 1987, p. x.

161. Richard Majors, "Cool Pose: A Symbolic Mechanism for Masculine Role Enactment and Coping by Black Males," in Majors and Gordon, *The American Black Male,* p. 253.

162. William Julius Wilson, *The Truly Disadvantaged,* pp. 25–26; William Julius Wilson, "The Urban Underclass in Advanced Industrial Society," in Paul Peterson, ed., *The New Urban Reality,* The Brookings Institution, Washington, DC, 1985, p. 137.

163. U.S. Bureau of the Census, *Statistical Abstract of the United States: 1994,* p. 80. Among white families with children below the poverty line in 1991, 51 percent were female headed. U.S. Bureau of the Census, *Current Population Reports,* Series P-60, No. 181, *Poverty in the United States: 1991,* U.S. Government Printing Office, Washington, DC, 1992, pp. 7–8.

164. Garfinkel and McLanahan, *Single Mothers and Their Children,* pp. xix, 14–15, 30.

165. According to historian Steven Ruggles, the proportion of black children who lived without one or both parents in 1880 was 30 percent, compared with a white rate of 13 percent. The black rate remained roughly constant until 1960, after which both the black and the white rates began to climb. See Steven Ruggles, "The Origins of African-American Family Structure," *American Sociological Review* 59, No. 1 (1994), p. 140. See also U.S. Bureau of the Census, *Statistical Abstract of the United States: 1994,* p. 66.

166. Sidney Kronus, *The Black Middle Class,* Charles E. Merrill, Columbus, 1971, p. 10.

167. Garfinkel and McLanahan, *Single Mothers and Their Children,* p. 7.

168. Elijah Anderson, *Streetwise: Race, Class and Change in an Urban Community,* University of Chicago Press, Chicago, 1990, pp. 92–93, 112–113, 119; Elijah Anderson, "Neighborhood Effects on Teenage Pregnancy," in Jencks and Peterson, *The Urban Underclass;* Elijah Anderson, "Caught in the Welfare Web," *Crisis,* March 1994.

169. The destructive socialization practices of the black underclass are vividly portrayed (although less clearly analyzed) in the work of Carl Nightingale, *On the Edge: A History of Poor Black Children and Their American Dreams,* Basic Books, New York, 1993, pp. 79–107.

170. Julianne Malveaux, "Popular Culture and the Economics of Alienation," in Wallace, *Black Popular Culture,* p. 206.

171. Bell Hooks, *Yearning: Race, Gender and Cultural Politics,* South End Press, Boston, 1990, p. 76.

172. "Not for Her," *Insight,* September 13, 1992, p. 18.

173. Jordan, *Technical Difficulties,* pp. 22, 73–74.

174. Cole, *Conversations,* pp. 99, 140.

175. Cited in Bonnie Angelo, "The Pain of Being Black," *Time,* May 22, 1989, p. 122; see also Ann Hulbert, "Poor Conceptions," *The New Republic,* November 12, 1990, p. 21.

176. William Julius Wilson, *The Declining Significance of Race,* University of Chicago Press, Chicago, 1980; Wilson, *The Truly Disadvantaged.*

177. Douglas Massey and Nancy Denton, *American Apartheid: Segregation and the Making of the Underclass,* Harvard University Press, Cambridge, 1993.

178. "I see no reason why these cultural traits, which may be deeply ingrained and extremely difficult to eradicate, should not be classed as unjust injuries." Boxill, *Blacks and Social Justice,* p. 157.

179. Cornel West, "Nihilism in Black America," *Dissent,* Spring 1991, pp. 221, 223.

180. Cornel West, *Race Matters,* Beacon Press, Boston, 1993, p. 57.

181. In addition to West's *Race Matters,* see Cornel West, *Keeping Faith: Philosophy and Race in America,* Routledge, New York, 1993.

182. For a detailed account of the views of many of the black reformers, see Joseph Conti and Brad Stetson, *Challenging the Civil Rights Establishment: Profiles of a New Black Vanguard,* Praeger Publishers, Westport, CT, 1993.

183. See, e.g., Manning Marable, "Clarence Thomas and the Crisis of Black Political Culture," in Toni Morrison, ed., *Race-ing Justice, En-gendering Power.* Marable's essay is an attack on Stephen Carter, Juan Williams, Orlando Patterson, and William Raspberry for saying positive things about Clarence Thomas and what he stands for.

184. Shelby Steele, *The Content of Our Character,* St. Martin's Press, New York, 1990, p. 169.

185. Mark Mathabane and Gail Mathabane, *Love in Black and White,* Harper-Collins, New York, 1992, p. 178.

186. Orlando Patterson, "Race, Gender and Liberal Fallacies," *New York Times,* October 20, 1991.

187. Hugh Price, keynote address at National Urban League Convention, Indianapolis, July 24, 1994; see also Steven A. Holmes, "A Rights Leader Minimizes Racism as a Poverty Factor," *New York Times,* July 24, 1994, p. A-14.

188. "Can Colin Powell Save America?" *Newsweek,* October 10, 1994, p. 26; see also "Powell on Powell: I Talk to All of America," *U.S. News and World Report,* September 20, 1993; Pete Hamill, "A Confederacy of Complainers," *Esquire,* July 1991, p. 26.

189. Clarence Thomas, Savannah State College Commencement Address, Savannah, Georgia, June 9, 1985.

190. Stephen Carter, *Reflections of an Affirmative Action Baby,* Basic Books, New York, 1991, p. 62.

191. Cited in "The Hidden Hurdle," *Time,* March 16, 1992, p. 44.

192. William Raspberry, "He's a Racist—the Easy Answer," *Washington Post,* June 6, 1990; William Raspberry, "Challenging Blacks to Become Producers in the Marketplace," *Issues & Views,* Summer 1989, p. 12.

193. Thomas Sowell, *Ethnic America,* Basic Books, New York, 1981, p. 296.

194. Colin Powell, Fisk University Commencement Address, Nashville, Tennessee, May 4, 1992; see also Colin Powell, "The Poverty of Values," *The World & I,* July 1992, p. 102.

195. Randall Kennedy, "Blacks and Crime," *Wall Street Journal,* April 8, 1994.

196. Glenn Loury, *One by One from the Inside Out: Essays and Reviews on Race and Responsibility in America,* Free Press, New York, 1995, pp. 72, 184.

197. Anne Wortham, *The Other Side of Racism,* Ohio State University Press, Columbus, 1981, p. 339.

198. Orlando Patterson, *Ethnic Chauvinism,* Stein and Day, New York, 1977, pp. 155–56.

199. William Raspberry, "The Civil Rights Movement Is Over," *Washington Post,* February 25, 1987, p. A-23.

200. Acknowledging departures from the merit standard, Kennedy writes, "The proper response to that reality is not to scrap the meritocratic ideal, but to abjure all practices that exploit the trappings of meritocracy to advance interests that have nothing to do with the intellectual characteristics of the subject being judged." Randall Kennedy, "Racial Critiques of Legal Academia," *Harvard Law Review* 102 (1989), p. 1807.

201. Steele, *The Content of Our Character,* p. 116.

202. Stanley Crouch, *Notes of a Hanging Judge: Essays and Reviews 1979–1989,* Oxford University Press, New York, 1990, p. 64.

203. Cited by Juan Williams, "The Seduction of Segregation," *Washington Post,* January 16, 1994; see also Michael Meyers, "Blacked Out in the Newt Congress," *Washington Post,* November 20, 1994, p. C-1.

204. Juan Williams, "The Movement Continues," in Peter Collier and David Horowitz, eds., *Second Thoughts About Race in America,* Madison Books, Lanham, MD, 1991, p. 34.

205. Clarence Page, "Will the Force Again Be with the NAACP?" *Washington Times,* February 28, 1992.

206. Loury, *One by One from the Inside Out,* p. 36.

207. Cited by John Kasarda, "Why Asians Prosper Where Blacks Fail," *Wall Street Journal,* May 28, 1992.

208. Alan Keyes, *Masters of the Dream: The Strength and Betrayal of Black America,* William Morrow, New York, 1995.

209. Orlando Patterson, "Blacklash," *Transition,* Issue 62, 1993, pp. 7, 25.

210. Stanley Crouch, "Role Models," in Collier and Horowitz, *Second Thoughts About Race in America,* p. 61.

Chapter 13. *The End of Racism*

1. Zora Neale Hurston, *Dust Tracks on a Road,* HarperPerennial, New York, 1991, p. 240.

2. William Julius Wilson, *The Truly Disadvantaged: The Inner City, the Underclass, and Public Policy,* University of Chicago, Chicago, 1987, p. 11.

3. "If all racial discrimination were abolished today, the life prospects facing many poor blacks would still constitute major challenges for public policy." Gerald David Jaynes and Robin M. Williams, *A Common Destiny: Blacks and American Society,* National Academy Press, Washington, DC, 1989, p. 4.

4. E. Franklin Frazier, *The Negro Family in the United States,* University of Chicago Press, Chicago, 1939, p. 487.

5. "When we react to the rumor of inferiority by avoiding intellectual engagement, and when we allow our children to do so, black people forfeit the opportunity for intellectual development which could extinguish the debate about our capacities, and set the stage for group progress." Jeff Howard and Ray Hammond, "Rumors of Inferiority," *The New Republic,* September 9, 1985.

6. Michael Massing, "Ghetto Blasting," *New Yorker,* January 16, 1995, p. 36.

7. Andrew Hacker, *Two Nations: Black and White, Separate, Hostile, Unequal,* Ballantine Books, New York, 1992, p. 218.

8. An example of this rhetoric is Joe Feagin and Hernan Vera's assertion that despite her incendiary rhetoric, "Sister Souljah is not the problem—she is only a messenger with bad news about the state of white racism." Joe Feagin and Hernan Vera, *White Racism: The Basics,* Routledge, New York, 1995, p. 131.

9. Daniel Patrick Moynihan, "Defining Deviancy Down," *The American Scholar,* Winter 1993, pp. 17–30; see also Charles Krauthammer, "Defining Deviancy Up," *The New Republic,* November 22, 1993, pp. 20–25. Krauthammer develops a corollary to the Moynihan thesis: not only is "the deviant declared normal," but "the normal is unmasked as deviant."

10. Gertrude Himmelfarb, *The De-Moralization of Society,* Alfred A. Knopf, New York, 1995.

11. Judy Mann, "Let's Refrain from Attacking the Poor," *Washington Post,* November 23, 1994, p. D-19.

12. The American founders understood this. As Gordon Wood writes, in the founders' view, "A republic was such a delicate polity precisely because it demanded

an extraordinary moral character in the people. Every state in which the people participated needed a degree of virtue, but a republic which rested solely on the people absolutely required it." See Gordon Wood, *The Creation of the American Republic, 1776–1787,* W. W. Norton, New York, 1972, p. 68.

13. Christopher Jencks, *Rethinking Social Policy: Race, Poverty and the Underclass,* Harvard University Press, Cambridge, 1992, p. 145.

14. Anthony Appiah, *In My Father's House: Africa in the Philosophy of Culture,* Oxford University Press, New York, 1992, p. 45.

15. Jencks, *Rethinking Social Policy,* p. 41.

16. Gary S. Becker, *The Economics of Discrimination,* University of Chicago Press, Chicago, 1971.

17. Michael Kinsley, "The Spoils of Victimhood," *New Yorker,* March 27, 1995, p. 66.

18. James Fallows, *More Like Us,* Houghton Mifflin, New York, 1989, p. 49.

19. Theodore Cross, "Suppose There Was No Affirmative Action at the Most Prestigious Colleges and Graduate Schools," *Journal of Blacks in Higher Education,* No. 3 (Spring 1994), pp. 44–51.

20. Andrew Kull, *The Color-Blind Constitution,* Harvard University Press, Cambridge, 1992, p. 223.

21. Orlando Patterson argues that "our traditional liberal conception that one simply creates opportunities and assumes everything will work itself out . . . works very well for most people, including black immigrants, but the problem with black Americans is unique." Orlando Patterson, "American Dilemmas Revisited," *Salmagundi,* Fall 1994–Winter 1995, p. 42. See also Nathan Glazer, "Race, Not Class," *Wall Street Journal,* April 5, 1995, p. A-12.

22. Cited in "A Race-Neutral Helping Hand," *Business Week,* February 27, 1995, p. 121.

23. Hugh Davis Graham, "Race, History and Policy: African Americans and Civil Rights Since 1964," *Policy History,* Pennsylvania State University Press, Vol. 6, No. 1, 1994, p. 34.

24. Itabari Njeri, "Sushi and Grits: Ethnic Identity and Conflict In a Newly Multicultural America," in Gerald Early, ed., *Lure and Loathing: Essays on Race, Identity and the Ambivalence of Assimilation,* Penguin, New York, 1993, p. 40.

25. See, e.g., Jim Sleeper, *The Closest of Strangers,* W. W. Norton, New York, 1990; Wilson, *The Truly Disadvantaged*; Cass Sunstein, "Voting Rites," *The New Republic,* April 25, 1994; Rod Dreher, "Kemp Urges Affirmative Action Based on Economics," *Washington Times,* February 20, 1995, p. A-1; Clarence Page, "Salvation Based on Need," *Washington Times,* February 21, 1995, p. A-16.

26. Richard Posner, *The Economics of Justice,* Harvard University Press, Cambridge, 1981, p. 360.

27. Richard Epstein, *Forbidden Grounds: The Case Against Employment Discrimination Laws,* Harvard University Press, Cambridge, 1992.

28. Jennifer Roback, "The Separation of Race and State," *Harvard Journal of Law and Public Policy,* No. 1 (Winter 1991), p. 58.

29. Leon Wieseltier, "Taking Yes for an Answer," *Time,* February 28, 1994, p. 28.

30. John Courtney Murray, *We Hold These Truths,* Sheed and Ward, New York, 1960, p. 49.

31. At the same time, I agree with Rosalie Pedalino Porter that for immigrants whose first language is not English, the best option is one of "keeping one's native language for informal, conversational use in the home and neighborhood and developing a high degree of English-language fluency and literacy for work, schooling, and contacts outside the community." See Rosalie Pedalino Porter, *Forked Tongue: The Politics of Bilingual Education,* Basic Books, New York, 1990, p. 204.

32. T. S. Eliot, "Notes Toward the Definition of Culture," in T. S. Eliot, *Christianity and Culture,* Harcourt Brace Jovanovich, New York, 1939, p. 101.

33. "Debating a Proposed Hands-Off Policy," *Philadelphia Inquirer,* May 24, 1992, p. A-3; "Short Arms of the Law," *New York Times,* May 24, 1992.

34. George M. Fredrickson, "No Foreigners Need Apply," *New York Times Book Review,* August 22, 1993, p. 17.

35. Charles Taylor, *Multiculturalism and "The Politics of Recognition",* Princeton University Press, Princeton, 1992, p. 62.

36. Robert Bellah, "Civil Religion in America," in Russell Richey and Donald Jones, eds., *American Civil Religion,* University of Chicago Press, Chicago, 1974.

37. Sacvan Bercovitch, "Commemorating 1492," *Tikkun* 7, (September-October 1992), p. 61.

38. Rodolfo de la Garza, *Latino Voices: Mexican, Puerto Rican and Cuban Perspectives on American Politics,* Westview Press, Boulder, 1992; Peter Skerry, *Mexican Americans: The Ambivalent Minority,* Free Press, New York, 1993; Alejandro Portes and Ruben Rumbaut, *Immigrant America: A Portrait,* University of California Press, Berkeley, 1990.

39. In Europe, by contrast, many Turkish and Moroccan immigrants insist on living by an Islamic code that flouts some of the principles of liberal pluralism, provoking a nativist backlash that has clear racist and fascist undertones. See, e.g., Anthony Hartley, "Europe's Muslims," *The National Interest,* Winter 1990–1991, pp. 57–66.

40. Cited by Bill Moyers, *A World of Ideas,* Anchor Books, New York, 1990, Volume 2, p. 88.

41. Kenji Hakuta, *Mirror of Language: The Debate on Bilingualism,* Basic Books, New York, 1986, p. 167.

42. Alejandro Portes and Robert L. Bach, *Latin Journey: Cuban and Mexican Immigrants in the United States,* University of California Press, Berkeley, 1985, p. 91.

43. Alejandro Portes and Min Zhou, "Should Immigrants Assimilate?" *The Public Interest,* Summer 1994.

44. Marcus Lee Hansen, *The Problem of the Third Generation Immigrant,* Augustana Historical Society, Rock Island, IL, 1938, pp. 9–10; see also Marcus Lee Hansen, "The Third Generation in America," *Commentary,* November 1952.

45. Orlando Patterson, "Context and Choice in Ethnic Allegiance: A Theoretical Framework and Caribbean Case Study," in Nathan Glazer and Daniel Patrick Moynihan, eds., *Ethnicity: Theory and Experience,* Harvard University Press, Cam-

bridge, 1985; see also Orlando Patterson, *Ethnic Chauvinism: The Reactionary Impulse,* Stein and Day, New York, 1977, p. 103.

46. Alan Wolfe, "The Return of the Melting Pot," *The New Republic,* December 31, 1990, p. 29; see also Mary Waters, *Ethnic Options: Choosing Identities in America,* University of California Press, Berkeley, 1990.

47. For some competing views, see George Borjas, *Friends or Strangers: The Impact of Immigrants on the U.S. Economy,* Basic Books, New York, 1990; Donald Huddle, "Dirty Work: Are Immigrants Only Taking Jobs That the Native Does Not Want?" *Population and Environment,* No. 6 (July 1, 1993); Donald Huddle and David Simcox, "The Impact of Immigration on the Social Security System," *Population and Environment,* No. 1 (September 1, 1994); Ben Wattenberg and Karl Zinsmeister, "The Case for More Immigration," *Commentary,* April 1990, pp. 19–25; Julian Simon, "The Nativists Are Wrong," *Wall Street Journal,* August 4, 1993; Center for the New American Community, "Index of Leading Immigration Indicators," Washington, DC, November 1994.

48. Richard Alba, "Assimilation's Quiet Tide," *The Public Interest,* Spring 1995, p. 17; "Mixed Babies," *American Demographics,* June 1994, p. 39.

49. Cited by Lawrence Wright, "One Drop of Blood," *New Yorker,* July 25, 1994.

50. People for the American Way, *Democracy's Next Generation: A Study of American Youth on Race,* survey by Peter Hart Research Associates, Washington, DC, 1992, pp. 12–19, 95–100; see also Charlotte Steeh and Howard Schuman, "Young White Adults: Did Racial Attitudes Change in the 1980s?" *American Journal of Sociology* 98, (September 1989), pp. 340–67.

51. Eugene Rivers, "On the Responsibility of Intellectuals in the Age of Crack," *Boston Review,* September–October 1992.

52. Ralph Ellison, *Shadow and Act,* Random House, New York, 1964, p. 271.

53. Cited by Paul Klebnikov, "Showing Big Daddy the Door," *Forbes,* November 9, 1992, p. 154.

54. As Orlando Patterson writes: "Blacks now face a historic choice. To survive, they must abandon their search for a past, must indeed recognize that they lack all claim to a distinctive cultural heritage, and that the path ahead lies not in myth-making and historical reconstruction, which are always doomed to failure, but in accepting the epic challenge of their reality. Black Americans can be the first group in the history of mankind who transcend the confines and grip of a cultural heritage, and in so doing, they can become the most truly modern of all peoples—a people . . . whose style of life will be a rational and continually changing adaptation to the exigencies of survival at the highest possible level of existence." See Orlando Patterson, "Toward a Future That Has No Past," *The Public Interest,* Spring 1972, pp. 60–61.

55. Frederick Douglass, *Life and Times of Frederick Douglass,* Collier Books, New York, 1962, p. 289.

56. Frantz Fanon, *Black Skin, White Masks,* Grove Weidenfeld, New York, 1967, pp. 8, 10.

57. The first black millionaire, Madame C. J. Walker, made her fortune selling skin dye and hair-straightening cosmetics to blacks. "We wanted to be light-skinned

so bad," one activist recalls, "we would walk in the shade." See Audrey Edwards and Craig Polite, *Children of the Dream,* Doubleday, New York, 1992, p. 17.

58. Frederick Douglass, "The Nation's Problem," in Howard Brotz, ed., *Negro Social and Political Thought, 1850–1920,* Basic Books, New York, 1966, pp. 316–17.

59. W. E. B. Du Bois, *The Souls of Black Folk,* Penguin Books, New York, 1982, p. 11; see also W. E. B. Du Bois, *The Gift of Black Folk,* Kraus-Thomson, Millwood, NY, 1975, p. 139.

INDEX